anita beck

CLINICAL HANDBOOK OF PSYCHOLOGICAL DISORDERS

CLINICAL HANDBOOK OF PSYCHOLOGICAL DISORDERS
A Step-by-Step Treatment Manual

Edited by

David H. Barlow
State University of New York at Albany

The Guilford Press
New York   London

© 1985 The Guilford Press
A Division of Guilford Publications, Inc.
200 Park Avenue South, New York, N.Y. 10003

Printed in the United States of America

Library of Congress Cataloging in Publication Data
Main entry under title:

Clinical handbook of psychological disorders.

Includes index.
1. Behavior therapy—Handbooks, manuals, etc.
I. Barlow, David H. [DNLM: 1. Mental Disorders
—therapy.   2. Psychotherapy. WM 420 C641]
RC489.B4C584   1985   616.89'1   84-19314
ISBN 0-89862-648-X

For Beverly A. Barlow

If we have been successful . . . [these cases] . . . will show that we devise interventions by drawing on a relatively coherent theoretical framework of applied science. At the same time, tuning specific thrusts to specific individuals remains, in part, something of a performing art.—TED AND RENATE ROSENTHAL (Chapter 3, this volume)

CONTRIBUTORS

David H. Barlow, PhD, Center for Stress and Anxiety Disorders, and Department of Psychology, State University of New York at Albany, Albany, New York

Aaron T. Beck, MD, Center for Cognitive Therapy, Department of Psychiatry, University of Pennsylvania, Philadelphia, Pennsylvania

Steven E. Boone, PhD, Rehabilitation Research and Training Center, UCLA School of Medicine, Los Angeles, California; West Los Angeles Veterans Administration Medical Center—Brentwood Division, Los Angeles, California

Kelly D. Brownell, PhD, Department of Psychiatry, University of Pennsylvania School of Medicine, Philadelphia, Pennsylvania

Clyde P. Donahoe, PhD, Rehabilitation Research and Training Center, UCLA School of Medicine, Los Angeles, California; West Los Angeles Veterans Administration Medical Center—Brentwood Division, Los Angeles, California

Edna B. Foa, PhD, Department of Psychiatry, Temple University School of Medicine, Philadelphia, Pennsylvania

John P. Foreyt, PhD, Diet Modification Clinic, Baylor College of Medicine, Houston, Texas

David W. Foy, PhD, Rehabilitation Research and Training Center, UCLA School of Medicine, Los Angeles, California; West Los Angeles Veterans Administration Medical Center—Brentwood Division, Los Angeles, California

Jerry M. Friedman, PhD, Department of Psychology. State University of New York at Stony Brook, Stony Brook, New York

Douglas R. Hogan, PhD, Private practice, Garden City Park, New York

Neil S. Jacobson, PhD, Department of Psychology, University of Washington, Seattle, Washington

Stephen A. Maisto, PhD, Department of Psychology, Vanderbilt University, Nashville, Tennessee

Barbara S. McCrady, PhD, Center of Alcohol Studies and Graduate School of Applied and Professional Psychology, Rutgers University, Piscataway, New Jersey

Renate H. Rosenthal, PhD, Department of Psychiatry, University of Tennessee College of Medicine, Center for the Health Sciences, Memphis, Tennessee

Ted L. Rosenthal, PhD, Department of Psychiatry, University of Tennessee College of Medicine, Center for the Health Sciences, Memphis, Tennessee; Adult Psychiatry and Alcohol and Drug Unit, MidSouth Hospital, Memphis, Tennessee

Gail Steketee, MSW, Department of Psychiatry, Temple University School of Medicine, Philadelphia, Pennsylvania

Ira Daniel Turkat, PhD, Department of Psychology, University of North Carolina at Greensboro, Greensboro, North Carolina

Maria T. Waddell, PhD, Center for Stress and Anxiety Disorders, and Department of Psychology, State University of New York at Albany, Albany, New York

Charles J. Wallace, PhD, Rehabilitation Research and Training Center, UCLA School of Medicine, Los Angeles, California; West Los Angeles Veterans Administration Medical Center—Brentwood Division, Los Angeles, California

Lisa F. Wood, PhD, Department of Psychology, University of Washington, Seattle, Washington

Jeffrey E. Young, PhD, Department of Psychiatry, College of Physicians and Surgeons, Columbia University, New York, New York

PREFACE

This book represents a distinct departure from any number of recent books reviewing advances in the treatment of psychological disorders. Such a book only became possible during the last several years; it is based on the premise that we now have a technology of behavior change that necessarily differs from disorder to disorder. This technology consists of a variety of techniques or procedures with more or less proven effectiveness within a given disorder. Naturally we have more evidence for the effectiveness of these treatments with some disorders than for others. This book is also based on the assumption that considerable clinical skill is required to apply this technology most effectively. Thus, this book is *not* another review of therapeutic procedures for a given problem with recommendations for future research. Rather, it is a detailed description of actual treatment protocols in which experienced clinicians implement the technology of behavior change in the context of the 10 most frequently encountered adult disorders.

This book was motivated by countless clinical psychology graduate students, psychiatric residents, and other mental health professionals either in training or in practice asking, "But how do I do it?" Realizing that there is no source in which one can find step-by-step treatment protocols that one can use as a guide to practice, this book attempts to fill that void. To accomplish this purpose a number of specific topics are common to all chapters. Each chapter begins with a brief review of our knowledge of the specific disorder, followed by a description of the particular model or mini-theory that guides the technology utilized with the disorder in question. This model, or mini-theory, typically answers the question: What particular facets of the disorder should be assessed and treated? While clinical application always dilutes theoretical models, clinicians will recognize behavioral and systems approaches as the predominant theoretical context. This is followed by a description of the typical setting in which the treatment is carried out. This varies from disorder to disorder, ranging from the more usual office setting to the home environment of the patient. Similar detailed descriptions of the social context of treatment (e.g., the importance of the involvement of family or friends) as well as therapist and client variables that are important within the context of the particular problem are discussed. For example, therapist variables that may be important in implementing techniques for treating agoraphobia or marital distress are described. In addition, the implications for treatment of client variables such as dependency and unassertiveness in many agoraphobics or minimal social functioning in chronic mental patients are discussed. This is followed by a detailed description of the actual step-by-step process of assessment and treatment, liberally sprinkled, in many chapters, with transcripts of therapy sessions. Important components of this process are the specifics of the rationale given the patient before treatment as well as typical problems that arise during the implementation of the technology. Where data exist, information on clinical predictors of success or failure are provided.

In accomplishing the rather ambitious goals described above, I was very fortunate in having leading clinicians and researchers document in some detail how they actually treat their patients. Thus, all of the contributors, of necessity, are experienced and effective clinicians. It will be obvious from the length of the chapters alone that the amount of work that went into this book is much greater than that required for the usual contributed chapter. It was particularly gratifying that many of these authorities reported that for the first time they were writing about how they actually applied their technology and that the number of details they had to include were far beyond their expectations. My hope is that practicing clinicians and clinical students everywhere will benefit from acquaintance with these details.

My thanks, once again, to Sallie Morgan who has stayed with me through 16 years of long hours, deadlines, and endless revisions of manuscripts, and to Chris Adler and Bill Sanderson for compiling what we all hope will be a useful index to the book. Finally, this book is dedicated with love and respect to Beverly, who participated fully in the realization of a dream.

David H. Barlow
Nantucket Island
August 1984

CONTENTS

**CLINICAL HANDBOOK OF
PSYCHOLOGICAL DISORDERS**

AGORAPHOBIA

DAVID H. BARLOW AND MARIA T. WADDELL

This chapter describes the implementation of our detailed treatment protocol for agoraphobia. This protocol is distinguished by the direct involvement of the spouse in all aspects of treatment. As with all chapters, the emphasis is on the session-to-session interaction as well as various clinical strategies necessary for implementing the techniques. This detailed description is provided in the context of the treatment of a small group of agoraphobic women and their husbands. Although only one case is presented, the woman (called "Ginny") actually represents a composite of the women in the group in order to illustrate the range of difficulties encountered in using this treatment protocol. In our view the attention to the social and interpersonal context of treatment represented here by the inclusion of the spouse illustrates a rapidly growing trend, whatever one's theoretical orientation. In fact, a knowledge of the family or social "system" in which therapy is administered would seem extremely important for both treatment and maintenance of therapeutic gains across a wide range of problems. This trend is evident throughout this book, but strategies for including the spouse or significant other in treatment are specifically described in Chapter 2 on obsessive–compulsive disorders, Chapter 5 on alcoholism, Chapter 6 on obesity, Chapter 7 on marital distress, and Chapter 8 on sexual dysfunction. While clinicians and investigators in the latter two areas have been utilizing these strategies for years, only recently has their use begun to spread to the treatment of other problems. After a brief description of the advantages of utilizing this approach in treating agoraphobia, the remainder of the chapter is devoted to a detailed description of assessment and treatment in this context using our newly developed protocol—D. H. B.

INTRODUCTION

Everyone knows what it means to be nervous or anxious. These experiences are a part of modern life. In fact, complaints of anxiety, in many cases reaching severe proportions, are among the most common problems presenting to health practitioners. If one looks at the number of people seeking help for anxiety from general medical practitioners, this problem dwarfs other emotional or behavioral problems. One study revealed anxiety as the fifth most common reason for visits to a primary care physician, ranking only behind preventative examina-

David H. Barlow and Maria T. Waddell. Center for Stress and Anxiety Disorders, and Department of Psychology, State University of New York at Albany, Albany, New York.

tion, hypertension, lacerations and trauma, and pharyngitis and tonsillitis (Marsland, Wood, & Mayo, 1976). It is also important to note that these numbers represent only those people whom primary care physicians recognize as having anxiety. We now know that severe anxiety and panic often present to health practitioners as any one of a number of other problems that may mask the primary anxiety disorder. To take one of the most important examples, in a recent study over two-thirds of patients presenting to a clinic for problem drinking were found to be self-medicating an anxiety problem (Mullaney & Trippett, 1979). This finding fits with the experience of clinicians treating addictive behaviors, particularly alcoholism, where reports of taking a drink to calm oneself are very common.

These preceding statistics refer only to those seeking help. If one examines the prevalence of severe anxiety in the general population through survey methodology, the numbers become even larger. For example, one poll using reliable sampling methodology and conservative definitions revealed that 30%–40% of the general population suffered from the presence of anxiety, with greater prevalence in females (Shepherd, Cooper, Brown, & Kalton, 1966).

Agoraphobia is one of the more severe anxiety disorders. The name was first suggested by Westphal (1871) to describe a condition where walking through open spaces or through empty streets provoked a great deal of anxiety. Nevertheless, most people, including many health practitioners, would not have recognized this term as recently as 15 years ago due to a lack of familiarity with the syndrome (Mavissakalian & Barlow, 1981). Indeed, the term "agoraphobia," as suggested by Westphal (1871) has not helped since agoraphobics really do not fear open spaces or market places so much as they do their own internal sensations of fear or panic. In fact, a description first presented by Benedikt (1870), 1 year before Westphal, is far more appropriate. He suggested the name *platzschwindel* (dizziness in public places; see Mathews, Gelder, & Johnston, 1981). For what agoraphobics fear is dizziness or the symptoms of fear itself. Hence, the well-known and accepted characterization of agoraphobia as fear of fear. In keeping with our Greek traditions, another name that would be more appropriate than agoraphobia would be "panphobia." Pan, of course, was the Greek god with a nasty habit of hiding along the roadside until a group of early Greek travelers would appear and then jumping out and scaring them literally to death. Hence the term "panic" and "panphobia," describing as it does a fear of intense anxiety, would also seem more appropriate than agoraphobia.[1]

Nevertheless, agoraphobia is a relatively rare condition when compared to the more prevalent anxiety disorders such as generalized anxiety disorder. But it is an important problem to study and to learn how to treat, because agoraphobia is the one anxiety disorder that subsumes all of the important clinical features associated with the remaining anxiety disorders. Approximately 75% of agoraphobics tend to be women, and the onset occurs in late adolescence or early adulthood (Agras, Chapin, & Oliveau, 1972; Marks & Herst, 1970; Snaith,

---

1. We are indebted to Ron Ley for this observation.

1968). Prevalence estimates have varied. Agras, Sylvester, and Oliveau (1969), after surveying the population of a small city, Burlington, Vermont, estimated the prevalence at approximately 6 per 1000. Another recent estimate places the prevalence at 12 per 1000 (Uhlenhuth, Balter, Mellinger, Cisin, & Clinthorne, 1981). However, using somewhat less rigorous definitions, others have estimated the prevalence as high as 260 per 1000 (Langer & Michael, 1963). These vast differences probably represent conservative versus liberal definitions of the presence of agoraphobia symptoms since general anxiety, panic, and other agoraphobic-like symptoms seem to be on a continuum, with the most severe manifestations of this disorder, leading to disability and housebound status, found only at the extreme end of the continuum. Once again, this illustrates the variety of anxiety-like features present in agoraphobics.

For example, almost all agoraphobics are nervous, apprehensive, vigilant, and complain of a variety of somatic symptoms often associated with anxiety. For this reason, if they did not avoid a variety of situations they could easily be classified in the new DSM-III category of generalized anxiety disorder. For this reason, also, the majority of agoraphobics, much like the majority of all people suffering from anxiety disorders, visit first of all their primary care physician's office where they are administered thorough physicals and—unless the physician is particularly well informed about anxiety disorders—minor tranquilizers. In addition to being generally anxious, agoraphobics almost always have discrete and acute episodes of anxiety that we have come to refer to by the term "panic," described above. If the somatic symptoms associated with generalized anxiety disorder have not brought them to their physician's office, then almost certainly the panic will, for it is most often attributed by clients to heart attacks or other cardiovascular disturbances that agoraphobics presume will certainly lead to death. For this reason, many agoraphobics suffering their first panic will rush to the nearest emergency room.

Features of other subcategories of anxiety disorders listed in the DSM-III are also shared by agoraphobics. Since agoraphobics are often traumatized by their first panic experience, usually occurring during late adolescence or early adulthood, it is very common to see them reliving this nightmare symbolically in their dreams. In addition, they often anticipate and dread a re-experience of the initial panic in a variety of situations that are similar to, or on a generalization gradient with, the situation in which the panic first occurred. These phenomena resemble posttraumatic stress disorder (PTSD) that we are seeing so frequently in our veterans and others who undergo a traumatic experience such as a natural disaster or a rape.

Any clinician who has dealt with agoraphobics has also observed occasional intrusive unwanted thoughts that could be categorized as obsessional. Often these thoughts are associated with the catastrophic consequences of panic, such as thoughts of dying, losing control, fainting in the midst of a crowded store, or becoming incontinent. But equally often, these thoughts may be quite independent of the central feature of agoraphobia. For example, in our clinic we find that a large majority of our agoraphobic women with children have mild to moderate obsessive thoughts of harming or killing their children, particularly if left alone with them for a long period of time. Any clinician who has come across this phenomenon knows that it is often one of the last clinical features to emerge during the treatment of female agoraphobics, since it is virtually impossible for them to admit to anyone that they are entertaining these horrific and frightening thoughts; a state of affairs that, of course, is probably responsible for their becoming obsessive in the first place (Rachman & Hodgson, 1980).

Finally, almost all agoraphobics have a variety of social and evaluative fears as well as specific fears embedded within the broad range of avoidance and fear of panic attacks that characterizes agoraphobia. Thus, while social phobics fear being humiliated or otherwise embarrassing themselves while doing something in public, such as speaking, eating, or writing, agoraphobics also very often report these fears along with their basic fear of panic attacks. Thus, the successful treatment of agoraphobia is important to every clinician because it must encompass procedures that are applicable to almost all features of anxiety in general, something with which every clinician who sees a number of clients has to contend. Despite the long history of writings on agoraphobia, only during the 1960s did the clinical entity of agoraphobia become well delineated and increasingly recognized as a syndrome in its own right (Mavissakalian & Barlow, 1981). An exciting progression of research, however, that actually began with the publication of Wolpe's famous book (1958), has allowed clinical investigators to discover efficient and effective treatments for agoraphobia, particularly during the past decade (Mavissakalian & Barlow, 1981). While these treatments take a variety of forms, they can all be described as exposure-based; that is, the major active ingredient involves arranging to have the agoraphobic exposed to situations that are frightening and also commonly avoided so as to "reality test" the lack of actual danger. However, it now seems that the manner in which this basic therapeutic ingredient is delivered makes a great deal of difference, and that very divergent rates of clinical improvement will be obtained, depending on the manner of delivery.

Methods of Treatment

The purpose of this chapter is not to review in a scholarly fashion the treatments for agoraphobia. However, before outlining in detail our couples treatment of agoraphobia protocol, it will be helpful to review briefly the current status of the treatment for agoraphobia and, therefore, the reasons for our treatment of agoraphobia. (For in-depth, scholarly reviews of the treatment of agoraphobia see Chambless & Goldstein, 1982; Marks, 1981; Mathews et al., 1981; Mavissakalian & Barlow, 1981; O'Brien & Barlow, 1984; and Thorpe & Burns, 1983.)

Agoraphobia can be treated successfully by one of the following formats: first, direct exposure and, second, indirect exposure. Direct exposure involves arranging for the client to be exposed to feared situations—such as walking or driving away from a safe place or a safe person, crowded shopping centers, and the like—in a structured way. This structure can involve either a sudden, intense, prolonged exposure, or a more gradual, self-paced type of exposure. Naturally, these two forms of exposure occur on a continuum. When exposure is delivered intensely, it is often termed "flooding *in vivo*" or "prolonged *in vivo* exposure." Most usually this involves taking one or more agoraphobics to a local shopping mall and remaining with them for up to 4 hr or more while they experience and eventually habituate to intense anxiety. Typically the therapist or therapy aide accompanying the agoraphobics to the shopping mall will gradually withdraw to insure maximal anxiety during this experience. Often the therapist is an assistant or an ex-phobic who is trained in facilitating this type of activity (Marks, 1981). Direct exposure can also occur on a graduated basis and in its "mildest" form not require the presence of a therapist or a therapy aide. For example, the client can be requested to move up a hierarchy of fear-producing situations very gradually, in a self-paced manner, either with or without the help of a therapist or a family member. This can also be done on the instructions of a therapist, with the patient reporting back to the therapist each week to discuss progress (e.g., Mathews *et al.*, 1976).

The second type of exposure, indirect exposure, is most often delivered in imagination or symbolically, such as through the use of films with fear-arousing cues. Systematic desensitization is included in this category since this procedure is characterized by gradual imaginal presentation of a hierarchy of feared stimuli paired with relaxation. Other imaginal procedures, such as imaginal flooding, which is the more "intense" variety of indirect exposure, could be included here (Mavissakalian & Barlow, 1981).

A number of early studies demonstrated the superiority of direct exposure to indirect exposure (e.g., Barlow, Leitenberg, Agras, & Wincze, 1969; Emmelkamp & Wessels, 1975; see Mavissakalian & Barlow, 1981). Furthermore, early studies looking at outcome immediately after the conclusion of treatment concluded that the intensive variety of direct exposure, most often called prolonged *in vivo* exposure, was more effective than gradual or spaced exposure (Foa, Jameson, Turner, & Payne, 1980; Stern & Marks, 1973). However, the picture changes considerably if one looks at the outcome of treatment at follow-up points of 3–6 months. At this point any differences disappear, since either more graduated, self-paced direct exposure or even indirect exposure techniques produce therapeutic gains that catch up to those produced by prolonged *in vivo* exposure (Mathews *et al.*, 1976; Mathews, Teasdale, Munby, Johnston, & Shaw, 1977; Munby & Johnston, 1980). Klein, Zitrin, Woerner, and Ross (1983) found that self-paced exposure taking place in the context of supportive therapy, delivered within a phobia clinic, was as effective as indirect exposure (systematic desensitization) at follow-up. Klein *et al.* (1983) point out, correctly we think, that any treatment encouraging systematic exposure, whether gradual or intense, imaginal or *in vivo*, is likely to produce significant therapeutic gains eventually, particularly if these treatments are delivered within the context of a phobia clinic where demands for being brave and facing up to the feared situations are implicit.

In any case, the outcome of exposure-based treatments is fairly consistent when one examines a number of different studies conducted by clinicians in various parts of the world. If dropouts are excluded, the best estimates of outcome indicate that from 60%–70% of those agoraphobics completing treatment will show some clinical benefit and that these effects will be maintained, on the average, for periods of 4 years or more (Emmelkamp & Kuipers, 1979; Jansson & Ost, 1982; McPherson, Brougham, & McLaren, 1980; Munby & Johnston, 1980). In view of the consistency of this outcome and the fact that the effectiveness of this approach has been demonstrated repeatedly in controlled experimentation when compared to no treatment or some good placebo (e.g., Mathews, 1978; Mavissakalian & Barlow, 1981; O'Brien & Barlow, 1984), this development represents one of the success stories of psychotherapy. Nevertheless, having demonstrated that this approach is successful, investigators are beginning to examine its limitations. It is now becoming increasingly apparent that outcome from these treatments is characterized by many examples of failure, relapse, and limited clinical improvement. For example, one major problem most often overlooked in the treatment of agoraphobia is dropouts. An updated review of a large number of studies indicates that the median dropout rate from exposure-based treatments is 12%, with rates from 25%–40% recorded when drugs are added to exposure-based treatments (Jansson & Ost, 1982; Zitrin, Klein, & Woerner, 1978, 1980). Furthermore, data reflecting success rates of 60%–70% are also reflecting the fact that 30%–40% of all agoraphobics who complete treatment fail to benefit. Of the remaining 60%–70%, a substantial percentage may not reach clinically meaningful levels of functioning. For example, Marks (1981) reported that only 3 of 65 clients (4.6%) were completely symptom free at follow-up, as determined by assessors' clinical ratings. McPherson et al. (1980) reported that among clients who showed some improvement following behavioral treatment, only 18% who were reached at follow-up rated themselves as being completely free of symptoms. Finally, Munby and Johnston (1980) observed relapses occurring in as many as 50% of clients who had benefitted clinically, although in most cases these clients were eventually able to return to a level of clinical improvement previously reached in treatment.

Furthermore, it now seems possible that direct exposure, carried out in an intensive fashion as it often is, may be less effective than previously assumed, and might even be detrimental if viewed in a broader context. For example, returning to the issue of dropouts, intensive *in vivo* exposure, administered over a short period of time, seems to produce a dropout rate considerably higher than the median 12% (e.g., Emmelkamp & Ultee, 1974; Emmelkamp & Wessels, 1975). Marks (1978) even reports that 23% of a large group of agoraphobics refused this very drastic treatment before beginning. On the other hand, a more gradual self-initiated exposure program, carried out over a longer period of time with a cooperative partner in the environment, produces a very low dropout rate (Jannoun, Munby, Catalan, & Gelder, 1980; Mathews et al., 1977). Another disadvantage of direct, intensive exposure is the sometimes deleterious effect of dramatic behavioral changes following *in vivo* exposure on the interpersonal system of the client, particularly the spouse (e.g., Hafner, 1977; O'Brien, Barlow, & Last, 1982). Since at least 75% of agoraphobics are women, the majority of whom are married, these effects most often show up in the husband (Mavissakalian & Barlow, 1981). In addition, it has been observed consistently that continued progress after treatment is terminated does not occur with intensive, therapist-assisted, direct exposure. This is a serious problem since we have already noted that improvement most often is far less than desired. Other investigators suggest that therapist-assisted, direct exposure may produce a dependence on the therapist which in and of itself precludes further improvement once a therapist is absent (e.g., Mathews et al., 1977). Finally, this approach is associated with a higher relapse rate than less intensive, graduated treatments (Hafner, 1976; Jansson & Ost, 1982).

There are two therapeutic approaches, however, that do seem to enhance the results of exposure-based treatments, at least initially. The first is the use of antidepressants such as tricyclics and monoamine oxidase (MAO) inhibitors that target the reduction of panic (Zitrin, 1981). In one of the best studies to date, Zitrin et al. (1980) report that some clinical improvement was noted in approximately 70% of a group receiving exposure in vivo, which is typical of results found around the world, but that this improvement, as rated by the therapist, increased to 92% with the addition of imipramine. However, both dropouts and relapses were very high in this study. At 6-month follow-up, approximately 65% of each group remained clinically improved if one looks at therapist ratings. If one subtracts dropouts, then the percentage of those showing some clinical improvement drops to 49% for each group at 6-month follow-up, somewhat below the typical outcome of exposure-based treatment calculated in a similar fashion. Zitrin, Klein, Woerner, and Ross (1983) report a similar comparison between imaginal exposure (systematic desensitization) with and without imipramine (other groups were also involved in this comparison). Once again, results from completers at posttreatment measurement revealed an advantage to imipramine; but, at follow-up, when one subtracts dropouts, 54% of the imaginal exposure group improved compared to 52% of the imaginal exposure plus imipramine group.

Another approach that seems to enhance treatment, without some of the disadvantages of the pharmacological approaches noted above, is the addition of a spouse or other concerned family member or friend to a more gradual self-paced treatment protocol. For example, Hand, Lamontagne, and Marks (1974) noted that agoraphobics treated in what became a cohesive group, stayed in touch with one another and supported each other after treatment, evidently resulting in further improvement. Mathews et al. (1977), in the uncontrolled clinical trial mentioned above, included spouses of agoraphobics as cotherapists and noted that over 90% were much improved at the end of treatment, with improvement continuing at follow-up. Munby and Johnston (1980) conducted follow-ups of a series of studies carried out by the same group of investigators and noted that the treatment in which spouses were directly included produced continuing improvement and results that were superior at a 4- to 9-year follow-up to those from agoraphobics treated in separate clinical trials, but more intensively and without spouses. Sinnott, Jones, Scott-Fordham, and Woodward (1981) also noted that agoraphobics treated as a group, who were all taken from the same neighborhood, were superior on many outcome measures to a group composed of agoraphobics from diverse geographical regions who presumably did not meet, socialize, or generally support each other during or after therapy. It seems likely that the reason for greater improvement lies in support and motivation for continued "practice" in facing feared situations between sessions and after treatment is over. Facilitation of practice between sessions may also account for the long-term success of indirect (imaginal) exposure or more gradual direct exposure when compared to more direct intensive exposure. This may explain Klein et al.'s (1983) observation that any therapy delivered in the context of a phobia clinic with implicit demands for facing feared situations or "practicing" should have some effect. Arranging conditions where agoraphobics are likely to continue to practice on their own may then result in continued improvement when compared to direct, intensive, short-term, therapist-accompanied treatments where gradual individual practice is not specifically taught, and dependence on the therapist may result (Jannoun et al., 1980). If facilitating practice and exposure between sessions is as important as it seems, then it may be helpful if another agoraphobic lives nearby; but the most logical motivating agent is the spouse, who is most intimately involved with the problem to begin with. Also, in view of the fact mentioned above that agoraphobia often arises during stressful situations, such as periods of marital disruption, including the spouse in treatment may produce an additional advantage by addressing some of the stressful interpersonal issues that may have contributed to initial panic as well as its maintenance.

Finally, more graduated, home-based treatments where patients proceed at their own pace within the context of a structured treatment program produce significantly less dropouts than the more intensive, prolonged, exposure *in vivo* or the pharmacological treatments. For example, Mathews et al. (1977), Jannoun et al. (1980), and our recent study, described below (Barlow, O'Brien, & Last, 1984), all recorded dropout rates of under 5%. This type of outcome statistic is often overlooked when one considers treatment efficacy, but is receiving increased attention from psychotherapy researchers (Barlow & Wolfe, 1981).

Interpersonal Context of Treatment

The growing evidence supporting practice between sessions as the critical therapeutic ingredient, no matter what one does during sessions, is paralleled by a growing research emphasis on the social context of agoraphobia, and, in particular, the relation of agoraphobia to marital adjustment. Evidence from this area also suggests possible detrimental effects of prolonged *in vivo* exposure.

For many years, of course, interpersonal relations and particularly marital relationships have been considered important in the development and maintenance of agoraphobia (Agulnik, 1970; Andrews, 1966; Fry, 1962; Goldstein, 1970; Goldstein & Chambless, 1978; Lazarus, 1966; Webster, 1953; Wolpe, 1970).

Goldstein and Chambless's (1978) conceptualization that "complex agoraphobia"—agoraphobia that is not secondary to a drug experience or physical disorder—virtually always develops in a climate of marked interpersonal conflict has received wide attention. Individuals with low levels of self-sufficiency experience conflict concerning a desire to escape from an unsatisfactory marriage on the one hand, and fears of independence on the other. This produces anxiety and panic. Although this reanalysis has not yet been empirically validated, it does seem to be consistent with the clinical picture of many female agoraphobics.

Some clinicians and researchers have also suggested that interpersonal factors, particularly the quality and pattern of the client's marriage, may have an important influence on the client's response to treatment and that, conversely, treatment-produced change in phobic symptomatology may significantly affect the client's marriage and other interpersonal relationships. For example, many clinicians report that husbands and/or marriages deteriorate with increased independence of the agoraphobic wife, resulting in problems such as suicidal attempts by husbands and extreme pressure on wives to return to their dependent role (Hafner, 1977; Hudson, 1974). In an interesting paper by Hafner (1979), he describes seven cases of agoraphobic women married to abnormally jealous men. Such men equate improvement of their wife with sexual infidelity (since they are now able to go out alone, they must be having affairs with other men). In these cases, also, improvement on the part of the wives was associated with increased morbidity in their husbands. Bland and Hallam (1981), however, reported that treating agoraphobia has little effect on marital adjustment *per se*, but Milton and Hafner (1979), looking at the effects of treatment on marital relationships, found that couples who were initially maritally dissatisfied did not improve in these areas. Thus, the picture is mixed when one examines the effects of treatment on marriages, although there are many concrete examples of harmful effects.

In examining the other side of this coin, Hafner (1977, 1979; Milton & Hafner, 1979) has presented evidence of the deleterious effect of marital problems on the response to behavioral treatments of agoraphobia. For example, Milton and Hafner (1979) reported that agoraphobics with unsatisfactory marriages, defined as those couples in the lower half of a median split on a measure of overall marital adjustment, were less likely than patients with satisfactory marriages to improve following intensive, prolonged, *in vivo* exposure treatment. Patients with unsatisfactory marriages were also more likely to relapse during the 6-month follow-up period. Similar results were reported by Bland and Hallam (1981), although Emmelkamp (1980) reported that levels of marital satisfaction did not seem to predict outcome. The implication here, of course, as noted by Bland and Hallam (1981), is that poor marriages may be associated with less favorable outcome since spouses may be less likely to provide spontaneous support and encouragement to their partners during treatment and follow-up and that clients may be less likely to accept such support even if offered.

What is common about the Bland and Hallam and the Hafner studies, as well as other clinical studies where marked deterioration in marriages and spouses' mental health have been noted after changes in agoraphobia (Hafner, 1977; Hudson, 1974), is that treatment was therapist-supervised, included prolonged exposure *in vivo*, and usually lasted no more than 2 weeks. Spouses were not involved in any way. This intensive intervention, particularly when completed in as little as 2 weeks, would seem inevitably to impact on any social system, particularly a marriage, and it is only common sense that this influence would be negative since major changes in the spouse's role, to which he has presumably become adapted, are occurring beyond his control. One possibility is that including spouses actively in treatment and spreading out treatment over a longer period of time to allow practice to occur between sessions may not only result in more substantial improvement in a greater number of clients, with further continuation of this improvement beyond therapy, but might also avoid resulting marital dissatisfaction so often observed previously.

During the past several years, through the support of the National Institute of Mental Health (NIMH), we have tested the effectiveness of a graduated, direct exposure treatment protocol that includes the husband as an active participant in treatment. This treatment consists of 12 sessions that take place in our clinic and are attended by groups of four or five agoraphobics and their husbands. Results from this clinical trial indicate that agoraphobics who engage in a self-paced, exposure-based treatment that was graduated in nature and without the direct participation of a therapist, did significantly better if their spouses were included, compared to a group treated identically without their spouses (Barlow, O'Brien, & Last, 1984). In this study, 86% (or 12 of a group of 14 clients treated in this manner) responded clinically, closely replicating the uncontrolled clinical trial reported by Mathews *et al.* (1977). Furthermore, as noted above, only 1 out of 28 clients dropped out of this treatment protocol, yielding a dropout rate of 3%. Finally, although data are still undergoing final analysis, the influence of this treatment on marital adjustment seems uniformly positive (O'Brien *et al.*, 1982). A detailed presentation of this treatment protocol, as applied to a composite of several women undergoing this treatment during the past several years in our clinic, comprises the remainder of this chapter.

THE CONTEXT OF THERAPY

Setting

Our treatment is delivered in a conveniently located phobia and anxiety disorders clinical setting. The majority of the actual patient contact takes place in a comfortable group therapy room with a capacity of approximately 15 people. Thus, the largest group that we see will consist of 6 agoraphobics and their spouses and 1 or 2 therapists, for a total of 14 people in the room at any one time. A location near a downtown area does have an advantage since one is able to assess the severity of agoraphobia in a standardized fashion. Since the middle 1960s (e.g., Agras, Leitenberg, & Barlow, 1968), we have asked agoraphobics to walk from what is, or has become, a safe place such as a clinic to an increasingly crowded downtown area. We first did this in Burlington, Vermont, but we have been able to arrange a similar course in every setting where we have treated agoraphobics. This type of arrangement is now common in phobia clinics, and will be described in more detail in the assessment section of this chapter, not only for assessment purposes but also as part of therapy. Naturally, many compromises must be made along the way. We have had clients with various physical disabilities who have been unable to walk, and therefore we have driven them into more frightening situations. Also, we have treated agoraphobics in rather rural settings where it has not been possible to walk to a more crowded area. Nevertheless, simply walking away from a safe place is often a useful assessment, and a setting where this can be arranged is helpful.

We have not limited our treatment settings to clinics or hospitals in which we were located. In at least one instance, an agoraphobic woman arranged for one of our staff to see a group of six agoraphobics in one of the meeting rooms of her church located in a small town. This was very convenient since all the agoraphobics lived within a mile of the church and could reach this destination if accompanied by their husbands or friends. The church also provided a convenient base from which to begin a walk into the village area.

Finally, regardless of the specific location of treatment, we have found it very helpful to make a home visit, whether the goals of treatment are clinical or clinical research. In our own treatment protocol, the home visit is an important measure of change, since we assess systematically the client's ability to accomplish five difficult tasks in her local neighborhood. This procedure is also described in the section on assessment. However, whether one is systematic about a home visit or not, something is often learned. For example, in one case a client who presented herself as suffering only moderately from agoraphobia was discovered to be unable to enter her back porch or even the far side of her kitchen. In fact, she was limited to moving around in two and a half rooms in her house. Since her husband did not come in to verify her initial report, her optimistic account of the severity of her agoraphobia might have gone undetected for a while, therefore hampering progress in therapy. In another case a woman was able to travel moderately within her neighborhood but was unable to enter a drugstore that was within one block of her home. After discovering this on the home visit, the woman reported that the configuration of fluorescent lights in the drugstore made entering impossible and, therefore, an extreme case of light sensitivity so often found clinically in agoraphobics became an important issue in treatment.

Clinically, of course, one is not too interested in how a client does at the clinic or surrounding area since, in most cases, he or she is unlikely to return there again. The primary and overriding goal in any therapy is to make a client comfortable and mobile in his or her own environment, and getting a "feel" for this environment, even if it is some distance away from the clinic or treatment setting, can be very helpful clinically.

Social Factors

Social factors, of course, are extremely important in our own approach to treatment since it is basically a couples treatment where the spouse is heavily involved. Some of the reasons for this were described in the introduction, and the actual process of this therapy will be described below, so we will not belabor those issues here. In clinical work, however, a spouse is not always available. In other cases a noncooperative spouse will not come to therapy, although this seems to be much rarer than one would expect. In these cases we try to enlist some other significant person in the client's environment. We do this for several reasons. First, there is evidence that attempting to carry out our protocol for any extended period of time, as is necessary, may not be effective in the absence of a helping partner (Holden, O'Brien, Barlow, Stetson, & Infantino, 1983). One option in these cases, of course, would be to bring the client to a clinic setting and do intensive, *in vivo* exposure. But we have already discussed the potential advantages of our treatment protocol. Therefore, we try to bring a "partner" in if we can. In some cases the partner has been an older child, usually someone 18 years or older. In almost all of the cases we have treated, where a child was involved, it was a mother–daughter combination where the mother was the agoraphobic. This mother–daughter partnership has worked quite well. Even in cases where the daughter works, we have found her to be motivated to accompany her mother on the various types of exercises described below in the section on intervention. If the agoraphobic is in a particularly distressed marital situation, a mature child also has the advantage of being aware of the family situation and working around it. Nevertheless, there are advantages in attempting to involve the noncooperative spouse if at all possible.

In another case, a woman in her late 50s who found it simply impossible to work with her husband, but whose marital adjustment was otherwise within normal limits, chose to work with a very close friend her own age. In this rather unusual case, the husband came to all sessions in the typical treatment protocol described below, but the friend accompanied the agoraphobic client for all practices. Much to our surprise, this worked out extremely well, and at a 3-year follow-up the woman, who was quite severe to begin with, had recovered completely. With the spouse in attendance, there is much more flexibility to work with the variety of issues that arise in a marriage relative to agoraphobia, but in a pinch someone else may do.

Patient Variables

The experimental analysis of patient variables that may be important in treatment is very new in the area of agoraphobia as it is in most areas of psychopathology, and therefore our knowledge is limited. What we do know, as described in the introduction, is that the typical agoraphobic is a woman with a somewhat passive personality with an onset of panic occuring in late adolescence or early adulthood in the context of some stressful situation. There are many atypical agoraphobics, however. In our own clinic the ratio of women to men runs as high as 90 : 10, in contrast to the usual 75 : 25 figure quoted in the literature. Other clinics also seem to report this 90 : 10 ratio (e.g., Goldstein, 1982). Nevertheless, we do treat males routinely. Since we do not get too many males in our clinic, at first we were reluctant to include one male in a group of four or five female agoraphobics. Previously we would wait until we had at least two males so they could keep each other company and so that their wives could utilize the group process to deal with issues that might be unique to wives of agoraphobic husbands. But we now treat males as they come into the clinic, even if they are the only male in the group, and we have found that this does not seem to present any particular problems.

A variety of patient variables have been hypothesized to influence the process or outcome of treatment. One important variable is the severity of depression in an agoraphobic client presenting for treatment. For example, Zitrin *et al.* (1980) noted that depression predicted a particularly poor outcome, and Foa, Steketee, and Milby (1980) have found that depression also affects outcome in obsessive compulsives. Nevertheless, in our own recently completed trial of couples treatment of agoraphobia (Barlow, O'Brien, & Last, 1984) we did not find that level of depression (as measured by the Beck Depression Inventory) predicted outcome. In this experiment severely depressed women, that is, with scores over 30 on the Beck Depression Inventory, did as well as those with little or no depression. Thus it would not be possible to say at this time that severe depression would contraindicate treatment.

Another variable thought to influence outcome is marital adjustment, and this literature has been discussed in the introduction. Naturally, couples treatment of agoraphobia deals directly with this particular issue. Finally, a body of literature is developing that discusses individual differences in agoraphobics in terms of their somatic versus experiential experience of anxiety (Barlow, Mavissakalian, & Schofield, 1980; Lang, 1968; Vermilyea, Boice, & Barlow, in press). When these two response systems diverge, that is, if treatment decreases subjective or experiential aspects of anxiety but not physiological or somatic aspects, then the client is said to be demonstrating desynchrony between response systems. In clinical research the most common pattern of desynchrony seems to be continued high physiological or autonomic nervous system responding, accompanied by reports of decreased fear measured subjectively. Some investigators think that this may predict relapse (Barlow *et al.*, 1980; Grey, Rachman, & Sartory, 1981). Nevertheless, there is no firm evidence at this time. However, in our own recent trial (Barlow, O'Brien, & Last, 1984), we have five clients who could be considered failures since they improved either very little or not at all. At least three of these clients continually complained of somatic sensations that they found intolerable. Their somatic complaints did not seem qualitatively different from the usual and customary agoraphobic concerns over heart attacks, and the like, but they did seem to differ in intensity. It is possible that this subgroup of agoraphobic patients may need a direct therapeutic attack on the somatic aspects of their anxiety using, for example, relaxation therapy intensively delivered or possibly even pharmacological agents. This question also awaits further scientific inquiry.

Therapist Variables

Very little can be said about therapist variables at this time. In one study (Jannoun *et al.*, 1980) therapist differences were found in the treatment of agoraphobia, but it was not clear just what the differences were. In our own clinic we routinely substitute inexperienced therapists for experienced therapists in the course of our treatment protocol, so that one therapist might run the first three sessions and a second therapist run the second three sessions, depending on availability, scheduling, and so on. While we have not evaluated this strategy systematically, we cannot see any differences clinically and we get few if any complaints from the patients as long as they are aware that this will be happening and they know who the therapists are. For this reason we try to have all people who may act as therapists attend the first session, with future attendance dependent on schedules. Naturally, some facility at working with couples would seem necessary in our treatment protocol, but none of our therapists is considered to be an expert in marital therapy.

ASSESSMENT

Classification

Recognizing an agoraphobic does not seem to be particularly difficult. Recently we have developed a structured interview, the Anxiety Disorders Interview Schedule (ADIS), for diagnosing the major anxiety disorders as outlined in DSM-III (DiNardo, O'Brien, Barlow, Waddell, & Blanchard, 1983). Of all of the major anxiety disorders in DSM-III, a classification of agoraphobia with panic attacks was agreed upon most often by two clinicians in our clinic interviewing a patient independently on two different occasions. The kappa statistic was .857, which is very high indeed. While clinicians in practice would not routinely want to administer this structured interview, which was designed primarily to differentially diagnose subcategories of anxiety disorders as well as to rule out affective disorders and other major problems, those working in phobia or anxiety disorder clinics may well wish to adopt some of the carefully worded questioning developed in this interview over the period of a year.[2]

One of the reasons the diagnosis is fairly straightforward is that agoraphobia is particularly well defined in terms of initial classification in DSM-III. The criteria are as follows: (1) The individual has marked fear of, and thus avoids being alone or in, public places from which escape might be difficult or help not available in case of sudden incapacitation (e.g., crowds, tunnels, bridges, public transportation); (2) there is increasing constriction in normal activities until the

---

2. Copies of the Anxiety Disorder Interview Schedule (ADIS) along with instructions for its use are available at cost from the Phobia and Anxiety Disorders Clinic, 1535 Western Avenue, Albany, NY 12203.

fears or avoidance behavior dominate the individual's life; (3) the symptoms are not due to a major depressive episode, obsessive–compulsive disorder, paranoid personality disorder, or schizophrenia (American Psychiatric Association, 1980). In DSM-III agoraphobia is subdivided into two categories; specifically, agoraphobia with panic attacks and agoraphobia without panic attacks. A panic attack is defined as the occurrence of a "rush" of anxiety accompanied by specific physiological sensations (e.g., palpitations, difficulty breathing, paresthesias). One usually looks for the panic to reach a peak fairly quickly (i.e., 15 min or less). In addition, these attacks are likely to occur, at least some of the time, unpredictably; that is, without the "trigger" of a phobic stimulus or stressor. In the following paragraphs we will say a bit more about determining the presence of panic as well as how to assess it. Suffice it to say that recognizing panic does not seem to present a problem, and when questioned most patients will readily recognize what you are talking about. On the other hand, recent evidence indicates that panic is an ubiquitous phenomenon occurring at least occasionally across all anxiety disorders as well as major affective disorders (Barlow, 1983; Barlow, Blanchard, Vermilyea, Vermilyea, & DiNardo, 1984).

In fact, in our clinic we almost never see an agoraphobic without features of panic. Out of 41 agoraphobics seen during a period of 1 year in our clinic, only 1 fit the diagnosis of agoraphobia without panic attacks, and even this particular classification was questionable. Other phobia and anxiety disorder clinics around the country are reporting the same results. Do not expect to see too many agoraphobics without panic.

Although agoraphobia seems to be easy to recognize, there are still some problems with assessment. Many people that we see in our clinic seem to have the features of agoraphobia with panic, but have only limited avoidance behavior. For example, one client in our clinic recently reported that she was able to get around pretty well, particularly if a friend accompanied her, but she was unable to drive outside of a 5-mile radius surrounding her home. In this case avoidance was not widespread, nor were most normal activities constricted, but there was a very specific pattern of avoidance. It is always possible that someone like this might be classified as a simple driving phobic rather than an agoraphobic. The difference here is that a driving phobic is afraid of having a panic attack while driving. Fortunately it does not make too much difference for behavioral clinicians who will then proceed with their behavioral analysis and design an individualized treatment, determining along the way if more "agoraphobic-like" behaviors and emotions appear. The more usual case is that a patient will present with extremely variable patterns of avoidance and anxiety. That is, several months ago they were really doing well, whereas at present they have an increasing pattern of avoidance that is making it difficult for them to even go to work. Often this variable pattern of avoidance occurs against a background of chronic anxiety with occasional panics, and at times it is difficult to decide whether the proper classification is agoraphobia with panic, or generalized anxiety disorder, or panic disorder. This distinction would be fairly important, because presently the psychosocial interventions for these disorders are quite different. For generalized anxiety disorder or panic disorder a combination of relaxation and cognitive therapy has the most empirical support at this time (e.g., Barlow, Cohen, *et al.*, 1984), while for agoraphobia you would concentrate more on the avoidance behavior utilizing panic management procedures, as described below in the section on intervention. The key, once again, is determining whether a fear of panic resulting in avoidance behavior is the major problem at present.

Another common coexisting problem in agoraphobics is depression. Nevertheless, as noted above, we have not found depression, even in fairly severe form, to interfere with response to our particular treatment described in this chapter. Others have, however (e.g., Zitrin *et al.*, 1980), and clinicians may want to make a judgment on whether a severe primary depression should be treated before tackling the agoraphobia or *vice versa*. One aspect that we consider in making this decision is the chronology as well as the severity of the two disorders. If a severe primary depression had its onset well before the onset of the agoraphobia, then one might consider dealing with the depression first to see if the agoraphobia lifts on its own; sometimes this happens clinically, although there is not too much data on the relationship between these disorders. On the other hand, if the agoraphobia preceded the depression, then it would seem clinically logical to treat the agoraphobia first.

With these considerations in mind, it is possible to begin the process of assessing agoraphobia. Following initial classification as determined during an interview, there is always the process of behavioral analysis. While classification will give the clinician some very good clues on what specific aspects of problematic behaviors to assess, the behavioral analysis is the actual process of assessing each client individually as they appear rather than assuming that every client stereotypically fits the features as described in the broad and general classification schema. This process is outlined in detail in a recent book (Barlow, 1981; Nelson & Barlow, 1981). For purposes of this chapter, behavioral assessment simply means that each client's behavior is carefully observed, measured, and analyzed. More importantly, relationships between these problematic behaviors and environmental or organismic variables that may be maintaining them are continually sought. This is really something that most clinicians do anyway; it is just that behavioral assessment and analysis formalizes the process and ensures a continuing close interaction between the process of assessment and treatment until the case is terminated.

Another hallmark of behavioral assessment is a comprehensive approach to measuring problems that occur in what has been termed the three major response systems. These response systems are commonly referred to as behavioral or motoric, cognitive or subjective, and physiological or somatic (Barlow, 1981; Lang, 1968, 1977). In phobia in general, and agoraphobia in particular, the application is particularly clear. The behavior one must carefully assess is avoidance behavior, the subjective or cognitive features of agoraphobia include reports of and the experience of fear, while the physiological or somatic component refers most often to autonomic nervous system reactivity accompanying fear, such as increased heart rate, respiration, and other physiological signs of arousal. Behavioral assessment, then, looks at all three of these components of fear as they relate to each other and as they relate to particular features of each individual's environment. For example, and as illustrated below, two patients meeting the general classification of agoraphobia may present with very different sets of problems depending on their individual life circumstances. An elderly woman living in a third-floor walk-up in an urban area will obviously have different problems with different goals for treatment than a male with a large family living in a rural area who must drive 30 miles round trip to work each day. With these considerations in mind, it is possible to outline the actual steps of assessment, beginning with the specifics of the clinical interview.

The Clinical Interview

We have already mentioned the existence of the ADIS. Once again, administration of this schedule would not be necessary in every clinical setting, particularly those settings where clinicians are seeing patients with a wide variety of disorders. Nevertheless, we will recommend some of the specific questions from this structured interview that pertain to agoraphobics. Naturally, some special considerations apply when interviewing potential agoraphobics as opposed to other disorders. Agoraphobics will most often be terrified of the first interview. For those patients who have difficulty leaving their house in order to come to a clinic or office setting, they will anticipate this visit for hours, days, or even weeks in advance. We have had patients who have tried to get to our clinic only to turn around and go back home after coming within sight of the door. Most often these people have to be accompanied by a spouse or friend, and this alone will require some special logistical considerations in getting them to the interview. Occasionally we will make a home visit to do the first interview, but we try to avoid this if at all possible since we are at a considerable advantage if it is demonstrated that the patient can make it to the clinic.

Therapy often begins during the first 10 min of this initial interview, when some clients will report experiencing a "full-blown" panic. Naturally the experienced clinician will interrupt the proceedings only to say that he or she is well aware of how the client is feeling before continuing on with specific questions and will make every attempt to get the client to focus on the material at hand. While it may appear that the clinician is simply proceeding with the interview, the secondary purpose of diverting the patient's attention from the panic to questions of the moment will have its therapeutic effect.

In terms of the structure of the initial interview, we have recommended the graduated funnel approach (Nelson & Barlow, 1981) for obtaining information. This approach initially involves asking relatively global questions about many areas of the individual's life, including such topics as presenting complaints, existence of other problems, history, and functioning in major areas such as family, marital relationships, and so on. Following the initial broad inquiry, the interviewer gradually focuses on and asks more detailed questions about issues and problems that have been identified as requiring further information. As any clinician knows, it is not at all uncommon to discover that the client's initial complaints are not his or her primary concerns, but that more serious problems exist in other areas of functioning. In the special case of agoraphobia, occasionally clients will present with agoraphobia when, in fact, a severe obsesssional process, a psychotic process, or perhaps even unrelated substance abuse is more prominent.

To assess for agoraphobia, we use the sequence of questions from the ADIS (DiNardo *et al.*, 1983) shown in Figure 1-1. (The ADIS is continually undergoing revision and this is a sample of the current version.) The first series of questions assesses for this existence of panic with the potential of establishing a diagnosis of panic disorder; these are followed by the agoraphobia section of the interview.

Once the interviewer establishes the strong possibility of an agoraphobic problem, several other areas should be covered during the initial interview. These areas usually involve issues that are frequently correlated with phobic and agoraphobic disorders. While exploring the specific patterns and severity of avoidance behaviors, one should be particularly concerned about the degree of reliance on a safe place or a safe person, with particular emphasis on the identity of this person or these people who are considered safe. Most often it is a spouse, but occasionally it is another family member or a friend. A "safe" person, of course, means that the agoraphobic feels comfortable in going places with this person that would be impossible to go to either alone or with other people not considered safe. Usually, of course, a person is considered "safe" because he or she knows about the agoraphobia, and even if he or she does not approve, as is the case with some spouses, the agoraphobic feels that this person would take the agoraphobic to the hospital or be able to help in some way if the agoraphobic were incapacitated by panic. Another issue in examining the pattern of avoidance behavior is the variability across time, which is examined directly in the interview. Almost all agoraphobics report that they experience good days on which they are more active and avoid less as well as bad days when they may end up totally housebound. Many female clients report that they are at their worst immediately before or during menstruation. In fact, this seems to us clinically to be part of a pattern where the occurrence of any heightened physiological sensations, for whatever reason, in men or women may bring the possibility of impending panic to mind and therefore increase general levels of anticipatory anxiety.

One problem that is quite variable across agoraphobics is depersonalization or derealization (feelings of unreality on the ADIS). In our experience, only a minority of agoraphobics report this problem, but when they do, it is usually reported as the prominent feature of panic and often requires some special therapeutic attention. Finally, every clinician will want to examine the pattern of cognitions associated with panic and avoidance behavior. Initial questions on this topic are specified on the ADIS. For agoraphobics, several issues frequently arise. First of all, despite the increasing publicity given to agoraphobia in popular magazines and newspapers, many agoraphobics have avoided seeking

FIGURE 1-1. Panic disorder and agoraphobia sections of the Anxiety Disorders Interview Schedule.

PANIC DISORDER

1. (Have you had times when you have felt a sudden rush of intense fear or anxiety or feeling of impending doom?)

YES   NO

If YES, or if there is any uncertainty about the existence of panics, continue inquiry. Otherwise skip to Generalized Anxiety Disorder.

How long on the average does it take for the rush of anxiety to peak? _____
(in minutes)

How long does the panic last on the average? _____
(in minutes)

Frequency of Panics

(In the past year, how many panics have you had?) _____

(When were they most frequent this year?) _____

(During the period when they were most frequent, how frequent were they?) _____

_____

(When were they the most frequent ever?) _____

(How frequent were they then?) _____

(During the past month, how frequent have they been?) _____

Severity/Symptoms of Panics

Then ask the severity for each symptom at each of the time periods above. (For example: Have you experienced dyspnea [difficulty breathing] during these attacks in the past month? How severe was it? How about in the past year when the attacks were the most frequent [not past month?]? How severe was it then? How about during the time the panics were the most frequent ever? How severe?) Continue inquiry with each symptom and rate severity on a 0–4 scale.

0	1	2	3	4
/	/	/	/	/
None	Mild	Moderate	Severe	Very severe/ grossly impaired

Panic Attacks: Rate symptoms using the scale above.

Past year	Most frequent	Past month	
_____	_____	_____	Dyspnea—difficulty breathing
_____	_____	_____	Palpitations
_____	_____	_____	Chest pain or discomfort
_____	_____	_____	Choking or smothering sensations
_____	_____	_____	Dizziness, vertigo, or unsteady feelings
_____	_____	_____	Feelings of unreality
_____	_____	_____	Paresthesias—tingling or prickling sensations
_____	_____	_____	Hot or cold flashes
_____	_____	_____	Sweating
_____	_____	_____	Faintness
_____	_____	_____	Trembling or shaking
_____	_____	_____	Fear of dying, going crazy, or doing something uncontrolled during an attack

(What thoughts do you have before/during?) _____

_____

Situations in Which Panic Occurs

(In what situation(s) have you had these feelings?) _____

_____

(continued)

FIGURE 1-1. (*Continued*)

If patient indicates situation-specific panics (public speaking, driving, heights, etc.), further inquiry is necessary to assess presence of panics that occur while at home alone or unpredictably in a variety of situations.
(Have you had these feelings come "from out the blue" or in situations where you did not expect them to occur?) _____

2. *History*
   (Tell me about your first panic.)
   (When did it happen?) _____
   (Where were you?) _____
   (With whom?) _____
   (How did it start?) _____

   (Where you under any life stress? What was happening in your life at the time?) _____

   (Do you remember having similar feelings (perhaps milder) any time before this?) _____

   (Describe your *worst* panic attack?) (What made it the *worst* attack?) _____

3. (Have you had periods when you didn't have them, either because you could control them or you didn't worry about them?)
   If YES,

(When?) from–to (month and year)	(What was going on in your life? How did you get over it?) That is, Did stressor let up or did person develop coping strategy?	(How did they come back? Changes in life circumstances?) Stressor-related?

4. (How do you handle the panics now?) _____

AGORAPHOBIA
(Do you feel panicky in any situations, or avoid them because you might be unable to leave in case you felt faint or panicky?)

YES   NO

Specify range of activity (e.g., time spent in situation, how often, distance from home) and factors affecting ability to enter or stay. Specify range of activity when alone and when accompanied and write in spaces provided. Use scale below to rate fear and avoidance.

0	1	2	3	4
/	/	/	/	/
No avoidance or escape; no fear or anxiety	Occasional avoidance or escape; mild fear	Moderate avoidance—may enter alone; moderate fear	Severe avoidance—rarely alone, must be accompanied; severe fear	Very severe avoidance—never enters even with safe person; very severe fear and panic

(How much fear do you experience in these situations?) (How often do you avoid such situations?)

			Rating	
	Range of activity alone	Range of activity accompanied	Fear	Avoidance
Driving				
Riding in car				
Grocery stores				
Mall				
Crowds				
Public transportation				
Bus				
Plane				
Taxi				
Waiting in line				
Walking (how far?)				
Elevators				
Being at home				
Public places				
Movies				
Restaurants				
Theaters				
Auditoriums				
Church				
Enclosed places				
Tunnels				
Small rooms				
Open spaces				
Parks				
Squares				
Work				
Other				
Other				

If no evidence of fear and avoidance of any of these situations is obtained, skip to Simple Phobia.

Note any special conditions, objects, or rituals that patient uses to enable himself or herself to enter feared situations: carrying items such as a bottle of beer or soda, medication, special objects such as books, printed relaxation instructions, umbrellas, or other objects; or avoiding certain foods and drinks.

(Are there any sorts of things you carry with you, or things you do just before going out that help you feel more comfortable?) _____

(continued)

FIGURE 1-1. (*Continued*)

(What do you feel will happen to you if you are stuck in a situation that you commonly avoid?) Heart attack, stroke, pass out, scream, go crazy, lose control, embarrass self, etc. _____

(What do you usually do when you have a panic attack or high anxiety?) Escape, call for help, stick it out, never go anywhere that might create anxiety, etc. _____

(Do you have fluctuations in where and how far you can go due to things like:) Specify and get example; specify if better or worse.

Time of day _____   Sickness/illness _____
Day of week _____   High stress _____
Interpersonal conflict _____   Other _____
(Do you have a "safe person"?) _____ Who? _____

History and Course
This information may overlap with information obtained under Panic Disorder. If it overlaps, note where information may be found.
(When did you first begin avoiding these situations?) _____

(Do you remember the first time that you felt you couldn't go into _____ or had to get out?) (Where were you?) _____

(Whom were you with?) _____
(How did you feel?) Check for panic. _____

If PANIC: (Had you had any panicky feelings prior to this?) _____

(Were you experiencing any life stesses at the time?) _____

(Have there been periods in your life since this first time when you could enter these situations without panic or in spite of it?)

Check for remission, exacerbations, and precipitants.

Period	(What was going on in life: how did you get over it?)	(What happened when it came back?)

If there have been remissions, precipitant of current episode:
(How did the problem get started again?) _____

out health professionals because they think that they are the only person in the world with such symptoms and fears and that diagnosis will mean very quick institutionalization in the nearest state hospital. Once relieved of this concern, thoughts of impending catastrophic consequences associated with anxiety and panic most often fall into one or two categories. First, some agoraphobics will report that if they fall prey to their panic while away from their safe place or person, they will eventually lose control and "go crazy" or "go insane." Second, others report that the ultimate catastrophic consequence is severe physical problems, usually a "heart attack" followed by death.

Finally, the most important part of the assessment, as mentioned above, is a determination of the functional relationship between avoidance behaviors, cognitive patterns, and the experience of anxiety on the one hand and associated internal or external cues on the other hand. This is the well-known "functional analysis" in which maladaptive behaviors and feelings are related to specific events, resulting in an individual and idiosyncratic pattern of responses. It is this determination, over and above the initial classification, that is necessary for the clinician to individually tailor a standardized set of therapy principles to the patient who is undergoing assessment. This goal is achieved through the administration of the following more or less standard set of assessment instruments.

Self-Report Measures

Fear and Avoidance Hierarchy

Following directly from the clinical interview, an idiosyncratic fear and avoidance hierarchy of 10 situations is developed in our clinic with each patient, and we strongly recommend this procedure whenever agoraphobics are treated clinically since it forms one of the most convenient ways of assessing progress from the point of view of the patient. This hierarchy is usually constructed at the second session after the initial interview, and in our clinic is combined with one of the behavioral measures—the behavioral walk—to be described later in this discussion. This hierarchy, in fact, will also play a prominent role in treatment since items from it will be assigned for "homework" during treatment. The patient is not specifically informed of this beforehand, however, since the explanation will be accompanied by a complete rationale for treatment and since prior information might cause the patient to withhold reporting difficult items in his or her environment for fear of being "forced" to do the items before he or she is ready. In developing the hierarchy, the clinician should utilize information from the structured interview as well as from the patient's report during his or her appointment. The clinician may begin by saying, "I know from your last interview that you're having difficulty getting to a number of places. Could you tell me some of the things that you would like to do that are currently difficult or impossible for you?" Generally the patient will then list places or tasks that he or she is unable to go to or complete, but which the patient feels should be part of his or her daily life. The clinician then uses these reports, as well as items noted during the interview, to develop 10 items or situations that have particular relevance for the patient. For example, if the patient wanted to be able to go to the local mall and also felt that he or she should be able to do the grocery shopping, or go to a small store a few blocks from home, all of these items would be included. Ultimately all of these items would be rated on a scale of 0–8, where 0 represents no anxiety and 8 represents the probability of extreme anxiety and panic. One of the items lower on the hierarchy might be driving to a small store only two blocks from home and then back again. For others, in order to derive items that will be rated a 2 or 3 on the hierarchy, simply walking outside the door and down to the end of the front walk might be sufficient. Items higher in the hierarchy may include traveling longer distances and/or visiting places that are typically crowded, such as malls or restaurants during the lunch hour. Other typically difficult items are waiting in lines at banks or at checkout counters in grocery stores. It is very important to have a wide variety of items, in terms of anxiety ratings, on the hierarchy. For very severe patients, it might be necessary to break down individual trips to get a variety of anxiety ratings. For example, if simply walking down the front walk would be rated a 3, then walking or driving half way to a nearby small store may be a 5, going into the store may be a 6 or a 7, and so on. Thus, each step involved in "getting there" must be included. By breaking the items down more thoroughly, clients will not have a sense of failure from attempting items that are too difficult for them too early in treatment. On the other hand, it is also important to include the most difficult items on the severe end of the hierarchy that will comprise some of the ultimate important goals for the patient.

One must be careful to only include items in this hierarchy that can, in fact, be accomplished during routine practice sessions and do not depend on external circumstances. Therefore, one should try not to include items such as shopping during the Christmas rush, going on vacation, or going to the movies, which depend on time of year or the schedule of a movie theater. Other items that are dependent on circumstances may include attending a neighbor's party or going to dinner at a friends. Naturally, these items will be addressed during treatment as they arise, but should not be part of this initial hierarchy.

Patients often have difficulty compiling this hierarchy for a number of reasons, and therefore it must be constructed with the help of the therapist. However, after a bit of initial practice most therapists are able to accomplish this goal in as little as 20 minutes. An example of a typical hierarchy developed for the case to be described is presented later in this chapter (see Figure 1-3, p. 33).

Weekly Records

Critically important both for research purposes and clinically, weekly records are the self-monitoring of information on the type and amount of outside activity that patients are involved in each day. Not only do these weekly records serve as tangible evidence of improvement, but they also highlight areas where additional work is needed. Agoraphobics, in general, tend to catastrophize and minimize gains, thereby becoming easily discouraged. If the therapist has a record of actual improvement, this can then be used in a very positive way in therapy to point out important gains.

We provide a form for our patients on which they can keep this information, which we call the "Weekly Record." These particular forms were worked out after several years of trial and error in order to make it as easy as possible for the agoraphobic to provide all of the clinically relevant information. These forms, as we actually use them in our clinic, are presented later in this chapter (see Figures 1-4 and 1-5, pp. 34, 35, and 37).

Once again, if it is at all clinically feasible, the importance of this self-monitoring is apparent. Time and time again in our own clinical work, accurate record keeping by the agoraphobic at the time of the activity, or at least on the same day, has provided important information that often seems routine to the patient and/or his or her spouse or family member and therefore is not reported at weekly sessions. Provision of this information helps the clinician to do the most thorough job, along with the patient, in overcoming all of the individualized aspects of the agoraphobic problem in that patient's own environment. Naturally there are occasional problems when clients cannot seem to fit in the duties involved in filling out the form on a daily basis, although we have found that this occurs only in a small minority in our clinic. Our way of handling this is first to emphasize the importance of the daily record at the initial session. Second, we have at least 1 and sometimes 2 weeks of practice with the forms during assessment before treatment begins. Third, we examine systematically the records as they are handed in, particularly during the first few weeks, and provide detailed, corrective feedback on the accuracy and completeness of the record at the time of the session, highlighting in a very positive way full compliance with the record-keeping activity. For more detailed information on the incorporation of self-monitoring into all aspects of clinical practice see Barlow, Hayes, and Nelson (1984).

Questionnaires

For research purposes, we also administer a number of paper-and-pencil questionnaires that we find useful. These, of course, are very helpful and easy to administer periodically, and we recommend several for routine inclusion in any treatment program for agoraphobia. Foremost among these would be the Fear Questionnaire (Marks & Mathews, 1979). This questionnaire is a very brief, one-page form that yields three major scale scores where one can examine relative severity of phobic response as compared to some standardized norms. The three scales are agoraphobia, social phobia, and blood and injury phobia. This questionnaire is reproduced in Figure 1-2.

Filling out this questionnaire initially provides the clinician with yet another vantage point for classification and initial assessment, and filling it out after treatment provides further objective evidence of extent of improvement. Since many agoraphobics are depressed, we also administer routinely the Beck

FIGURE 1-2. Fear Questionnaire.

Name: _____ Age: _____ Sex: _____ Date: _____

Choose a number from the scale below to show how much you would avoid each of the situations listed below because of fear or other unpleasant feelings. Then write the number you chose in the box opposite each situation.

0	1	2	3	4	5	6	7	8

Would not avoid it		Slightly avoid it		Definitely avoid it		Markedly avoid it		Always avoid it

1. Main phobia you want treated (describe in your own words) .... □
2. Injections or minor surgery .... □
3. Eating or drinking with other people .... □
4. Hospitals .... □
5. Traveling alone by bus or coach .... □
6. Walking alone in busy streets .... □
7. Being watched or stared at .... □
8. Going into crowded shops .... □
9. Talking to people in authority .... □
10. Sight of blood .... □
11. Being criticized .... □
12. Going alone far from home .... □
13. Thought of injury or illness .... □
14. Speaking or acting to an audience .... □
15. Large open spaces .... □
16. Going to the dentist .... □
17. Other situations (describe) .... □

Leave blank → □ □ □ □
Ag + Bl + Soc = Total
2-16

Now choose a number from the scale below to show how much you are troubled by each problem listed, and write the number in the box opposite.

0	1	2	3	4	5	6	7	8

Hardly at all		Slightly troubled		Definitely troubled				Very severely troubled

18. Feeling miserable or depressed .... □
19. Feeling irritable or angry .... □
20. Feeling tense or panicky .... □
21. Upsetting thoughts coming into your mind .... □
22. Feeling you or your surroundings are strange or unreal .... □
23. Other feelings (describe) .... □

□ Total

How would you rate the present state of your phobic symptoms on the scale below? Circle one number between 0 and 8.

0	1	2	3	4	5	6	7	8

No phobias present		Slightly disturbing/ not really disabling		Definitely disturbing/ disabling		Markedly disturbing/ disabling		Very severely disturbing/ disabling

Depression Inventory (Beck, Ward, Mendelson, Mock, & Erbaugh, 1961). We felt that treating agoraphobia almost always has a large and positive effect on depression, as reflected by major decreases in scores on the Beck Depression Inventory. This form is very easy to administer, is available in most clinicians' offices, and is useful for monitoring levels of depression. Finally, since one of the major purposes of our clinical program is to look at the marital context of agoraphobia, we administer a number of self-report and direct observational measures of marital status. This would not be necessary for most clinicians, who would probably nevertheless want to administer at least one questionnaire of marital adjustment since, as noted above, this seems important clinically. The measure most widely in use these days is the Dyadic Adjustment Scale (see Spanier, 1976), which gives a good idea of overall marital adjustment. The cutoff score in common use for discriminating a relatively poorly adjusted marriage from a better adjusted one is a mean score of 97 for the husband's and wife's ratings. Any score below this may indicate that the therapist will have to keep a close eye on marital issues during treatment. Since there is, as yet, no evidence of the interaction of personality variables with the treatment of agoraphobia, we do not utilize any personality tests. Naturally, this may change in the future if research demonstrates that different personality types or disorders predict outcome.

Behavioral and Physiological Measures

We have already described the behavioral walk taken by all of our clients as a standardized behavioral measure of severity of agoraphobia. Once again, we find this a useful exercise since most clients do much better on this behavioral walk than they estimate they will do before attempting it. It provides a ready assessment of how anxiety is experienced so that the therapist can examine in some detail, after the walk is over, for relative presence of somatic versus cognitive aspects of anxiety, and the like. Furthermore, it does not consume a great deal of time and therefore is easy to implement if the clinic or treatment location is in a suitable area.

Nevertheless, of the two behavioral measures we employ, we would have to say that clinically the more important is the home visit. This assessment was referred to above, and the reasons for its importance need not be belabored here. In our setting the second session of the assessment process is devoted to the behavioral walk as well as the construction of the hierarchy. This then sets the stage for the home visit, which occurs during the third session. Since the hierarchy has already been constructed and consists of situations in the patient's home environment, items for the home visit are chosen from this hierarchy of 10 situations. For the last several years we have chosen five of these situations that represent a range of activities but yet can be accomplished in a period of 1 hr to 1½ hr. Once again, examining the hierarchy presented above, items actually chosen for the home visit in the case described later in this chapter included items 2, 6, 8, 9, and 10, since these represented a range of activities but were easily attempted. Naturally, after each item is attempted, careful examination of how the client experiences anxiety provides a great deal of information. Hierarchy items always specify whether the agoraphobic is accompanied or not. For most patients, it makes a great deal of difference whether they do something accompanied or alone, and the therapist is always a "safe" person. Therefore, ratings of anxiety are greatly affected.

In terms of procedures, patients are told to attempt only those items that they are willing to, with instructions that they may stop at any time. It is very rare for patients to refuse to attempt at least some of the hierarchy items, and this is not typically viewed as a highly aversive assessment procedure, even though anxiety may escalate markedly during the tasks. For scoring purposes, 1 represents a refusal to attempt the task, 2 indicates an attempt followed by an escape, and 3 means the task was completed. As with the behavioral walk, patients are always asked for anxiety ratings on a 0–8 scale. Clients report both the average rating for the task as well as the maximum rating experienced during the task. These ratings as well as the number of items completed can also be compared to the patient's posttreatment performance as another measure of improvement.

The physiological assessment in our clinic is conducted using a portable pulsemeter during the behavioral walk (see Holden & Barlow, 1984; Vermilyea *et al.*, in press). Since this portable pulsemeter connects directly onto the upper abdominal area, with leads appropriately placed to pick up heart rate, it is very convenient for recording ambulatory heart rate. We provide a permanent record of this heart rate by connecting up this relatively inexpensive pulsemeter to a small microcassette recorder which, along with the pulsemeter itself, is carried in a pocket or purse. Nevertheless, we will not describe this procedure further since at the present time there is only preliminary evidence, noted above, that physiological measures such as heart rate during anxiety-provoking tasks are correlated in any way with outcome. Other difficulties, however, make the use of these measures problematic at this point in time (Holden & Barlow, 1984). We would expect further information to be available within the next 2–3 years.

TREATMENT

Treatment in our clinic is conducted according to a fairly detailed treatment protocol developed for clinical research purposes. This protocol is derived from research findings from around the world suggesting treatments or treatment components that contribute to long-term success in dealing with agoraphobia. Much of this literature was reviewed at the beginning of the chapter.

Specifically, our treatment protocol consists of eight weekly 90-min group discussion sessions followed by four biweekly 90-min group discussion sessions, for a total of 16 weeks. All of these weekly group sessions are attended by both the agoraphobic and his or her spouse or, as noted above, occasionally another relative or close friend. Naturally there are occasions when one or the other partner cannot make the session. But at the beginning of treatment we make a point of describing the format for the treatment sessions and ensuring that everyone can make every session, barring unforseen emergencies.

The basic component of treatment, of course, is a prearranged schedule of exposure or confrontation with difficult situations. For reasons described above this is not done in a prolonged way or intensely, but is best characterized as a self-initiated, graduated exposure carried out with the help of the spouse or partner entirely in the client's own environment. We ask the spouse (or the partner) to come because there is now evidence that the effects of treatment are facilitated by this working together on overcoming agoraphobic fears (Barlow, O'Brien, & Last, 1984) and that significant obstacles to the program can be overcome if a helpful therapeutic agent exists in the client's own environment. The transcript below will illustrate the variety of relationship issues that arise as one tries to deal with this very difficult problem.

Finally, as noted above, the very graduated nature of the exposure-based exercises and the presence of a therapeutic agent in the environment seem to combine to ensure compliance with the program, reduce dropouts to a minimum, and facilitate progress past the point of termination of formal treatment sessions. For this reason, all patients are told that treatment will actually take 1 year, although we will only be meeting in groups during the first 16 weeks. This helps them to avoid the expectation that they should be "cured" at the end of 16 weeks (which was an expectation our patients had before we instituted the "1 year" instructions no matter how often we discouraged it) and to instill very early the notion that the couple will be continuing to work on the problem after group sessions are over.

Of course, it should be possible to treat the couple "alone." Nevertheless, there is evidence in the literature on the facilitative and supportive nature of groups, and our own clinical experience indicates that these agoraphobic women often become fast friends, calling each other frequently and generally providing additional support to each other as they go about conquering their fears. Occasionally this is not the case. In our initial 14 women treated with their husbands (Barlow, O'Brien, & Last, 1984), one of the failures reported feeling very much out of place in the group. It is possible that she would have done better with individualized treatment.

Finally, in addition to arranging for exposure exercises dealing with issues of compliance and instilling appropriate therapeutic expectations, some additional techniques are present in our protocol. The first is cognitive restructuring, which in our protocol combines the use of self-statement training (Meichenbaum, 1977), and paradoxical intention (Ascher, 1980). These methods are well known to most clinicians and will be illustrated in detail in the case transcript as they are used with agoraphobics. As previously noted, there is, of course, no evidence that these techniques contribute in any clinically significant way to the treatment of agoraphobia, but we are not sure that all the evidence is in, since it is very difficult area to investigate indeed (Last, Barlow, & O'Brien, 1984). Furthermore, our patients seem to derive great comfort clinically from use of the cognitive procedures, and therefore we are continuing to include them for the time being. Another series of techniques to be found in the following illustration can be classified as panic management procedures, such as deep breathing through the nose, to be used when panic occurs. Once again, these procedures have not been evaluated specifically for their contributions to treatment. Including them as part of the treatment protocol, however, seems to increase compliance with the exposure exercises for at least some of our patients, since they report that they feel at least somewhat more in control if panic occurs.

Treatment Protocol Outline

In this section a brief outline of the treatment protocol is presented. The actual illustration of the application of this protocol will occur in the next section. During the first session introductions are made, and each client is invited to report general background information about his or her problem, discussing both when the experiences of agoraphobic problems or panic attacks began and how he or she is currently functioning. Spouses are also invited to comment. Typically this is somewhat difficult, particularly for the client who begins, but the ice is soon broken as everyone realizes they are experiencing remarkably similar feelings. Just after this recitation—which can often take 10 min or more for each person with frequent interruptions of "That's what I felt too" from others—clients and spouses are given information about the nature of anxiety in general and agoraphobia in particular as well as the process of treatment. We emphasize that treatment will require both the agoraphobic and the spouse to participate in many activities between therapy sessions and that spouses will learn to serve as "coaches" and "confidants" for their agoraphobic partner. We also reiterate that daily records of activities and practice sessions outside of the home are necessary.

Session 2 includes a review of the treatment rationale, further explanations of the nature of anxiety, and a discussion of how the experience of anxiety is currently viewed by the patient. This is followed by a discussion of each agoraphobic's activities and any anxiety experienced while participating in these activities during the past week. The session ends with a brief explanation of the role of cognitions in anxiety and the therapist instructs agoraphobics to begin attending to thoughts that occur during anxiety-provoking situations. This is in preparation for Session 3, during which the therapist introduces cognitive coping skills in the form of coping self-statements. As in Session 2 and all subsequent sessions, Session 3 begins with a brief description by each patient of activities during the past week. The therapist then introduces the rationale for the coping technique and instructs clients on its uses, employing actual events during the past week as reported by agoraphobics as examples. Patients are then asked to begin using this technique and the first homework assignment is given, which consists of practicing the lowest hierarchy item. Session 4 and all following sessions include discussion of the week's activities, encouragement, and further instruction on using cognitive and exposure techniques to further progress. Throughout these sessions the therapist assists spouses in understanding and implementing their role as facilitators and offers further explanations of anxiety when the need arises. In addition, the therapist will attempt to foster more adaptive communication techniques between the partners if poor communication or other relationship issues are interfering with progress.

The following transcript is based on detailed notes recorded in anticipation of writing this chapter during group treatment, conducted by the two authors, of five agoraphobic women and their husbands. The case actually represents a composite of the experiences of all five couples as they worked together to overcome their fears. In this way a much larger variety of experiences, representing most issues that arise in treating agoraphobics with this protocol can be presented. Based on our clinical experience over the past 5 years, the situations encountered are very typical and should anticipate most problems and issues that arise as clinicians attempt to utilize these procedures in their practice.

CASE STUDY

Patient

The following (composite) agoraphobic patient was referred by her physician to our clinic for treatment of panic attacks and an inability to go out of the house alone. At the time of referral, Ginny (a pseudonym) was a 35-year-old housewife and mother living in a middle-class suburban area. She had been unable to work outside of the home for the past 5 years because of her anxiety problems.

During the structured interview, Ginny reported that her problems began about 5 years previously. At that time she was recently married, and she and her husband had just moved to this area after her husband was transferred. Ginny stated that her husband's job was very demanding, requiring him to be away from home several nights each week. She often felt lonely and deserted. She attempted to make friends with her neighbors but they were very busy as well. She reports that they began having marital difficulties surrounding her feelings of abandonment and her husband's feelings that she was too demanding. Although he had initially not wanted her to go to work, he agreed to let her attempt to find a job so that she would have something to do to fill her time.

Ginny found a job as an elementary school secretary and reported having enjoyed it; however, her marital problems continued to escalate and she had made only a few friends at work. She continued to feel lonely a great deal. She reported that her husband disapproved of her working full-time and complained that she was not home enough, which resulted in further arguments between them. Ginny was beginning to feel more and more pressured by her husband, but she did not want to stop working, especially since she was beginning to feel tense and nervous when she was home alone.

She reported that her first panic attack occurred during this time. She and her husband were out to dinner with a few of his new business associates and their wives. She was feeling out of place and uncomfortable with these people and wishing that the evening would end. She became light-headed and thought that she was about to faint. She then reported becoming cold and sweaty with increased respiration and heart rate. She became very frightened, feeling certain that she was about to lose control. She was unable to remain at the restaurant but instead insisted that her husband take her to the hospital where they examined her, gave her some Valium, and sent her home. Although she was afraid that she might be going crazy, she also thought that there must be something seriously physically wrong. She had three complete physicals that year, each with a different physician. Each physician recommended psychiatric or psychological help. She began therapy with four different therapists, but felt that none understood her problem and she became convinced that she must be crazy. One morning, while attempting to get to work, she experienced a particularly bad panic and immediately returned home, calling in sick. Although she intended to try to return to work the next morning, when the time came she could not do so.

Various medications, including Valium, were prescribed over the years, and recently she had begun taking Valium again (5 mg twice during the day and 10 mg at bedtime). Although she carried her Valium with her at all times and even found that she must keep the empty pill bottle with her during those rare times when she ran out of medication, she reported that her condition had continued to deteriorate. Her avoidance had escalated to the point that she had difficulty on some days just going out to her mailbox. She tried to hide her avoidance pattern from friends and neighbors as much as possible. She would often arrange for rides for her children (a boy aged 10 years and a girl aged 8 years) with neighbors, but if one child was taken sick at school she would call a taxi rather than go to school herself. While her close friends and neighbors were aware of this problem, she was very adept at inventing various reasons for avoidance to other friends and relatives. She reported decreased self-esteem and confusion over why she was unable to improve. She claimed that her life was very restricted and did not feel that she would ever be able to work again.

She thought that her friends and her husband had never understood her anxiety feelings and had given up on her. She reported, in fact, that no one had been able to understand how she felt. At the time of referral, she was averaging approximately four panic attacks each week; some even occurring while at home without any obvious precipitating event.

In addition to her agoraphobic problems, she reported problems with mild depression that coincided with increases in anxiety over the preceding 5 years. The periods of depression varied from mild to moderate depending on how much and how often she was able to leave the house during the week. It seemed, then, that her depression was secondary to her anxiety problems but was resulting in additional complications since it further decreased her motivation to leave the house.

Assessment

Following her structured interview she was classified according to DSM-III criteria as agoraphobic with panic attacks. She was then contacted and her second appointment at the clinic was scheduled. After the treatment program was explained, consent forms were signed and her hierarchy completed (Figure 1-3). She was then asked to attempt the 1-mile walk. She became very anxious and frightened. She reported fears of having a panic attack and being unable to return to the clinic to get help. It was pointed out to her that it was not necessary for her to complete the entire walk, but she was encouraged to at least attempt the first couple of stations. Although she was still very anxious, she agreed to make an attempt. She did much better than she had anticipated, completing 10 of the 20 stations. Although her anxiety was still high (a 6 on the scale), she was very pleased with her accomplishment. She then completed the questionnaires, which further substantiated her diagnosis and our estimate of the severity of her depression.

At the end of this assessment she was given the Weekly Record with an explanation of how to complete the two different forms. One of these weekly records, Form A (Figure 1-4), requires that the client record his or her anxiety rating at four specified times each day. (Figure 1-4 is chosen from a week early in therapy.) The interviewer asks the client about his or her "typical" routine and then together they decide on four approximately evenly divided times during the day when the patient will record his or her anxiety rating. (This provides a useful

FIGURE 1-3. Phobias: Fear and avoidance.

Rate the degree to which you tend to avoid situations because of the fear or unpleasant feelings associated with them. Briefly describe the feared situations.

For each, write the applicable number in the space provided.

0	1	2	3	4	5	6	7	8
/	/	/	/	/	/	/	/	/
Do not avoid—no anxiety	Hesitate to enter situation but rarely avoid it— slightly/ somewhat anxious		Sometimes avoid situation— definitely anxious		Usually avoid situations —markedly or very often anxious		Invariably avoid situation— very severe /continuous anxiety; near panic	

	Description	Rating
1. The worst fear	Driving to the mall and going in to shop	8
2. The second worst fear	Going into K-Mart alone	7
3. The third worst fear	Going to grocery store for week's groceries	7
4. The fourth worst fear	Going to the park and walking around	6
5. The fifth worst fear	Going to visit friends	6
6. The sixth worst fear	Driving alone a short distance outside of your safe area	6
7. The seventh worst fear	Going to a restaurant for lunch or dinner	5
8. The eighth worst fear	Going grocery shopping for about 15 minutes	5
9. The ninth worst fear	Going to a small store near home and buying a few items	4
10. The tenth worst fear	Walking up to the corner	3

FIGURE 1-4. Weekly Record, Form A

Name: Ginny   Group: _____   Week # 3

Anxiety Ratings:

0	1	2	3	4	5	6	7	8
/	/	/	/	/	/	/	/	/
Complete relaxation	Very slight anxiety	Slight anxiety	Some anxiety	Moderate anxiety	Definite anxiety	Much anxiety	Very much anxiety	Maximum discomfort

Daily ratings of anxiety—include rating and the time recorded:

Date and Day:	8/1/—	8/2/—	8/3/—	8/4/—	8/5/—	8/6/—	8/7/—
Morning	9 a.m./3	8 a.m./2	9 a.m./3	8 a.m./3	8 a.m./7	9 a.m./3	8 a.m./2
Afternoon	10 a.m./3	1 p.m./3	2 p.m./3	12 p.m./3	1 p.m./3	12 p.m./3	1 p.m./3
Evening	7 p.m./6	6:30 p.m./2	7 p.m./2	6 p.m./3	7. p.m./3	6 p.m./3	6 p.m./2
Bedtime	11 p.m./3	11 p.m./3	12 a.m./2	11 p.m./3	12 a.m./3	11 p.m./5	11 p.m./3

On the following, using the above scale, list incidents that you would rate as "4" or above: For any incident that you would label as "panic," PLEASE put a "P" after your Maximum Anxiety Rating.

Date	Time of onset	Time ending	Situation of increased anxiety or anxiety attack (Please describe)	Maximum anxiety (and "P" if applicable)	Anxiety at ending time	Non-anxiety-provoking/ nonstressful	Anxiety-provoking/ stressful	Comments
8/1/—	10 a.m.	11 a.m.	Went into grocery store with my daughter.	7(P)	3		√	I always have trouble going without my husband, but I had to get a few things for my daughter.
8/1/—	6:30 p.m.	7:30 p.m.	Sitting watching TV.	6	3	√		
8/2/—	8 p.m.	8:15 p.m.	Had just arrived at friends' home.	4	3		√	
8/3/—	6:20 p.m.	6:35 p.m.	Husband left me alone in the store.	4	3		√	
8/5/—	7:30 a.m.	9:30 a.m.	Just getting breakfast ready at home. Husband went to work and kids out to play.	7(P)	3	√		
8/5/—	2 p.m.	3 p.m.	Kids and I went to post office.	5(P)	3	√		
8/6/—	10:30 p.m.	11:30 p.m.	Husband and I had an argument.	7(P)	3		√	Made me angry. I don't know why I got anxious.

measure of background, or general, anxiety level.) Then, it is explained that in addition the patient should record any episodes of anxiety that he or she would rate as 4, moderate anxiety or above. This information is also recorded on the Form A Weekly Record. For those episodes of 4 or more, the client is to write down the date, time, and anxiety rating at the beginning and end of each episode, a brief description of the situation, whether the situation was stressful or nonstressful, and whether he or she would note this as a panic attack. It is explained that this information will be useful during the treatment sessions and will also help the patient to become more knowledgeable about his or her anxiety. (This form provides a great deal of information for research but can also be useful clinically. It can provide a concrete example of improvement and can help identify problematic situations.)

The second Weekly Record form, Form B, requires that the patient record the time he or she spends out of the house, indicating which items were assigned for practice and which were not (Figure 1-5). It is explained that each time the patient leaves the house he or she is to record the date, time, and each place visited. For each location and for traveling the patient is instructed to record the amount of time spent in each and the amount of time alone. Finally, the patient is to record his or her anxiety rating for each and the time upon returning home.

Although these forms are thoroughly explained, most patients have some difficulties completing them at first. Considering the amount of information required, this is to be expected. Patients are asked to call the clinic with any questions and their forms are checked weekly for problems in record keeping. Ginny, as with most clients, experienced some difficulties. With Form A (Figure 1-4), she had problems remembering to diligently record all the information, especially the time when the episode ended and whether it would be considered a panic attack. She reported confusion about what we meant by "ending time" until it was explained to her that this meant when her anxiety went below 4. She was also unclear that for rating an episode as a "panic" we wanted her to use *her* criteria and not ours. Her final problem was not always feeling comfortable recording on either form in some situations, particularly when other people were around. We told her that she could, at those times, record the information on a separate sheet of paper and then copy this onto the forms later. However, it was stressed to her that she must write this information down at the time so that it would be accurate. She felt that she would be able to do this.

Form B (Figure 1-5) posed some additional problems. Ginny tended to put all locations for time out of the home together as one time out, without noting separate times at each place. She would also give multiple anxiety ratings but was not certain which times these referred to. The form was re-explained to her, and once she became more familiar with what was expected, these problems were eliminated.

Her next assessment was a home visit. Five items were chosen from her hierarchy by the clinician prior to the appointment. The clinician then explained that she would be asked to do some tasks that might cause her anxiety; however, she was informed that at any time if she felt unable to complete the task or too

FIGURE 1-5. Weekly Record, Form B.

Name: ____Ginny____   Weekly Record: (____8/1/—____ to ____8/7/—____)

*Please put a "√" by any activity that was an assigned practice for this week.

Date	Time left home	Time returned home	List each activity (including transportation) and place traveled to while away from home*	Total time spent	Time alone	Anxiety rating (0–8) Maximum	Anxiety rating (0–8) Average
8/1/—	9:45 a.m.	10:30 a.m.	I drove to grocery store near my home and returned home. (√)	30 min	None	7(P)	5
8/2/—	12 noon	12:20 p.m.	Went for a walk around the block.	20 min	20 min	3	3
8/2/—	7:30 p.m.	9:30 p.m.	Husband, kids, and I went to visit friends.	2 hr	None	4	3
8/3/—	6:00 p.m.	7:00 p.m.	I drove (with my husband in the car) to the grocery store. We went in together, but I shopped alone for 15 minutes. We stayed together in store for about 15 more minutes. (√)	1 hr	15 min	4	3
8/5/—	2:30 p.m.	2:20 p.m.	I then drove to the gas station and back home. Kids and I went to the post office.	20 min	None	5	5
8/7/—	12:30 p.m.	1:00 p.m.	I went to store with kids. (√)	30 min	15 min	3	3

37

fearful, she should just say so and she could stop. The purpose of the test, it was explained, was to see how fearful she was in a number of different situations but that it was her choice to attempt the tasks that are requested. The first item on the hierarchy that was chosen was to walk to the corner near her home. She was asked if she would be willing to attempt this and she agreed, somewhat relieved that she was asked to do something she felt she could do. She completed this item with a reported maximum anxiety rating of 2. She was then asked if she would attempt to drive to the store a block and a half from her home and go in and buy a few items. She agreed and reported a maximum anxiety rating of 5. She also agreed to go into a nearby grocery store to shop for 15 min. She was extremely surprised that her anxiety was lower then she expected, a maximum of 4. Although she was feeling very good about her accomplishments, she did not want to attempt the next two requested items, driving alone outside of her safe area for a few blocks or going into K-Mart alone. Therefore, this behavioral assessment was complete; she was reminded that treatment would begin in 2 weeks, and it was requested that she continue maintaining her weekly record.

Treatment Transcripts

The following dialogue represents actual examples of the process of therapy during the 12 therapy sessions. Once again, these examples actually occurred but are placed in the context of a composite patient to illustrate both therapy techniques and typical problems that occur while treating an agoraphobic client with this protocol. Although the transcript presents only interaction with one agoraphobic and her spouse, similar interactions with the remaining two to five couples would also occur in each session. Each session lasts approximately 1½ hr.

Session 1

This first session begins with the introduction of group members to one another and to the therapist.

THERAPIST: During this treatment program I will discuss information with you about anxiety and instruct you in the use of skills to help you deal with your anxiety. In addition, spouses will learn to serve as coaches and facilitators so that during and after the initial 12-session program they can take a more active role in helping their agoraphobic partner overcome problems with anxiety. Following the initial 12 sessions, I will meet with you periodically during the coming year to check on your progress and to help you with any problems that may occur. Now, I would like each of you to discuss how your problems began and how you currently view your problems. [This is done in order to increase group cohesiveness and to help group members realize that others have similar problems. A common complaint among agoraphobic clients is that they believe that no one else feels like they do.] Ginny, would you like to begin?

GINNY: I first noticed problems with agoraphobia about 5 years ago when I was going through a lot of changes in my life. I had recently married and we moved to a new town. My first panic attack occurred one evening when my husband and I were out to dinner with some of his new business associates and their wives. I was feeling trapped and uncomfortable and did not feel that I was making the proper impression. It seemed no one was paying any attention to me or even looking at me. I felt like I was going to faint, my heart was pounding, and I got very cold and sweaty and began feeling as if I would lose all control. I thought I was going crazy and insisted that my husband take me to the hospital; of course they said nothing was wrong. From that night on things have been kind of up and down, but now I seem to be getting progressively worse. I can go to a few places with my husband but practically nowhere alone, except out to the mailbox and to the backyard. Even at home I sometimes get these "panics."

SPOUSE: Initially I thought she was sick and I told her she had better go to the doctor's. Then when he said it was just nerves, it seemed to me she should be able to do at least some of these things if she really wanted to. I mean, I get nervous too but I still have to do things. But I do hate to see her suffer. I used to try and force her to do things, but there were so many fights that after awhile I just started doing all of the shopping, errands, and so forth. Sometimes lately Ginny will want to try and go, but she usually ends up getting nervous, and I figure it's easier and quicker if I just do it myself, so Ginny usually stays home. I know that Ginny's the one that is suffering, but I'm really at my wit's end about how to help her.

G: I've always been a "nervous" person, but I'm not really sure why I have problems like this. I should be able to go to a grocery store and stand in line like everyone else but I can't even do that. Why do I have to be so scared all the time? I just can't understand why I have this.

T: Although there may be some good reasons for your first panic and the subsequent agoraphobia, identifying them is not important in overcoming this disorder. Therefore, even though it's very interesting, you need not be overly concerned about why this problem began. We will focus instead on helping you overcome it. As you know, you've just described the classic symptoms of agoraphobia. All agoraphobics have a fear of being in a place where help might not be quickly available. Almost all agoraphobics also feel a real lack of confidence in being able to manage or control their own reactions. They always think the worst is going to happen. Ginny says that she can go some places with her husband because she feels that he would be able to help her if she had a panic attack. But even when he's around there are many places and situations that are just too frightening to encounter. All of you have certain situations where you feel comfortable or people with whom you feel comfortable; for most of you it's being home or being with your husband, or perhaps one or two other good friends or relatives. For some of you, even your dog or young child may be enough company to ensure that you'll be able to accomplish more than you could alone. We will call these people and situations "safe people" or "safe situations."

We've already mentioned that we really don't need to know too much about why this started in order to treat it, but we do know that agoraphobia almost always begins during a very stressful period in your life, a time when a lot of things are happening in your life that are putting a lot of pressure on you. Things like getting married, getting divorced, moving, going through financial difficulties, or having trouble with your kids or your parents are typical kinds of situations that can put some pressure on you. Sometimes it's a lot of little things that add up so that it is hard to remember any one big thing, but all of these things cause stress. We have found that during periods such as this people get very "nervous" to begin with and stay that way over a long period of time, and it doesn't take much before a full-blown panic attack might occur. During periods when you're *not* under a lot of pressure or stress, these same situations probably wouldn't make any difference, but during times of stress if you're nervous anyway you're susceptible to having these panics.

The other factor that is important is how "high strung" you are to begin with. This seems to be something that runs in families. In other words, if you have a mother or a father who tends to be kind of high strung and nervous, chances are you will be. About half of all people tend to be more or less high strung, so this is not at all unusual. But, from what we've learned, it seems you have to have this kind of personality in order to be susceptible to stress and ultimately agoraphobia. In any case, when you have that first rush or panic, no matter what sets it off, your mind is unable to account for this sudden intense physiological reaction. Therefore, it is only human nature that you invent a reason to account for it. Unfortunately, the two most common reasons are "I must be having a heart attack," or "I must be going crazy." Naturally, the first thing you want to do is to get out of the situation where this is occurring. Since there is no question that you're going to feel better as soon as you get home and relax, the feeling of relief that you get only ensures that the next time it happens you'll also go home as fast as you can and that you tend to avoid those situations or places where you were when it first happened.

G: I find as I get worse that I can go to fewer and fewer places. In fact, on my "bad days" now I can't even go out to the mailbox and even being home alone I have panic attacks.

T: What seems to be happening is that your anxiety is beginning to generalize to more situations. Have you ever had the experience of seeing someone on the street who you don't know but because they have certain features that remind you of a close friend, maybe without your even being aware of a resemblance, you are immediately attracted to this stranger? Avoidance behavior develops in the same way. You have a panic attack in a particular situation that contains many different cues or stimuli, some of which are common to other situations. These cues can remind you of the anxiety that was experienced in the other situation and cause an increase in anxiety and even a panic attack. With each new situation additional cues are associated with anxiety, which can result in even more situations becoming anxiety-provoking; some of the cues may even be normal physical changes inside your body. In order to alleviate symptoms of anxiety, the person often leaves or escapes the situation. For awhile this works in decreasing the anxiety, because anxiety is time-limited and goes away eventually anyway. Therefore, leaving anxiety-provoking situations becomes associated with relief and within time the individual will begin avoiding in order to not experience the anxiety at all.

As you begin to confront your anxiety, which we're going to teach you how to do, you may find that you feel worse because you are no longer avoiding certain situations. However, this temporary increase in discomfort should be viewed as a positive sign. It is the first step toward getting better. It is a sign that improvement is beginning because you are going to drain the power of the machine that turns on when you experience anxiety. We will discuss this further during the next session.

Session 2

The therapist begins with a brief review of the treatment rationale presented in Session 1.

THERAPIST: As we said last week, treatment is going to take 1 year. During these next 11 sessions over the coming 15 weeks, we will learn specifically how everyone can deal with their fear and overcome it. At the end of this time, some of you will be quite a bit better while others will also be better, but maybe not as far along. This isn't important. What is important is that you take what we've learned and use it consistently over the full year. If you do this, then you're going to feel very differently at the end of the year than you do now.

The last time we also talked about treatment consisting of changing what you do and what you think about what you do. It is important not only to practice confronting situations you're now avoiding but to change your way of thinking about any anxiety that you feel. Anxiety is a combination of behavioral and cognitive factors accompanied by physiological changes. These physiological changes are not harmful, although they may seem so to you. It is the way you interpret these physical responses that causes them to be so terrifying. After pleasurable exercise, such as playing tennis, you may experience increases in respiration and heart rate, sweating, muscular tension, and even lightheadedness; these will not be interpreted as danger signals but, instead, as the result of your increased physical activity. In fact, you might even feel refreshed. When these same responses occur now, you interpret them as danger signals. But it is important to remember that it is your interpretation of them that causes you to label these responses as dangerous. Now, before we begin discussing your past week, I want to point out to you again that it is very important for you to keep careful records of your activities on your weekly records. We will use these in later sessions and they will help you to become more confrontive with your anxiety. How did you do during the past week?

GINNY: I had a pretty bad week. In fact, part of the reason was because of keeping this record. It makes me more anxious to have to write down my anxiety rating and what I'm about to do. If I'm going to do something, I just want to run out and do it as fast as possible. I don't want to have to think about it.

T: I understand that it may be difficult for you, but not thinking about your anxiety is just another way of avoiding dealing with it. It is important for you to begin to stop all avoiding and this includes beginning to notice your anxiety level both before and during something that might be difficult. It may be hard, but this is another part of learning to deal with your anxiety. On your weekly record you stated that you went into a small store alone for 10 minutes and that your anxiety rating was 7 [on a scale of 0, no anxiety, to 8, panic]. Tell us about how you did.

SPOUSE: Well, I thought she did pretty well. Early in the morning Ginny said she was going to go to the store and she seemed very determined about it and ended up going. Two weeks ago if she had made those plans in the morning she would have become so nervous she wouldn't have done it.

G: I didn't feel that I did that well at all because I got so upset, more upset than I expected. It's just a little store near my home and I thought this was going to be a good day for me, a low-anxiety day, but I felt awful at the store.

T: It's not how you feel that is important at this point. What is important is that you did it.

S: It didn't look like you were having a hard time.

G: Well, I was, and it should have been easier.

T: The more you do this task and others, the easier it will be for you. You have been avoiding so many situations for such a long time and now you are trying to change this. So, you can expect your anxiety to be high for awhile. This should not concern you. Remember, you're going to feel worse before you feel better. In fact, feeling worse is going to be a sign that you're getting better because it will mean that you're doing more things, avoiding less, and confronting your anxiety. If you don't come into these sessions and say that you felt badly during the week, then I'll begin to think you haven't really been doing your homework. If you come in and say "I felt terrible," then that's a sign to me that you've been going out and facing a lot of things that are difficult for you and learning to confront your anxiety in a healthy way. So, one of the important lessons to remember early in treatment is that feeling worse is good and it's a sign you're getting better. Now I would like you to try and identify what thoughts you had before and during your trip to the little store.

G: I only know that before I went I was certain that I couldn't do it, but felt well enough to try. Then, once I was in the store, I got so upset that I just knew that I had to get out. I can't remember any other thoughts.

T: Don't be concerned if it is difficult for you to identify your thoughts at first. It does take practice to identify your thoughts, especially when you are anxious. That's a very good start of identifying negative thoughts that increase your anxiety. We will continue to try and identify thoughts associated with anxiety in the coming weeks. Most thoughts related to anxiety are negative and catastrophic-type thoughts. These are thoughts such as, "I can't handle this anxiety," or "If I stay here, I'm going to go crazy." They are thoughts that center around negative statements about yourself or statements that predict terrible consequences. As you become more aware of these thoughts, you will begin to see how they are related to increasing your anxiety.

I would also like you to try to take a more objective view of the fear that you experience. Your anxiety is like a machine that is fueled by avoidance and fear, and this means any avoidance, even the reluctance to "think" about anxiety you mentioned earlier. Each time you go into a situation and escape or each time you avoid a situation or use some "distracting" cognitions to avoid anxious thoughts, you are adding fuel to the machine, giving it more power. Every little thing you do to avoid feeling uncomfortable is a way of wrestling with or fighting the machine. Every time you fight to turn off the machine it gets worse. Your job now is to drain this machine of its power by just accepting it and going with it instead of fighting it and fueling it. This week, I want you to pay particular attention to what thoughts you are having during anxiety-provoking situations.

Session 3

THERAPIST: During this session we will be discussing coping self-state-ments. But, before I begin explaining this to you, let's discuss what happened during the past week.

GINNY: I did a few things this week. I did go over to a friend's house with my husband and kids and to the post office with my kids. I didn't have too much anxiety while I was out, but I had a lot of problems worrying beforehand about what might happen. I kept thinking that I wouldn't be able to handle what I needed to do, especially when I had to go to the store. I tired going into that small store alone again and it really scared me. I just kept telling myself that I might get really nervous because it might be too hard for me to do. I asked Jack [spouse] about it and he was fairly helpful because he said, "Don't go if you don't want to." But then it seemed like there was a lot of pressure on me. I knew that I could just fall apart or go crazy if I had to wait in line. If I didn't go crazy, I did think that I would probably pass out or something. But, when I got to the store, it wasn't as bad as I had expected.

T: It's very good that, even though you were very frightened, you went ahead and did the task. Those fearful thoughts you reported are related to what we call anticipatory anxiety and this type is a "what if" kind of thought, which is one of the types of thoughts that need to be changed in order to help decrease your anxiety. One of the skills we are going to discuss is changing your scary thinking. We will do this through the use of what we call coping self-statements. These are statements that you can say to yourself to help you to deal with your anxiety. You have seen how negative self-statements can increase your anxiety, such as your "what if" thoughts. Well, in the same way, coping self-statements can help to decrease your anxiety. [Clients are then given a copy of a four-stage model of coping self-statements and instructed on their use.]

Coping Self-Statements

1. *Stage of preparing for a stressor*
   - What is it I have to do?
   - I can develop a plan to deal with it.
   - I can manage this situation.
   - No negative self-statements; just think rationally.
   - Don't worry. Worry won't help anything.
   - Remember that avoiding feared situations only makes my fears worse. I have to approach what I fear to learn to cope with anxiety.

2. *Stage of confronting and handling a stressor*
   - One step at a time. I can meet this challenge.
   - Don't think about fear, just about what I have to do. Stay relevant.
   - I can handle the situation.
   - This anxiety is what the doctor said I would feel. It's a reminder to use this situation as a way to learn to cope with anxiety.

3. *Stage of coping with the feeling of being overwhelmed*
   - Keep the focus on the present; what is it I have to do?
   - When fear comes, just pause.
   - I was supposed to expect my fear to rise.
   - I feel my fears rising and I accept it as a fact.
   - Let me label my fear from 0 to 10 and watch it change.
   - It's not the worst thing that can happen.
   - Don't run away.
   - If I stay here, in time my anxiety will certainly decrease.
   - This is an opportunity for me to learn to cope with my fears.
   - I can do what I have to do in spite of anxiety.
   - My anxiety won't hurt me.

Reinforcing Self-Statements

- It worked; I was able to do it.
- Wait until the group hears about this.
- It wasn't as bad as I expected.
- I made more out of the fear than it was worth.
- My negative thoughts—that's a large part of the problem. When I control my negative thoughts and anticipations, I control my fear.
- This experience will help me practice again in the future.
- It's getting better each time I use the procedure.
- I'm really pleased with the progress I'm making.
- I *can* learn to overcome my fears!

T: A coping self-statement is a specific thought or self-statement designed to help you deal constructively with or manage a potentially difficult task or situation. As previously discussed, negative catastrophic thoughts can either make you anxious or make whatever you are feeling worse. It's the "thinking" part of the anxiety and it gears you up to start avoiding even before you begin, and certainly while you're doing something. If you're saying to yourself, "If I do this I may die," then almost certainly you're also already thinking about ways to avoid the feelings or the situations that are going to cause your death. But, once again, this only adds fuel to the machine. As you've probably learned, it is possible to identify cognitions that occur in stressful situations or when anxious. It is also possible to consciously change these thoughts. You can replace the negative thoughts that contribute to anxiety with coping, constructive thoughts that help to keep anxiety under control and help you to deal with anxiety. You should attend to your thoughts whenever anxiety is experienced, being particularly alert to negative, catastrophic, "what if" types of thoughts. If any negative thoughts are identified that will probably occur, they should be replaced with relevant coping self-statements. For example, thoughts such as, "My heart is pounding and my chest hurts. I must be having a heart attack," can be replaced with such thoughts as "I'm experiencing anxiety. It's very (or extremely) uncomfortable, but nothing serious is going to happen to me."

SPOUSE: That sounds like what I used to tell her. I used to say, "Don't worry about it, you'll be OK," but it didn't seem to do any good and sometimes would make her worse.

T: A lot of the procedures we're going to be using are just good common sense, Jack. What's going to be different is that we're going to be very systematic and very comprehensive. Many agoraphobics and their spouses have done the right thing some of the time, but usually end up filling the machine up with fuel again the next hour. It's hard to make progress that way.

G. I always tell myself that I can't stand this anymore and that I have to get out of whatever situation I'm in at the time. How would I change this?

T: Those thoughts could be replaced with such statements as "I *can* handle this. I will stay and wait for the anxiety to decrease."

G: But, I don't know if this will work for me.

T: It will take some time and practice to learn to use this procedure effectively. The negative thoughts have a lot of power because you have used them for a long time and it will take time to unlearn these anxiety-provoking ways of thinking. However, with some work, it can be done. Let me explain this a little further.

We conceptualize anxiety as a four-stage process. The process of dealing with anxiety or with a stressful situation or experience should be seen as a series of four steps or stages: preparing for a stressor (or anxiety), confronting or dealing with a stressor, coping with feelings of being overwhelmed by a stressor, and evaluation of and rewarding oneself for coping attempts.

At least some of the time, you know in advance that a stressor is coming up. For example, you may have a dentist's appointment in three days or you know you have to travel someplace that may be stressful in a short while. [Examples that are relevant to couples in the group are always used.] Occasionally you may even know in advance that internal feelings, such as certain physical sensations, may occur, at least at a certain time in the future. For example, certain people feel tired or faint at about the same time each day. Other individuals can predict that they will feel certain internal physical feelings whenever they go to work or, as you have mentioned, when you go to crowded stores. In a sense, then, these internal sensations can be predicted in advance, and this is when you would use Stage 1—preparing ahead for a stressor.

When the stressful situation actually is encountered, for example, being at the dentist's for an appointment, or being in a crowded store, the goal is to remain focused on the task or situation, not to anticipate what *might* happen in 5 minutes or in an hour but to use coping self-statements and logically analyze the situation, which we'll discuss in future treatment sessions. When confronting a stressful situation, accept the anxiety that occurs, don't fight it or try to suppress it because fear of fear is often the biggest problem. Try to identify antecedent situations and/or cognitions that precede anxiety. Adopting a task-oriented approach such as "What can I do to deal with this situation?" or telling yourself to take one step at a time and focus on the situation will be helpful. Do not become preoccupied with anxiety or your internal feeling state. The third stage involves coping with feelings of being overwhelmed, or what some people call "panic." This stage does not always occur, but it is important to practice dealing with it so that you can prepare for what to do if you feel extremely panicky or overwhelmed. You need to recognize this as a separate stage. Most people do not feel overwhelmed *every* time they feel anxious, but sometimes you may feel overwhelmed. When this occurs, try to remain in the situation. View this as an opportunity to practice changing behaviors and thoughts regarding panic. You should attempt to use your coping self-statements and try to reevaluate the situation and your reaction, attempting to be more logical about what is occurring. This is not easy to do when panicky, but with practice you will be able to do this. You could ask yourself if you are overreacting to the external situation and/or to your internal feelings of anxiety. Attempt to stay focused on the present and recognize you probably can function even when experiencing panic. Another important step is to remember to breathe though your nose. When agoraphobics are overwhelmed and panic, often they breathe too quickly or hyperventilate. This increases scary physical sensations. But breathing deeply through your nose prevents this. Extreme anxiety will be time-limited; your anxiety level will come down given sufficient time (but remember, this may be gradual and take some time, so don't become discouraged). Don't struggle with the anxiety or "demand" that you feel calm or relaxed; accept the anxiety and wait for it to decrease. Struggling with anxiety often just adds energy to it and makes it last even longer. Remember to focus on the task at hand and your thoughts, and to breathe through your nose.

After dealing with stressors and/or experiencing anxiety, look back over the experience to see what you can learn from it. This is the fourth stage and is very important. "Evaluate" your attempts to cope with the situation. Did you remember to try to cope, to try some of the strategies learned during treatment? What seemed to help? What didn't? What could you have done differently or better? These are all examples of the questions you can ask yourself. It is very important not to expect perfection or success on every try. This is a relearning process and takes time; so you need to recognize even small gains. Reward yourself for your attempts and progress through rewarding self-statements such as, "That was a good try!," "I handled that very well!," and "I'm learning how to deal with anxiety!" Praising yourself is an important skill that will increase the likelihood of further coping attempts and further progress. Don't expect miracles or to be able to eliminate all anxiety. In order to use the coping self-statements effectively, you must practice. This involves, first of all, learning the coping self-statements. Please read the coping self-statements sheet frequently over the next week to become as familiar as possible with them. At first, using the coping self-statements may seem artificial or awkward. This is not unusual in learning any skill, such as how to hold and swing a racquet when first learning to play tennis. It is often helpful to try to develop your own coping self-statements using the sheet as an example. The coping self-statements must be consciously used at first. But, gradually they are likely to become more habitual and automatic, so that you will have learned to respond to stress with constructive thoughts rather than negative thoughts. At the present time, you are probably more accustomed to saying negative thoughts because you have been doing so for a long time. Therefore, it is like trying to break a bad habit and replace it with a good one. Since negative self-statements have been practiced and learned over many years, it will take time and effort to learn how to use coping self-statements in a skilled manner. So, be certain not to belittle gradual progress, but to praise yourself for all gains, regardless of how small they may seem.

(*To the spouse.*) You will be taking part in some of the practice sessions. This will enable you to help your spouse learn to use these skills. More specifically, you can say some of these statements out loud when your partner begins to report anxiety during practice sessions. Help your partner to remain as objective as possible. And, you too must remember that this is a difficult process and that overcoming agoraphobic problems will take a great deal of work.

During the next week, I want you to begin attempting to change your negative thoughts. Remember, in order to do so, you and your spouse must first become very familiar with the examples of coping statements that you have been given. Notice what negative, catastrophic thoughts that you are saying to yourself and change these using the examples you've been given or positive coping statements that you develop yourself. Don't become discouraged—just begin working on this relearning process. It is also important for the spouses to remember to coach their partner in this new way of thinking. I want you to begin practicing your first hierarchy item at least three times this week and one of these practices should be with your spouse. Remember, at least three times and at least one with your spouse.

Session 4

THERAPIST: You've spent a lot of time up until now trying to avoid or suppress anxiety. Now it's time to change this way of dealing with your anxiety. Instead of avoiding and fighting your anxiety, which fuels your "machine," we are going to invite the machine to turn on until it runs out of fuel. This machine is really nothing more than a collection of negatively emotionally charged memories that you have come to fear. By facing these fearful memories you decrease the power that they have over your present behavior and thoughts. You may experience an increase in your anxiety as you work on draining the machine of its power, but this is to be expected and nothing to be concerned about. During treatment you can expect ups and downs, but even the downs are part of getting better. What has been happening during the past week?

GINNY: This week I did a little better. I cut down on my medication. It's been bothering me to take it. Taking pills makes me feel very out of control. So, I like the feeling of gaining some control again. I've been trying to use the coping statements and it's pretty hard, but I did decide to come to the meeting regardless of whether I felt bad or not.

T: That's very good. It's going to be helpful to you in the coming weeks to try and maintain that attitude about your anxiety. It is also important to give yourself credit for every step, no matter how small, that you take toward dealing with your anxiety.

G: I still feel like I should be able to do more than I do. The little things like walking to the corner anyone should be able to do.

SPOUSE: The thing I can't understand is why it's so scary one day and not bad the next. If Ginny can do it one day, why can't she do it everyday? If she wants to go to the beauty shop or to visit friends she seems to be able to do that, but when she thinks about going to the store you would think that we live in a dangerous area and that she'd be mugged.

T: I know it's hard to understand if you haven't experienced the intense fear that often follows from the experience of panic attacks. However, for your wife it's just as frightening as living in a very dangerous area where one is risking their life to go out. It might help you to think of it this way.

G: It is like that. He doesn't understand that it really is that scary for me. I do feel like I'm going to die sometimes.

S: I know you say that, but objectively you know it isn't true. They've told you what to do, so why can't you stop thinking about it this way?

G: You make it sound so easy. If that was all I had to do, I would have already done it!

T: (*To the spouse.*) It is a very difficult pattern to change, Jack, and it will take some time. It can be done, but you will need to change *your* thinking as well. Your wife will need all the support she can get from you while she tries to make these changes. It will be important for you to think of every step she takes as a major accomplishment because for someone with agoraphobia it *will* be a big step. If she walks to the corner, you must help her learn to give herself credit and to feel that she is making changes and accomplishments every step of the way. Agoraphobia is very unpredictable. Some things that would seem that they should be harder to do are actually easier. On some days the same task can be either easier or harder, depending on a lot of things. A lot of people think that agoraphobics must be faking because of these inconsistencies, but it's the nature of the problem.

S: I've never really thought of it that way. It's hard to understand why it's so terrifying for her, but I will try to understand and notice what she does.

T: That should be helpful to both of you during this difficult time. So, is it agreed that you will both try and remember to reward each small step? (*Both spouse and client agree.*) Good, now let's continue discussing what's been going on this week.

G: Well, I did say I was doing a little better, but it's hard to reward myself for this; and, plus, other things that shouldn't be hard often are.

T: Well, why don't you give me an example?

G: OK, it was even hard for me to come here tonight. I felt like I couldn't breathe while we were driving here tonight. I tried to tell myself that it was just the anxiety and it would go away, but it didn't work. I tried to distract myself by looking at billboards and other things along the side of the road. Then I tried to force some air in and make my heart stop beating fast. I kept trying to change my thoughts. I tried harder and harder, and the harder I tried the worse my anxiety got. My heart started pounding and I thought that I would have a heart attack.

T: I understand that these physical sensations can be very frightening. But, it's going to be important to remember what we said earlier. These are just physical sensations that are similar to the effects of exercise. It appears that the problem was that you were fighting the anxiety or trying too hard to suppress it. Fighting the anxiety is a way of avoiding and fueling the machine with your fears. You were trying too hard to make it go away instead of accepting it. The thoughts will take awhile to change and you can expect your progress in changing them to be slow. You need to give yourself time to change your way of thinking and to learn to accept instead of resist the anxiety.

G: I try, but it's so hard and I just can't believe that these symptoms, as you call them, are not going to hurt me. It's not all in my head like my husband thinks. They really happen.

T: As you say, they are not "all in your head." Your body is responding to a "dangerous" situation, and that is why the physical sensations or symptoms occur, because you view the situation as dangerous in some way. It is a very difficult task to change this view because your body's response makes it seem as if there really is danger. Therefore, it becomes a vicious cycle of your thoughts keying off your body's defenses and your body's responses increasing the intensity of the thoughts, and then the body increases the intensity of the response. This can escalate to the point where you have a full-fledged panic attack. Changing this pattern is no simple matter, but it can be done in time. Just be patient and continue to work hard. What kinds of things did you attempt in the past week?

G: I did my homework assignment, walking up to the corner. I did it twice alone and once with Jack. I got really nervous when I was alone, but it wasn't too bad with my husband. I went out a few other times. I went to a friend's house again with Jack for a couple of hours and we went to the store together, but I couldn't wait in line at all and I thought that I would pass out the whole time that I was in the store. I did the things that I had to do, but I felt horrible. I didn't enjoy myself at my friend's home. I just kept wanting to get out of there. What good does it do to keep going places and doing things if I'm so nervous that I feel horrible?

T: Remember, we said that what is important is what you do—not how you feel. [This needs to be repeatedly stressed because clients focus so intensely on how they feel and give too much importance to the symptoms.] Feeling better will come later. For now, just work on doing your homework and going out regardless of how you feel or how anxious you get. As I've mentioned before, you may actually feel worse for awhile, that's part of getting better. (*To the spouse.*) How do you feel your wife did on her homework exercises?

S: She did OK, but she constantly complains about her feelings. I can't stand it anymore. Some days it seems like that's all she talks about.

G: (*To the spouse.*) But you never listen; sometimes you don't even respond. You just don't care how I feel.

S: I care, but I can't stand hearing about it anymore. What do you expect me to do? I can't make you feel better, and talking about it all the time just upsets me too.

T: It is not uncommon for couples to experience a great deal of tension due to agoraphobic problems, and especially when treatment begins. This may be a difficult time for both of you. The symptoms can result in becoming very concerned about well-being and result in the spouse feeling very frustrated because he doesn't feel that he can help. (*To the spouse.*) But, you can help by not becoming overconcerned. These symptoms are a result of anxiety, not from a physical illness. You can help Ginny to develop a more objective view of the anxiety. This can be accomplished by helping her to focus on whatever task she is actually doing and suggesting and providing coping self-statements and encouragement. You can serve as a coach to your agoraphobic partner and, in doing so, help her to improve. Although I realize it is difficult, it is also important for you, Ginny, to not continue complaining about the anxiety. Your focus should be on how you are doing, not how you are feeling; focusing on the symptoms fuels the machine and often increases the intensity of the symptoms. You are putting your energy into the anxiety instead of into what you are trying to accomplish. It may prove helpful if you attempt to stop yourself when you first notice that you are complaining about your symptoms. Many agoraphobics are continually scanning their bodies for symptoms, but when you do this you are focusing your attention in on yourself instead of focusing on the outside world, and you're bound to notice something. I want you to start changing your focus this week while you work on your next hierarchy item.

Session 5

THERAPIST: To date we have discussed the basic methods that we feel you should use to deal with anxiety. I know it is harder to do than it sounds, but, with work, you can see real improvement by following these methods. We are going to focus on the difficulties that you encounter in different situations and on helping you change your attitude about panic and avoidance. This change in attitude will be geared toward helping you to learn to accept your anxiety. I want you to begin welcoming anxiety and viewing it as an opportunity to practice. By welcoming and thereby accepting the anxiety, you will be draining the machine of its fuel. During the coming weeks you can expect a great deal of anxiety as your machine runs continually as you try to drain it. Remember, this is to be expected. During the early weeks, you will probably find this experience very unpleasant, but you can deal with the anxiety that you will experience. How have things been going during the past week?

GINNY: Well, according to my diary I've been doing fine, if that's how you want to look at it, but my anxiety is worse. My machine is running all the time.

T: Good, that is what it should be doing. What is important is that you are doing more.

SPOUSE: She really does seem worse. Even I'm getting concerned.

T: As I've told you before, at first your spouse will feel worse as she exposes herself to more situations. (*To Ginny.*) You will feel worse before you feel better. It's kind of like your anxiety is having a temper tantrum because it's not getting its way, because you're not attending to it right away when it kicks up. But, if you're consistent and continue to "ignore" it, it will go away. When you learn to accept the anxiety and stop fighting it, you will drain the machine and eventually the anxiety will decrease.

G: But, that's really hard to do. The symptoms are terrible and I'm feeling so anxious, even at home now.

T: Instead of viewing these experiences as something horrible, try to think of them as opportunities to practice your new skills. Why don't we examine some of your experiences this past week?

G: I walked to the end of the block several times and it wasn't horrible except once, but that time my anxiety was so high I didn't think I would make it back home.

T: That was your best homework session because it gave you the best opportunity to deal with your anxiety. Next time, start using your coping statements at low anxiety levels and continue throughout, then you can use it as a more complete training experience. The more anxiety you experience, the more you will realize that it will not hurt you, and the more often you use your statements the sooner you will learn to change to more adaptive thinking. Can you identify any thoughts or anything that happened the time you became so anxious while walking?

G: One of my neighbors was outside and I was afraid that they would come up and speak to me and I would have to talk with them. I'm afraid that I would have to stand there and talk to them and I couldn't get away. I'd be trapped and I might not be able to speak at all, or something terrible like that. This has been a problem for me for some time. I'm really afraid that someone will speak to me when I'm alone and anxious.

S: Sometimes we'll cross the street just to avoid seeing anyone.

T: Those are catastrophic kinds of thoughts again. It's good that you noticed them, but let's try to change them. You don't know for a fact that you won't be able to speak or that, if you couldn't, your neighbor would think you were crazy. Instead, what could happen is that you could have a pleasant conversation and your anxiety may actually be low. How could you change these statements to more adaptive ones?

G: I could think that everything will be fine.

T: Yes, but is that something you believe?

G: No, I'm pretty sure that I won't be.

T: Well, it's important that the coping statements you use be ones that are believable. For example, you could say, I might not be as uncomfortable as usual when I speak to my neighbor. So, I'll try it this time and if I get anxious, it will be a good practice session for me.

G: I could try saying that and it might work.

T: Well, how about trying it out here first. If Sallie [another group member] would be willing to pretend to be your neighbor (*Sallie agrees*), then you could pretend that you're out for a walk and attempt to speak to her. Would you be willing to try that?

G: Well, I guess I could try, but it sounds awfully silly.

T: It's a little difficult to get into, but if you really try you might find that it doesn't seem so silly and that it serves as a useful practice. OK, I want Sallie to stand over here and, Ginny, you come walking out from there. Good. Now, just pretend you're on your street at home.

SALLIE: Good morning, Ginny. How are you today?

G: Good morning. I'm feeling OK. It's really a pretty day isn't it?

S: Yes, it is. Where are you going?

G: Well, I . . . um . . . I'm just going for a little walk. Good-bye.

S: That was really good!

T: You both did very well. How about telling us what kinds of things you were thinking?

G: Well, it wasn't so bad. I was surprised that I felt kind of comfortable with it. It scared me a little when Sallie asked me where I was going. I'm always afraid that people, especially ones that I don't know well, will ask me questions that I won't be able to answer or that I'll sound stupid. But, I told myself to just stay focused on what I was doing and that this would be a good practice for me. Maybe I will try it at home, but it's still scary.

T: We won't expect it not to be scary yet, but with practice it will become less and less frightening for you. You may also find that as you do more, you will feel more confident and become less afraid of what other's will think of you. [It is very common for agoraphobic patients to be overly concerned about how other people will view them.] When you do try talking to neighbors, let us know how you did. Now, what else happened this week?

G: I worked in the garden and got really tired. You know, muscles sore and short of breath. I can tell the difference between physical exhaustion and anxiety, but I can't tell the difference between a virus and anxiety. I thought I had a virus this week but my husband insisted that it was anxiety.

T: It's very good that you can tell the difference between physical exertion and anxiety. The symptoms are very similar and many people get the two confused. With the physical exertion, you labeled your feelings differently. With a virus, it's harder to do because you can't identify an external cause. As you become more objective about your anxiety, you will be able to tell the difference between physical illness and anxiety. During the next week, I want you and your spouse to put more effort into viewing the anxiety objectively and using the coping self-statements. For the coming week, your item is to go grocery shopping for about 15 minutes. Why don't you do this twice alone and once with your spouse, and continue talking. In fact, try talking to whomever you meet and let us know how you did next time.

Session 6

THERAPIST: (*Following opening greetings to group.*) Last week I asked you and your spouse to work on viewing the anxiety more objectively. How did this go during the past week?

GINNY: I think I did pretty well. We've changed some things. My husband has been helping me. He's been reading the coping self-statements to me when I get anxious. One thing that I discovered really drives me nuts is having him ask me, "How do you feel?" when I'm not anxious. When I feel bad I want to tell him about it, but if I feel OK and he asks me how I feel, I start scanning my body and it makes me worse.

T: What would you like your husband to say at times when you are dealing with anxiety?

G: Anything but "How do you feel?" Maybe he could ask where I am on my scale.

T: (*To spouse.*) Would this be OK?

SPOUSE: Sure, I've been trying to pay more attention to her anxiety. I know how she looks when she's really bad and I'm learning to identify when she's moderately anxious as well. I already starting asking her what her level was and trying to catch her when her anxiety starts rising so that she will notice it and work on dealing with and accepting it. Plus, if she notices it at the lower levels, then I can help her, but once it gets too high there's no way to reach her.

T: That is very true. Once the anxiety gets too high you cannot focus on the outside world well at all because so much of your attention is focused inward on the symptoms. Your machine won't tolerate interruptions and it takes over at these times. So, by catching the anxiety before it gets out of control, you can realize what negative things you are saying to yourself and use the coping/ accepting kinds of skills that we have discussed. It's very good that you have been working as a team and that you [the spouse] have been helping your partner view her anxiety more objectively by asking her what her level is and then supplying statements that are more rational than what she typically uses.

G: It really has helped. I realized I've been saying a lot of things to myself that have been making me worse. I've been trying to tell myself that it's just anxiety and that it won't really hurt me. I still get scared, though.

T: Still being frightened is not unusual at this point. It is a fear of fear as well as of the panic attacks that the fear brings on. You've made a good start on changing your attitude. Why don't you tell us about some of your experiences this week?

G: Well, I kept up the walking. You know, you were right. It is getting better. The more I do it, the easier it becomes. The best time was when my husband went with me and said coping statements to me. I went to the small store near my home and it went fine. I also went to the grocery store and once stayed for half an hour and it wasn't any worse than 15 minutes. The time by myself wasn't so great, but not as bad as I expected. I got up to a 5 but it only lasted a few minutes. I'd really like to try some extra things next week.

T: We'll go to the next item on your hierarchy and add that to what you've been doing. So, next week you will begin driving alone outside of your safe area. It has been a very long time since you have done this so we will take it slow at first. How far past your area would you like to begin?

G: The most I've driven in a year is the two blocks to the store. How about a couple of extra blocks?

T: That will be fine, remember to do it at least once with Jack. I also want you to continue walking and going to the store.

Session 7

THERAPIST: How have things been going this week?

GINNY: Well, I started out OK this week. I did fine talking to my neighbors. But things have gotten bad for me again. I just want to stay in the house. My anxiety is high all the time.

T: What is your anxiety level right now?

G: I guess about a 3.

T: What was the highest level you've experienced today?

G: Oh, I don't know, maybe a 5 or 6. It hasn't been quite as bad today. I guess it hasn't been that high all the time, but it seems that way when I think about it. [It is common for agoraphobics to exaggerate, especially in retrospect. Therefore, it is important to help them be as specific and objective as possible.]

T: Now it sounds like you're beginning to think more rationally about the anxiety. Saying to yourself that the anxiety has been high all week is an example of a catastrophic self-statement. These kinds of statements, as we've discussed before, fuel the machine and also make it difficult for you to deal rationally with the anxiety. Why don't you try again to describe your anxiety for the week?

G: Well, it was high and I felt bad—worse than usual. . . . OK, if I think about it calmly, I guess I would say that my anxiety was higher more often this week than last week.

T: That's very good—a much more rational statement. This statement, compared to your earlier statement, illustrates the difference between objectively describing a situation and catastrophizing. Why don't we review what's been happening this week?

SPOUSE: I think part of the problem this week is that she's been doing too much too fast. She felt good last week and then decided to do all kinds of things this week.

G: Well, I did do quite a bit and I was doing well. So, one day I decided to go to the mall across town. It's about a 40-minute drive, but I was sure I could do it. I started getting anxious but decided to do it anyway. I wasn't too bad until I got to the mall. They were having a big sale and it was very crowded. I went in anyway and had a terrible panic attack. I was so scared that I went to the phone and called my husband to come and get me. I thought I'd go crazy before he got there and I forgot to use my breathing and focusing exercises for dealing with panic. It turned out to be a real mess. I've been so scared that I haven't been out alone since that day.

T: It sounds like your husband may be correct. I know it's tempting when you're getting better to do more and more. But, it's also important to do new things in a step-wise fashion. That's why we start with your easiest item and work our way up to the harder ones. What you did was something that was at the top of your hierarchy and you couldn't stay. There's nothing wrong with being an 8 on your scale if you are sure you can stay, but if you have to leave that undoes a lot of good. It's perfectly understandable that you would flee such an overwhelming situation, but these are possible reasons why you've been having more problems ever since then. The "escape" added a little more fuel to the machine.

G: Yes, that does make sense, but I just feel that more is expected of me since I've been doing a little better. My husband is part of the reason that I overdid things this week. He thinks that because I can do one thing, that I should be able to do a lot more.

S: I have not expected you to do too much. I've been trying to be understanding about how you've been feeling and just encourage you.

G: Well, it feels like you expect more of me than I can do. Just because I can go to a mall store successfully doesn't mean I can go to the grocery store alone for all those things you wanted.

S: OK, so I shouldn't have asked you to go, but I didn't feel well that day and it didn't seem too much to ask; besides, you're supposed to be going into more situations to expose yourself to anxiety so you can learn to deal with it.

G: But I want to be the one to pick the situation! I don't want you acting like you can just expect everything from me now. I'm not ready for all that pressure. Plus, what about that party in 2 weeks? (*To the therapist.*) He wants me to go to a party with 200 people where I can't leave once I get there. And now he tries to say he's not pressuring me.

S: It's important that we go to this. You don't know how you're going to feel. This party could mean a promotion for me. Can't you do something for me? I've put up with your problems for years. I'm tired of making excuses for you. We could leave after an hour or so, if you really had to go—as usual! Look, I've tried to be understanding and I'm trying to work with you and coach you, but sometimes I need some support from you, too.

T: This might be difficult for your wife to do right now, but since it seems to be so important, let's see if we can find a way to work this out. I realize, as I'm sure your wife does, that agoraphobic problems affect everyone in the family and this often makes it even harder for the agoraphobic. It can often result in feeling very guilty so that requests to do more seem like a great deal of pressure. This is usually because the agoraphobic, especially in treatment, is putting a lot of pressure on herself to do more.

G: I do feel very guilty about the sacrifices my family has had to make because of my fears. Most of the time I feel badly about the effects this has had, especially on my husband. I feel like I've made his life so much harder and that, because of me, we haven't been able to do what other couples do. It's been a big strain on all of us.

S: It's been difficult at times, but I didn't realize you felt so badly. It hasn't been that hard on us, especially now that you're working on this problem. The kids and I are very proud of you. We all want to help. I guess in some ways I have been making it harder for you. It's just that some things seem so important that I want us to do them, even though I realize that it might be hard.

T: You stated before that the two of you could leave this party after an hour or so, could it be a shorter time than that?

S: I guess we could leave after half an hour—if we had to do so.

T: How would you both feel about this: You agree to go for a very short period of time because this is a difficult task for your wife. (*To Ginny.*) Then, you agree to stay for say one half hour, regardless of your anxiety, and then any time after that, if your anxiety goes, say, to a 7, you and your husband will leave. The two of you can use this time to practice the coping techniques and it would be a good opportunity for your husband to practice his coaching skills. (*To the spouse.*) It would be important, of course, for you to give your spouse a great deal of support, both before and during this party.

G: If he will help me and stay with me, I'll try it. But, he's got to really help me and stick to the agreement.

S: I can do that. I'm willing to agree to those terms.

T: Fine, so during the week practice the coping techniques with coaching. This will also be helpful in learning to deal with anticipatory anxiety. So, although in general I want you to slow down a bit, this is a special circumstance and let's try to deal with it the best we can. (*Couple agrees.*) Have there been any other things that have occurred during the week that are causing problems for you?

G: Well, there is something else. In fact, it's a problem that I've had for the past year and I've been afraid to bring it up because it sounds so crazy. I have really strange thoughts when I'm home alone with the kids sometimes. I wasn't having the thoughts very often until this bad episode. Now I've had them a lot.

T: It's not unusual when you're very anxious to have unusual thoughts and experiences. But, they can be very frightening.

G: They are frightening. I can't believe that I can think this way. I have bad thoughts about my children. It happens when I'm anxious and they won't be quiet or are doing something to get on my nerves. The other day I was trying to cook dinner and the kids were fighting and wouldn't listen to me. Well, . . . I had this knife in my hand . . . I was cutting up meat. Anyway, I thought that if I got anymore out of control that I would stab them. It scared me to death. Now I think about this a lot and get really anxious when I'm alone with them.

T: It is perfectly natural to have these thoughts occasionally, although it takes a lot of courage to admit them. Everyone has thoughts like these occasionally. People who tend to be anxious, such as agoraphobics, however, often get very frightened by these thoughts. What happens is that they tend to treat them as if they're actually going to do them. That is, what's really frightening you is that you think that there's a danger of your losing control and actually taking the knife and stabbing one of your children. If you weren't very anxious and nervous to begin with, these types of thoughts whenever you get annoyed or irritated would just go in one ear and out the other. That is, you'd hardly even notice them. We all have thoughts like that occasionally, but most of the time we just never really notice them and go about our own business. Your problem, then, is not that you're having the thought, it is that you're reacting to it and trying to suppress it. That is, you're fighting or wrestling with it just like you do with the anxiety machine. Therefore, you need to treat these thoughts just like you treat your machine. That is, just ignore it and focus on the next thing you're doing rather than worrying about the thought and whether you'll carry it out or not. If you can do this, then these thoughts won't bother you anymore. [In our experience, these minor obsessional episodes are common, but are easily handled by strategies such as that outlined above. Naturally, in the fully developed obessional process it is more severe and the problem will need much more systematic attention. See Chapter 2.] Now, for next week, I want you to work on the low-level hierarchy items that were assigned previously.

G: Even these will be hard for me now.

T: Don't worry ahead of time. There may be times when you attempt these tasks that you might experience anxiety, but it's not important if you experience the anxiety, but how you deal with it. Remember to continue your practice— just a little more slowly—and continue to work on your coping techniques both when alone and with your husband's help.

Session 8

THERAPIST: (*Following greetings.*) How did your exercises go during the past week?

GINNY: I did much better than last week. I experienced some anxiety problems but did the tasks anyway. I drove again. I started first with my husband because I was so scared. He helped me identify my thoughts, and once I changed some I did better. I went from a 5 to a 3. But, the next time that I was able to do this alone I was really anxious for hours ahead of time—about a 6 or 7. I didn't do too badly after I got started, but beforehand I was so anxious I almost didn't complete my tasks. The anxiety is improving when I'm actually doing things, but I'm still having problems when I think about doing them. What I tried once was just doing something on the spur of the moment; now, that was the best time.

T: Possibly it was the time that you experienced the least anxiety, but it was not what I would view as your best exercise. You see, what was happening was that you were still avoiding. This time you were avoiding the anticipatory anxiety. As you continue to avoid less situations, it is also important to not avoid anxiety. The key is not escaping but accepting your anxiety and doing so by objectively viewing what occurs, changing your thinking patterns, and experiencing the successes that come with continued practice. Your current coping techniques of avoidance only work for a short time and cause you many problems. It is a bad habit that needs to be changed. Everytime you avoid the anxiety, remember, you are feeding the machine. Your job now is to drain the machine. I'd like you to begin dealing with your anticipatory anxiety as you have done with the anxiety you experience in fearful situations.

I realize that it is uncomfortable—sometimes extremely so—to experience anxiety. But, as I've told you before, you will feel worse before you feel better. It is a step toward recovery. In the process of improving, what we typically see is that first you do more and feel worse. Then, you feel better while in an anxiety-provoking situation, but your anticipatory anxiety increases. Finally, this too will improve. These are the steps you can expect as you work toward overcoming your agoraphobic problems. So, I want you to keep working on both your anticipatory and situation-specific anxiety.

G: It's hard to remember all of those things when you are experiencing anxiety. I guess I would still rather avoid having to feel anxious. It's so frightening.

T: Experiencing anxiety is a part of life. It happens to everyone at one time or another.

SPOUSE: That's true, even I have had panic attacks occasionally, but I just don't pay any attention to them. I had a big presentation to do in front of a lot of people. I was really scared and I felt all the things that my wife talks about, but I knew why it happened and I wasn't really afraid of the symptoms. They made sense to me.

T: Yours is not an uncommon experience. Everyone experiences anxiety, and so our goal here is not to eliminate those feelings forever, but to help you learn to deal with the anxiety and to overcome your fears. It takes a lot of time and work but you are making progress and you must keep that in mind.

G: Yes, I guess I am doing better. We even went to the movies this week for the first time in years.

T: That's very good. Tell us how you did.

G: Well, when we were driving to the theater, my husband kept asking me what my thoughts were and what my level was. I guess he could tell that I was pretty apprehensive and scared.

S: Yes, I could tell, but she did really well. The anxiety got pretty high, around 6, but she was still able to identify thoughts and we worked on coming up with more realistic ways of thinking about it.

G: My anxiety level kept going up and down, but the highs didn't last too long. When we got to the theater, the parking lot was really crowded and it went up again, but I continued to use the coping and focusing and breathing, and I went in and even enjoyed the movie. He's getting to be a much better coach and doesn't seem to be pressuring me as much.

T: It sounds as though you are using the coping procedures very effectively and that the two of you are working as a team. You should be very pleased with yourselves. For the next week, I'd like you to do the next item on your hierarchy and to continue doing the good job that you have done in the past week. I also want you to schedule your tasks for each day ahead of time so that you will have the opportunity to deal with the anticipatory anxiety. The upcoming party will also be helpful in this area. The two of you can work on any anticipatory anxiety you experience.

Session 9

THERAPIST: How did your teamwork approach go during the past week?

GINNY: Really well. We even worked together on the anticipatory anxiety. It's still pretty hard to deal with, though.

T: You needn't be concerned. Remember, the anticipatory anxiety is the last to improve. Just keep working and rewarding yourself. Don't be discouraged if it takes some time.

G: But, we only have three more sessions and I'm scared because I should be so much better by now.

T: You are right on schedule. Even though we only have three more sessions of the initial twelve, this is a 1-year treatment program. You and your husband will take over where we leave off, and I will meet with you periodically throughout the next year to check on your progress. Overcoming your patterns of dealing with anxiety takes a long time and you can't expect overnight cures. Give yourself time and encouragement and you will continue to improve. Over the course of the next year, you can expect to have ups and downs, times when you are more anxious, but this is to be expected. So, if you have difficult times, remember that you are still learning and you needn't become unduly distressed.

G: Well, I guess I still want the anxiety to go away because I don't even want to think about feeling worse—ever.

T: That's understandable, but remember, you are trying to learn to accept the anxiety, not fight it or find ways to ward it off. Just try to remember to accept it and learn to live with and work with anxiety. How did the party go?

G: Really great! I couldn't believe it. My husband spent a lot of time with me beforehand; I would tell him my thoughts and he would help me think more objectively. We stayed for 3 hours. There were times I thought I might have to leave, but the anxiety would only stay high for a few minutes at a time. It really helped knowing that he would help me and wouldn't pressure me if I wanted to leave.

SPOUSE: She did a great job! I was really pleased. She's right—I am getting to be a better coach.

T: It sounds like you both did a very good job. What else have you been doing?

G: I've been doing so good this week. I feel so much better and am doing so much more. I went into K-Mart and shopped—I did great. I never thought I'd be able to do that again. I've been busy all week and I really am proud of myself. However, I did have one experience this week when I did not deal well with my anxiety.

S: That was when we were at her parents' house—she just can't say "no" to them and then she gets anxious. I think it's because she's angry that she gets so upset.

T: Why don't you describe what happened?

G: Well, my parents are always asking me to do things. I guess I feel like I have to do what they want, but I don't always want to and hate to tell them this. I'm always trying to please them and sometimes I guess I do get really angry. I didn't realize it before. This Sunday I had a horrible panic attack while I was at their home. I didn't want to be there. We had other things that I wanted to do and I felt trapped and, yes . . . angry.

T: What would happen if you told your parents that you had other things to do?

G: Well, I guess that I'm afraid that they will get angry with me, but maybe that's better than doing all these things that I don't want to do. It's a pretty scary idea to owe them so much.

S: But, you do a lot for them. You don't have to do everything. You've always been afraid of feeling angry.

T: It sounds like this is another area that you avoid. But this time it is an emotional one. Why don't you experiment this week; instead of doing things others want that you don't, try saying "no."

G: Well, it won't be easy, but I'll try. Doing new things is pretty scary to me.

T: That's your machine talking, feeding you anticipatory anxiety. When you feel angry or any strong emotion, you will experience a physiological change. It sounds like you've been interpreting this as anxiety.

G: That may be what I am doing.

T: Well, this week let's try facing up to this emotion and maybe learn to differentiate anger from anxiety. I also would like you to continue your good work on exposing yourself to situations and your excellent teamwork.

Session 10

THERAPIST: You look a little distressed this week.

GINNY: I am very upset. I feel like I've had a complete relapse. Everything is terrible.

T: Why don't you tell me what's been happening this week?

G: My husband was in an accident. He's been in the hospital, that's why he isn't here tonight. He spilled boiling water on his legs and he is being treated for the burns. He's going to be OK. He's home now but not feeling well. Surprisingly, I did fine during the emergency. I couldn't believe how calm I was. I got him to the hospital and I was in control until I found out that he would be alright and then I fell apart. My anxiety was a 7 or 8 for 2 days. I feel terrible now, too. My level is a 6. It's hopeless, I'll never get better.

T: It is not unusual when under extreme stress to respond with this kind of anxiety, especially for someone who has learned this way of responding to stress.

G: But, I was fine during the most stressful time. It wasn't until I knew my husband would be alright that I fell apart.

T: That is not an uncommon reaction. You apparently were not focusing on yourself during the emergency, but were, instead, responding in a very appropriate manner to what needed to be done. However, after the emergency had passed, you had time to focus on yourself. Could you describe for us what you mean by "fall apart?"

G: My anxiety was suddenly an 8. I thought I was going to collapse. All my muscles ached and then my heart started pounding and I thought that I was going to have a heart attack or pass out. I was so sure that I wasn't going to survive.

T: Physiologically, your symptoms are not difficult to explain and it has nothing to do with going crazy or having a heart attack. If you consider the degree of stress that you were under, your responses up to a point were what one would expect. The feeling that you would collapse could be explained both by the fact that you were relieved and also that you had kept your muscles tensed for such a long period of time, which also accounts for the muscular aches. Unfortunately, it doesn't sound like you interpreted these symptoms in this way.

G: No, I didn't, I got scared—I was scared anyway because I was so concerned about my husband, plus I was going to be alone with the kids for days. I started worrying about everything.

T: As your catastrophizing escalated, so did your anxiety symptoms. So, you see, your panic attack can easily be explained in this situation.

G: Well, I can see that now, but why have I been so bad ever since?

T: If you think about this, I imagine you could answer that question for yourself. Your fears of the anxiety and of being alone could easily account for the increase in your experience of anxiety.

G: That makes sense because I was scared and afraid of getting worse again with my husband gone. But, I even had a panic attack that woke me up, and I wasn't dreaming or anything.

T: Well, it is possible that you were having a bad dream that you don't remember, but it is also possible that you experienced a "spontaneous" panic attack. These can occur sometimes for no apparent reason, but can be coped with in the same manner as any other increase in anxiety. Let's spend a few minutes focusing on what happened before your husband's accident.

G: I was doing really well. I did additional driving and was able to deal with what anxiety I did experience. Oh, I also told my parents that I really didn't want to do something. They didn't take it too well at first but finally agreed to do it themselves. I was really proud of myself. I was a little anxious, about a 3, when I decided to tell them, but then I got angry and this time I was able to keep the anxiety and anger separate. That made me feel much better about myself.

T: It sounds like you were doing very well.

G: Yes, but that was then and now I feel like I can't cope with anything.

T: Well, let's start with what you just said, that you can't cope with anything. Is that really true?

G: Well . . . no, but it feels that way.

T: That is negative talk, the kind of talk that results in your becoming anxious. Actually, it sounds to me like you've been coping with many things and doing a very good job of it.

G: I haven't been doing a good job the last few days.

T: During times of extreme stress, everyone's anxiety increases. So, it is not unusual for you to have been experiencing a very difficult time. However, now it is time to begin focusing on changing your thoughts and your behavior and to stop fueling your machine.

G: Well, I can try.

T: It may be hard, especially following such a stressful period, but you have done it before and I'm sure that you can deal with your anxiety now. I'd like you to continue with what you've been doing and add your next hierarchy item for this week.

Session 11

THERAPIST: (*To the spouse.*) I'm glad to see you back. How are you feeling?

SPOUSE: Physically, much better, but I've been kind of depressed. Some of the depression is probably because of the injury, but some of it is because my wife is getting so pushy.

GINNY: I am not pushy. Just because I can do more things now and don't want to do everything you say doesn't mean I'm pushy.

S: Well, it seems pretty pushy to me. You used to be quieter . . . more accepting. Definitely easier to get along with.

G: That's because I felt bad all the time. I didn't want to make things any worse for you so I was always trying to make you happy, just like with my parents. I don't want to always do things whether I want to or not.

S: You don't seem to need anybody anymore. I want you to be able to do things, but now you act like you don't care whether I'm in the house or not.

G: I don't feel that way at all. I just don't need you as much and I don't want to be that dependent anymore.

S: Well, regardless, I'm starting to worry about our relationship. It's not the same anymore.

T: It is not uncommon for couples to experience a period of adjustment when so many changes are occurring in their relationship. Your wife's independence has probably been further accentuated by your accident and the fact that you have been required to depend on her recently.

S: Yes, it's been very strange to have her doing things for me. I guess it has made her seem more independent than ever. It's not that I don't want her to get better or to be able to do things. But, I want her to still need me, too. I guess I don't want everything to change. It's kind of frightening.

T: Yes, it can be frightening and the two of you will need to work on adjusting your relationship now that it's changing. It will take some time for you to feel secure with your wife's added freedom, but, in time, it won't be so unsettling for you and you can feel more secure with the relationship.

G: I didn't understand that he was feeling this way. I still need him, but how I need him is changing and I like the way it's changing. I guess I can try to help him understand this. (*To the spouse.*) I didn't mean for you to feel insecure. It doesn't mean that I don't care or don't need you. I think our relationship is getting better. We talk more, don't we?

S: Yes, and in some ways I feel that it's getting better, but these changes are hard to get used to.

T: In time you will both adjust to the changes, especially if you do communicate about how you're feeling. I'm very glad to hear that your wife is doing so much better.

S: So am I. We did do a lot of things together this week and she even did all the shopping by herself.

G: Yes, I did all the grocery shopping. I was really proud of myself. I'm having some anxiety in stressful situations, but most of the time it isn't too bad. When we went out to dinner, the anxiety peaked at an 8, but only for a few minutes. I was able to deal with it and we had a good time. I went to K-Mart again too and did just fine.

T: It sounds like you are doing a great job. You have your last hierarchy item to attempt this week.

G: That's kind of scary, it's the one I messed up before by trying it too early.

T: You do have some negative memories about that, but deal with it as you would any other situation—both the anticipatory anxiety and any anxiety you experience in the mall.

G: My anticipatory anxiety is finally starting to get better. OK, I'll try it a few times.

Session 12

THERAPIST: How have things been going this week?

GINNY: I did really well going to the mall. I went twice on my own and once with my husband. I went with him first. He coached me every step of the way and I remembered that when I went on my own.

SPOUSE: She did very well. She even shopped all three times; but, you know, this is getting expensive!

G: That's alright, it feels great. It really surprises me—all the things I can do. A lot of things I don't even think about anymore. I just go and do them. I never thought I'd be able to do that.

It is kind of scary now, though, because treatment ends tonight. I'm afraid that I will go back to the way I was before.

T: This is a hard session for everyone. But, treatment is not really ending tonight. Remember, this is only the end of the first 12 sessions. I will be seeing you periodically during the next year. As I've said in the past, there will be ups and downs and there may be times that you feel you are doing badly, but that is all part of getting better.

G: I still don't want to feel badly, I guess.

T: Of course not, no one does, but anxiety and stress are parts of life for everyone. You are learning to deal with this when it occurs, but for you, as for everyone else, it will occur. Since you have learned in the past to cope with anxiety by avoiding, this pattern may occur very temporarily, again, but you have the skills and knowledge to prevent this from becoming a chronic pattern. So, don't become frightened if you have an occasional down day, they will occur, but that's all they are. You are well on your way to overcoming your anxiety problems, but you must keep working on this.

G: I'll try, but it is really scary to feel that you are out there on your own.

S: But, I think it's easier for me to work with her now if there's a problem.

T: That's exactly what we want you to do. Your wife will need your help. Recall that when we began I told you that you would be trained to take over where we leave off. You have learned to become a good coach and your help during the next year is crucial. We will have booster sessions starting monthly for a while and then less frequently as time progresses, but the two of you will be doing the work.

G: But, there are still things that I haven't done that are scary for me. For example, I have to be in a wedding in a few months and there are other things too, like taking long trips.

T: Just approach everything the way you have learned to do during these sessions. Begin new things in a graded fashion if necessary. Remember to use your coping skills for both anticipatory anxiety and for anxiety in the stressful situation and you will do fine. Your husband can help you to do this, especially if there are times you forget or times you feel the need to have reminders. You are not all alone, although I think you can manage pretty well on your own now. We will see you again in a month and in the meantime I want you to keep working on improving skills. You have come a long way and, even if you do have an occasional difficult time, you will have all the gains that you have made so far to help you through those times.

A CONCLUDING NOTE

Typically, in our program the group is seen 2 or 3 weeks after the last session and then with decreasing frequency. Most couples will come to the first session and then will drift away as they are able to handle their own lives increasingly on their own. As noted in the Introduction, occasionally a relapse will occur, most often precipitated by some extremely stressful life situation, but even the most severe relapses can be handled in two to three sessions if contact is made immediately. In other cases, couples who have moved away and then relapsed have written to us that they have relapsed, but with the help of their family, and perhaps contact with another mental health professional, have been able to work back through the program much more quickly than the first time, even if their "relapse" lasted as long as 6 months. The literature reviewed at the beginning of the chapter, as well as our own experience, indicates the "relapse" happens but does not last, since improvement reported by most clinics around the world is maintained at 4–10 years after treatment.

Nevertheless, it is only fair to remind the reader of several factors also reviewed in the beginning of the chapter. A substantial number of people do not achieve optimal functioning, and yet another proportion show no improvement whatsoever. Much work remains before we are able to identify individual predictors of failure or only partial improvement, which will allow us to tailor treatment more closely to individuals. In our own program we are becoming much more heavily involved in the relationship aspects of dealing with agoraphobia, whether it be with the spouse or, less frequently, some other member of the family. We have come to believe that while exposure-based treatments may be the *sine qua non* of any successful treatment, more fully optimal responding from a much larger percentage of clients may come about through important changes in the dominant personal relationships in these people's lives. We will know a lot more about this in the coming years.

References

Agras, W. S., Chapin, H. N., & Oliveau, D. C. (1972). The natural history of phobia. *Archives of General Psychiatry, 26*, 315–317.

Agras, W. S., Leitenberg, H., & Barlow, D. H. (1968). Social reinforcement in the modification of agoraphobia. *Archives of General Psychiatry, 19*, 423–427.

Agras, W. S., Sylvester, D., & Oliveau, D. (1969). The epidemiology of common fear and phobia. *Comprehensive Psychiatry, 10*, 151–156.

Agulnik, P. L. (1970). The spouse of the phobic patient. *British Journal of Psychiatry, 117*, 59–67.

American Psychiatric Association. (1980). *Diagnostic and statistical manual of mental disorders* (3rd ed.). Washington, DC: Author.

Andrews, J. D. W. (1966). Psychotherapy of phobias. *Psychological Bulletin, 66*, 455–480.

Ascher, L. M. (1980). Paradoxical intention. In A. Goldstein & E. B. Foa (Eds.), *Handbook of behavioral interventions: A clinical guide* (pp. 266–322). New York: Wiley.

Barlow, D. H. (1983, October). *The classification of anxiety disorders.* Paper presented at "DSM-III: An Interim Appraisal" conference sponsored by the American Psychiatric Association, Washington, DC.

Barlow, D. H. (Ed.). (1981). *Behavioral assessment of adult disorders.* New York: Guilford.

Barlow, D. H., Blanchard, E. B., Vermilyea, J. A., Vermilyea, B. B., & DiNardo, P. A. (1984). *The phenomenology of generalized anxiety in the anxiety disorders.* Manuscript submitted for publication.

Barlow, D. H., Cohen, A. S., Waddell, M. T., Vermilyea, B. B., Klosko, J. S., Blanchard, E. B., &

DiNardo, P. A. (1984). Panic and generalized anxiety disorders: Nature and treatment *Behavior Therapy, 15,* 431–449.

Barlow, D. H., Hayes, S. C., & Nelson, R. O. (1984). *The scientist-practitioner: Research and accountability in clinical and educational settings.* New York: Pergamon.

Barlow, D. H., Leitenberg, H., Agras, W. S., & Wincze, J. P. (1969). The transfer gap in systematic desensitization: An analogue study. *Behaviour Research and Therapy, 7,* 191–197.

Barlow, D. H., Mavissakalian, M., & Schofield, L. (1980). Patterns of desynchrony in agoraphobia: A preliminary report. *Behaviour Research and Therapy, 18,* 441–448.

Barlow, D. H., O'Brien, G. T., & Last, C. G. (1984). Couples treatment of agoraphobia. *Behavior Therapy, 15,* 41–58.

Barlow, D. H., & Wolfe, B. E. (1981). Behavioral approaches to anxiety disorders: A report on the NIMH-SUNY, Albany, research conference. *Journal of Consulting and Clinical Psychology, 49,* 448–454.

Beck, A. T., Ward, C. H., Mendelson, M., Mock, J., & Erbaugh, J. (1961). An inventory for measuring depression. *Archives of General Psychiatry, 4,* 561–571.

Benedikt, V. (1870). Uber Platzschwindel. *Allgemeine Wiener Medizinische Zeitung, 15,* 488.

Bland, K., & Hallam, R. S. (1981). Relationship between response to graded exposure and marital satisfaction in agoraphobics. *Behaviour Research and Therapy, 19,* 335–338.

Chambless, D. L., & Goldstein, A. J. (Eds.). (1982). *Agoraphobia: Multiple perspectives on theory and treatment.* New York: Wiley.

DiNardo, P. A., O'Brien, G. T., Barlow, D. H., Waddell, M. T., & Blanchard, E. B. (1983). Reliability of DSM-III anxiety disorder categories using a new structured interview. *Archives of General Psychiatry, 40,* 1070–1075.

Emmelkamp, P. M. G. (1980). Agoraphobics' interpersonal problems: Their role in the effects of exposure in vivo therapy. *Archives of General Psychiatry, 37,* 1303–1306.

Emmelkamp, P. M. G., & Kuipers, A. C. M. (1979). Agoraphobia: A follow-up study four years after treatment. *British Journal of Psychiatry, 134,* 352–355.

Emmelkamp, P. M. G., & Ultee, K. A. (1974). A comparison of "successive approximation" and "self-observation" in the treatment of agoraphobia. *Behavior Therapy, 5,* 606–613.

Emmelkamp, P. M. G., & Wessels, H., (1975). Flooding in imagination vs. flooding in vivo: A comparison with agoraphobics. *Behaviour Research and Therapy, 13,* 7–15.

Foa, E. B., Jameson, J. S., Turner, R. M., & Payne, L. L. (1980). Massed vs. spaced exposure sessions in the treatment of agoraphobia. *Behaviour Research and Therapy, 18,* 333–338.

Foa, E. B., Steketee, G., & Milby, J. B. (1980). Differential effects of exposure and response prevention in obsessive–compulsive washers. *Journal of Consulting and Clinical Psychology, 48,* 71–79.

Fry, W. F. (1962). The marital context of an anxiety syndrome. *Family Process, 1,* 245–252.

Goldstein, A. J. (1970). Case conference: Some aspects of agoraphobia. *Journal of Behavior Therapy and Experimental Psychiatry, 1,* 305–313.

Goldstein, A. J. (1982). Agoraphobia: Treatment successes, treatment failures, and theoretical implications. In D. L. Chambless & A. J. Goldstein (Eds.), *Agoraphobia: Multiple perspectives on theory and treatment* (pp. 183–213). New York: Wiley.

Goldstein, A. J., & Chambless, D. L. (1978). A reanalysis of agoraphobia. *Behavior Therapy, 9,* 47–59.

Grey, S. J., Rachman, S., & Sartory, G. (1981). Return of fear: The role of inhibition. *Behaviour Research and Therapy, 19,* 135–144.

Hafner, R. J. (1976). Fresh symptom emergence after intensive behaviour therapy. *British Journal of Psychiatry, 129,* 378–383.

Hafner, R. J. (1977). The husbands of agoraphobic women: Assortative mating or pathogenic interaction? *British Journal of Psychiatry, 130,* 233–239.

Hafner, R. J. (1979). Agoraphobic women married to abnormally jealous men. *British Journal of Medical Psychology, 52,* 99–104.

Hand, I., Lamontagne, Y., & Marks, I. M. (1974). Group exposure (flooding) in vivo for agoraphobics. *British Journal of Psychiatry, 124,* 588–602.

Holden, A. E., & Barlow, D. H. (1984). *Heart rate and heart rate validity recorded in vivo in agoraphobics and non-phobics.* Manuscript submitted for publication.

Holden, A. E., O'Brien, G. T., Barlow, D. H., Stetson, D., & Infantino, A. (1983). Self-help manual for agoraphobia: A preliminary report of effectiveness. *Behavior Therapy, 14,* 545–556.

Hudson, B. (1974). The families of agoraphobics treated by behaviour therapy. *British Journal of Social Work, 4,* 51–59.

Jannoun, L., Munby, M., Catalan, J., & Gelder, M. (1980). A home-based treatment programme for agoraphobia: Replication and controlled evaluation. *Behavior Therapy, 11,* 294–305.

Jansson, L., & Ost, L. (1982). Behavioral treatments for agoraphobia: An evaluative review. *Clinical Psychology Review, 2,* 311–337.

Klein, D. F., Zitrin, C. M., Woerner, M. G., & Ross, D. C. (1983). Behavior therapy and supportive psychotherapy: Are there any specific ingredients? *Archives of General Psychiatry, 40,* 139–153.

Lang, P. J. (1968). Fear reduction and fear behavior: Problems in treating a construct. In J. M. Shlien (Ed.), *Research in psychotherapy* (Vol. III). Washington, DC: American Psychological Association.

Lang, P. J. (1977). Imagery in therapy: An information processing analysis of fear. *Behavior Therapy, 8,* 862–886.

Langer, T. S., & Michael, S. T. (1963). *Life stress and mental health.* New York: Macmillan.

Last, C. G., Barlow, D. H., & O'Brien, G. T. (1984). Cognitive change during behavioral and cognitive–behavioral treatment of agoraphobia. *Behavior Modification, 8,* 181–210.

Lazarus, A. A. (1966). Behavior rehearsal vs non-directive therapy vs advice in effecting behavior change. *Behaviour Research and Therapy, 4,* 209–212.

Marks, I. M. (1978). *Living with fear.* New York: McGraw-Hill.

Marks, I. M. (1981). *Cure and care of neuroses: Theory and practice of behavioral psychotherapy.* New York: Wiley.

Marks, I. M., & Herst, E. R. (1970). A survey of 1200 agoraphobics in Britain: Features associated with treatment and ability to work. *Social Psychiatry, 5,* 16–24.

Marks, I. M., & Mathews, A. M. (1979). Brief standard self-rating for phobic patients. *Behaviour Research and Therapy, 17,* 263–267.

Marsland, D. W., Wood, M., & Mayo, F. (1976). Content of family practice: A data bank for patient care, curriculum, and research in family practice—526,196 patient problems. *Journal of Family Practice, 3,* 25–68.

Mathews, A. (1978). Fear reduction research and clinical phobias. *Psychological Bulletin, 83,* 390–404.

Mathews, A. M., Gelder, M. G., & Johnston, D. W. (1981). *Agoraphobia: Nature and treatment.* New York: Guilford.

Mathews, A. M., Johnston, D. W., Lancashire, M., Munby, M., Shaw, P. M., & Gelder, M. G. (1976). Imaginal flooding and exposure to real phobic situations: Treatment outcome with agoraphobic patients. *British Journal of Psychiatry, 129,* 363–371.

Mathews, A. M., Teasdale, J., Munby, M., Johnston, D., & Shaw, P. (1977). A home-based treatment program for agoraphobia. *Behavior Therapy, 8,* 915–924.

Mavissakalian, M., & Barlow, D. H. (Eds.). (1981). *Phobia: Psychological and pharmacological treatment.* New York: Guilford.

McPherson, F. M., Brougham, L., & McLaren, S. (1980). Maintenance of improvement in agoraphobic patients treated by behavioural methods—a four-year follow-up. *Behaviour Research and Therapy, 18,* 150–152.

Meichenbaum, D. H. (1977). *Cognitive-behavior modification: An integrative approach.* New York: Plenum.

Milton, F., & Hafner, J. (1979). The outcome of behavior therapy for agoraphobia in relation to marital adjustment. *Archives of General Psychiatry, 36,* 807–811.

Mullaney, J. A., & Trippett, C. J. (1979). Alcohol dependency and phobias: Clinical description and relevance. *British Journal of Psychiatry, 135,* 565–573.

Munby, J., & Johnston, D. W. (1980). Agoraphobia: The long-term follow-up of behavioural treatment. *British Journal of Psychiatry, 137,* 418–417.

Nelson, R. O., & Barlow, D. H. (1981). Behavioral assessment: Basic strategies and initial procedures. In D. H. Barlow (Ed.), *Behavioral assessment of adult disorders* (pp. 13–43). New York: Guilford.

O'Brien, G. T., & Barlow, D. H. (1984). Agoraphobia. In S. M. Turner (Ed.), *Behavioral treatment of anxiety disorders* (pp. 143–185). New York: Plenum.

O'Brien, G. T., Barlow, D. H., & Last, C. G. (1982). Changing marriage patterns of agoraphobics as a result of treatment. In R. DuPont (Ed.), *Phobia: A comprehensive summary of modern treatments* (pp. 140–153). New York: Brunner/Mazel.

Rachman, S., & Hodgson, R. J. (1980). *Obsessions and compulsions.* Englewood Cliffs, NJ: Prentice-Hall.

Shepherd, M., Cooper, B., Brown, A. C., & Kalton, G. W. (1966). *Psychiatric illness in general practice.* London: Oxford University Press.

Sinnott, A., Jones, R. B., Scott-Fordham, A., & Woodward, R. (1981). Augmentation of *in vivo* exposure treatment for agoraphobia by the formation of neighborhood self-help groups. *Behaviour Research and Therapy, 19,* 339–347.

Snaith, R. P. (1968). A clinical investigation of phobias. *British Journal of Psychiatry, 114,* 673–697.

Spanier, G. B. (1976). Measuring dyadic adjustment: New scales for assessing the quality of marriage and similar dyads. *Journal of Marriage and the Family, 10,* 15–28.

Stern, R., & Marks, I. M. (1973). Brief and prolonged flooding: A comparison in agoraphobic patients. *Archives of General Psychiatry, 28,* 270–276.

Thorpe, G. L., & Burns, L. E. (1983). *The agoraphobic syndrome: Behavioural approaches to evaluation and treatment.* Chichester, England: Wiley.

Uhlenhuth, E. H., Balter, M. B., Mellinger, G. D., Cisin, I. H., & Clinthorne, J. (1981, December). *Quasi-diagnostic symptom clusters: Correlates and relations to drug use.* Paper presented at the 20th annual meeting of the American College of Neuropsychopharmacology, San Diego, CA.

Vermilyea, J. A., Boice, R., & Barlow, D. H. (in press). Rachman and Hodgson (1974) a decade later: How do desynchronous response systems relate to the treatment of agoraphobia? *Behaviour Research and Therapy.*

Webster, A. (1953). The development of phobias in married women. *Psychological Monographs, 67,* 1–18.

Westphal, C. (1871). Die Agoraphobia: Eine neuropathische Erscheinung. *Archiv für Psychiatrie und Nervenkrankheiten, 3,* 384–412.

Wolpe, J. (1958). *Psychotherapy by reciprocal inhibition.* Palo Alto, CA: Stanford University Press.

Wolpe, J. (1970). Identifying the antecedents of an agoraphobic reaction: A transcript. *Journal of Behavior Therapy and Experimental Psychiatry, 1,* 299–304.

Zitrin, C. M. (1981). Combined pharmacological and psychological treatment of phobias. In M. Mavissakalian & D. H. Barlow (Eds.), *Phobia: Psychological and pharmacological treatment* (pp. 145–173). New York: Guilford.

Zitrin, C. M., Klein, D. F., & Woerner, M. G. (1978). Behavior therapy, supportive psychotherapy, imipramine, and phobias. *Archives of General Psychiatry, 35,* 307–321.

Zitrin, C. M., Klein, D. F., & Woerner, M. G. (1980). Treatment of agoraphobia with group exposure in vivo and imipramine. *Archives of General Psychiatry, 37,* 63–72.

Zitrin, C. M., Klein, D. F., Woerner, M. G., & Ross, D. C. (1983). Comparison of imipramine hydrochloride and placebo. *Archives of General Psychiatry, 40,* 125–139.

2

OBSESSIVE–COMPULSIVE DISORDER

GAIL STEKETEE AND EDNA B. FOA

A number of significant advances have been made in the treatment of these extraordinarily difficult patients in just the last 5 or 10 years. In this chapter, two of the world's leading experts report on the application of these advances and the various pitfalls one encounters in translating research findings into practice. It will not take the reader long to see that successful therapy for this problem is markedly different both in structure and content from the usual therapeutic approaches. Intensive daily sessions involving both imaginal as well as direct *in vivo* practice in dealing with difficult situations seems essential, as is enlisting the cooperation of significant others in the home environment. The importance of involving significant others continues a theme first described in Chapter 1 wherein spouses or other people close to the person with the problem become an important and integral part of treatment.

In this chapter, the most complete assessment package yet reported is described. This package includes specific scales, most of which were developed by the authors, that are included in the appendices. These will be easily incorporated into an assessment and treatment program by clinicians, particularly after reading the section on interviewing the patient, which describes in some detail, through transcripts of interviews, the "flow" of the assessment process. Finally, the chapter also includes brief and up-to-date summaries of behavioral, cognitive, and biological theories or models of obsessive–compulsive disorders along with a summary of alternative treatments (e.g., surgical, pharmacological) and evidence for their effectiveness.—D. H. B.

DEFINITION

The description of obsessive–compulsive disorder has changed little since it was first introduced by Esquirol in 1838. An obsessional symptom is typically described as a "recurrent or persistent idea, thought, image, feeling or movement which is accompanied by a sense of subjective compulsion and a desire to resist it, the event being recognized by the individual as foreign to his personality and into the abnormality of which he has insight" (Pollitt, 1956, p. 842). Variously labeled obsessional state, obsessional neurosis or illness, and obses-

Gail Steketee and Edna B. Foa. Department of Psychiatry, Temple University School of Medicine, Philadelphia, Pennsylvania.

sional–compulsive disorder, the current DSM-III (1980) appellation "obsessive–compulsive disorder" had been most commonly employed in recent writings (e.g., Emmelkamp, 1982; Foa, Steketee, & Ozarow, 1985; Insel, 1982; Marks, 1981a; Salzman & Thaler, 1981).

Obsessive–compulsive disorder includes both cognitive and behavioral aspects. Conventional formulations of this disorder typically refer to thoughts, images, and impulses as obsessions, while repetitious overt actions are defined as compulsions or ritualistic behavior. This modality-based distinction poses conceptual problems that become apparent when the functional relationship of the symptoms to anxiety is considered. For example one patient experienced as much discomfort from physical contact with chicken soup as from the mere thought of it. Both arouse anxiety, yet one is a cognitive event and the other behavioral. He relieved the former discomfort by washing, an overt ritual, and the latter by the thought "Palmolive," a cognitive ritual. In a second case the number "3" provoked anxiety in the patient while the number "7" reduced it. Although both are identical in form, they serve quite different purposes. These observations point out the inadequacies of the traditional definitions and suggest that alternative conceptualizations are needed.

The above considerations have led Foa and Tillmanns (1980) to propose a definition of obsessions and compulsions based on the functional relationship between obsessive–compulsive symptoms and anxiety. According to their model, "obsessions" or "ruminations" are defined as thoughts, images, or actions that *generate* anxiety. Compulsions, on the other hand, are conceived of as attempts to *alleviate* the anxiety aroused by the obsessions; they take the form of either overt actions or covert, cognitive ("neutralizing") events; both are functionally equivalent (Rachman, 1976).

Obsessive–compulsive disorders have usually been classified according to the nature of the ritualistic behavior, namely washing and/or cleaning, checking, and less frequent forms such as repeating and ordering. Case examples of the most common manifestations, washing and checking rituals, and their associated obsessional thoughts are given below.

Case 1. Sara is a 33-year-old married female, with two children. She felt contaminated (a nonspecific feeling of being dirty, accompanied by extreme anxiety and discomfort) when in contact with her mother. Her symptoms started 10 years prior to treatment when she was pregnant with her second child and her mother had touched her once in order to feel the movements of the fetus. Sara felt highly anxious immediately after that touch and was relieved after a normal shower. She came for treatment when she felt contaminated by everything that could have been even remotely in contact with her mother: persons living in the area where her mother lived, persons who were in contact with her mother, mail from the area where her mother lived, and so forth. She avoided contaminated places and controlled her husband's and children's movements to avoid being contaminated through them. In spite of all attempts to avoid contamination, Sara needed to actively clean herself. The washing activity gradually increased to include about 50 hand washings, three 30-min showers and several hours of cleaning various objects in her environment each day.

Case 2. Mike, a 32-year-old patient, performed checking rituals that were preceded by a fear of harming other people. When driving, he had to stop the car often and return to check whether he had run over people, particularly babies. Before flushing the toilet, he had to check to be sure that a live insect had not fallen into the toilet, since he did not want to be responsible for killing a living thing. At home he repeatedly checked to see that the doors, stoves, lights, and windows were shut or turned off so that no harm, such as fire or burglary, would come to his family due to his negligence. He particularly worried about his 15-month-old daughter, repeatedly checking the gate to the basement to be sure that it was locked. He did not carry his daughter while walking on concrete floors in order to avoid killing her by accidentally dropping her. Mike performed these and many other checking rituals for an average of 4 hr a day. Checking behavior started several months after his marriage, 6 years prior to treatment. It increased 2 years later, when his wife was pregnant with their first child, and continued to get worse over the years.

A shortcoming inherent in the traditional classifications mentioned above is their failure to bear on treatment strategies. To remedy this situation, Foa *et al.* (1985) proposed a classification system that rests on the types of cues that evoke anxiety and the type of activity (cognitive or overt) that reduces it. This classification will be briefly discussed here and its implications for treatment will be considered later in the chapter.

All obsessive–compulsives manifest internal fear cues, that is, intrusive thoughts, images, or impulses. These may be triggered by contact with *external cues*, such as a contaminated object or the locking of a door; they may also arise without apparent external events. A further distinction can be made with respect to the presence or absence of fears of *disastrous consequences*. For instance, the thought "Did I lock the door properly?" may be associated with the fear of a rapist invading one's home; the spontaneous image of Jesus's penis may give rise to a fear of going to hell. On the other hand, the intrusive thought "Is my hand contaminated?" may elicit discomfort in the absence of any concern with possible aversive consequences.

Thus, obsessions can be divided into several kinds: (1) presence of intrusive cognitive material, external fear cues and fears of disasters; (2) presence of intrusive material and external cues (in the absence of disasters); and (3) presence of intrusive material and fear of disasters (in the absence of external cues). A fourth type, intrusive cognitive material with neither external cues nor fear of disasters, is theoretically possible, but we have not observed patients with such obsessions, nor have we come across such reports in the literature.

How can rituals be classified? If all rituals are anxiety reducing, the type of ritual (e.g., washing, checking) becomes irrelevant since it does not lead to differential treatment. A more useful approach is to categorize compulsions on the basis of their mode (e.g., cognitive or behavioral). Although these two classes do not differ in their functional relationship to anxiety, they do carry different treatment implications as discussed in Foa *et al.* (1985).

The combination of the above classifications of obsessions and compulsions yields eight types of obsessive–compulsives; these are shown in Figure 2-1.

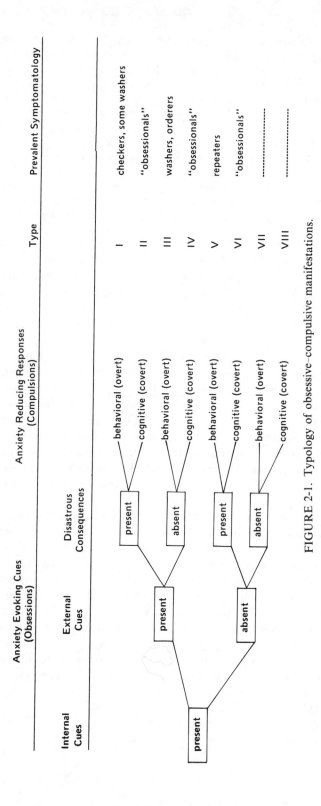

FIGURE 2-1. Typology of obsessive–compulsive manifestations.

As mentioned, only six types have been observed. It should be noted that a patient may experience more than one type of obsessive–compulsive manifestation. Similarly, a given obsession may be associated with both covert and overt rituals. As seen in Figure 2-1, the second, fourth, and sixth types are all distinguished by the absence of overt rituals. Patients manifesting this pattern have been labeled as "obsessionals"; they may vary, however, with respect to whether or not their obsessions include external cues and/or anticipated disasters. Type one, overt compulsions triggered by both external cues and fears of future disasters, is found in nearly all patients with checking rituals and in many of those with washing and cleaning rituals. The third type, obsessions triggered by external cues without feared consequences, is prevalent in patients with ordering rituals and is also found among those with washing rituals. The fifth type represents obsessions triggered by internal cues and by fears of future disasters; it is most often observed in patients who exhibit repeating rituals.

Obsessive–compulsive disorder is distinguished from compulsive personality (referred to by some as anal retentive personality) by the presence of discreet, intrusive, upsetting thoughts and repetitive stereotyped actions that are ego alien. Although the orderliness, rigidity, indecisiveness, and perfectionism characteristic of the compulsive personality style is sometimes present in individuals with an obsessive–compulsive disorder, it is by no means an essential element. Indeed, Lewis (1957) noted that "in no psychiatric condition is there a more obvious association between illness and preceding personality than here, yet we meet people with severe obsessional symptoms whose previous personality revealed no hint of predisposition" (p. 2). Supporting Lewis's observation is the finding that only 25% of (Rosenberg, 1967) a sample of obsessive–compulsives exhibited such traits. Guidano and Liotti (1983) have suggested that only some of the compulsive personality traits (e.g., conscientiousness, scrupulosity in moral matters, overestimation of details, rigidity, perfectionism, and uncertainty in making decisions) may be associated with obsessive–compulsive symptoms. Other characteristics such as orderliness, cleanliness, obstinacy, punctuality, and parsimony may be unrelated. Thus, although a relationship between traits and symptoms has traditionally been claimed, its nature and extent is unclear (Pollack, 1979; for review see Slade, 1974).

THEORETICAL MODELS

Behavioral Theory

Mowrer's (1939) two-stage theory for the acquisition and maintenance of fear and avoidance behavior has been commonly adopted to explain phobic and obsessive–compulsive disorders. Further elaborated by Dollard and Miller in 1950 and again by Mowrer in 1960, this theory postulates that first a neutral event becomes associated with fear by being paired with a stimulus that by its nature provokes discomfort or anxiety. Through an associative process concrete objects as well as thoughts and images acquire the ability to produce discomfort. In the second stage of symptom development, escape or avoidance responses are developed to reduce the anxiety or discomfort evoked by the various conditioned stimuli and are maintained by their success in doing so. Because of extensive generalization, many of the fear-provoking situations of obsessive–compulsives cannot readily be avoided. Passive avoidance behaviors, such as those utilized by phobics, are rendered ineffective in controlling anxiety. Active avoidance patterns in the form of ritualistic behaviors are then developed.

Support for the fear acquisition stage of this model is inadequate (e.g., Rachman & Wilson, 1980). The majority of patients cannot recall conditioning events associated with symptom onset. Onset does, however, often follow stressful life events, which Watts (1971) has suggested may serve to sensitize the individual to cues that have an innate tendency to elicit fear. Teasdale (1974) proposed that anxiety responses learned during early experiences may be enhanced by stress. In the same vein Rachman (1971) posited that for obsessive–compulsives, a state of heightened arousal could lead to sensitization of thoughts that have special significance for the individual. Related to these notions is Eysenck's (1979) theory that brief exposure to upsetting events that are above the tolerance threshold of an individual will produce sensitization; fear will then be acquired. Accordingly, individuals who are more highly arousable physiologically may be prone to developing anxiety disorders. There is evidence to suggest that obsessive–compulsives are indeed more physiologically reactive to threat anticipation than normals (Boulougouris, 1977). However, these data were obtained after symptom onset, and arousability may have been the effect rather than the cause of the obsessive–compulsive disorder. Nonetheless, it is not unreasonable to presume that heightened physiological arousal combined with a general stressor and with specific fear cues may produce such symptoms.

Whereas factors related to the acquisition of an obsessive–compulsive disorder are still largely unclear, there is evidence to suggest that obsessions give rise to anxiety/discomfort and compulsions reduce it. Ruminative thoughts were found to increase heart rate and deflection of skin conductance more than neutral thoughts (Boulougouris, Rabavilas, & Stefanis, 1977; Rabavilas & Boulougouris, 1974). Likewise, contact with contaminated objects resulted in increased heart rate and subjective anxiety (Hodgson & Rachman, 1972), as well as skin conductance level (Hornsveld, Kraaimaat, & van Dam-Baggen, 1979). A series of experiments with washers and checkers revealed that in most instances anxiety decreased following the performance of a ritual after deliberate provocation of an urge to ritualize (Hodgson & Rachman, 1972; Hornsveld et al., 1979; Roper & Rachman, 1976; Roper, Rachman, & Hodgson, 1973).

Cognitive Theories

In an attempt to explain obsessive–compulsive symptoms, Carr (1974) proposed that such individuals have abnormally high expectations of unpleasant outcomes; that is, they overestimate the risk of negative consequences for a variety of actions. He noted that obsessional content typically includes exaggerations of the normal concerns of most individuals—health, death, other's welfare, sex, religious matters, performance at work, and the like. Similarly, McFall and Wollersheim (1979) stressed the erroneous beliefs of obsessive–compulsives. These included the idea that one must be perfectly competent in all endeavors to be worthwhile, the belief that failure to live up to perfectionistic ideals should be punished, and the belief that certain magical rituals can prevent catastrophes. Such mistaken beliefs, the authors suggested, lead to erroneous perceptions of threat, which in turn provoke anxiety. The obsessive–compulsive's tendency to devalue his or her ability to deal adequately with such threats compounds the dysfunctional process. The resulting feelings of uncertainty, discomfort and helplessness are reduced through magical rituals, which are viewed by the patient as the only available method for coping with the perceived threat, since he or she lacks other more appropriate coping resources.

Beech and Liddell (1974) proposed that ritualistic behaviors are maintained not only to reduce immediate discomfort, but also to address the obsessive–compulsive's need for certainty before terminating an activity. Guidano and Liotti (1983) have suggested that a strong belief in perfectionism and in the potential for a correct solution to all situations characterize these patients.

Experimental findings lend some support to the above assertions. Obsessive–compulsives were observed to catalogue events discretely without being able to link concepts integratively, thus creating "islands of certainty" amidst confusion in an effort to control and predict events (Makhlouf-Norris, Jones, & Norris, 1970; Makhlouf-Norris & Norris, 1972). Reed found that obsessive–compulsive thinking was characterized by underinclusion or overspecification of concepts (Reed, 1969). He attributed their doubt and indecision to a distrust of their own conclusions (Reed, 1968). Consistent with these findings, Persons and Foa (1984) observed that ritualizers utilized overly specific concepts in their thought patterns with respect to both obsessional and neutral cues. An analogue study of college students scoring high on the Maudsley Obsessive–Compulsive Inventory (MOCI) checking subscale indicated that such individuals had poorer recall for prior actions and greater difficulty distinguishing real from imagined events than did subjects who had low scores (Sher, Frost, & Otto, 1983). These findings suggest that memory deficits in checkers may motivate repetitious checking behavior. A greater tendency of obsessive–compulsives than other psychiatric patients to request a repetition of information before rendering a decision was observed by Milner, Beech, and Walker (1971). Volans (1976) found similar trends although the differences in experiment failed to reach significance.

The above findings suggest that obsessive–compulsives are more rigid, perfectionistic, and doubting, requiring excessive amounts of information to make a decision, only to distrust their choice. These observations must be interpreted with some caution, however, since several of the studies included individuals deemed to have a compulsive personality style rather than an obsessive–compulsive disorder.

Foa and Kozak (1985) conceptualized anxiety disorders as specific impairments in affective memory networks. They adopted Lang's (1979) bio-informational theory, which states that fear exists as an information network (prototype) in memory that includes information about feared *stimuli,* fear *responses,* and their *meanings.* This information network is conceived of as a program for fear behavior itself, which occurs when the affective memory is accessed or activated. Neurotic fears, proposed Foa and Kozak, differ structurally from normal fears. The former are characterized by the presence of erroneous estimates of threat, unusually high negative valence for the threatening event, and excessive response elements (e.g., physiological, avoidance, etc.). In addition, neurotic fear structures are distinguished by their resistance to modification. This persistence may reflect failure to access the fear network, either because of active avoidance or because the content of the fear network precludes spontaneous encounters with situations that evoke anxiety in everyday life. Additionally, anxiety may persist because of some impairment in the mechanism of change. Cognitive defenses, excessive arousal with failure to habituate, faulty premises, and erroneous rules of inference are all impairments that would hinder the processing of information necessary for changing the fear structure.

Foa and Kozak (1985) suggested that several forms of fear occur in obsessive–compulsives. The patient who fears contracting venereal disease from public bathrooms and washes to prevent this has a fear structure that includes excessive associations between the stimuli (bathroom) and the anxiety responses as well as mistaken evaluations about the harm from the stimulus situation. For other obsessive–compulsives, fear responses are associated with mistaken meaning rather than with a particular stimulus. For example, patients who are disturbed by perceived asymmetry and who reduce their anxiety by rearranging objects do not fear the objects themselves, nor do they anticipate disaster from the assymmetry. Rather, they are upset by their view that certain arrangements of stimuli are "improper."

Although these authors suggest that no one form of fear structure is common to obsessive–compulsives, these patients all share an impairment in the interpretive rules for making inferences about harm. Typically, obsessive–compulsives base their beliefs about danger on the *absence* of discomfiting evidence and often fail to make inductive leaps about general safety from specific disconfirmations regarding danger. Consequently, although rituals are performed to reduce the likelihood of harm, they can never really provide safety and therefore must be repeated. In observing obsessive–compulsive checkers, one is impressed by what seems to be a memory deficit for their own actions *vis à vis* danger situations. However, a patient's doubt about the status of the just-checked gas burners, may reflect impairment in evidential rules for inferring danger.

Biological Factors

Several biological factors have been implicated in the development of obsessive–compulsive disorders. The number of reports appearing in the literature on monozygotic twins concordant for this disorder far exceeds chance expectations, thus pointing to a possible genetic factor in its etiology (Black, 1974). However, none of the concordant pairs were reared apart, and thus the influence of environment cannot be extracted from these reports. Moreover, discordance for the disorder in identical twins has also been found (Parker, 1964). Further, although parents and siblings of obsessive–compulsives show a significantly higher incidence of this disorder in contrast to psychiatric controls, its overall occurrence is low: Only 8% of parents and 7% of siblings showed such symptoms (Black, 1974). It seems apparent that gentic transmission can account for only a small portion of the variance in explaining the etiology of obsessive-compulsive disorders.

Seeking to delineate the neurological bases of obsessional neurosis, Pavlov (1934) extrapolated findings from observations of the stereotypic behavior of dogs in his laboratory. He proposed that whereas stereotypical and perseverative actions are due to a "pathological inertness" in the motor area of the cortex, obsessions and compulsions might result from a "similar inertness in other (cerebral) cortical cells in relation to sensations, feelings and conceptions" (p. 190). Such phenomena might result, he thought, from disease, intoxications, or occasional "accentuation of one or other of our emotions" (p. 193). The intensity of the inertness may determine the severity of the symptom, with hallucinations representing the extreme.

In contrast to the speculative nature of Pavlov's proposals, other authors have documented the occurrence of organic manifestations exhibited by obsessive–compulsive patients. Schilder (1938) reported on seven cases in which organic symptoms were evident, including tremor, facial rigidity, and excessive hyperactivity. Referring to Lewis's (1935) report on three cases of obsessive–compulsive neurosis with childhood histories of encephalitis, Shilder suggested that brain lesions might be implicated in the development of this disorder. Compared to normals, higher rates of birth abnormalities (Guirdham, 1972; Capstick & Sheldrup, 1977) and neurological illnesses (Grimshaw, 1964) have also been noted in obsessive–compulsives. Abnormal electroencephalogram (EEG) patterns were observed by Pacella, Polatin, and Nagler (1944); Flor-Henry, Yendall, Koles, and Howarth (1979); and Shagass, Roemer, Straumanis, and Josiassen (1984). These findings may implicate biological factors as directly causative of obsessions and compulsions. Alternatively, physical impairments indirectly may give rise to psychological deficits, which in turn lead to the development of further physical symptoms.

REVIEW OF TREATMENTS

Obsessive–compulsive disorders have long been considered among the most intractable of the neurotic disorders. As recently as 1960, Breitner noted that "most of us are agreed that the treatment of obsessional states is one of the most difficult tasks confronting the psychiatrist and many of us consider it hopeless" (p. 32). Indeed, traditional psychotherapy has not proven effective in ameliorating obsessive–compulsive symptomatology (Black, 1974). In a sample of 90 inpatients, Kringlen (1965) found that only 20% had improved at a 13- to 20-year follow-up. Somewhat more favorable results were reported by Grimshaw (1965); 40% of an outpatient sample were much improved at a 1- to 14-year follow-up.

Behavioral Treatments

Some improvement in the prognostic picture was evident with the introduction of behavioral methods derived from learning theory models. A detailed review of findings from case reports and controlled studies is available in Foa *et al.*, (1985). A summary is presented here.

If obsessions evoke anxiety/discomfort that is subsequently reduced by compulsions, then treatment should include anxiety-reducing procedures and/ or methods for blocking the reinforcement embedded in the performance of the rituals. Procedures aiming at both have been developed.

Aversion Procedures: Punishing the Obsessive–Compulsive Symptoms

Aversive methods are based on the principle that when an aversive event follows immediately upon the occurrence of a particular behavior, that behavior will be suppressed. Procedures such as shock treatment, thought stopping, snapping of a rubber band on the wrist, and covert sensitization have been applied to both obsessions and compulsions with mixed results. The use of *electrical shock* following reported obsessive thoughts has fared best; improvement was evident in six of seven patients in single case reports (Kenny, Solyom, & Solyom, 1973; McGuire & Vallance, 1964) and in four of six patients who participated in a controlled study (Kenny, Mowbray, & Lalani, 1978).

Although early case reports of *thought stopping* seemed promising, the outlook dimmed with subsequent controlled investigations in which gains were evident in only 8 of 24 patients (Emmelkamp & Kwee, 1977; Stern, 1978; Stern, Lipsedge, & Marks, 1975). To date the use of *covert sensitization* has been examined in only one case report (Wisocki, 1970). Thus, although these procedures have produced gains in some patients, their overall success rate has not exceeded that of traditional psychotherapy.

In another operant procedure, *aversion relief*, termination of an electrical shock (relief) was associated with the onset of a taped narrative of the patient's anxiety arousing obsessive thoughts. In this way, obsessions were negatively reinforced. Two series of single case studies indicated that 9 of 16 patients were improved at follow-up (Solyom, & Kingstone, 1973; Solyom, Zamanzadeh, Ledwidge, & Kenny, 1971). Other investigators reported less success when a similar technique was applied to ritualistic behavior (Marks, Crowe, Drewe, Young, & Dewhurst, 1969; Rubin & Merbaum, 1971).

In summary, the effects of procedures aimed at suppression of obsessive–compulsive symptoms are equivocal. The best results were obtained by Solyom and his colleagues with the use of aversion relief treatments for obsessions. Further testing of this procedure in controlled studies with a larger sample is needed before its efficacy can be established.

Reducing Anxiety and Discomfort

Procedures aimed at reducing the anxiety associated with obsessions have also been applied to obsessive–compulsives. Foremost among these procedures is systematic desensitization in which a state of relaxation is repeatedly paired with brief presentations of anxiety-provoking circumstances that are introduced in a gradual manner. As anxiety to obsessions decreases with this procedure, the compulsive behavior would be expected to extinguish automatically since it would no longer be needed for its anxiety reducing properties. Although reports indicate that his treatment is effective for *some* obsessive–compulsives, overall, desensitization has produced benefit in only 30%–40% of single-case reports (Beech & Vaughn, 1978; Cooper, Gelder, & Marks, 1965). To date, the efficacy of this technique with obsessive–compulsives has not been tested in controlled trials.

In an effort to promote habituation or reduction of anxiety to feared obsessional situations, investigators have utilized a variety of procedures involving prolonged exposure. One such technique, *paradoxical intention*, requires the patient to deliberately increase the frequency or intensity of the obsessional thought in an exaggerated and often humorous fashion (e.g., imagining that one is the "greatest mistake maker in the world" (Gertz, 1966). In two series of case reports utilizing this technique, the results were somewhat encouraging with 9 of 16 patients improved (Gertz, 1966; Solyom, Garza-Perez, Ledwidge, & Solyom, 1972); no controlled investigations have been reported.

Limited success has been achieved with *flooding in imagination* or its variant, *implosion*. In this procedure the therapist narrates a detailed image incorporating the patients' obsessional thoughts, images, impulses, and associated feelings. Although two case studies report benefits with this method (Broadhurst, 1976; McCarthy, 1972), comparative investigations show gains in only 6 of 10 patients (Emmelkamp & Kwee, 1977; Steketee, Foa, & Grayson, 1982). In another variant of exposure, *satiation*, the therapist prompts patients to repeatedly verbalize or write brief summaries of their obsessive thoughts for periods of up to 1 hour. Stern (1978) observed that only two of his seven patients improved with this method. An alternate version, *overt satiation*, was tested with three obsessionals using the aid of a "surrogate therapist," usually the spouse (Vogel, Peterson, & Broverman, 1982). Although all three case improved rapidly, the authors noted that three additional patients failed to benefit because of inadequate compliance either from the patient or the surrogate therapist.

In examining the differential effects of thought stopping and prolonged imaginal exposure, Emmelkamp and Kwee (1977) found that two patients failed to improve regardless of the treatment applied and three improved equally with either procedure. By contrast, Stern (1978) reported that two of seven patients who received exposure (satiation) improved, whereas none benefitted from thought stopping. It seems, then, that although some patients have benefited from each of the above described procedures, their overall efficacy has not been very impressive.

If, as suggested previously, obsessive–compulsive symptomology is composed of obsessions that evoke anxiety and compulsions that reduce it, then treatment should consist of techniques directed at decreasing the former and blocking the latter. Interventions directed at both symptoms simultaneously would be expected to yield a more successful outcome. In the foregoing studies rarely did investigators attempt to treat both types of symptoms differentially. An exception was aversion relief, in which emission of rituals was followed by the application of electrical shock, which was terminated upon exposure to the obsessions; treatment was successful in the two cases reported (Marks, Crowe, Drewe, Young, & Dewhurst, 1969; Rubin & Merbaum, 1971). Another treatment program that addressed both obsessions and compulsions, exposure and response prevention, has proven highly successful and has become the treatment of choice for this disorder. A summary of the research on this procedure follows.

Exposure and Response Prevention

Employing prolonged exposure to obsessional cues with strict prevention of ritualistic behavior, Meyer (1966) reported a successful outcome in two cases. Later reports indicated that this treatment regimen was highly successful in 10 of 15 cases and moderately so in the remaining 5; only two relapses occurred after a 5- to 6-year period (Meyer & Levy, 1973; Meyer, Levy, & Schnurer, 1974). Not surprisingly, such remarkable results with a severely dysfunctional group of patients provoked considerable interest in this treatment program. Variants of this method have now been examined in many controlled and uncontrolled studies. Findings have been remarkably consistent: Approximately 65%–75% of more than 200 patients who have undergone this procedure were improved and stayed so at follow-up. (See Foa et al., 1985, and Rachman & Hodgson, 1980, for detailed reviews of these studies.)

Briefly, the treatment consists of repeatedly exposing the patient for prolonged periods (45 min to 2 hr) to circumstances that provoke discomfort. Typically, exposure is graded so that moderately disturbing situations precede more upsetting ones. Ten to twenty daily sessions are held. Patients with washing rituals are required to touch their particular "contaminated" objects; those with checking compulsions are exposed to situations that evoke urges to check (e.g., exiting through the door, using the stove). They are requested to refrain from ritualizing regardless of the strength of their urges to do so. Details of this treatment regimen are provided later in this chapter.

The effects of treating obsessions and compulsions with exposure only, response prevention only, or their combination was examined by Foa and her colleagues (Foa, Steketee, Grayson, Turner, & Latimer, 1984; Foa, Steketee, & Milby, 1980; Steketee, Foa, & Grayson, 1982). At both posttreatment and follow-up, combined treatment was clearly superior to the two individual components employed separately. The component treatments produced differential benefits; exposure affected primarily the anxiety to contaminants and response prevention impacted mostly on ritualistic behavior. The superiority of employing both procedures simultaneously was thus established.

The advantage of exposing patients to feared circumstances in actual practice (i.e., *in vivo*) rather than in imagination has been demonstrated for simple phobics. For obsessive–compulsives and for agoraphobics the picture is less clear. If *in vivo* exposure is superior, it is only marginally so. (For a review see Mathews, 1978.) Moreover, if it is important to include exposure to *all* types of fear cues, then patients who fear disastrous consequences from contact with external cues (e.g., contracting a disease from bathroom germs or being responsible for the outbreak of a fire) should improve more when imaginal exposure is included in the behavioral treatment. Therefore, Foa, Steketee, Turner, and Fisher (1980) tested the effects of combined *in vivo* and imaginal exposure versus *in vivo* exposure only. Although at the end of treatment no differences between groups were observed, the former was superior in maintaining gains. This finding suggests that for those patients who have thoughts of future harm as an important feature of their obsessive ideation, the addition of imaginal exposure is indicated.

It is commonly noted that obsessive–compulsive symptoms produce a decline in the general functioning of those afflicted with this disorder. In addition to interference in work, home management, social, and leisure activities, these symptoms often produce conflict in marital relationships. As Marks (1981b) noted, however, "the presence of severe marital problems is not a contraindication for exposure treatment" (p. 590). Examining the relative effects of marital therapy and exposure and response-prevention treatment in obsessive–compulsives with disturbed marriages, Cobb, McDonald, Marks, and Stern (1980) found that marital treatment improved only the marital relationship whereas exposure treatment improved both the obsessive–compulsive symptoms and the marriage. It should be noted, however, that the latter treatment was less successful with patients whose obsessions revolved around excessive sexual jealousy. In four such cases, the addition of other behavioral procedures including marital therapy proved necessary (Cobb & Marks, 1979).

Assertiveness training has also been employed to treat six patients with obsessions about harming others, which were hypothesized to reflect social anxiety (Emmelkamp & Van de Heyden, 1980). Assertiveness training was found to be at least as effective as thought stopping. Given the generally poor results with the latter procedure and the specificity of the obsessions selected for this study, the general utility of assertiveness training as a treatment for obsessive–compulsive symptoms remains in question.

Cognitive Psychotherapy

Cognitive psychotherapy is founded on the assumption that thoughts and beliefs play a causal role in emotion and behavior. Cognitive interventions represent attempts to modify thoughts, belief systems, and irrational ideas and are for the most part delivered in conversation-like form. Only one study assessed the effects of cognitive therapy with obsessive–compulsives. Studying 15 patients Emmelkamp, van der Helm, van Zanten, and Plochy (1980) compared graded exposure *in vivo* with exposure preceded by self-instructional training. Treatment produced significant improvement in both groups; no differences between conditions were found at posttreatment or at follow-up. The authors concluded that the cognitive technique did not enhance the efficacy of exposure.

The failure of the procedure employed in the above study does not necessarily mean that cognitive treatment should not be implemented with obsessive–compulsives. If Foa and Kozak (1985) are correct in proposing that these patients have impairments in the rules by which they process information, then one might expect cognitive techniques to be beneficial. Such techniques, however, should be tailored to the specific cognitive deficits of this disorder.

The literature on the use of exposure and response prevention with obsessive–compulsives clearly indicates that this program produces successful outcome exceeding that of any other psychotherapeutic procedure. At present, then, this method is the preferred treatment for this disorder.

Pharmacological Treatment

A large variety of pharmacological agents, both anxiolytic and antidepressant, have been employed in an effort to remedy obsessive–compulsive symptoms. Included among the drugs administered to this population are the tricyclics (e.g., imipramine, clomipramine, doxepin); the benzodiazepines (e.g., chlordiazepoxide, diazepam); monoamine oxidase (MAO) inhibitors (e.g., clorgyline, phenelzine); and major tranquilizers (e.g., chlorpromazine, haloperidol). For reviews see Sternberg (1974) and Ananth (1976).

Uncontrolled studies and case reports clearly indicate that tricyclic antidepressant drugs reduced depressive symptomatology in obsessive–compulsive patients. Their effects on obsessive–compulsive symptoms are less clear (Ananth, 1977; Cammer, 1973; Freed, Kerr, & Roth, 1972; Geissman & Kammerer, 1964). More recently specific antiobsessive properties have been attributed to the tricyclic antidepressant clomipramine. In double blind trials this drug has been found to reduce ruminations and rituals more effectively than placebo (Karabanow, 1977; Marks, Stern, Mawson, Cobb, & McDonald, 1980; Thoren, Asberg, Cronholm, Jornestedt, & Traskman, 1980) and than the MAO inhibitor clorgyline (Insel, Alterman, & Murphy, 1982). A clear superiority of clomipramine over other tricyclics in reducing obsessive–compulsive symptoms has not yet been demonstrated. Comparing the effects of clomipramine and doxepin on obsessive–compulsives, Ananth and Van den Steen (1977) concluded that the former yielded superior results. Inspection of their results, however, casts doubt on this conclusion: Clomipramine reduced depression and general anxiety more than did doxepin, but not obsessive–compulsive symptoms. Likewise no significant differences were detected between clomipramine and nortriptyline (Thoren *et al.*, 1980).

Whether the apparent effects of clomipramine are due to a direct antiobsessive action or are secondary to its antidepressant properties is the subject of current controversy. Supporting the latter view are findings from a subset of 20 obsessive–compulsives (10 most depressed and 10 least depressed) in the Marks *et al.* (1980) study: Only the depressed patients showed drug effects on obsessive–compulsive symptoms. By contrast, both Thoren *et al.* (1980) and Insel *et al.* (1982) failed to find pretreatment depression ratings predictive of response to
• clomipramine. Negating the mediating role of depression in the effects of clomipramine on obsessional symptoms are the findings that nontricyclic antidepressants (MAO inhibitors) have not been as effective as the tricyclics (Insel *et al.*, 1983; Sternberg, 1974). A more defnitive test of the role of depressive symptoms in determining the response of obsessive–compulsives to tricyclics is currently underway in our laboratory at Temple University.

The value of combining pharmacotherapy and behavioral procedures has been examined in four group studies, all employing clomipramine. In an uncontrolled study, Neziroglu (1979) treated 10 patients with clomipramine followed by behavioral treatment. Clomipramine was effective, decreasing symptoms over baseline by 60%. A further improvement of 18.7% was observed after behavioral treatment. Unfortunately, the level of depression was not measured and thus its role in the drug action cannot be assessed.

Sookman and Solyom (1977) compared the effects of clomipramine with those of behavioral treatment. The authors concluded that clomipramine was as effective as behavioral treatment in reducing ruminations but less effective in ameliorating rituals. No statistical tests were conducted on the data and, again, measures of depression were not collected. Amin, Ban, Pecknold, and Klinger (1977) also examined the effects of clomipramine and behavior therapy in the following groups: clomipramine and behavior therapy, clomipramine and simulated therapy, and behavior therapy plus placebo drug. However, the number of subjects (three, two, and three respectively) was too small to provide reliable information about differential treatment effects. Moreover, the behavioral procedure selected by the authors, desensitization, has not proven effective with obsessive–compulsives.

A large controlled study in which the effects of clomipramine and behavioral treatment (exposure *in vivo* and response prevention) were compared was conducted by Marks *et al.* (1980). Forty obsessive–compulsive patients were assigned to the following groups: (1) clomipramine followed by behavioral treatment; (2) clomipramine followed by placebo psychotherapy (relaxation) and then by behavior treatment; (3) placebo drug followed by behavioral treatment; and (4) placebo drug followed by placebo psychotherapy and then by behavioral treatment. Patients with primary depression were excluded from the study. The results indicated that clomipramine alone effected improvement on both mood scales and measures of obsessive–compulsive symptoms; the application of behavioral treatment was followed by additional significant improvement on most behavioral measures but not on mood scales.

The above reports do not clarify the role of depression in the effects of clomipramine on obsessive–compulsives. From the evidence to date, Asberg, Thoren, and Bertilssen (1982) have concluded that "in patients with . . . severe obsessive–compulsive illness who are also dysphoric, clomipramine appears to be the drug of choice. It can be tried also in patients who are not dysphoric, but the effect is not equally convincing" (p. 20). Because of the high rate of relapse on withdrawal from clomipramine (Ananth, 1977; Insel *et al.*, 1983; Marks *et al.*, 1980; Thoren, *et al.*, 1980) and the relatively moderate improvement it produces (40% for Insel *et al.*, 1983, and 42% for Thoren *et al.*, 1980), therapy by exposure and response prevention remains the treatment of choice. The addition of clomipramine or other tricyclics may be indicated for patients who exhibit symptoms of marked depressions.

Psychosurgical Procedures

Several surgical procedures have been employed to treat obsessive–compulsive symptoms including leucotomy (e.g., Pippard, 1956; Sargent, 1962), tractotomy (e.g., Bridges, Goktepe, Maratos, Browne, & Young, 1973), and cingulectomy (e.g., Lewin, 1960). Of these, leucotomy appears to the most successful procedure. Leucotomized obsessive–compulsives fared better than nonleucotomized matched patients: At a 5-year follow-up, 50% of the former and 23% of the latter were much improved on target symptoms (Tan, Marks, & Marset, 1971). Using a stereotactic limbic leucotomy procedure, Mitchell-Heggs, Kelly, and Richardson (1976) reported that patients with obsessive–compulsive symptoms were more affected by the surgery than those with chronic anxiety (89% and 66% respectively). Depressed patients benefited less from the procedure than obsessionals whose response matched that of schizophrenics. A later report on 100 patients substantiated these findings (Mitchell-Heggs, Kelly, Richardson, & McLeish, 1978).

More recently, Tippin and Henn (1982) found that five obsessive–compulsives whose chronic symptoms had not responded to drugs, psychotherapy, or behavior therapy (type unknown) were considerably improved by a modified leucotomy procedure. Patients in this and other studies (e.g., Bailey, Dowling, & Davies, 1975) evidenced continued improvement at follow-ups ranging from 1 to 7 years. Summarizing findings from six studies of leucotomy with obsessive–compulsive patients, Tippin and Henn (1982) suggest that as many as 69 of 110 patients were improved or symptom free and required no further intervention; an additional 20 were moderately improved.

ASSESSMENT

Ideally, measurement of obsessive–compulsive symptomatology should assess obsessions and compulsions separately. Assessment of obsessions should include information about external fear cues, internal fear cues (thoughts, images, or impulses) and thoughts of disastrous consequences. The degree of discomfort/

anxiety associated with obsessional content should also be measured on physiological and cognitive indices. The amount of passive avoidance behavior associated with obsessional thoughts must also be appraised. Additionally, both overt and cognitive compulsions should be separately assessed.

Whereas global measures of obsessive–compulsive symptoms have proven useful in assessing treatment effects (e.g., Foa, Grayson, *et al.*, 1983; Marks *et al.*, 1980), in order to better understand the mechanisms underlying various treatment procedures, measures of specific manifestations are essential. Several instruments to assess obsessions, anxiety, avoidance, and compulsions have been developed, largely for research purposes; however, reliability and validity have been investigated for only a few. Available measures include Likert-like scales for self, therapist, and assessor ratings, inventories, behavioral observations, and physiological measurements.

Measures of Obsessions and Associated Anxiety

The frequency and severity of obsessions are rarely measured. More often, fear or anxiety associated with obsessions have been evaluated. Rabavilas and Boulougouris (1974) observed that physiological responses (heart rate and skin conductance) increased during elicitation of patients' obsessive fantasies and employed these responses to evaluate treatment effects.

More common are attempts to rate the main fears associated with obsessions (e.g., contact with toilets) on Likert-like scales that have been adopted from studies on phobias (Watson & Marks, 1971). The difficulty with such measures is that they are more suitable for washers, whose main fear component is contact with discrete external stimuli. They are less appropriate for checkers, whose obsessive thoughts are centered primarily on fears of potential catastrophies. To evaluate this aspect of the obsession, we have developed two measures: The Cues for Urges to Ritualize (CUR) Inventory (Appendix A) assesses the three aspects of obsessive content, internal cues, external cues, and expected consequences. The Thought Inventory (Appendix B) aims at studying the specific consequences feared by the patient and their intensity.

Measures of Avoidance

To measure passive avoidance, we have developed an Exposure Test (Appendix C), in which the patient is asked to approach his or her most feared situation as closely as possible in discrete steps. The number of uncompleted steps constitutes a measure of avoidance and the level of subjective discomfort experienced during each step forms an additional measure of obsessional anxiety. A similar behavioral avoidance test has also been used by other investigators (Marks, Hodgson, & Rachman, 1975). This measure can be of immediate value to the therapist in obtaining direct information about the extent of the avoidance and associated discomfort.

Measures of Compulsions

Behavioral measures of target rituals have been employed to assess the frequency and duration of ritualistic behavior (see Appendix D). The patient is requested to record the number of minutes spent on compulsive activity. Although this measure has been employed in several studies and appears to be sensitive to treatment effects (Emmelkamp & Kraanen, 1977; Foa, Steketee, & Milby, 1980), it is not without problems. Some patients are noncompliant when asked to record rituals throughout an entire day. On the other hand, time sampling may not accurately reflect the ritualistic behavior, since many obsessive–compulsives can easily delay the emission of rituals. The discomfort of most obsessive–compulsives in being observed when engaging in compulsive actions renders the use of objective observers to record rituals potentially distorting. In addition to the above difficulties, self-monitoring by itself has been shown to produce significant changes in target symptoms (e.g., Nelson, 1977).

To overcome such difficulties, Mills, Agras, Barlow, and Mills (1973) introduced a mechanical device that registered the number of occasions on which a patient approached the sink in his or her hospital room. This method requires that all washing take place in one location. An additional drawback is that when only frequency is recorded, the severity of the ritualistic symptoms can be grossly distorted, since some patients wash rarely but for very long periods. Given that both of these behavioral recording methods suffer from shortcomings, the convenience of the self-monitoring procedure obviously renders it more useful for clinical practice.

Despite problems of reliability and validity, daily completion of a Behavioral Measurement Chart (Appendix D) provides useful insight into the patient's daily routine and daily fluctuations in ritualistic behavior. This information may help generate hypotheses about external influences on compulsive behavior.

Standardized Inventories

Of the standardized instruments devised to evaluate obsessive–compulsive symptoms, the Leyton Obsessional Inventory (LOI; Cooper, 1970) has been the most widely used. It employs a card sort procedure of 69 items to obtain four scores: symptom, trait, resistance, and interference. This instrument discriminates obsessive–compulsives from normals, house-proud housewives, and depressives and has adequate test–retest reliability (see Emmelkamp, 1982, for review). It has been criticized for its inadequacy in detecting important obsessive–compulsive symptoms such as intrusive thoughts and washing rituals and for the interdependence of its four scales. Further, correlations between the Leyton and other measures of obsessive–compulsive symptoms have been highly variable across studies (Rachman, Marks, & Hodgson, 1973; Marks et al., 1975). A shortened 20-item paper-and-pencil version of this inventory, the Lynnfield

Obsessional–Compulsive Questionnaire was developed to circumvent the cumbersome administration procedure required by the Leyton and to better tap obsessional ruminations (Allen & Tune, 1975). Despite evidence of its satisfactory reliability and validity, this version has not been widely adopted.

Both obsessional traits and symptoms are assessed by the Sandler–Hazari Obsessionality Inventory (Sandler & Hazari, 1960). In contrast to the Leyton, this measure failed to discriminate patients from controls and therefore is of questionable validity (see Emmelkamp, 1982, for review). An Obsessive–Compulsive Checklist (Philpott, 1975) has been used to evaluate degree of impairment in 62 daily activities. It was later shortened to include 39 items (Marks, Hallam, Connolly, & Philpott (1977). Like the Leyton, this measure is usually administered by an assessor. It has been found to detect changes following treatment (Insel *et al.*, 1982, with the long version; Marks *et al.*, 1980, with the short version). More recently, Hodgson and Rachman (1977) have developed the Maudsley Obsessive–Compulsive Inventory (MOCI), which is composed of 30 true–false questions concerned exclusively with symptom dimensions. In addition to a general obsessive–compulsive score, this inventory yielded five subscales: checking, cleaning, slowness, doubting-conscientiousness, and ruminating were identified. It was found to have adequate validity and reliability (Rachman & Hodgson, 1980). Its focus on symptoms to the exclusion of traits has rendered this instrument useful in the assessment of treatments directed at symptoms.

Two inventories that measure psychopathology—the Minnesota Multiphasic Personality Inventory (MMPI) and the Hopkins Symptom Checklist (HSCL; Derogatis, Lipman, Rickels, Uhlenhuth, & Covi, 1974) or its newer relative, the Symptom Checklist-90 (SCL-90; Derogatis, 1977)—yield what have been labeled obsessive–compulsive subscales. The validity of both scales has been questioned. Doppelt (1983) has found that neither scale elevation nor code (personality) types of the MMPI predicted outcome for obsessive–compulsives. Obsessive–compulsives were found to differ from other neurotics on the obsessional scale of the HSCL, but a cutting score that correctly identified a satisfactory percentage of the patients could not be found (Steketee & Doppelt, in preparation). Further, this scale failed to correlate significantly with standardized measures of obsessive–compulsive symptoms.

INTERVIEWING THE PATIENT

The first interviews with the obsessive–compulsive patient have a dual purpose: establishing a diagnosis and collecting information pertinent to treatment planning. We have suggested that obsessions are defined by the specific cues that give rise to anxiety. These are classified as external cues (e.g., tangible objects), internal cues (e.g., images and impulses), and worries about future consequences. Also defining obsessive–compulsive symptoms are patterns of avoidance, which may be grouped into passive and active (ritualistic) forms. The latter can be further subdivided into overt or covert (cognitive) compulsions. As will be discussed later, information pertaining to each of these dimensions will determine the treatment procedure to be used. Later interviews may focus on environmental and social variables that may affect treatment progress or maintenance of gains. A discussion of the type of information sought in the initial interviews follows. An outline of the topics to be covered is provided in Appendix E.

External Fear Cues

For the vast majority of obsessive–compulsives, certain external cues generate anxiety. The interviewer should solicit highly specific information about such cues in an attempt to identify the basic sources of concern. Washers who fear public toilets may or may not fear toilets in their own home, public doorknobs, railings, and so on. Contamination "travels" and objects become contaminants through contact (which may be quite remote) with the source of contamination. It is impossible to understand the patient who fears contact with leather items, animals, and neckties without the knowledge that all these items are contaminated only to the extent that they are associated with "maleness."

Identification of the source of fear is important not only in comprehending the patient's conceptual structure but also in determining treatment: to achieve successful outcome, habituation to the source of fear is essential. Often, when treatment does not include confrontation with this source a relapse will occur. For example, a patient who feared her hometown was treated with systematic exposure and response prevention 3000 miles away from the town. Treatment consisted of exposure to items that had been contaminated by direct or indirect contact with the hometown. Because she lived so far from this town, however, direct exposure to it was not implemented. She continued to avoid her hometown despite a move to a city within 150 miles of it. Within a year new items associated with the hometown started to disturb her again until a complete relapse was evident. It was not until she was repeatedly exposed (for prolonged periods) to her hometown that she experienced lasting improvement.

In this case the source of fear was readily identified by the patient; in other cases it is quite obscure. Detailed investigation of the onset of the fears and the various current contaminants eventually enables the clinician to identify the source contaminant. The following dialogue is illustrative of this process.

THERAPIST: Can you tell me why you wash so much?

PATIENT: My car is dirty. Every time I use the car I have to wash a lot so that I don't spread it all around.

T: What is it about the car that is dirty?

P: I'm not sure, I just know it feels dirty to me and everything in it is dirty. I have to be very careful about cleaning it.

T: What else besides the car and the things that touch the car are dirty?

P: Some of my furniture.

T: What furniture?

P: There's a cupboard and a table.

T: If you clean them well will they be clean?

P: I can clean the dishes that are in them and that's OK, but I can't seem to get the furniture itself clean enough.

T: What about the car? Can you clean it?

P: No, I can never get it clean enough but I keep from spreading it by cleaning the things in it. I wash the clothes I wear and I shower after I was in the car.

T: And you don't know why the car feels dirty?

P: No, I'm sorry.

T: When did it all start?

P: About 7 years ago when I lived in a basement apartment in New York. It was flooded with a sewage back-up.

T: What happened?

P: I cleaned it but it never felt really clean like it used to. I moved after 4 months because I never got used to the dirty feeling.

T: Did the furniture that bothers you come from that apartment?

P: Yes, I think so.

T: Did you have the car then too?

P: Yes.

T: Do you have any other things from that apartment?

P: No, I got rid of them. But I couldn't afford to get rid of everything.

T: Would you feel contaminated by sewers in general?

P: No. That never occurred to me.

T: What would happen if I asked you to go back to your apartment?

P: I could never do that.

T: So the thing you are most afraid of is to return to your apartment. Is it that the furniture and your car are dirty because of that apartment?

P: Maybe, I didn't think about it.

Unlike the washer's fears, with checkers, it is less important to identify the external fear cues that elicit urges to check since for them the source usually lies in the feared consequences attendant upon exposure to the feared situations if rituals are not performed. They will be discussed below.

Internal Fear Cues

Anxiety/discomfort may be generated by internal cues, that is, thoughts, images, or impulses that are disturbing, shameful, disgusting, or horrifying. Such cues may include number sequences, impulses to stab one's child (which may be triggered, in turn, by external cues such as knives or scissors), thoughts that one's spouse may have an auto accident on the way home, images of having sex with Christ, or impulses to expose one's genitals. Some obsessive–compulsives may respond with anxiety to internal bodily sensations such as tachycardia, minor pains, or swallowing if these are interpreted as signals for impending physical disease (e.g., heart attack, choking, cancer). When the latter concerns are accompanied by elaborate checking rituals, they are classified as obsessive–compulsive; when patients who are concerned with physical illness confine their anxiety reduction activity to frequent contact with physicians, they are diagnosed as hypochondriacal.

Patients who are reluctant to disclose their "shameful" obsessions, can be encouraged with direct questions, a matter-of-fact attitude, and, if necessary, reassurance that 85% of normal individuals also have such unwanted ideas (Rachman & DeSilva, 1978).

THERAPIST: You've told me that there are certain thoughts that make you feel you have to wash. Can you tell me about them?

PATIENT: I wash if I pass Fifth Street.

T: Why? What is it that makes you wash? What are your thoughts?

P: I can't talk about it.

T: I really need to know about them. It's important for your treatment.

P: I've never told them to anyone. I can't make myself say them. They're really awful. You wouldn't want to talk to me if you knew.

T: We all have thoughts we're ashamed of, mostly sexual or religious ones. Or sometimes we get urges to hurt someone and this can be pretty upsetting. Are your thoughts similar to any of the ones I just mentioned?

P: I really don't want to say.

T: I understand your reluctance to share thoughts you yourself don't approve of, but I'm afraid the treatment will not be good enough if we do not take into consideration what upsets you most. Remember, every one of us gets shameful thoughts. I promise that I will continue to talk to you even after you tell me about them.

P: I'm afraid that if I talk about them they might come true.

T: As you yourself know, it's unlikely that saying them will not make them come true. But in any case, even if it were remotely possible, you will have to take this risk in order to get better.

Fears of Harm

Often the external and internal cues for discomfort are associated with anticipated harm, which for some may be the primary source of discomfort. Although the details vary from patient to patient, most washers fear disease, physical debilitation, or death to themselves or others to whom they might spread the contamination. Most checkers seek to avoid being responsible for an error that will either lead to physical harm (e.g., leaving the stove on and burning the house down) or psychological harm (e.g., setting the table incorrectly and eliciting criticism from a significant other; writing "I am a homosexual" on a check and thereby losing others' respect). Those with repeating rituals are concerned that their upsetting thoughts will come to pass (e.g., an accident happening, losing control and stabbing someone, punishment from God). For some the feared disaster is vague: "I do not really know what will happen if I don't wash. I just feel that something terrible will happen to my family."

Not all patients fear an environmental disaster. In our experience about half of the washers deny any concern about physical harm stemming from contamination. Rather, it is the intense unpleasant emotional state that they find intolerable. Without their rituals they fear that the experience of high anxiety will be unending and will ultimately destroy them emotionally. This sort of fear may be viewed as a special type of anticipated harm.

Strength of the Belief in Harm

Foa (1979) has observed that assigning high probabilities to feared consequences (i.e., having "overvalued ideas") was associated with failure. Therefore, information about the strength of the belief becomes important when one considers treatment. While most patients are aware of the senselessness of their fears, when questioned carefully a rare few will assert that the disasterous consequences they anticipate (e.g., dying from contact with a leukemic patient's waterglass) will in fact occur. Overvalued ideators may require cognitive manipulations to correct their misconceptions and to convince them of the need to accept the seemingly high risk in exchange for a normal lifestyle.

To assess the strength of the patient's belief, one can pursue the following line of questioning:

THERAPIST: Logically, how likely is it that you will get cancer if you touch a person with cancer and you don't wash? What is the percent likelihood that this will actually happen? Give me a number from 0 to 100.

PATIENT: Oh, it feels really dangerous.

T: I'm not asking you about your feelings. I know that you "feel" that it's dangerous or you wouldn't go to the lengths you do to avoid these situations. Ignore your feelings for a moment and just use logic. How likely is it that you'll get cancer from touching Mrs. Blackwell [a co-worker who had a recent mastectomy]?

P: Not that high, maybe 40%.

T: You mean that of 10 people who touch her, 4 will get cancer?

P: No, that's not right. If you put it like that, its probably less than 1%.

Most obsessive–compulsives will respond in the above manner. The following dialogue is typical of overvalued ideators:

PATIENT: If I go to a cancer hospital and I touch my children without washing real well, they will get cancer.

THERAPIST: How certain are you that they'll get it?

P: One hundred percent.

T: How likely is it that I'd get cancer if I went there?

P: I'm not sure, probably less than my kids. I'm not sure I'd get it either. We're probably stronger than they are. But I'm sure they would get it.

T: So you believe that cancer is transmitted by direct touch. You must know that there isn't any medical evidence for this.

P: I know. I've talked to experts and I've read many articles on the subject. But medicine doesn't know everything and I'm sure that 5 years from now they will find out that I was right.

Avoidance and Rituals

Both active and passive forms of avoidance behavior are exhibited by obsessive-compulsives. Whenever possible, obsessive–compulsives, like phobics, seek to passively avoid situations that provoke discomfort. Most avoidance patterns are obvious (e.g., refraining from using public toilets, shaking hands, touching garbage, using the stove, and taking out the trash). More subtle forms of avoidance include such actions as sidestepping brown spots on the sidewalk (possible dog feces), touching doorknobs at their less-used base with fingers only (to be washed later), sitting forward on chairs to avoid the spot that others usually use, and wearing only slip-on shoes to avoid having to touch laces or buckles. Since even minor avoidances prevent *full* exposure to the fear cues, they may serve to maintain that fear and thus may reduce treatment efficacy.

Active forms of avoidance, that is, ritualistic behavior, have already been discussed. These consist of washing, cleaning (including wiping with alcohol or spraying with antiseptic cleaner), checking, repeating actions, placing objects in a precise order, and repeatedly requesting reassurance. For some, anxiety is also reduced by cognitive rituals such as praying, thinking "good" thoughts, and mentally listing events. The functional relationship of each ritual to the fear cues and to passive avoidance behaviors should be ascertained. If a relationship cannot be identified, then the diagnosis of obsessive–compulsive disorder should be questioned and the possibility of psychotic thinking processes should be considered. Stereotyped ritualistic behaviour is sometimes observed in schizophrenics.

History of Main Complaint

A detailed account of the events surrounding the onset of the current symptoms may provide clues about variables associated with maintenance of symptoms. Although postulated intrapsychic conflicts are not incorporated in behavioral theories of obsessive–compulsive symptoms, it is important to identify existing interpersonal or intrapersonal conflicts since they may increase the general level of stress, which in turn may further aggravate current symptomatology.

Often onset is associated with some stressful event such as childbirth, death of a significant other, or marriage. Such events may not play a direct part in etiology of the disorder but they may raise the general level of stress so that preexisting psychological impairments are manifested overtly. Once evident, obsessive–compulsive symptoms may continue even when these stressors are resolved. But if the stress continues, it may impair the patient's ability to effectively process therapeutic experiences or to maintain treatment gains. It is therefore important to explore whether the onset stressor still exists at the time of treatment. For example, a patient whose obsessive–compulsive symptoms began after a premarital sexual encounter continued to denegrate herself for it. While not the immediate focus of treatment, her attitudes and attendant emotional upset about this event required attention after the successful treatment of her obsessions and rituals.

Many patients arrive with an extensive history of unsuccessful psychotherapeutic efforts and are anxious to tell the therapist about previous treatments. A detailed inquiry about previous therapy is particularly necessary in the case of patients who failed to benefit from an exposure and response-prevention program. From failed attempts the therapist may learn how to avoid prior pitfalls.

Mood State

Both depressive and anxious mood states have been identified as prognostic factors in the outcome of behavioral treatment with obsessive–compulsives (Boulougouris, 1977; Foa, 1979; Foa, Steketee, Grayson, & Doppelt, 1983; Marks et al., 1980). Severely depressed patients were less likely to benefit from treatment and evidenced more relapse, whereas for mildly depressed patients treatment was more often highly successful. With regard to general anxiety, those who showed low anxiety benefited from treatment; patients with severe anxiety were equally likely to succeed or fail (Foa, Steketee, et al., 1983).

Because of their relationship to treatment outcome, mood states, especially depression, should be carefully assessed. Attempts to reduce adverse mood states before treatment, either by drugs or psychological means (e.g., cognitive therapy), may enhance the efficacy of the behavioral program. Depression can be assessed by administering the Beck Depression Inventory (Beck & Beamesderfer, 1974) or the Hamilton Depression Scale (Hamilton, 1960). A variety of inventories are available to measure anxious mood state, including the Spielberger State–Trait Anxiety Inventory (Spielberger, Gorsuch, & Lushene, 1970) and the Taylor Manifest Anxiety Scale (Taylor, 1953).

The above strategem for assessment was not meant to be a comprehensive guide for interviewing a psychiatric patient. Rather, it is a guide for the specific information required for conducting exposure and response-prevention treatment with an obsessive–compulsive. Obviously, the clinician will also want to assess mental status and collect information about general life history, especially as it bears on current symptomatology.

TREATMENT

Selection of Procedure

As noted earlier, obsessive–compulsive symptoms can readily be viewed as consisting of obsessions that give rise to discomfort and avoidance and compulsive behaviors that reduce it. If we are to effectively treat this syndrome, we must select therapy procedures for each of these two sets of symptoms. Which treatment methods, then, should be applied to which manifestations and under what conditions? Table 2-1 delineates the obsessive–compulsive manifestations and specifies which method of treatment is appropriate for each.

Treatment of Obsessions

For the treatment of external obsessive cues, several choices are available. *In vivo* procedures are preferred because of their seeming superiority over imaginal ones for such concrete cues (Emmelkamp & Wessels, 1975; Rabavilas, Boulougouris, & Stefanis, 1976). Because of its questionable efficacy with this disorder, desensitization is not recommended for obsessive–compulsives. Rather, exposure *in vivo* (flooding in practice) is the treatment of choice for reduction of anxiety generated by external fears cues. Research has demonstrated that for most patients the speed with which increasingly anxiety-provoking cues are presented matters little (Hodgson, Rachman, & Marks, 1972). Since patients prefer to be gradually introduced to their most feared situation, a five- or six-step hierarchy usually is employed. The use of a model who demonstrates contact with the disturbing situation has not been found to enhance the effectiveness of exposure (Rachman *et al.*, 1973). However, since some patients report that modeling is helpful, the therapist should demonstrate contact with feared situations whenever indicated.

Longer periods of exposure have been shown to be more advantageous than brief interrupted ones (Rabavilas *et al.*, 1976). No research has been conducted on the optimal time period for exposure, however, nor do we know at what point to terminate an exposure session. For obsessive–compulsives discomfort begins to dissipate after 30–60 min, and this reduction continues for about 90 min (Foa & Chambless, 1978; Rachman, DeSilva, & Roper, 1976). Consequently, sessions of 1–2 hr are recommended.

The anxiety associated with internal cues and anticipated future disasters has been reported to improve following a variety of procedures including imaginal flooding, satiation, paradoxical intention, systematic desensitization, and aversion relief. Of these, imaginal flooding appears to be the most versatile in enabling the therapist to incorporate many cues into a single imaginal sequence. Should the patient's obsessive thoughts or images be quite circumscribed, however, techniques such as satiation, in which a brief obsessional phrase is repeatedly evoked, may also be used. Paradoxical intention addresses mainly the disastrous content of the obsessions; it is usually practiced briefly in the office and is employed primarily as a homework procedure.

Self-exposure procedures have also proven effective for this disorder (Emmelkamp & Kraanen, 1977). For motivated patients the therapist's presence during exposure may not be needed.

TABLE 2-1. The Relationship between Obsessive–Compulsive Manifestations and Treatment Interventions

| | Obsessive–compulsive manifestations | | | | |
| | Anxiety-evoking cues (obsessions) | | | Anxiety-reducing responses (compulsions) | |
Treatment interventions	External	Thoughts, images, impulses	Disastrous consequences	Behavioral	Cognitive
Exposure procedures	Prolonged exposure *in vivo*	Imaginal flooding	Imaginal flooding (imɔlosion)		
	Desensitization *in vivo*	Systematic desensitization	Aversion relief		
	Exposure with para-doxical instruction	Aversion relief	Satiation		
		Satiation	Paradoxical intention		
		Paradoxical intention			
Blocking procedures				Response prevention	Thought stopping
					Aversion by shock
					Aversion by rubber band

Treatment of Compulsions

As for phobics, the passive avoidance of obsessive–compulsives is blocked whenever deliberate exposure is instituted. However, exposure does not automatically eliminate overt compulsions. To this end response prevention, which is considered to be the treatment of choice for compulsions, is implemented. Although aversion therapy had produced successful outcomes in several reported cases, applications, of this procedure with sexual deviates were found to result in a high rate of relapse, particularly when appropriate alternative sexual behaviors are not available to the patient (see Brownell & Barlow, 1980, for review). It is possible that aversion may facilitate the effectiveness of response prevention, but to date no research on the combination of the two procedures has been conducted.

The degree of strictness of the response prevention has varied across studies, ranging from normal handwashing and no supervision to complete abstinence from washing for several days at a time under continuous supervision. The amount of supervision does not seem to impact strongly on outcome, perhaps because motivated patients comply with treatment instructions without supervision and unmotivated ones will circumvent them.

Cognitive rituals are more difficult to treat, possibly because their emission is less under the patient's control than that of overt rituals. Techniques such as thought stopping, aversion treatment, and distraction are potentially helpful. But information about the actual efficacy of these methods for covert compulsions is not yet available. In using blocking procedures caution must be exercised to avoid the inclusion of anxiety-provoking obsessions among the target cognitive rituals. Exposure rather than blocking procedures should be applied to obsessions in order to facilitate habituation of the associated anxiety.

A frequently unrecognized form of ritualistic behavior is repeated requests for reassurance. A patient fearful of her daughter gaining access to pills kept in the medicine cabinet was in the habit of repeatedly asking: "It's OK if I leave them there if they have safety caps on, isn't it?" Reassurance from the therapist quieted her only briefly, whereupon she would begin to doubt that she had closed the safety caps properly and request repeated confirmation that her technique in closing the caps was proper. In her case response prevention consisted of refusal to provide reassurance. Not all requests for information or reassurance are compulsions; only when they become stereotyped and repetitive is corrective action required.

Implementation of Procedures

In the following section we will discuss how to conduct exposure and response-prevention treatment. This will include a description of the setting, the social context, relevant therapist and client variables, and the sequence of treatment. A case study will illustrate the application of specific procedures. In an effort to provide information to the therapist who is inexperienced with either obsessive–compulsive patients or the application of exposure treatment, we have included illustrations of various complications that may arise in the course of treatment and proposed suggestions for solving them.

Overview

The treatment program consists of three stages, an information-gathering period, an intensive exposure and response-prevention phase, and a follow-up maintenance period. These are summarized below.

INFORMATION-GATHERING PERIOD

For most patients, 3–6 hr are sufficient for collecting information about obsessions, compulsions, history of the problem, and general life history and for planning the treatment program with the patient. For local patients, these sessions are usually held weekly; for those who come from long distances, fewer sessions of longer duration are planned. In the latter cases, it is suggested that an evaluation interview be scheduled initially to obtain general information about current symptomatology and to assess motivation level and appropriateness for behavioral treatment. The treatment program should be discussed in sufficient detail with the patient so that he or she is not surprised during the active treatment phase by the implementation of exposure and response prevention.

During these preliminary sessions, the therapist delineates the content of imaginal flooding scenes, the objects or situations to be confronted *in vivo* and the rituals to be prevented. The setting, home or hospital, is selected, and individuals are designated to assist the patient in his or her assignments and to support the patient when difficulties arise between sessions. It is important that supervisors have a good relationship with the patient and demonstrate a supportive attitude toward the treatment undertaking. Similarly, in the hospital only those nurses, aides, or other medical personnel with whom the patient feels most comfortable should be selected as assistants. It is important that the therapist instruct the aides in the patient's presence in order to avoid misunderstandings.

TREATMENT PERIOD

In our program, patients are usually seen for 15 treatment sessions scheduled on every weekday. Clinical observations suggest that massed sessions produce better results than do spaced sessions. We suggest a minimum of three sessions each week. Treatment may be extended if significant progress is evident, and the remaining discomfort is be expected to decrease with 1 or 2 weeks of further therapy. There is a point, however, where the therapeutic efforts have diminishing returns. Rachman *et al.* (1979) observed that 30 sessions were only slightly better than 15 sessions of exposure. If 20 treatment sessions produce minimal results, it is doubtful that additional sessions will be of benefit. When patients manifest several rituals and several sources of anxiety, treatment should aim at one or two major rituals and associated obsessions for maximal gain; remaining symptoms can be treated later.

A typical therapy session proceeds as follows: The first few minutes are spent in discussion of the patient's current mood, urges to ritualize, and prior homework assignment. Unexpected upsetting events are also attended to at the beginning of the session. In the remaining time, procedures directed at anxiety reduction are implemented. First, the patient is exposed in fantasy to descriptions of the situations, objects, or thoughts (including thoughts of future harm) that provoke fear and discomfort. Patients are instructed to imagine the content of the verbal description as vividly as possible and to allow themselves to feel as if they were actually in these situations. Subjective levels of anxiety on a scale of 0–100 are monitored approximately every 10 min. Typically, subjective anxiety increases gradually and then decreases. Imaginal exposure is terminated when a substantial reduction in discomfort is observed. As noted earlier, this occurs usually within 1 hr but may require up to 2 hr.

We recommend that a series of five different scenes be prepared, each including increasingly more disturbing content. The least-disturbing scene should be introduced in the first session. When this scene ceases to generate a high level of anxiety, the next one is introudced and so forth until the most disturbing image no longer produces discomfort. An example of a typical scene is provided in Appendix F. An example of the sequence of imaginal exposure images for a washer and for a checker are given in Appendices G and H, respectively.

Following imaginal exposure, the therapist confronts the patient in a graded sequence with items or situations that provoke discomfort. When indicated the therapist models contact with the items. Whenever possible the objects or situations are selected to correspond to those presented imaginally in the same session. Exposure *in vivo* should continue until a substantial reduction in anxiety is achieved. In successive sessions more disturbing items are added to previous ones; the most anxiety-provoking situations are typically presented by the sixth session. Examples of the sequence of *in vivo* exposure for a washer and a checker are given in Appendices I and J, respectively.

For washers, all nonessential washing and cleaning is eliminated except for one 10-min shower every 5th day. Dishwashing and other activities necessitating contact with water should be conducted with gloves or assigned to someone else during the intensive phase of treatment. Checkers are permitted one check only of items that normally are checked after use, such as stoves and door locks. Other objects judged not to require routine checking (e.g., unused electrical appliances, discarded envelopes) may not be checked. Infractions of these rules are to be recorded on the daily self-monitoring form and are discussed in the beginning of the next session. Rules for implementation of response prevention for washers and checkers are given in Appendix K.

In the last few sessions of treatment, the patient should be introduced to rules of "normal" washing, cleaning, or checking. Response-prevention requirements are relaxed to enable the patient to return to what we consider to be a normal routine. For washers this would include one 10-min shower daily and handwashing before meals, after bathroom use and after handling grimy, greasy, or sticky objects. Initially, any washing should be followed immediately by reexposure to contaminants. Also, the therapist may wish to continue some restrictions, particularly when strong urges to wash are still present. For example, patients whose obsessions were focused on bathroom germs may be allowed to wash normally except after bathroom use for several weeks after completion of intensive treatment.

MAINTENANCE PERIOD

Following the intensive treatment phase, the therapist may prescribe a self-exposure maintenance regimen to ensure periodic contact with previously avoided situations and to prevent a return to former avoidance patterns. For example, a patient who fears "leukemia germs" would be asked to engage routinely in activities he or she had previously avoided, such as touching all doorknobs, using public facilities including bathrooms, waiting areas, restaurants, and so on. Additionally, he or she would be required to visit the waiting area of a cancer hospital, first weekly and then biweekly until discomfort was minimal and washing rituals were under control.

For many patients, normal work and/or leisure activities have been severely curtailed by the obsessive avoidance patterns. These must be reestablished and new ones developed to fill the time that becomes available when hours of ritualizing are decreased to only a few minutes each day. This may entail interpersonal skills training for those who are deficient in this area. Marital or family therapy may be required by some patients to improve communication patterns. Partners who have participated in the ritualistic behavior of the patients need to rehearse refusal of such requests while at the same time encouraging and supporting the patient.

Maintenance treatment typically requires weekly sessions for periods varying from a few months to more than a year. The duration depends on the level of treatment functioning. In our center, a follow-up self-help group meeting weekly at minimal cost has provided needed support for maintenance exposure activities, as well as a source of regular interaction for the more socially insolated individuals.

Therapeutic Setting

It is generally advisable to allow patients to remain in their normal environment whenever possible throughout therapy. If employed, the patient is encouraged to continue to work. Some patients have established a lifestyle of extensive passive avoidance, thus circumventing the need to ritualize. For instance, one housewife had insisted that her family not eat meals at home for fear of food crumbs entering the house and attracting bugs. This avoidance of normal use of the home for meals had been established by her in order to end 10 hr of cleaning each day. It continued for several years so that at the time of treatment she could not recall how she had behaved before all food was banished from the home. Returning to routine eating at home was necessary in order to obtain information about anxiety levels to "contaminants," avoidance patterns, and rituals. This information was in turn incorporated into the treatment program.

Maintenance of the patient's usual routine and living situation during intensive treatment is particularly important for those checkers and washers whose fears are triggered by their feelings of responsibility in their own home environment. Hospitalization may create an artificially protected setting, particularly for checkers who may not feel responsible for their surroundings and hence fail to experience their usual urges to check. Hospitalization is reserved, then, for patients who live too far to commute for frequent sessions or who lack an appropriate supervisor in the home to aid in treatment. On rare occasions, when the family interaction is so disturbed that living at home is deemed detrimental to progress in treatment, hospitalization or a temporary alternative living situation should be considered.

Social Context

Early in the data-gathering phase, the therapist is advised to initiate at least one session in which important family members (typically the spouse–partner or parents) attend. Family members' attitudes toward the patient's symptoms and toward treatment, as well as their interactions with the patient can be assessed *vis-à-vis* their potential impact on the therapeutic process. If the relationship is deemed sufficiently positive to expect that the relative or friend could be a helpful supervisor during treatment, then further meetings can be scheduled prior to and during treatment to explain the role of therapeutic aide and assign supervisory tasks.

Depending on the symptomatology, some patients may require assistance from several individuals in their environment such as spouse, parents, friends, and even clergy. One young man who sought to behave exactly according to God's wishes in all major and minor details of his life required the consultation of a clergyman of his faith to verify that according to biblical writings he could forego prayers before departing on a subway ride, before brushing his teeth, on greeting a friend, and so on. In another case a woman continually requested reassurance from her husband, parents, and doctor that she had properly performed her motherly duties of protecting her child's health. In this case interviews with her parents and spouse and a call to her doctor were needed to enlist their support in the appropriate handling of refusals of her requests.

Similarly, for hospitalized patients regular consultation with nursing staff who are involved in assisting with the treatment regimen is needed. In our experience, the attitude of such staff toward the patient and his or her treatment will strongly affect the patient's experience with the hospital setting. Placing a patient on a ward in which staff are not sympathetic to the patient's struggles with anxiety or to the importance of following the treatment plan obviously will be detrimental to outcome.

Therapist Variables

Intensive treatment via exposure to feared situations and blocking of the ritualistic behavior provokes considerable stress for patients. Their willingness to undergo such "torture" attests to their strong motivation. Such a treatment regimen requires that the therapist maintain a careful balance between pressuring the patient to proceed and sympathizing with his or her discomfort. Findings from a study by Rabavilas, Boulougouris, and Perissaki (1979) indicate that respectful, understanding, encouraging, explicit, and challenging therapists were likely to achieve positive outcomes, whereas permissiveness and tolerance were associated with poor prognosis. The behavior of obsessive–compulsive patients during treatment spans the gamut from extreme cooperation to blatant manipulation. To some extent, knowing when to push, when to confront, and when to be flexible is a matter of good observational skills and judgment based on experience. As much as possible, however, the therapist should exhibit an attitude that counteracts the harshness of the treatment program, while still adhering to the regulations established at the outset of therapy. The following verbatim material illustrates this point.

The patient has been asked to touch a chocolate bar (a highly contaminating item for her) in her third treatment session.

PATIENT: There's no way that I'm going to touch that. I haven't been near a Milky Way in years.

THERAPIST: I know how upset you must feel. On the other hand avoiding for all these years has not been all that productive for you. How about if we start by putting it on the arm of your chair?

P: I won't like it, but if I don't have to touch it, it's OK.

T: (*Puts the candy bar way on the arm of the chair. Patient moves to one side.*) You know that when you touched other things you were afraid of, you ended up feeling less concerned about it after a while. I want you to use this memory now and touch the chocolate bar with the tip of your fingers.

P: I said I won't do it. The other things were much easier. I can't do it! I can't touch it!

T: Remember at the beginning we agreed that you would follow instructions, even when it's very difficult. It's important that you touch the chocolate today because tomorrow it won't be any easier. Now reach over and touch it with your finger. (*She hesitates.*) Go ahead, you can do it. (*She touches it reluctantly.*)

T: That's great. You see, it hasn't killed you! Now before you lose your courage, put your whole hand on it. (*Patient hesitates and looks extremely uncomfortable, but touches it with several fingers.*) You're doing fine. Make sure your entire hand is contaminated. Good. Now I want you to hold it in both hands.

A study by Emmelkamp and Kraanen (1977) compared exposure treatment planned by a therapist but carried out without his or her presence to exposure with the therapist present. Results showed that both were equally effective. Such findings should not be taken to indicate that the therapist is superfluous to the treatment process; they merely suggest that the patient can carry out the therapist's assignments without his or her presence. Given the difficulty that many patients exhibit when first prevented from ritualizing after exposure, the therapist's presence during the first few exposure sessions seems strongly advisable. Homework assignments between sessions may be sufficient to provide the patient with a needed sense of self-mastery and attribution of gains to his or her ability to control his or her own actions. Fading of the therapist's participation toward the end of the treatment program may further enhance the patient's self-efficacy. As noted by Emmelkamp and Kraanen (1977), the self-exposure group tended to maintain their gains better than did the therapist-exposure group. Fading of the therapist presence may then increase the likelihood of long-term success.

Patient Variables

Of primary importance among factors affecting the patient's ability to benefit from treatment is their *level of motivation.* A courageous attitude is essential to the undertaking of a strict exposure and response-prevention regimen. Patients must feel that their symptoms are sufficiently intolerable and unacceptable to them that they justify considerable discomfort at the present in order to benefit in the long run. Often, patients are pressured into seeking therapy by family members and agree to undergo treatment in order to appease the family, rather than because of their own inability to tolerate their symptoms. Such patients improve in the short run but are likely to lose treatment gains over time.

Several factors may affect patients' motivation. An expectation that treatment will benefit them is, of course, essential. It can be enhanced by a clear explanation of the mechanisms by which such treatment operates. After ascertaining that treatment by exposure and response prevention is indicated for a patient, the following rationale is provided:

During treatment I will ask you to touch things that are disturbing to you, such as toilet seats in public bathrooms, and you won't be allowed to wash or clean yourself. I know that this will be very hard for you, but there is a good reason for asking you to do it. In a way I'm asking you to do the opposite of what you have been doing. So far you've done your best to avoid contamination and when that didn't work you washed. As a result, you've never permitted yourself to find out that nothing would have happened if you hadn't washed. If I expose you to toilet seats and don't let you wash, you will find out that your beliefs about the consequences of touching toilet seats are wrong. Also, you'll find out that even when you don't wash, in time you'll feel less upset and the feeling of dirtiness will decrease. For these reasons it is important that we reverse your habits, although it will be very difficult for you. I'll try to help you through it in whatever way is needed.

It is unreasonable to expect that treatment of 1-month duration, albeit intensive, will completely ameliorate obsessive–compulsive symptoms. Leading clients to expect total absence of symptoms is likely to result in disappointment that in turn may cause relapse. Rather, patients should be told that their anxiety will diminish to manageable levels and that their urges to ritualize will be more readily controllable. They should therefore expect that symptoms will improve but that maintenance of their gains will require continuous effort.

Motivation will also be affected by "secondary gains" accruing from the patient's symptoms. Young adults, fearful of living independently of their parents and of managing a career and social life alone, may have much to gain by remaining symptomatic, unless convinced of their need and ability to master these life tasks. Similarly, individuals receiving financial support for psychological disability may be reluctant to lose such benefits.

As noted earlier, the patient's *mood state* may also impact on his or her ability to benefit from exposure and response-prevention treatment. Marked depression is likely to interfere with the ability of some to habituate to feared situations, perhaps by increasing the patient's sensitivity to highly anxiety-provoking obsessional cues (Foa, Grayson, *et al.*, 1983). It may be that when patients are exceedingly fearful, they are incapable of processing the information that is inherent in the exposure situation, and thus discomfort persists unabated (Foa & Kozak, 1985). Antidepressant medication or cognitive therapy for depression may facilitate responsiveness to behavioral treatment for depressed individuals. High general anxiety was also found to hinder treatment efficacy for some individuals although not for others (Foa, Grayson, *et al.*, 1983). Given the present state of knowledge, we suggest that if patients are highly anxious or highly depressed and do not evidence anxiety reduction during the first two or three sessions of exposure treatment, anxiolytic or antidepressant medications should be tried.

A further stumbling block in treatment, as noted previously, is the patient's *belief system* regarding the likelihood that the feared consequences will in fact materialize. Those who firmly believe that their worst fears will come to pass if they fail to protect themselves by ritualizing have been observed not to habituate to feared contaminants across exposure treatment sessions (Foa, 1979). Unfortunately, reliable and valid measures of the degree of conviction have not yet been developed, and little is known about effective treatment manipulations for this difficulty.

CASE EXAMPLE OF A TREATMENT PROGRAM

In this section we will demonstrate through verbatim material the process of gathering information relevant to treatment, planning the treatment program, and conducting exposure sessions.

Case Description

June, a 26-year-old married woman who had just completed her bachelor's degree in nursing, sought treatment for a severe washing and cleaning problem. She was extremely agitated in the first interview and described herself as "crying a whole lot" during the previous 6 weeks. She arrived in the company of her husband of 6 months and her sister-in-law, whom she considered a good friend. Previous treatment by systematic desensitization, major and minor tranquilizers, and cognitive restructuring had proved ineffective. June had been unable to seek employment as a nurse due to her symptoms.

The above information was collected at June's initial evaluation for participation in treatment by exposure and response prevention. After ascertaining the absence of psychosis, drug and alcohol abuse, or organic disorders, she was appointed a therapist (Steketee).

Information Gathering

Information is usually gathered in the following sequence: Present symptomatology and history of symptoms are explored in the first and second sessions; personal and family history are discussed in the third session; the fourth session is devoted to treatment planning. Deviations from this sequence are sometimes necessary, especially when the description of symptoms leads to the elaboration of events in the patient's personal and family history.

Current Symptomatology

The therapist seeks information about the obsessional content, including external and internal fear cues, beliefs about consequences, and information about passive avoidance patterns and types of rituals. Because *rituals* are the most concrete symptom, it is often convenient to begin the inquiry by asking for a description of this behavior.

THERAPIST: I understand from Dr. F that you are having a lot of difficulty with washing and cleaning. Can you tell me more about the problem?

PATIENT: I can't seem to control it at all recently. I wash too much. My showers are taking a long time, and my husband is very upset with me. He and my sister-in-law are trying to help, but I can't stop it. I'm upset all the time and I've been crying a whole lot lately [she is on the verge of tears] and nothing seems to help.

T: I see. You look upset right now. Please try to explain what your washing has been like in the past few days so I can understand. How much washing have you been doing?

P: Much too much. My showers use up all the hot water. And I have to wash my hands, it seems like all the time. I never feel clean enough.

T: About how long does a shower take? How many minutes or hours would you say?

P: About 45 minutes I guess. I try to get out sooner. Sometimes I ask Kenny to make me stop.

T: And how often do you take one?

P: Usually only twice, once in the morning and once at night before bed, but sometimes if I'm really upset about something I could take an extra one.

T: And what about washing your hands? How much time does that take?

P: You mean how many times do I wash?

T: How long does it take each time you wash your hands and how often do you wash your hands in a day?

P: Um, maybe 20 times a day. It probably takes me 5 minutes each time, maybe more sometimes. I always have the feeling they're not really clean, like maybe I touched them to the side of the sink after I rinsed and then I think they're dirty again.

The therapist now has some basic information about the most prominent rituals. Some further questioning will clarify whether *other compulsions* are also in evidence.

THERAPIST: Do you do anything else to make yourself feel clean?

PATIENT: Yes, I alcohol things. I wipe things with alcohol, like the car seat before I sit down.

T: Do you wipe yourself with alcohol?

P: No, only things that I think are dirty.

T: Can you tell me how much you do that?

P: I use about a bottle of alcohol a week.

Here the therapist must chose whether to inquire about what objects she cleans or to ask about possible *additional rituals*. The therapist chose to continue the inquiry about ritualistic actions, and to turn to the subject of "contaminants" as soon as this is completed.

THERAPIST: OK, can you think of any other things that you do to clean yourself or other things around you that you feel are dirty?

PATIENT: That's all I can think of right now.

T: What about other kinds of what we call "compulsive" type of activities? Do you have to check or repeat things over and over?

P: No, except when I wash if I don't feel it's enough. Then I wash again.

T: No other repetitive actions besides washing?

P: Nope.

Since this patient does not appear to have multiple types of ritualistic behaviors, the therapist can now turn to the *obsessional content. External cues* are usually solicited first.

THERAPIST: What are the things that make you feel you want to wash. For instance, why do you wipe the car seat with alcohol?

PATIENT: I think that maybe I got dog dirt on it when I got in from before, or Kenny might have.

T: From your shoes?

P: Yes, I also worry about the hem of my dress touching the seat. I've been worrying that my shoe could kick my skirt hem or when I step up a step like to go in a building, the dress could touch the step.

T: A dress like this? [June is wearing a dress that comes to just below her knee. The likelihood that it could have touched a curb or sole of her shoe is very slim.]

P: Yes.

T: Has your skirt ever had dog dirt on it?

P: I don't think so, but in my mind I think that maybe it could have gotten some on it. I suppose it would be hard for that to happen, wouldn't it?

Thoughts that highly improbable events might have occurred are common in obsessive–compulsive disorders. Such distortions may be the result of intense anxiety. Doubts about "safety" often lead to requests for reassurance or to rituals. Reassuring June that her dress is unlikely to be soiled would be counter-therapeutic since it perpetuates the neurotic fears. Rather, the therapist proceeds to inquire further about the obsessional content.

THERAPIST: Is dog "dirt" the most upsetting thing that you worry about?

PATIENT: Probably. Yes, I think so, but bathroom germs are pretty bad too.

T: What sort of germs?

P: From toilets. You know, when you go to the bathroom.

T: Urine and feces?

P: Yes, urine doesn't bother me as much as the other.

T: Why?

P: Because I learned in nursing school that it's almost sterile. I had a hard time in the course about microbiology because it upset me to try to learn about bacteria and microorganisms. They make it sound like there are all kinds of germs everywhere that are real dangerous. I didn't learn it very well; I tried to avoid thinking about it.

The patient has indicated that *cues regarding the potential harm* that may derive from contact with feces may be a prominent feature of her obsessions. The therapist questions her further to ascertain their place in the symptomatology.

THERAPIST: Are you afraid of diseases that could come from feces?

PATIENT: Yes, I guess so. The thing of it is, though, I know other people don't worry about it like I do. To them, you know, they just go to the bathroom and wash their hands and don't even think about it. But I can't get it out of my head that maybe I didn't get clean enough.

T: If you didn't wash enough, would you get sick or would you cause someone else to get sick?

P: Mostly I worry that I'll get sick, but sometimes I worry about Kenny too.

T: Do you worry about a particular kind of disease?

P: I'm not sure. Some kind of illness.

It is not uncommon for patients who fear harm that may ensue from not ritualizing to be unable to identify a specific feared consequence. Checkers often fear they will forget or throw out something important, but they do not always know exactly what this will be. Repeaters may fear that something bad will happen to a loved one but often cannot specify what particular disaster will befall them. However, many obsessive–compulsives do fear specific consequences (e.g., blindness, leukemia). At this point, the therapist may either choose to complete the inquiry about concrete cues or pursue the investigation about the feared consequences and the belief that such harm is indeed likely to occur. The latter course is chosen here.

THERAPIST: Let's say that you did actually touch dog feces or human feces and you weren't aware of it, so you didn't wash to remove it. What is the likelihood that you or Kenny would really get seriously ill?

PATIENT: Well, I feel like it really could happen.

T: I'm asking you logically now. I'm sure that emotionally you feel it could happen, but I'm asking what you believe in your head. I mean out of 10 times of touching feces, how often will you get sick?

P: Oh, I know it's pretty unlikely, but sometimes it seems so real.

T: Can you put a number on it? What's the percent chance that if you touched a small amount of feces and didn't wash that you'd get sick?

P: I'd say low, less than 25%.

T: That means that one time in every four, you'd get sick.

P: No, that's not right. I guess it's really less than 1%.

From the above dialogue it is clear that June does not exhibit "overvalued ideation," although her first estimate was high. A true "overvalued ideator" would have assigned higher probabilities (usually over 50%) and would insist on the accuracy of his or her estimate even in the face of persistent questioning.

THERAPIST: OK. Now, besides disease, what else could happen if you got feces on you?

PATIENT: I suppose I'm also afraid of what other people might think if I got dog feces on my shoe or on my dress. Somebody would see it or smell it and think it was really disgusting and I was a dirty person. I think I'm afraid they would think I'm not a good person.

The therapist would then question her further about this feared consequence, inquiring about the probability of others evaluating her character negatively because she had feces on her dress. The material regarding feared consequences is collected for later inclusion in the imaginal flooding scenes. To conclude the inquiry about the nature of the obsessions, the external feared stimuli remain to be further elucidated.

THERAPIST: Besides dog and human feces and toilets, what else can "contaminate" you? Is it OK if I use the word "contaminated" to describe how you feel if you handle these things?

PATIENT: Yes, it's like I can feel it on my skin, even if I can't see it. Uh, I also get upset if I see "bird do" on my car.

T: Bird droppings? The whitish spots?

P: Yeah. I have to hold my skirt close to me when I get in or out of the car so it doesn't touch the outside of the car.

Here the patient also provides information about avoidance behaviors associated with her contaminants. The therapist will note this and return later to ask about additional avoidance patterns.

THERAPIST: OK, bird do, what else?

PATIENT: Dead animals, like on the roadside. I feel like the germs, or whatever it is, get on the tires from the pavement and get on the car. Even if I don't run over it. Like it's spread around the street near it.

T: What do you do if you see a dead animal?

P: I swerve wide around it. Once I parked the car and as I got out, I saw this dead cat right behind the car. I had to wash all my clothes and take a shower right away. I was really a mess that day.

T: It sounds like that was very difficult for you. . . . Is there anything else besides dead animals that contaminates you?

P: I can't think of any. There are lots of places I avoid now but that's because of what we just talked about.

The experienced therapist will question the patient further about other items that are likely to be contaminated because of their potential relationship to the ones June has already noted.

THERAPIST: What about trash or garbage?

PATIENT: Yeah, that bothers me. And I also avoid gutters on the street.

T: What's in the gutter that upsets you?

P: Dead animals, I guess. And then the rain spreads the germs down the street. Also rotten garbage. It's really dirty. Sometimes the gutters are really disgusting.

T: Um hum. Are you afraid you could get sick from dead animals and garbage?

P: Yes, it's like the toilets or dog dirt.

In order to prepare for an exposure program in which objects are presented hierarchically with respect to their ability to provoke discomfort, the patient is asked to rank his or her major contaminants.

THERAPIST: Now, let's make a list of the main things that upset you. I'm going to ask you how uncomfortable you would be on a 0–100 scale if you touched the thing I'll name. Zero indicates no discomfort at all and 100 means you'd be extremely upset, the most you've ever felt.

PATIENT: OK.

T: What if you touched dog dirt?

P: And I could wash as much as I wanted?

T: No, let's say you couldn't wash for a while.

P: One hundred.

T: A dead animal.

P: Also 100.

T: Bird do on your car.

P: That depends on whether it is wet or dry.

T: Tell me for both.

P: One hundred wet and 95 dry.

T: Street gutter.

P: Ninty-five.

T: Garbage in your sink at home.

P: Not too bad. Only 50. But, the trash can outdoors would be 90.

T: Why the difference?

P: Because the inside of the trash can is dirty from lots of old garbage.

T: I see. What about a public toilet seat?

P: That's bad. 95.

T: Car tires?

P: Usually 90. But if I just passed a dead animal they'd be 99.

T: What about a doorknob to a public bathroom?

P: The outside knob is low, like 40. But the inside knob is 80 because people touch it right after they've used the bathroom and I've seen that some don't wash their hands.

T: I understand. How about grass in a park where dogs are around?

P: If I did walk in the grass, it would be about 80 or 85, but I don't usually do it. I also have a lot of trouble on sidewalks. You know, the brown spots on the concrete. I guess most of it is just rust or other dirt, but I think maybe it could be dog dirt.

T: How much does that bother you?

P: To step on a brown spot? About 90. I always walk around them.

The therapist will continue in this vein until a list of 10–20 items is formed. These will be ordered from low to high in preparation for treatment by exposure. Items equivalent with regard to their disturbance being are grouped together.

Considerable information about *avoidance patterns* has emerged from the above interview about fear cues. More details can be obtained by asking the patient to describe step-by-step a typical day's activities from the time he or she washes up until bedtime. For June we were particularly concerned with bathroom routines, her shower, use of the toilet, handling of towels and dirty clothes, and dressing and putting on shoes. Additional information about avoidance patterns can be ascertained by inquiring about other routine activities such as shopping, eating out, house cleaning, preparing meals, working, and so on. The following dialogue exemplifies the degree of detail desired:

THERAPIST: June, in order for us to plan your treatment carefully, I need to know what you avoid in your daily routine. Why don't you start by describing what you do first when you wake up.

PATIENT: I go to use the bathroom first.

T: Nightgown on or off?

P: I take off my nightgown because I don't want it to touch the toilet. That way it's clean at night after I shower.

T: Go on.

P: I go the toilet. I suppose I use a lot of toilet paper because I don't want to get anything on my hand. Then I have to shower after a bowel movement.

T: How do you get ready to shower?

P: I have to put a new towel on the rod near the shower. I don't like it to touch anything before I use it. Oh, and I put my slippers facing the door, near the shower so I can put them on without stepping on the bathroom floor when I get out of the shower. Then I get into the shower.

T: You said you shower for 45 minutes. Why does it take so long?

P: I have to wash myself in a special order and I count how many times I wash each part. Like I wash my arm four times. That's why it takes so long.

T: What is the order you use?

P: First I wash my hands, then my face and hair and then I go from the top down.

T: What about the genital and anal area? [This area should disturb this patient most since she feels contamination from urine and fecal "germs."]

P: Oh yes, those are last, after my feet.

Such a detailed description helps the therapist to anticipate possible avoidance by the patient during treatment and to break these patterns with specific instructions. Supervision of normal washing behavior at the end of treatment will address June's tendency to count and to order her washing.

Assessment

After the initial session of information gathering, it is advisable to introduce self-monitoring of frequency and duration of compulsions.

THERAPIST: Before our next session, I'd like you to record all the washing and cleaning that you do, including wiping things with alcohol. You can use this form [see Appendix D]. Please write down every time you wash, how long you washed, what made you wash, and how anxious you were before you washed. This kind of record will help us identify any sources of contamination you've forgotten, and we can also use it to measure your progress during treatment.

PATIENT: Do you want me to write in each space for each half hour?

T: No, only when you wash or use alcohol.

P: OK.

Other standardized measures, such as the Maudsley Obsessive–Compulsive Inventory or Beck Depression Inventory, are given to the patient for completion at the end of the first session.

History of Symptoms

At the next session the therapist seeks information about the onset of the problem with particular reference to the presence of specific stressors at the time and whether these stressors are still present.

THERAPIST: How long have you been washing like this?

PATIENT: It started about 2 years ago in my first year of nursing school. It wasn't real bad right away. It started with the city. I had to go into the city to classes and the city seemed real dirty.

T: Did nursing have something to do with it?

P: Maybe. I was under a lot of tension. I had to quit working as a secretary and it was pretty hard without an income and a lot of school bills. My mother and dad weren't much help. And then we started to learn all the sterilizing techniques and I already told you about the course in microbiology.

T: Did it gradually get worse?

P: Mostly, but I did notice that it was a lot worse after a rotation on surgery where I was really worried about germs contaminating the instruments. That's when I started to wash more than usual.

T: Did you seek help at that time?

P: I was already seeing Dr. W at the University, and he tried to help.

T: You were already in treatment with him? For what reason?

P: He was helping me with an eating problem. I had anorexia. I'd been seeing him for about a year when the washing started.

T: Anorexia? Did treatment help?

P: Yes, I was down to 85 pounds and I'm up around 105 now. He mostly asked me to increase my weight every week and he did "cognitive therapy" I think it's called.

T: I see. What about the washing problem?

P: He tried the same type of therapy, but it didn't work for that. That's why I'm here. My sister-in-law heard about it and Dr. W said I should go.

Indeed, the available cognitive procedures have not been found effective with obsessive–compulsives.

THERAPIST: What about drugs? Were you ever given medication for this problem?

PATIENT: I take Valium now. It hasn't stopped the washing so far. Sometimes I think it calms me down a little, but I still get awfully upset.

T: Have you tried any other treatments?

P: Only for the anorexia. I went to another counseling center at the university for about a year, but that didn't really help at all.

June's history is unusual only in the relatively recent onset of her symptoms. The mean duration of symptoms for a sample of 72 patients studied at Temple University was 11.1 years (Foa, Grayson, et al., 1983). Other centers in England and Holland report similar figures. June's treatment history of unsuccessful trials of various psychotherapeutic and pharmacological treatments is typical. Since previous failure with nonbehavioral treatments has not been found to influence outcome with exposure and response prevention, the clinician should not be discouraged by such a history. However, because of a possible skeptical attitude about the value of treatment, the therapist should provide the patient with a clear rationale for exposure and response-prevention treatment along the lines discussed earlier and demonstrated below.

THERAPIST: Before I continue to collect more information about your problem, let me tell you about your treatment.

PATIENT: I was wondering what I'd be doing in therapy here.

T: The treatment is called exposure and response prevention. That means that we'll expose you gradually to the things you've described to me that you're afraid of, like door handles to bathrooms and toilet seats and bird do. We'll do this in hour and half sessions every weekday and I'll assign you homework to do similar things between therapy sessions.

P: You mean I have to touch them, even dog dirt?

T: Yes, in order to get over these kinds of fears, people must learn to confront what they're afraid of and stay with it until the discomfort decreases.

P: Even if I did, it would probably take me a year to get used to it.

T: Remember, you didn't used to feel like this about dog dirt. When you were younger, did you ever step in dog dirt and just wipe it off on the grass and go on playing?

P: Yeah, I forget that. I didn't even think about it then.

T: To get you back to this point, we need to expose you directly to what you're afraid of. Now, there's a second part to treatment. I'm also going to ask you not to wash for 5 days at a stretch. No handwashing or showering for 5 days and then you get a 10-minute shower; then you have to wait another 5 days again to wash.

P: You're kidding! If I could do that I wouldn't be here. How can I not wash? Every day I resolve to stop, but I always give in. You mean I wouldn't be able to wash after I use the bathroom or before I eat? Other people wash after they use the toilet. Why can't I just wash less, like normal people do?

T: Other people don't have this kind of problem. Every time you wash you feel a bit better, less "contaminated" and less anxious. Right?

P: Yes.

T: If you wash, even briefly whenever you feel "contaminated," you never get a chance to learn that the feeling of contamination would go down by itself without washing. If you are really very anxious, it might take awhile, even several hours, before you felt better, but you will eventually feel better. But, even brief washings every few hours will reinforce your idea that you have to wash to feel better.

P: But why 5 days? I could shower once a day.

T: For the same reason. You'd still feel relief even if you waited 24 hours between washings. And that would strengthen your belief that you need to "decontaminate" by washing yourself. You must learn to use soap and water to feel clean and fresh, but not to "decontaminate" yourself.

P: I think I understand. I know I shower now to get the things I'm afraid of off my body. I used to shower just to get sweat and dirt off and feel nice. I'm still not sure I could stand it though, not washing for that long.

T: You will need to make a commitment before we start that even though you feel very uncomfortable and even quite upset at times, you won't wash. This treatment is very demanding. I'll try to help you as much as I can by planning the treatment so you know what to expect each day and by supporting you whenever you need it. Someone will have to be available to help supervise you any time you need it. Between sessions you can always call me here or at home if a problem comes up. I know the treatment won't be easy for you, but I'm sure you can do it if we make sure you have the support you need to get through the hard parts.

At this point, a commitment is not requested. Rather, the patient should be aware of what will be required of him or her so that he or she can adjust to these expectations and plan activities during the treatment period accordingly. The patient should make the necessary arrangements for attending treatment at least 3 days each week for a period of the 3–4 weeks. It is important that the therapist not minimize the difficulty of the treatment regimen, so the patient is prepared to struggle and enters treatment with a readiness to mobilize inner resources.

The history of the patient is usually taken in the third and fourth sessions. Since the process of collecting such histories for obsessive–compulsives does not differ from other psychiatric patients, details are not provided here.

Treatment Planning

During the fourth interview a treatment plan is composed by the patient and therapist, and a commitment to follow the therapist's instructions is secured.

THERAPIST: OK, now. I want to discuss our plan for each day during the first week of therapy. It's clear that we need to expose you both in imagination and in reality to the things that bother you, which we talked about in our first sessions. As I said already we'll also limit your washing. The scenes you will imagine will concentrate on the harm that you fear and the actual exposures will focus on the things that contaminate you. Restricting your washing will teach you how to live without rituals. In imagination you will picture yourself touching something you're afraid of, like toilet seats, and not washing and then becoming ill. We can have you imagine going to a doctor who can't figure out what's wrong and can't fix it. That's the sort of fear that you have, right?

PATIENT: Yes, that and Kenny getting sick and it being my fault.

T: OK, so in some of the scenes, you'll be sick and in others Kenny will get sick. Should I add that other people blame you for not being careful? Is this what you're afraid of?

P: Yes, especially my mother.

T: OK. We'll have her criticize you for not being careful enough. Can you think of anything else we should add to the image?

P: No, that's about it.

T: We can compose the scenes in detail after we plan the real exposures, since in each session I'd like to use the same items for both the images and the actual exposure. Let's review the list of things you avoid or are afraid to touch in order to make sure that the items are in the right order. Then we'll decide what to work on each day. OK?

P: OK. (*June goes over the list, which includes such items as trash cans, kitchen floor, bathroom floor, public hallway carpet, plant dirt, puddles, car tires, dried dog "dirt," and bird "do." Changes are made as needed.*)

T: Good. Now let's plan the treatment. On the first day we should start with things that are below a 60. That would include touching this carpet, doorknobs that are not inside bathrooms, books on my shelves, light switches, and stair railings. On the second day, we'll do the 60- to 70-level items, like faucets, bare floors, dirty laundry, and the things on Ken's desk. (*The therapist continues to detail sessions 3–5 as above, increasing the level of difficulty each day.*) In the 2nd week we will repeat the worst situations like gutters, tires, public toilets, bird do, and dog dirt, and we'll also find a dead animal to walk near and touch the street next to it.

On rare occasions, direct confrontation with a feared object may have some likelihood of producing harm, for example pesticides or other chemicals. In such cases, judgment should be exercised to find a middle ground between total avoidance and endangerment. With chemicals, for example, patients are exposed to small quantities that are objectively nonharmful. In June's case the therapist decided that direct contact with a dead animal was not called for and that stepping on the animal's fur with her shoe and then touching the shoe sole constituted sufficient exposure.

THERAPIST: How does this plan sound?

PATIENT: The 1st week is OK, but I'm really scared about the 2nd week. I'm not sure I will be ready to do that by then.

T: I can't force you to do it and it wouldn't help if I did. You have to be prepared to grit your teeth and just do it. It will get easier but it really is hard at first. Remember, I will be there with you.

P: Yes, I know it. I feel like I don't really have a choice anyhow. This washing is crazy and I'm disgusted with myself. I suppose I'm as ready as I'll ever be.

T: Good. Now remember, I'll ask you to keep touching whatever we are working on that day for another 4 hours at home. But you will already have done it with me so I don't think it will be too hard. I take it that you talked to Kenny about assisting us with supervising, since I saw him out in the waiting room.

P: Yes, he said that that's fine. He wanted to know what he should do.

T: Let's call him in. Did you talk to your sister-in-law about being available when Kenny is at work during the day?

P: Yes, she was really good about it but she couldn't come today because of the kids.

T: If it's difficult for her to come, I could talk to her on the phone. Why don't you go get Kenny now.

Treatment

The patient was seen for 15 treatment sessions, which were held every weekday for a period of 3 weeks. During the 4th week the therapist visisted her twice for 4 hours each time at her home. During these visits the therapist contaminated her entire house and exposed her to objects that provoked discomfort at home and in her neighborhood. Thereafter, once weekly follow-up sessions were instituted to ensure maintenance of gains and to address any other issues of concern to her.

As discussed earlier, treatment begins with exposure to moderately difficult items on the hierarchy and progresses to the most disturbing ones by the beginning of the 2nd week. The major feared items are repeated during the remainder of the 2nd and 3rd week. The following sequence, which occurred on the 6th day of treatment, is exemplary of this process.

THERAPIST: How was your weekend?

PATIENT: Not that great. I suppose it was as good as I could expect. I took my shower Friday night and I was so nervous about finishing in time I don't even know if I washed right.

T: Most people feel the same way the first time they do it. Remember though, you aren't supposed to wash "right," just to wash. Did Ken time it?

P: Yes, he called out the minutes like you said, "5, 7, 9," and then "stop."

T: You stopped when he said to?

P: Yes, but it sure wasn't easy.

T: I know. I'm really pleased that you were careful to follow the rules.

P: I have pretty much decided that this is my chance to get better so I'm trying my best.

T: Good. I am glad you feel so positive. How was the homework?

P: I touched the floor and the soles of my shoes and the cement. It is all written on the daily sheet there. On Saturday, I went to my sister's so I could play with the kids like we said. They stepped on me when I sat on the floor and I tried to touch their bottoms when I held them. On Sunday Kenny and I went to the park. I didn't sit in the grass but I did walk around and touched my shoes afterward.

T: The soles?

P: Yeah. We also went downtown and I threw some things in the trash cans and pushed them down and tried to touch the sides. It's sort of hard because I felt conspicuous but I did it anyway.

T: That sounds really good. I'm glad to hear it. How about your doormat and going into the garden?

P: I did the doormat and I stood in the garden, but I couldn't touch the dirt. The neighbor's dog always runs all over. I know I should have touched it but I just couldn't get up the courage.

T: Well, you did do so many other things. Let's go outside today and do it together so it will be easier for you to walk in the garden when you go home.

P: OK.

T: How are you and Kenny doing?

P: He got mad on Friday night after the shower because I started to ask him how he showered and if I was clean enough. I think I nagged him too much so he lost his temper. We just watched TV, and after a while we talked a bit and he sort of apologized for getting mad. But I understand; I ask too many questions. Otherwise the rest of the weekend was OK.

T: Well, it's unfortunate that Ken got mad but it's good that he didn't answer your questions. He's not supposed to reassure you about cleanliness.

P: I think he has a hard time knowing when to answer me and when not to. I am not real sure either, so if you could talk to him before Wednesday when I shower again. . . .

T: That's a good idea. I'll call him after we're done with today's session. Now, today we'll start with the scene about you driving your car to an appointment with me and you get a flat tire and have to change it. The cars splash the puddle near you and it lands on the car and on you. Then you notice a dead animal when you walk behind the car and it's right behind you. You feel really contaminated. You feel uncomfortable and also like you have to use the bathroom. You walk to the gas station nearby to see if they can fix the tire and you have to urinate so badly that you have to use their restroom. They agree to fix the tire if you remove it and bring it to them because otherwise they are too busy. Of course that means you have to handle the tire which is contaminated by the dead animal. We'll add some bird do on the street and on the sidewalk too. Then, later you start to feel sick and you feel like it's from the dead animal. Sound awful enough?

P: Yup. Ugh. That one is really bad. Do I have to? Never mind, I know the answer.

T: OK. I want you to close your eyes now and imagine that you are driving your car on West Avenue. . . .

Note that the therapist checks the patient's assignment from the previous day to verify that she has completed it and has not engaged in avoidance. This provides an opportunity to reinforce efforts at self-exposure. It is important to keep track of completion of homework, since patients do not always volunteer information about omissions. They will, however, admit failure to comply if directly asked and are likely to carry out the next assignment if reinforced adequately.

With regard to the conflict between June and Kenny, it is our experience that, like Kenny, most family members are quite willing to help. Difficulty may, however, arise when they are unable to help without becoming upset, thereby increasing the patient's tension. Providing them with an opportunity to ventilate their frustration and at the same time coaching them may reduce familial tension.

Since the imaginal scene had already been planned with the patient, it posed no surprises for her. It is presented for up to 1 hr, or until a substantial decrease in anxiety is evident. Next, the patient is confronted *in vivo* with situations like those included in the fantasied scene:

THERAPIST: It's time to do the real thing now. I looked for a dead animal by the side of the road yesterday and I found one about a mile away. I think we should go there.

PATIENT: Yuck, that's terrific. Just for me you had to find it.

T: Today's our lucky day. You knew we were going to have to find one today anyhow. At least it's close.

P: Great.

Humor is encouraged and can be quite helpful if the patient is capable of responding to it. It is important that the therapist not laugh *at* but rather *with* the patient.

THERAPIST: (*Outside the office.*) There it is, behind the car. Let's go and touch the curb and street next to it. I won't insist that you touch it directly because it's a bit smelly, but I want you to step next to it and touch the sole of your shoe.

PATIENT: Yuck! It's really dead. It's gross!

T: Yeah, it is a bit gross, but it's also just a dead cat if you think about it plainly. What harm can it cause?

P: I don't know. Suppose I got germs on my hand?

T: What sort of germs?

P: Dead cat germs.

T: What kind are they?

P: I don't know. Just germs.

T: Like the bathroom germs that we've already handled?

P: Sort of. People don't go around touching dead cats.

T: They also don't go running home to shower or alcoholing the inside of their car. It's time to get over this. Now, come on over and I'll do it first. (*Patient follows.*) OK. touch the curb and the street, here's a stone you can carry with you and a piece of paper from under its tail. Go ahead, take it.

P: (*Looking quite uncomfortable.*) Ugh!

T: We'll both hold them. Now, touch it to your front and your skirt and your face and hair. Like this. That's good. What's your anxiety level?

P: Ick! Ninety-nine. I'd say 100 but it's just short of panic. If you weren't here, it'd be 100.

T: You know from past experience that, this will be much easier in a while. Just stay with it and we'll wait here. You're doing fine.

P: (*A few minutes pass in which she looks very upset.*) Would you do this if it wasn't for me?

T: Yes, if this were my car and I dropped my keys here, I'd just pick them up and go on.

P: You wouldn't have to wash them?

T: No. Dead animals aren't delightful but they're part of the world we live in. What are the odds that we'll get ill from this?

P: Very small I guess. . . . I feel a little bit better than at first. It's about 90 now.

T: Good! Just stay with it now.

The session continues for another 45 min or until anxiety decreases substantially. During this period conversation focuses generally on the feared situations and the patient's reactions to it. The therapist inquires about June's anxiety level approximately every 10 min.

THERAPIST: How do you feel now?

PATIENT: Well, it is easier, but I sure don't feel great.

T: Can you put a number on it?

P: About 55 or 60 I'd say.

T: You worked hard today. You must be tired. Let's stop now. I want you to take this stick and pebble with you so that you continue to be contaminated. You can keep them in your pocket and touch them frequently during the day. I want you to contaminate your office at work and your apartment with them. Touch them to everything around, including everything in the kitchen, chairs, your bed, and the clothes in your dresser. Oh, also, I'd like you to drive your car past this spot on your way to and from work. Can you do that?

P: I suppose so. The trouble is going home with all this dirt.

T: Why don't you call Ken and plan to get home after he does so he can be around to help you. Remember, you can always call me if you have any trouble.

P: Yeah. That's a good idea. I'll just leave work after he does. OK. See you tomorrow.

This scenario illustrates the process of *in vivo* exposure. The therapist answers clearly the questions raised without detouring from the essential purpose of the session, exposure to the feared contaminant. After the initial increase the anxiety may begin to drop relatively quickly for some patients and may require longer for others. As noted previously, it is advisable to continue the exposure until the patient appears visibly more at ease and reports a substantial decrement in anxiety (40% or 50%).

After 10–15 sessions the patient's reported anxiety level is expected to decrease considerably. At the 15th session, June reported a maximum discomfort of 70 Subjective Units of Discomfort (SUDs) (still somewhat high although reduced from 99 SUDs), which lasted for a few minutes. Her minimal anxiety was 35 SUDs. Her average anxiety level during this session was 45 SUDs. Ideally, by the end of treatment the highest level should not exceed 50 SUDs and should drop below 20 SUDs at the end of the session. In June's case more follow-up sessions were required because anxiety was still quite high.

To facilitate a transition to *normal washing and cleaning behavior*, the therapist instituted a "normal washing" regimen, which included a 10-min shower daily and 30-s hand washing not to exceed six times on the following occasions: before meals, after bathroom use, and after touching greasy, sticky, or visibly dirty objects. This was prescribed for the last weekend of June's intensive treatment.

When the therapist arrived for a *home treatment session* the next week, the following conversation ensued:

THERAPIST: How did it go over the weekend?

PATIENT: Not too bad. But I got sort of upset Saturday. We went to a picnic and there were several piles of dog dirt around. I had on my flip-flops and I wanted to play volleyball. You can't in flip-flops so I went barefoot.

T: That's great! I'm glad to hear it.

P: Yeah, but then I got really upset about going home and carrying it into the apartment. I did it, I walked all over barefoot and with the flip-flops but I worried about it for another whole day, till I talked to Kenny about my thoughts on Sunday around noon. I felt better when he said he wouldn't worry about it. It seems like I feel guilty or something, like the house isn't clean enough. But lately if he says it is, I've been able to take his word for it.

T: Well, in time you'll be able to make this kind of judgment yourself. How about your washing and cleaning?

P: It was all right. I washed for half a minute before I ate and after volleyball because it was dusty. I deliberately didn't wash when I got home because I felt bad and I knew if I did, it would be to "decontaminate" myself. I showered Saturday night and I did feel relieved but I knew I should go and walk around barefoot and touch the floors I'd walked on. So I did that.

T: That's great! It sounds like you handled it fine. I'm really pleased. You avoided washing when it would mean reducing feelings of contamination and you exposed yourself when you felt concerned about germs. That's excellent. Now, let's go over the problem situations that still need work here at home. What things still disturb you?

P: The basement. I haven't done much with the kitty litter box and old shoes that I threw down there a year ago because they got contaminated. The closet still has some contaminated clothes. And I still worry about the backyard some. Also the porch. Pigeons have been perching on the roof and there are droppings on the railing now so I thought I'd wait until you came to do that.

T: OK. Let's start low and work up. Which is easiest?

P: The basement and closets.

T: Fine, down we go.

Exposure to contaminants during the home visit is conducted in the same manner as during treatment sessions. Typically, home sessions last longer, from 2 to 4 hr until all "dirty" items are touched and "clean" places are contaminated. These visits should be repeated if the patient expresses considerable concern about his or her ability to adopt a permanent regimen of nonavoidance.

Follow-up sessions should be scheduled as needed to ensure that gains are maintained. For some patients, one or two follow-up sessions are sufficient; for others, weekly sessions are needed for several months. June was seen weekly until she experienced a setback following the development of a new obsession. She became concerned about hitting a pedestrian while driving. Thoughts that she "might have hit someone" intruded, particularly after turning a corner or glancing in the mirror to change lanes. Once evoked, they persisted for several hours. To overcome this new problem, the therapist directed her to increase her driving and refrain from retracing her steps or looking in the mirror to check for casualties. June was told that she could stop her car only if she knew for certain that she hit someone. Thoughts that it "might" have occurred were to be ignored. To reduce June's anxiety about having obsessions (e.g., "Oh, my God, here it is again, this is terrible") she was advised to expect occasional recurrences of obsessive thoughts. The frequency of obsessions about hitting someone decreased from several each day to once weekly after 3 weeks of self-exposure; the associated anxiety diminished from 95 to 50 SUDs or less.

Of the several germ-related fears, only that of dog feces partially recurred. Fears of public bathrooms and dead animals remained low. The therapist felt that the fear of dog feces had received insufficient attention during treatment. To address this return of fear, June was seen three times a week for 1-hour exposure sessions in which she touched brown spots on the sidewalk and walked near and eventually stepped on dog feces. Homework consisted of going to parks, walking on sidewalks without looking, stepping on dog feces and wiping her shoes, petting dogs, touching her shoe soles, her doormat, and stepping on the grass where she thought dogs had been. This treatment continued for 4 weeks and was reduced to twice a week for an additional 3 weeks. Thereafter, June came once weekly for another 6 weeks during which self-exposure was assigned and everyday concerns were dealt with. News media coverage of herpes led to a brief concern about public toilets, but this dissipated within a few days.

In the dialogue below, the therapist reviews with June her progress at a 9-month follow-up.

THERAPIST: I'd like to know how you feel compared to when you first came here 9 months ago.

PATIENT: I'm definitely a lot better. But, I still have some bad days when I worry a lot about something, and I get down on myself. But when I remember how upset I was last summer and all that washing I did, it's really a whole lot better. Maybe about 80% better. I'm not ready to be a floor nurse yet, but the job I got after treatment is pretty good for now. Kenny and I are doing fine except he's real sensitive if I bring up one of my fears. I wish he'd just listen and say "OK" or something instead of looking worried about me. It's like he's afraid I'm going to get upset again. It makes it hard to talk freely but sometimes he does handle it fine. I really can't complain, he's been through a lot too when I was really a mess last year and before that.

T: I'm glad to hear you feel so much better. You look a lot more at ease. You laugh more now. I don't know if you recall, but you never did in the beginning.

P: I remember.

T: What's left now, the other 20%?

P: Obsessions I guess. I can still worry about driving over someone. Mostly it lasts less than 15 minutes, but now and then it hangs on through an evening.

T: How often?

P: Once every week or two I think. And I still have an urge to avoid walking on the grass in parks. Like I'm hyper alert. I do it pretty often, but I'm self-conscious.

T: You mean you have to remind yourself not to avoid dog feces?

P: Yeah. And I tend to see things in black and white, all good or all bad. I catch myself feeling guilty for dumb things like eating dessert after a full meal. I can stop it but it's like I'm out to punish myself or think badly about what I did. I have to watch out for it. Still, the thoughts are nothing like they used to be. I can have fun now. And work is pretty absorbing, so I can go whole days without getting down on myself for something. Will I always do that?

T: Maybe to some extent. We know that you have a tendency to obsess. Most people who have had an obsessive–compulsive problem say that the rituals and urges to do them decrease more quickly than the obsessive ideas. You might have disturbing thoughts for a while, but you can expect them to become less frequent if you're careful not to attempt to control them through rituals or by avoiding things. Can you handle that?

P: I suppose so. They're not a lot of fun, but I feel like I'm living a normal life again. I suppose everyone has some problems to deal with.

Rarely do patients report complete remission of all obsessions. It is unrealistic to lead a patient to expect that 4 weeks of treatment will result in a total absence of obsessions and rituals. They should expect some struggle with obsessions and urges to ritualize. Strategies for coping with such occasional difficulties should be rehearsed.

COMPLICATIONS DURING TREATMENT

June exhibited few of the common diffculties that can arise during treatment by exposure and response prevention. Potential problems are discussed in this section.

Noncompliance

Despite June's initial concerns about her ability to tolerate confrontation with contaminants and at the same time comply with the demands of response prevention, she followed the treatment regimen. In this respect, June is typical of most obsessive–compulsives who elect to participate in this program. However, while only a few patients fail to abide by the agreed-upon rules, a larger number try to slightly bend them. Failure to resist rituals and persistence in avoidance patterns lead, of course, to poor outcome.

It is extremely rare for a patient to actively conceal ritualistic activity from the therapist. If ritualizing continues the patient should be confronted with the implications of conduct for treatment outcome. If noncompliance persists treatment should be discontinued with the understanding that the patient may return when he or she is prepared to follow the treatment regimen. It is preferable to stop treatment than to continue under unfavorable conditions where failure is likely to occur, leaving the patient hopeless about future prospects for improvement.

While direct violation of response-prevention instructions is relatively rare, the replacement of prohibited rituals with less obvious avoidance patterns is quite common. For example, one woman found that the use of hand lotion served to "decontaminate" her almost as successfully as did the previously employed washing. Inadvertently, she disclosed the anxiety-reducing properties of the lotion to her therapist who, of course, banned its use. Other examples of replacement rituals include brushing off hands and blowing off "germs." These can be discovered by direct questioning. Although they may be only minimally intrusive, these rituals must be prevented for the patient to learn that anxiety decreases in the *total absence* of rituals.

Another problem is posed by individuals who carry out the required exposure without ritualizing but continue to engage in unreported and sometimes unnoticed passive avoidance behaviors. Examples include placing "contaminated" clothing back in the closet for a second wearing but making certain it does not touch the clean garments; and delaying entry or departure from a public bathroom until another person heads for the door, thereby eliminating the need to touch the doorknob. Such behaviors reflect an ambivalent attitude toward treatment and in this respect they are predictors for failure. Their persistence hinders habituation of anxiety to feared situations and may leave the patient with the erroneous belief that such avoidance protects him or her from harm. Failure to give up avoidance patterns also calls for a reevaluation of continuation in treatment.

Emergent Fears

Rarely do new fears emerge during treatment. In June's case new obesssions emerged as preexisting ones declined. Foa and Steketee (1977) reported three cases in which the reduction of anxiety to contaminants was followed immediately by the development of new fears. However, their content was related to the original fears. The authors suggested that the new fears had been too anxiety provoking to admit to conscious awareness, and that as they became less arousing through generalization from treated fears, they entered awareness. June's new obsessions, however, can less easily be viewed as an extension of her original fears. It is possible that the underlying dimension that connected concern with cleanliness and fear of harming pedestrians was the fear of being a "bad person." The prospect of being dirty was less anxiety provoking than the idea of being a murderer and was, therefore, admitted to awareness. A possibly related childhood memory is June's mother's assertion that June's excema on her arms, legs, and face was the "bad" in her coming to the surface. The fear of being a "bad person" seems to have been reinforced by a strict religious upbringing and a view of God as punitive. In adolescence June recalled making a personal vow to be a "responsible person." The obsessive–compulsive symptoms, both cleanliness and carefulness in driving, can be viewed as an effort to keep her vow.

Familial Patterns

Family members have typically experienced years of frustration with the patient's symptomatology. It is not surprising that some are impatient, expecting treatment to result in total symptom remission; when that does not happen they are disappointed and angry. Although basically supportive, June's husband became quite concerned when during the 3rd week of treatment she became panicky after cleaning off pigeon droppings from her front porch. Reassurance by the therapist that occasional anxiety attacks are to be expected and do not reflect failure allayed his concerns.

Conversely, some family members continue to protect the patient from formerly upsetting situations. Years of accomodation to the patient's peculiar requests have established habits that are hard to break. The husband who was accustomed to enter his home through the basement where he immediately removed his clothes and showered for his wife's sake may find it disconcerting to enter through the front door and toss his overcoat on the couch. Similarly, he is likely to find himself continuing to perform a variety of "contaminating" household activities that he has come to regard as his responsibility. The above familial patterns may offset progress in treatment or interfere with maintenance of gains and may require the application of family therapy.

Functioning without Symptoms

Many obsessive–compulsives have become nonfunctional as their symptomatology occupied an increasingly large proportion of their time. Successful treatment leaves them with a considerable void in their daily routine. Assistance in the development of new skills and the planning of both social and occupational activities should be the focus of follow-up therapy in these cases.

A complicating factor is the patient's concern that the new ventures may fail, which often prevents him or her from acquiring necessary skills or making needed overtures. For example, one patient who responded well to exposure and response prevention found himself with nearly 12 free hours each day that had been devoted to ritualistic activity. He was too frightened to resume his social and professional activities, which he had deserted 12 years before. His therapist referred him to a day treatment center where he could develop social skills and relieve interpersonal anxiety. Within a year, he took a job, although at a lower level than his former professional work. Failure to resume a functional lifestyle would most likely have resulted in relapse.

CONCLUSION

The treatment program described here effects marked improvement in most obsessive–compulsive ritualizers. Seventy-five percent of cases maintain their benefit over time. The example provided in this chapter was that of a washer, largely because the description of the washers' treatment program is more straightforward. The results with checkers are not less favorable, although planning a therapy program for them requires some ingenuity. For example, a patient who feared shaming her husband by mistakenly writing that he was a homosexual was requested to write "Jerry Smith is a homosexual" on blank checks and pieces of scrap paper that were strewn about in public places. An example of response prevention for a checker is provided by a patient who checked his food for sharp objects (e.g., glass) that could harm him. In this case, blindfolded eating was instituted.

A problem specific to checkers arises when their rituals are performed only in an environment for which they feel responsible. For them, other settings do not adequately trigger urges to ritualize. The individual who repeatedly checks doors and windows to protect his or her family from burglary does not concern himself or herself with such responsibility in the hospital. There, he or she assumes, it is the nurse's duty to protect patients. In such cases treatment should be conducted in the patient's natural environment.

In this chapter we have described what we consider to be the optimal treatment for obsessive–compulsives: intensive treatment for a short period of time followed by weekly sessions if needed. The concentrated efforts required during the intensive treatment phase may not be feasible for the therapist in clinical practice. It is possible that three sessions each week would be sufficient to achieve satisfactory results; our clinical experience suggests that once-weekly sessions are not adequate. The clinician for whom the allocation of even 6 hr each week is not possible may enlist assistance from paraprofessionals for exposure *in vivo* treatment. Alternatively, two therapists may share the intensive phase of treatment, with one assuming the coordinating role. At times we have simultaneously treated two patients with similar symptoms, thus economizing on the therapist's time.

Two patient characteristics have been observed to interfere with treatment success, severe depression and overvalued ideation. For patients who evidence severe depression, the use of antidepressants or other therapy for depression (e.g., cognitive treatment) is indicated before implementation of exposure and response prevention. In our experience the prognosis for overvalued ideators is more bleak. Most made little or no progress during the intensive behavioral treatment phase. Those who continued in treatment eventually evidenced some improvement, but the number of sessions required was very large. In the absence of potent methods for altering their belief system, behavioral programs appear to have little to offer such individuals.

Although most patients show immediate improvement after exposure and response prevention, about 20% relapse. Data from our studies suggest that patients at greatest risk for relapse are those who were only moderately improved at the end of treatment (Foa, Grayson, *et al.*, 1983). It seems, then, that the therapist should not be content with partial success. When a pattern of slow but consistent gains is evident, additional intensive treatment should be considered for the partially improved.

Another variable that seems associated with relapse is the absence of adequate follow-up treatment. Patients from out of town who could not continue regular contact with their therapist were found to be particularly prone to lose their gains. Follow-up treatment should focus on both systematic reinforcement of a nonritualistic lifestyle and helping the patient overcome obstacles to normal functioning.

Although our effectiveness in treating obsessive–compulsive disorders is satisfactory, it should be noted that 25% of patients who have approached us refuse to partake in the profferred treatment. An additional 25% fail to benefit as we noted earlier. Therefore, complacency with these techniques is not justified. Methods for increasing motivation and an understanding of the mechanisms that underlie improvement will hopefully enhance our efficacy.

APPENDIX A: CUES FOR URGES TO RITUALIZE (CUR) INVENTORY—W

Name: _____   C ____ E ____ I ____

Date: _____

This questionnaire inquires about what triggers your urges to clean or wash. Some people wash or clean in order to prevent harm such as disease, death, punishment, or criticism from happening to themselves or to someone else. Others do not fear any particular harm but simply feel anxious or tense while in contact with certain things. Still others want to wash because of disturbing thoughts, impulses, or images that pop into their heads. Please read each statement carefully and circle the answer that best describes your experiences.

	True	False
1. Repeated unpleasant thoughts make me want to wash or clean.	T	F
2. My washing or cleaning is not intended to protect me or anyone else from harm.	T	F
3. My washing or cleaning is not caused by coming into direct contact with some objects.	T	F
4. I feel uncomfortable if I touch certain things or substances and don't wash or clean.	T	F
5. I'm not afraid that anything bad will happen to me or to someone else if I don't wash or clean.	T	F
6. I'm afraid that something bad will happen to me or to someone else unless I wash or clean.	T	F
7. My need to wash or clean does not result from disturbing images that pop into my head.	T	F
8. I feel that touching certain objects may be dangerous for me or someone else.	T	F
9. My washing or cleaning is not triggered by touching certain things or substances.	T	F
10. My washing or cleaning is not triggered by impulses to do unacceptable things.	T	F
11. I feel that washing or cleaning might protect me or someone else from harm.	T	F

12. Impulses to do unacceptable things are the source of my washing or cleaning.   T   F

13. The possibility that I might have touched a certain object makes me want to wash or clean.   T   F

14. I do not feel a need to wash and clean when I might have touched a particular object.   T   F

15. There is no danger in touching the objects that cause me to wash or clean.   T   F

16. I do not have repeated unpleasant thoughts that make me feel a need to wash or clean.   T   F

17. I feel a need to wash or clean when I come into direct contact with some objects.   T   F

18. Disturbing images that pop into my head cause me to feel that I need to wash or clean.   T   F

APPENDIX B: THOUGHT INVENTORY

Name: _____

Date: _____

When confronted with highly feared situations people may find themselves having various thoughts and feelings. Some are listed below. If you recognize any of these thoughts as being on your mind when you confront your most feared object or situation, check the appropriate box on the left-hand side.

For each item you checked, please rate the strength of the thought using the scale below:

0	1	2	3	4
Very weak thought	Weak	Moderate	Strong	Very strong thought

Put your rating (0–4) on the line at the right of each box you checked.

Check if it worries you right now

Circle rating for each checked item

_____   1. High anxiety should be avoided.   0 1 2 3 4

_____   2. If this does not work, I will be worse off than before.   0 1 2 3 4

_____   3. If I persist at it, I'll get better eventually.   0 1 2 3 4

_____   4. If I can do it once, I can do it again.   0 1 2 3 4

_____   5. Even if I do it once, I won't necessarily be able to do it again.   0 1 2 3 4

_____   6. High anxiety is harmful.   0 1 2 3 4

_____	7. Nothing terrible is going to happen.	0	1	2	3	4
_____	8. I will get extremely anxious and I might go crazy.	0	1	2	3	4
_____	9. High anxiety won't really hurt me.	0	1	2	3	4
_____	10. People should be able to put up with reasonable anxiety.	0	1	2	3	4
_____	11. All my life I've been prone to anxiety and this tendency doesn't change.	0	1	2	3	4
_____	12. Even if I get extremely anxious, I will not go crazy.	0	1	2	3	4
_____	13. Even if I find it difficult in the beginning, I'll get better in time.	0	1	2	3	4
_____	14. I am not by nature a fearful person.	0	1	2	3	4
_____	15. People need to confront their fears in order to get rid of them.	0	1	2	3	4
_____	16. Even if I do it, it wouldn't help me.	0	1	2	3	4
_____	17. Facing my fears will not change them.	0	1	2	3	4
_____	18. Something terrible might happen.	0	1	2	3	4
_____	19. I will not be able to stop worrying that some harm could come to me or others.	0	1	2	3	4
_____	20. I will be overwhelmed by anxiety.	0	1	2	3	4
_____	21. If I continue to confront my fears, eventually I will stop worrying.	0	1	2	3	4
_____	22. Even if I get very anxious, it won't overwhelm me.	0	1	2	3	4

Which of the following unpleasant consequences do you find yourself worrying about right now?

_____	23. Contracting a serious disease (e.g., cancer).	0	1	2	3	4
_____	24. Someone else getting seriously ill.	0	1	2	3	4
_____	25. Myself dying.	0	1	2	3	4
_____	26. Someone else dying.	0	1	2	3	4
_____	27. Being responsible for a serious mistake.	0	1	2	3	4
_____	28. A fire breaking out.	0	1	2	3	4
_____	29. Fainting.	0	1	2	3	4
_____	30. Having a bad accident happen to me.	0	1	2	3	4
_____	31. Someone else having a bad accident.	0	1	2	3	4
_____	32. Bad luck happening to me.	0	1	2	3	4
_____	33. Bad luck happening to someone else.	0	1	2	3	4
_____	34. Losing control of my actions.	0	1	2	3	4
_____	35. Having a heart attack.	0	1	2	3	4
_____	36. Being criticized or ridiculed by others.	0	1	2	3	4
_____	37. Attacking and harming someone else.	0	1	2	3	4
_____	38. An intruder breaking into my home, car, etc.	0	1	2	3	4
_____	39. Failing to prevent a loved one from being harmed.	0	1	2	3	4
_____	40. Going to hell or being punished by God.	0	1	2	3	4

_____	41. Ruining my reputation.	0	1	2	3	4
_____	42. Ruining another person's reputation.	0	1	2	3	4
_____	43. Forgetting something important.	0	1	2	3	4
_____	44. Harm happening to me.	0	1	2	3	4

APPENDIX C: OBSESSIVE-COMPULSIVE EXPOSURE TEST

Name: _____

Date: _____   Rating period: _____

Exposure item: _____

On a scale of 0–100, please rate anxiety/discomfort reported by the patient in each step below. If the patient is able to touch the object, have him or her hold it and record the anxiety level until it no longer increases.

Anxiety/discomfort

		Anxiety/discomfort
1.	4 ft	_____
2.	2 ft	_____
3.	1 ft	_____
4.	6 in	_____
5.	1 in	_____
6.	1 finger (1 s, clean hand)	_____
7.	Whole hand (1 s)	_____
8.	30 s	_____
9.	1 min	_____
10.	2 min	_____

EXPOSURE TEST PROTOCOL (read verbatim)

It is important to measure how difficult it is for you to encounter the things you fear at different points during the program, and how uncomfortable you get when you encounter them. Therefore, we will do what we call an exposure test with the thing that bothers you most.

We still start by placing the item you fear most 4 ft away from you. I will then ask you to approach it gradually in steps as close as you can. I will guide you through one step at a time. But you may stop the test at any point that it becomes too difficult. I will ask you to rate your anxiety on the 0–100 scale after each step. 0 indicates no anxiety/discomfort and 100 indicates panic level anxiety/discomfort.

1. Let's start now with your standing 4 ft from (name item).
   (Therapist indicates spot but DOES NOT PRECEDE patient. Wait 5 s and get rating.) Please rate you current level of anxiety.

2. Please stand 2 ft from (name item).
   (Proceed as in Step 1.)
3. As above for 1 ft.
4. Please hold your hand (uncontaminated) 6 in from (name item).
   (Demonstrate 6 in with a nonfeared item. Get rating as above.)
5. As above for 1 in.
6. Please touch (name item) like this.
   (Demonstrate 1 finger touch with nonphobic object. Get rating.)
7. Now please touch (name item) again but keep touching it for as long as you can even while I get your ratings.
   (Begin timing at touch. Request ratings at 30, 60, 120 s, then have patient withdraw hand.)

At end of test:
We are done now. It really is important to measure your progress this way.

Answer queries about stopping the test with: Try to complete as many steps as feel comfortable without pushing yourself into great difficulty (suffering, distress).

APPENDIX D: SELF-MONITORING OF RITUALS

Name: _____   Date: _____

Ritual A: _____   Ritual B: _____

In the second column of the table below, please describe the activity or thought that evokes a ritual. In the third column record the anxiety/discomfort level (0–100). In the fourth column write the number of minutes you spend in performing rituals during the time stated in Column 1.

Time of day	Activity or thought that evokes the ritual	Discomfort (0–100)	Number of minutes spent on rituals	
			A	B
6:00–6:30 a.m.				
6:30–7:00				
7:00–7:30				
7:30–8:00				
8:00–8:30				
8:30–9:00				
9:00–9:30				
9:30–10:00				
10:00–10:30				
10:30–11:00				
11:00–11:30				
11:30–12:00				
12:00–12:30 p.m.				
12:30–1:00				

1:00–1:30 p.m.
1:30–2:00
2:00–2:30
2:30–3:00
3:00–3:30
3:30–4:00
4:00–4:30
4:30–5:00
5:00–5:30
5:30–6:00
6:00–6:30
6:30–7:00
7:00–7:30
7:30–8:00
8:00–8:30
8:30–9:00
9:00–9:30
9:30–10:00
10:00–10:30
10:30–11:00
11:00–11:30
11:30 p.m.–6.00 a.m.

Total

APPENDIX E: GUIDELINES FOR PLANNING A TREATMENT PROGRAM

I. Information Gathering
   A. Obsessions
      1. External Cues
         Specifically elicit information about objects or situations that provoke high anxiety or discomfort (e.g., urine, pesticides, locking a door).
      2. Internal Cues
         a. Inquire about *thoughts, images, or impulses* that provoke anxiety, shame or disgust (e.g., images of Christ's penis, number of impulses to stab one's child).
         b. Inquire about *bodily sensations* that disturb the patient (e.g., tachycardia, pains, swallowing).
      3. Consequences of External and Internal Cues
         a. Elicit information about possible harm that can be caused by the *external object or situation* (e.g., disease from touching a contaminated object, burglary if a door is not properly locked).

      b. Elicit fears about harm caused by *internal cues*
- from thoughts, images, or impulses (e.g., "God will punish me. I may actually stab my child").
- from bodily sensations (e.g., "I'll lose control").
- from the long-term experience of high anxiety (e.g., "This anxiety will never go away and I'll always be highly upset").

    4. Strength of Belief System

Assess the degree to which the patient believes that his or her feared consequences may actually occur; that is, what is the objective probability that confrontation with feared cues will actually result in psychological or physical harm?

B. Avoidance Patterns
    1. Passive Avoidance

Gather a list of all situations or objects that are avoided (e.g., using public bathrooms, stepping on brown spots on the sidewalk, carrying one's child on a concrete floor, driving). Attend to subtle avoidance practices (e.g., touching doorknobs on the least-used surface, driving at times of least traffic).

    2. Rituals

List all ritualistic behaviors including washing, cleaning, checking, repeating an action, ordering objects, requesting reassurance, and cognitive rituals (e.g., praying, neutralizing thoughts, "good" numbers). Many patients exhibit more than one type of compulsion.

Pay attention to subtle rituals such as the use of "Handiwipes" or lotion to decontaminate hands. Wiping as a short version of a washing ritual.

    3. Relationship between Avoidance Behaviors and Fear Cues

Ascertain the functional relationship between the fear cues and the avoidance associated with it.

C. History of the Main Complaint
    1. Events associated with onset.
    2. Fluctuations in the course of symptoms and events associated with remission and recurrence of symptoms.
    3. Prior coping with symptoms prior treatment efforts and resultant effects.

D. Mood State
    1. Depression

Assess the level of depression by clinical interviews and inventory (e.g., Beck Depression Inventory or Hamilton Depression Scale).

Consider antidepressant medication or cognitive therapy for depressed ratings prior to behavioral treatment.

    2. Anxiety

Consider ameliorating procedures such as anxiolytic drugs. If used, fade their use near the end of treatment.

E. General History

Include information about relationship with parents, siblings and peers, educational achievements, employment history, dating history, sexual experiences, marital relationship, and medical history.

II. Treatment Program

A. Decision to Hospitalize

During intensive treatment the patient is likely to be temporarily under high stress. Hospitalization should be considered for those who live alone or are in a stressful familial relationship.

B. The Use of Prolonged Exposure

1. *In vivo* exposure for external objects or situations that evoke high levels of anxiety.

2. Imaginal exposure

a. When *in vivo* exposure is practically impossible.

b. When the feared catastrophes constitute a major component of the patient's fear model. In these cases imaginal exposure is used in combination with *in vivo* exposure.

3. Suggestions for Exposure Treatment

a. All designated exposure items are arranged hierarchically according to the SUDs (Subjective Units of Discomfort) levels they evoke and are presented in ascending order beginning midway. That is, if the top item evokes 100 SUDs, exposure commences with items at a 50-SUD level; if the top item evokes 80 SUDs, a 40-SUD item is presented first.

b. A given item should be presented until the anxiety level provoked is reduced by half.

c. An exposure item should be repeated until it evokes no more than minimal anxiety.

d. Frequent sessions should be implemented preferably three or more times each week.

e. Ideally, the intensive treatment program should be terminated when the most feared item has been confronted and provokes only mild anxiety. If substantial gains are not evident after 15 sessions, continuation of intensive treatment should be questioned.

f. Regularly scheduled follow-up sessions are recommended to consolidate treatment gains.

g. For motivated patients, detailed instructions for self-exposure may be sufficient. If the relationship between spouses or family members is good, they can be actively involved in the treatment program.

III. Homework

A total of 4 hr of exposure homework is assigned. For patients whose treatment includes imaginal exposure, a tape of that day's fantasy exposure is made for later replay at home; an additional 3 hr of *in vivo* exposure is also assigned.

IV. Response Prevention

A. Washers are usually permitted one 10-min shower every 5th day and no handwashing except under unusual circumstances during the first 2 weeks of treatment. Thereafter, to facilitate learning of normal washing, the therapist may permit one 10-min shower each day and 30-s handwashings after bathroom use, before meals, and when hands are visibly dirty or greasy.

B. Checkers are allowed one brief check of items that are normally checked after use (e.g., stove, door locks) and no checking of items that are not typically checked by most people.

C. Supervisors at home or in the hospital should not use force to prevent ritualizing, but report infractions to the therapist.

APPENDIX F: EXAMPLE OF AN IMAGINAL EXPOSURE SCENE

I want you to imagine the following scene as vividly as you can, as if is actually happening, and to let yourself experience the feelings as you imagine. Imagine that you are sitting here in the chair, and I am with you. The door opens and your mother comes in. She enters the room, she sees you, and she says, "I'm glad to see you. It's been a long time." She comes to you, and she touches you. She wants to hug you. Your mother is astonished that you let her hug you, and she says, "I can't believe that I am allowed to hug my daughter again." Now you feel the contamination spreading all over you. You can feel her hands on your back. And you begin to feel that it will never go away. It can never be washed off. You would like your mother to leave and you want to take a shower or a bath so you can feel clean again. You can't say anything. You can't move, you are overwhelmed by the feeling of being contaminated. Your mother is standing beside you, and she is holding your hand and you can feel how she becomes even more contaminating. You would like her to take her hand off. She is asking you, "Are you afraid of me?," and you would like to explain to her how much afraid of her you are, but you don't say anything. You just let her hold your hand and let her hug you. You let her sit beside you, very close, and she is contaminating you. You can feel the contamination all over your body. You wish you could run out and scream and never come in contact with her again. But you stay here, you stay beside her as she contaminates you more and more. You feel the burning spots on your back and hands. It is the feeling of contamination, creeping up your arms, creeping up your face, it's all over your body.

You try to keep your hand close to your body to make sure that the parts that are not contaminated now will remain clean. But it is spreading over your whole body. And your mother is still beside you, still contaminating you. She is contaminating you more and more. She is telling you something but you can't really listen to her. You are so upset, your heart is beating, you can feel your heart beating really fast. You feel as though you are going to faint. But something forces you to stay and listen to her. You would like to run to the next room, but you realize that you have to face the fact that you can't avoid your mother any longer. You feel trapped. She will never go away, she will go on contaminating you forever, more and more. You will never feel free again. You have the urge to leave the room and to forget everything about your mother. But her touch is everywhere on your body. How are you feeling now?

APPENDIX G: EXAMPLE OF THE SEQUENCE OF IMAGINAL EXPOSURE FOR WASHERS (15 SESSIONS)

The patient, Steve, felt contaminated by feces, urine, sweat, and contact with others. He feared contracting a debilitating disease. Each treatment session included exposure in imagery to contaminants and disastrous consequences.

Scene 1. Steve was asked to imagine touching newspapers, doorknobs, and other objects, all of which fell into the range of 50–60 SUDs. He was also asked to imagine that after touching these objects, he contracted hepatitis and became seriously ill.

Scene 2. Steve was asked to imagined touching of newspapers and doorknobs with the addition of sweat. Fears of disease and debilitation are incorporated as above.

Scene 3. The patient was requested to imagine contact with newspapers, door-knobs, sweat, and toilet seats from public bathrooms along with feared disastrous consequences.

Scene 4. Steve imagined contact with newspapers, doorknobs, sweat, toilet seats, and urine. Feared consequences were incorporated into the scene.

Scene 5. Steve imagined contact with items from Session 4 with the addition of feces from a soiled piece of toilet paper. Feared diseases and their effects were focused upon in detail.

Additional scenes were constructed as needed to include fears described by Steve. Imagined contact with the three most disturbing contaminants under various circumstances was continued during each treatment session and lesser contaminants were included periodically until they no longer evoked discomfort. Each session was taped on a cassette recorder and given to the patient to be played again at home that day.

APPENDIX H: EXAMPLE OF THE SEQUENCE OF IMAGINAL EXPOSURE FOR CHECKERS (15 SESSIONS)

The patient, Mike (described on p. 71), received the following imaginal treatment sequence:

Scene 1. Mike was asked to imagine that he neglected to check the stove and the lights and consequently his home caught fire during the night, resulting in the destruction of his home.

Scene 2. The patient was instructed to fantasize that he flushed the toilet without watching, discovering that he had drowned a pet gerbil in the toilet.

Scene 3. Mike was asked to imagine a scene in which he leaves the basement gate open and his daughter falls down the stairs, suffering serious injury.

Scene 4. Mike was instructed to imagine that he carried his daughter on a concrete floor and dropped her due to his carelessness, causing her serious injury and hospitalization.

Scene 5. Mike imagined a scene that he drives on the highway and finds himself pursued by a police officer who arrests him for a hit-and-run offense in which he injured three people.

Exposure in imagination to the above scenes continued for the remainder of treatment. When considerable habituation was evident for a given scene, the next one was introduced. Scenes were tape-recorded during the session and homework consisted of playing them back.

APPENDIX I: EXAMPLE OF THE SEQUENCE OF EXPOSURE *IN VIVO* FOR WASHERS (15 SESSIONS)

The following hierarchy was constructed for Steve (see Appendix G): feces = 100 SUDs; urine = 90 SUDs; toilet seats in public bathrooms = 80 SUDs; sweat = 75 SUDs; newspapers = 60 SUDs; doorknobs = 50 SUDs. These items all have in common the ability to cause disease.

During *in vivo* exposure treatment, the following sequence was pursued:

Session 1. Steve walked with the therapist through the building, touching doorknobs, especially those of the public restrooms and holding each for a period of several minutes.

Session 2. Steve held doorknobs and newspapers.

Session 3. Steve held newspapers and doorknobs. Contact with sweat was introduced by having him place one hand under his arm and the other inside his shoe.

Session 4. Exposure began with newspapers and sweat. Toilet seats were added by having the patient sit next to the toilet and place his hand on the seat.

Session 5. Exposure began with contact with sweat and toilet seats. Urine was then introduced by having Steve hold a paper towel soaked in his own urine specimen collected that morning.

Session 6. Exposure included urine, toilet seats, and sweat with the addition of fecal material (a piece of toilet paper lightly soiled with his own fecal material). Homework focused on feces, urine, and toilet seats.

Sessions 7–15. Daily exposure to the highest three items was continued.

Homework focused on the objects used during that day's treatment session. Weekend homework mirrored Friday's exposure. Periodic contact with lesser contaminants continued throughout.

APPENDIX J: EXAMPLE OF THE SEQUENCE OF EXPOSURE *IN VIVO* FOR CHECKERS (15 SESSIONS)

For Mike (see p. 71 and Appendix H) the hierarchy was as follows: driving on highways without retracing route = 100 SUDs; carrying daughter on concrete floors = 85 SUDs; daughter playing near open basement gate = 75 SUDs; flushing toilet with cover closed = 70 SUDs; opening doors and windows without checking = 60 SUDs; turning lights and stove on or off without checking = 50 SUDs.

Exposure *in vivo* was conducted in the patient's home as follows:

Session 1. Mike was required to turn the lights on and off once, to turn the stove on and off once, and to open and close doors and windows once. After each action he was required to leave the room immediately and focus his attention on his failure to check these objects. This procedure was repeated throughout the session using different switches and windows.

Session 2. Exposure to situations from Session 1 was repeated with the addition of repeated flushing of the toilet without looking into the toilet bowl.

Session 3. Exposure to above situations was continued. In addition Mike was instructed to open the gate to the basement and allow his daughter to play near the gate without his supervision.

Session 4. Mike was exposed to all situations presented on the previous day with the addition of carrying daughter on the concrete floor.

Session 5. After initial exposure to previous situations, Mike was instructed to drive alone on the highway without retracing his route. He reported to the therapist every 20 min.

Sessions 6–15. Exposure to all of the above situations under various conditions was continued, with particular emphasis on the most difficult items. Homework was assigned daily. It consisted of practicing with situations that were introduced during the treatment sessions.

APPENDIX K: RULES FOR RESPONSE PREVENTION

WASHERS

During the response-prevention period, the patient is not permitted to use water on his or her body (i.e., no handwashing, rinsing, wet towels, or wash cloths are permitted). The use of creams and other toiletry articles (bath powder, deodorant, etc.) is permitted except where use of these items reduces contamination. Shaving is done by electric shaver. Water can be drunk or used to brush teeth with care not to get it on the face or hands. Supervised showers are permitted every 5 days for 10 min each, including hair washing. Ritualistic washing of specific areas of the body (e.g., genitals, hair) is prohibited.

At home response prevention is supervised by relatives or friends who are instructed to be available to the patient should he or she have difficulty controlling a strong urge to wash. The patient is to report any such concern to the supervisor, who will remain with the patient until the urge decreases to a manageable level. Observed violations of response prevention are reported to the therapist. The supervisor is to attempt to stop such violations through firm verbal insistence, but no physical force is used and arguments should be avoided. Faucets can be turned off by the supervisor if the patient gives prior consent to such a plan. Showers are timed by the supervisor but no direct observation of showering behavior is made.

In the hospital response-prevention rules are identical to those described above. Supervisors are nurses and aides previously instructed according to the above rules. Violations should be handled quietly but firmly and reported to the therapist. Physical restraint will not be used but faucets may be turned off according to the patients' previous request. Showers are conducted as above.

CHECKERS

Beginning with the first session of exposure and response prevention, the patient is not permitted to engage in any ritualistic behavior. Normal checking is permitted (e.g., one check of door locks).

At home response prevention is conducted under the supervision of relatives or friends. The supervisor is instructed to be available at the patient's request whenever an urge to check is difficult to resist. The supervisor is to stay with the patient until the urge decreases to a manageable level. Force is not used, but any violations of response prevention are reported to the therapist.

In the hospital patients receive rules for response prevention identical to those described above. Supervisors are nurses and aides previously instructed according to the above rules. They are to assist the patient by remaining with him or her whenever an urge is reported to be very difficult to resist. Force and arguments are avoided but all violations are reported to the therapist.

For patients judged to be highly motivated, response prevention may be implemented without supervision.

Acknowledgments

Preparation of this chapter was supported by Grant MH31634 awarded to Edna B. Foa by the National Institute of Mental Health.

References

Allen, J. J., & Tune, G. S. (1975). The Lynfield Obsessional/Compulsive Questionnaire. *Scottish Medical Journal, 20*(Suppl. 1), 21–24.

American Psychiatric Association. (1980). *Diagnostic and statistical manual of mental disorders* (3rd ed.). Washington, DC: Author.

Amin, M. D., Ban, T. A., Pecknold, J. C., & Klinger, A. (1977) Clomipramine (Anafranil) and behavior therapy in obsessive–compulsive and phobic disorders. *Journal of International Medical Research, 5*, 33–37.

Ananth, J. (1976). Treatment of obsessive–compulsive neurosis: Pharmacological approach. *Psychosomatics, 17*, 180–184.

Ananth, J. (1977). Treatment of obsessive–compulsive neurosis with clomipramine (Anafranil). *Journal of International Medical Research, 5*(Suppl. 5), 38–41.

Ananth, J., & Van den Steen, N. (1977). Systematic studies in the treatment of obsessive–compulsive neurosis with antidepressants. *Current Therapeutic Research, 21*, 495–501.

Asberg, M., Thoren, P., & Bertilsson, L. (1982). Psychopharmacologic treatment of obsessive–compulsive disorder. *Psychopharmacolgy Bulletin, 18*, 13–20.

Bailey, H. R., Dowling, J. L., & Davies, E. (1975). Cingulotomy and related procedures for severe depressive illness: Studies in depression, IV. In W. H. Sweet, S. Obrador, & J. G. Martin-Rodriguez (Eds.), *Neurosurgical treatment in pain and epilepsy*. Baltimore: University Park Press.

Beck, A. T., & Beamesderfer, A. (1974). Assessment of depression: The depression inventory. In P. Pichot (Ed.), Psychological measures in psychopharmacology. *Modern Problems of Pharmacopsychiatry, 7*, 151–169.

Beech, H. R., & Liddell, A. (1974). Decision making, mood states, and ritualistic behavior among obsessional patients. In H. R. Beech (Ed.), *Obsessional states*. London: Methuen.

Beech, H. R., & Vaughn, M. (1978). *Behavioural treatment of obsessional states.* New York: Wiley.

Black, A. (1974). The natural history of obsessional neurosis. In H. R. Beech (Ed.), *Obsessional states.* London: Methuen.

Boulougouris, J. C. (1977). Variables affecting the behaviour modification of obsessive–compulsive patients treated by flooding. In J. C. Boulougouris & A. D. Rabavilas (Eds.), *The treatment of phobic and obsessive–compulsive disorders.* Oxford: Pergamon Press.

Boulougouris, J. C., Rabavilas, A. D., & Stefanis, C. (1977). Psychophysiological responses in obsessive–compulsive patients. *Behaviour Research and Therapy, 15,* 221–230.

Breitner, C. (1960). Drug therapy in obsessional states and other psychiatric problems. *Diseases of the Nervous System, 31*–35.

Bridges, P. K., Goktepe, E. O., Maratos, J., Browne, A., & Young, L. A. (1973). A comparative review of patients with obsessional neurosis and with depression treated by psychosurgery. *British Journal of Psychiatry, 123,* 663–674.

Broadhurst, A. (1976). It's never too late to learn: An application of conditioned inhibition to obsessional ruminations in an elderly patient. In H. J. Eysenck (Ed.), *Case histories in behavior therapy.* London: Routledge & Kegan Paul.

Brownell, K. D., & Barlow, D. H. (1980). The behavioral treatment of sexual deviation. In E. B. Foa & A. Goldstein (Eds.), *Handbook of behavioral interventions.* New York: Wiley.

Cammer, L. (1973). Antidepressants as a prophylaxis against depression in the obsessive–compulsive person. *Psychosomatics, 123,* 663–674.

Carr, A. T. (1974). Compulsive neurosis: A review of the literature. *Psychological Bulletin, 81,* 311–318.

Capstick, N., & Seldrup, J. (1977). Obesssional states: A study in the relationship between abnormalities occurring at the time of birth and the subsequent development of obsessional symptoms. *Acta Psychiatrica Scandinavia, 56,* 427–434.

Cobb, J. P., & Marks, I. M. (1979). Morbid jealousy featuring as obsessive–compulsive neurosis: Treatment by behavioral psychotherapy. *British Journal of Psychiatry, 134,* 301–305.

Cobb, J., McDonald, R., Marks, I., & Stern R. (1980). Marital versus exposure therapy: Psychological treatments of co-existing marital and phobic–obsessive problems. *Behavioural Analysis and Modification, 4,* 3–16.

Cooper, J. (1970). The Leyton obsessional inventory. *Psychological Medicine, 1,* 48–64.

Cooper, J. E., Gelder, M. G., & Marks, I. M. (1965). Results of behavior therapy in 77 psychiatric patients. *British Medical Journal, 1,* 1222–1225.

Derogatis, L. R. (1977). *SCL-90: Administration, scoring and procedures manual—I for the R(evised) version.* Baltimore: Johns Hopkins University School of Medicine, Clinical Psychometrics Research Unit.

Derogatis, L. R., Lipman, R. S., Rickels, K., Uhlenhuth, E. H., & Covi, L. (1974). The Hopkins Symptom Checklist (HSCL): A self-report symptom inventory. *Behavioral Science, 19,* 1–19.

Dollard, J., & Miller, N. E. (1950). *Personality and psychotherapy: An analysis in terms of leraning, thinking and culture.* New York: McGraw-Hill.

Doppelt, H. (1983). *A typological investigation of the MMPI scores of clients with an obsessive–compulsive disorder and the relationship of their MMPI scores to behavioral treatment outcome.* Unpublished doctoral dissertation, Adelphi University.

Emmelkamp, P. M. G. (1982). *Phobic and obsessive–compulsive disorders: Theory, research and practice.* New York: Plenum.

Emmelkamp, P. M. G., & Kraanen, J. (1977). Therapist-controlled exposure *in vivo:* A comparison with obsessive–compulsive patients. *Behaviour Research and Therapy, 15,* 491–495.

Emmelkamp, P. M. G., & Kwee, K. G. (1977). Obsessional ruminations: A comparison between thought-stopping and prolonged exposure in imagination. *Behaviour Research and Therapy, 15,* 441–444.

Emmelkamp, P. M. G., van der Helm, M., van Zanten, B. L., & Plochy, I. (1980). Contributions of self-instructional training to the effectiveness of exposure *in vivo*: A comparison with obsessive–compulsive patients. *Behaviour Research and Therapy, 18,* 61–66.

Emmelkamp, P. M. G., & Van de Heyden, H. (1980). The treatment of harming obsessions. *Behavioural Analysis and Modification, 4,* 28–35.

Emmelkamp, P. M. G., & Wessels, H. (1975). Flooding in imagination and flooding *in vivo*: A comparison with agoraphobics. *Behaviour Research and Therapy, 13,* 7–15.

Esquirol, J. E. D. (1838). *Des maladies mentales* (Vol. II). Paris: Baillière.

Eysenck, H. J. (1979). The conditioning model of neurosis. *The Behavioral and Brain Sciences, 2,* 155–199.

Flor-Henry, P., Yendall, L. T., Koles, Z. J., & Howarth, B. G. (1979). Neuropsychological and power spectral EEG investigations of the obsessive–compulsive syndrome. *Biological Psychiatry, 14,* 119–130.

Foa, E. B. (1979). Failure in treating obsessive–compulsives. *Behaviour Research and Therapy, 17,* 169–176.

Foa, E. B., & Chambless, D. L. (1978). Habituation of subjective anxiety during flooding in imagery. *Behaviour Research and Therapy, 16,* 391–399.

Foa, E. B., Grayson, J. B., Steketee, G. S., Doppelt, H. G., Turner, R. M., & Latimer, P. R. (1983). Success and failure in the behavioral treatment of obsessive–compulsives. *Journal of Consulting and Clinical Psychology, 51,* 287–297.

Foa, E. B., & Kozak, M. J. (1985). Treatment of anxiety disorders: Implications for psychopathology. In H. Tuma & J. D. Mazer (Eds.), *Anxiety and the anxiety disorders.* Hillsdale, NJ: Erlbaum.

Foa, E. B., & Steketee, G. (1977). Emergent fears during treatment of three obsessive–compulsives: Symptom substitution or deconditioning? *Journal of Behavior Therapy and Experimental Psychiatry, 8,* 353–358.

Foa, E. B., Steketee, G., Grayson, J. B., & Doppelt, H. G. (1983). Treatment of obsessive–compulsives: When do we fail? In E. B. Foa & P. M. G. Emmelkamp (Eds.), *Failures in behavior therapy.* New York: Wiley.

Foa, E. B., Steketee, G., Grayson, J. B., Turner, R. M., & Latimer, P. (1984). Deliberate exposure and blocking of obsessive–compulsive rituals: Immediate and long term effects. *Behavior Therapy.*

Foa, E. B., Steketee, G., & Milby, J. B. (1980). Differential effects of exposure and response prevention in obsessive–compulsive washers. *Journal of Consulting and Clinical Psychology, 48,* 71–79.

Foa, E. B., Steketee, G. S., & Ozarow, B. J. (1985). Behavior therapy with obsessive–compulsives: From theory to treatment. In M. Mavissakalian, S. M. Turner, & L. Michelson (Eds.), *Obsessive–compulsive disorders: Psychological and pharmacological treatments.* New York: Plenum.

Foa, E. B., Steketee, G., Turner, R. M., & Fisher, S. C. (1980). Effects of imaginal exposure to feared disasters in obsessive–compulsive checkers. *Behaviour Research and Therapy, 18,* 449–455.

Foa, E. B., & Tillmanns, A. (1980). The treatment of obsessive–compulsive neurosis. In A. Goldstein & E. B. Foa (Eds.), *Handbook of behavioral interventions: A clinical guide.* New York: Wiley.

Freed, A., Kerr, T. A., & Roth, M. (1972). The treatment of obsessional neurosis. *British Journal of Psychiatry, 120,* 590–591.

Geissmann, P., & Kammerer, T. (1964). L'imipramine dans la nevrose obsessionelle: Etude de 30 cas. *Encephale, 53,* 369–382.

Gertz, H. O. (1966). Experience with the logotherapeutic technique of paradoxical intention in the treatment of phobic and obsessive–compulsive patients. *American Journal of Psychiatry, 123,* 548–553.

Grimshaw, L. (1964). Obsessional disorder and neurological illness. *Journal of Neurological and Neurosurgical Psychiatry, 27,* 229–231.

Grimshaw, L. (1965). The outcome of obsessional disorder, a follow-up study of 100 cases. *British Journal of Psychiatry, 111,* 1051–1056.

Guidano, V. F., & Liotti, G. (1983). *Cognitive processes and emotional disorders.* New York: Guilford.

Guirdham, A. (1972). *Obsession.* London: Neville Spearman.

Hamilton, M. (1960). A rating scale for depression. *Journal of Neurological and Neurosurgical Psychiatry, 23,* 56–62.

Hodgson, R. J., & Rachman, S. (1972). The effects of contamination and washing in obsessional patients. *Behaviour Research and Therapy, 10,* 111–117.

Hodgson, R. J., & Rachman, S. (1977). Obsessional–compulsive complaints. *Behaviour Research and Therapy, 15,* 389–395.

Hodgson, R. J., Rachman, S., & Marks, I. M. (1972). The treatment of chronic obsessive-compulsive neurosis: Follow-up and further findings. *Behaviour Research and Therapy, 10,* 181–189.

Hornsveld, R. H. J., Kraaimaat, F. W., & van Dam-Baggen, R. M. J. (1979). Anxiety/discomfort and handwashing in obsessive–compulsive and psychiatric control patients. *Behaviour Research and Therapy, 17,* 223–228.

Insel, T. R. (1982). Obsessive–compulsive disorder—five clinical questions and a suggested approach. *Comprehensive Psychiatry, 23,* 241–251.

Insel, T. R., Alterman, I., & Murphy, D. L. (1982). Antiobsessional and antidepressant effects of clomipramine in the treatment of obsessive–compulsive disorder. *Psychopharmacology Bulletin, 18,* 115–117.

Insel, T. R., Murphy, D. L., Cohen, R. M., Alterman, M. A., Kilts, G., & Linnoila, M. (1983). Obsessive–compulsive disorder: A double-blind trial of clomipramine and clorgyline. *Archives of General Psychiatry, 40,* 605–612.

Karabanow, O. (1977). Double-blind controlled study in phobias and obsession. *Journal of International Medical Research, 5,* 42–48.

Kenny, F. T., Mowbray, R. M., & Lalani, S. (1978). Faradic disruption of obsessive ideation in the treatment of obsessive neurosis: A controlled study. *Behavior Therapy, 9,* 209–221.

Kenny, F. T., Solyom, L., & Solyom, C. (1973). Faradic disruption of obsessive ideation in the treatment of obsessive neurosis. *Behavior Therapy, 4,* 448–451.

Kringlen, E. (1965). Obsessional neurotics, a long term follow-up. *British Journal of Psychiatry, 111,* 709–722.

Lang, P. J. (1979). A bio-informational theory of emotional imagery. *Psychophysiology, 6,* 495–511.

Lewin, W. (1960). Symposium on orbital undercutting: Selective leucotomy. *Proceedings of the Royal Society of Medicine, 53,* 732–734.

Lewis, A. (1935). Problems of obsessional illness. *Proceedings of the Royal Society of Medicine, 29,* 325–336.

Lewis, A. (1957). Obsessional illness (R.M.P.A. lecture). *Acta Neuropsiquiátrica Argentina, 3,* 323–334.

Makhlouf-Norris, F., Jones, H. G., & Norris, H. (1970). Articulation of the conceptual structure in obsessional neurosis. *British Journal of Social and Clinical Psychology, 9,* 264–274.

Makhlouf-Norris, F., & Norris H. (1972). The obsessive–compulsive syndrome as a neurotic device for the reduction of self-uncertainty. *British Journal of Psychiatry, 121,* 277–288.

Marks, I. M. (1981a). Review of behavioral psychotherapy, I: Obsessive–compulsive disorders, *American Journal of Psychiatry, 138,* 584–592.

Marks, I. M. (1981b). *Cure and care of the neuroses.* New York: Wiley.

Marks, I. M., Crowe, E., Drewe, E., Young, J., & Dewhurst, W. G. (1969). Obsessive–compulsive neurosis in identical twins. *British Journal of Psychiatry, 15,* 991–998.

Marks, I. M., Hallam, R. S., Connolly, J., & Philpott, R. (1977). *Nursing in behavioral psychotherapy.* London: Royal College of Nursing of the United Kingdom.

Marks, I. M., Hodgson, R., & Rachman, S. (1975). Treatment of chronic obsessive–compulsive neurosis by *in vivo* exposure: A 2 year follow-up and issues in treatment. *British Journal of Psychiatry, 127,* 349–364.

Marks, I. M., Stern, R. S., Mawson, D., Cobb, J., & McDonald, R. (1980)). Clomipramine and exposure for obsessive–compulsive rituals. *British Journal of Psychiatry, 136,* 1–25.

Mathews, A. M. (1978). Fear-reduction research and clinical phobias. *Psychological Bulletin, 85,* 390–404.

McCarthy, B. W. (1972). Short term implosive therapy: Case study. *Psychological Reports, 30,* 589–590.

McFall, M. E., & Wollersheim, J. P. (1979). Obsessive–compulsive neurosis: A cognitive behavioral formulation and approach to treatment. *Cognitive Therapy and Research, 3,* 333–348.

McGuire, R. J., & Vallance, M. (1964). Aversion therapy by electric shock: A simple technique. *British Medical Journal, 1,* 151–153.

Meyer, V. (1966). Modification of expectations in cases with obsessional rituals. *Behaviour Research and Therapy, 4,* 273–280.

Meyer, V., & Levy R. (1973). Modification of behavior in obsessive–compulsive disorders. In H. E. Adams & P. Unikel (Eds.), *Issues and trends in behavior therapy.* Springfield, IL: C. C. Thomas.

Meyer, V., Levy, R., & Schnurer, A. (1974). A behavioural treatment of obsessive–compulsive disorders. In H. R. Beech (Ed.), *Obsessional states.* London: Methuen.

Mills, H. L., Agras, W. S., Barlow, D. H., & Mills, J. R. (1973). Compulsive rituals treated by response prevention. *Archives of General Psychiatry, 38,* 524–527.

Milner, A. D., Beech, H. R., & Walker, V. J. (1971). Decision processes and obsessional behaviour. *British Journal of Social and Clinical Psychology, 10,* 88–89.

Mitchell-Heggs, N., Kelly, D., & Richardson, A. (1976). Stereotactic limbic leucotomy—a follow-up at 16 months. *British Journal of Psychiatry, 128,* 226–240.

Mitchell-Heggs, N., Kelly, D., Richardson, A., & McLeish, J. (1978). *Further experience of limbic leucotomy.* Unpublished manuscript.

Mowrer, O. (1939). A stimulus–response analysis of anxiety and its role as a reinforcing agent. *Psychological Review, 46,* 553–565.

Mowrer, O. (1960). *Learning theory and behavior.* New York: Wiley.

Nelson, R. O. (1977). Methodological issues in assessment via self-monitoring. In J. D. Cone & R. P. Hawkins (Eds.), *Behavioral assessment: New directions in clinical psychology.* New York: Brunner/Mazel.

Neziroglu, F. (1979). A combined behavioral–pharmacotherapy approach to obsessive–compulsive disorders. In J. Oriols, C. Ballus, M. Gonzalez, & J. Prijol (Eds.), *Biological psychiatry today.* Amsterdam: Elsevier/North Holland.

Pacella, B. L., Polatin, P., & Nagler, S. H. (1944). Clinical and EEG studies in obsessive–compulsive states. *American Journal of Psychiatry, 100,* 830–838.

Parker, N. (1964). Close identification in twins discordant for obsessional neurosis. *British Journal of Psychiatry, 110,* 496–504.

Pavlov, I. P. (1934). An attempt at a physiological interpretation of obsessional neurosis and paranoia. *Journal of the Mental Sciences, 329,* 187–197.

Persons, J. B., & Foa, E. B. (1984). Processing of fearful and neutral information by obsessive–compulsives. *Behaviour Research and Therapy, 22,* 259–265.

Philpott, R. (1975). Recent advances in the behavioral measurement of obsessional illness. Difficulties common to these and other instruments. *Scottish Medical Journal, 20*(Suppl.), 33–40.

Pippard, J. (1956). Discussion: Obsessional–compulsive states, the surgical treatment of obsessional states (abridged). *Proceedings of the Royal Society of Medicine, 49,* 846–849.

Pollack, J. M. (1979). Obsessive–compulsive personality: A review. *Psychological Bulletin, 86,* 225–241.

Pollitt, J. (1956). Discussion: Obsessive–compulsive states (abridged). *Proceedings of the Royal Society of Medicine, 49,* 842–845.

Rabavilas, A. D., & Boulougouris, J. C. (1974). Physiological accompaniments of ruminations, flooding and thought-stopping in obsessive patients. *Behaviour Research and Therapy, 12,* 239–243.

Rabavilas, A. D., Boulougouris, J. C. & Perissaki, C. (1979). Therapist qualities related to outcome with exposure *in vivo* in neurotic patients. *Journal of Behavior Therapy and Experimental Psychiatry, 10,* 293–299.

Rabavilas, A. D., Boulougouris, J. C., & Stefanis, C. (1976). Duration of flooding sessions in the treatment of obsessive–compulsive patients *Behavior Research and Therapy, 14,* 349–355.

Rachman, S. (1971). Obsessional ruminations. *Behaviour Research and Therapy, 9,* 229–235.

Rachman, S. (1976). The modification of obsessions: A new formulation *Behaviour Research and Therapy, 14,* 437–443.

Rachman, S. J., Cobb, J., Grey, S., McDonald, B., Mawson, D., Sartory, G., & Stern, R. (1979). The behavioural treatment of obsessional–compulsive disorders with and without clomipramine. *Behaviour Research and Therapy, 17,* 462–478.

Rachman, S., & DeSilva, P. (1978). Abnormal and normal obsessions. *Behaviour Research and Therapy, 16,* 233–248.

Rachman, S., DeSilva, P., & Roper, G. (1976). The spontaneous decay of compulsive urges. *Behaviour Research and Therapy, 14,* 445–453.

Rachman, S., & Hodgson, R. (1980). *Obsessions and compulsions.* Englewood Cliffs, NJ: Prentice-Hall.

Rachman, S., Marks, I. M., & Hodgson, R. (1973). The treatment of obsessive–compulsive neurotics by modelling and flooding *in vivo. Behaviour Research and Therapy, 11,* 463–471.

Rachman, S. J., & Wilson, G. T. (1980). *The effects of psychological therapy,* Oxford: Pergamon Press.

Reed, G. F. (1968). Some formal qualities of obsessional thinking, *Psychiatria Clinica, 1,* 382–392.

Reed, G. F. (1969). "Underinclusion"—a characteristic of obsessional personality disorder, II. *British Journal of Psychiatry, 115,* 787–790.

Roper, G., & Rachman, S. (1976). Obsessional–compulsive checking: Experimental replication and development. *Behaviour Research and Therapy, 14,* 25–32.

Roper, G., Rachman, S., & Hodgson, R. (1973). An experiment on obsessional checking. *Behaviour Research and Therapy, 11,* 271–277.

Rosenberg, C. M. (1967). Personality and obsessional neurosis. *British Journal of Psychiatry, 113,* 471–477.

Rubin, R. D., & Merbaum, M. (1971). Self-imposed punishment versus desensitization. In R. D. Rubin, H. Frensterheim, A. A. Lazarus, & C. M. Franks (Eds.), *Advances in behavior therapy.* New York: Academic Press.

Salzman, L., & Thaler, F. H. (1981). Obsessive–compulsive disorders: A review of the literature. *American Journal of Psychiatry, 138,* 286–296.

Sandler, J., & Hazari, A. (1960). The "obsessional": On the psychological classification of obsessional character traits and symptoms. *British Journal of Medical Psychology, 33,* 113–122.

Sargent, W. (1962). The present indication for leucotomy. *Lancet, 1,* 1197.

Schilder, P. (1938, May). The organic background of obsessions and compulsions. *American Journal of Psychiatry,* 1397–1416.

Shagass, C., Roemer, R. A., Straumanis, J. J., & Josiassen, R. C. (1984). Distinctive somatosensory evoked potential features in obsessive–compulsive disorder. *Biological Psychiatry, 19,* 1507–1524.

Sher, K. K., Frost, R. O., & Otto, R. (1983). Cognitive deficits in compulsive checkers: An exploratory study. *Behaviour Research and Therapy, 21,* 357–364.

Slade, P. D. (1974). Psychometric studies of obsessional illness and obsessional personality. In H. R. Beech (Ed.), *Obsessional states.* London: Methuen.

Solyom, L., Garza-Perez, J., Ledwidge, B. L., & Solyom, C. (1972). Paradoxical intention in the treatment of obsessive thoughts: A pilot study. *Comprehensive Psychiatry, 13,* 291–297.

Solyom, L., & Kingstone, E. (1973). An obsessive neurosis following morning glory seed ingestion treated by aversion relief. *Journal of Behavior Therapy and Experimental Psychiatry, 4,* 293–295.

Solyom, L., Zamanzadeh, D., Ledwidge, B., & Kenny K. (1971). Aversion relief treatment of obsessive neurosis. In R. D. Rubin, J. P. Brady, & J. D. Henderson (Eds.), *Advances in behavior therapy*. New York: Academic Press.

Sookman, D., & Solyom, L. (1977). Effectiveness of four behaviour therapies in the treatment of obsessive neurosis. In J. C. Boulougouris & A. D. Rabavilas (Eds.), *The treatment of phobic and obsessive–compulsive disorders*. Oxford: Pergamon.

Spielberger, C. D., Gorsuch, R. L., & Lushene R. G. (1970). *The state–trait anxiety inventory*. Palo Alto, CA: Consulting Psychologists Press.

Steketee, G., Foa, E. G., & Grayson, J. B. (1982). Recent advances in the treatment of obsessive–compulsives. *Archives of General Psychiatry, 39,* 1365–1371.

Steketee, G., & Doppelt H. (in preparation). *Use of the Hopkins Symptom Checklist in the measurement of obsessive–compulsive symptoms*.

Stern, R. S. (1978). Obsessive thoughts: The problem of therapy. *British Journal of Psychiatry, 133,* 200–205.

Stern, R. S., Lipsedge, M. S., & Marks, I. M. (1975). Obsessive ruminations: A controlled trial of thought-stopping technique. *Behaviour Research and Therapy, 11,* 659–662.

Sternberg, M. (1974). Physical treatments in obsessional disorders. In H. R. Beech (Ed.), *Obsessional states*. London: Methuen.

Tan, E., Marks, I. M., & Marset, P. (1971). Bimedial leucotomy in obsessive–compulsive neurosis: A controlled serial enquiry. *British Journal of Psychiatry, 118,* 155–164.

Taylor, J. A. (1953). A personality scale of manifest anxiety. *Journal of Abnormal and Social Psychology, 48,* 285–290.

Teasdale, Y. D. (1974). Learning models of obsessional–compulsive disorder. In H. R. Beech (Ed.), *Obsessional states*. London: Methuen.

Thoren, P., Asberg, M., Cronholm, B., Jornestedt, L., & Traskman, L. (1980). Clomipramine treatment of obsessive–compulsive disorder, I: A controlled clinical trial. *Archives of General Psychiatry, 37,* 1281–1285.

Tippin, J., & Henn, F. A. (1982). Modified leukotomy in the treatment of intractable obsessional neurosis. *American Journal of Psychiatry, 139,* 1601–1603.

Vogel, W., Peterson, L. E., & Broverman, I. K. (1982). A modification of Rachman's habituation technique for treatment of the obsessive–compulsive disorder. *Behaviour Research and Therapy, 20,* 101–104.

Volans, P. J. (1976). Styles of decision making and probability appraisal in selected obsessional and phobic patients. *British Journal of Social and Clinical Psychology, 15,* 305–317.

Watson, J. P., & Marks, I. M. (1971). Relevant and irrelevant fear in flooding—A crossover study of phobic patients. *Behavior Therapy, 2,* 275–293.

Watts, R. (1971). *An investigation of imaginal desensitization as an habituation process*. Unpublished doctoral dissertation, University of London, Great Britain.

Wisocki, P. A. (1970). Treatment of obsessive–compulsive behavior by covert sensitization and covert reinforcement: A case report. *Journal of Behavior Therapy and Experimental Psychiatry, 1,* 233–239.

3

CLINICAL STRESS MANAGEMENT

TED L. ROSENTHAL AND RENATE H. ROSENTHAL

The reader will find this chapter both unique and an extremely important contribution to clinical practice. Any generally practicing clinician probably sees more of the types of problems illustrated in this chapter than all other problems combined. The Rosenthals correctly conclude that stress not only cuts across most diagnostic categories but also includes in its manifestations problems very similar to those found in the anxiety state categories, specifically generalized anxiety disorder and panic disorder. For example, in the very detailed and fascinating case study presented near the end of this chapter, describing an individual undergoing severe stress, the reader will witness a full-blown panic disorder developing part way through treatment, only to be remediated in large part by further reductions in the patient's stressful life style. It is no coincidence that current psychosocial treatment approaches to generalized anxiety disorder and panic disorder are very similar.

This chapter is not another repetition of the mechanics of relaxation training or the technology of biofeedback or self-statement training. Rather, it is a comprehensive clinical description of the art of putting these procedures together that evolves from a deep appreciation of the authors' biobehavioral perspective. The Rosenthals' clinical expertise is nowhere more evident than in the variety of ways in which they introduce and describe the numerous techniques and lifestyle changes that are so important to complex stress management programs. There is little question that their clinical methods enhance the probability of compliance with these sometimes difficult procedures. Finally, everyone reading this chapter will be indebted, as are the Rosenthals, to the patient himself, who wrote a long soliloquy on not only the experience of stress, but also the process of clinical stress management from the patient's point of view. This report provides a perspective that will be invaluable to practicing clinicians.—D. H. B.

INTRODUCTION

The recognition of the burdens that stress can exert on human life and the efforts to ease such problems are concerns that have long preceded scientific inquiry. Philosophers living in troubled times, such as the Greek Stoics and later Montaigne in France, sought to devise personal philosophies that would spare

Ted L. Rosenthal and Renate H. Rosenthal. Department of Psychiatry, University of Tennessee College of Medicine, Center for the Health Sciences, Memphis, Tennessee. Ted L. Rosenthal is also affiliated with the Adult Psychiatry and Alcohol and Drug Unit, Jack Morgan, MD, Medical Director, MidSouth Hospital, Memphis, Tennessee.

the individual excessive preoccupation with the social woes of their respective eras. The word "stress" is, itself, very old. It probably entered Middle English as a variant form of the noun "distress." That meaning probably grew together with an Old French word, *estrèce*, which meant straits, narrowness, and oppression. Over time, these two streams of meaning fused together to signify hardship, adversity, or affliction. It was also early recognized that such burdens need not be overt in nature but may instead rest on mental or vicarious duress. For example, Spenser's *Faerie Queene*, written in 1590, contains a sentence illustrating observational arousal. In modern English, it is as follows: "Because of his heavy stress, the war-like Damsel was sad herself and sore empassioned." In more general terms, we shall use the word stress to mean *strain upon personal endurance*. As such, stress may manifest itself purely in subjective, phenomenological forms, purely through physiologic malfunction, but most often as a biobehavioral disruption.

An Overview of Stress-Related Conditions

Unlike agoraphobia or schizophrenia, some stress is an inevitable part of normal, everyday living and purely stress-produced problems are not often identified as a coherent clinical entity. The obvious exception involves traumatic stress of exceptional kinds, which might overpower most people so exposed. Examples include military combat and civilian bombardment during wartime, major catastrophes such as fires, floods, airplane or railroad crashes, earthquakes, and personal assaults such as rape or incarceration in concentration camps. In the nomenclature of the American Psychiatric Association's (1980) *Diagnostic and Statistical Manual of Mental Disorders* (DSM-III), symptoms resulting from such disastrous experiences are classified as *posttraumatic stress disorders*. They are confined to reactions prompted by clear-cut, extraordinary stressors; their prevalence is not known, partly because it will depend on the degree of international upheaval or accidental calamity befalling the victims; and, rape aside, their acute manifestations mainly confront clinicians who work in military, mass casualty, and emergency room settings. Perhaps a more commonly encountered acute stress reaction occurs when extraverted, "characterological" or "acting-out" personalities paint themselves into quandries by ill-considered, rash conduct and then face situational stress prompted by loss of job, divorce proceedings, or the criminal justice system. Such crises aside, these individuals are not the usual clientele seeking stress-management or psychotherapeutic services.

Much more common are cases that would fall, diagnostically, in the DSM-III categories of *adjustment disorder* and *anxiety states*, especially *generalized anxiety disorder, psychological factors affecting physical condition* (such as migraine headache and diverse pain symptoms), and often, also, *affective disorders* and *substance abuse disorders*—especially when the person becomes addicted to, or dependent upon, alcohol for its sedative (i.e., stress-reducing) properties. In the same vein, stress-related pain disorders often result in drug addiction (Valium, Librium, Darvon, Talwin, to name just a few). Having acknowledged these categorical groupings, we will not pursue them in further detail. The reason is that stress elements contribute to, or exacerbate, a host of medical illnesses that include cardiovascular disease, ulcer, rheumatic and orthopedic problems, gynecologic difficulties, and reactions to reduced or lost physical function. Finally, there are many "perfectly normal" persons—competitive executives, harassed housewives, and submissive Caspar Milquetoasts are stereotyped illustrations—who seek and need stress management. For them, successful intervention can both improve the experiential quality of their lives *and* serve a preventive health role to fend off or delay physical maladies they might otherwise develop. In short, stress may turn up nearly anywhere and the clinician's task is to aid the person to curb and cope with such strains within the particular context of life facing that overtaxed individual.

Many stress-related complaints are identical to or overlap common symptoms of anxiety. These include such subjective manifestations as tension, chronic arousal, fatigue, discouragement, and worry. Physical symptoms may involve tightness, cramps, or "butterflies" in the stomach (i.e., "bad gut feelings," including loose bowels); similar tenseness or discomfort in the musculoskeletal system; tension headaches; and such "nervous" symptoms as fidgeting, tapping fingers or foot, sweaty palms, and dry throat. Lifestyle manifestations that also overlap anxiety symptoms include shortened temper or impatience—becoming more thin-skinned or getting "bugged" too easily—reduced sexual activity, and emotional outbursts or a frequent combat to restrain them.

Other symptoms of stress we commonly observe may occur in a "classical" anxiety picture, but are not its prototypic ingredients. These complaints include a pattern of hypervigilance or chronic "red alert" in which the patient over-prepares before each "crisis" or challenge and rehashes it excessively afterwards; the patient broods or ruminates about stressful events, which then endure much longer in subjective time than their duration in objective time, whether pain, a performance challenge, or an interpersonal confrontation is at issue. Patients report difficulty in shifting attention, in remembering, and especially in concentrating upon just one thing at a time. There is a sense of having "too many balls in the air to juggle" and a longing for "peace of mind" or "relaxation." Sleep functions are almost always disturbed. A minority sleep excessively "for escape" and do not want to get out of bed much of the time. A majority have various insomniac problems. Their sleep is restless; it is hard to fall asleep, to stay asleep, to sleep deeply or soundly, and to awake refreshed. They have substantial difficulty dismissing the pressures of the day and unwinding from those strains without chemical assistance. Hence, they often increase their reliance on alcohol or other drugs in order to relax. There is reduction in the perceived importance of recreation and leisure activities, and sometimes in normal socializing with friends. Many have never engaged in regular physical exercise; those who formerly did, decrease or give up exercising. They report decline in their sense of humor; they laugh or smile less often than in the past. We observe that their total pace of life and self-demands are excessive (and verge toward "perfectionism").

As a result, their overall functioning appears out of reasonable balance and reflects behavioral discord rather than harmony in their rhythm of living. Spouse, kin, or friends typically agree the patient is not living in a balanced manner and has "gotten worse" compared to previous adjustment.

Why Take a Biobehavioral Stance?

The simplest factual conclusion from the available data is that Descartes's distinction between "mind" and "body" is a false dichotomy. Mental and physiological processes interpenetrate intimately. Their complex reciprocal relationships permeate all facets of normal regulation and are especially evident in stress-related problems. Since Selye's (e.g., 1950, 1951, 1956) work, the literature has burgeoned. We will not presume to review it in detail. Novaco's (1979) fine chapter on stress and anger control provides an overview of the historical material, and Turk and Genest (1979) discuss further relationships with the regulation of pain. Our present goals are (1) to show why contributory, multivariate causation, rather than a linear stimulus–response (S-R) view best fits the data, (2) to illustrate such a conception from research on affective disorder, and (3) to sketch some of the new evidence—emerging at an accelerating pace—that suggests conjoint, biobehavioral events as the determinants of stress-related clinical complaints.

Causal Networks

Science is a conservative enterprise. Among its esthetic priorities is a bias toward parsimony, that is, that the "simplest" possible explanation is to be preferred. This tradition has fostered a preference for univariate models that are still cherished by many psychologists and psychiatrists, especially those interested in studying animal models of human behavior. However, such views become increasingly strained by evidence of elective, interpretive acts that can steer conduct into multiple, alternative options and can recycle covert processes of evaluation and memory search when decision making so requires. The bulk of the data indicate that human cognition is governed by complex, executive acts that mediate between overt stimuli and responses (see Rosenthal, 1984a; Rosenthal & Bandura, 1978; Rosenthal & Zimmerman, 1978; Zimmerman, 1983). It is somewhat ironic to note that such a view of human self-regulation—resisted by peripheralistic thinkers in behavioral science—has more readily gained acceptance by "hard" scientists. For instance, the astronomer Sagan (1978, p. 240) writes: "Each human being is a superbly-constructed, astonishingly compact, self-ambulatory computer, capable on occasion of independent decision-making and real control of his or her environment."

In psychology a network-like reciprocity among external stimulus conditions, the individual's covert processes (including values, experienced physiological feedback such as arousal states, and acts of judgment), and overt conduct is probably best exemplified by Bandura's (1977a, 1982a, 1983) social learning theory. It has rejected a univariate view of causation, at base, because such a view clashes too sharply with the available evidence; the cited references present in detail the reasoning that supports a multivariate conception. Thus, the cognitive context of a procedure will determine whether or not it is effective and, in some cases, whether or not it is even utilized. A simple example involves dysphoric but religious patients. They rejected guidance imagery cast in secular form, but benefited when equivalent content was tied to the teachings of Jesus (Propost, 1980). Another instance involves the introduction of contrasting comparison standards, which serve as benchmarks for assessing one's own competence. In turn, when such benchmarks diverge, so can the overt actions they steer, as shown by a study that varied the perceived degree of a model's handicap. One group of submissive clients was given a description of a profoundly unassertive person who was labeled as "typical." For a second group of submissive peers, the "typical" comparison model was depicted as mildly inhibited. A behavioral test promptly followed. It required each client to confront assertively a feisty adversary by telephone. As predicted, the clients whose model was severely submissive far surpassed those given the mildly submissive model on multiple behavioral measures (Hung, Rosenthal, & Kelley, 1980). Thus, this study illustrates how acts of judgment—based on subjective inferences drawn from contrasting modeled standards—can alter overt performance.

In short, the strains on univariate, S-R explanations have grown too stark for such analyses to remain parsimonious. A much more complex framework appears necessary. Moreover, many pivotal human decisions are governed by coincidence or situational accidents in ways not readily handled by views based on simplistic determinism (Bandura, 1982b). Here are two obvious examples: A chance encounter at a party with an attractive and datable person can then determine the course of one's subsequent marital and familial experiences. Computer assignment to different sections of the same course, but taught respectively by a boring versus a captivating lecturer, can greatly influence a student's choice of careers and hence steer years of occupational and financial experience. The foregoing issues will be further illuminated by research that traces relationships between genetic constitution and mood or conduct disorders, relationships among neuroendocrine events and molar behavior, and relationships across hierarchical levels of physiological organization. In all these spheres, psychological stress and biological variables will share an intimate reciprocity of causation.

Depression as a "Final Common Pathway"

We have collaborated on research for some years with our colleague, Dr. Hagop Akiskal. He has taught us his conception of major affective disorder (and certain subaffective dysthymias) as the clinical resultant or "final common pathway" that manifests the interacting, reciprocal impact of neurochemical, genetic, personality, and stressful life event components. Phrased differently, such affective illnesses as pronounced, melancholic depressions are assumed to occur when a threshold is crossed by a combination of biological, psychological, and situational strains acting conjointly. Akiskal's theory is one form of a *stress–diathesis* (i.e., constitutional vulnerability) approach and, in its network-like, multivariate stance, it shows an affinity with the reasoning of Bandura's social learning theory.

Thus, in especially vulnerable individuals, a full-blown depression may be triggered by relatively trivial stressors. Akiskal conceives such persons to have high genetic penetrance for affective illness, and the evidence that mood disorders run in some family bloodlines now appears beyond dispute (see Akiskal, 1979; Akiskal *et al.*, 1980; Akiskal & Webb, 1978). At the other extreme, some conspiracies of circumstance—such as debilitating chronic diseases, for example, multiple sclerosis, loss of kidney function—invite affective risk for all but the most steadfast souls. Thus, crisis reactions in cancer (unlike surgery) patients did not abate when studied for 15 weeks (Gottesman & Lewis, 1982). Likewise, a profound personal loss, such as the death of a beloved spouse, will spur depressive episodes in many persons. DSM-III classifies such despondency as *uncomplicated bereavement*, noting: "A full depressive syndrome frequently is a normal reaction to such a loss, with feelings of depression and such associated symptoms as poor appetite, weight loss, and insomnia" (American Psychiatric Association, 1980, p. 333).

However, most often a complex tissue of *biobehavioral* variables will kindle affective dysfunction. As elements of an interlocking system, they may compound jointly to cross the threshold igniting melancholia, or some may temper others to stave off major depression. Stressful life events, and perceptual–cognitive biases that magnify the subjective impact of any stressor, can be potent arsonists to inflame people who are vulnerable because of genetically transmitted affective temperaments, because of fragile adjustment to living, because of unusual situational demands—such as occupations that entail protracted working with little rest or irregular shifts whose switches tax bodily harmonies—or because of all such covariant strains upon endurance acting in concert (Akiskal, 1979; Depue, 1979; Rosenthal & Rosenthal, 1983). Many illustrative examples could be given. Here are just a few. In some chronic depressions, patients display malaise that initially appears to stem from pessimistic personal philosophies or cynical, jaded attitudes. Yet they improved if given medication (e.g., desimipramine or nortriptyline) often assumed to alter brain chemistry. A significantly larger proportion (30%) of these tricyclic-responsive depressives had blood relatives who had met the criteria for depressive disorder than did depressives (3.3%) who proved nonresponsive to pharmacotherapy. More striking was the difference between the responder ("subaffective dysthymic") and nonresponder ("characterologic depression") groups when tested in the sleep laboratory, and compared to unipolar melancholics and nondepressed controls. The mean rapid-eye-movement (REM) latency of the responders was 57.6 min, very close to that for the full-blown unipolar depression patients, 59.0 min, and suggesting some underlying physiologic concordance. The nonresponders showed a much longer (and highly statistically significant difference) REM latency mean of 98.8 min, which was indistinguishable from that for nonde-pressed controls, 101.0 min. In stark contrast, the characterologic but depressed nonresponders showed very much greater developmental assault, and they abused sedative–hypnotic drugs and/or alcohol (60%) more than did the dys-thymic responders (10%). For instance, during their formative years, loss of at least one parent occurred more often among characterologic (60%) than dys-thymic (25%) depressives. Abuse of alcohol and the deviant parental modeling thus created was much more frequent in the families of characterologic (53%) than dysthymic (10%) patients. Thus, although the dysthymics had significantly more major depressions in their family histories, there was no difference in the proportion of dysthymics (30%) and characterologic depressives (27%) whose kin had committed suicide. Finally, the characterologic group's proportion of growing up in homes where *both* parents met criteria for some psychiatric diagnosis (47%) far exceeded the dysthymics' (10%). Here, then, were two groups of patients who presented depressive complaints. In the dysthymics, the evidence suggested that their symptoms were associated with a genetic vulnera-bility to affective disturbance, which responded to tricyclic medication. Genetic contributions seemed much weaker spurs to depression in the characterologic group, which in turn had endured greater developmental upheaval typified by the stresses of stormy, unstable modeling by parents and more frequent loss of one or both parents before age 15 years. It is noteworthy that these social learning history stressors resulted in unfavorable clinical outcomes (based on both psycho- *and* pharmacotherapies) more often for the characterologic (30%) than for the dysthymic (5%) depressive patients (Akiskal, King, Rosenthal, Robinson, & Scott-Strauss, 1981; Akiskal *el al.,* 1980; Rosenthal, Akiskal, Scott-Strauss, Rosenthal, & David, 1981).

A final illustration involves research conducted on a Danish sample. Here, too, interactive biobehavioral relationships were found between "acting-out" and affective disorders as a joint function of upbringing, lineage, and sex of patient. The sons of alcoholics showed higher rates of alcoholism but no greater psychopathology—regardless of where they were raised—compared to a control group. The daughters of alcoholics, *if* placed in adoptive homes, were more prone to alcoholism, yet *not* to depression than the general population, but they did not differ in these respects from control adoptees. Yet when raised by their biological parents, daughters of alcoholics developed significantly more depres-sions. As compared to adopted controls' parents, their mothers were more often described as having depressions and personality disorders, and their fathers more often manifested antisocial or conduct disorders. Hence, for the daughters but not the sons of alcoholics, characterologic instability depended most strongly on the social learning context and the sorts of developmental experien-ces it provided (Goodwin, Schulsinger, Knop, Mednick, & Guze, 1977a, 1977b). For further examples showing how both nature and nurture may interpenetrate in the depressive disorders, see Brown (1979) and Paykel (1979). A recent treatment study shows that self-control therapy *plus* desimipramine was supe-rior to either intervention alone (Roth, Bielski, Jones, Parker, & Osborn, 1982;

and compare Friedman, 1975; Weissman, 1978; Weissman *et al.*, 1979). In an important paper Depue and his colleagues discuss issues of diathetic threshold and data supporting genetic involvement in the major affective disorders from a biobehavioral perspective (Depue *et al.*, 1981).

Biobehavioral Linkages with Stress

New evidence, emerging rapidly, combines to indicate that the network of psychophysiological reciprocal causation is better unified but more complexly interwoven than was conceived by the dominant thinking of the past. Here is an illustrative potpourri: Among unipolar melancholics who showed fairly regular diurnal variations in mood (usually attributed to the uptake and release times of catecholamines), memories of unhappy experiences were more likely to be retrieved at more depressed times of day, when most past experiences were rated as more negative. Happy memories were more frequent at less depressed times of day, when the hedonic tone of most past experiences was rated more favorably (Clark & Teasdale, 1982). Untangling causal skeins is especially difficult with individual patients. There are new data showing that changes in weather can alter the density of small positive ions in the air and thereby raise irritability and shift mood among ion-sensitive persons (Charry & Hawkinshire, 1981). Variation in the intensity of photic stimuli—as occurs when the amount of daylight undergoes seasonal changes—also can affect mood in humans (Wehr, Wirz-Justice, Goodwin, Duncan, & Gillin, 1979). More generally, the clinical impact of circadian rhythms may be greater than formerly assumed (Goodwin & Wehr, 1982). Yet sleep disturbances are among the most common and debilitating of stress-related complaints. Even among chronic insomniacs without other known disorder, the distinction between bodily and mental factors proved difficult. Most often, they claimed their wakeful stirrings were prompted by a combination of cognitive and somatic cues. For those able to make a sharp cleavage, cognitive dominated over somatic intrusions (Lichstein & Rosenthal, 1980). However, the material opening this paragraph suggests that the content of cognition and its affective tone may, at times, be determined by physiologic events. Once more, we come full circle to the impasse created by efforts to divorce mind from body.

It further appears that the endocrine and immune systems are linked bidirectionally and influence each other (Besedovsky & Sorkin, 1977.) When the customary innervation of the sympathetic nervous system is interrupted, such departures from typical activation can diminish or block protective immune responses. Also, changes in neuroendocrine secretion serve to modulate or control the processes of the immune system to a much greater extent than previously assumed (Besedovsky, Del Ray, Sorkin, Da Prada, & Keller, 1979). Both perceptually mediated and tissue-mediated stress reactions can trigger similar biochemical changes conveyed through sympathetic messages that result in detrimental hormone alterations. Perhaps most striking is Riley's (1981) conclusion that resultant decline in immune function can lead to attack by usually latent viruses that stimulate cancer and can reduce resistence to newly deviant cancer cells and to other pathophysiologic events that are ordinarily held at bay by an immune system operating at its full capacity. Reciprocally, a combination of muscle and guided imagery relaxation methods was tested on cancer patients to reduce the aversiveness of their chemotherapy. The relaxation group surpassed control patients in reduced anxiety and nausea *and* lower physiological arousal (as measured by pulse rate and systolic blood pressure) during chemotherapy and also experienced less severe and less protracted nausea at home afterward (Lyles, Burish, Krozely, & Oldham, 1982).

In discussing stress in the workplace, McLean (1982) concurs that much research (cited therein) confirms that psychosocial stressors alter the levels of diverse body chemicals, hormones, and organic processes as well as subjective reports of anxiety and dysphoria. Likewise, various medical therapies—tricyclic antidepressants, lithium, and electroconvulsive therapy (ECT)—that have been used with success in treating affective disorders can all change the permeability of the blood–brain barrier, which in turn seems to be regulated by adrenergic (sympathetic) signals from the central nervous system (Preskorn *et al.*, 1981). Moreover, there may be closer interconnections among neural peptides and cognitive functions than previously suspected. For instance, attentional responses, especially deficits in somatosensory attention, have been related to levels of opioid peptides and this endorphin-mediated process is also associated with abnormal perception of pain (Davis, Buchsbaum, & Bunney, 1980). A longstanding hypothesis has been that stress may trigger depression by depleting or altering the neuroamine balance (e.g., Anisman & Zacharko, 1982). Whatever the actual mediating events, some involvement of neurotransmitter deviancy in the major affective psychoses seems highly likely. Reciprocally once again, new research suggests that experiential events and self-referent subjective perceptions can stimulate adrenergic activity and thereby influence the release of catecholamines (Bandura, Reese, & Adams, 1982). It is on the massive bulk of converging evidence that we base our conviction that stress is best viewed in *biobehavioral* terms. If from now on we emphasize the psychological aspects, we do so for discursive convenience. (For an overview of resaerch on the physiologic consequences of stress, as mediated through pituitary secretion following emotional activation of the adrenal cortex, see Riley, 1981). No matter how better-evolved future theory may refine the picture, it now seems probable that biobehavioral influences that form a network-like system engage in a surprising amount of two-way communication across the experiential, neurophysiological, and cellular levels of organization in the human being.

Exacerbation Cycles

In order to vividly grasp our conception of stress and how it can snowball (discussed in the following section), it is necessary to epitomize the evolution of vicious cycles. Henceforth, we intend to write mainly as practicing clinicians and suspect a shift in prose style will accompany this shift in viewpoint. Before we embark on clinical material, it seems germane to illustrate how normal persons, through no obvious fault of their own, can encounter "a run of bad luck"— apparently accidental in nature (Bandura, 1982b)—which then mushrooms into stress—laden personal quandries. To do so, we will engage in some limited self-disclosure as we sometimes do with patients *when appropriate.*

Catch 23

We try to practice what we preach. For several years we have biked and jogged on an almost daily basis, deriving much pleasure from our unambitious but regular exercise regimen. One morning while biking before work in a secluded, low-traffic residential area, one of us had a freak accident. We later learned that a chance, structural failure led to the front wheel brakes suddenly locking the front wheel. There was no warning. Tossed over the handlebars with the pavement approaching fast, to avoid neurosurgery one braces the fall with one's hands and wrists. X-rays disclosed no fractures, but the ligaments were badly torn in both wrists. To avoid further strain bicycle riding, but not jogging, had to be suspended during several weeks of recuperation. This apparently led to some weakening of the thoracic muscles that are toned by biking, and while rising from a chair an awkward motion triggered a major charley horse at the union of thorax and hip. This created considerable pain, required several days on prescribed muscle relaxant medication, and precluded resort to Jacobsonian relaxation exercises when ordinarily called for.

In this context there descended another stressor. We had hired a contractor to convert a stone and masonary garage into a small guest house, creating a self-contained efficiency unit for rental. Our contractor phoned the city to check on feasibility and was told the conversion was legal since an extant room that was part of the garage had been used for rental long before the current zoning restrictions. We decided to proceed, invested considerable money to do so, but when all the major first-phase work was completed, the city inspector delivered a bombshell technicality: Yes, we could do the expansion and conversion. No, we could not add a kitchen since this would make the structure a separate dwelling. Hence, we had to settle for a refrigerator and some storage cabinetry as a dinette but no stove, no kitchen sink, and definite prospects of much less rent than anticipated. One of us despaired of recovering our investment; the other took a wait-and-see, "one-day-at-a-time" stance. Upon virtual completion we had a very handsome but kitchen-free conversion and sought a suitable and hopefully long-term tenant.

By chance we mentioned our cottage to a colleague who does free-lance editorial work in her spare time. She surprised us by expressing interest for her own use: Her home was overflowing with manuscripts and she wanted a convenient, inexpensive workplace to rent as a noncommercial office. At that point only some final steps of plumbing remained, namely, to join a new exterior waterline to the revamped interior plumbing. We showed her the pristine, converted cottage; it delighted her, and a lease was signed during registration week, when social events to welcome incoming medical students required several very long evenings. Usually, as we teach our patients to, we would have rested and piddled that weekend to compensate for an especially heavy work week. Unfortunately, long in advance, all of Saturday and Sunday until noon had been promised to a friend from out of town. His family was planning to move to Memphis. He had come to look at some possible homes and wanted our advice and companionship while scouting them. We did reserve Sunday from noon on as "down time." We did ease through the exploration at a fairly gentle pace, but by noon Sunday, our orthopedically injured spouse was already very weary and feeling some reinflammation in the charley horse. We proceeded to unwind as planned, reading the paper and petting our dogs. Soon after, the phone rang. It was an out-of-town patient facing a sudden and legitimate crisis: Without warning, and after 12 years of marriage, the patient's spouse—who had psychiatric problems which might or might not explain the decision—had asked for a divorce. In short, this led to several lengthy phone conversations throughout the afternoon and evening, plus some cramping and discomfort in the tender musculature.

Imagine oneself in the same situation, arriving at the office Monday morning to be greeted by the following note from our colleague–tenant: "Did you say the plumber was finished? The reason I ask is that he didn't plug the hot water heater in, and I didn't want to—also, he left a horrible mess. He got hand- and footprints all over the paint, and he took down a couple of panels in the back room and put them back up very haphazardly, with cracks and a lot of greasy handprints. He also left piles of rubble in the bathroom. I started vacuuming but gave up after I filled the only bag I had with me. He also got black gunk all over the bathroom carpet (Is it new? It sure doesn't look it now!). In any case, thought you'd want to know about this, and didn't want you to think I had been climbing the walls in dirty boots."

Not only muscle tension, but blood pressure rose sharply. The charley horse throbbed. One feared both embarrassment at disappointing a friend and concern lest a mutually beneficial rental arrangement for our cottage be jeopardized. An angry phone call to the contractor (who had chosen the plumber) ensued, stipulating that the problems be corrected at the plumber's expense. After viewing the carnage, our trustworthy contractor became equally incensed, accepted responsibility to correct the mess, and the matter was turned over to him. However, in the process of events a nearly healed muscle injury was reactivated and recovery was delayed substantially.

Some firsthand compassion for patients with pain complaints, and firsthand experience with the intimate connections between external stressors and internal complications (e.g., angry arousal, muscle tension and pain, somewhat maintained by inability to totally dismiss the matter from mind) were gained from this experience. Many morals could be drawn from the foregoing. The moral we favor for readers to draw is "Let he who is free from sin cast the first stone."

CONCEPTUALIZING STRESS

From the preceding example, one can foresee that we view typical, clinically significant stress to involve multiple strains whose impact on people is *cumulative*. At some cumulative value that person's capacity to withstand the "slings and arrows of outrageous fortune" starts to be overtaxed and give way. If the sum of stressors mounts higher, personal adjustment and biobehavioral harmonies deteriorate progressively—probably at an accelerating rate beyond the person's "threshold of endurance." This will occur whether cumulative stress is generated by physical debility, accident, interpersonal clash(es), or by unwise conduct, all acting in various combinations in concert. How a person perceives the source(s) may influence attributional processes and hence alter the perceived weights the person assigns elements drawn from diverse sources; but all combine cumulatively to strain endurance. We are also fairly sure that, past some individualized threshold duration, the *chronicity* of the composite stressors has more a multiplying than an additive impact on net strain. One may liken our view to a river system at flood. The excess of water stems from major streams *and* minor tributaries, but the longer the flooding persists, the faster the flood damage progressively rises until maximal damage is reached. (A more comprehensive sample of our relatively "formal" theorizing, as we teach it to patients, is embedded in the clinical case portions of this chapter.)

This is not to imply that patients usually share our "multiple-strains" view at referral. Far more often the person has singled out *one* as *the* problem, or confines self-assessmentt to the few heaviest burdens, and minimizes the roles of all other, but perceptually more trival, stressors. For instance, some patients with stress-related somatic complaints (e.g., gastrointestinal discomfort, hyperventilation syndrome) insist that *nothing* has happened that can explain their symptoms in terms of stressful events. These people search for *major* disasters (deaths, bankruptcies, divorces, etc.) as "psychological" events. They tend to completely dismiss cumulative strains of a "minor" sort whose erosive impact builds and builds. One must often supply factual tutoring on the issues before the patient starts to grasp the concept. Such people tend to interpret drains wrought by "little things" as weakness, failure, or moral shortcomings; they need the therapist's persuasion and blessing to include "small" vexations in their self-assessments. Yet *collectively* these "minor" woes may create as much or more biobehavioral "friction" than what the patient judges to be the most irksome, "squeakiest" wheel(s). Paradoxically, the minor strains may be easiest to allay and the major strains the most refractory to change. Still, in our cumulative view, if resolving "easy" problems reduces the sum enough, the patient may become able to tolerate major burdens that can only be partly or slightly abated.

Hence, our assessment goals are very broad. We seek to gain a detailed grasp of the person's physical status, career situation, lifestyle, social and heterosocial relationships, and also the person's value system, aspirations, *and* subjective perceptions of the assets and liabilities impinging multiple facets of living.

Illustrative examples aplenty will be presently supplied. The reader will note that—if we indeed practice what we preach—considerable clinician time, and therefore service costs, will be involved. Unlike some demonstrably helpful programs, we taken few shortcuts and "make haste slowly." This is not to deny that brief, highly structured, "technique-oriented," efforts at stress management can prove constructive, especially in the short run.

For instance, a recent study with patients suffering from ischemic heart disease found that a combination of training in (1) stretching/relaxation exercises, (2) meditation of various sorts, and (3) *imposed* dietary changes (i.e., a vegan diet virtually devoid of animal products) intensively applied within a *restricted* communal environment designed to ensure compliance to the treatment regimen had very encouraging results: As compared to untreated controls, less than 1-month intensive group treatment led to a 44% increase in duration of exercise, a 55% increase in total physical work expended, some improved cardiac status, a 91% reduction in the frequency of episodes of angina as measured by patient self-reports, and a 20.5% decrease in plasma cholesterol levels (Ornish *et al.*, 1983). However it remains an open question how long these changes will endure—especially those in diet affecting plasma cholesterol levels —once the patients return to their natural home, career, social, and nutritional environments. Thus, we seek to tune both assessment and treatment to the individual, on a case-by-case basis, although some diagnostic and intervention elements are nearly always provided. This stance implies a "luxury" level of service delivery, which may abridge the general applicability of some of our routine emphases, and which is best understood from a brief panorama of the settings within which we practice.

CONTEXT, PATIENT, AND THERAPIST VARIABLES

We both work in multiple settings. Our stress management *program* is part of the Department of Psychiatry, University of Tennessee College of Medicine. Its widest preventive health, industrial, and research goals are *inter*disciplinary and affiliated with the Departments of Community Medicine (including Preventive Cardiology) and Obstetrics–Gynecology among others. This program is young, begun in 1981, and such large-scale endeavors are still in the planning or early data-gathering stages. The Stress Management Clinic (SMC), equally young, has already seen and treated a goodly number of cases, delivering services to both physician- and self-referred patients. Our staff of licensed psychiatrists and clinical psychologists currently averages over 16 years of clinical experience (apart from Psychiatry Residents and Psychology Interns who may take part for educational purposes). We are *not* an "eclectic" group since we span diverse orientations, and in many ways we each maintain our own perspectives. Yet we are fortunate in enjoying mutual respect and we readily consult among ourselves and with other colleagues. Thus the "typical" amalgam of services an SMC patient receives will doubtless depend on the treating clinician. The views herein expressed, and the case material later presented, draw on the present writers' experiences.

SMC patients are typically seen in consulting rooms at the University of Tennessee Doctors' Office Building, which houses other medical specialities on other floors. Since most patients have earlier seen their physicians there, and referral to us keeps cases within an integrated health care system, we suspect that the overall quality of patient care in such settings is exceptional. Reciprocally, the setting integrates us into patients' medical care rather than fostering a "mind versus body" dichotomy. These SMC cases are largely confined to private sector patients, affluent enough to pay for "elective" services, or who are covered by "generous" health insurance. *All* SMC fees collected funnel into a Psychiatry Department educational fund. Hence, at the SMC, the patients are virtually all nongeriatric, gainfully employed, verbal, ambitious, bright, and intellectually curious.

In sharp contrast, through different channels, we each see another population of patients with stress-related problems in various *non*-SMC contexts. These include patients with gasteroenterologic or cardiovascular illness seen for consultations requested by their physicians at *their* offices or in the hospital, inpatients with alcohol and drug problems involving elements of stress, and outpatients seen for consultation or treatment at various units of the Department of Obstetrics–Gynecology, such as its Pelvic Pain Clinic or at a physician's individual office. Some of these patients bitterly resent the premise that something nonphysical can be "wrong with them." Thus, one may begin as a consultant who is "blessed" by their physician and—depending on how and how deftly one executes that role—only eventually will some of these patients entertain and maintain office visits to the psychiatry facility. Demographically, most of these patients are quite unlike the SMC clientele. A fraction of them are low-socioeconomic-status, public-sector cases. A majority are "blue-collar," lower middle-class people who are neither psychologically minded nor—in light of the dominant cultural values of our Mid-South locale—favorably disposed to traffick with any of the "shrinking" professions.

Hence, between us, we encounter most of the spectrum of stress-related complaints. The patients' ages, careers, economic, and educational levels vary widely, and a fair proportion of cases reside in outlying rural communities (in Arkansas, southern Missouri, Mississippi, and Tennessee) for which Memphis is the primary referral center for specialized services. At one pole are cases in which stress is a contributory aspect of such major medical illness as post-bypass-surgery cardiovascular patients with high risk of mortality. At the opposite pole are persons seen primarily for stress-related symptoms or concerns about the long-term, future dangers to their health of a stressful lifestyle. Most cases fall between these extremes. They have some degree of physical illness or display its early warning signs, and their clinical management requires active collaboration with psychiatric and nonpsychiatric physicians. Thus our settings and perspective at work must be seen as actively participating in a *medical* community.

We need not, however, confine service delivery to hospital, clinic, or office. If some *in vivo* technique, such as participant modeling, seems called for, we will take that patient to the actual driving, height, or other phobic cue milieu to reduce the given fear as *part* of overall treatment. Likewise, if proper assessment requires *in vivo* behavioral observations, those will be performed. Not all, but most, of our patients are usually seen individually, but virtually always spouse, kin, friends, and other significant interaction partners are brought into treatment and, to the extent possible, enlisted as allies to help foster progress. We are not doctrinaire. As pragmatic clinicians, we will call on a host of resources, such as clergymen, attorneys, financial counselors, physical therapists, teachers, and, in some instances, our own personal friends having special expertise, *so long as* (1) such consultants are needed to help in the case; (2) we have the patient's consent to enlist them; and (3) we have no reason to doubt that the consultant(s) will adhere to our own very strict standards about maintaining the patient's confidentiality. For this same reason, diverse but trivial details have been altered throughout the case material later presented, in the effort to safeguard the identities of the patients we serve in a confidential capacity.

ASSESSMENT

In our view, the old adage that "action without thought is like shooting without aim" is particularly germane to clinical work. As a result, we usually conduct intensive pretreatment evaluations. Often, aspects of intervention (e.g., advice and encouragement about the helpful effects of regular physical exercise) begin during the assessment process. Often too, spouse, child(ren), and other important social partners are seen—separately from if necessary, but preferably, conjointly with—the patient being assessed. Consultations with physicians to determine the patient's physical status and limitations are nearly always obtained if the patient is self-referred or has not had a thorough physical exam within the past year. In a number of cases, these routine precautions have led to early detection and prompt treatment of such illnesses as incipient gout and hypertension in people not referred to us by a physician. Further such cautionary tales will emerge in the case material.

Invariably, we take a detailed history, which usually entails a minimum of 2 hr. As indicated by the nature of the patient's presenting problems (and the information supplied by the referring physicians who are the main sources of our caseloads), we may continue into extensive developmental, social, or sexual histories. Alternatively, when scrutiny of such current adjustment factors as residential arrangements, work schedule and duties, marital communication, and the like, seem important, those are pursued in depth. Initial assessment only ends when the treating clinician is content there is sufficient understanding of the patient's situation that a formulation to steer initial intervention can be made. That formulation, as a tentative treatment plan, ordinarily is recorded as the concluding section of each SMC evaluation. In reality, however, assessment continues throughout treatment in the form of feedback, new developments, collateral contacts, and the patient's discovering—or growing willing to disclose—information not supplied during initial assessment. In turn, these emergent data help refine the scope and content of intervention.

If individually needed, we may administer any number of psychodiagnostic devices, ranging from the Beck Depression Inventory to the old, but still-useful, Vineland Social Maturity Scale: The latter's special virtue is that is comprises a hierarchically graded set of work-sample items. Most of these the clinician can readily verify from direct observation or such documentary evidence as degrees earned, books published, and memberships in various community service capacities, for example, on the Board of the Arthritis Foundation, of the Memphis Arts Council, an officer of the PTA, and so on.

Typically, however, we now routinely administer just three self-report devices, (1) which are given before and after treatment at least, and sometimes also at "milestones" during treatment or follow-up and (2) whose special merits require some discussion. The first is the Eysenck Personality Questionnaire (EPQ; Eysenck & Eysenck, 1975). This is a 90-item (yes–no) inventory, which unfortunately is still mainly standardized on British samples. However (and unlike, e.g., the MMPI), it is a true "personality" inventory with each item contributing to only one of four scales. Three are the major dimensions of personality that Eysenck and others have extracted by repeated factor-analytic and contrasted-groups studies. In descending order of variance explained per factor, they are: (I) N (predisposition to develop emotional arousal); (II) E (Introversion–Extraversion, not only in common parlance terms of low-to-high "people-seeking" but also bearing on such cognitive aspects as ability to maintain attention and concentration); and (III) P (best characterized as "tough-mindedness" or stylistic tenacity). The final scale, L, is construed as a Lie scale but preliminary work suggests it also helps identify persons at risk for certain kinds of biobehavioral complaints (e.g., pelvic pain) as the result of over-scrupulous, constricted attitudes and self-expectations. We obtain the Eysenck data because (1) they allow us to make comparisons with a "trait" view of personality toward which, despite reservations, we think an open mind is best maintained, (2) they fall into a coherent theoretical view of personality and, unlike MMPI scores, are not drenched with grossly symptomatic content, and (3) since many of our patients are, psychiatrically, either within normal limits or at the lower rungs of major disorders, the EPQ seems a better yardstick to map the level of manifest psychopathology typical among our patients. Finally, its brevity (most patients complete it in less than 15 min) suggests to us that it may yield more honest—and hence more valid—responses than do instruments whose lengths exhaust, frustrate, or anger many respondents.

Both remaining instruments have been developed for our clinical and research needs, and are still undergoing progressive refinement. The Leisure Interests Checklist© (LIC) consists of 135 categorically organized potential activities or diversions presented in a randomized order. For each, the person must check own degree of interest, from "very much" to "not at all," on a simple, 4-point scale. This is illustrated by the first page of the LIC, which is presented as Figure 3-1. The list continues across a host of diverse recreational options. On the final page, the respondent is asked to select his or her five favorite interests and, for each, to estimate how many hours presently are spent engaged in each activity per week.

We use the LIC in a variety of ways. First, it helps us to pinpoint *potential* diversions, congenial to the person, that can become intervention targets. Likewise, it serves as a cognitive aid to remind patients about former pasttimes they have allowed to slip from their lives. Our goal is to cultivate some noncompetitive, low-stress buffers to counteract having attention preoccupied with lofty performance standards, worries, self-doubts, and other kinds of self-referent thinking that both maintains excessive arousal *and* expands the subjective duration of actual stressors (e.g., harrassment at work) manyfold when the person broods about them (sometimes nearly incessantly) at home. By and large, we find few patients whose range of interests is truly constricted. Instead, they usually have plentiful interests of a soothing nature but rarely take the time to pursue those because they give recreation a low personal priority. Hence the second use of the LIC is to try to gauge if the person is devoting more time to recreation (or to *nonarousing* activities) than when first assessed. Any clinician who has sought to alter habitual lifestyles knows it is no mean feat to accomplish such transformations. Nor will one's first efforts to convey the benefits of recreation—which we liken to lubricants or shock-absorbers in running a car— often attain the desired impact. Usually one must teach (in part with case or personal examples as a form of modeling), persuade, cajole, remind, and sometimes nag before the message starts to be translated into action. Our usual caution is along these lines: "Don't expect to notice the value of more physical exercise and low-key amusements in less than 4–6 weeks. You've got to give it a fair trial. But then you, not I, can be the judge of how well regular exercise and more recreation do or don't pay for themselves in terms of how you feel and how well you can handle your duties." We generally repeat the LIC at plausible milestones as one yardstick of the patient's change or lack of change in time allocation. The third main use for the LIC is to locate common interests between patient and spouse or family, or to detect previous common ground that has been let go fallow. We have grown accustomed to hearing that spouses have tried but failed repeatedly to identify mutually enjoyable activities. Yet it has become commonplace for us to discover unrecognized shared interests if each partner completes an LIC independently and we then match up items jointly in the "very much" and "much" interest categories as tentative common ground. For instance, despite over 20 years of essentially happy marriage, only such *systematic* scrutiny disclosed that (1) unbeknowst to each, both spouses enjoyed reading or studying history and walking in municipal parks and (2) their former frequency of jointly valued theater- and movie-going had (among other diversions) been allowed to decline sharply. These activities then became some of the first targets for enhanced mutual play.

The BAROMAS© scales were jointly developed with Professor Albert Bandura and are our first attempt to apply the reasoning and methodology of his germinal work on self-efficacy (e.g., Bandura, 1977b, 1978, 1982a, 1983) to

LEISURE INTERESTS CHECKLIST (Form B)

For every activity listed on the left, mark the space on the right that best tells how interested you are in that activity, when you are YOUR NORMAL, TYPICAL self.

YOUR Amount of Interest

	Very Much	Much	A Bit	Not at All
1. Decorating and painting around the house	___	___	___	___
2. Looking at maps, travel folders and tour books	___	___	___	___
3. Finding bargains at sales and auctions	___	___	___	___
4. Betting and gambling	___	___	___	___
5. Astrology, horoscopes, the Zodiac	___	___	___	___
6. Visiting caves, waterfalls, scenic wonders	___	___	___	___
7. Making jewelry, baskets, statues	___	___	___	___
8. Breeding or training animals for shows or competition	___	___	___	___
9. Learning about other religions	___	___	___	___
10. Planning trips, excursions, and outings	___	___	___	___
11. Making jams, jellies, preserves, pickles, etc.	___	___	___	___
12. Attending circuses and rodeos	___	___	___	___
13. Going to Church groups and Church social activities	___	___	___	___
14. Being in a wine tasting or wine study group	___	___	___	___
15. Growing house plants	___	___	___	___
16. Science hobbies like astronomy and nature study	___	___	___	___
17. Raising pets	___	___	___	___
18. Visiting with relatives	___	___	___	___
19. Doing things with your child(ren) or grandchild(ren)	___	___	___	___
20. Doing things with your neighbors	___	___	___	___
21. Flower or vegetable gardening	___	___	___	___

FIGURE 3-1. Sample of the LIC items.

the phenomenological and lifestyle manifestations of stress. Self-efficacy involves a person's self-perception and confidence about being able to execute successive items arranged in a task hierarchy from easiest to hardest. One of the 10 current BAROMAS scales is presented as Figure 3-2. Some of the others— derived from the same *idiographic* measurement strategy—include ability to place on hold an allegedly urgent phone call for varying amounts of delay, to engage in regular physical exercise for increasing durations, and *without* resort to alcohol or other drugs, to unwind oneself (from 0%–100%) after a long hard day and then to attain increasing lengths and depths of sleep.

Two clinical examples will illustrate some of the other BAROMAS scales and will convey far better than discourse the sorts of changes we observe on our three, "routine," repeated self-report devices. The first case was seen for a combination of job-related pressures, somewhat exacerbated by rather perfectionistic self-standards, plus the massive burdens on self and family wrought by the spouse's episodic but major psychiatric illness. The patient was treated at the SMC (by the strategy soon to be exemplified) for some 7 months. On the EPQ (which fell *entirely* within normal limits on both administrations) there were no

FIGURE 3-2. Sample of the BAROMAS scales.

BAROMAS* (Form 1)

10	20	30	40	50	60	70	80	90	100
Quite uncertain				Moderately certain					Certain

Reducing time pressures	Can do	Confidence
Comfortably goof off (e.g., daydream, watch the clouds, piddle around, meditate, doodle) for 5 min	_____	_____
Comfortably goof off for 10 min	_____	_____
Comfortably goof off for 15 min	_____	_____
Comfortably goof off for 30 min	_____	_____
Comfortably goof off for 45 min	_____	_____
Comfortably goof off for 1 hr	_____	_____
Comfortably goof off for 1½ hr	_____	_____
Comfortably goof off for 2 hr	_____	_____
Comfortably goof off for 2½ hr	_____	_____
Comfortably goof off for 3 hr	_____	_____
Comfortably goof off for 4 hr	_____	_____
Comfortably goof off for 5 hr	_____	_____
Comfortably goof off for 6 hr	_____	_____
Comfortably goof off for 7 hr	_____	_____
Comfortably goof off all day	_____	_____

*The Bandura–Rosenthal Metrics for Assessing Stress. These instruments were developed by joint collaboration between the Department of Psychiatry, University of Tennessee College of Medicine, and the Department of Psychology, Stanford University. The use of these instruments for purposes of scientific research is explicitly allowed without need to request permission from the copyright holders.

ALL OTHER RIGHTS FOR ALL OTHER PURPOSES ARE STRICTLY RESERVED

©Albert Bandura, Virginia Bandura, Renate Rosenthal, and Ted L. Rosenthal, 1981.

changes on *N* or *P*. There were equivocal trends (i.e., shifts of more than 1 *SD*) toward less Extraversion on *E* and more candor on *L* (the Lie scale). On the LIC there was virtually no change (16 hr/week) devoted to recreation. However, the *allocation* of time was different. Initially, the patient reported no regular physical exercise, but after treatment 2.5 hr of swimming plus jogging in a typical week were reported. Among the patient's BAROMAS changes were: (1) a *realistic reduction* is perceived confidence of 20% and 50%, respectively, on the next last and final items (akin to Figure 3-2) concerning tolerating telephone urgency; at first, 100% confidence was claimed on all items but failed to cohere with other clinical data; (2) a substantial (*overall* gain of 190%) increase in perceived confidence about coping with emotional tension and stress; (3) an *overall* gain of 330% in ability to "goof off" comfortably; initially, the longest duration entertained was 1 hr with a confidence rating of 30%, but after treatment 2½ hr "goofing off" was given a confidence rating of 50%; (4) an overall gain of 210% in physical exercise; initially, the most exercise deemed feasible was 1 hr three times each week with a confidence rating of 50% but, after treatment, confidence—consistent with the LIC changes—rose to 100%, and 1 hr four and five times each week were judged at 50% and 40% respectively. Perhaps most striking were the reported gains in being able to set task priorities and execute them *without* worry about or interference from other tasks held in abeyance. On that 22-item (amount of potential change is a function of number of items to assess change) self-efficacy scale there was a 790% confidence increase reported in ability to effectively deploy attention to focus without interference upon the task at hand as compared to pretreatment judgments.

A second SMC patient is still in treatment, but has been reassessed some 4.5 months after it began. This person was self-referred for a combination of realistic financial concerns prompted by the present harsh economic climate *plus* a lifelong tendency to set stringent, highly perfectionistic self-standards and to keep feelings concealed. The patient occupies a kind of "Atlas" role toward many family members and friends. There is much mutual love but, although offering support to others, the patient was very reticent to seek aid and comfort from loved ones. This patient's EPQ scores were also *entirely* within normal limits; for the interval measured, the only change noted was a 1.5 *SD* drop in *P* ("tough-mindedness"). The LIC shows a rise in recreation time in a typical week from 12 to 28 hr. More striking is the shift away from such "passive" diversions as reading, to more "active" and social activities such as aerobic exercises and communion with family members; tallied from this perspective, the rise in overt athletic and social involvement becomes +22 hr/week. On the BAROMAS, some of the judgments of *overall* increases in confidence were (1) 385% in tolerating telephone urgency, (2) 100% in being able (Figure 3-2) to "goof off" comfortably, and (3) 70% in being able to set priorities and then keep attention focused on the chosen task. There was also a 190% *decrease* in self-judged ability to unwind at the end of a long hard day without chemical assistance. The patient and we interpret that change as a more informed and realistic view of the degree that mental and muscular tension have been burdens than was recognized at initial assessment. Some of this self-perceived progress has been corroborated by the spouse, but both agree there remains ample room for further improvements.

Note that we use our measures as working benchmarks rather than "true" quantities. After sufficient refinements, we plan to subject the then-evolved versions of the measures to validation studies. However, ample data already support the empirical validity of self-efficacy scales under controlled conditions (e.g., Bandura, 1982a, 1983; Rosenthal, 1984a) and our main clinical concern has been to make a start toward measures that seem to point us in the key directions—some of which, at first blush, may seem ephemeral—faster than interview or trial-and-error. For this pragmatic aim, tuned to the individual patient, we (and our SMC colleagues) have been quite pleased with the information yield from the BAROMAS and the LIC, *especially* when the clinician and the patient discuss the self-report ratings (at each administration) in some depth to clarify and particularize concrete details, which in turn will often then become specific intervention targets.

INTERVENTION

The time now arrives to attempt to exemplify how we actually work with stress-laden people. An extended case study eventually will be presented below. First we must turn to the critical task that follows assessment: How we strive to share our conceptual perspective with a representative, if not "typical," patient. The research data supporting the role of organized introductions to treatment are elsewhere discussed in depth (Rosenthal, 1980).

Orienting the Patient

If the reader were in our offices for therapy *and* on assessment manifested some composite of the problems we have come to expect, one would hear us speak along the following lines: "Probably the most important concepts to grasp about stress are, first, that stress is inevitable and stems from no one thing. Instead, what gets to a person is a batch of pressures—some larger and some smaller—adding together. Let me show you what I mean." At this point we would introduce the first of two schematics we have devised to aid us, which is presented as Figure 3-3.

We would then make the point that disruptive stress is the net result of too many stressors operating for too long, which creates habitual overload on "one's turbine." As a result, reducing stress to a manageable and then to an harmonious degree will entail making a *variety* of changes—some harder and some easier—whose combined effects will reduce the overflow on "one's turbine."

The second main point one must grasp involves the nature of vicious cycles (introduced earlier), which then escalate or become self-maintaining. To help convey the concept to lay patients, our second schematic (Figure 3-4) depicts how, whatever the composite of perceived stressors, maladaptive strategies

ONCE THE TURBINE IS MOVING TOO FAST REDUCE THE FLOW FROM ANY COMBINATION OF SOURCES

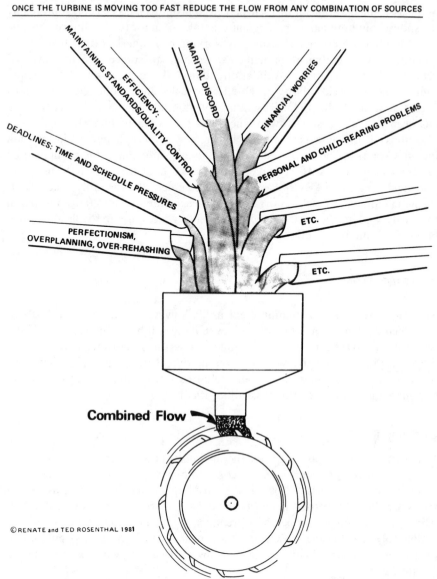

FIGURE 3-3. Combined flow stress turbine diagram.

PROBLEM – (E.G. FAILURES, PERSONAL LOSSES, FRIGHTENING EVENTS, TIME–PRESSURE, INSULTS, ETC.)

PERCEIVED STRESSOR: ANGER, FEAR, WORRY, SELF–DOUBT, NEGATIVE ANTICIPATIONS. THESE, IN TURN CREATE FURTHER DIFFICULTIES IN BODILY EFFECTS, MENTAL FOCUS, THOUGHT AND MEMORY AND CONSTRUCTIVE "ESCAPE" AS SHOWN

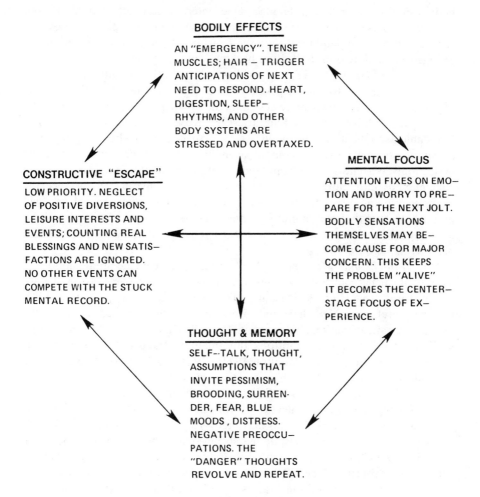

BODILY EFFECTS

AN "EMERGENCY". TENSE MUSCLES; HAIR – TRIGGER ANTICIPATIONS OF NEXT NEED TO RESPOND. HEART, DIGESTION, SLEEP– RHYTHMS, AND OTHER BODY SYSTEMS ARE STRESSED AND OVERTAXED.

CONSTRUCTIVE "ESCAPE"

LOW PRIORITY. NEGLECT OF POSITIVE DIVERSIONS, LEISURE INTERESTS AND EVENTS; COUNTING REAL BLESSINGS AND NEW SATIS– FACTIONS ARE IGNORED. NO OTHER EVENTS CAN COMPETE WITH THE STUCK MENTAL RECORD.

MENTAL FOCUS

ATTENTION FIXES ON EMO– TION AND WORRY TO PRE– PARE FOR THE NEXT JOLT. BODILY SENSATIONS THEMSELVES MAY BE– COME CAUSE FOR MAJOR CONCERN. THIS KEEPS THE PROBLEM "ALIVE" IT BECOMES THE CENTER– STAGE FOCUS OF EX– PERIENCE.

THOUGHT & MEMORY

SELF–TALK, THOUGHT, ASSUMPTIONS THAT INVITE PESSIMISM, BROODING, SURREN– DER, FEAR, BLUE MOODS , DISTRESS. NEGATIVE PREOCCU– PATIONS. THE "DANGER" THOUGHTS REVOLVE AND REPEAT.

EACH PART OF THE STRESS REACTION CAN TURN ON AND "FEED" EACH OTHER PART. THIS CAN BECOME A REPEATED VICIOUS CYCLE, WITH ONE PART MAKING ALL THE OTHERS WORSE.

© RENATE and TED ROSENTHAL 1980

FIGURE 3-4. Vicious cycle of exacerbating stressors diagram.

invite disruption in four key spheres: These interconnect and, like increasing critical mass, can exacerbate each other.

These four nodes (which are depicted in space to maintain parallelism with the prior schematic, as a "close-up view" of the turbine) are (as capsuled on Figure 3-4) as follows:

1. Bodily Effects. Whether a danger is real, or is merely so perceived, one's body will not know the difference. One enters a state of "red alert" and overtaxes diverse biological functions such as sleep and digestion. The correct self-perception of impaired rest (and the weariness it can cumulatively produce) or digestive malfunction itself often becomes an added source of worry.

2. Mental Focus. The research evidence showing that attentional processes serve as the gateway to what is actively made "figure versus ground" in subjective experience is elsewhere reviewed in detail (e.g., Bandura 1977a, 1983; Rosenthal, 1982; Rosenthal & Bandura, 1978; Rosenthal & Zimmerman, 1978). For clinical application, the point we seek to convey is that keeping one's attention *on* such stressful content as how well or poorly one is meeting perfectionistic aspirations prevents redirecting one's attention *off* the arousing content and onto more calming content. We often give as an instance the common patient error of "trying to fight" broodings and arousal by "will power." We note that one cannot fight any tangible or mental adversary without directing additional attention toward it, thereby maintaining its salience and protracting its duration.

3. Thought and Memory. In light of emergent evidence that mood and emotional valence can systematically alter access to, and retrieval from, memories in storage (see Clark & Teasdale, 1982, and Rosenthal & Rosenthal, 1983, for further references), we have pulled out these facets as a separate node. We inform the patient that fearful or pessimistic self-talk (see Turk, Meichenbaum, & Genest, 1983) and assumptions that magnify dangers and reduce self-perceived competence (see Bandura, 1977b, 1978, 1983) come to operate like self-fulfilling prophecies, which create the very dire outcomes they intend to ward off. For patients who have difficulty grasping how habitual mental sets in effect prepare one to define new events in old ways, we often tell a few "set-breaking jokes." For readers who may vigorously doubt the reality of all such mental phenomena as sets, despite massive evidence showing their importance in regulating cognition (see Rosenthal, 1980), we will present one such example, capsuled by Professor Albert Bandura who shared it with us as "the epic poem now making the rounds of San Francisco." We ask that the next few phrases be spoken out loud: "Roses are red. Violets are blue. I'm schizophrenic and so am I." One may anticipate that patients often ask further questions or seek further illustrations and we work actively to satisfy their requests.

4. Constructive "Escape." Here we go into the role of (noncompetitive) and, usually, not overly thrill-laden) leisure activities as mental buffers analogous to lubricants or shock absorbers for an automobile. Once the four nodes in our thinking on exacerbation cycles have been grasped and clarified for the patient as needed, we then *particularize* our theoretical perspective. We draw on the material in the patient's own history, LIC, and BAROMAS, as exemplars of the manifestations of stress and unwise lifestyle and cognitive style patterns that invite strain *for that individual.* At base, we are performing a teaching function when we orient a patient.

Indeed, more often than not, we allow SMC patients to read their own evaluations based on assessment, clarify any technical jargon they fail to understand clearly, and present them with a copy of the assessment report for mnemonic purposes. More often than not too—unless specifically contraindicated or resisted—we try to bring the person's spouse or other special interaction partner to the next session. We then review the foregoing steps both as a way to recruit the spouse as an ally by sharing and demystifying our goals *and* to assure that the message extends to the primary partner in the patient's social support system. Often, disclosing all or some of the burdens the patient has striven to "spare" loved one(s) is the first critical step in facing the issues squarely. As lagniappe, the conjoint session(s) devoted to this purpose continue to aid most patients to actively process and hence to understand and remember better (see Rosenthal, 1984a; Rosenthal & Zimmerman, 1978) some rather complicated material, which, despite our best efforts to make concrete by personal illustrations, remains quite abstract as a conceptual synthesis.

A simple example of the foregoing issues will be given shortly. Let the reader recall that people in our region are typically reluctant to seek psychiatric and psychotherapeutic services. In part, this is because of the dominant value orientation of the Mid-South area. In part, despite its size, Memphis remains more a burgeoning rural capital than the metropolis it might seem to be from Chamber of Commerce statistical evidence of growth. There is ample, if soft, survey and anecdotal evidence that urban and rural communities differ in both the nature of dominant stressors and in their respective priorities. Thus, for the United States, such informal or quasi-systematic data, drawn from many sources, *converge* to suggest that rural populations are (1) more fatalistic, (2) more family oriented and less willing to disclose a relative's "quirks" to "outsiders," (3) in general more conservative, and (4) less informed of and more dubious about psychotherapeutic efforts than are urban citizens (for an in-depth review of this literature, which offers consistency in lieu of adequate methodology, see Falcone & Rosenthal, 1982; for a capsule of the most recent publications, see Bachrach, 1983).

In addition, it is our strong clinical impression (although not substantiated by systematic data) that the patient population in our region is more likely to express psychological distress in terms of somatic complaints. Many of our patients present initially with physical symptoms and seem genuinely surprised to find out that chronic (often minor, but cumulative) stresses are at the root of their "chief complaint."

What thus must be recognized henceforth is that our intervention modes have become tuned to our cultural matrix. An act that plays well in Peoria or Memphis will very likely require stylistic transliteration if it is to be applied in San Francisco or Boston.

In the Memphis cultural context, then, consider the job-related complaints of a patient in a two-career household. This man had made a number of job-related changes that required residential shifts. At first, the wife was supportive but had grown less tolerant of the prospect of moving the family and readjusting her own career options when the patient continued to complain of unacceptable pressures in the current work setting. In-depth discussions revealed that there was slim realistic chance of altering the work strains directly. Yet the patient had come to blame *all* dissatisfactions on the work situation but ignored other relevant factors: For instance, that schedule changes to accommodate the wife's career needs were depriving the patient of much-needed diversions. Thus, what had formerly been a half-day free each week—open for the husband to engage in hobbies—had been eroded due to the spouse's office schedule. As a result, the patient's prior respite was now filled with child-care duties. In turn, the wife was discouraged by (and hence nonsupportive of) the patient's stresses since those portended still another dislocation for the family. However, she was blind to the extra-job strains (which the patient failed to perceive or mention)—such as increased responsibilities bought at the cost of leisure time—that contributed to the patient's discontent.

Hence, two kinds of efforts were made: First, to help the wife as well as the patient understand how the lost free half-day was a "penny wise, pound foolish" marital strategy and further, that there were real, legitimate, yet not easily alterable reasons for patient's unhappiness at work. Second, to find a way to abate the patient's job frustrations with minimal familial and financial disruption and without jeopardizing the patient's job security during very hard economic conditions. This was attempted by encouraging the patient to discuss the work strains with a superior in the organization, who proved far more compassionate and helpful than the patient's apprehensive predictions. (The superior had once held the patient's post and knew its stressors first-hand.)

To the patient's surprise, the superior concurred with a tentative plan we had jointly evolved: The patient's organization had, as a standing policy, an arrangement to fund advanced training in exchange for later "payback" time, conditional on concurrence by higher echelons. Could the patient acquire further schooling (at a substantial fraction of current wages, paid by the employer) and later return to compatible but more advanced duties whose context would dispel a number of frustrations currently prominent? The answer, in principle, was a resounding "yes." The highly placed supervisor was very satisfied with this tentative solution and promised strong support for it. In turn, the wife was more tolerant of such a temporary dislocation than would have been the case if permanent change loomed once more for the family. Although the time to enact this resolution still lies in the future, optimism about a strategy each partner can accept has raised morale for both the patient and spouse. This will likely make it easier for both partners to endure burdens that now appear time limited, rather than permanent. Note that the solution strategy emerged from our efforts to orient both patient *and* spouse by personalizing for them—in concrete form drawn from the details of their life—the conception of stress discussed earlier, after the assessment phase was completed.

The Process of Treatment

We surmise that our approach to treating stress is more comprehensive than a number of other conceptualizations. Yet we have no newly minted *techniques* for reducing stress to share. Elements of commonality among most, so-called, "cognitive–behavioral" approaches are pervasive, and "unique" aspects are far more the exception than the rule (see Rosenthal, 1982, 1984a). Let us illustrate this claim by examining two significant aspects of overlap among the myriad of extant "relaxation" methods. The techniques in question would span (1) Jacobson's (1938) progressive muscle relaxation and (2) his more recent (1964) *self-operations* procedures. Also included would be (3) Benson's (1975) relaxation method, (4) autogenic training and related techniques, (5) the various forms of symbolic relaxation or guided positive imagery, and diverse techniques that derive from Eastern culture such as (6) yoga, (7) various kinds of "mental discipline" taught as part of the martial arts, and (8) transcendental or other meditation regimens. Our colleague, Dr. Neil Edwards, has shown us that (9) the Lamaze birth-easing system, whereby extensive practice before delivery allows the spouse–coach to draw the attention of the mother in labor away from the pains during delivery, should clearly qualify for inclusion. Likewise, (10) the "self-instructions" methods pioneered by Meichenbaum and now being applied to patients with pain complaints (e.g., Turk *et al.*, 1983) also involve more than an awareness of patient's self-statements; it is necessary for the patient to generate new self-instructions and conduct that are *incompatible with* prior, maladaptive patterns. The foregoing listing could be augmented with many further technique instances. However, in common, all seem to induce a relatively calm state whose intensity will depend on such desiderata as the patient's *ability* to attain vivid mental images—not all people are capable of clear visual imagery—*diligence* in rehearsing the technique, and eventual *competence* in utilizing the method. Another common vector among all such procedures is that each can, potentially, draw the patient's attention away from stress-laden cues, shift it instead toward calmer content, whether positive or neutral in valence, and thereby *distract* the patient from habitual mental sets that invite preoccupation with personal stressors. There is ample experimental evidence that distraction can reduce, if not always remove, states of arousal (see Rosenthal, 1980). In the same vein physical exercise that is vigorous yet appropriate for the patient, if pursued on a regular basis and does *not* elicit competitive arousal, may more swiftly and robustly decrease arousal so long as exercise becomes part of the person's lifestyle (e.g., Bahrke & Morgan, 1978). Reciprocally, there is evidence that arousal states invite an attentional focus on negative, self-referent content (e.g., Wegner & Giuliano, 1980).

Therefore, our conceptual perspective permeates our clinical behavior. We assume that "half a loaf is better than none" and strive to aid patients to make and maintain changes that are the most appealing or least aversive to that specific individual. For example, a patient who defies all usual efforts to begin some type of needed exercise program may require the redefinition or "embedding" of the task in a new context. Often, exercise that is resisted on an individual basis may be accepted if turned into a family undertaking or a parental duty. Thus, the patient may be more amenable to parent–child hiking, swimming, or biking if they are seen as ways to foster the child's recreational skills (in spheres that bear on popularity and social acceptance) or bodily well-being. One father who was evasive about gymnasium facilities in his smallish town promptly "discovered" the low-cost and nearby YMCA when the task was made family and not personal exercise. As do the media ads about hypertension ("Do it for the loved ones in your life."), we are not above mobilizing "Jewish guilt" (e.g., "What will your wife and children do if you keep on this way, straining your body but refusing to get it in better shape, which means dangers of heart attack, ulcer, and so forth?") if that seems requisite.

Apart from those just mentioned, we may weave a host of techniques together to clothe a patient's treatment needs. These elements include guidance to promote proper self-assertiveness and emotional expression (often curtailed by cultural mores that favor stoic constriction of feelings), Novaco's (1979) extension of assertion training to the management of maladaptive anger, and cognitive restructuring laced with much exemplary modeling: Very often our patients display a developmental heritage of stern parental modeling that creates excessively stringent self-standards, perfectionistic expectations (anything less than one's very best is equated with failure), and—in men—an exaggerated, stereotypic view of masculinity, which is frequently perceived as an obligation to compete with male peers in any context, whether at work, on the golf-links, or in conversation. We do what seems apt to counteract such imbalanced personal philosophies. In one case of this sort, the patient described how, during adolescence, he had been much influenced by his father's values, which epitomized those "macho" standards just discussed. The patient then spontaneously asked for the therapist's views on such matters, that is, competing with others. Despite its obvious "psychodynamic" affinity, the therapist took this opening as a golden opportunity to exemplify more tolerant and moderate self-standards, for instance, that one may well seek utmost excellence in a few very high-priority spheres of life, but not across the board. That opening, presented by serendipity, has borne two anecdotal fruit: First, the patient has without prompting continued to pose to the therapist similar questions drawn from developmental experience, and the therapist continues to demonstrate more moderate stances than taken by the patient's father. Second, the patient's own problems and concerns have had a cautionary impact on how the patient is changing his style in rearing his young son. It is amusing and highly gratifying to hear this person recount anecdotes of diminished stringency toward the boy (e.g., "Son, as long as you did your best, that's all that counts. Nobody's perfect and we're all better at some things and worse at others"). In his parental solicitude, the patient is actively reworking the content emphases modeled by the therapist, and thereby increasing the robustness of their storage and their ease for self-utilization (e.g., Rosenthal, 1984a). From the foregoing, it should be evident that much *teaching* by diverse formats and a substantial share of therapeutic social influence (Rosenthal, 1980) are virtually always ingredients when we treat and especially for the more refractory cases with long track records of a stressful lifestyle and an Atlas-like self-conception.

Probably more than most of our clinical brethren, we worry about and work hard to enhance the technical quality of our guidance messages in terms of their format and structure. Social learning theory views cognition as an active, ongoing, synthesis of information—weighted for perceptual salience and personal relevance—which undergoes progressive refinement by experiential feedback and inferential reasoning (Bandura, 1977a, 1982a, 1983; Rosenthal, 1984a; Rosenthal & Bandura, 1978; Rosenthal & Zimmerman, 1978). Hence, we do our best to cast our messages in vivid forms and to enlist multiple channels to convey the same core meanings. In practice, this concern with effective communication leads us to use humor (as noted earlier), analogies, parables, rhymes, and other slogans (e.g., "slower not lower standards"), mnemonic devices including assignments to keep records, logs, or to self-monitor some conduct under intervention, and often visual or spatial cognitive aids such as diagrams, sketches, and maps. There are profuse and convergent research data to support the worth of such aids to information processing (e.g., Rosenthal, 1984a, 1984b; Rosenthal & Davis, 1983; Rosenthal & Zimmerman, 1978).

Here are some concrete examples: Given our clientele, we have grown more adept at supplying, when needed, such scriptural maxims as the following: "Do unto others as you would unto yourself," and then explaining that, (confirmed by consultation with clergy of several denominations), the verse does *not* mean doing for others but ignoring or neglecting oneself. Likewise, we often invoke, and elaborate upon, "Make a joyful noise unto the Lord." and "God helps those who help themselves."

Since many of our SMC patients are worried by the correct perception that their cognitive competence has suffered (as the result of arousal-produced interference), we often sketch and explain the graphic statement of the Yerkes–Dodson law. With performance = response = coping on the ordinate and stress = anxiety = arousal = striving on the abscissa, we first show the general relationship that, as arousal rises, performance mounts to some asymptote and then declines. We next show that, for tasks of low complexity, much arousal is required before performance deteriorates. We then conclude by showing and explaining that, for the high complexity tasks of greatest interest to our patients—such as preparing and presenting sales-promotions, analyzing system problems in their organizations, diagnosing their patients, and so on—the curve rises very quickly to asymptote and then drops steeply as arousal increases. Not only is this a scientifically factual capsule of the cognitive interference the patients notice and brood about in themselves, but it also proves very reassuring to most patients that the problems are neither mysterious to us, nor should they assume such arousal-based interference need continue permanently. Finally, by giving them hope of progress *and* specifying some of the steps they need take to redress their overaroused "cruising speed," we usually observe an increase in their perceived self-efficacy to achieve, and thus to earnestly undertake, the changes we recommend (see Bandura, 1977b, 1978, 1983).

There seems little doubt that some of our thrusts to change overtaxed lifestyles for the better are unorthodox. We maintain and actively update what amounts to a file of inexpensive local restaurants that serve appetizing food. We also keep tabs on which of them offer take-out services and which remain open late or on days when most competitors are closed, for example, Mondays. Providing information of this nature allows single patients and working couples with limited incomes to reduce their routine culinary duties. Instead, at least now and then, they can phone ahead before leaving work and have a meal ready to take home, or they can stop and dine on work nights with no need to prepare food or do dishes themselves. For more affluent patients, the options are broader. We keep informed about the quality of catering services in our town, and can recommend good ones since we both enjoy cooking and restrict our kudos to caterers whose products we have tested ourselves. Especially with female patients, we offer compromise solutions to abate conflicts between the wish to achieve lofty culinary standards and the burdens of meeting epicurean criteria themselves when they throw a dinner party. One compromise is for the host(ess) to create one or two dishes of distinguished quality but to purchase the remaining courses from the restaurant or caterer that prepares them. Another compromise is to learn some simple but appealing recipes for gracious living with little effort. Here for dessert are three concrete illustrations: to serve a variety of good cheeses with fruit in season as do the French very often; to buy "deluxe" ice cream available in speciality shops and merely top it with canned cherries soaked in brandy (in a jar in the refrigerator) ahead of time so that just assembling the dish, and touching a match to it, creates flaming cherries jubliee; to melt high-quality chocolate in a double-boiler and let the guests dip fresh fruit, such as strawberries or chunks of pineapple, into the chocolate themselves. We do not hold back our own recipes but reproduce and offer to our patients copies of those our friends most often request, such as salad dressing and orange soufflé, if they are quick and popular. In this context, we sometimes can "sneak in" excellent dishes that are lower in cholesterol than those the patient knows best.

In a very different sphere of intervention, here are some further down-to-earth examples. The terrain of Memphis is exceedingly monotonous. Except for the Mississippi River itself, the floodplain it drains can make few claims to scenic grandeur. This paucity in geologic diversity has led to a local stereotype that varied topography for hiking or sight-seeing requires nearly a day's travel time to reach the Ozark, Ouachita, or Smoky Mountains. Consider that most of our patients need to abandon sedentary patterns, to learn to take time for recreation, and to increase tolerance for nonbusiness, non-task-oriented pursuits. Since they rarely "have enough time" to drive to the mountains, they often invoke the monotonous landscape to excuse procrastination and failure to implement earnestly our exhortations. We retort by informing them about Crowley's Ridge. It lies due west, less than an hour's drive, consists of wind-blown topsoil now anchored by vegetation, and runs some 200 miles north to south but only a mile or so wide. It contains farms, ranches, and fruit orchards and its high, rolling land is admirable for walking, biking, or riding horses. It gives a welcome relief that contrasts sharply with the local habitat both in elevation and foliage and is especially lovely when the fruit trees blossom in the spring and when the leaves turn brilliant colors in autumn. Since most Memphians somehow maintain ignorance about the ridge (which, oddly, is not shown on many maps of this region), we can offer new vistas for patients who truly believe the only changing landscapes lie hundreds of miles away. We can also "call the bluff" of people who use our flat habitat as an excuse for inactivity.

In like vein, we keep informed about interesting places to tour near Memphis, have maps at the office of nearby sites one can easily visit in a weekend, and provide patients with duplicates of the maps and, sometimes, detailed routes of places to explore. We also stay abreast of "off-beat" audience events in town. These are numerous but usually not well publicized. Some of the best only occur once each week (such as bluegrass and country music fests) and take place in remote quarters (such as union local halls) to keep costs down. Others only run one or a few nights. Some are regular series but are best enjoyed by advance subscription because few seats are available at the box office for the most rewarding performances.

The foregoing reasoning would obviously shift in a different habitat. For instance, in a crowded, much larger metropolis, one could apply the same principles but alter the concrete tactics: Since we have lived in some very large cities, we can appreciate how their formidable traffic jams can make someone reluctant to fight the other drivers for a change of scene out of town. These obstacles can render anyone's wanderlust inert. Yet there are ways to circumvent the congestion. One might suggest the patient depart when the city is sleeping, before sunrise, and postpone breakfast until out in the hinterlands, and so on. Likewise, most cities have a multitude of inexpensive short tours, often sponsored by the Audobon Society, the Sierra Club, and similar groups of nature lovers. Travel is usually by comfortable chartered bus and hence devoid of stressful driving for passengers. It usually demands some concerted research to learn about such offerings, and stress-laden people frequently will not do that homework but will utilize it if their therapist supplies the information. Further, especially for lonely patients, travel of this sort is a good way to meet people (including potential dating partners) who share at least some mutual interests. In undertaking to fill the role of travel or recreational consultant, a therapist can model solutions that harassed, overworking "worrywarts'" rarely devise on their own. The result is to enrich the quality of life for a clientele sorely in need of play and amiable distractions.

Log Jams

Just as a missing horseshoe nail can immobilize the horseman and invite loss of a battle, sometimes obstacles to desirable change may stem from barriers rarely discussed in texts on therapeutic management. Identifying and clearing these "log jams" may be prerequisite to fostering constructive alterations in lifestyle and conduct. To remove log jams, the therapist must have a lucid and coherent grasp of the contexts and patterns of the patient's daily living. Not infrequently, the actual realities are ill conveyed by interview procedures. A simple example involves the case of Gary (presented in detail below). No verbal interchange could tell as vividly as did two visits to observe his coaching activities the degree of intense, sustained arousal he manifested before, during, and after his team met another in competition. A more intricate illustration concerns a family, treated some years past, whose distress and impaired familial interaction persisted "mysteriously" despite repeated office visits. We suspected a log jam, and arranged a series of observations in the home. The "detective work" paid off. Only by penetrating the natural environment could we learn that each of the half-dozen children had a black-and-white television in their rooms; the parents did also. Yet another television, but color, situated in the living room had turned common "family" space into a combat arena. Much of what should have been time for family recreation was spent either arguing about which program should be shown in the living room, or was spent in isolation, glued to the television in family members' private spaces. The discovery that multiple video sets were fragmenting mutual interaction led to proscribing televiewing beyond strict time limits that protected conjoint socialization. Only then did progress become possible.

Some additional case examples follow: Impending divorce will often evoke provocations and retaliations from both estranged spouses. Thus, one patient's career demanded promptly answering sudden phone calls summoning the person to fill in at work with no advance preparation when on call. The vengeful ex-spouse exploited this responsibility by using the telephone to harass the patient (despite legal counsel to the contrary) by calling in the wee hours, breaking into the patient's already fragile sleep, and enticing the patient into angry disputes. The patient's exhaustion was thus increased and in turn was exacerbated by the desire to retaliate against the spouse's aural *blitzkrieg*. Further, spouse's intrusions kept patient's mental focus on issues (such as how to handle the children, who were the objects of a custody fight, and what impact would divorce have on the children) that were worrisome enough to the patient without the spouse's inflammatory ploys. The telephone battles were largely circumvented by advising the patient to obtain a recording and answering device. Not only could the patient screen and answer legitimate phone calls deserving prompt response and ignore the ex-spouse's tactics to foment controversy, but the legal and custody-related implications of having the spouse's adversary rhetoric recorded as potential courtroom evidence led to sharp curbing of the ex-spouse's telephone intrusions.

At times, parental distress caused by the misadventures of wayward offspring blocks the parent's capacity to cope with his or her own serious problems. There seems little recognition by our patients that "acting-out" character or personality disorders have a poor prognosis for positive change. As earlier discussed, family ties are strong here, and hence, so are the temptations to conceal a child's major provocations or, once disclosed, to give the delinquent progeny "one more chance" despite dubious and longstanding track records of drug abuse, theft, promiscuity, and deception. Hence, with extremely acting-out offspring, we periodically have the painful task of trying to help the parent(s) accept his or her own inability to "straighten out" the miscreant. In an exemplary case a cardiovascular patient—at serious risk of mortality after open-heart surgery—resisted (despite excellent rapport) making many needed changes including a reduction in heavy daily alcohol consumption. It *eventually* emerged that the patient and an adult child, residing at home, were locked in chronic combat due to the child's acting-out escapades. The child's history strongly suggested an antisocial personality, and we used the DSM-III description of this disorder and its poor prognosis to assist the patient and spouse to renounce their efforts to salvage the child and instead to take more active steps to "cultivate their own garden." Only when a joint plan (in consultation with the referring cardiologist) was collectively devised to encourage the miscreant to leave town, and that move elsewhere was accomplished, did progress occur: At that point the patient rather swiftly achieved lifestyle changes that had previously seemed "impossible." However, when the breakup of a romance returned the child to the parental home, progress ceased and some gains were partly undone, for example, some resumption of drinking to excess. Over time, a fraction of the lost ground was regained. This was aided by arranging for the erring child to sleep often at the homes of kin, many of whom lived close by, to reduce conflictual parent–child interactions. As a result, the patient was able to deal rather well with a series of major illnesses that befell siblings, and which were further strains on an aged parent the patient needed to protect from undue anxiety. Despite these sudden burdens, the patient's consumption of alcohol presently remains lower, and the patient's ability to handle crises is visibly greater than before treatment began.

A further instance of how critical data may only emerge well after the start of treatment, when patients develop sufficient trust in their therapist, concerns the ways that material goods may tyranize their owners by preempting personal space. The couple being seen were bright, vivacious people who interpersonally and economically were free of noteworthy problems. For some time we had been urging the wife to increase recreation to counteract her domestic burdens. She concurred with this strategy yet, to our vexation, and for no evident reason, hobby projects at home, toward which she had expressed strong interest, were never implemented. Eventually, and with much embarrassment, the couple made a confession: Despite their mutual wish for the wife to take up the hobbies jointly discussed, their large home lacked enough space to do so. Indeed, a horde of accumulated possessions engulfed floor and surface space in every room. Many of the objects had economic value but rarely were put to use. Somehow they had "gotten into the rut" of enduring the spatial encroachment which, in turn, prevented the initiation of the hobbies selected. Only when the spouses were repeatedly exhorted to identify the surplus objects, and to sell them by holding a yard sale, did new recreation commence. Despite both partners' early reluctance to dispose of the intruding clutter, they each expressed relief once it was gone. Moreover, after the sale, the wife's routine chores, which had been oppressing her, were lightened since there was no longer need to clean, wax, dust, and otherwise tend the superfluous possessions.

A different type of log jam we frequently encounter involves taking a step the patient desires to take, judges as necessary, and may spontaneously propose as the obvious course of realistic action but still does not undertake. We are excluding here fears of being able to enact the behavior, or of suffering from the consequences of so behaving, as problems that fall outside the self-evident terrain of log jams. Instead, there is usually a too-stringent definition of one's own responsibility or a clearly overscrupulous concern about "selfishness." Might the patient hurt somebody valued who consistently prevents the patient from attaining obviously legitimate desires or satisfactions? Here are two examples. The first involved a very appealing person who had performed unusually well—compared to peers—until the death of a beloved close relative. This deprived the patient of a key source of emotional support, nurturance, and companionship. The loss was especially critical because of a tangled love relationship with a partner who may have had sterling virtues but who, in our judgment, was unusually self-absorbed, truly selfish, or both. The nub of the thing was that a protracted engagement had continued for years. The partner persisted in maintaining a vague, evasive stance when the patient (whose career required city living) asked that they "fish or cut bait" about marrying. There were always excuses about why the partner could not set a date for joining the patient. In turn, the patient was lonely and craved heterosocial companionship. From a scrupulous conception of betrothal, the patient had refrained from all "dating in the meanwhile." The nub of resolution grew from repeated discussions about realistic versus quixotic definitions of "responsibility." Once the patient comprehended the extent of the self-imposed ethical "straight jacket" and its deleterious effects, we jointly agreed there were not many options. In essence, the choices were to confront the out-of-town, now-and-then fiancée, or to explore on an *experimental*, "test" basis, how it would feel to ask others out. The patient opted for the latter plan, began dating and by chance quickly encountered a partner whose charms far surpassed those of the indecisive fiancée. To the patient's surprise, despite some short-term petulance, the ex-fiancée did not seem vastly undone when the patient announced wedding plans to another. At last follow-up the patient was doing very well and the marriage was very happy.

A second example is given in capsule form: As the result of repeated intrusions by a most stubborn grandparent, a couple was actively exploring job possibilities in another state. Yet they were reluctant to raise directly with the offender how these intrusions were self-defeating and were building up to deprive both grandparents of easy access to the couple and their children, all of whom were much-loved and much-needed by their elders. When it became clearer that continued, silent preparations to move far away were "cutting off nose to spite face," for all concerned (rather than "considerate"), it became possible to enhance joint accommodation. Reluctantly and imperfectly, the elders agreed to and adhered to some specific limits on how they might and might not impinge on the privacy of the younger generation and its perogatives for parental decision making. At last contact the situation was less than idyllic but much more tolerable than previously. The couple was spared a major move not really wanted, and the grandparents were spared the departure of loved ones whose companionship and proximity were mainstays of their social support network. Note that the foregoing illustrations concerned issues in which a *consensus* of clinicians and citizens would likely agree with the fairness of the resolutions adopted. Such ethical clarity is not always the case.

TRUE ISSUES OF VALUES

Fairly often we find ourselves engaging in what at base are philosophical discussions with our patients. The topics will concern value judgments that are difficult for the patient to make but for which, we too, are not appropriate as mentors because no consensus can be invoked as a yardstick. The topics encompassed are manifold. They include what kinds of sexual activities are "normal" or "legitimate," and how soon after a relationship commences is erotic intimacy "appropriate" or "seemly." (If strong religious convictions are involved, we may get the patient's pastor, or clergy of the same denomination, to consult on matters of doctrine. Or we may encourage the patient to pose the quandry, in "abstract" if not personal terms, to trusted friends.) The sphere of values may instead concern what is "fair" to an interaction partner, such as a lover, estranged spouse, or overly demanding friend. Decisions about abortion, entering marriage or seeking divorce, making financial or career plans and changes, and choosing schools for children all would fall into the category of value judgments except insofar as matters of fact or consensus are present, for instance, helping the patient obtain informed assessments about the social atmosphere, academic quality, and extracurricular offerings of one school as compared to another. Otherwise, in the domain of value judgments, we proceed as do most conventional psychotherapists. We strive to help patients consider the issues in full, to explore the options feasible, but to reach their own best decisions without allowing our personal biases to narrow their value judgments. We do caution that, for some decisions, there is no one "right" answer but rather that "There are many mansions in the Kingdom of the Lord," or, in its transliteration from the German, "God's zoo is big."

Some Illustrative Case Vignettes

Shortly, we shall present in detail the complex case of Gary. First, here are a few capsules of cases, seen briefly or easily summarized, to suggest the variety of patients and some of the intervention problems we encounter.

Case 1

Mr. A was a graduate student, referred by his physician for examination anxiety in the face of competitive academic pressures. In all but one respect (below), Mr. A presented what seemed a fairly clear-cut but very severe fear of being examined on written or oral tests. Initial treatment consisted of a combination of systematic desensitization (including thorough instruction in deep muscle relaxation), cognitive restructuring to reduce "catastrophic" anticipations, and guidance to make some badly needed study and lifestyle changes (e.g. to resume some recreational activities and to take breaks when arousal mounted too high while studying). In struggling with his worries and school pressures, Mr. A had ceased all diversions, most notably, physical exercise, which he enjoyed but felt expendable while "under the gun" scholastically yet which could help him to "work off" some of his excessive tension. He showed partial improvement on the foregoing regimen.

However, Mr. A continued to complain of intense physiological arousal (e.g., profuse sweating) and terror-laden dreams before exams. Search for further psychosocial conflicts, stressors, or other problems still undisclosed failed to yield any clues. Rather, the symptom picture suggested physiological involvement. Hence, Mr. A was referred to a psychiatric colleague who had special interests and expertise in neuroendocrine disturbances. As a result, Mr. A was placed on beta-blocking medication. His remaining symptoms—apparently due to catecholamine disturbance—dropped sharply, then disappeared, and have never recurred.

Case 2

Mrs. B was a housewife in her mid-30s, the mother of two young children. She was referred by her cardiologist for an enduring obsessive concern that she was about to have a "heart attack." The initial symptoms appeared about a year before her referral to us, and sounded like a classic panic episode (with flushing, faintness, and intense fear of "going crazy" during that first attack). A complete workup at that time had disclosed no physical problems of note apart from mitral valve prolapse—for which Mrs. B was treated with Inderal (propranolol). Her initial panic-like state did not recur, but she remained hugely preoccupied with her health and kept complaining of diverse symptoms including tightness in the chest, numbness and tingling sensations, loss of concentration, fatigue, insomnia, and general dysphoria. A psychiatrist had treated her with monoamine oxidase (MAO) inhibitors and group psychotherapy but these only brought minimal benefit.

When she came to us, she had discontinued the MAO inhibitors, was quite apprehensive about starting another psychological–psychiatric type of therapy, and voiced skepticism that "talking about her problems" could help her. Over time she had developed the habit of taking her pulse every few minutes to check on her heartbeats, and she seemed geniunely scared about her health status. A thorough psychosocial assessment revealed that Mrs. B had been and still was under a great deal of stress. The events that led up to her initial panic attack included: (1) a recent move here from another state; (2) a son who required special private schooling, which severely drained family income; and (3) serious job problems for her husband. At her urging and insistence, he had taken a post that allowed him to remain in town and to spend more time with the family, unlike his prior job which entailed much travel. Mrs. B soon concluded that the husband was unhappy in his new career, a problem he denied while taking an attitude of "Let's not dwell on it. Everything will be OK." Mrs. B shared her adjustment strains in a very worried tone of voice, interspersed with many sighs and frequent comments about bodily sensations. It soon grew evident that she was hyperventilating quite severely and that most of her somatic complaints might stem from this habit. An attempt to instruct her in relaxation techniques proved futile. She remained inattentive, "hysteroid" in style, and preoccupied with her physical sensations, hence warding off the relaxation cues. In contrast, when we discussed hyperventilation at length, she spontaneously made good progress in controlling her breathing rate and sighing. Despite her early pessimism, she also reported significant relief from "just being able to sit down and talk about these things."

Therefore, using a fairly traditional, supportive psychotherapy approach, the first eight or so sessions were, in essence, largely "ventilation." She was given, and availed herself of, the chance to express and share burdened feelings that she kept to herself for many years. Her somatic symptoms diminished in this phase. However, she continued to avoid *all* physical exertion lest she provoke a sudden recurrence of chest pain. In her own words: "How do I know I won't croak." She was in no way agoraphobic. She traveled freely by car, socialized readily, and took care of light household duties, but she consistently avoided any activity that might "stress her heart." (Her father's death from a sudden heart attack several years previously may have sensitized her to heart-related dangers.) No amount of reassurance seemed able to abate her worries.

After consulting with her cardiologist, we sent Mrs. B to a physical therapist who is familiar with treating chronic pain patients who also present phobic-like avoidance of physical exertion. The colleague saw her for some 4 weeks in office visits thrice weekly. She was taught an exercise regimen, which she enacted very well and without distress under supervision. As her tolerance for exercising grew, she became willing to try short walks and to implement her exercise program at home. She soon gained confidence that she would not "croak" and, soon after, to our complete surprise announced she was taking steps to apply for a part-time job. Several months later, she expanded her working to full-time to increase her contribution to the family budget. At last contact she was doing well at work and at home. She had regained her self-confidence and was glad once more to view herself as a productive member of the household.

Case 3

Mr. C was referred by his cardiologist after assessment for heart disease proved negative. As had Mrs. B, the patient initially had presented himself in a panic-like state, flushed, with racing pulse, and was quite convinced that he was verging on a heart attack. Unlike Mrs. B, those symptoms did not persist, and he was very open to the idea that his complaints were stress related. He was willing and eager to consider lifestyle changes, and he mainly desired professional guidance to make needed alterations efficiently. He described his life as happy and fulfilling. His marriage was good, his social network was ample and gratifying, and he claimed high satisfaction with his job. However, the company employing him had undergone a reorganization, which placed enormous pressure on Mr. C and some colleagues. They were required to engage in frantic, repeated air travel from coast to coast for a number of months. During this interval, he had neglected personal needs for recreation, "down time," and peace. He freely admitted having pushed himself to the breaking point.

Beyond those just described, initial assessment failed to disclose further problems. Mr. C completed our self-report devices at home, after his first visit, at which time his wife independently answered an LIC too; since Mr. C voiced concerns lest new diversions reduce his limited time with his family, we sought leisure activities of interest to both spouses. At the second visit he reported taking "to heart" the content thrust exemplified in the assessment measures: He was at pains to ensure "goofing off comfortably" when at home—where he had begun to rely on a telephone recorder to protect him from intrusion except when *he chose* to be available. He was also cultivating the attitude of leaving his work "on the doorstep" at the end of the day, so he could enjoy his wife and children. As directed, after their LICs were completed, the spouses compared them and thereby discovered some common interests neither had known were mutual. Hence, they had spontaneously enrolled in a class to permit joint recreation. (We take it as a good prognostic indicator when patients implement "obvious" steps on their own. Reciprocally, when someone fails to heed the "handwriting on the wall," despite our urging, this is a warning sign that the source(s) of noncompliance need further exploration.) Mr. C had experienced no symptom recurrence and displayed optimism about the future. At the third visit progress continued. Their "better-balanced" lifestyle agreed with all family members and the patient felt they could continue a "saner" way of life on their own. A follow-up contact 2 months later showed continued progress. Since no additional problems could be detected, no further visits were scheduled, Mr. C was instructed to telephone if unforeseen difficulties, or the need for more guidance, arose. When last contacted some 10 weeks later, Mr. C was doing well, had joined a spa and lost 10 lb, had no recurrence of the initial symptoms, and described the situation for himself and the family as happy and content.

Case 4

Mrs. D was in her mid-20s, a factory worker and mother of three children, who was married to a mechanic. Her gasteroenterologist referred her after discharge from the hospital for an episode of gastrointestinal complaints, which her physician felt probably stemmed from stress and strain. Most notable was vomiting. Mrs. D complained, "I just can't keep my food down. It just comes back up." She denied vigorously any and all stressors. Note that *no* evidence suggested her vomiting was purposely induced for weight control. There also was no history of binge eating. Her attribution was that she simply "gets this way now and then." Such common protestations notwithstanding, assessment proceeded on the premise that she experienced but did not detect various burdens. Thus, it emerged that her days were replete with many duties and self-imposed responsibilities above and beyond the tasks necessitated by her job and by tending her spouse, children, and home. The therapist was astonished that she had kept going as well as she had, given her litany of extra chores. She "enjoyed," and was dedicated to, taking the role of "listening ear and leaning post" for a host of sisters, brothers, and cousins who lived nearby in a small, rural community. When asked if *she* exclusively must be the one to minister to all these nurturance-seeking kinfolk, she appeared to be taken aback. She had never before really considered "setting limits" for others' demands as a means of self-preservation. She had grown into the role of "everyone's mother," and had not contemplated shedding or shortening that heavy mantle. She was told "On Doctor's Orders," that she must learn to strike a more realistic balance: She must refuse some of the least-reasonable demands from kin. She must first fulfull her duties to children and spouse, and must also reserve some time for herself. Her response was equivocal. She listened attentively, seemed to ponder the issues, but would not commit herself to follow the strategy outlined for her.

It is often the case with out-of-town patients (especially in the winter), who are hospitalized in Memphis and seen for consultation then or just afterward, that no regular series of appointments can be arranged. For such instances, as with Mrs. D, our role is confined to crisis intervention. We try to "strike while the iron is hot," propose the main lines of what steps seem indicated, and hope the patient will follow through despite our inability to maintain continuing office visits. Sometimes little can be accomplished on such a sporadic basis. Sometimes there is initial progress and subsequent "backsliding" which may or may not eventuate in regular appointments, depending on pragmatic realities and the patient's desires. However, with Mrs. D, the feedback was positive. She was phoned several months after the last face-to-face contact and asked how was she doing? Her answer was "fine." She reported she had decided to set some limits on demands from kin and had implemented that plan. She felt the changes had helped her considerably. She was holding down her food and denied any further episodes of throwing up.

Case 5

Her physician referred Mrs. E, a married woman in her mid-30s, for multiple somatic complaints (headaches, neck pain, stomach ache) and trouble concentrating; these symptoms had plagued her for 2 yr. She was taking antidepressants and minor tranquilizers, prescribed by an out-of-town practitioner, but decided to change doctors when she realized she was growing dependent on the tranquilizers.

Mrs. E married when she was very young; she and her husband were both inexperienced sexually. Their life together consisted of hard work and many responsibilities. Sexual experimentation remained a low priority for her until her husband became briefly infatuated with another woman. At that point, Mrs. E realized that she was very sexually inhibited, was eager to improve, yet at the same time, felt very guilty about sexual experimentation. She was poorly informed about sexuality, held very rigid ideas of what was "normal," but wanted to learn more and thus enrich her marriage. As a good, conservative Christian, she was at pains to point out that she did not want to engage in erotic activities contrary to biblical teachings. In our opinion her sexual fears and their effect on the marital relationship were at the very core of her distress. Her husband repeatedly reassured her that "the other woman" was a mistake of the past, but she felt nagging insecurity about her adequacy as a wife and her chances to keep her husband's sexual interest.

Given Mrs. E's religious convictions, we were reluctant to recommend sexual experiments that might conflict with her interpretation of scriptures. We knew many of her inhibitions involved cultural value judgments rather than biblical prohibitions. Not being theologians ourselves, we called in a consultant. One of our colleagues, herself a conservative Christian, referred us to a book by a respected Christian counselor that openly addressed the issues gnawing at the patient. Using scriptual references throughout, the book gives explicit and concrete guidance about sexual practices, while dispelling various myths, and advocating erotic sensuality as a wholesome pleasurable exchange between spouses. After reading the book, Mrs. E became able to talk freely, without embarrassment, about her own sexual difficulties, which proved rooted in some traumatic early experiences. She no longer invoked religion as an excuse to avoid experimentation. Rather, she asked us to help her overcome her fears, recognizing that the bedroom pursuits her husband desired did not contravene the teachings of the Bible. The upshot has been positive. Her anxiety is much reduced, the couple's sex life appears better, and their interpersonal intimacy more generally has improved, e.g., she now often accompanies her husband on business trips she formerly avoided from fear of sexual opportunities if alone with her husband. If we have been successful, the foregoing cases will show that we devise interventions by drawing on a relatively coherent theoretical framework of applied science. At the same time, tuning specific thrusts to specific individuals remains, in part, something of a performing art.

A MAJOR MIDCOURSE CORRECTION: THE CASE OF GARY

We now present the case longest in treatment with either of us. We shall henceforth call the man "Gary." We owe Gary multiple debts: He has taught us a great deal about stress, alerting us to some of its subjective manifestations rarely expressed by less-articulate people. He thus has aided us to grasp and to plumb the content domains reflected in the BAROMAS and LIC inventories. He has both consented for his case to be presented in detail and has prepared his first-person overview of therapy for inclusion below. Since his treatment now appears "in the home stretch" toward a successful outcome, it seems most timely to review it for illustrative purposes.

Case Synopsis

In all, Gary has been seen for some ninety 90- to 120-min sessions, since late summer 1980 when a psychiatric colleague referred him for stress management. With no prior psychiatric history, Gary had started to have anxiety attacks after watching two peers struck down by coronary occlusions. At referral he was age 50. Initial evaluation disclosed a concern with heart attacks since (1) developing a hiatal hernia in 1968, (2) witnessing the two heart attacks, and (3) enduring the newly emergent anxiety episodes. Gary's own account provides further background. Session one introduced progressive relaxation. The exercises disclosed how "tight" were his muscles, his difficulty surrendering "control" of them, and how manifest muscular tension cohered with verbal reports of a hypervigilant pattern of chronic alertness or overactivation, with brooding about *potential* anxiety and anticipating dire consequences to follow commonplace deeds.

The first 6 months of therapy seemed uneventful and positive in course. He diligently practiced muscle exercises and calm relaxation scenes. We made a start helping him comprehend how his parents had modeled stringent standards (e.g., "Anything worth doing is worth doing well."), which he had acquired only too well, and how such self-driving expectations had endured into adulthood, become habitual, and led him to set excessive goals and accept too many responsibilities rather than farming them out to others or just refusing them. Coupled with a too-fast-paced, customary "cruising speed," he invited the hypervigilant, "fast idle" pattern that was "dry kindling" when added stressors descend suddenly as is inevitable in human life. He began to make some progress in "goofing off" more and adopting a less-pressured schedule. By then he reported his wife's positive reactions to his therapy. She had been shy about a joint session, but agreed to one in early October. She stated he was "overscheduling" himself less, fidgeting in his sleep less often, and was taking in stride "minicrises" that formerly would have loomed larger.

Next, we introduced a debits versus credits notion of balancing heroic efforts by compensatory "down time." Gary showed signs of change, for example, when a World Series game got him too excited, he turned it off at the sixth inning; he did not force himself to watch until it ended. We discussed taking breaks at work or during highly arousing events, and some "common sense" ways to keep the hernia quiescent, for example, avoid tight clothing and confining positions that may cramp his midsection—especially after eating—and such foods as bacon that invited hernial flare-ups. We also turned to the years 1956–

1962, which began with his father's cerebrovascular accident (CVA), leading to mental incompetence, institutionalization, and eventual death. Hence, frequent drives to the parents' distant home to aid in family matters fell to Gary, strains increased by hurt from the still-birth of one of twin girls. In retrospect, Gary saw how long he had run a "red ink" balance, ignoring its warning signs of cumulative stress and fatigue. He disliked the "tough guy who must say 'no' to subordinates" career role. Otherwise, his early years in labor relations were very rewarding but his self-pacing was frantic. For example, within 5 days, he achieved the following frantic "hat trick": Drove to City A to pick up a car, drove it to the airport and flew to City B for a half-day business meeting, returned and drove to City C, flew from there to City D for a conference where he got a lift faster than expected to City E and hence changed motel and flight reservations to catch a plane back to City C, slept there 5 hr and then completed the long drive home.

Late in 1980 we began examining how organizational changes had rendered his labor relations post more draining and less satisfying than formerly. After many discussions, treatment took as a focal thrust having Gary explore within his firm any openings for a "horizontal" transfer to a desirable, but less stressful, position. General progress was muted by a deluge of unforeseeable crises ("78 wasp stings") and by refusal to shed or "let George do" any of the team coaching whose stressful impact was observationally confirmed when we attended two meets. We also started to discuss his grief—sometimes experienced but usually suppressed—about his mother's aging and diminished vigor. The effort was made to help him actively contrast "mother-then" (his images of her past capacity and conduct) with "mother-now" (to feel more calm with, and compassion for, her declining competence). Things went "too" well. By mid-January 1981, Gary seemed to have gotten overconfident. The progress note states: "He continues with a dazzling concatenation of multiple stressors: moving his mother, dealing with the labor union, a taxing labor relations inquiry, two weddings for his children, a pregnant bird-dog near whelping, and so on. I used the illustration that, by perceived contrast, after months of 100 MPH, slowing down to 75 MPH *seems* easy, even if that pace strains a vehicle designed to cruise at 50 MPH." Efforts were made to slow Gary down further and to realize that having "two kids leave the nest will take more out of you than you're reckoning on." These "braking" efforts seemed effective; Gary reported more "goofing off" and less fast-paced self-scheduling.

Most fortunately, just the sort of horizontal move he sought within his firm became a feasible prospect. By late February 1981, much progress seemed evident. We were considering reducing sessions to once biweekly, and prematurely noted "Everything is going well; approaching termination." We scheduled a "closing" conjoint with the wife, who confirmed that "All is going well." She noted visible improvement in his attitude, willingness to rest and "woolgather," physical condition (e.g., no more belching), and self-pacing. A follow-up visit to the colleague who had referred Gary gave this optimistic view: "He is doing very well." Sessions were reduced to one every 3 weeks and a progress note emphasized: "Next time check if Gary is sticking with *maintenance* muscle relaxation (thrice weekly). He has learned to take breaks when 'on hold' for phone calls (not working as before), and has postponed several elective meetings to more convenient times." At about that point, "Murphy's law" asserted itself.

Gary expected a less-pressured job and a shorter work year to start in summer, but a host of woes descended in concert. His office was assigned to take responsibility for a troubled subsidiary. His mother was suddenly hospitalized, forcing an emergency air flight and much worry on Gary. Most agonizing was an employee—whom he had "groomed and brought along"—charging that Gary and the firm were guilty of "discrimination" when the person was passed over for promotion. In fact, the accuser lacked some openly available educational requirements for that job description, and someone with far better credentials had applied and been hired. Nonetheless, Gary was deeply hurt to have his motives questioned and was further burdened by an Equal Employment Opportunities Commission (EEOC) hearing, which entailed much paperwork, when the disgruntled accuser lodged a formal EEOC complaint. Treatment was scheduled weekly or biweekly in April and May to help Gary handle the emotional arousal provoked by the impending hearing and the accuser's distrusting, hostile attitude. Excerpts from progress notes reflect the flow of events: (4/1) "Urged he not take signs of being overtaxed as 'routine costs of doing business' but must make up by more 'black ink.'" (4/14) "Saw [Gary] for 'emergency' re: job complaint. Seems to be taking pressures in better stride and not expecting miracles of self." (4/21) "Work crisis continues but at abating intensity. We discussed the emotional, logistical, and ethical issues involved." (5/7) "Work crisis has an apparent solution that can't be fully implemented till mid-June or so. Gary must endure, and allow for, the special burdens on him of his former closeness and intimacy with, and affection for, the complaining employee until then; he agrees." (5/19) "Yet another tangle in the work problem. Internecine intrigue keeps conflict alive. Hopefully, the crux may resolve before this week is out. Gary is managing well, given the amount of real-life stress and its chronicity." (5/25) "Worst all over. Gary was exhausted and slept most of weekend. He felt 'down' today so we discussed postcrisis letdown and his need to recuperate."

Empathically, one may sense Gary's weariness by this point: He felt it but did not fully grasp it, despite warnings that *much* down time was needed. He showed overoptimism, undertook too much, increased his use of the prescribed Ativan, yet grew concerned by his reliance on it. He broached discontinuing its use. The therapist replied "we'll cross that bridge when we come to it, after things settle down," and urged him to take a long weekend. He did, but despite this respite he remained very weary after months of cumulative strain. He reported a mild but evident anxiety spell and *much* hiatal hernia pain. On 6/16, we jointly agreed to this strategy: "(1) Will have his internist check his hernia. (2) Gary will take a 1-day vacation each week, to shorten work demands until he starts an extended vacation in July. (3) His wife or child will accompany him on the long trip to his mother's home, after her discharge from hospital there, to do the driving and help share burdens. (4) Gary will minimize activities during free time and treat himself as a 'semi-invalid' to recuperate before the long July vacation. (5) He will defer deciding about a planned out-of-town speaking trip some days hence; a decision to go (versus to cancel) will require his wife's joint agreement."

Notes from the next four sessions reflect benefits from this curtailed schedule: (6/25) "In nearly all respects has followed advice, reduced activity, made recuperation first priority and, as a result, feels much better." (7/2) "Good progress toward recuperating." (7/7) "Very definite progress. Seems to have regained the lost ground plus, in the process, has learned more about fine-tuning own self-pacing as a function of ebb and flow of external stresses." (7/22) "Progress continues. More realistic about (1) allowing for emotional reactions (especially of loss, e.g., eventually of mother, but proximally when they visit children in Wyoming—rarely seen due to distance from Memphis), (2) pacing himself on the trip, and (3) about turning down untimely invitations to speak at conferences when already booked solid." At that point, Gary and his wife left for the vacation trip to Wyoming.

They returned some weeks later with mainly good news: The trip went well and Gary had put to use some 75%–80% of the guidance given him beforehand. Before the therapist's concerns about the forthcoming coaching season could be raised, Gary raised the issue himself. Starting his new job duties plus the strains of coaching boded ill for "balanced" living. The provisional, joint solution was (1) to appoint an associate coach to spare Gary some duties and (2) close monitoring of how much "down time" would it cost to "pay for" the positively valenced, exciting coaching role? The answer was not long in coming. Team practice began in late September, and we worked on Gary taking a "wait and see" stance about how draining coaching would prove. Other issues targeted after vacation were (1) to monitor and record when and why he took Ativan for several months before asking his physician to permit discontinuing it, (2) to prepare himself for his aged mother's inevitable passing, for which scene practice while relaxed was one technique enlisted, and (3) to redefine his role and duties, both to self and others, from "Daddy" to "Granddad."

The coaching quandary came to a head in late October, as shown by progress note extracts: (10/21) "Saw [Gary] in crisis. He awoke 4 A.M. with anticipatory anxiety (as earlier foreshadowed) at resuming coaching burdens. Has determined to turn all but administrative-logistical duties over to associate and bow out. Is relieved at his decision but can see there will be mourning over leaving that 'Daddy' role, since he helped found the league. Yet is much more realistic about heeding warning signals than prior." (10/27) "Much discussion of 'mourning' since his decision to quit coaching. His wife feels he is 'in better touch' with himself than for as long as she's known him. We discussed 'R & R' and 'Elder-Statesman/Granddad' options that may evolve presently." He continued to do well but to voice familiar concerns throughout autumn: (11/24) "Still needs to deal more fully with certain issues, for example, mother's aging and eventual passing." (12/7/81) "Continued difficulty 'letting go' and retiring from coaching role, that is, being 'Granddad' versus 'Daddy.'" By this phase self-monitoring disclosed some tendency to take Ativan "preventively," to ward off *anticipated* arousal rather than "as needed" and the therapist grew concerned about this facet. By and large, Gary coped well with the host demands of the holidays. He started expressing a wish to attend team meets as a spectator; we agreed to wait some 3 weeks and then see how well he tolerated attending part of a meet. In late January 1982, Gary recognized he still harbored some fear of a heart attack. We began a short course of desensitization to habituate that arousal, with further scene practice assigned as homework. He also visited the cardiac stroke unit for *in vivo* counterarousal practice. Most disturbing were Gary's worries about a collectively planned "cut-down" schedule for Ativan. We discussed, and agreed, that referral to a colleague expert in substance detoxification was in order. At about the same time, his internist discovered Gary had strained a disk and, by favoring it posturally, might be creating midsection discomfort that seemed to be, but was not, hernia pain. A physical therapist then entered the case for the disk-related problems. For the moment, no arousal to heart failure cues (e.g., on television) was evidenced.

Early in March the physician in charge of withdrawing Gary from Ativan began careful outpatient detoxification. Gary had *always* adhered to the dosage prescribed but appeared sensitive to that medicine and had grown dependent on it. A rocky period of some 6 weeks transpired, during which our contacts mainly addressed the discomforts wrought by physical symptoms of withdrawal. Yet Gary's attitude stayed positive. He felt he had made vast lifestyle changes and that, once detoxified, it would mark "turning the last corner." When the drug was fully withdrawn, Gary visited his mother, took her geriatric limitations in good stride, and began to actively resume camping and fishing diversions without hernial complaint. His optimism and self-confidence rose and, by June, he saw "no major mountains left to climb." He seemed to have mastered his "catastrophizing" tendency to perceive one "spike" of arousal as the harbinger of an anxiety attack, which such self-referent worries can ignite as a kind of self-fulfilling prophecy. We agreed to cut back sessions in light of a pending vacation, and not to resume for some 2 months unless needed. Lying ahead of Gary was a much-craved wilderness fishing trip in Canada, whose prospect he was relishing. Then the next boom descended.

Before the trip with old comrades, there was a spate of frantic and sleepless preparatory festivity. Gary departed exhausted and, while "in the bush," had a frank panic attack (details are in Gary's own account following). Yet again, he was told in depth how "ignoring gentle messages from his body invites thunderclaps of retaliation." The next several sessions were aimed at helping Gary understand, and hence cease worrying about, the Canadian "catastrophe," but his self-confidence was badly shaken. He became disposed to "wrap himself in cotton wool," despite guidance that "balance, not hibernation" was called for. He also reported continual vulnerability to startle at any sudden cue—a new development that made the therapist wonder about catecholamine changes as the result of aging. "It's a definite shot of adrenaline that's occurring," Gary said, "Even very simple, normal kinds of things that happen by surprise." It appeared the trauma in Canada had really knocked his self-efficacy to perform any usual task "for a loop." Thus (7/27), he reported "I have some fears of being afraid that I didn't used to have," and (8/3) "He let himself get upset by a combination of some overstrain plus mental dwelling on doubts, vulnerability, and negative feeling states. We thus focused on the causation, and resolution, of the 'afraid-to-be-afraid' dynamic as it relates to arousal cycles. Have urged and prompted *moderation* and balance between 'sprinting,' which is self-driving, and cotton-wool retreat." Index cards to record triggers to arousal spikes and his ability to follow criteria to guide decisions about accepting versus avoiding a given activity were supplied. He was having difficulty grasping the differences among things he "needs" versus "wants" versus "ought" to do, which became the focus of our next few sessions (during which it emerged that Gary had greatly truncated muscle relaxation exercises, and was refreshed in practicing them properly). We then tried a frontal attack on his "fear of fear" ruminations (and newer, driving concerns) by a series of desensitization sessions. By the end of August he was able to resume such diversions as brief fishing trips and a Labor Day trip to visit children for which (1) he was guided to take low-traffic toll roads; (2) he was given a mnemonic card to distinguish "overprotective apprehension" (which calls for completing a balanced and wanted action) from "close calls" or subtle judgments (which imply accepting any chosen option), and (3) his wife would do all driving unless he actively *wanted* to take the wheel.

There seems little doubt (see Gary's account) that his diminished efficacy led him to decide against undertaking even routine challenges with "fear-of-fear" arousal erupting into anxiety attacks in the autumn. The therapist was in a quandary as to how to elicit *reasonable* activity and began to suspect that Gary had a fear of death that had been periodically raised, but had been denied each time. It puzzled the therapist why a man who had lived so exemplary a Christian life should fear dying, and this topic became focal when Gary had severe anxiety attacks in October 1982. Progress note excerpts trace the therapist's efforts to discern if dying *per se*, a sense of serious illness real or imagined, a combination, or what, lay at the bottom of things (for which purpose, Gary was sent to the most meticulous diagnostician known to the therapist). (10/13) "[Gary] has had resurgence of panic. I suspect fear of dying or fear of insidious illness. He will obtain a complete physical exam tomorrow and will ponder in depth why he appears so fearful of dying." (10/25) "Has been found physically normal and healthy for his age. This also rules out catecholamine problems. Agrees he has 'blocked' facing the prospect of death and now will do reading and thinking on the subject to make peace with the cosmic order and improve own self-perceptions and perspective in that light. Also, he grants that the self-triggering exacerbation cycle—states he sees it now—is built on anxious apprehensions about his self-efficacy to accomplish any task calmly."

At about that point we seemed to have finally turned the corner: (11/1) "[Gary] has made visible progress. Is reducing anxious apprehension, withdrawal, and 'surrender.' For example, he *initiated* a short camping trip with a buddy and it went well." (11/8) "Is doing well despite a trip and need to handle things alone with wife out of town." (11/17) "Substantial progress reported, including (1) seeking companionship from which he had withdrawn, (2) coping successfully with diverse stressors, (3) decrease in degree and frequency of arousal manifestations, and (4) making active efforts to achieve peace with his mortality and eventual death." (12/2) "Participated more, and more spontaneously, in a training activity and enjoyed same. He took distorted TV 'smear' directed against his firm in good stride: 'I couldn't have done it 2–3 weeks ago; it's an important milestone.'" (12/14/82) "General progress continues including (1) reduced concern with death and (2) realization that his direct observations of dying had been largely confined to his father's protracted and awful decline via a serial cycle of strokes across some 19 months. Hence, he had miscoded catastrophe and misery as prime exemplars of the category *Death*." (1/3/83) "General progress continues." (1/17) "Essential progress continues—able to attend a meet of his former team." However, protracted apparent strain in the thoracic region led to further referrals, discussed in Gary's account. With progress at last seeming stable, sessions were scheduled less often in February 1983. (2/17) "Definite progress continues: Physical exam last week found diastolic BP had dropped to 84 after hovering about 90–92 the past 4 years. Has taken numerous minor stressors in stride, and also a major stress episode when his son and daughter-in-law were burglarized. He was able to unwind well that night 'even though some months back I couldn't have dreamed of going to help them,' as he and his wife had done." (2/28) "Substantial progress handling diverse demands but, especially, the final meet of the league tourney he had founded and formerly coached." It is now germane to present Gary's report of the course of his treatment through his own eyes.

The Patient Speaks

I was truly one who had "made it." As the director of a labor relations division at a major organization near Memphis, I had a national reputation, was past president of our national association, was requested as a seminar participant from coast to coast, and did a great amount of consulting. My family life could not have been better. I had an ideal marriage of 26 years and our four children had all turned out well. Two had graduated from and two were enrolled in college. Three of the children had excellent marriages, and the fourth was approaching her wedding day.

On the civic side, I had served as Clerk of the Elders of our church, chaired special task forces for area-wide church groups, served on a local school board, on a YMCA board, and had been a boy-scout leader. I was an avid fisherman and camper who had enjoyed many a wilderness trip. Our family had spent several camping and travel vacations together. Although, not on easy-street, the combination of my salary with my wife's salary (she is an accomplished science teacher) allowed us to be quite comfortable, particularly now that the college bills were beginning to decline. We looked forward to long and happy careers.

In the spring of 1979, it all started to come apart. The winter and early spring of that year had been quite stressful. At work I had changed bosses, beaten back the first major unionization drive for our employees, responded to several government investigations, and continued in general at my usual frantic pace. Professionally, our national association had just fired its executive director and I played the major peace maker around the country. In February my 81-year-old mother had just sold our family home (400 miles from me) and moved into an apartment in her home city. I had reinvested the money from the sale of her home and was managing a trust for her. Our next-youngest child was married in March and our youngest daughter was planning a wedding in August. I had coached a sports team representing our firm for 24 years, and the winter of '79 was more hectic than usual as we went undefeated the entire year until losing in the semifinals of a prestigious tournament to a team we had defeated easily during the year.

My problems began in April following a dismissal hearing which I was managing, in which the supervisor had a heart attack during the actual hearing. I handled that emergency quite well, but the next week I seemed to fall apart. I wanted to withdraw from many activities, even very simple ones, as I just could not face issues anymore. I recall trying to conduct a workshop and finally stopping my talk and leaving. My hiatal hernia, which had been an off-and-on problem since 1968, cranked up most dramatically.

Shortly afterwards I was on a camping canoe trip for our sports team. I had responsibility for purchasing all of the food and for being camp cook, an assignment that I relished and enjoyed. I was miserable almost all of the weekend and my hiatal hernia gave me constant pain and trouble. I did not want to eat, and I had trouble driving. I did not want to participate in any of the activities, even the most simple ones.

The following Monday I had trouble handling the most routine of phone calls. Ironically, I was due to see my internist for my annual physical examination that very week. I reviewed all of the recent events with my physician, who gave me an even more thorough physical examination than usual. Everything checked out fine and the physician prescribed a light dosage of Ativan tranquilizer (4 mg daily) for me to use to get over some of my anxiety problems. We had to immediately reduce the daily dosage to 1½–2 mg as it was obvious that I was very sensitive to the drug. The medication worked, and by midsummer I was virtually off the Ativan and everything seemed normal again.

The rest of 1979 went fine. I would use the Ativan on rare occasions on an "as needed" basis averaging about 10–15 mg each month.

One year later, in August of 1980, I fell apart again. The work year had been even more turbulant. We had undergone a very major Federal Labor Relations compliance review and had many other problems. I had moved my mother into a new apartment in her home city. My wife's mother died. Our first grandchild was born. I began having anxiety problems again. The hiatal hernia flared up, and I had trouble handling stressful situations. Again I wanted to withdraw or run away from the problems; again I could not face even the simplest of tasks. Some examples follow: On a routine phone call in which I was asked to answer the simplest of questions (something that would normally be a piece of cake), I would get so nervous and uptight that I would put the person on hold to compose myself before giving the answer. Then I would take several minutes to recover from the ordeal. To make a presentation or to run a staff meeting (tasks that I used to handle with pleasure and with ease) was sometimes next to impossible. These were not everyday occurrences, but would vary and gradually increased in regularity. Many days I would seem "normal," while other days I would be anxious and tense and unable to function. I began the use of Ativan on a regular basis once again, using about 1.5 mg, daily. Although it helped a little, this time it did not have the former effect and the problems continued.

In early September of 1980, I was referred to one of the Drs. Rosenthal —the therapist (Th)—for treatment for my anxiety and for stress management. I was a very scared person at this time. To not be able to function as I had for 50 years (at breakneck speed doing everything for everybody, solving problems quite easily, and thoroughly enjoying every bit of it) was extremely traumatic. I also feared for my health as a result of my hiatal hernia problem and the pain that it produced.

Th taught me relaxation exercises, which I began doing at home. Th also taught me to transfer traumatic thoughts to relaxation scenes whenever the anxious moments arose. Th began a very slow and gentle recap of my work and personal history. Th identified the fact that I had been driving myself at a 90 MPH rate and then dropped to a cruising speed of 70, which I thought was slow enough for recovery. I began to understand that recreation at breakneck speed was almost as stressful as those things that clobbered me at the office. I thus learned that positive stress can be almost as damaging as negative stress. This took a long time to sink in. I had run the recreation side of my life in the same manner as I ran my office. On the weekend camping and fishing trip (which I averaged about once a month during the spring, summer, and fall), I had to be the total manager, that is, buying the food, serving as cook and fishing guide, in addition to fishing 10 hr a day myself. I truly enjoyed this, and had no idea how much of an impact this was having on my system. I went about church and civic work the same way, and coached my sports team with the same intensity.

Th worked from September through December to get me to understand the need to slow down and move at a slower pace, to learn that an unplanned weekend at home doing nothing could be not only valuable but a lot of fun. I learned the need of down time which really meant "down," not changing to something that was diversionary. I learned the need for "black ink" when things at the office or my personal life had piled up "red ink." During the winter of 1981 I was much improved. The quality of life was on a real upswing and I really did slow down. At least I thought I slowed down from my former pace.

In January my boss began talking about the possibility of his changing positions within our firm and having me joining him. I jumped at this possibility as it would spare me the crunch of the labor relations post and all of its stress. (I would not have recognized the need for this 6 months before.) By March it was certain that I would be changing positions sometime during the summer. In addition, by special arrangement, I would work on a 10-month basis instead of 12 so that I would have 2 months off in the summer (our slowest season). This was another way to reduce the stress of work. Since all but one daughter had finished college and she was in her last year we could afford the salary reduction.

In the spring of 1981, before I could change positions, some extremely stressful things occurred. Our office had the labor relations of a small subsidiary firm added to its responsibility. I was involved with a major EEOC complaint aimed directly at me personally. My 83-year-old mother was rushed to the hospital in her hometown with a salt imbalance problem and I made a quick round-trip flight to handle the emergency. Upon dismissal from the hospital 10 days later, she joined my wife and me at our home for about a month. Finally, in early June after I had tied down most of the knots in changing positions (announcements to the staff and the filling of some vacant staff positions), I had another downturn. On a visit to our headquarters building for a casual meeting with the person I was reporting to in the interim, I had an anxiety attack in the basement. Although I was there on an unannounced visit with no problems to discuss, I simply could not get on the elevator and meet the appointment. I ended up sitting on the basement steps hyperventilating with my hiatal hernia in great pain. Finally, I was able to take a few steps and I walked back to my office, taking a circuitous route to try and calm down. I told my secretary to hold all calls and immediately relaxed on a couch. Several hours later I had recovered and began to function normally.

Two days later I had a similar occurrence, although it was not as acute. This occurred on a fishing trip on a lake about 70 miles from home. My fishing partner and I had completed a successful afternoon of bluegill fishing and were going to enjoy a couple of hours of early evening bass fishing. As we began, I suddenly became extremely anxious and could not even pick up my fishing rod. We immediately headed for shore, my fishing buddy loaded the boat by himself, and we headed for home. I recovered on the trip back.

When Th heard of this, it was immediately suggested that I reduce my work load to a 4-day work week. In addition, I eliminated all activities and commitments in the evenings and on weekends. I worked only 4 days and would piddle and relax during the evenings and over a long 3-day weekend. No special activities or outings were planned for any of the weekends. Surprisingly, I not only learned that it was OK to take it easy and do nothing, but actually learned to enjoy and appreciate such marvelous down time.

At the end of the summer, my wife and I took a 3-week camping trip to Wyoming. The trip included a 5-day stay in Yellowstone National Park. The ground rules for this trip were totally different than any we had taken in the past. Instead of cranking out 500–700 miles each day, we traveled between 200 and 300 miles daily before settling down for a long evening's camp time, then broke camp in a relaxed manner the next morning. My wife did 75%–80% of the driving, a total reversal of past roles. I changed positions in September 1981 and learned to appreciate a much less stressful position. I really enjoyed working at a less frantic pace in my new role.

Our sports team began practicing in late September. In late October we had a practice game scheduled with a rival team whose players were in town to attend a meeting. The morning of this game a curious thing happened. When I arose that morning, I had some stress and anxiety signs for the first time in several months. I suddenly realized for the first time in my life that I no longer wanted to coach the team. This was totally different than what had occurred for the previous 26 years as I always looked forward eagerly to each game. It was as if something or someone was telling me to stop coaching. I immediately called my assistant coach and indicated that I was sick, would not be able to attend that night, and that he would have to handle the team. The next day I discussed with him what my problems were, asked him if he would take the team for the season and then discussed this with a vice-president of our firm. Before the week was over I had divested myself of all coaching responsibility but did agree to stay and handle scheduling arrangements for the team as well as other business matters. I also agreed to continue directing an end-of-the-year tournament involving many teams from several neighboring states, a tournament which had been running for 26 years and originally had been my brain child.

At Th's suggestions I did not attend the opening game of the season. I finally made the fourth game of the year, a trip which almost turned into a disaster. The game was a close one, but more than that I was anxious from the start, an anxiety that became worse as the game went along. This anxiety did not relate to how well the team was doing, but rather to whether or not I could stand sitting there watching them play with all of the nervous signs in place in my head. Finally, at Th's suggestion, I would go to games arriving at half-time and leaving whenever I felt like it. By this method I was able to work back to the start of a game and by midseason I was able to enjoy attending them.

By February 1982 the lifestyle change that Th had brought to me really began to pay off. I had slowed down, was enjoying a new quality of life, was on a regular exercise program (I would swim a quarter of a mile during the noon hour each day) and felt fine most of the time. However, both Th and I noticed with curiousity that I would still get small dosages of anxiety at certain times that made no sense whatsoever. This might occur when I was out walking the dogs, when I was at home in the evening reading or simply enjoying some music. In tracing the problem, we realized that I had developed a dependency on Ativan. I had been taking about 1½ tablets (equaling 1½ mg) of Ativan on a more or less regular basis since the summer of 1980 and was averaging 50 mg of Ativan each month. Although this was a very light amount and was taken by prescription, it was obvious that I was suffering from symptoms of Ativan withdrawal. They would occur when I had not taken any Ativan for a day or two. This theory was reinforced when the taking of Ativan would eliminate symptoms 30 min later. As a result, Th referred me to a friend, a physician who is a drug specialist, and he began a withdrawal program for me. This program began on March 1, and I must say I now have sympathy for anyone who must go through withdrawal from any drug. I was away from my desk for a month and had all of the usual withdrawal problems such as no sleep, the shakes, alternate chills and hot flashes, loss of appetite, and the absolute inability to even move from the living room couch to answer the door bell. By early April I was back to work on a part-time basis. This was incrementally stretched out until I returned to work full-time in May. By late May I was driving an automobile again and felt back to normal. At that point I made a huge mistake. I took all of the positive signs after withdrawal as well as discussions with Th about reducing the visits with Th to a caretaker capacity to mean that I was "cured." This caused a disaster.

Eight of us were involved in a wilderness fly-in fishing trip in central Canada in late June. I had flown into this lake before and eagerly looked forward to getting back into this wonderful country. Instead of taking the long drive to the northwestern site, I flew to Duluth to be picked up en route. As a matter of fact I thought that by flying instead of driving, by taking it "easy," I could do just about anything I wanted to do. I really set myself up long before we left. For those who have never participated in this type of activity, it is hard to imagine the "high" that one works up prior to such a trip. I did nothing to control this and as a matter of a fact did not even recognize the symptoms. Several old friends who were going on the trip arrived in town a few days ahead of time and we had nothing but a series of pregame pep rallies prior to the trip. I planned all the menus and helped to assist in the purchasing of all of the supplies for the trip. Although I planned to do very little of the cooking, I found myself in the kitchen for most of the meals the first 2 days that we were in the bush. In addition I served as fishing guide and father figure, among other unplanned chores.

The second night in our wilderness cabin I was really clobbered. This time it was a panic attack of the worst magnitude. Symptoms included extremely fast heart rate and breath rate, alternate chilling and sweating, hyperventilation, plus sheer terror. This occurred about midnight. Two of my friends carried me into the cook house and helped me get through the night by placing their sleeping bags next to me and by reassuring me the rest of the night. I stayed in the bunk all of the next day. By the end of the third day in camp I was beginning to feel a little bit better but with no strength. I spent the next 4 days piddling around camp, poking the fire, gently walking the beach, and reading a couple of books. During the remainder of our stay, my total fishing time was 1 hr. We were taken out on schedule by float plane after 6 days, and I flew back from Duluth, rather than coming back by automobile as planned.

Th was able to review with me all of the reasons why this panic attack happened. I had done everything much beyond normal limits and had forgotten the draining effects of positive stress. This, combined with the fact that we were 200 miles from any medical help, set the wrong "rotors" in motion. I spent the summer recovering from this episode. Since this was my first summer on my new schedule, all of the things that I had planned to do went totally by the boards as I just stayed home and took it easy.

At the end of July two other problems occurred. At a church meeting about 80 miles from home I was involved in a volunteer consulting visit about business matters. I experienced another anxiety attack, which I was able to work off by removing myself from the meeting. Then 2 days later I had a morning anxiety attack. This one was the result of working in the yard too much the night before and then getting up to go fishing the next morning with very little sleep and without enough black ink accumulated. (It seems that I would never learn.) Although I recovered quickly from both of these anxiety attacks, the second one was followed about 12 hr later by probably the best shedding of tears that I have ever experienced. Th placed me on a very reduced program which had me minimize movies or television, reading exciting novels, watching sporting events (which I dearly love), or doing anything that could be stimulating.

I returned to work in mid-August and was glad to begin being productive again. However, I was experiencing some unusual pain or tension around my rib cage. I had been using Tegament to control the hiatal hernia (since the Ativan withdrawal process) and it seemed to be under control. Thinking that these problems were related to the hiatal hernia, a gastroenterologist gave me a complete, thorough check-up. It turned out the problems were not hernia related. In reviewing all this Th discovered that I had forgotten all about his relaxation exercises and had not done them properly for well over a year. In defense of Th, he had periodically asked if I was doing them, and I thought that I was, but I found out that I was completing only a small portion of them. I then began doing relaxation exercises both morning and evening on a very regular basis and have continued to this day.

As we began to make arrangements for the 1982–1983 sports' season, I realized that these preparations were getting me extremely nervous and anxious, even though I would not be coaching. Therefore, I made the decision to totally divorce myself from the team in its entirety and turned over its management to someone else. This was very difficult to do since this team had been *my* show for 27 years, but it was essential to do it, and I am much relieved that this is no longer any responsibility of mine. I did not go to a game until late in the season, and then only because I wanted to, not out of any sense of responsibility.

Although I was feeling better, without realizing it I was setting myself up for another disaster. This was caused by a pendulum swing in the exact opposite direction. For my entire life I have done everything at top speed, have gotten involved in all kinds of activities, and have wanted to be in charge of everything. Now I was just the opposite, was not involved with church work or civic activities, not attending sporting events, and had reduced my outdoor activities to very minor amounts. I did not attend movies, plays, or concerts. I was going to work and returning home and that was all. In essence I had cut myself off from everything. I hit bottom in early October and had three anxiety attacks in a row. One was at a Sunday evening choral service and the other two were on the following Tuesday morning. Although of short duration, the best way to characterize them was sheer terror. Although hyperventilation did not occur, the heart and breath rates did rise, I perspired heavily, and was overcome with extreme nervousness. I was at a point where I could not stand to be by myself. Simply being alone at night while my wife went shopping, or the 30-min span from the time my wife left home in the morning to teach school and my daughter picked me up in the morning was unbearable. In addition, I had lost all confidence in doing anything, for example, going to church, going to any social event of any type, any outdoor outing, or even making a trip to the store by myself. I was literally afraid of such things as a barking dog at night, sirens in the dark, rain on the roof, or any other unusual noises. All of these symptoms were new and were not present at any other time during my illness. This was truly the most terrifying time of all. Until one loses control of oneself and becomes afraid of oneself he or she does not know what real fear is.

Th suggested several techniques that helped tremendously. Whenever I felt anxiety beginning I would use the relaxation exercises if at all possible. If not, I would use relaxation scenes and try in some manner to change the tape inside my head. If I could mentally switch gears from myself to something else, this would always help. At Th's suggestion, by carrying index cards I was able to combat my nerves and not let it get away from me. Whenever the rotor would get running too fast, I would put down the time, place, and event that caused the problem. This would help me understand it and greatly diminish the anxiety. It was also a good mechanism for reviewing the problems with Th. In addition, and also at Th's suggestion, I went to an internist for the most thorough physical examination of my life. I came through this with flying colors, and this helped to greatly diminish the anxiety.

Th discovered that I had a real fear of death. The idea of dying had never really occurred to me and I had always blocked the thought of my death out of mind. Th suggested that I meet with my minister to discuss the entire problem with him. These meetings are continuing and have been quite fruitful. I have also done more praying than I have ever done in my lifetime. In addition, Th has had me visit some very beautiful Memphis cemeteries as we realized that I had not been in a graveyard in years. I am beginning to understand that death is not necessarily painful, but can be a very beautiful and a very natural milestone that will happen in everyone's life.

I began to understand that my total withdrawal from society plus the fear of my own death was causing a "fear of fear," which in many ways was the hardest thing that I had to get over. I used some other techniques Th suggested, which allowed me to get into a more normal relationship with people. Both my wife and I made every effort to schedule an occasional event for me during the evening or weekend (with moderation, of course). Although I was swimming a quarter of a mile at noon everyday, I was doing it in solitude and then eating a snack lunch by myself. I made it a point to always talk to somebody else that I could join for lunch just to chat with. I made a point of getting out to visit the units of our firm and meeting many of my old friends from time to time. Little by little things began to improve. Th helped me to be very patient.

Now in February 1983 my confidence is much better, and I am well on the way to recovery. I can fish again, enjoy the out of doors, our social and church life is back to normal (moderate, though). I can get up in front of a group and speak, work with the staff in our division, and watch "Hill Street Blues" on television. I find that I can sleep much better at night. My wife says that I sleep soundly and do not flip around nor move constantly as I used to. My hiatal hernia is under complete control and unless I eat something I shouldn't, it is better than it has been in 15 years. Although I still get nervous under extreme stress, the anxiety is not there.

In December of 1982 and February 1983, I began two treatments involving a health care delivery team, which was greatly improved my entire picture. I was diagnosed in December as having a temporomandibular joint (TMJ) problem. This is actually a dental occlusion problem that had been developing for many many years, but until I underwent a great amount of stress the symptoms were not prevalent. The symptoms included headaches, buzzing of the ears, aching jaws, aching upper teeth, and muscle twitches under one eye. A dentist began treating this problem in December by the use of a splint which I wear while sleeping at night to realign the occlusion and by ultrasound treatments on the face. In addition I apply wet heat to each jaw area for 30 min each day. These treatments have helped a great amount.

In February I was referred to a physical therapist who specializes in working with TMJ problems. Apparently, as one gets older, one's posture acclimates to the occlusion problem and unless the physical therapist is able to rework the posture, the muscle problems will continue. Since July of 1982, I have had some very bad thoracic muscle problems, which appear to be strained thoracic muscles due to extreme tenseness. My physical therapy diagnosis included cervical dysfunction, including tightness in suboccipital region, and the midcervical in the upper thoracic region. This dysfunction was both joint and muscular. I also had some muscle imbalance along the cervical spine and in the upper quarter of my body, particularly in the upper thoracic region. I have now been working with a physical therapist for 3 weeks and can already sense some very marked improvement in the problem areas.

Another item that should be mentioned is the very important lifestyle changes that were epitomized in some weekend experiences of mine in late February 1983. On Thursday of that week, my daughter and my wife were appearing as chorus members in a local opera company's production. I went to the opening performance on Thursday night after a full day of work and was extremely tired by the time the long opera closed at 11:30. I thoroughly enjoyed it but it just wore me out. By the time my wife and daughter had changed clothes and gotten out of their make-up and I got to bed it was 1:00 a.m. I rejected an option of going out to eat with the cast and went on home to bed. I had indicated to my office that I might wait as late as noon to come in on Friday. I got up around 7:30, piddled around the house that morning, went and got a haircut, and arrived at the office at 11:00. At that time I received a phone call from two of my former players who were currently coaching the team. They asked me to go to lunch with them to discuss some unusual problems they thought they might be facing in the meet that night. Our team was in the opening round of the tournament that I had managed for so many years. After the enjoyable lunch I indicated to them that I might or might not be at the meet that night, depending upon how I felt. By 7:30 that evening the decision was made for me as I was bone tired and went to bed to get a good 12-hr sleep.

The next day our team was playing the semifinals of the tournament. I went to the meet and enjoyed it very much, indicating that I might or might not be back for the evening finals. I also had the option of going fishing Sunday afternoon, called my fishing partner around supper time and we determined that we would not go the next day because of what looked like poor weather conditions. I already made up my mind that I would either go to the tournament final, or go fishing, but not both. Since we were not going fishing, I went on to the finals which our team won and I enjoyed it very much. As they were giving out all of the trophies after the meet, I got a very pleasant surprise. The tournament director indicated that the tournament committee had established a permanent trophy in my name to be given to the team displaying the best sportsmanship and asked me to come up front to present it. I enjoyed this very much and was able to do so without any problems of stress. I then simply piddled around the following Sunday and was able to come back and go to work in a normal manner on Monday. The important points here were at no time did I overschedule or get overcommitted as to what I was going to do during what *could* have been a very long and hard weekend. I simply took each situation as it came along, making the decision at the appropriate time.

I have much to be thankful for. I have learned that prestige, power, and money are not all that important. I have truly learned a moderate lifestyle that allows me to enjoy a new and better qualify of life. The firm is able once again to make use of my knowledge, ability, and long experience. I have a very marvelous marriage of over 30 years, a very delightful and understanding wife, four super kids, four fine in-law children, and three lovely grandchildren. I am looking forward to the golden years as a gray panther (a bald panther would be better) with much relish!

CONCLUSION

The case of Gary reflects a number of key issues raised at the outset of this chapter. First and foremost, the interplay among external or contextual events *and* a person's self-evaluative reactions jointly affect what the person experiences and performs. With Gary it is of interest that the physical therapist now treating him for TMJ and related cervical and upper thoracic strains believes those muscular problems could not have been improved until Gary had achieved a better-balanced lifestyle and more skill at modulating the pressures we have sought to teach him to deal with. In a personal communication (dated March 17, 1983), that therapist wrote: "In summary, Gary has suffered from postural dysfunction over the years and when his stress level is increased the 'pain' will come on. Basically, our treatment consists of moving the areas that are tight, strengthening the areas that are loose, and correcting posture. . . . Gary has responded well. I believe this is due to him handling his lifestyle and stress very well." Note that stress-triggered maladaptive responses also include the bio-mechanical hazards just mentioned.

The precise mechanisms governing how attributional and self-attributional processes steer a given instance of conduct are not fully known. Nor is there reason to assume their serial ordering and comparative impact need be identical across a range of patients, or across multiple situations for the same patients. Gary's eager, guarded, or strongly avoidant reactions to the prospect of a wilderness camping trip covaried respectively with his perceived self-efficacy to manage those activities with comfort, minor anxiety, or the danger of panic episodes looming in his mind. What does seem clear is that environmental and phenomenological influences interlock to guide subjective as well as overt activity. The reciprocal interplay among self-reactions and measurable, biobehavioral performances has been found in both children (Gelfand & Hartmann, 1982) and adults. Self-expectations can be altered by experimental directions (Shaw & Blanchard, 1983), by performance feedback (Bandura & Cervone, 1983), or by multiple sources of guidance cues that, in concert, can augment or attenuate each other (Bandura, 1983; Rosenthal, 1980). Without necessarily isolating the day-to-day balance of dominant mechanisms, we feel the events of Gary's case epitomize multivariate causation. We further believe that no lock-step regimen of techniques would have proven salutary given that Gary's course was strongly affected by chance events (the unfortunately timed EEOC charges brought by the disgruntled employee, "78 wasp stings" coming all together, etc.) and both his and the therapist's errors in correctly perceiving what would be a workable cruising speed for him. Certainly, one is hard-pressed to blame a patient when a common anxiolytic drug (Ativan) is prescribed and taken in approved dosage yet leads to unforeseeable dependency.

As elsewhere discussed (e.g., Rosenthal, 1982, 1984a; Rosenthal & Rosenthal, 1983), few *elements* of our conceptual stance are truly novel; some were discussed by the ancient Greeks and, likely, by their intellectual forebears as well. The goal of clinical theory is to supply a working map to spare therapists and patients the costs of rediscovering partly familiar terrain anew, and to emphasize the major landmarks to be negotiated as well as some of the viable paths for meeting those goals. Since aspects of each human situation remain unique, we assume some idiosyncratically aimed exploration is inevitable no matter which conceptual "map" one adopts. Ours is not perfect nor complete, but it seems to be serving our patients and us well.

Early in this chapter, we discussed some of the scientific evidence that favors the sort of biobehavioral, stress–diathesis thinking we advocate. Although much of those data are quite new, it would be presumptuous to imply that a recognition of linkages between stress and illness is some recent development. The hypothesis, if not the empirical data, is part of all our cultural heritage. It seems fitting to close with a concrete example. The Prussian general Carl von Clausewitz was on a Polish battle campaign in 1831. A cholera epidemic developed and spread westward across Poland toward his headquarters in Posen. His loving wife became aware of the danger. She wanted to join him in

Posen to care for him should he fall ill. He in turn was an equally devoted spouse and did not wish her to take the risk. Here, in Paret's (1976) translation, is part of his letter forbidding her to come:

Do you believe that I would take you to a battle? And yet that would be no more than an intensification of this sudden danger [i.e., cholera]. . . . In this brief illness during which physicians and surgeons constantly attend one, nursing by ladies is almost out of the question in any case. And don't you believe that I am ten times more likely to fall victim to the disease when I am afraid of infecting you than when I have no need to worry? No, if anything protects me, it is my complete composure. Next door is a room for transient visitors. Yesterday evening, when I was already in bed, I heard someone vomit violently; what could be more natural than to think of cholera, and yet I fell asleep at once. (p. 422)

Despite the objective hazards, he was more concerned to prevent the subjective stress he anticipated that his wife's presence—making her vulnerable to the disease—would arouse in him.

Acknowledgments

This chapter is dedicated to Al Bandura, who showed us the city, performed chi-square dances at critical times, and has always been a steadfast friend and teacher. The Tennessee Department of Mental Health and Mental Retardation, J. D. Brown, MD, Commissioner, and the Memphis Mental Health Institute, R. D. Fink, MD, Superintendent, are gratefully acknowledged for funding to the first author that partly supported completion of this chapter.

References

Akiskal, H. S. (Ed.). (1979). Affective disorders: Special clinical forms. *Psychiatric Clinics of North America, 2* (Whole No. 3), 417–629.

Akiskal, H. S., King, D., Rosenthal, T. L., Robinson, D., & Scott-Strauss, A. (1981). Chronic depressions: Clinical and familial characteristics in 137 probands. *Journal of Affective Disorders, 3*, 297–315.

Akiskal, H. S., Rosenthal, T. L., Haykal, R. F., Lemmi, H., Rosenthal, R. H., & Scott-Strauss, A. (1980). Characterological depressions: Clinical features of "dysthymic" verusus "character-spectrum" subtypes. *Archives of General Psychiatry, 37*, 777–783.

Akiskal, H. S., & Webb, W. L. (Eds.). (1978). *Psychiatric diagnosis: Explorations of biological predictors.* New York: SP Medical & Scientific Books.

American Psychiatric Association. (1980). *Diagnostic and statistical manual of mental disorders* (3rd ed.). Washington, DC: Author.

Anisman, H., & Zacharko, R. M. (1982). Depression: The predisposing influence of stress. *The Behavioral and Brain Sciences, 5*, 89–137.

Bachrach, L. L. (1983). Psychiatric services in rural areas: A sociological overview. *Hospital and Community Psychiatry, 34*, 215–226.

Bahrke, M. S., & Morgan, W. P. (1978). Anxiety reduction following exercise and meditation. *Cognitive Therapy and Research, 2*, 323–334.

Bandura, A. (1977a). *Social learning theory.* Englewood Cliffs, NJ: Prentice-Hall.

Bandura, A. (1977b). Self-efficacy: Towards a unifying theory of behavioral change. *Psychological Review, 84*, 191–215.

Bandura, A. (1978). Reflections on self-efficacy. *Advances in Behaviour Research and Therapy, 1*, 237–269.

Bandura, A. (1982a). Self-efficacy mechanisms in human agency. *American Psychologist, 37,* 122–147.

Bandura, A. (1982b). The psychology of chance encounters and life paths. *American Psychologist, 37,* 747–755.

Bandura, A. (1983). *Social foundations of human thought and action.* Unpublished manuscript, Stanford University, Stanford, CA.

Bandura, A., & Cervone, D. (1983). Self-evaluative and self-efficacy mechanisms governing the motivational effects of goal systems. *Journal of Personality and Social Psychology, 45,* 1017–1028.

Bandura, A., Reese, L., & Adams, N. E. (1982). Microanalysis of action and fear arousal as a function of differential levels of perceived self-efficacy. *Journal of Personality and Social Psychology, 43,* 5–21.

Benson, H. (1975). *The relaxation response.* New York: William Morrow.

Besedovsky, H. O., Del Rey, A., Sorkin, E., Da Prada, M., & Keller, H. H. (1979). Immunoregulation mediated by the sympathetic nervous system. *Cellular Immunology, 48,* 346–355.

Besedovsky, H. O., Sorkin, E. (1977). Network of immune–endocrine interactions. *Clinical and Experimental Immunology, 27,* 1–12.

Brown, G. W. (1979). The social etiology of depression—London studies. In R. A. Depue (Ed.), *The psychobiology of the depressive disorders: Implications for the effects of stress* (pp. 263–289). New York: Academic Press.

Charry, J. M., & Hawkinshire, F. B. W. (1981). Effects of atmospheric electricity on some substrates of disordered social behavior. *Journal of Personality and Social Psychology, 41,* 185–197.

Clark, D. M., & Teasdale, J. D. (1982). Diurnal variation in clinical depression and accessibility of memories of positive and negative experiences. *Journal of Abnormal Psychology, 91,* 87–95.

Davis, G. C., Buchsbaum, M. S., & Bunney, W. E., Jr. (1980). Alterations of evoked potentials link research in attention dysfunction to peptide response symptoms of schizophrenia. In E. Costa & M. Trabucchi (Eds.), *Neural peptides and neuronal communication* (pp. 473–487). New York: Raven Press.

Depue, R. A. (Ed.). (1979). *The psychobiology of the depressive disorders: Implications for the effects of stress.* New York: Academic Press.

Depue, R. A., Slater, J. F., Wolfsetter-Kausch, H., Klein, D., Goplerud, E., & Farr, D. (1981). A behavioral paradigm for identifying persons at risk for bipolar depressive disorder: A conceptual framework and five validation studies. *Journal of Abnormal Psychology* (Monograph), *90, 381–437.*

Eysenck, H. J., & Eysenck, S. B. (1975). *Manual: Eysenck Personality Questionnaire.* San Diego, CA: Educational and Industrial Testing Service.

Falcone, A. M., & Rosenthal, T. L. (1982). *Delivery of rural mental health services.* Cleveland, OH: Synapse, Inc.

Friedman, A. S. (1975). Interaction of drug therapy with marital therapy in depressive patients. *Archives of General Psychiatry, 32,* 619–637.

Gelfand, D. M., & Hartmann, D. P. (1982). Response consequences and attributions: Two contributors to prosocial behavior. In N. Eisenberg-Berg (Ed.), *The development of prosocial behavior* (pp. 167–196). New York: Academic Press.

Goodwin, D. W., Schulsinger, F., Knop, J., Mednick, S., & Guze, S. B. (1977a). Alcoholism and depression in adopted-out daughters of alcoholics. *Archives of General Psychiatry, 34,* 751–755.

Goodwin, D. W., Schulsinger, F., Knop, J., Mednick, S., & Guze, S. B. (1977b). Psychopathology in adopted and nonadopted daughters of alcoholics. *Archives of General Psychiatry, 34,* 1005–1009.

Goodwin, F. K., & Wehr, T. A. (Eds.). (1982). *Circadian rhythms in psychiatry.* Pacific Grove, CA: Boxwood Press.

Gottesman, D., & Lewis, M. S. (1982). Differences in crisis reactions among cancer and surgery patients. *Journal of Consulting and Clinical Psychology, 50*, 381–388.

Hung, J. H. F., Rosenthal, T. L., & Kelley, J. E. (1980). Social comparison models spur immediate assertion: "So you think you're submissive?" *Cognitive Therapy and Research, 4*, 223–234.

Jacobson, E. (1938). *Progressive relaxation.* Chicago: University of Chicago Press.

Jacobson, E. (1964). *Anxiety and tension control.* Philadelphia, PA: Lippincott.

Lichstein, K. L., & Rosenthal, T. L. (1980). Insomniacs' perceptions of cognitive versus somatic determinants of sleep disturbance. *Journal of Abnormal Psychology, 89*, 105–107.

Lyles, J. N., Burish, T. G., Krozely, M G., & Oldham, R. K. (1982). Efficacy of relaxation training and guided imagery in reducing the aversiveness of cancer chemotherapy *Journal of Consulting and Clinical Psychology, 50*, 509–524.

McLean, A. A. (1982). Improving mental health at work. *The Psychiatric Hospital, 13*, 77–83.

Novaco, R. W. (1979). The cognitive regulation of anger and stress. In P. C. Kendall & S. D. Hollon (Eds.). *Cognitive–behavioral interventions: Theory, research, and procedures* (pp. 241–286). New York: Academic Press.

Ornish, D., Scherwitz, L. W., Doody, R. S., Kesten, D., McLanahan, S. M., Brown, S. E., De Puey, E. G., Sonnemaker, R., Haynes, C., Lester, J., McAllister, G. K., Hall, R. J., Burdine, J. A., & Grotto, A. M. (1983). Effects of stress management training and dietary changes in treating ischemic heart disease. *Journal of the American Medical Association, 249*, 54–59.

Paret, P. (1976). *Clausewitz and the state.* New York: Oxford University Press.

Paykel, E. S. (1979). Recent life events in the development of the depressive disorders. In R. A.Depue (Ed.), *The psychobiology of the depressive disorders: Implications for the effects of stress* (pp. 245–262). New York: Academic Press.

Preskorn, S. H., Irwin, G. H., Simpson, S., Friesen, D., Rinne, J., & Jerkovich, G., (1981). Medical therapies for mood disorders alter the blood–brain barrier. *Science, 213*, 469–471.

Propost, L. R. (1980). The comparative efficacy of religious and non-religious imagery for the treatment of mild depression in religious individuals. *Cognitive Therapy and Research, 40*, 167–178.

Riley, V. (1981). Psychoneuroendocrine influences on immunocompetence and neoplasia. *Science, 212*, 1100–1109.

Rosenthal, T. L. (1980). Social cueing processes. In M. Hersen, R. M. Eisler, & P. M. Miller (Eds.)., *Progress in behavior modification* Vol. 10, (pp. 111–146). New York: Academic Press.

Rosenthal, T. L. (1982). Social learning theory. In G. T.Wilson & C. M. Franks (Eds.), *Contemporary behavior therapy: Conceptual and empirical foundations* (pp. 339–363). New York: Guilford Press.

Rosenthal, T. L. (1984a). Cognitive social learning theory. In N. S. Endler & J. McVicker Hunt (Eds.), *Personality and the behavior disorders* (rev. ed., pp. 113–145). New York: Wiley.

Rosenthal, T. L. (1984b). Some organizing hints for communicating applied information. In B. J. Gholson & T. L. Rosenthal (Eds.), *Applications of cognitive–developmental theory* (pp. 149–172). New York: Academic Press.

Rosenthal, T. L., Akisal, H. S., Scott-Strauss, A., Rosenthal, R. H., & David, M. (1981). Familial and developmental factors in characterological depressions. *Journal of Affective Disorders, 3*, 183–192.

Rosenthal, T. L., & Bandura, A. (1978). Psychological modeling: Theory and practice. In S. L. Garfield & A. E. Bergin (Eds.), *Handbook of psychotherapy and behavior change* (2nd ed., pp. 621–658). New York: Wiley.

Rosenthal, T. L., & Davis, A. (1983). *Cognitive aids in teaching and treaching.* Unpublished manuscript, University of Tennessee College of Medicine, Memphis.

Rosenthal, T. L., & Rosenthal, R.H. (1983). Stress: Causes, measurement, and management. In K. Craig & R. J. McMahon (Eds.), *Advances in clinical behavior therapy* (pp. 3–26). New York: Brunner/Mazel.

Rosenthal, T. L., & Zimmerman, B. J. (1978). *Social learning and cognition.* New York: Academic Press.

Roth, D., Bielski, R., Jones, M., Parker, W., & Osborn, G. (1982). A comparison of self-control therapy and combined self-control therapy and antidepressant medication in the treatment of depression. *Behavior Therapy, 13,* 133–144.

Sagan, C. (1978). *Broca's brain.* New York: Random House.

Selye, H. (1950). *Stress—the physiology and pathology of exposure to systemic stress.* Montreal: Acta Inc.

Selye, H. (1951). *First annual report on stress.* Montreal: Acta Inc.

Selye, H. (1956). *The stress of life.* New York: McGraw-Hill.

Shaw, E. R., & Blanchard, E. B. (1983). The effects of instructional set on the outcome of a stress management program. *Biofeedback and Self-Regulation, 8,* 555–565.

Turk, D. C., & Genest, M. (1979). Regulation of pain: The application of cognitive and behavioral techniques for prevention and remediation. In P. C. Kendall & S. D. Hollon (Eds.), *Cognitive-behavioral interventions: Theory, research, and procedures* (pp. 287–318). New York: Academic Press.

Turk, D. C., Meichenbaum, D., & Genest, M. (1983). *Pain and behavioral medicine: A cognitive-behavioral perspective.* New York: Guilford.

Wegner, D. M., & Giuliano, T. (1980). Arousal-induced attention to self. *Journal of Personality and Social Psychology, 38,* 719–725.

Wehr, T. A., Wirz-Justice, A., Goodwin, F. K., Duncan, W., & Gillin, J. C. (1979). Phase advance of the circadian sleep–wake cycle as an antidepressant. *Science, 206,* 710–713.

Weissman, M. M. (1978). Psychotherapy and its relevance to the pharmacotherapy of affective disorders. From ideology to evidence. In M. A. Lipton, A. Di Mascio, & K. F. Killam (Eds.), *Psychopharmacology—a generation of progress* (pp. 1313–1321). New York: Raven.

Weissman, M. M., Prusoff, B. A., Di Mascio, A., Neu, C., Goklaney, M., & Klerman, G. L. (1979). The efficacy of drugs and psychotherapy in the treatment of acute depressive episodes. *American Journal of Psychiatry, 136,* 555–558.

Zimmerman, B. J. (1983). Social learning theory: A contextualist account. In C. J. Brainerd (Ed.), *Recent advances in cognitive-developmental theory* (pp. 1–46). New York: Springer.

4

DEPRESSION

AARON T. BECK AND JEFFREY E. YOUNG

One of the most important developments in psychosocial approaches to emotional problems has been the success of cognitive therapy for depression. It is now well known that this approach is as good or better than other approaches such as drugs for treating depression, and this chapter presents a very detailed version of the latest rendition of cognitive therapy.

Employing a variety of well-specified cognitive and behavioral techniques, cognitive therapy is also distinguished by the detailed structure of each session with its specific agendas and the very deliberate and obviously effective therapeutic style of interacting with the patient through a series of questions. Finally, the authors underscore very clearly the importance of the collaborative relationship between the therapist and patient, and outline specific techniques to achieve that collaborative state so that the patient and therapist become an investigative team. Many of these concepts and procedures should be very useful to clinicians treating any number of problems in addition to depression.—D. H. B.

OVERVIEW

Depression is the most common presenting problem encountered by mental health professionals. A variety of approaches have been applied to the treatment of depression, and most recently there has been an increasing emphasis on short-term psychotherapies for depression (Rush, 1982). Short-term approaches that have received the greatest attention in outcome research include behavior therapy, interpersonal psychotherapy, brief psychodynamic therapy, and cognitive therapy (Bergin & Lambert, 1978).

Despite the tremendous advances in psychotherapy for depression, pharmacotherapy remains the standard against which other treatments are compared. Recent research suggests that cognitive-behavior therapy is at least as effective as tricyclic antidepressants in the treatment of nonbipolar, depressed outpatients (Rush, Beck, Kovacs, & Hollon, 1977; Beck, Rush, Shaw, & Emery, 1979; Blackburn & Bishop, 1979, 1980; McLean & Hakstian, 1979). The efficacy of the cognitive–behavioral approach with depression is especially striking in light of a number of studies in the past showing that traditional psychotherapies

Aaron T. Beck. Center for Cognitive Therapy, Department of Psychiatry, University of Pennsylvania, Philadelphia, Pennsylvania.

Jeffrey E. Young. Department of Psychiatry, College of Physicians and Surgeons, Columbia University, New York, New York.

are only slightly more effective than pill placebos in reducing depressive symptomatology (Hollon & Beck, 1978).

COGNITIVE MODEL OF DEPRESSION

The cognitive model assumes that cognition, behavior, and biochemistry are all important components of depressive disorders. We do not view them as competing theories of depression, but rather as different levels of analysis. Each treatment approach has its own "focus of convenience." The pharmacotherapist intervenes at the biochemical level; the cognitive therapist intervenes at both the cognitive and behavioral levels. Our experience suggests that when we change depressive cognitions, we simultaneously change the characteristic mood, behavior, and (we presume) biochemistry of depression.

Our focus in this chapter will be on the cognitive disturbances in depression. According to this theory, negatively biased cognition is a core process in depression. This process is reflected in the "cognitive triad of depression": depressed patients typically have a negative view of themselves, of their environment, and of the future. They view themselves as worthless, inadequate, unlovable, and deficient. Depressed patients view the environment as overwhelming, as presenting insuperable obstacles that cannot be overcome, and as continually resulting in failure or loss. Moreover, they view the future as hopeless; they believe their own efforts will be insufficient to change the unsatisfying course of their lives. This negative view of the future often leads to suicidal ideation and actual attempts.

Depressed patients consistently distort their interpretations of events so that they maintain negative views of themselves, the environment, and the future. These distortions represent deviations from the logical processes of thinking used typically by people. For example, a depressed woman whose husband comes home late one night may conclude that he is having an affair with another woman, even though there is no other evidence supporting this conclusion. This example illustrates an "arbitrary inference"—the patient has reached a conclusion that is not justified by the available evidence. Other distortions include all-or-nothing thinking, overgeneralization, selective abstraction, and magnification (Beck et al., 1979).

According to the cognitive model, an important predisposing factor for many patients with depression is the presence of early negative schemas. The child learns to construct reality through his or her early experiences with the environment, especially with significant others. Sometimes these early experiences lead children to accept attitudes and beliefs that will later prove maladaptive. For example, a child may develop the schema that no matter what he or she does, his or her performance will never be good enough. These schemas are usually out of awareness, and may remain dormant until a life event (such as being fired from a job) stimulates the schema. Once the schema is activated, the patient categorizes, selects, and encodes information in such a way that the failure schema is maintained. Negative schemas, therefore, predispose depressed patients to distort events in a characteristic fashion, leading to a negative view of themselves, the environment, and the future.

The focus of cognitive therapy is on changing depressive thinking. These changes may be brought about in a variety of ways: through behavioral experiments, logical discourse, examination of evidence, problem solving, role playing, and imagery restructuring, to name just a few. The remainder of this chapter will elaborate on these techniques and their application in clinical practice.

CHARACTERISTICS OF THERAPY

Cognitive therapy with adult depressed outpatients is usually undertaken in the therapist's office. It has most frequently been applied in a one-to-one setting, with just the patient and therapist. Group cognitive therapy has been successful with many depressed outpatients, although we have not yet had enough experience in group settings to know with which patients groups will prove desirable. It is not unusual to involve spouses, parents, and other family members in the course of treatment. They might be used, for example, to provide information that will help patients test the validity of their thinking regarding how others in the family view them. Moreover, "couples therapy" based on the cognitive model is often very effective in relieving depression related to chronic interpersonal problems.

In our clinical experience, a number of therapist characteristics contribute to effective cognitive therapy. First, cognitive therapists should ideally demonstrate the "nonspecific" therapy skills identified by other writers (e.g., Truax & Mitchell, 1971). They should be able to communicate warmth, genuineness, sincerity, and openness. Second, the most effective cognitive therapists seem to be especially skilled at seeing events through the patient's perspective (accurate empathy). They are able to suspend their own personal assumptions and biases while they are listening to depressed patients describe their reactions and interpretations. Third, skilled cognitive therapists can reason logically and plan strategies. They are not "fuzzy" thinkers. In this respect they resemble good trial lawyers, who can spot the sometimes subtle flaws in another individual's reasoning, and skillfully elicit a more convincing interpretation of the same events. Cognitive therapists plan strategies several steps ahead, anticipating the desired outcome. Fourth, the best practitioners of this approach are active. They have to be comfortable taking the lead, providing structure and direction to the therapy process.

We do not yet know which patient characteristics are related to success in cognitive therapy. Our experience suggests that several subtypes of depressives seem less amenable to short-term cognitive therapy. These include patients with hallucinations or delusions; schizoaffective disorders; impaired memory functioning (e.g., organic brain syndromes); borderline personality structures; and severe endogenous depressions. With these patients, cognitive therapy may be helpful over a longer period of time, often in combination with pharmacotherapy, milieu treatment, or extra support from the environment.

Certain patient characteristics are predictive, in our experience, of a more rapid response. Patients who are appropriately introspective; can reason abstractly; are well organized and good planners; are conscientious about carrying out responsibilities; are employed; are not excessively angry, either at themselves or at other people; are less dogmatic and rigid in their thinking; can identify a clear precipitating event for the depressive episode; and have close relationships with others often show faster improvement in depressive symptoms through cognitive therapy.

COLLABORATION

Basic to cognitive therapy is a collaborative relationship between patient and therapist. When the therapist and patient work together, the learning experience is enhanced for both and a cooperative spirit is developed that contributes greatly to the therapeutic process. Equally important, the collaborative approach helps to ensure compatible goals for treatment and to prevent misunderstandings and misinterpretations between patient and therapist. Because of the importance of the collaborative relationship, we place great emphasis on the interpersonal skills of the therapist, the process of joint selection of problems to be worked on, regular feedback, and the investigative process we call collaborative empiricism.

Interpersonal Qualities

Since collaboration requires that the patient trust the therapist, we emphasize those interpersonal qualities that contribute to trust. Warmth, accurate empathy, and genuineness are desirable personal qualities for the cognitive therapist, as for all psychotherapists. It is important that the cognitive therapist not seem to be playing the *role* of therapist. The therapist should be able to communicate, verbally and nonverbally, that he or she is sincere, open, concerned, and direct. It is also important that the therapist not seem to be withholding impressions or information, or evading questions. The therapist should be careful not to seem critical or disapproving of the patient's perspective.

Rapport between patient and therapist is crucial in the treatment of depressed patients. When rapport is optimal, patients perceive the therapist as someone who is tuned in to their feelings and attitudes, is sympathetic and understanding, and is someone with whom they can communicate without having to articulate feelings in detail or qualify statements. When the rapport is good, both patient and therapist feel comfortable and secure.

A confident professional manner is also important in cognitive therapy. Therapists should convey relaxed confidence in their ability to help the depressed patient. Such confidence can help counteract the patient's initial hopelessness about the future. Since the cognitive therapist must sometimes be directive and impose structure, especially in the early stages of treatment, it is helpful to maintain a clear sense of confident professionalism.

Joint Determination of Goals for Therapy

In the collaborative relationship the patient and therapist work together to set therapeutic goals, determine priorities among them, and set an agenda for each session. Problems to be addressed over the course of therapy include specific depressive symptoms (e.g., hopelessness, crying, difficulty concentrating) and external problems (e.g., marital difficulties, career issues, child-rearing concerns). Priorities are then jointly determined in accordance with the amount of distress generated by a particular problem and how amenable to change the particular problem is. During the agenda-setting portion of each therapy session (discussed in detail in the next section), therapist and patient together determine the items to be covered in that session. Through this collaborative process, target problems are selected on a weekly basis.

The process of problem selection often presents difficulties for the new cognitive therapist. These include failure to reach agreement on specific problems to focus on, selection of peripheral concerns, and the tendency to move from problem to problem instead of persistently seeking a satisfactory solution to only one problem at a time. Because the problem selection process entails both structuring and collaboration on the part of the therapist, considerable skill is necessary.

Regular Feedback

Feedback is especially important in therapy with depressed patients; it is a crucial ingredient in developing and maintaining the collaborative therapeutic relationship. The cognitive therapist initiates the feedback component early in therapy by eliciting the patient's thoughts and feelings about many aspects of the therapy, such as the handling of a particular problem, the therapist's manner, and homework assignments. Since many patients misconstrue therapists' statements and questions, it is only through regular feedback that the therapist can ascertain whether he or she and the patient are on the same "wavelength." The therapist must also be alert for verbal and nonverbal clues to convert negative reactions.

As part of the regular feedback process, the cognitive therapist shares the rationale for each intervention mode. This helps to demystify the therapy process and facilitates the patient's questioning the validity of a particular approach. In addition, when the patients understand the connection between a technique or assignment the therapist uses and the solution of a problem, they are more likely to participate conscientiously.

The third element of the feedback process is for the therapist to check regularly to determine whether the patient understands his or her formulations. Patients sometimes agree with a formulation simply out of compliance, and depressed patients frequently exhibit both compliance and reluctance to "talk straight" with the therapist for fear of being rejected, criticized, or of making a mistake. The therapist must therefore make an extra effort to elicit feelings or wishes relevant to compliance (e.g., anxiety about rejection, wish to please) from the patient and must be alert for verbal and nonverbal clues that the patient may not indeed understand the explanations.

As a regular part of the feedback process, at the close of each session the cognitive therapist provides a concise summary of what has taken place and asks the patient to abstract and write down the main points from the session. The patient keeps this summary for review during the week. In practice, the therapist uses capsule summaries at least three times during a standard therapeutic interview: in preparing the agenda, in a midpoint recapitulation of the material covered up to that point, and in the final summary of the main points of the interview. Patients generally respond favorably to the elicitation of feedback and presentation of capsule summaries. We have observed that the development of empathy and rapport is facilitated by these techniques.

Collaborative Empiricism

When the collaborative therapeutic relationship has been successfully formed, the patient and therapist act as an investigative team. Though we elaborate on the investigative process later, it is appropriate to introduce it in the context of the collaborative relationship. As a team, patient and therapist together approach the patient's maladaptive cognitions and underlying assumptions in the manner that scientists approach questions: Each thought or assumption becomes a hypothesis to be tested and evidence is gathered that supports or refutes the hypothesis. Events in the past, circumstances in the present, and possibilities in the future are the data that constitute evidence, and the conclusion to accept or reject the hypothesis is jointly reached by subjecting the evidence to logical analysis. Experiments may also be devised to test the validity of particular cognitions. The cognitive therapist need not persuade patients of illogicality or inconsistency with reality since patients "discover" their own inconsistencies. This guided discovery process is a widely accepted educational method and is one of the vital components of cognitive therapy.

THE PROCESS OF COGNITIVE THERAPY

We will here attempt to convey a sense of how cognitive therapy sessions are structured and a sense of the course of treatment. Detailed discussion of particular techniques follows this section.

The Initial Sessions

A main therapeutic goal of the first interview is to produce some symptom relief. Relief of symptoms serves the patient's needs by reducing suffering and also helps to increase rapport, collaboration, and confidence in the therapeutic process. Symptom relief should be based on more than rapport, sympathy, and implied promise of "cure," however, so the cognitive therapist seeks to provide a rational basis for reassurance by attempting to define a set of problems and demonstrating some strategies for dealing with them.

Problem definition continues to be a goal in the early stages of therapy. The therapist works with the patient to define specific problems to focus on during therapy sessions. The cognitive therapist does this by obtaining as complete a picture as possible of the patient's psychological and life situation difficulties. The therapist also seeks details concerning the depth of depression and particular symptomatology. Cognitive therapists are especially concerned with how the patients see their problems.

Once the specific problems have been defined, the patient and the therapist establish priorities among them. Decisions are made on the basis of amenability to therapeutic change and centrality of the life problem or cognition to the patient's emotional distress. In order to help establish priorities effectively, the therapist must see the relationships among particular thoughts, particular life situations, and particular distressing emotions.

Another goal of the initial session is to illustrate the close relationship between cognition and emotion. When the therapist is able to observe the patient's mood change (e.g., crying), he or she points out the alteration in affect and asks for the patient's thoughts just before the mood shift. The therapist then labels the negative thought and points out its relationship to the change in mood. The therapist initially gears homework assignments toward helping the patient see the intimate connection between cognition and emotion.

A frequent requirement in the early stage of therapy is to socialize the patient to cognitive therapy. Particularly if they have previously undertaken analytically oriented or Rogerian therapies, many patients begin cognitive therapy expecting a more insight-oriented, nondirective therapeutic approach. The cognitive therapist can facilitate the transition to a more active and structured one by maintaining a problem-oriented stance, which often entails gently interrupting patients who tend to speculate about the sources of their problems and seek interpretations from the therapist.

Finally, the therapist must communicate the importance of self-help homework assignments during the initial session. Therapists can do this by stressing that doing the homework is actually more important than the therapy session itself. The therapist can also provide incentive by explaining that patients who complete assignments generally improve more quickly. The nature and implementation of self-help homework assignments are considered in further detail in a later section of this chapter.

The Progress of a Typical Therapy Session

Each session begins with the establishment of an agenda for the session. This insures optimal use of time in a relatively short-term, problem-solving therapeutic approach. The agenda generally begins with a short synopsis of the patient's experiences since the last session, including discussion of the homework assignment. The therapist then asks the patient what he or she wants to work on during the session and often offers topics to be included.

When a short list of problems and topics has been completed, the patient and therapist determine the order in which to cover them and, if necessary, the time to be allotted to each topic. There are several issues to be considered in establishing priorities, including stage of therapy, severity of depression, likelihood of making progress in solving the problem, and potential pervasiveness of effect of a particular theme or topic. The cognitive therapist is sensitive to patients' occasional desires to talk about something that seems important to them at the moment, even if such discussion seems not to be productive in terms of other goals. This kind of flexibility characterizes the collaborative therapeutic relationship.

After these preliminary matters have been covered, the patient and therapist move on to the one or two problems to be considered during the session. The therapist begins the discussion of a problem by asking the patient a series of questions designed to clarify the nature of the patient's difficulty. In doing so, the therapist seeks to determine whether maladaptive assumptions, misinterpretations of events, or unrealistic expectations are involved. The therapist also seeks to discover whether the patient had unrealistic expectations, whether the patient's behavior was appropriate and whether all possible solutions to the problem were considered. The patient's responses will suggest to the therapist a cognitive–behavioral conceptualization of why the patient is having difficulty in the area concerned. The therapist will now have discerned the one or two significant thoughts, assumptions, images, or behaviors to be worked on. When this target problem has been selected, the therapist chooses the cognitive or behavioral techniques to apply and shares their rationale with the patient. The specific techniques used in cognitive therapy are explained in the following sections of this chapter.

At the close of the session, the therapist asks the patient for a summary, often in writing, of the major conclusions drawn during the session. The therapist asks for the patient's reactions to the session in order to ascertain whether anything disturbing was said and in order to forestall any delayed negative reactions following the interview. Finally, the therapist gives a homework assignment designed to assist the patient in applying the particular skills and concepts from the session to the problem during the following week.

Middle and Later Sessions

While the structure of cognitive therapy sessions does not change during the course of treatment, the content often changes significantly. Early sessions are aimed to overcoming hopelessness, identifying problems, setting priorities, socializing the patient to cognitive therapy, establishing the collaborative relationship, demonstrating the relationship between cognition and emotion, labeling errors in thinking, and making rapid progress on a target problem. Therapy is initially centered on the patient's symptoms, with attention given to behavioral and motivational difficulties. Once the patient shows some significant changes in these areas, the emphasis shifts to the content and pattern of the patient's thinking. In the later sessions, the therapist and patient discuss the basic assumptions seen to result in vulnerability to depression.

In contrast to the initial sessions, middle and later sessions center on problems that demand greater probing to understand and change. More specifically, in an early session the therapist might use behavioral techniques to encourage the patient to become more active; in a later session he or she might work with the automatic thought "I'll never be able to advance in my career" or "No one can ever love me." In general, middle sessions focus on more complex problems that often involve several dysfunctional thoughts and behaviors. The therapist works to help the patient integrate concepts learned in earlier sessions. The homework assignments that are given require continual repetition and the application of specific rational responses to dysfunctional thoughts.

In the later sessions, when the patient is feeling less depressed, the therapist and patient turn from specific thoughts about particular problems to more general assumptions about self and life. Such "silent" assumptions as "Unless I perform perfectly I am a failure" and "You never get what you want in life" often underlie many of the patient's problems. These maladaptive assumptions are the rules and formulas by which developing individuals learned to "make sense" of the world, and the assumptions continue to determine how they organized perceptions into cognitions, set goals, evaluated and modified behavior, and understood events in their lives. Cognitive therapy aims at counteracting the effects of maladaptive assumptions and replacing learned techniques and methods with new approaches. If the maladaptive assumptions themselves can be changed, the patient will become less vulnerable to future depressions.

In the later sessions, the patient assumes increased responsibility for identifying problems, coming up with solutions, and implementing the solutions through homework assignments. The therapist increasingly assumes the role of advisor or consultant as the patient learns to implement therapeutic techniques without constant support. As the patient becomes a more effective problem solver, the frequency of sessions is reduced, and therapy is eventually discontinued.

COGNITIVE TECHNIQUES

The specific cognitive techniques provide points of entry into the patient's cognitive organization. The cognitive therapist uses techniques for eliciting automatic thoughts, testing automatic thoughts, identifying maladaptive assumptions, and analyzing the validity of maladaptive assumptions to help both therapist and patient understand the patient's construction of reality. In applying specific cognitive techniques in therapy, it is important that the therapist work within the framework of the cognitive model of depression. Each set of techniques will be discussed in turn.

Eliciting Automatic Thoughts

Automatic thoughts are those thoughts that intervene between outside events and the individual's emotional reactions to them. They often go unnoticed because they are part of a repetitive pattern of thinking and because they occur so often and so quickly. We rarely stop to assess their validity because they are so believable, familiar, and habitual. The patient in cognitive therapy must learn to recognize these automatic thoughts for therapy to proceed effectively. The cognitive therapist and the patient make a joint effort to discover the particular thoughts that precede such emotions as anger, sadness, and anxiety. Therapists use questioning, imagery, and role playing to elicit automatic thoughts.

The simplest method to uncover automatic thoughts is for the therapist to ask patients what thoughts went through their minds in response to particular events. This questioning provides patients with a model for introspective exploration that they can use on their own when the therapist is not present and after the completion of treatment.

Alternatively, when the patient is able to identify those external events and situations that evoke a particular emotional response, the therapist may use imagery by asking the patient to picture the situation in detail. The patient is often able to identify the automatic thoughts connected with actual situations when the image evoked is clear. In this technique, the therapist asks patients to relax, close their eyes, and imagine themselves in the distressing situation. Patients describe in detail what is happening as they relive the event.

If the distressing event is an interpersonal one, cognitive therapists can utilize role playing. The therapist plays the role of the other person in the encounter, while patients play themselves. The automatic thoughts can usually be elicited when patients become sufficiently engaged in the role play.

In attempting to elicit automatic thoughts, the therapist is careful to notice and point out any mood changes that occur during the session and to ask the patient's thoughts just before the shift in mood. Mood changes include any emotional reaction, such as tears or anger. This technique can be especially useful when the patient is first learning to identify automatic thoughts.

Once patients become more familiar with the techniques for identifying automatic thoughts, they are asked to keep a Daily Record of Dysfunctional Thoughts (Beck *et al.*, 1979; see Figure 4-1), in which they record the emotions and automatic thoughts that occur in upsetting situations between therapy sessions. In later sessions they are taught to develop rational responses to their dysfunctional automatic thoughts and to record them in the appropriate column. The therapist and patient generally review the Daily Record from the preceding week near the beginning of the next therapy session.

Eliciting automatic thoughts should be distinguished from the interpretation process of other psychotherapies. In general, the cognitive therapist works only with those automatic thoughts mentioned by patients. Suggesting thoughts to patients may undermine collaboration and might inhibit patients from learning to continue the process on their own. As a last resort, however, when

DATE	SITUATION Describe: 1. Actual event leading to unpleasant emotion, or 2. Stream of thoughts, daydream, or recollection, leading to unpleasant emotion.	EMOTION(S) 1. Specify sad/ anxious/ angry, etc. 2. Rate degree of emotion, 1–100.	AUTOMATIC THOUGHT(S) 1. Write automatic thought(s) that preceded emotion(s). 2. Rate belief in automatic thought(s), 0–100%.	RATIONAL RESPONSE 1. Write rational response to automatic thought(s). 2. Rate belief in rational response, 0–100%.	OUTCOME 1. Rerate belief in automatic thought(s), 0–100%. 2. Specify and rate subsequent emotions, 0–100.

Explanation: When you experience an unpleasant emotion, note the situation that seemed to stimulate the emotion. (If the emotion occurred while you were thinking, daydreaming, etc., please note this.) Then note the automatic thought associated with the emotion. Record the degree to which you believe this thought: 0% = not at all; 100% = completely. In rating degree of emotion: 1 = a trace; 100 = the most intense possible.

FIGURE 4-1. Daily Record of Dysfunctional Thoughts.

nondirective strategies fail, the cognitive therapist may offer several possible automatic thoughts, asking the patient whether any of the choices fit.

Even when many efforts to elicit automatic thoughts have been made by the therapist, sometimes the thought remains unavailable. When this is the case, the cognitive therapist tries to ascertain the particular meaning of the event that evoked the emotional reaction. For example, one patient began to cry whenever she had an argument with her roommate and friend. Efforts to elicit automatic thoughts proved unsuccessful. Only after the therapist asked a series of questions to determine the meaning of the event did it become clear that the patient connected having an argument or fight with the end of a relationship. Through this process, the therapist and patient were able to see the meaning that triggered the crying.

Testing Automatic Thoughts

When the therapist and patient have managed to isolate a key automatic thought, they approach the thought as a testable hypothesis. This "scientific" approach is fundamental to cognitive therapy, in which the patient learns to think in a way that resembles the investigative process. Through the procedures of gathering data, evaluating evidence, and drawing conclusions, the patient learns firsthand that one's view of reality can be quite different from what actually takes place. By designing experiments that subject their automatic thoughts to objective analysis, patients learn how to modify their thinking because they learn the *process* of rational thinking. Patients who learn to think this way during treatment will be better able to continue the empirical approach after the end of formal therapy.

The cognitive therapist approaches the testing of automatic thoughts by asking patients to list evidence from their experience for and against the hypothesis. Sometimes, after considering the evidence, patients will immediately reject the automatic thought, recognizing that it is either distorted or actually false.

When previous experience is not sufficient or appropriate to test a hypothesis, the therapist asks the patient to design an experiment for that purpose. The patient then makes a prediction and proceeds to gather data. When the data contradict the prediction, the patient can reject the automatic thought. The outcome of the experiment may, of course, confirm the patient's prediction. It is therefore very important that the therapist not assume the patient's automatic thought is distorted.

There are some automatic thoughts that do not lend themselves to hypothesis testing through the examination of evidence. In these cases, there are two options available: therapists may produce evidence from their own experience and offer it in the form of a question that reveals the contradiction; or the therapist can ask a question designed to uncover a logical error inherent in the patient's beliefs. The therapist might say, for example, to a patient who is sure he cannot survive without a close personal relationship, "You were alone last year and you got along fine, what makes you think you can't make it now?"

In testing automatic thoughts, it is sometimes necessary to refine the patient's use of a word. This is particularly true for global labels such as "bad," "stupid," or "selfish." What is needed in this case is an operational definition of the word. To illustrate, a patient at our clinic had the recurring automatic thought, "I'm a failure in math." The therapist and patient had to narrow down the meaning of the word before they could test the thought. They operationalized "failure" in math as being unable to achieve a grade of "C" after investing as much time studying as the average class member. Now they could examine past evidence and test the validity of the hypothesis. This process can help patients to see the all-inclusiveness of their negative self-assessments and the idiosyncratic nature of many automatic thoughts.

Reattribution is another useful technique for helping the patient to reject an inappropriate self-blaming thought. It is a common cognitive pattern in depression to ascribe blame or responsibility for adverse events to oneself. Reattribution can be used when the patient unrealistically attributes adverse occurrences to a personal deficiency such as lack of ability or effort. The therapist and patient review the relevant events and apply logic to the available information to make a more realistic assignment of responsibility. The aim of reattribution is not to absolve the patient of all responsibility, but to examine the many factors that help contribute to adverse events. Through this process, patients gain objectivity, relieve themselves of the burden of self-reproach, and can then search for ways to solve realistic problems or prevent a recurrence. Another strategy involving reattribution is for the therapist to demonstrate to patients that they use stricter criteria for assigning responsibility to their own unsatisfactory behavior than they use in evaluating the behavior of others. Cognitive therapists also use reattribution to show patients that some of their thinking or behavior problems can be symptoms of depression (e.g., loss of concentration) and not signs of physical decay.

When the patient is accurate in identifying a realistic life problem or skill deficit, the cognitive therapist can use the technique of generating alternatives, in which therapist and patient actively search for alternative solutions. Because the depressed person's reasoning often becomes restricted, an effort to reconceptualize the problem can result in the patient's seeing a viable solution that may previously have been rejected.

It should be noted that the cognitive techniques outlined above all entail the use of questions by the therapist. A common error we observe in new cognitive therapists is an exhortative style. We have found that therapists help patients to change their thinking more effectively by using carefully formed questions. If patients are prompted to work their own way through problems and reach their own conclusions, they will learn an effective problem-solving process. We will elaborate on the use of questioning in cognitive therapy later in the chapter.

Identifying Maladaptive Assumptions

Maladaptive assumptions are the themes connecting the automatic thoughts of patients across situations and over time. They govern, for example, what patients consider right or wrong in judging themselves and others. The therapist can discern these patterns only through careful observation; although some themes can be found in the beliefs of many depressed patients, each individual patient has a unique set of personal rules. Time and effort are required to uncover and modify the specific maladaptive assumptions of a particular patient.

While it is usually fairly easy for most patients to learn to identify their automatic thoughts, it is more difficult for them to identify the underlying assumptions. These assumptions are much less accessible. Some typical unarticulated assumptions include, "In order to be happy, I must be wealthy" and "If I don't have a husband, I'm nobody." While everyone has underlying rules, maladaptive assumptions differ from adaptive ones in being rigid and excessive. They are framed in absolute terms, are unrealistic, and are used too frequently and inappropriately.

Maladaptive assumptions are especially problematic when individual patients have to cope with events that expose their unique vulnerabilities, such as acceptance and rejection, health and sickness, or gain and loss. For example, a patient who held the belief that he had to be perfect placed a high value on career performance. He assessed his own worth on the basis of how well he could accomplish work tasks and how many goals he could achieve. When he was laid off from his job, he believed that he no longer had any value as a person and became severely depressed. In order to identify maladaptive assumptions, cognitive therapists listen for themes that radiate through different situations or problem areas.

When the therapist believes he or she has identified a particular maladaptive assumption, he or she can make a list of several related automatic thoughts that the patient has already expressed and ask the patient to abstract the general rule that underlies the thoughts. If the patient cannot do this, the therapist uses a technique similar to the questioning used in the testing of automatic thoughts: The therapist appeals to the patient's logic by suggesting a plausible assumption, listing the thoughts that follow from it, and asking the patient if the assumption seems to fit. During the questioning process, the therapist is careful not to influence the patient's response. The therapist should be open to the possibility that his or her plausible assumption is not necessarily correct and be ready to join the patient in an effort to find a more accurate statement. Again, it is precisely this kind of flexibility that characterizes optimal collaboration between therapist and patient in cognitive therapy.

A priority in the later stages of cognitive therapy is to help patients identify and challenge those particular maladaptive assumptions that contribute to their vulnerability to depression. For both practical and therapeutic reasons, the patient must be actively involved in this process. In order to emphasize the importance of altering maladaptive assumptions, the therapist can tell the patient that even though depressive symptoms have abated, vulnerability to depression often remains unless these beliefs are identified and changed.

Analyzing the Validity of Maladaptive Assumptions

Identifying a maladaptive assumption is the first major step toward changing it. Sometimes patients see its absurdity or maladaptiveness immediately once the thought is verbalized and thus no longer hidden. The process of identification itself may be helpful, since many assumptions have never been tested or questioned by patients.

Questioning the patient is generally the most effective approach to modify maladaptive underlying assumptions. While the therapist could offer numerous counterarguments, patients do not seem to change their beliefs based on the number of counterarguments, but because a particular argument makes sense to them. One or two new ways of looking at a situation are often instrumental in changing long-held beliefs.

One approach to modification, once an assumption has been uncovered, is for the therapist to ask the patient if the assumption seems reasonable. If the patient does not see the problems inherent in the assumption, the therapist asks questions designed to reveal them. For example, if a patient believes he or she should put effort into everything, the therapist can disclose, through a series of questions, the problem of putting effort into relaxation.

An effective alternative approach to questioning the logic and consequences of a maladaptive assumption is to have the patient gather evidence against the assumption, either alone or in collaboration with the therapist. The cognitive therapist is careful not to argue with the patient; instead, the therapist seeks to guide and collaborate with the patient in the process of developing evidence. Challenges to the patient's assumptions should be offered in the form of questions and suggestions of alternative assumptions, not in the form of a lecture or argument. When possible, the therapist should work to support the patient's adaptive beliefs since adaptive beliefs can sometimes be effectively used to counter maladaptive ones.

Therapists can also help patients question their assumptions by working with them to make a list of the advantages and disadvantages of modifying the assumption. When the list has been completed, the therapist and patient can discuss the consequences of altering the assumption or weigh the long-term and short-term advantages and disadvantages of particular maladaptive assumptions.

Finally, the behavioral strategy known as "response prevention" can sometimes be used effectively to help patients move beyond their assumptions about what they should ideally do in a given context. Once the rule has been disclosed, an experiment is designed to test what would happen if the patient acted contrary to the "should." The patient predicts the result, carries out the experiment, and discusses the results with the therapist. It is often helpful to subdivide the experiment into discrete graded tasks so the patient can try less threatening changes before more difficult ones.

BEHAVIORAL TECHNIQUES

Behavioral techniques are used throughout the course of cognitive therapy but are generally concentrated in the earlier stages of treatment. Behavioral techniques are especially necessary for those more severely depressed patients who are passive, anhedonic, socially withdrawn, and unable to concentrate for extended periods of time. By engaging the patient's attention and interest, the cognitive therapist tries to induce the patient to counteract withdrawal and become more involved in constructive activity.

The therapist selects from a variety of behavioral techniques those which will help the patient cope more effectively with situational and interpersonal problems. Through homework assignments, patients implement specific procedures for dealing with concrete situations or for using time more adaptively.

The cognitive therapist uses behavioral techniques with the goal of modifying automatic thoughts. For example, a patient who believes "I can't stay with anything anymore" can modify this thought after completing a series of graded tasks designed to increase mastery. The severely depressed patient is caught in a vicious cycle in which a reduced activity level leads to negative self-label which, in turn, results in even further discouragement and consequent inactivity. Intervention with behavioral techniques can enter and change this self-destructive pattern.

The most commonly used behavioral techniques include scheduling activities that include both mastery and pleasure exercises, cognitive rehearsal, self-reliance training, role playing, and diversion techniques. The scheduling of activities is frequently used in the early stages of cognitive therapy to counteract loss of motivation, hopelessness, and excessive rumination. The therapist uses an activity schedule for planning activities hour-by-hour, day-by-day (see Figure 4-2). Patients maintain an hourly record of the activities that they engaged in. Activity scheduling also helps patients obtain more pleasure and a greater sense of accomplishment from activities on a daily basis. The patients rate each completed activity (using a 0–10 scale) for both mastery and pleasure. The ratings usually contradict patients' beliefs that they cannot accomplish or enjoy anything anymore. In order to assist some patients in initiating mastery and pleasure activities, the therapist sometimes finds it necessary to subdivide an activity into segments ranging from the simplest to the most difficult and complex aspects of the activity. We call this the "graded task" approach. The subdivision enables depressed patients to undertake tasks that were initially impossible and thus provides proof of success.

Cognitive rehearsal entails asking the patient to picture or imagine each step involved in the accomplishment of a particular task. This technique can be

Note. Grade activities *M* for mastery and *P* for pleasure 0–10.

		Mon.	Tues.	Wed.	Thurs.	Fri.	Sat.	Sun.
Morning	6–7							
	7–8							
	8–9							
	9–10							
	10–11							
	11–12							
Afternoon	12–1							
	1–2							
	2–3							
	3–4							
	4–5							
	5–6							
	6–7							
	7–8							
	8–9							
Evening	9–10							
	10–11							
	11–12							
	12–6							

Remarks:

FIGURE 4-2. Weekly Activity Schedule.

especially helpful with those patients who have difficulty carrying out a task that requires successive steps for its completion. Sometimes impairment in the ability to concentrate creates difficulties for the patient in focusing attention on the specific task. The imagery evoked by the cognitive rehearsal technique helps the patient to focus and helps the therapist to identify obstacles that make the assignment difficult for the particular patient.

Some depressed patients rely on others to take care of most of their daily needs. With self-reliance training, patients learn to assume increased responsibility for routine activities such as showering, making their beds, cleaning the house, cooking their own meals, and shopping. Self-reliance involves gathering increased control over emotional reactions.

Role playing has many uses in cognitive therapy. It may be used to bring out automatic thoughts through the enactment of particular interpersonal situations, such as an encounter with a supervisor at work. Role playing may also be used, through homework assignments, to guide the patient in practicing and attending to new cognitive responses in problematic social encounters. A third use of role playing is to rehearse new behaviors. Thus, role playing may be used as part of assertiveness training and is often accompanied by modeling and coaching.

Role reversal, a variation of role playing, can be very effective in helping patients test how other people might view their behavior. This is well illustrated by a patient who had a "humiliating experience" while buying some clothes in a store. After playing the role of the clerk, the patient had to conclude that she had insufficient data for her previous conclusion that she appeared clumsy and inept. Through role reversal, patients begin to view themselves less harshly as "self-sympathy" responses are elicited.

Finally, the therapist may introduce various diversion techniques to assist the patient in learning to reduce the intensity of painful affects. The patient learns to divert negative thinking through physical activity, social contact, work, play, and visual imagery. Practice with diversion techniques also helps the patient gain further control over emotional reactivity.

QUESTIONING

As we have stressed throughout this chapter, questioning is a major therapeutic device in cognitive therapy. A majority of the therapist's comments during the therapy session are questions. Single questions can serve several purposes at one time, while carefully designed series of questions can help the patient consider a particular issue, decision or opinion. The cognitive therapist seeks through questioning to elicit what patients are thinking; the therapist tries to avoid telling patients what he or she believes they are thinking.

In the beginning of therapy, questions are employed to obtain a full and detailed picture of the patient's particular difficulties. They are used to obtain background and diagnostic data; to evaluate the patient's stress tolerance, capacity for introspection, coping methods, and so on; to obtain information about the patient's external situation and interpersonal context; and to modify vague complaints by working with the patient to arrive at specific target problems to work on.

As therapy progresses, the therapist uses questioning to explore approaches to problems, to help the patient to weigh advantages and disadvantages of possible solutions, to examine the consequences of staying with particular maladaptive behaviors, to elicit automatic thoughts, and to demonstrate maladaptive underlying assumptions and their consequences. In short, the therapist uses questioning in most cognitive therapeutic techniques.

While questioning is itself a powerful means of identifying and changing automatic thoughts and maladaptive assumptions, it is important that the questions be carefully and skillfully posed. If questions are used to "trap" patients into contradicting themselves, patients may come to feel that they are being attacked by the therapist or manipulated. Too many open-ended questions can leave patients wondering what the therapist expects of them. Therapists must carefully time and phrase questions to help patients recognize their thoughts and assumptions and to weigh issues objectively.

SELF-HELP HOMEWORK ASSIGNMENTS

Rationale

Regular homework assignments are very important in cognitive therapy. When patients systematically apply what they have learned during therapy sessions to their outside lives, they are more likely to make significant progress in therapy and to be able to maintain their gains after termination of treatment. Homework assignments are often the means through which patients gather data, test hypotheses, and thus begin to modify maladaptive assumptions. In addition, the data provided through homework assignments help to shift the focus of therapy from the subjective and abstract to more concrete and objective concerns. When the patient and therapist review the previous week's activities during the agenda-setting portion of the interview, they may do so quickly, and the therapist can draw relationships between what takes place in the session and specific tasks, thereby avoiding tangents and side issues. Homework assignments further the patient's self-reliance and provide methods for the patient to continue working on problems after the end of treatment. Cognitive therapists emphasize the importance of homework by sharing with patients their rationale for assigning homework in therapy. They are also careful to explain the particular benefits to be derived from each individual assignment.

Assigning and Reviewing Homework

The cognitive therapist designs each assignment for the particular patient. The assignment should be directly related to the content of the therapy session so that the patient understands its purpose and importance. Each task should be clearly articulated and very specific in nature. Near the end of each session, the assignment is written in duplicate, with one copy going to the therapist and one to the patient.

Some typical homework assignments include reading a book or article about a specific problem, practicing diversion or relaxation techniques, counting automatic thoughts on a wrist counter, rating activities for pleasure and mastery on the activities schedule, maintaining a Daily Record of Dysfunctional Thoughts, and listening to a tape of the therapy session.

During the therapy session, therapists ask for patients' reactions to homework assignments. They ask, for example, whether the assignment is clear and manageable. In order to determine potential impediments, the therapist may ask the patient to imagine taking the steps involved in the assignment. This technique can be especially helpful during the earlier stages of therapy. The patient assumes greater responsibility for developing homework assignments as therapy progresses through the middle and later stages.

It is essential that the patient and therapist review the previous week's homework during the therapy session itself. If they do not do this, the patient may conclude that the homework assignments are not important. During the first part of the therapy session, the therapist and patient discuss the last week's assignment, and the therapist summarizes the results.

Difficulties in Completing Homework

When patients do not complete their homework assignments, or do them without conviction, cognitive therapists elicit automatic thoughts, assumptions, or behavioral problems that may help both therapist and patient understand where the difficulty resides. The therapist does not assume that the patient is being "resistant" or "passive–aggressive." When the difficulties have been successfully identified, the therapist and patient work collaboratively to surmount them. It is, of course, common for patients to have difficulties in completing homework, and we will consider some of the typical problems and ways to counteract them.

When patients do not understand the assignment completely, the therapist should explain it more fully, specifying his or her expectations in detail. Sometimes using the behavioral technique of cognitive rehearsal (described above) can be helpful in such situations.

Some patients believe that they are naturally disorganized and cannot maintain records and follow through on detailed assignments. The therapist can usually help invalidate such general beliefs by asking patients about other circumstances in which they make lists; for example, when planning a vacation or shopping trip. The therapist can also ask these patients whether they could complete the assignment if there were a substantial reward entailed. This kind of question helps make the patient recognize that self-control is not the problem; rather, the patient does not believe that the reward is great enough. When the patient comes to see that the problem is an attitudinal one, the therapist and patient can proceed to enumerate the advantages of completing the assignment.

More severely depressed patients may need assistance to structure their time so that homework becomes a regular activity. This can generally be accomplished by setting a specific time each day for the homework assignment. If necessary, the patient and therapist can set up a reward or punishment system to make sure that the homework gets done. For example, patients can reward themselves for doing the assignment with a special purchase or punish themselves for not doing it by not watching a favorite television program.

Some patients are afraid of failing the assignments or of doing them inadequately. In these cases, the therapist can explain that self-help assignments cannot be failed: Doing an assignment partially is more helpful than not doing it at all, and mistakes provide valuable information about problems that still need to be worked on. In addition, since performance is not evaluated, patients cannot lose if they view the activity from a more adaptive perspective.

Sometimes patients believe their problems are too deeply embedded and complex to be resolved through homework assignments. The therapist can explain to these patients that even the most complex undertakings begin with and consist of small concrete steps. Some writers, for example, resolve their "writers' blocks" by taking the attitude, "If I can't write a book, I can at least write a paragraph." When enough paragraphs have been written, the result is a book. The therapist and patient can consider the advantages and disadvantages of the patient's believing that problems cannot be solved by doing homework. Or the therapist can ask the patient to experiment before reaching such a conclusion. In those instances where the patient believes that he or she has not made enough progress, and therefore that the homework is not helpful, the therapist can detail the progress the patient has made or can help the patient see that it may take more time before substantial change can be perceived.

When patients seem to resent being given assignments, the therapist can encourage them to develop their own assignments. The therapist might also offer the patient alternative assignments from which to choose, making one of the alternatives noncompliance with homework assignments. If patients choose noncompliance, the therapist can help to examine the consequences of that choice. Still another strategy is to present patients with a consumer model of therapy: Patients have a certain goal (overcoming depression) and the therapist has a means of achievement to offer; patients are free to use or reject the tools, just as they are free to buy or not buy in the marketplace.

When patients believe that improvement can be made just as readily without homework, therapists have two options. They can offer their own clinical experience that most patients who held that opinion were proven wrong and progressed more slowly in therapy. The other option is to set up an experiment for a given period of time, during which patients do not have to complete assignments. At the end of the predetermined period, the therapist and patient can evaluate the patient's progress during that time interval. Once again, it is important that the cognitive therapist keep an open mind: some patients do indeed effect significant change without formally completing homework assignments.

SPECIAL PROBLEMS

The novice cognitive therapist often makes the error of staying with the standard method outlined above even if it is not working very well. The cognitive therapist should be flexible enough to adapt to the needs of patients and to the several special problems that commonly arise in therapy. We have grouped these special problems into two categories: difficulties in the therapist–patient relationship, and problems in which the therapy itself seems not to be working.

Problems in the Therapist–Patient Relationship

The first set of problems concerns the therapist–patient relationship itself. When the therapist first perceives a patient to be dissatisfied, angry, or hostile, it is imperative that the therapist present the patient with these observations. The therapist can then ask about the accuracy of the observations, the patient's feelings, and thoughts the patient has about the therapist. It is essential that therapists be aware that many interventions can be misinterpreted by depressed patients in a negative way.

With problems of misinterpretation, therapists approach the thought in the same way that they approach other thoughts: They work with the patient to gather data and search for alternative accounts of the evidence. Difficulties in the therapist–patient relationship can generally be resolved through dialogue. There are times when therapists may need to tailor behavior to the particular needs of the individual patient. For instance, therapists may become freer with self-disclosure and personal reactions to meet the needs of patients who persist in seeing the therapist as impersonal. Similarly, therapists can make a point of checking formulations of the patients' thoughts more frequently to meet the needs of patients who continue to believe the therapist does not understand them.

It is imperative in situations like these that the therapist not assume that the patient is being stubbornly resistant or irrational. Cognitive therapists collaborate with patients to achieve a better understanding of patients' responses. The reactions themselves often provide data regarding the kinds of distortions patients make in their other social and personal relationships. The patients' responses therefore give the therapist the opportunity to work with patients on their maladaptive interpretations in relationships.

Problems with the Rate of Progress

A second set of problems occurs when the therapy appears not to be working even when patients conscientiously complete homework assignments and the collaborative relationship seems successful. Sometimes problems stem from inappropriate expectations on the part of the patient—or unrealistic expectations on the part of the therapist—regarding the rapidity and consistency of change. When therapy seems not to be progressing as quickly as it "should," both patient and therapist must remember that ups and downs are to be anticipated in the course of treatment. It is important for therapists to keep in mind that some patients simply progress more slowly than others. The therapist or patient, or both, may be minimizing small changes that have indeed been taking place. In this case the therapist can emphasize the small gains that have been made and remind the patient that large goals are attained through small steps toward them.

At times, patients' hopelessness can lead them to invalidate their gains. Therapists should seek to uncover the thoughts and maladaptive assumptions that contribute to the pervasive hopelessness. In these cases, therapists must work to correct mistaken notions about the process of change and about the nature of depression before further progress in therapy can occur.

In some cases where therapy seems not to be working successfully, it may be that some of the therapeutic techniques have not been correctly used. Problems often arise when patients do not really believe the rational responses or are not able to remember them in times of emotional distress. It is important that the therapist determine the amount of belief the patient has in the rational responses and help the patient use the new responses as closely as possible to the moment when the automatic thought occurs. To the patient who does not fully believe a rational response, the therapist can ask the patient to take an experimental stance, to take the new belief and "try it on for size." The patient who cannot think of answers because of emotional upset should be told that states of emotional distress make reasoning more difficult and that thoughts such as "If this doesn't work, nothing will" can only aggravate the problem. Patients should be assured that they will be able to think of rational responses more readily with practice.

Another problem deriving from the misapplication of cognitive therapy techniques occurs when the therapist uses a particular technique inflexibly. It is often necessary for the therapist to try out several behavioral or cognitive techniques before finding an approach to which the patient responds well. The cognitive therapist must stay with a particular technique for a while to see if it works, but he or she must also be willing to try an alternative technique when it becomes apparent that the patient is not improving. To give a specific example, behavioral homework assignments are sometimes more helpful with particular patients, even though the therapist has every reason to predict in advance that cognitive assignments will be more effective.

In some instances where it appears that little progress is being made in therapy, it turns out that the therapist has selected a tangential problem. The cognitive therapist should be alert to this possibility, especially during the early stages of therapy. When there appears to be little or no significant change in depression level, even when the patient seems to have made considerable progress in a problem area, the therapist should consider the possibility that the most distressing problem has not yet been uncovered. A typical example of this kind of difficulty is the patient who presents difficulty at work as the major problem when it turns out that marital problems are contributing significantly to the work difficulties. The real issue may be withheld by a patient because it seems too threatening.

Finally, cognitive therapy is not for everyone. If the therapist has tried all available approaches to the problem and has consulted with other cognitive therapists, it may be best to refer the patient to another therapist, either with the same or a different therapeutic orientation.

Regardless of why therapy is not progressing satisfactorily, cognitive therapists should attend to their own cognitions. They must maintain a problem-solving stance and not allow themselves to be influenced by their patients' despair or to see themselves as incompetent. Hopelessness in patient or therapist is an obstacle to problem solving. If therapists can effectively counteract their own negative self-assessments and other dysfunctional thoughts, they will be better able to concentrate on helping patients find solutions to their problems.

CASE STUDY

In the case study that follows, we will describe the course of treatment for a depressed woman seen at our clinic. Through the case study we will illustrate many of the concepts described earlier in this chapter, including the eliciting of automatic thoughts, the cognitive triad of depression, collaborative empiricism, structuring a session, and feedback.

Assessment and Presenting Problems

The patient, whom we will call Irene, phoned the Center for help because she had heard about cognitive therapy on a local radio show. Irene recognized that she was experiencing many of the symptoms of depression described on the program.

She went through the typical assessment procedure at the Center, which consists of 1½ hr of a standard clinical interview and an additional 1½ hr of paper-and-pencil testing.

The intake interviewer reported that Irene was a 29-year-old Caucasian woman, living with her husband and two young children. She was a high school graduate who had stopped work after marrying. Irene described her major problems as depression (for the past few years), difficulty coping with her children, marital conflict, and a sense of "being kept back" by her husband. In terms of her marriage, Irene said she felt stigmatized because her husband had just been released from a drug abuse center. Furthermore, her husband had just been laid off from work and was thus unemployed. He refused to participate in marital counseling with her.

Irene said she had been socially isolated since her marriage, although she reported having had normal friendships as a child and teenager. One factor that she felt made it difficult for her to socialize with other women in the neighborhood was her belief that they looked down on her because she had such poor control over her children and because of her husband's drug record.

The interviewer diagnosed the patient as having major depressive disorder on Axis I and dependent personality on Axis II. Her test scores verified the diagnosis of depression. Irene's Beck Depression Inventory (BDI) score was 29, placing her in the moderate-to-severe range of depression. Her most prominent depressive symptoms included: guilt, self-blame, loss of pleasure, irritability, social withdrawal, inability to make decisions, fatigue, difficulty motivating herself to perform daily functions, and loss of libido. Her Young Loneliness Inventory score (Young, 1982) was 30, indicating an extremely high degree of loneliness. We use this scale because we have observed clinically that depression is often related to lack of satisfaction with interpersonal relationships. The Young Inventory is similar in format to the Beck Depression Inventory and assesses the extent to which patients are distressed by the absence of various types of friendships and intimate ties. Irene also received a high score on the Dysfunctional Attitude Scale (DAS; Weissman & Beck, 1978). We use the DAS to assess the most frequently observed maladaptive underlying assumptions. Careful analysis of patient responses to this scale are often useful to the therapist in identifying key assumptions that can later become targets of treatment, as described earlier in this chapter.

First Session

Irene was treated initially by the first author (Beck). Since an intake interview had already been completed by another therapist, Beck did not spend time reviewing symptoms in detail or taking a history. The session began with Irene describing the "sad states" she was having. Beck almost immediately started to elicit her automatic thoughts during these periods[1]:

THERAPIST: What kind of thoughts were you having during these 4 days when you said your thoughts kept coming over and over again?

PATIENT: Well, they were just—mostly, "Why is this happening again"— because, you know, this isn't the first time he's been out of work. You know, "What am I going to do"—like I have all different thoughts. They are all in different things like being mad at him, being mad at myself for being in this position all the time. Like I want to leave him or if I could do anything to make him straighten out and not depend so much on him. There's a lot of thoughts in there.

T: Now can we go back a little bit to the sad states that you have. Do you still have that sad state?

P: Yeah.

T: You have it right now?

P: Yeah, sort of. They were sad thoughts about—I don't know—I get bad thoughts, like a lot of what I'm thinking is bad things. Like not—there is like, ah, it isn't going to get any better, it will stay that way. I don't know. Lots of things go wrong, you know, that's how I think.

T: So one of the thoughts is that it's not going to get any better?

P: Yeah.

T: And sometimes you believe that completely?

P: Yeah, I believe it, sometimes.

T: Right now do you believe it?

P: I believe—yeah, yeah.

T: Right now you believe that things are not going to get better?

P: Well, there is a glimmer of hope but it's mostly . . .

T: What do you kind of look forward to in terms of your own life from here on?

P: Well, what I look forward to—I can tell you but I don't want to tell you. (*Giggles.*) Um, I don't see too much.

---

1. The case transcript from which this material was excerpted has been copyrighted by the Center for Cognitive Therapy and is reproduced by permission from the Center.

T: You don't want to tell me?

P: No, I'll tell you but it's not sweet and great what I think. I just see me continuing on the way I am, the way I don't want to be, like not doing anything, just being there, like sort of with no use, that like my husband will still be there and he will, you know, he'll go in and out of drugs or whatever he is going to do, and I'll just still be there, just in the same place.

By inquiring about Irene's automatic thoughts, the therapist began to understand her perspective—that she would go on forever, trapped, with her husband in and out of drug centers. This illustrates the hopelessness about the future that is characteristic of most depressed patients. A second advantage to this line of inquiry is that the therapist introduced Irene to the idea of looking at her own thoughts, which is central to cognitive therapy.

As the session continued, the therapist probed the patient's perspective regarding her marital problems. The therapist then made a decision not to focus on the marriage as the first therapeutic target, since it would probably require too much time before providing symptom relief. Instead, the therapist chose to focus on Irene's inactivity and withdrawal. This is frequently the first therapeutic goal in working with a severely depressed patient.

In the sequence that follows, the therapist guides Irene to examine the advantages and disadvantages of staying in bed all day:

PATIENT: Usually I don't want to get out of bed. I want to stay there and just keep the covers up to my head and stay there, you know. I don't want to do anything. I just want to be left alone and just keep everything out, keep everything away from me.

THERAPIST: Now, do you feel better when you get under the covers and try to shut everything out?

P: Yeah.

T: You do feel better?

P: Yeah, I feel better that way.

T: And so how much time do you spend doing that?

P: Now, lately? I don't get to do it too much because I have two kids. I don't ever really get to do it all that much. I would love to do it more. It would help. I mean I feel safe, sort of secure, like they are over on the other side of the wall and they are not near me.

T: Now after you have spent some time in the covers, how do you feel about yourself?

P: If I'm laying there, I don't know.

T: Let's say afterwards?

P: Afterwards? I don't usually have any bad feeling about—oh yeah, I do, I feel like, Oh Christ, you've been laying there doing nothing, you should have been doing this, you should have been doing that, you should have got up and done something, whatever it is I was suppose to do. You know, even when I'm there, I'm not making any solutions to any problems, I'm just there.

T: On the one hand you seem to enjoy and on the other hand afterwards you're a little bit critical of yourself?

Note that the therapist does not try to debate or exhort Irene to get out of bed. Rather, through questioning, he encourages her to examine more closely her assumption that she is really better off in bed. This is the process we call collaborative empiricism. By the second session, Irene had reexamined her hypothesis about remaining in bed:

PATIENT: About staying in bed versus getting up, I thought about that the other day. I thought when I told you—like I said something about like keeping the bad things away from me. Like when I was under the covers or just staying in bed they weren't really kept away from me. Like I always felt like I was always beating them down, I always had to ward them off. I don't know. I thought I told you it made me feel better to stay there, but I don't know if it really did. I don't think it did now that I am thinking about it.

THERAPIST: It is funny then that when you talked about it your recollection was that it actually was comforting, but that sometimes happens with people. It happens to me too. I think that something is really good that's not so hot when I actually check it out.

Returning to the first session, after some probing by the therapist, Irene mentioned that cognitive therapy "is like my last hope." The therapist used this as an opportunity to explore her hopelessness and suicidal thinking:

THERAPIST: What was going through your mind when you said "This is my last hope"? Did you have some kind of a vision in your mind?

PATIENT: Yeah, that if it doesn't work out that I don't think that I could take living like this the rest of my life.

T: If it doesn't work out, then what?

P: Then I wouldn't really care what happened to me.

T: Did you have something more concrete in mind?

P: Well, right this minute I don't think I could commit suicide but maybe if afterwards I thought there was nothing left, I could. I don't know though, I thought about suicide before but I have never been able to bring myself to do it. I've come close but I've never been able to succeed. I know little certain things stop me like my kids, I don't think—even though I sometimes think I'm not as good a mother as I could be—I think they would be a lot worse off with my husband. I think it would destroy some other people, like my mother if I did something like that, you know. That is what I think mainly stops me, my children and my mother. Just that they would—I guess I'm afraid that if I did something like that, maybe my mother would feel that she failed somewhere, which is not true, I don't think, and just about my kids. I couldn't trust my husband with my kids. I think it would really—even though I'm messed up—I think that he would mess them up more.

T: Now these are some of the reasons for not committing suicide, now what are some of the reasons why you wanted to, do you think?

P: Because sometimes it is just hopeless, there are no solutions, there's no—it continues constantly the same way, all the time.

The therapist wants the patient to feel as free as possible to discuss suicidal thoughts; thus, he tries hard to understand both the reasons for her hopelessness and the deterrents. After determining that she had no imminent plans to make an attempt (although she had made an attempt a couple of years earlier), the therapist said he would work with her to solve the problems in her life now and also "work things out inside you own head." He then asked her to select a small problem that they could work on together:

THERAPIST: Now is there any other smaller decisions that you could make that would affect your life right away?

PATIENT: I don't know. Well, I guess just trying—like for a long time I have been wanting to go out and do other things, like I don't know, join something, feel like I'm a part of something, you know, and I haven't been able to do it. I don't know if it's financial why I haven't been able to do it. I mean that is the excuse I come up with but I think sometimes it is not financial, sometimes it's just I don't get up and do it.

T: Well is there some specific group that you have in mind you could join?

P: I don't know. (*Giggles.*) I guess that is another decision I can't make. I think like everything interests me and nothing interests me.

T: Why don't we make a list and see what happens—a mental list? What are some of the things you would be interested in doing?

P: Tennis, I have been wanting to do that for a long time.

T: Now does this involve joining a tennis team?

P: Yeah, well that is what I would want to do.

T: Well, do you know people who belong to it?

P: No, I know other people but they don't belong to it in Philadelphia. Well, they do but I guess . . .

T: How would you go about finding out about a tennis team?

P: You would only have to go down to the nearest tennis court and that's it.

T: What would happen when you went down there?

P: I don't know. I have never been on one.

T: Well, what do you think you could do when you got there?

P: I guess you just—I don't know how many people are in one group. I don't know if you have to have a whole group go down with you and say OK we want to be a team, but I guess there are some people who are short of the whole group and then you could get on that team. You know, I guess.

T: Well, how could you get that information?

P: I guess if I went down there.

T: Do you think you could get the information if you went down there?

P: Yeah.

T: You could find out then whether you join as individuals or groups or how many, if they need somebody to fill in?

P: Yeah, uh-huh.

T: How do you feel about doing that?

P: Kind of stupid. (*Giggles.*)

T: Does it seem so trivial?

P: Yeah, it seems like well why didn't I just do it before.

T: Well, you probably had good reasons for not doing it before. Probably you were just so caught up in the hopelessness.

P: Right, right.

T: When you are hopeless you tend to deny, as it were, or cut off possible solutions. Remember when your husband lost his job, you said that you refused to accept the fact that he would get compensation?

P: Right.

T: When you get caught up in hopelessness then there is nothing you can do, is that what you think?

P: Yeah.

T: So then rather than be down on yourself because you haven't gone over before, why don't we carry you right through?

This excerpt illustrates the process of graded tasks that is so important in the early stages of therapy with a depressed patient. The therapist asked the patient a series of questions to break down the process of joining a tennis league into smaller steps. Irene realized that she had known all along what to do but, as the therapist pointed out, her hopelessness prevented her from seeing possible solutions:

PATIENT: First steps are really hard for me.

THERAPIST: First steps are harder for everybody, but that's why there is an old expression "A journey of a thousand miles starts with the first step."

P: That's very true.

T: Because that step—it's very important to take the first step. Then after taking the first step, and second step, and third step and so on. So all you have to do is take one and you don't have to take giant steps.

P: Well, yeah, I can see that now. I don't think I seen it before. I think before I was thinking every step was just as hard as the first step and maybe it's not that way at all, maybe it's easier.

In the second session, Irene reported success:

PATIENT: I called about the tennis and they said just to come in and give them your name. That's all you had to do, just come in and give them your name, which was really easy to do. It would have been a first step. I was surprised that it was so easy. I guess I thought it was going to be a lot harder, but it wasn't.

At the end of the first session, the therapist helped Irene write out an activity schedule for the coming week. The activities were quite simple, such as taking the children out, visiting her mother, reading a book, going shopping, and checking out the tennis team. Finally, the therapist asked her for feedback about the session and about her hopelessness:

THERAPIST: Do you have any reactions?

PATIENT: I know I went through stages from happy to sad to happy to sad to happy to sad.

T: Where are you at now?

P: Where am I at now? Half-decent.

T: Half-sad/half-happy?

P: No, a little more happier than I am sadder.

T: Now it may be that when you leave you'd be thinking that we haven't really worked on the big problems, and you have to have a way to answer that.

P: I guess I'll just say it will take a little more time.

Second Session

In the second session, the therapist began by collaborating with Irene to set an agenda. She wanted to discuss an argument she had with her husband and to deal with her feelings of inferiority; the therapist added the issue of activity versus inactivity to the agenda. They then reviewed the previous homework. Irene had carried out all the scheduled activities and had also listed some of her negative thoughts in between sessions. Her BDI score had dropped somewhat. (Patients routinely fill out the BDI before each session so that both the patient and the therapist can monitor the progress of treatment.)

Irene then shared her list of negative thoughts with the therapist. One concern was that she had cried during the first session:

PATIENT: Well, I know you are a professional but I felt like I was changed from one mood so easily to another. Like that sort of—when I interpreted it to myself, I felt like I could be manipulated and that was like—I don't know, I don't want to be easily led.

THERAPIST: Well, that's good. You had the thought then that I was manipulating you, that I was somehow pushing the buttons and turning the knobs?

P: Well, yeah.

The therapist offered Irene an alternative perspective:

THERAPIST: I would say just that I wasn't intending to manipulate you, that you yourself are not so gullible that you were easily manipulated. It is just that the way we were going through the interview, we were hitting some points that were sensitive and other points that were not so sensitive and when we talked about the negatives, you felt worse and when we talked about some positive things, then you felt better or perhaps when you were able to work through some particular problem, get on top of it, made you feel better. Then we go on to another problem, you feel worse. So it was just the nature of the interview rather than having anything to do with you being weak and me being overpowering, manipulative. But that was very good, and going through this explanation again not only to give you the information but to show you how to cope with the negative thoughts.

This is an illustration of how a cognitive therapist can utilize events during the session to teach patients to identity their automatic thoughts and to consider alternative interpretations.

Irene next discussed her argument with her husband, and specifically her thought that maybe she should leave him. She and the therapist agreed that it might be better to wait until her depression lifted a little before trying to make such a major decision. We often recommend that depressed patients postpone major decisions until they are able to regain a realistic perspective on their lives.

The therapist provided a summary of the two key themes he had identified from listening to Irene's automatic thoughts about her husband and about therapy. The first theme was her fear of being controlled by other people (including the therapist); the second was that other people did not care about her. In the segment that follows, the therapist explains how he arrived at the conclusion that caring is an important schema for her:

THERAPIST: Like for instance, when you say the way your husband treats you, it sounded as though you were really bothered about his lack of concern for your feelings and wishes.

PATIENT: Yeah, yeah.

T: I don't want to make too much out of this at the moment, but you also said that after your second baby was born you had the feeling that nobody cared for you, namely, your family.

P: Well, I don't know what happened, I can't remember the circumstances of what happened.

T: But whatever it was, this was the upshot.

P: Yeah.

T: So one of the things that seizes you, can really grab hold and make you feel terrible, is this whole notion that nobody cares, and that even that you are so sensitive in that one area that you thought that we were just using you as a guinea pig here and they were just interested in seeing how I work and not interested in you, the clinic wasn't interested in you, and I wasn't interested in you. So again it seems to be this notion of people who are important not caring. Is that correct?

P: Yeah, in most instances, yeah.

T: In all the instances I have mentioned.

P: Yeah.

T: Well, what this tells us is that you have to be alert to the sense that they don't care because this can really make you feel bad. It may not even be correct. If you found out, for instance, that your mother does care, so that you are wrong in thinking that but still the thought came through very strongly and your current thought is that we don't care, or it was.

About halfway through the session, the therapist asks the patient for feedback thus far:

THERAPIST: Now at this point, is there anything that we have discussed today that bothered you?
PATIENT: That bothered me?
T: Yeah.
P: Uh, I'm feeling stupider and stupider as we go along.
T: That is important, OK. Can you . . .
P: Well, I'm trying not to but I don't know.
T: Well, if you are, you are. Why don't you just let yourself feel stupid and tell me about it.
P: Well, I just feel that I should be recognizing all these things, too.

This comment led to identification of a third key theme: that Irene had been viewing herself as increasingly dumb for the past few years. By this point, however, the patient was beginning to catch on to the idea of answering her thoughts more rationally. After the therapist pointed out the negative thought in the excerpt above, the patient volunteered:

PATIENT: I know what to do with the thought, "I'm stupid for not recognizing these things myself."
THERAPIST: What are you going to do with it right this minute?
P: I am going to say—"Well, you are the professional, you are suppose to see these things."
T: Right, you'd fire me if I didn't see them. Right?
P: I didn't think of that but (laughs) . . . no, I wouldn't fire you. I wouldn't fire anybody.
T: So what you are saying is that since I am professionally trained I can see certain things. The other thing is that other people are objective and can often see things in us much more readily than we can in ourselves. It just happens to be a fact of human nature.
P: Yeah.

The same automatic thoughts arose again later in the session, when Irene felt stupid for not knowing the answer to one of the therapist's questions. In the extended excerpt below, the therapist helps her set up an experiment to test the thought, "I look dumb":

THERAPIST: OK, now let's just do an experiment and see if you yourself can respond to the automatic thought and let's see what happens to your feeling. See if responding rationally makes you feel worse or makes you feel better.

PATIENT: OK.

T: OK, why didn't I answer that question right? I look dumb. What is the answer to that? What is the rational answer to that? A realistic answer?

P: Why didn't I answer that question? Because I thought for a second that was what I was suppose to say and then when I heard the question over again, then I realized that was not what I heard. I didn't hear the question right, that is why I didn't answer it right.

T: OK, so that is the fact situation. And so is the fact situation that you look dumb or you just didn't hear the question right?

P: I didn't hear the question right.

T: Or it is possible that I didn't say the question in such a way that it was clear.

P: Possible.

T: Very possible. I'm not perfect so it's very possible that I didn't express the question properly.

P: But instead of saying you made a mistake, I would still say I made a mistake.

T: We'll have to watch the video and see. Whichever. Does it mean if I didn't express the question, if I made the mistake does it make me dumb?

P: No.

T: And if you made the mistake, does it make you dumb?

P: No, not really.

T: But you felt dumb?

P: But I did, yeah.

T: Do you feel dumb still?

P: No.

The preceding exchange demonstrates the use of reattribution. At first, the patient attributed her difficulty answering him as evidence that she was stupid. As a result of the guided discovery approach, she reattributed the problem to one of two factors: either she didn't hear the question right or the therapist did not ask the question clearly enough. At the end of the experiment, Irene expressed satisfaction that she was finally recognizing this tendency to distort her appraisals:

PATIENT: Right now I feel glad. I'm feeling a little better that at least somebody is pointing all these things out to me because I have never seen this before. I never knew that I thought that I was that dumb.

THERAPIST: So you feel good that you have made this observation about yourself?

P: Right.

After summarizing the main points of the second session, the therapist assigned homework for the coming week: to fill out the Daily Record of Dysfunctional Thoughts (see Figure 4-1) and the Weekly Activity Schedule (with mastery and pleasure ratings) (see Figure 4-2).

Third Session

By the beginning of the third session, Irene's mood had visibly improved. She had joined a tennis league with her sister, and had begun to respond more rationally to her automatic thoughts about being dumb. In fact, she was practicing her cognitive therapy skills by helping a friend with a similar problem of self-blame. The primary agenda item Irene chose to work on was "how I back away from other people." She described an incident in which a neighbor was taking advantage of her, but she could not assert herself. In discussing her thoughts, Irene expressed a maladaptive underlying assumption that interfered with her behaving assertively:

PATIENT: I want to be a nice person. I don't want to cause a lot of trouble. I don't want to be fighting with everybody constantly. But I don't like myself when I give in too much too.
THERAPIST: Well, is it possible to be a nice person without giving in all the time?
P: I guess.

The therapist continued probing to understand why the patient believed that a nice person cannot get angry or be assertive. As the discussion progressed, it became obvious that, while in the abstract the patient could see that she was not necessarily bad because she got angry, in real-life situations Irene nevertheless felt she was wrong. The therapist's task next was to help the patient bring her rational thinking to bear on her distorted thinking *in the context of a concrete event*. At the therapist's request, Irene then described an argument in which she yelled at a nieghbor with good justification, yet felt she was bad. The therapist helped her use logic to evaluate her underlying assumption:

THERAPIST: You had the thought "I was wrong to get mad at her, to yell at her." It seems likely that you believe that thought and that the thought was right and that you were wrong. And since you thought that thought was right, you then had to wish to withdraw behind your hat, as it were.
PATIENT: Right.
T: Now, let's look at it. Do you think that thought is correct?
P: No, I don't see how it could have been correct.
T: So according to your own values, you don't think that it is wrong to stick up for your rights?
P: Right.

T: And do you think that you were sticking up for yourself when she called the cops for a car that is blocking her car?

P: Well, the car shouldn't have been blocking her car . . .

T: That wasn't—the question was, should she have called the cops?

P: No, I didn't call the cops when she put her car in the middle of both driveways.

T: Right. So, do you think that it is natural for anybody to get mad at someone who calls the cops over something like that?

P: Wait, what was that?

T: Let me put it again. Do you think it was natural for you to get mad in that situation?

P: Yeah.

T: OK, so you don't see anything wrong in getting mad?

P: No.

T: No. And yet you have the thought right after that that it was wrong to get mad and to yell at her?

P: Yeah, I did have that thought.

T: OK, now this is one of the problems. If you want to get over this sense of giving in all the time, one of the things that you can do is to look for this thought—I was wrong to do such and such a thing—and refer back to this conversation that we are having now and decide for yourself whether, indeed, you were wrong. Now if every time you asserted yourself in that particular way, you think—I was wrong to do that—you are going to feel bad and then you are not going to want to assert yourself again. Is that clear?

P: Uh-huh.

T: So we have to decide here and now, do you indeed think that you were wrong to assert yourself with her?

P: No.

T: Now the next time you get the thought—I was wrong, I shouldn't have said that, I shouldn't have stood up for my rights—how are you going to answer that thought?

P: If I was wrong? I wasn't wrong and I should stick up for my rights.

T: Now are you saying that because that is the answer or because you really believe it?

P: No, I believe it. I did the right thing there, I think. I did the right thing there. I did the right thing.

The therapist followed this discussion with a technique called "Point–Counterpoint" to help Irene practice rational responses to her automatic thoughts even more intensively. In this excerpt the therapist expresses the patient's own negative thinking, while she tries to defend herself more rationally:

THERAPIST: Now I am going to be like the prosecuting attorney and I'll say "Now I understand you were yelling at your neighbor because she called the cops. Is that true?"

PATIENT: Yeah.

T: Now it seems to me that that was a very bad thing for you to do.

P: No, it wasn't.

T: You don't think it was?

P: No, I should have hit her.

T: Well, you can sit there and say you should have hit her. I thought you said before that you wanted to be a nice person.

P: I was a nice person when I didn't call the cops when she blocked the driveway.

T: I know, but now you are saying that you are going to go out and hit her.

P: No, I wouldn't hit her. I wouldn't hit her unless she hit me.

T: Well, but still you yelled at her.

P: I yelled at her, yeah.

T: It doesn't seem to me that nice people yell at other people.

P: Well, I am still a nice person, but she did something wrong and I had to do something wrong.

T: Well, how can you still be a nice person if you yell at people?

P: How can you still be a nice person? You just are. You are a nice person. It is just that a nice person gets mad too.

T: You say a nice person gets mad too?

P: When somebody does something wrong to them.

T: Where did you ever get that idea that nice people get mad when they are wrong?

P: When the other person is wrong? Where did I get that idea? It's true.

T: You really believe that's true?

P: Yeah, nice people are the same as everybody else.

T: So, nice people can get mad?

P: Uh-huh.

Finally, the therapist returns to the underlying assumption and asks the patient how much she believes the new perspective:

THERAPIST: If you get mad, you are not a nice person. How do you believe that?

PATIENT: No.

T: Do you believe it partially?

P: Umm, no. Well, they don't get mad for nothing. They get mad when there is a reason.

T: OK, so right now would you say that you believe—now what about the belief—let's put it the other way, the belief that you can get mad and still be a nice person. How much do you believe that?

P: A hundred.

T: 100%?

P: Yeah.

    T: You are sure 100%, not 90% or 80%?
    P: No, I think 100%.

For the remainder of the third session, Irene and the therapist reviewed other instances of non-assertiveness to reinforce the main point of the session: that nice people can behave assertively and sometimes even get mad. The session ended with a summary of the main issues raised in the first three sessions.

Summary of the Initial Sessions

In the first three sessions, the therapist laid the groundwork for the remainder of treatment. He began immediately by teaching Irene to identify her negative automatic thoughts. By doing that the therapist began to understand her feelings of hopelessness and explored her suicidal ideation. By identifying her thoughts in a variety of specific situations, he was able to deduce several key themes that later proved central to Irene's thinking: the belief that other people did not care about her, that she could be easily controlled by others, that she was dumb, and that she would not be a nice person if she asserted herself. The therapist made especially skillful use of the patient's thoughts during the therapy session to help Irene see that she was distorting evidence about the therapeutic interaction and coming to the inaccurate conclusion that she was easily manipulated and dumb.

    Beyond identifying thoughts and distortions, the therapist guided Irene to take concrete steps to overcome her inactivity and withdrawal: he asked her to weigh the advantages and disadvantages of staying in bed; broke down the task of joining a tennis group into small, manageable steps; and worked with her to develop an activity schedule to follow during the week.

    Finally, the therapist employed a variety of strategies to demonstrate to Irene that she could test the validity of her thoughts, develop rational responses, and feel better. For example, during the course of the three sessions, the therapist set up an experiment, used reattribution, offered alternative perspectives, and practiced the Point–Counterpoint technique.

    One final point we want to emphasize is that the primary therapeutic mode was questioning. Most of the therapist's comments were in the form of questions. This helped Irene to evaluate her own thoughts outside of the session and prevented her from feeling attacked by the therapist.

    By the end of these initial sessions, Irene reported being more optimistic that her life could change. She was then transferred to another cognitive therapist, Dr. Judith Eidelson, for the remainder of treatment. (This transfer had been explained to the patient before she saw Dr. Beck.)

Later Sessions

The first issue Eidelson dealt with was Irene's belief that she was stupid. The patient began to fill out the Daily Record of Dysfunctional Thoughts and

gathered evidence that she was not as stupid as she believed. In fact, Irene brought up the possibility of taking a college course.

There were several obstacles: (1) Her husband had never given her keys to either their car or their house; (2) she did not have enough money to take the course; and (3) she worried that her husband would try to punish her if she tried to become more independent.

Dr. Eidelson set up several experiments with Irene to test a series of beliefs: that her husband would punish her; that she would fail at a job even if she could get one; and that she would fail a college-level course.

Through graded tasks, Irene asked her husband about obtaining keys, joined the tennis league, and began socializing with friends. Although her husband felt rejected and accused her of being stupid, he never took any active steps to stop her, despite her predictions. Irene then got a job as a waitress and again, contrary to her expectations, she was very successful and received a great deal of positive feedback on the job. Soon after getting the job, Irene enrolled in a sociology course and received a grade of A. At each step in the sequence, Irene would identify her automatic thoughts and respond to them, before taking the next step toward independence.

During the final sessions of therapy, the patient raised the issue of leaving her husband. The therapist worked with Irene to evaluate several thoughts and assumptions: (1)"Somehow he'll change and the marriage will work"; (2) "Marriage is a lifetime commitment"; (3) "I can't manage on my own"; and (4) "Leaving him would represent a failure to me." Irene eventually discarded each of these beliefs as invalid or unlikely, and decided to end the marriage. Shortly thereafter, Irene terminated therapy. She felt confident about herself and her decision, and her BDI score was in the normal range. The patient was successfully treated in 20 sessions.

CONCLUSION

There is mounting evidence that cognitive therapy is an effective, short-term treatment for adult outpatients with nonbipolar depressions. Cognitive therapy teaches patients to elicit their automatic thoughts, underlying assumptions, and early schemas. These cognitions are then "put to the test" by examining evidence, setting up *in vivo* experiments, weighing advantages and disadvantages, trying graded tasks, and employing other intervention strategies. Through this process, patients begin to view themselves and their problems more realistically, feel better, change their maladaptive behavior patterns, and take steps to solve real-life difficulties. These changes take place as a direct result of carefully planned, self-help assignments at home.

Throughout the treatment, cognitive therapists maintain a collaborative alliance with their patients. They are very active in structuring the session, yet go to considerable lengths to help patients reach conclusions on their own. The therapist serves as a guide, helping the patient maneuver through a labyrinth of dysfunctional cognitions that need to be reevaluated.

References

Beck, A. T., Rush, A. J., Shaw, B. F., & Emery, G. (1979). *Cognitive therapy of depression.* New York: Guilford.

Bergin, A. E., & Lambert, M. J. (1978). The evaluation of therapeutic outcomes. In S. L. Garfield & A. E. Bergin (Eds.). *Handbook of psychotherapy and behavior change: An empirical analysis* (2nd ed., pp. 139–190). New York: Wiley.

Blackburn, I., & Bishop, S. (1979, July). *A comparison of cognitive therapy, pharmacotherapy, and their combination in depressed outpatients.* Paper presented at the annual meeting of the Society for Psychotherapy Research, Oxford, England.

Blackburn, I., & Bishop, S. (1980, July). *Pharmacotherapy and cognitive therapy in the treatment of depression: Competitors or allies?* Paper presented at the First World Congress on Behavior Therapy, Jerusalem, Israel.

Hollon, S. D., & Beck, A. T. (1978). Psychotherapy and drug therapy: Comparison and combinations. In S. L. Garfield & A. E. Bergin (Eds.), *Handbook of psychotherapy and behavior change: An empirical analysis* (2nd ed. pp. 437–490). New York: Wiley.

McLean, P. D., & Hakstian, A. R. (1979). Clinical depression: Comparative efficacy of outpatient treatments. *Journal of Consulting and Clinical Psychology, 47,* 818–836.

Rush, A. J. (Ed.). (1982). *Short-term psychotherapies for depression.* New York: Guilford.

Rush, A. J., Beck, A. T., Kovacs, M., & Hollon, S. (1977). Comparative efficacy of cognitive therapy and imipramine in the treatment of depressed outpatients. *Cognitive Therapy and Research, 1,* 17–37.

Truax, C. B., & Mitchell, K. M. (1971). Research on certain therapist interpersonal skills in relation to process and outcome. In A. E. Bergin & S. L. Garfield (Eds.), *Handbook of psychotherapy and behavior change: An empirical analysis* (pp. 299–344). New York: Wiley.

Weissman, A., & Beck, A. T. (1978). *Development and validation of the Dysfunctional Attitude Scale.* Paper presented at the annual meeting of the American Association of Behavior Therapists, Chicago. (Address requests to: Center for Cognitive Therapy, Room 602, 133 South 36th St., Philadelphia, PA 19104.)

Young, J. E. (1982). Loneliness, depression, and cognitive therapy. In L. A. Peplau & D. A. Perlman (Eds.), *Loneliness: A sourcebook of current theory, research, and therapy* (pp. 388–389). New York: Wiley.

5

ALCOHOLISM

BARBARA S. McCRADY

McCrady cogently notes in this chapter that the treatment of alcoholics is often an unrewarding enterprise. Not only is treatment a difficult undertaking, but working with alcoholics who are often uncooperative, or even disruptive to the life of a clinician, can be frustrating and depressing. Furthermore, treating alcoholism requires a broad and deep acquaintance with medical and social aspects of drinking as well as psychological interventions. On the other hand, there may be no greater reward than successfully working with a problem drinker who is then able to begin a new life. The development of the techniques described in this chapter, many of which are very recent in origin, has made this possible in an increasing number of cases, and McCrady, a very experienced clinician and clinical researcher, illustrates clearly and in considerable detail how these techniques are administered within the context of a typical case. McCrady takes note of the older conditioning and contingency management approaches and then, based on the most recent data, advocates a behavioral-systems model, which emphasizes the importance of the social environment. Once again, attention to the social context of treatment, particularly the role of the spouse or a significant other in treatment, is highlighted. In this vein McCrady discusses at some length the variety of setting variables that are important as well as the data available on the desirability of outpatient, partial hospitalization, or inpatient settings depending on the particular client with whom one is working. The actual components of treatment, consisting of detailed assessment, the acquisition of skills necessary for abstinence, as well as a discussion of the variety of skills needed to deal with the causes of drinking are outlined in enough detail to allow immediate implementation by a skilled clinician. Finally, as with any addictive behavior, the emphasis on maintenance strategies and their description may be one of the more important parts of the chapter. Clinicians dealing with alcoholics or problem drinkers should find these step-by-step descriptions, as well as a discussion of factors that may predict success or failure, invaluable in their practice.—D. H. B.

Clinicians generally have a negative view of alcoholism, and are pessimistic about its treatment (Knox, 1971). For medical personnel, these attitudes are often shaped by their early experiences in hospitals and inner-city emergency rooms, where they are exposed to alcoholics with long histories of treatment and failure and whose condition is complicated by chronic medical problems.

Barbara S. McCrady. Center of Alcohol Studies and Graduate School of Applied and Professional Psychology, Rutgers University, Piscataway, New Jersey.

For other professions, such as social work, early clinical contacts with alcoholics may be with family members who have been the victims of abuse, or who have suffered serious financial problems because of the family member who is alcoholic. Many clinical psychologists have clinical training sites in Veterans Administration (VA) hospitals, also populated by chronic and debilitated alcoholics. These early clinical experiences shape negative and pessimistic views about the treatment of alcoholism, which may be reinforced by supervisors who see alcoholism as untreatable. If the student goes to the literature, he or she might find articles suggesting that the one session of "advice" to stop drinking is as good as a year of comprehensive, multifaceted treatment (Edwards *et al.*, 1977).

In counterpoint to these negative stereotypes, this chapter will review some of the literature on the effectiveness of the treatment of alcoholism, and then discuss clinical issues involved in treatment and the behavioral treatment of persons with drinking problems. Treatment issues considered will go beyond behavioral models, because of the complex, multifaceted nature of alcoholism, which affects physical health, the social functioning of the person, and the emotional and behavioral functioning. The underlying assumption of the chapter is that alcohol abuse and alcoholism are treatable, challenging to treat, rewarding to treat, and that much of the frustration, anger and hopelessness that clinicians experience when dealing with this problem comes from their own unrealistic expectations about the process of treatment and recovery and from not having the therapeutic tools necessary to work with this difficult population.

BACKGOUND

Treatment Outcomes

Despite the broad visibility of the Edwards *et al.* (1977) study of advice versus treatment, a thorough reading of the treatment outcome literature suggests that treatment, on the average, is clearly more effective than no treatment for alcoholism. For example, in a comprehensive review of 384 studies of psychologically oriented treatments for alcoholism, Emrick (1975) found that treatment had little clear effect on rates of continuous abstinence 6 months after the completion of treatment, but that treatment did have a significant impact on helping clients to decrease the amount or frequency of their drinking.

Few treatment approaches have stood out as unequivocally better than any others. Those that have had the best success have actively involved the social system of the alcoholic, or have helped the alcoholic to construct or get involved in a new social system that would support abstinence. Thus, Hunt and Azrin's (1973) community reinforcement approach, and most marital therapy studies (e.g., Hedberg & Campbell, 1974; McCrady, Paolino, Longabaugh, & Rossi, 1979) have shown better outcomes than their individually oriented treatment controls. Surveys conducted by Alcoholics Anonymous (AA) (Leach & Norris,

1977) suggest that about 70% of those actively involved in AA for a year or more have good sobriety. These findings also point to the potency of social system interventions. Other research has found that persons referred to treatment with strong contingencies for obtaining treatment and maintaining abstinence (e.g., Haynes, 1973; Hore & Plant, 1981) have generally positive treatment outcomes. Finally, those who are willing to take disulfiram (Antabuse) also tend to have better outcomes than those who do not (Ritson, 1968).

Client–Treatment Matching

More important than the general question of whether or not treatment works or what treatment is the best, is the more complicated question of client–treatment matching. Pattison (in press) has suggested that the goals of the treatment intervention must be considered. For example, Librium is a highly effective medication for alleviating the symptoms of alcohol withdrawal, and for avoiding the development of major withdrawal syndrome (delerium tremens) (Kaim, Klett, & Rothfeld, 1969). Many forget that this is a treatment for one part of a person's alcohol problem. Similarly, when a person is housed in a 24-hr rehabilitation program, success is incredibly high—few people drink anything while in an inpatient setting (Longabaugh & Beatte, in press), even though many relapse quickly after leaving the hospital. Thus, many alcoholism treatments are highly effective for the goals they are directed toward and when properly implemented.

There are two recent discussions of patient–treatment matching that are important. Because the focus of the chapter is on clinical issues, these will be reviewed only briefly. Kissin and Hanson (in press) have suggested that assessment must cover the medical, social, and psychological areas, and that there are some research data suggesting the most appropriate interventions in each of these areas. For example, in decisions about the use of disulfiram in treatment, the presence of depressive symptoms seems to contraindicate the use of this medication, as depressive symptoms seem to be exacerbated, and patients tend to relapse. Similarly, patients who show depressive symptoms appear to respond well to treatment with lithium carbonate by significantly decreasing their drinking. Patients with certain patterns of psychological "traits" seem to respond better to verbal therapies than others. In general, the Kissin and Hanson model is practical in its focus, makes recommendations for treatment decisions based on statistical differences found in research studies, but provides less of a model for clinical decision making with the individual client.

A second approach to patient–treatment matching has been to develop a theoretical model that would guide assessment and treatment decisions. Longabaugh and Beattie (in press) have recently proposed a model that integrates several themes in the research literature. They posit five major variables: personal resources, alcohol dependency, investment in the social environment, the social environment's degree of support for alcohol dependence or alcohol health, and the social environment's degree of support of psychological health.

They suggest a complex set of interactions among these five sets of variables, and suggest that patient–treatment matching decisions be made in light of an assessment of these five blocks of variables.

While neither of the models described here is avowedly "behavioral" in its approach, each illustrates the complexity of treatment decision making and provides some kind of model that helps a clinician in making decisions about what variables to consider in the course of treatment.

Treatment Models

Treatment of alcoholism has derived from a number of theoretical models. The most commonly applied models include the disease model (Jellinek, 1951), psychodynamically based treatments (Blum, 1966), treatments derived from a systems theory perspective (Steinglass, 1976), and behavioral models (Nathan & Briddell, 1977). Since the emphasis in this volume is on the behavioral treatment of adult disorders, it is important to mention a few of the behavioral models that have been applied to alcoholism treatment before presenting the model used in this chapter. More extensive reviews of behavioral treatments for alcoholism are available (e.g., Hay & Nathan, 1982; Nathan & Briddell, 1977; Nathan & Lipscomb, 1979).

Early behavioral interventions were based on conditioning models, and involved the conditioning of an aversive response to the sight, smell, or taste of alcohol. Electrical and chemical aversion were most commonly used, with some modest successes (Voegtlin, 1940). These interventions still form the basis for some treatment programs, or are used as one element in broad-spectrum behavioral programs. A second model, used more recently, is primarily a cue exposure and extinction model (Blakey & Baker, 1980; Hodgson & Rankin, 1982). In these treatments the client is exposed repeatedly to cues associated with alcohol consumption and is prevented from drinking, or consumes modest amounts of alcohol, and is then prevented from consuming more alcohol. These interventions are designed to extinguish the subjective craving for alcohol and to therefore decrease or eliminate alcohol consumption. Case reports to date provide some promising results in this area.

Contingency management approaches have formed a second class of behavioral interventions in the alcoholism field. Limited contingency management programs have provided positive reinforcement or the avoidance of aversive consequences, contingent on abstinence or on taking disulfiram. These contingencies have been administered through the legal system (e.g., Haynes, 1973), through marital partners (e.g., P. Miller, 1972), or other significant systems. All of these interventions appear to have a high degree of effectiveness when utilized, but legal and ethical issues need careful consideration before such interventions are undertaken, many clients will not consent to such procedures, and the limited research in this area has not addressed the issue of maintenance of treatment gains after the formal contingencies are discontinued.

The alternative to these limited contingency management programs has been the more comprehensive "community reinforcement" model developed by Hunt and Azrin (1973; Azrin, 1976). In this approach to treatment, the client enters a world in which access to all significant reinforcers (job, friends or family, apartment, etc.) is contingent on abstinence. This approach has been applied to severely impaired, chronic alcoholics from the state hospital and has impressive results. However, it is extremely costly and time consuming to implement, and client consent is a major problem.

The third approach to behavioral treatment of alcoholism has derived from a social learning viewpoint. Programs of this variety have focussed on teaching alcoholics the skills necessary to stop or decrease their drinking, and focus on cognitive variables and behavioral skills training rather than on environmental manipulation or counterconditioning strategies. These approaches either teach alcoholics specific skills to facilitate abstinence or decreased drinking (e.g., W. Miller, 1978; W. Miller, Taylor, & West, 1980; M. Sobell & L. Sobell, 1973, 1976), or take the broader view of helping the alcoholic restructure his or her lifestyle in a way that is incompatible with abusive drinking (e.g., Marlatt & Gordon, 1985; P. Miller, 1982).

BEHAVIORAL-SYSTEMS MODEL

Elsewhere (McCrady & Hay, 1983) I have proposed a model for the assessment and treatment of alcoholism that integrates skills acquisition and reinforcement approaches to alcoholism treatment. In the model of assessment and treatment proposed here, a basic stimulus–organism–consequences (SORC) (Goldfried & Sprafkin, 1974) model is used to analyze drinking behavior. Thus, drinking is assumed to be cued by certain identifiable stimuli, and the drinking response is mediated by certain cognitive, affective, and physiological responses of the person to the eliciting stimulus. Immediate reinforcing consequences of alcohol consumption are seen as maintaining the drinking behavior, despite numerous delayed aversive consequences. In the behavioral-systems model this type of behavioral analysis is applied across a variety of interpersonal systems, so that the relationship between the individual's drinking and interactions with family, friends, employers, and co-workers is considered. In each of these systems, behaviors of the other person, interactions that cue drinking, responses of the other that reinforce the drinking response, as well as behaviors that punish drinking are all assessed. Table 5-1 illustrates the kinds of variables that might be included in a behavioral-systems analysis of a person's drinking.

Thus, treatment begins with assessing these various behavioral systems, and making decisions about what systems are most actively involved in the mainte-nance of the person's drinking. Further, each system is assessed for its potential for change in a direction that would support or reinforce the person's changed drinking behavior. Within each system, an assessment is made to determine

TABLE 5-1. Behavioral-Systems Matrix

	Antecedent	Organism	Response	Consequence
Individual	Time Place Visual cues Stress Problem-solving failure	Withdrawal symptoms Expectation of positive consequences Expectations of "loss of control"	Sip rate Frequency of drinking Amount Beverage Type	Initial decreases in anxiety or depression Forgetting Decreases in alcohol withdrawal Self-labeling as competent
Spouse	"Nagging" "Control"	(Retaliation fantasies) (Decreased self-efficacy) (Negative emotional states)	(Secret drinking) (Gulping drinks) (High ethanol content drinks) (Change drinking setting)	Reinforcing drinking Shielding from negative consequences Punishing drinking
Marital	Poor communication and problem-solving skills Coercive control behaviors Vague and inconsistent communications Marital problem areas	(Retaliation) (Expectations of increased skills) (Hopelessness)	?	Increase in affection Increased assertion Increased verbal output

Note. Elements in parentheses are speculative and have no current empirical support.

where in the behavioral chain interventions could be most easily or effectively introduced: in modifying or eliminating the stimulus; in teaching the client new cognitive, affective or behavioral responses to the existing stimulus; or in rearranging the consequences for drinking in that particular situation. The actual interventions, based on the assessment previously described, then combine skills training, cognitive structuring, stimulus control, consequence control, and contingency management procedures.

Before discussing how this kind of a model can be applied to the assessment and treatment of an actual alcohol abuser, it is important to emphasize that there are a number of clinical considerations that go beyond the actual treatment model and form the basis for good clinical decision making and clinical care for alcoholics, regardless of the treatment implementation model used. In the next section, several issues related to the treatment setting, social context of treatment, and client and therapist variables will be considered.

APPLICATIONS OF TECHNIQUES

Setting Variables

There are a number of settings available that are appropriate for the implementation of behavioral alcoholism treatment. These include inpatient residential settings, partial hospitals, outpatient clinics, and halfway houses. Unfortunately, the research literature provides little information to guide clinical decisions about the level of care appropriate for an individual client. For example, in studies of the effects of different lengths of inpatient care, no differences in treatment outcomes have been found when comparing different lengths of treatment (Mosher, Davis, Mulligan, & Iber, 1975; Page & Schaub, 1979; Stein, Newton, & Bowman, 1975; Willems, Letemendia, & Arroyave, 1973). Similarly, studies comparing the partial hospital and inpatient settings (Longabaugh et al., 1983; McCrady, Longabaugh, Fink, Stout et al., 1983; McLachlan & Stein, 1982) have found no significant differences in clinical outcomes after treatment in these two settings, but substantial cost savings for the partial hospital. In the area of patient–treatment matching, Orford and his colleagues (Orford, Oppenheimer, & Edwards, 1976) found that clients included in the Edwards et al. (1977) advice-versus-treatment study who showed signs of alcohol dependence did markedly better with treatment than with advice, while those with less severe alcohol problems did not receive an incremental benefit from treatment over advice. However, all such studies comparing level of care or length of treatment are limited by the fact that patients judged unsuitable for the least intense treatment provided by the study are often excluded, thus truncating the range of severity of problems, and limiting the value of the results.

While research data on treatment settings are of use, the clinician must make a decision with each individual client about what setting is most appropriate for the initiation of treatment. In making this decision, a number of factors need to be considered, including: the need for detoxification, medical status, past treatment history, the results of the client's previous attempts to stop drinking, what social supports and personal resources the client has, the client's initial attitudes about treatment, practical concerns, and the client's personal preference about the initial treatment setting. Each of these will be considered in turn.

Detoxification

If a client is physically addicted to alcohol, then he or she will experience alcohol withdrawal symptoms when decreasing alcohol consumption or stopping drinking. There are a number of signs that suggest that a client is addicted to alcohol (Femino & Lewis, 1980). Daily drinking, drinking regularly or intermittently throughout the day, and morning drinking all suggest an addictive drinking pattern. If the client reports awakening during the night with fears, trembling, or nausea, or experiences such symptoms first thing in the morning, these are suggestive of addiction. If the client does not drink for a day, then further withdrawal symptoms should appear, including tremulousness, nausea, vomiting, difficulty sleeping, and elevations in pulse, blood pressure, and temperature. Such symptoms usually begin with 5–12 hr after stopping or decreasing drinking. More severe withdrawal symptoms may also occur, including delirium, hallucinations, or seizures.

If a client has not consumed any alcohol for several days prior to the initial clinical contact, then concerns about alcohol withdrawal are not relevant. If the client has stopped drinking within the last 3 days, then the clinician can ask and observe whether he or she is currently experiencing withdrawal symptoms. If currently drinking, the clinician must rely on drinking history, drinking pattern, and the results of previous attempts to stop drinking to determine if detoxification will be necessary.

If a client needs detoxification, four alternative approaches are available: inpatient or partial hospital medical detoxification, inpatient nonmedical detoxification (e.g., O'Briant, 1974), or outpatient medical detoxification (e.g., Sausser, Fishburne, & Everett, 1982). Inpatient, medically assisted detoxification is essential if the client has a history of disorientation, delirium, hallucinations, or seizures during alcohol withdrawal, or is showing current signs of disorientation, delirium, or hallucinations. If a client does not have any of the above problems, but does not think that he or she can go through alcohol withdrawal without 24-hr supervision, a social setting detoxification setting would be appropriate. If the client has some social supports, then detoxification could be initiated on a partial hospital or outpatient basis. The choice between these two settings would be determined by how much support the person will need during withdrawal, and whether a structured program will be appropriate after the completion of withdrawal. If significant structure and/or support is needed, then the partial hospital would be preferable to an outpatient approach.

Medical Problems

As noted, when considering the best setting for detoxification, the presence of other medical problems should be considered. A cautious approach to the treatment of alcoholics dictates that every client should have a thorough physical examination and blood and urine studies at the beginning of treatment. The clinician should *routinely* include questions about physical health in the first contact with an alcoholic client, and if significant physical complaints are noted, the client should receive quick medical attention. Some alcoholic clients will have medical problems that require hospitalization, and if this is the case, then the hospitalization must begin the treatment.

Treatment History

After physical health issues have been considered, the clinician should consider the client's history of previous treatment. Some simple questions to consider are:

1. Has the client attempted outpatient treatment in the past, and been able to stop or decrease drinking successfully for a period of time? If so, then another attempt at outpatient treatment might be indicated.
2. Has the client dropped out of outpatient treatment in the past? If so, and there is no strong indication that any variables have changed in the interim, then a more intensive partial hospital or inpatient program might be most appropriate.
3. Has the client dropped out of, or drunk repeatedly while in a partial hospital treatment program? If so, then inpatient treatment might be indicated.
4. Did a client relapse immediately after discharge from an inpatient program? If so, then a partial hospital or outpatient setting might be more appropriate, as it may be that the relapse was associated with problems in generalization from the inpatient to the natural environment.

In general, behaviorally oriented treatments are most easily implemented in an outpatient, or partial hospital environment, because these settings facilitate the accurate assessment of cues for drinking, and the rehearsal of skills in the natural environment can begin early in the treatment (McCrady, Longabaugh, Fink, & Stout, 1983). However, if the client is unlikely to remain in treatment, or is likely to continue in an uncontrolled drinking pattern, then a 24-hr hospitalization is advisable.

Previous Attempts to Stop on His or Her Own

Many clients have stopped drinking on their own at some time, or have successfully cut down their drinking to quite moderate levels. It is important to determine whether or not a client has engaged in such attempts in the past, and the results of such attempts. If a person has successfully stopped on his or her own, even for 1–2 weeks, then the person is a better candidate for outpatient treatment than if he or she has always been unsuccessful in such attempts in the past and has begun drinking abusively after a few days.

Social Support Systems

This is a major variable to consider in deciding where to initiate treatment. If a client has some supports such as a spouse, an older child, a parent, close friends, a concerned employer, an AA sponsor, or some other person who is available on an almost daily basis, *and* who is preceived as an important source of support and reinforcement, *and* who may be willing to learn how to provide some of that support and reinforcement, then the client is a good candidate for some form of ambulatory treatment (partial hospital or outpatient). If the support appears to be potentially available, but the person or persons currently do not provide any such support, then the partial hospital is preferable. If a person is lacking in social supports, and has some of the other indicators for inpatient treatment indicated here, then inpatient treatment might be advisable. Alternatively, a halfway house might provide a good setting for treatment, especially for persons who do not currently have any social supports, and have not been successful at developing them in the past, even during periods of abstinence from alcohol.

Personal Resources

The next area to consider encompasses the client's personal psychological resources. Has this person been successful in other areas of life in setting goals, making changes in behavior, and completing tasks? If so, then outpatient treatment is more feasible than if the client has a history of not following through on decisions, not attaining goals that were desired. Another aspect of personal resources is the person's cognitive functioning. Continued, heavy alcohol consumption has significant effects on the drinker's memory and problem-solving and visual–spatial abilities. Some of this impairment recovers quickly after the cessation of drinking, while some impairment may persist for many months or even years (Goldman, 1983). Thus, the initial assessment should include some brief screening for cognitive deficits, and if such deficits are found, and the person is actively drinking, then a higher level of care might be considered. Otherwise, the learning, cognitive focus of treatment might be exceedingly frustrating for both client and therapist, because the client just would not be able to learn, retain, and use the information presented in treatment, until some of the most severe of the cognitive impairment is ameliorated.

Attitudes about Treatment

While this is a difficult area to assess, the factors of most concern are whether the client wants treatment at this time, and whether the client has a commitment to making changes through treatment. If a person is ambivalent about treatment, but willing to get involved, then sometimes a more intensive program is advantageous, as the program can provide a higher density of reinforcement for attending treatment and making changes than can occur in outpatient treatment. However, sometimes this ambivalence makes it impossible to treat a client in a more intensive partial hospital or inpatient program, because the person is not willing to disrupt his or her life to the extent required for such a program.

Practical Concerns

There are a number of practical concerns that should at least be mentioned. Does the person have a job? Can he or she get time off from work to attend a day hospital or inpatient program? Is this job in jeopardy? Is the employer willing to support treatment, or would any more absences mean a job loss? If so, then it would be unwise to recommend inpatient treatment if outpatient treatment seems at all likely to be successful. A second concern is the person's financial condition. Can he or she afford to take time off, and collect temporary disability (if sick time is not available), with the accompanying reduction in income? If not, outpatient treatment, or a partial hospital program that allows the person to work would be appropriate. Another kind of financial concern is the person's ability to pay for treatment. If health insurance covers inpatient treatment, but not partial hospitalization, then the former setting might be necessary even though not preferred, given the high costs of health care.

Other practical concerns revolve around transportation and child care. Can the client get to appointments if treatment begins on an outpatient basis? Is his or her driver's license suspended, and if so, can transportation be arranged? Is child care available if the person has to be hospitalized? If not, the day hospital setting becomes particularly advantageous.

There are a whole host of other, idiosyncratic practical concerns that the clinician must be sensitive to. Research suggests that alcoholics are more likely to become involved with and remain in treatment if their immediate needs are recognized (e.g., Chafetz *et al.*, 1962), so this becomes an important area when initiating treatment.

Personal Preference

Finally, the client's own preferences about the treatment must be carefully considered. If the client feels strongly about wanting to be in a hospital, then the clinician might be well advised to listen carefully to this request, even if the initial assessment suggests that outpatient treatment might be feasible. Similarly, if the client wants outpatient treatment, it might be attempted even if the clinician believes that more intensive treatment would be preferable.

General Considerations

In general, the selection of the initial treatment setting must be seen as a tentative decision. Often, an initial contract must be established that includes the client's preferred setting, but with some specification of the circumstances that would dictate a different level of care. For example, if the clinician believed that the client would find it extremely difficult to discontinue drinking on an outpatient basis, but this was the client's desire, then an initial contract might involve a plan for reducing and stopping drinking, teaching skills to support that plan, and a time limit. If the person were unsuccessful by the time specified, then the contract would be reviewed and alternative settings considered. Thus, while the initial setting decision is important, continuing to consider and discuss other treatment settings is an important early step in the treatment process.

Table 5-2 summarizes some of the indicators for each treatment setting dicussed in this section.

TABLE 5-2 Indicators for Treatment Settings

Setting	Criteria for use
Outpatient	No need for detoxification
	Already completed detoxification
	No previous treatment
	Able to discontinue or decrease drinking on own in the past
	Able to discontinue or decrease drinking with previous outpatient treatment
	Some social supports available
	Preference for outpatient treatment
Partial hospital	Previous failure of outpatient treatment
	Need for detoxification, with no history of complications during detoxification
	Trouble discontinuing or decreasing drinking on an outpatient basis
	Ambivalence about treatment
	Some social supports available
	Practical concerns (e.g., child care, need to work)
Inpatient	Need for continuously supervised detoxification
	Inability to abstain or decrease drinking with a lower level of care
	Acute medical or psychiatric problems requiring 24-hour care
	Lack of social supports
	Significant cognitive impairment
	Subjectively expressed need for hospitalization
Halfway house	Need for extended structure
	Slow cognitive recovery
	Lack of social supports for abstinent lifestyle

Social Context of Treatment

In this section the involvement of significant social systems will be considered. As reviewed previously, the literature on the treatment of alcoholism suggests that involvement of some significant social system is associated with positive treatment results. Thus, the clinician's first inclination should be to involve the spouse or some significant other in the treatment. As the functional analysis is completed, it should become clearer which persons are most important to involve, either because they are important cues for drinking, because they provide strong reinforcement for drinking, or because they can provide strong contingent reinforcement for stopping drinking.

There are a number of types of involvement of significant others including information, differential reinforcement for drinking and abstinence, emotional or practical support, relationship-focused treatment, treatment for the significant others, and/or helping the client access new social systems.

Information

Folklore in the alcohol field suggests that alcoholics tend to minimize or lie about their drinking and its consequences. The empirical literature is much less pessimistic, as a number of studies have shown that alcoholics in inpatient treatment provide accurate information about negative consequences associated with drinking (L. Sobell & M. Sobell, 1975; M. Sobell, L. Sobell, & Samuels, 1974). Studies comparing spouse and client reports of drinking behavior have shown that clients often report more drinking than do their spouses (McCrady, Paolino, & Longabaugh, 1978). However, there are a number of clinical considerations that support the involvement of someone else in the assessment and information-gathering process. First, clients are often referred to treatment or coerced into treatment by someone who has observed the adverse effects of their drinking. This process is often confusing and annoying to the client. Collecting information from the referring person, with the client present as well, helps the clinician and client understand the need for treatment.

Another reason that information from significant others is important is because of the effects of alcohol on memory. As noted earlier, alcohol consumption has a deleterious effect on memory functioning, and the client may forget important events that occurred while drinking. Recalling these events, and experiencing the emotional impact of them, can be important in motivating the person to remain in treatment and to make changes (Johnson, 1973). Having a significant person provide such information, in a supportive but factual way, can facilitate the treatment process.

Responses to Drinking and Abstinence

A second, and very different kind of social system involvement is in the establishment of a network that will provide differential reinforcement contingent on abstinence, and which will facilitate the immediate application of aversive consequences when the client drinks. Such reinforcement can be relatively simple, such as positive comments and encouragement from friends and family, or can involve the negotiation of detailed contracts, specifying the consequences of drinking. Such contracts may be negotiated with an employer who is willing to get involved and aware that the client has not been functioning on the job. Behaviors required of the client might be attending treatment on a regular basis, taking disulfiram under the supervision of the industrial nurse or personnel officer, reporting to an employee assistance program counselor on a regular basis, or coming to work sober and not drinking on the job. It should be noted, however, that such contingencies are not applied in most employee assistance programs (e.g., Hore & Plant, 1981). Contingencies can also be established with family members or friends, who would withdraw attention, or refuse to spend time with the person when drinking, but would continue to interact in positive ways when the person is not drinking.

A second component of the differential reinforcement notion is allowing the client to experience the naturally occurring aversive consequences of drinking. Many spouses protect the client from consequences of drinking, by covering for the person at work, doing their chores, lying to friends and family about the drinking, and so on (Orford *et al.*, 1975). Treatment interventions can teach the family member to allow naturally occurring consequences to be experienced by the client, thus increasing the punishers for drinking. This is an area of intervention heavily used by self-help organizations such as Al-Anon, but only more recently explored by behaviorally oriented clinicians (McCrady & Noel, 1982).

Decreasing Cues for Drinking

A third way that significant others can be involved in treatment is in helping to change their behaviors that cue drinking. For example, a spouse who "nags" the client about drinking, telling the person not to drink, or giving suggestions on how to not drink, may actually be engaging in behaviors that increase the person's desire to drink. Helping the spouse learn to identify such behaviors, learn about the relationship between these behaviors and the client's drinking, and learn alternative ways of discussing concerns about drinking may be another type of involvement.

Support for Not Drinking

Support is somewhat different from differential reinforcement, although both may be conceptualized as consequence control procedures. Support involves helping the client, upon request, to implement behavior changes. For example, if the client wants to talk about urges to drink and thinks that certain responses from another person would be helpful, providing these responses would be support. Or, if a self-management plan requires another person for its implementation (e.g., staying at a cocktail party for 1 hr instead of 3 hr), then compliance with these behaviors would constitute support.

Relationship Change

For many clients, there are important interactions with spouse, children, parents, or close friends that cue drinking behavior. Another type of involvement of the support system would be in relationship-focused treatment that would modify the problem interactions. This intervention could be behavioral marital or family therapy (e.g., McCrady & Noel 1982; O'Farrell, Cutter, & Fortgang, 1979) or parent skills training. Any of these treatments might be necessary for a particular client.

Significant-Other-Focused Treatments

Finally, many times family members have developed problems as a consequence of being involved with an alcohol abuser (Hingson, McCrady, & Walsh, 1984).

Spouses may have been battered during drinking episodes and need to learn ways to protect themselves during any future episodes. Spouses and children may blame themselves for the person's drinking, feel guilty, and have decreased their own level of functioning because of these reactions, and may need information and treatment to help them. While such interventions are beyond the scope of this chapter, it is essential for the clinician to be sensitive to the fact that the drinking has serious effects beyond the individual, and to be willing to provide treatment or referral for family members. As a general rule, I feel strongly that the clinician has an obligation to the family if abuse has occurred, and should not ignore the family's need for protection during treatment.

Accessing New Social Systems

For some clients, there are no social systems present that can be modified. For such clients it is important to access new systems that will provide differential reinforcement for drinking and abstinence or that will be incompatible with drinking. There are a number of groups that will provide strong support to a person for not drinking. Alcoholics Anonymous is the best known of these, but such groups as Drink Watchers or Women for Sobriety are alternative self-help groups. Many religious groups do not allow alcohol consumption, and serious involvement in such groups can also support abstinence. Pentacostal religions, Black Muslims, and fundamentalist Baptists are but a few examples.

Many group activities are also incompatible with drinking. Running, hiking, or bicycling groups are examples. Involvement in focussed intellectual activities can also serve such a focus. Unfortunately, alcohol can be involved with almost any activity, and the therapist and client need to look carefully at such activity groups to determine whether the group norm is drinking or not, and to seek out groups where drinking is not customary.

In summary, the decision about the social context of alcoholism treatment is a complicated one. The initial phases of assessment probably should involve at least one significant other. The results of this initial assessment should reveal who is a major cue for drinking, who reinforces drinking, and who is accessible for treatment involvement, either as a support or source of reinforcement for the client's behavior change. For some clients there are not readily accessible supports, and then new support systems must be systematically constructed with the client. These may be conventional support systems, such as AA, all-encompassing constructed reinforcement systems, such as in Hunt and Azrin's (1973) community reinforcement program, or systems that suit the client's individual needs.

Client Variables

There are a number of problems that alcohol abusers bring to treatment that the clinician needs to be aware of and sensitive to at the beginning of treatment. While some of the comments in this section are based on empirical research, many of these are derived from clinical observations. Thus, they are factors for the clinician to consider, and for the researcher to investigate. Five topics will be addressed in this section: emotional factors, cognitive factors, interpersonal relationship factors, medical issues, and social context issues.

Emotional

When a person begins to realize that his or her drinking is causing problems, he or she may have a variety of reactions. Most commonly, as negative consequences accumulate, the person begins to feel out of control of his or her life, and ashamed of the behaviors. At the same time, the things that the client is doing are unacceptable to his or her self-definition. Thus, financial or work irresponsibility, neglecting family, engaging in physical violence, or verbal abuse are all actions about which the person feels intense guilt and self-blame. The prospect of admitting these things to a stranger is frightening and embarrassing, making it difficult for clients to talk about drinking-associated problems. As many clients ascribe their problems to some kind of weakness of "will-power," and believe that if they were only "stronger" this would not have happened, they often blame themselves for their actions. Thus, clients are reluctant to be honest and are unusually sensitive to implied criticisms from the therapist when they are honest. The therapist can attenuate this problem by making some empathic comments such as, "I appreciate how difficult it is to talk about these things," by letting the client know that many of their actions are common patterns associated with alcoholism, and by listening to the client's descriptions of drinking behaviors in an accepting manner.

A second important factor is what is often called "ambivalence." There are a number of powerful reinforcers for continued drinking: Many of the aversive consequences are delayed, and some clients anticipate negative consequences of stopping drinking (such as loss of friends, loss of social contacts, or a personal sense of defeat). Thus, there are reinforcers for drinking and aversive consequences of abstinence that are on one side of this "ambivalence." At the same time, the aversive consequences of drinking are salient to the client, and he or she usually anticipates some reinforcers for abstinence, such as improved physical health, a sense of pride and accomplishment, or a renewed relationship with an estranged spouse. Thus, the client is in a classical double approach–avoidance conflict, and will show contradictory and sometimes unpredictable behaviors while in this conflict. The therapist must be aware of the conflict and acknowledge it but at the same time reinforce the side of the "ambivalence" that will keep the client in treatment.

A third emotional factor is that many alcoholic clients are depressed or anxious. Some of these affects are a result of the physiological effects of alcohol, while others are consequences of the guilt, shame, or fear described above. Whatever the etiology, such emotions may make it difficult for the client to provide information, to absorb information presented in treatment, or to implement homework assignments between treatment sessions.

Finally, many clients are afraid that treatment will not be successful. For some, these concerns stem from earlier unsuccessful attempts at treatment; for others it derives from their own sense of incompetence for having a drinking problem at all. Such concerns may lead to premature termination of treatment, or to an unwillingness to attempt behavior change procedures. Thus, clinicians must attempt to help the client understand something about the etiology of drinking problems, in order to remove some of the sense of personal weakness or failure, and also to assign homework that has high probability of success.

Cognitive

As noted earlier, many alcoholics will have subtle cognitive deficits, especially in the early weeks after the cessation of drinking. They may have trouble retaining information and may have particular difficulty with problem-solving tasks (Goldman, 1983). Information should be presented simply and redundantly. A single intervention should be repeated several times, written handouts should accompany treatment sessions, and homework assignments should be written out. The use of multiple modes of input may also be helpful, including verbal input, behavioral rehearsal, imagery techniques, and visually presented materials. While this is not necessary for all clients, those who do have deficits will become frustrated with treatment and may drop out quickly, rather than to experience this frustration and embarrassment. Unfortunately, the clinician may then conclude that the person was "not motivated" or "not ready" for treatment, rather than realizing that treatment was not correctly implemented.

Interpersonal

A third important client factor is the person's history of interactions with others about their drinking. Many alcoholics have been reinforced for verbal behaviors that are not helpful in treatment. For example, clients may be used to placating an angry spouse or employer after a drinking episode, promising it will never happen again. In addition, many clients have avoided aversive consequences of drinking episodes by lying and denying that it occurred. In treatment, when a client drinks, such behaviors are not helpful to the progress of therapy. The clinician, then, needs to teach the client that honest reports of drinking and developing strategies to decrease its reoccurrence are more appropriate; the clinician must shape these behaviors, rather then becoming annoyed at client promises or lies.

In sum, many of the verbal behaviors of alcoholics that clinicians find annoying or frustrating are understandable if the person's learning history is considered. With this perspective, such behaviors become problems to solve in the course of treatment, requiring the therapist to shape and teach a new set of verbal skills, rather than viewing these actions as "resistance" or "lack of motivation" for treatment.

Medical

Clinicians also need to be sensitive to the physical effects of heavy alcohol consumption. Even if a person does not have obvious medical problems, the effects of heavy drinking can be insidious and debilitating. Many people eat poorly while drinking, resulting in nutritional deficits, poor energy, or vague and diffuse physical discomfort. Many people also get very limited physical exercise when drinking, so their general muscle tone, cardiovascular fitness, and energy are poor. Treatment planning must consider these limitations, and programs of exercise or any interventions that require a good deal of stamina must be introduced gradually. Clients need to be reminded of simple things, such as eating properly and getting adequate sleep, as necessary prerequisites to being able to make major life changes.

Social Context

Finally, the therapist must assess whether the client has come to treatment voluntarily, or whether seeking treatment was motivated by some external force (such as the courts, the job, a spouse, or a friend). With externally motivated clients, one of the early tasks of treatment is both to support the contingencies that caused the person to seek treatment and to help the person begin to develop beliefs about his or her drinking that will support continuation in treatment.

Therapist Variables

Research on therapist variables in alcoholism treatment is scant. There has been some consideration of the differential effectiveness of professionals and paraprofessionals and of the comparative effectiveness of abstinent alcoholic versus nonalcoholic therapists. Findings are scant but suggest that paraprofessional and recovering alcoholic counselors have a positive role in alcoholism treatment, and they may enhance positive outcomes for certain kinds of clients (Argeriou & Manohar, 1978; Rosenberg, 1982). Data also suggest that such therapist variables as empathy (Emrick & Hansen, in press) are associated with better treatment success.

In addition to these research-based findings, there are certain attitudes and behaviors that the therapist should develop that appear to be conducive to successful treatment. First is a sense of empathy with the client. This involves some understanding of the client's subjective state, as described in the previous section, and an appreciation of the incredible difficulties involved in changing drinking behavior. It is helpful for any therapist who is going to work with alcoholics to personally give up some longstanding habit, such as smoking, overeating, running, reading, and the like. The therapist should keep a careful log of the behavior and a subjective account of the difficulties associated with the behavior change, especially noting relapse days. After several months of personal attempts at habit change, it is easier for a therapist to be empathic with alcoholics. In addition, therapists should attend some meetings of AA. Such meetings are important to many alcoholics who have successfully stopped drinking, and therefore the program should be understood. In addition, AA members tell stories about their drinking, their attempts at abstinence, and the problems and successes they encountered. Attending AA meetings is an excellent way of learning more about the subjective experience of being an alcoholic and helps the therapist to develop an appreciation of the pain involved in alcoholism and abstinence.

A second important therapist skill is the ability to discriminate between the person and the alcoholic behavior. Many of the things that a person does when drinking are socially inappropriate, and some are repugnant, illegal, or immoral. The therapist needs to be able to allow the client to describe such behaviors without feeling that the therapist is repulsed, but also without feeling that the therapist condones or accepts such behaviors. This is a delicate balance to achieve, especially when a client talks about drinking episodes in a joking manner. That joking may be the result of embarrassment or disgust with the drinking behavior or may indicate that the person does not believe that the behaviors are really that bad (which often occurs when a client has been coerced into treatment). In making this discrimination between the client and the drinking behavior, the therapist needs to encourage the client to talk about drinking behavior and sometimes needs to provide feedback about his or her own reaction to drinking associated actions. At the same time, the therapist needs to repeatedly communicate the belief that the client can develop the skills to modify the drinking and to modify some of these unacceptable actions. Thus, the stated or implied message to the client is, "You have done many things when drinking that are distressing to you and to the people around you. The fact that you are in treatment is a statement that you want to change some of these things. It is important to talk about things you have done when drinking, because by being aware of them, you will have a strong incentive to stop drinking and stop doing these things. Making changes will take time and a lot of work on your part, but I believe that you will be able to be successful if you stick with treatment and do the kinds of homework assignments that we develop." Thus the message must be positive about change but negative about the drinking-related behaviors.

A third extremely important therapist quality is the ability to be honest. Because of their discomfort and reinforcement history, it is hard for many alcoholic clients to be honest in treatment and in reporting drinking episodes, failed homework assignments, or their feelings and attitudes about being in treatment. The therapist must provide a positive model of honesty. The therapist should *never* ignore the smell of alcohol on a client's breath and should always review homework assignments in detail. Attending to these things teaches the client the importance of following through on commitments, the consequences of honesty, and increases the chances that the therapist and client will be able to identify problems and blocks to progress in treatment. While these comments may appear to obvious to behavioral clinicians, they are important to emphasize because so many alcoholic clients will, with great skill and persistence, attempt to avoid discussions of drinking or failed homework assignments.

Summary

This section has addressed the nonspecifics of therapeutic decision making and subjective factors that the clinician must be sensitive to in the initiation and implementation of treatment. The next section presents a detailed description of one case, which illustrates many of the assessment and treatment techniques used in skills-oriented behavioral treatment of alcoholism.

CASE STUDY

The following case study illustrates a number of applications of behavioral alcoholism treatment. It should be emphasized, however, that this is only one case, and it should not be seen as a blueprint for every case. The process of decision making will be made as explicit as possible, so that the reader will be able to use some of the same criteria for clinical decisions, even though the results of the decisions and the course of treatment may be very different.

Identifying Information

Mary sought treatment for her drinking problem after seeing an article in a local newspaper about a clinical research program for alcohol abusers and their spouses. One of her close friends had recently been involved in another alcoholism treatment program at the same hospital, so Mary was familiar with the facility and with the likelihood of positive treatment results.

Mary was a 49-year-old school teacher, married to Tom, a successful corporate executive, for 29 years. They had three children, David (25 years old), Stephanie (23 years old), and Mark (17 years old) who was the only one still at home.

Pretreatment Assessment

Assessment prior to the implementation of behavioral treatment techniques comprises several components including a clinical screening, general history, general problem assessment procedures, alcohol specific assessment procedures, and physical examination and laboratory studies.

Clinical Screening

The initial screening should be done when the client is sober, with a blood alcohol level of .05 mg% or less (M. Sobell, L. Sobell, & Vanderspek, 1979). If the client is intoxicated, the assessment should focus on the need for detoxification and ways to help the person get sober enough for further assessment, if immediate hospitalization is not warranted. If the person is sufficiently sober, the initial screening examines the client's reasons for seeking treatment, the presence of problems other than alcohol abuse, medical problems, drug use and abuse, and the need for detoxification.

Mary had made the initial phone contact with the treatment research project. She was scheduled for an initial interview within a few days and was asked to have her husband come as well. This latter was a criterion for the research component of the program, but also is my usual clinical practice if a client is married. At the initial meeting I began by explaining that the interview would have to begin with a breath test and that we would always begin this way. The purposes, I explained, were to be sure that Mary would have a clear head for the session and to encourage her to feel comfortable about honestly reporting any drinking. While the machine was warming up, we chatted about how they found out about the program and also how the machine worked. Breath testing could be viewed as a "police action." However, if the therapist presents it positively, the test effectively begins to set limits on the client's drinking, and provides a format for some education about alcohol. I discussed the .05-mg% limit, explaining that for a woman of Mary's size two drinks in the hour before the session would be sufficient to raise her blood alcohol level that high. Tom was interested in this information and asked also about how many drinks would lead to legal intoxication. I provided some information about blood alcohol levels and the rate of alcohol metabolism. Thus, in the first few minutes, I was able to impart information about alcohol and set a particular therapeutic tone for the session.

After the breath testing, which revealed that Mary had a blood alcohol level of zero, I explained that during this interview I wanted to get a chance to know what problems they had been having, and to try to determine together whether or not I could provide the appropriate treatment for them. In addition, there were some research criteria to meet, which are not relevant to this chapter.

This part of the interview began by asking "What were the main problems that led you to call?" Mary began to describe a number of problems. She was particularly concerned that she was drinking every day and that she was falling asleep quite early each evening (8:00–8:30 p.m.). She also felt that she was overly preoccupied with alcohol and drinking and constantly had to think about how to control her drinking, and she worried about how she would behave if she did drink. She no longer enjoyed going out to parties and other social events because of her worries about overdrinking. She did not like some of her actions when drinking, feeling that she became overly emotional and maudlin. When asked if there were any additional problems that concerned her, she also noted that she was having black outs after drinking, that her youngest son, Mark, was quite distressed about her drinking, that some of her friends were upset with her for things she said when drinking, and that she had noticed a lack of energy in the mornings.

To this point Tom had been quiet, so I asked him how he saw his wife's drinking problem. He responded that he didn't feel that his wife had much of a drinking problem; that the only things he had noticed were that she did not stop after three drinks, and that she had black outs. He indicated that her drinking had not affected him very much, but that he did get somewhat concerned when she would say that she could not remember what she had done at a party.

After this fairly brief description of the drinking problem, I indicated that I wanted to briefly ask questions about a number of areas to make sure that I understood all of the kinds of problems Mary and Tom were experiencing, and that we would return to a fuller discussion of the drinking in a little while. I then covered a number of areas, including history of hospitalizations and current medical problems, drug and medication use, treatment history, withdrawal symptoms, and brief screenings to assess cognitive functioning and other possible major psychiatric problems. This portion of the interview revealed that Mary had been hospitalized 5 years earlier with severe viral hepatitis, and had been confined to bed rest for several months following the hospitalization. As far as I could determine, her alcohol consumption did not play a role in the hepatitis, but one of the results of the illness was that her tolerance for alcohol was markedly reduced, so that two to three drinks had a major impact on her behavior. She also had had surgery to have a lump removed from her throat. The mass was benign, but she had been quite frightened at the time. She reported no current physical problems and had had a physical examination 3 months previously. I asked her to sign a release of information to obtain the results of that physical from her family physician, just to verify her report of her physical health status. Mary reported that she had never had any major emotional problems and had never been in treatment previously. She took some prescription medications for a sinus condition, and appeared to take this medication according to her prescription. She reported that she used no other medications, specifically responding "no" to questions about minor tranquilizers, amphetamines, cocaine, marijuana, and the like. Tom also reported no history of emotional problems or drug use or abuse.

Some brief screening questionnaires were integrated into this initial interview. The Mini-Mental Status Exam (Folstein, Folstein, & McHugh, 1975) includes 10 questions that screen for serious cognitive dysfunction. The examination is comprised of questions about orientation, having the client do serial-7 subtractions, a simple memory task, copying a figure, naming common objects, following a three-stage direction, and writing a sentence spontaneously. There are adequate norms for the test, which provides information about the person's overall cognitive functioning. Mary made no mistakes on the exam. In addition, I used several of the questions from the Present State Exam (Wing, Cooper, & Sartorius, 1974) to screen for psychotic disorders. She indicated that she experienced strong feelings of guilt, believing that when things went wrong they were always her fault. She did not show any other problems that would be indicative of depression, and this particular problem was noted for possible treatment intervention.

The final screening component of the interview was an assessment of whether or not Mary would experience alcohol withdrawal symptoms when she stopped drinking. To assess this, I asked a number of questions. First, she indicated that her last drink had been the previous evening, when she had had one glass of wine. Since it had been 20 hr since her last drink, she could have been expected to show some withdrawal symptoms, were she physically addicted to alcohol (withdrawal symptoms usually begin 5–12 hr after a person's last drink). I asked extensively about problems such as shaking, sweating, nausea, vomiting, diarrhea, having trouble sleeping the previous night, feeling excessive anxiety, or feeling confused. She said that the only problem she had experienced was some difficulty sleeping the previous night. I also questioned her about major withdrawal symptoms, such as seizures, hallucinations, and disorientation, and encouraged Tom to add any additional information. Since Mary did not have any withdrawal symptoms when she had previously stopped drinking, it seemed clear that she would not need to have a supervised alcohol detoxification and that she could begin treatment on an outpatient basis. While reviewing the symptoms of alcohol withdrawal, I also provided some information about physical addiction and withdrawal, as Tom and Mary were unfamiliar with these problems.

Drinking History

In taking the drinking history, it is important to begin to focus on patterns in the client's drinking, as a first step toward a functional analysis of drinking behavior. In addition, quantity is useful to assess, but not as crucial. Finally, a careful focus on the negative consequences of drinking is important. To assess drinking history and pattern, I used three assessment procedures: the Michigan Alcoholism Screening Test (MAST; Selzer, 1971), a 365-day drinking history, and a structured interview. The MAST was originally designed to screen for potential alcohol problems and covers a range of negative consequences of drinking. It asks all questions in the form "Have you ever. . . ?" and therefore must be followed up with interview questions to determine whether the problems identified are current or historical. Mary's score on the MAST was 9, which is in the problem range, but relatively low. She endorsed a number of concerns. She did not feel that she was a "normal drinker" because of her preoccupation with alcohol and because she felt that she was using alcohol as a reward. She also reported "feeling bad" about her drinking, trying to limit her drinking to certain times and places in an effort to control it, and said that she was not always able to stop drinking when she wanted. While the MAST did not add a good deal of further information to her clinical picture, it provided an efficient way of screening for a range of drinking-related problems (e.g., lost jobs, physical problems, work problems, arrests, drunk driving). Some clients will respond affirmatively to questions on the MAST that they had not previously mentioned in the clinical interview, thus providing a fuller picture of their drinking problems.

My drinking history interview covered several areas. The goal of such an interview is to obtain detailed information about drinking consequences in each of the client's major areas of life functioning including physical health, interpersonal relationships, occupational and financial functioning, and legal functioning. This interview revealed that Mary had never had marital problems because of her drinking and had never had a separation from her husband. She did note that one friend of hers had asked Tom if Mary had a drinking problem, but that only her son had actively complained about her drinking. She had been employed full-time as a teacher for the last 20 years and had not missed any work or ever lost a job because of her drinking. She felt that her effectiveness as a teacher was reduced because of her fatigue and occasional hangovers. Her personal income was the highest it had ever been, supporting the impression that her drinking had not led to any major deterioration in her job performance. She had never been arrested for anything, and was asked specifically about drunk driving or drunk and disorderly arrests and whether her driver's license had ever been suspended for alcohol-related reasons. She was also asked if she had ever had any car accidents and whether she had been drinking at the time of the accidents. She also had no physical complaints because of her drinking. In general, her concerns were quite specific to the emotional, subjective area, which is not uncommon for women alcohol abusers (McCrady, 1984).

Finally, a 365-day daily drinking history was obtained, using the time-line follow-back procedures developed by the Sobells and their colleagues (M. Sobell *et al.*, 1980). For research purposes, at least 6 months of data are necessary to obtain a representative baseline (McCrady, Duclos, Dubreuil, Stout, & Fisher-Nelson, in press), although for clinical purposes, the clinician might obtain a 3-month history, and then ask about periods during the year in which the client's drinking pattern was different. Since it is an awesome task to reconstruct one's drinking for each day of a year, the clinician needs to carefully explain the rationale for the interview. First, it is important to understand how much and how frequently the client has been drinking. This information is often helpful to the client in assessing the severity or extent of the drinking problem. Second, looking at daily drinking enables the client and clinician to identify patterns, as a way to develop an accurate understanding of cues associated with drinking and with abstinence. To obtain the history it is helpful to give the client or couple a calendar ahead of time and to ask them to fill in as many significant dates and events as they can recall. They should be encouraged to look at a calendar, appointment book, or checkbook for reminders, and a list of significant events can be provided (birthdays, anniversaries, weddings, funerals, parties, religious events, club events, vacations, family events, entertainment at home, births, doctors appointments, business trips or conventions, local political or union events, sports events, etc.). Mary's 365-day drinking history revealed that she had had only four abstinent days in the entire year, three of which were when she was camping. Her usual alcohol consumption was only one to two drinks each day, which, as noted, were enough to affect her significantly. She always drank more heavily at parties, when she and Tom would go out to dinner, on holidays, vacations, and weekends. She engaged in extremely heavy drinking (more than six drinks) three times during the year. One of these was at a teachers' party at the end of the school year; the second was at

Thanksgiving, when she was entertaining a large group of guests, and the third was associated with a plane trip to New York after some frightening experiences during a trip to Puerto Rico. Thus, the drinking history revealed that quantities were not a major problem, but the consistency of her drinking was clear, and certain patterns began to clearly emerge.

Other Life Areas

In addition to the drinking history, I routinely obtain some information about a client's general functioning in their marital relationships, with their children, in their work, and in how they spend their leisure time. Mary and Tom reported no significant marital problems. The positive interactions they had in the treatment sessions, Tom's immediate willingness to support Mary's decision to seek treatment and become involved himself, and very high scores on the Locke–Wallace Marital Adjustment Test (Locke & Wallace, 1959) (hers was 126; his was 138— well above the cutoff score of 100) all supported their initial reports of a happy marriage. Mary said that she had a warm, close relationship with each of her children. However, as she talked more, it was apparent that she would become quite upset whenever one of her children had a problem, as she would blame herself for this problem, thinking that if she had only been a better mother that her child would not have to experience any problems at all. She had some awareness that she was taking too much responsibility for her children's lives, but was not convinced that her beliefs were incorrect.

In the job area Mary said that she enjoyed her work. Two kinds of problems that she related to her drinking seemed to come up at work. The first was conflicts with other teachers and the administration around contract and union issues. She would feel angry about how a particular contract issue was being handled and would either say nothing, or, if she did speak up would find herself taking full responsibility for the problem, and then not get support from her fellow teachers. Both being unassertive and feeling unsupported were quite upsetting to her. The second kind of work stress was that Mary was usually assigned one problem class. She apparently had a reputation as being unusually good at handling problem students. However, when teaching these students, she would become tense, frequently getting headaches, becoming angry at the kids, and generally feeling that she was not as effective as she would like to be at these times. While in either of these work situations, she would be anticipating having a drink when she got home, to relax and forget about the day.

Finally, we talked about Mary's use of her free time and about her friends. Mary had one very close friend, Anne, whom she saw or talked to several times each week. They had been neighbors, and had learned how to drink together. They had continued to go out to lunch, or visit each other and drink until Anne went into alcoholism treatment. Mary continued to see her but no longer drank with her, because she felt that it would not be courteous to drink when Anne did not. Mary and Tom had a fairly large circle of friends who had frequent dinner or cocktail parties. Mary usually drank more heavily at these events, to feel at ease socially, and because she felt that she could then talk with "boring people" (which she felt she was obliged to do) and not be so bored herself. She thought that she was seen as a polite, nice person who never disagreed, and she could not imagine being any different at social events. She and Tom also travelled extensively, and she loved to read in her leisure time.

At this point in the assessment, I had some clear ideas about what problem areas were related to Mary's drinking, and I knew some of the aversive consequences of her drinking that served as reasons for her to want to stop, I knew that her medical status was good, and I knew there was no need for detoxification. In addition, she did not seem to have major problems in her life that had no functional relationship to her drinking, so it appeared that behaviorally oriented treatment to help her develop skills to maintain abstinence, and modify some of the problems that cued drinking would be appropriate treatment for her. She was highly motivated for treatment, and was acutely aware of the problems her drinking had caused, so it would not be necessary to focus treatment on motivational issues. She also had two extremely important supports for change in Anne, her abstinent friend, and in her husband. It seemed appropriate to have him continue in treatment with her, and to consider whether Anne's presence would be helpful at some point.

Treatment

Overview of Treatment

In general, treatment has to include several steps: (1) problem identification and general screening (discussed previously), (2) detoxification if necessary, (3) helping the client recognize the need to stop drinking and realize that skills acquisition is a necessary component of maintaining changed drinking status, (4) skills acquisition, and (5) maintenance of change.Skills acquisition includes the acquisition of specific strategies to not drink as well as more general coping strategies that will make long-term abstinence both possible and reinforcing. In addition, two further components need to be woven into the treatment on an ongoing basis—education about alcohol and its effects and reinforcement of the client's belief in the need to maintain abstinence. Since the issues of general problem identification and screening and detoxification assessment are discussed above, they will not be repeated here, but are noted to emphasize that these steps must be completed before intervention strategies should be initiated.

Identifying the Need for Abstinence

As discussed above, many clients have mixed feelings about whether or not they have a drinking problem and what is necessary in order to solve that problem. The extensive interviewing about negative consequences of drinking is an important first step in helping a person make a commitment to treatment and behavior change. With Mary there was no question that she knew she had a problem. With less-committed clients I often will make a list of negative consequences that we have identified and give it to the client. I will then have the client review the list several times each day, pairing the review with some high-frequency event such as smoking a cigarette or making telephone calls. I ask them to read the list at these times and think about each of the problems listed. This procedure is often quite powerful. The person increases the amount of time spent thinking that they do have a problem, and this sometimes results in a dramatic cognitive–affective shift.

The goal of this review is not to get a person to state, "I am an alcoholic" or to feel overwhelmed and powerless about their drinking (as in AA). Instead, the goal is to help the person identify sufficient reasons to want to continue in treatment and attempt behavior change procedures that are part of the treatment.

The second component of the initial phase of treatment is a discussion of drinking goals. While controlled drinking is used by many behavioral clinicians as an alternative to abstinence (e.g., Marlatt & Gordon, 1985; W. Miller, 1978; M. Sobell & L. Sobell, 1973, 1976), I think that controlled drinking should be viewed as a research issue rather than a part of routine clinical practice. Abstinence is a safe goal, as it is impossible to experience most negative consequences of drinking when abstinent. Clients must make an assessment of the importance of alcohol, compared to the myriad problems they have experienced when drinking. With some clients, it is helpful to present abstinence as a provisional decision, which the client will want to reevaluate periodically. My discussion of abstinence with Mary was as follows. (In all transcripts, M is Mary, T is Tom, TH is therapist. Mary often calls her husband by his nickname, Smitty.)

M: I'd like to clarify something with you, though, because I really think that maybe what I'm doing is, I might be hedging and be doing something dishonest to both me and to you. I really want to know what you think. I know that you're not here as a jailer or judge. What I've been trying to do is to say I don't have to stop drinking to myself. What I have to do is to stop drinking in a compulsive way. But I haven't said to myself, "I can never have another drink." I don't know if I should be doing this, or if I should just say to myself, "that's it—I can't have another drink." Or if I should say to myself, "I can handle one glass of wine if I go out to a nice restaurant—one glass of wine and not have another drink." Is that all dishonest? What I'm trying to get at, is that within the realm of the therapy or is that just dishonest?

TH: OK. I'm glad you're asking, because I'm not sure how clear I was about that in the beginning.

M: What I don't ever want to do again is drink compulsively or drink too much.

TH: OK. While you're in treatment, from my point of view the goal is to not drink any alcohol. Generally, if you're starting to get into trouble with alcohol it's a lot safer not to drink. It's hard to predict how much or how often you would have to drink to be compulsive again. It might be that having one drink every day would not lead you back into compulsive drinking, but it might be that having one drink every day and two drinks each evening of the weekend would lead you back into compulsive drinking. The boundaries are fuzzy between drinking and compulsive drinking, when you slide from one to the other. From my point of view, it's safer once you start to have problems to just say, "I'm not going to drink alcohol." As we go along in treatment, I'd like you to be abstaining from alcohol. You can stop and ask yourself that question periodically, "Do I want to be drinking at all? What would be the value of it?" I think because you haven't been physically addicted to alcohol that you need to be answering that question in a way that you feel comfortable with. But you need to abstain during treatment. Otherwise you're never going to know what it's like not to drink for a period of time. You know what it's like to drink compulsively; you know what it's like to drink moderately; you don't know as much about what its like to be an abstainer after having been a drinker. So you need to experience that in order to have the information to make your final decision about what you want to do. I come down on the very conservative side, saying that alcohol is pleasant, it gives some pleasant effects, sometimes it tastes good, it's nice socially, but compared to the risks that you're concerned about, why put yourself at risk. OK. So abstain during treatment and evaluate that question for yourself. We should discuss it periodically as you're going through, to see where you are in terms of your thinking.

   M: OK. That's good. I should have asked you the first time I came.

Skills Acquisition

BEHAVIORAL ANALYSIS (THREE SESSIONS)

After the initial commitment to treatment and abstinence is established, I begin to teach clients how to understand drinking as a learned behavior that is cued by identifiable antecedents, mediated by expectancies, and maintained by positive consequences. To do this, several techniques can be used. With Mary and Tom I began by explaining the concept of drinking as a learned behavior and used an already prepared sheet to help them learn the components of a behavior chain (Figure 5-1).

FIGURE 5-1. A client Triggers Sheet.

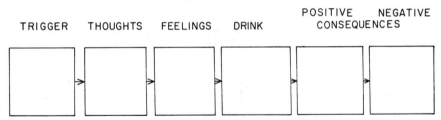

TH: We'll be spending time looking at your drinking and seeing what the systematic patterns are in it. We're going to use a specific format for looking at drinking situations. And I want to introduce you to that now. This sheet is entitled "Analyzing Drinking." Because that's what we're going to try to do—analyze the situations that go along with your drinking. We also call it a trigger sheet. Because what we're going to try to do is identify all kinds of triggers that go along with your drinking. Now a trigger is simply any situation, event, person, time that increases the probability that you will drink. A trigger is not something that makes you drink.

T: My coming home from work is a trigger.

TH: Right. Exactly. That's something that increases the probability that Mary would have a drink. Going to a dinner party would be a trigger. Being escorted onto the plane in Puerto Rico and having the cabin attendant say, "Would you have a drink?" This would be a trigger. They can be emotional and dramatic things, or simple, mundane things. But as long as they're things associated with drinking, that's the first thing that we'd want to identify. When we're looking for triggers, we're looking for a probability statement. They aren't things that guarantee that you're going to drink; if they guaranteed that you were going to drink, there'd be no point in treatment programs. And nobody could ever stop drinking because it would be 100% certain that you'd drink in those situations. When you encounter a situation where there's a trigger, you have a reaction to it—an internal reaction—that we call thoughts and feelings. You think about what's happening, you may have some emotional reaction, and part of that thinking may involve thinking about having a drink. So, for example, when you got on that plane in Puerto Rico, and the steward said "Would you like to have a drink?," I imagine you have had a whole series of thoughts and feelings. Is that fair to say?

M: Oh, yes. I had a lot.

T: Like—What a nice man . . .

M: Yes, he was, too.

TH: So, when he offered you the drink, you were thinking, "Oh, what a nice man," and "That's a good idea, I've got to relax."

M: That was my reward. I think I used it as a reward system more than even a relaxing system. Like I had done something really good or I had handled it good, I'd feel that at the end of the day I deserved a drink. I've put up with a great deal of pain-in-the-neck stuff at school, and I'd think of holding it out to myself like a carrot. Or, "Tonight I'll have a drink when Smitty comes home—that would be nice." I know I kind of used it as a reward in Puerto Rico.

TH: So, a situation comes up. You have thoughts and feelings and some of those thoughts relate to alcohol.

M: Obviously.

TH: And then you make a decision. Of course, I'm drawing out something that often happens quickly—in a second. And then you drink—a little or a lot. Now, as you'll notice, this is something that's happening across time. Usually the first things that happen when you drink are the positive consequences; basically you get some goodies from drinking.

M: Definitely.

TH: Like on the plane I imagine there was some relief in sitting back and having a drink. Were there other good things about that first drink, do you remember?

M: There was relief. I can't honestly say I liked the taste of drinking, except wine. It wasn't really the taste. I get the relaxation feeling. The feeling of—just before you get the feeling of getting high—the feeling of well-being. A feeling that you can handle things even if you normally would think it seemed hard. It's a false sense of security that you could handle anything. All the conventional things you feel when you drink.

TH: But you're in touch with these and it's important. Because a lot of times, for you, you can list a lot of negative things that go along with your drinking.

M: They come later, though. They come after the first one.

TH: I think you're reading my sheet here!

M: Well, I've lived with this and analyzed myself enough to know that the negatives come later. The positives are really there. If only I could stay there always. I'd love to be at that point that I could say that I never have to give up drinking. So I could stay with the positives that do come from one drink, or two drinks.

TH: So, as you just said, "The negatives come later."

M: Yes, they do come later.

TH: And we've talked a lot about those. There are a couple of things about this chain which I think are real important to think about. One is that sometimes the negative things can become triggers.

M: I agree. For instance, if I'm really upset. This is something that we've talked about before. How I say, "How bad was I last night? I must have embarrassed you by talking so much at that dinner party." Well, then I'm feeling so down about myself. This would be like on a Saturday or Sunday after a dinner party. "What a creep I am; I don't know how you can live with me. Why don't you get embarrassed when I do this and say, 'Mary!'" It gives me assurance which I don't believe. . . . So I will have a drink at lunchtime on a Saturday or Sunday. I will say, "I'll have a drink because I'm feeling so lousy so what's one more drink going to do. I already made a mess of the evening before in front of so many people." So I do know of the negative triggers. It's a trigger for me. The negative feelings can also keep me away—can avert me from drinking, too. The guilt is enough and I feel enough self-disgust. Then I won't drink too much for a long time. And I'll be very careful and try very hard to be perfect, the way I want to and congratulate myself when I haven't had more than I approve of drinking. So it can be both ways. So it can be an aversion sometimes. I can be so disgusted that I talk so much. Sometimes all I can remember is the sound of my own voice. You know, and Smitty says that wasn't the way it was at all. There were a lot of other people talking, and you were interesting, and people were listening to you and all. And I think how I bored them in every sense of the word. . . .

TH: One other thing that I wanted to mention about this; it's very important in terms of understanding why people keep drinking. That vicious circle thing. You've had courses in learning theory and things like that. We know, the most immediate consequence of the behavior is the one that's going to affect the future course of the behavior. One of the problems with drinking is the reinforcing consequences—the good things always come first. The punishment is delayed so it doesn't actively impact on your decision. The thing that's important is that *sequence* that happens. So one of the things we'll be doing later in treatment is helping you, in your head, to move the negatives up to help counter the thought, "Boy, a drink would taste good." And to be able, in your head, to try to move the positives away and the negatives up. Because the more the negatives are absolutely salient, the easier it is to not have a drink in any particular time. So, there's a lot of value of having things mapped out this way 'cause then we can start juggling around and figuring out how we can move things around in a way that it's easier not to drink. Overall, is that sequence pretty clear to both of you? Why don't we try to work one fairly simple example just to give you the hang of it.

Mary and Tom understood and accepted a behavioral view quite readily. As homework, I had them do several things to further their understanding of the behavioral chain and to help complete my assessment of cues for drinking. First, I introduced self-monitoring. Mary was given one card for each day of the week. She was told to carry the card with her at all times (W. Miller & Muñoz, 1976) and to make entries on the card if she had a drink, or if she experienced an urge to drink at any time. I emphasized that I did not want her to drink, but that if she did it would be important to be honest and record it so that we could learn what the situation was that cued the drinking, and could use that information to help her develop alternative strategies. She as instructed to record a drink before she consumed it, to measure drinks so that they were of a standard size (4 oz. of wine, 1 oz. shot of hard liquor, one 12-oz. beer), and not to have her glass refilled before she finished a drink. She was asked to enter urges any time she felt that she would like to have a drink. She was also asked to rate the intensity of that urge, using a 1–7 scale. Tom was also asked to make a daily estimate of Mary's urge intensity, and of whether or not he thought she drank. His recordings were used for research purposes, as a validity check, and also for clinical reasons. Spouse recording makes it explicit that the spouse is noticing whether or not the client is drinking. Without making this explicit, the spouse will still be observing and may try to surreptitiously let the therapist know when drinking occurs. In addition, asking the spouse to make subjective urge estimates helps the spouse pay attention to the client's subjective state and try to understand it, rather than being angry or unaware.

The second homework assignment was to have Mary and Tom both complete the Drinking Patterns Questionnaire (Zitter & McCrady, 1979). This questionnaire lists over 200 situations (external and internal) that clients have described as associated with drinking, and asks the client to check off which of these situations they believe is associated with their drinking. I also ask the spouse to complete the questionnaire for their perceptions of situations associated with drinking, as a way to obtain an observer's viewpoint.

The third homework was to have Mary work out some behavior chains on her own during the week. Over the course of 2 weeks, I asked her to do some chains that described past situations, and then to actually work out behavior chains at times when she was having an urge to drink. She worked out chains on several antecedents, including: (1) Tom having a drink when they were celebrating something together, (2) having her feelings hurt, (3) having wine poured into her glass at a dinner party, (4) having lunch with Anne and Anne was having a drink, (5) Thanksgiving, and (6) one of her children having a problem. Some of these behavior chains are illustrated in Figure 5-2.

The net effect of these homework assignments was to provide a comprehensive assessment of situations associated with Mary's drinking. Through the homework assignments Mary was also learning one self-control procedure for times when she wanted to drink—analyzing the feeling rather than drinking.

As a result of these homework assignments, it was apparent that there were several major problems associated with Mary's drinking that were quite suitable for behavioral interventions. First, some environmental control procedures were needed. Mary constructed environments that were highly conducive to drinking. For example, she would work so hard at holiday dinner preparations that she would want to drink. The numerous parties were an important antecedent, as were holidays and weekends. She also had a particular spot on her living room couch where she always sat when drinking. A number of self-management strategies were developed for these areas (see the following section). Second, Tom engaged in some behaviors that appeared to cue drinking and also tended to protect Mary from experiencing aversive consequences of her drinking, and this was a necessary area of intervention. Third, she was often with people who reinforced drinking, so it seemed to be important to maximize reinforcement of abstinence. Self-reinforcement and reinforcement from her husband, children, and Anne seemed most feasible.

The first set of interventions are ones that specifically would help Mary to not drink. The second set of interventions would be ones to help her with major problem areas that were associated with her drinking: her unrealistic expectations about having to be charming, perfect, and making everyone else happy; her lack of assertiveness; and her difficulties in relaxation, particularly in the classroom.

ABSTINENCE STRATEGIES (FIVE SESSIONS)

The first area of self-management planning was around holidays. Mary would prepare stuffed mushroom caps for 16 people for appetizers, have ham, turkey, and roast beef for dinner, and literally serve eight different desserts. She prepared everything herself and became exhausted in the process (especially since she had a full-time job to do in addition to all the preparations for entertaining). The self-management planning involved challenging her assumptions about what kind of a hostess she should be, as well as concrete ways of

TRIGGER →	THOUGHTS →	FEELINGS →	DRINK →	POSITIVE CONSEQUENCES →	NEGATIVE CONSEQUENCES
Wine poured into glass at dinner party	I would like the taste of wine I don't want to hurt the host I wouldn't want to get intoxicated	Anxiety about disappointing host Ambivalent about drinking	Drink	Tasted good, decreased anxiety, increased assertiveness, complimenting host	Lack of control, intoxication, black out, morning hangover
Holidays— preparing holiday meal	I've got to have everything perfect I'll have to prepare many desserts It's up to me to make everyone happy	Insecure Anxious Resentful Irritated	Drink	Anesthetizes feelings relating to holiday preparation	Guilt about drinking, angry at self, embarrassment about intoxication, hangover
Children's life problems	How have I failed, I must have been paying too much attention to my own life, I've created their problem through my neglect	Insecure Anger at self Guilty Responsible Depressed	Drink	Detachment from affect	Black out, increased guilt, self-contempt, hangover
Criticism from others or husband	I'd like to tell them off If I did I would be petty; maybe they're right	Angry Insecure Frustrated Inadequate	Drink	Detachment from affect, false sense of confidence, expressing her anger	Guilt, black out, hangover, insecure, regretful, shame

FIGURE 5-2. Mary's behavior chains.

decreasing her burden. When she first told me about the stuffed mushrooms, I gasped in amazement and said, "You've got to be kidding." I asked her to brainstorm, and she decided on decreasing the guest list, cutting out the stuffed mushrooms, serving only one kind of meat, and having only two desserts. Her comments about her planning illustrate the ways in which her thinking was beginning to change.

M: I'm not going to do that. Again it was that superwoman thing, the '50s. I was thinking of that this morning. I was reading an essay by Ellen Goodman. She was talking about the '50s women and how they were brainwashed to be supermoms, superwives, super everything, and I still—there are remnants of that I still cling to. One of them is my menu. I've seen it for a long time but couldn't just stop doing it. Even though I could see for years that this is ridiculous. The expectations of my guests overrode my own qualms. But now they don't. I think it's more important for me to stay sober than it is for them to have that many different kinds of dessert. I'm not going to feel sorry for myself and force myself into a position where the only way out is to drink, which is what I've been doing.

A second problem was dinner parties. We were able to identify several components of these situations that were problematic—the host pushing her to drink and she feeling that she couldn't refuse at this point, having wine served to her at dinner, and getting stuck talking to people whom she disliked. She and Tom decided that he would become her drink server, and that he would bring her club soda unless she explicitly asked him for something else. If wine was poured for her at dinner, I suggested that she could just leave it, or could refuse the wine completely. She felt that these ideas were not "gracious," but could not think of any alternatives. She explained that her friends were wine connoisseurs, and that not tasting their wine would be insulting and suggest that they had poor taste. She finally decided on two alternatives—putting the glass to her lips once, complimenting the host on the wine, and then putting it down, or surreptitiously giving her glass to Tom. I thought that both of these strategies were problematic, the first because once she had tasted the wine I suspected that it would increase the probability of her drinking more of it, and because it would create another uncomfortable situation if she did not drink it, because the host might ask her why she was not drinking any more of it. The second I thought might be difficult to implement, and that people might notice the switch, which would be embarrassing (a feeling she wanted to avoid). However, she settled on these strategies, and at the next party she used the putting the glass to her lips strategy with success.

After several weeks in treatment and several more parties, I asked Mary if she would consider refusing drinks more directly. I raised this because her concerns about other's views of her seemed to create problems, and because it seemed that hiding her abstinence might become increasingly uncomfortable, perhaps contributing to relapses. At this point, she was more amenable to direct ways of refusing. We brainstormed some ideas, and then role-played several times. I role-played a curious friend, who did not accept her initial refusals. She decided to first ask for an alternative beverage (club soda) and to say "I don't drink" if someone was persistent in pushing her. For friends she decided to say, "I've decided not to drink any more—its just a personal preference." I also included Tom in some of the role plays. Mary did not want Tom to "rescue" her from a difficult situation but said it would be helpful if he came over to join the conversation if Mary appeared to be on the spot. Much to her amazement, none of her friends said a thing when she asked for club soda at the next few parties, and she felt some relief that she was no longer trying to hide her nondrinking status.

For the third party problem—being stuck with boring people—Mary initially felt that she could not use any direct, assertive behaviors. She came up with some self-management plans such as deliberately seeking out people she liked as soon as she got to the party, or helping the hostess with food preparations in the kitchen. She thought that these were strategies she could implement, and I encouraged these, rather than suggesting that she might try more direct strategies, because I wanted to reinforce her planning and trying out new behaviors. Her strategy worked well, and she reported that she had no urges to drink at the dinner party she attended that week. In fact, she enjoyed herself immensely because she was not drinking and did not have to worry about whether or not she would overdrink and embarrass herself.

Two other areas I thought were important ones for self-management planning were the weekends and her favorite spot on the couch. The latter she insisted was no longer a problem. I suggested a simple self-control procedure, sitting in another chair or another part of the couch, but Mary was adamant. She stated that that spot allowed her to look out of her picture windows at a beautiful view, and that she did not want to give that up. She also stated that where she sat would not affect her drinking at all. I have found that many clients react as Mary did to simple kinds of self-control procedures, and it undermines the credibility of the treatment to push these too much if the client's initial reaction is negative. In considering the weekends Mary's behavior chain showed that she liked to drink on the weekend because she associated this with relaxing, having a sense of no responsibility, and feeling that she deserved some reward after working hard all week at school. As alternatives, she developed a number of ideas. These included spending more time reading novels, going out to lunch at a nice restaurant with Tom during the weekend, going for walks, or occasionally going into New York City to shop and go to the theater. Each of these plans had several components that were positive. First, while none were totally incompatible with drinking, they were not activities she normally associated with drinking. Second, they had high reward value to her, so they served as adequate substitutes for the rewards she had associated with drinking.

Self-management planning was carried out over two treatment sessions, with Mary trying out these plans during the week. While I did not continue to focus on self-management planning during later sessions, I would periodically check to see if she was continuing to use the plans we had developed, and continued to assess whether or not new situations were arising that were appropriate for self-management techniques.

The second area of skills acquisition related to abstinence was Tom's role in Mary's drinking. Initially, both Mary and Tom were unable to identify any ways in which they thought that Tom was involved in his wife's drinking. However, careful questioning revealed several important problems. First, Mary had been a nondrinker when she and Tom met. After many years of seeing him drink, she decided to begin to drink as well. She stated that she had felt left out when he drank and she did not. However, during that time, he had been drinking heavily, although without any problems, and would become high several times each week. It was this being high that led to her feeling left out. A second interaction between Tom's actions and Mary's drinking was the fact that they usually had a drink together when he got home from work. He had always mixed her a vodka and soda, without asking. A third way that Tom was involved was that he was somewhat protective of Mary when she was drinking. For example, when she had had three drinks in the evening, but was still awake, her speech would become quite slurred. If she received a phone call at that time, Tom would tell the caller that Mary was already asleep, rather than have her talk on the phone and later be embarrassed. As a result of being in treatment, Tom had decided to decrease the amount that he drank. He had done this prior to any discussion of the relationship between his and Mary's drinking, so we merely underlined that his change was helpful in decreasing a cue for her drinking. They also decided that he would ask her what she wanted to drink in the evening, rather than automatically fixing her a vodka, or a club soda. In this way, she would be making a decision about what she drank, rather than having her husband make the decision about her drink. Third, we discussed the possibility that protecting Mary from negative consequences of her drinking actually prolonged her drinking problem, as there were not many immediate aversive consequences if he protected her. To attempt to implement new behaviors even though Mary was not drinking, I used covert rehearsal techniques (Hay, Hay, & Nelson, 1977) with Tom, having him imagine that Mary had been drinking and that the phone rang. He imagined himself answering the phone, his uncertainty about whether or not he should call his wife to the phone, and then doing so. He was also asked to imagine how she looked and sounded on the phone, and to use covert reinforcement by thinking to himself that this would help her in the long run to want to be sober. He was not enthusiastic about this procedure, but rehearsed it several times during the week. Since Mary never drank during treatment, Tom did not get to engage in overt rehearsal of this skill.

Third, we looked at ways that Mary could receive more positive reinforcement for abstinence. She stated that Anne was already very enthusiastic about her not drinking, and that they had signed up for a course about alcohol and alcoholism, which they were going to take together. They also were having lunches and spent a good deal of time discussing some of their feelings about their previous drinking. Thus, it seemed that this relationship was one that explicitly was reinforcing her abstinence, and that the two of them were engaging in activities that would further reinforce her continued abstinence. I then raised the idea of Tom providing verbal or concrete reinforcement to her for not drinking.

TH: . . . Another part of being supportive is to give Mary positive feedback for the changes which she's making. I haven't heard the two of you talk about that so far, so I'm not sure whether that's happening yet or not.

M: No. I think I'm the only one giving me positive feedback and Mark is without verbalizing. He doesn't say, "Gee, I'm glad you're not drinking and I'm glad you're drinking tea or Sanka," but I'm getting a terrific amount of affection. Not that I didn't always get affection, because he's an affectionate person. But I can't say I was getting as much affection as I am now for the last few years. He hugs me and gives me kisses and says how much he loves me and what a terrific mother I am and that I'm the best mother in the world. I'm getting a lot of that and I know what's triggering that. He's so pleased; it's very obvious that he's thrilled. But then he's the only one of the children that ever really was subjected to it. So he's really the one who has the most to gain and had the most to lose. Mark's the one that lived with me. So I have found the way he's treating me right now definitely positive.

TH: (*To Tom.*) Have you noticed anything different with Mary? The way she looks or acts?

T: She's awake a lot.

TH: Is that good or bad?

T: Good. She used to go to sleep around 8:30. And now she stays up with the rest of the family.

TH: Anything else that you've noticed?

T: She's not cooking any better. Mary paints a horrible black picture of her behavior when she was drinking and it really wasn't that bad. But her problem was that she couldn't remember what it was like.

TH: What about after you'd go out? It sounds as though what would happen to you the next day is that you wouldn't remember and you would ask a lot of questions like "what did I say—wasn't I horrible?"

T: Yes, we've eliminated that.

TH: Do you now have a nice conversation about the party and the evening?

T: Now I can't remember (*laughing*). Mary gets mad at me when I can't remember. She'll ask what did he say or she say? And I'll say they talked about the Vietnam war and she was against it or he was for it. And I don't get that any more because now Mary is participating in the conversation.

TH: Is it any different when you're actually out together?

T: We've always enjoyed one another's company. . . . I enjoy her company more because I see her more.

TH: Do you compliment Mary, in general?

T: Very seldom.

TH: Is that a particular point with you not to?

T: No. I'm not a complimenter. It's the way I've been brought up.

TH: Would it be supportive to you in not drinking?

M: Not really because I'd be suspicious of it. He's right—it is the way he's been brought up. . . . I never had a doubt that Smitty thinks I look good or—those things I'm not insecure about. He tells me enough; he's not effusive, but he's not laconic like some husbands who don't give their wives any kind of approval or don't let them know how proud they are of them. He's not like that. I know how he feels. He lets me know enough. So I'm not insecure about that at all. I often sometimes question his taste. But I don't ever doubt the fact that he thinks I'm fine—even when I wasn't; but that's part of his nature, too. . . .

TH: So you're saying there's no discrimination from you about how you are, look, seem, act, feel, anything in relation to your drinking.

M: I don't see any. Maybe there is but I don't see any.

TH: Do you think that would be important?

M: I would like it if he'd say.

T: She expects her physical appearance to change because she hasn't had anything to drink. So I say, "Your nose isn't as red as it used to be." But I'd be lying, you know.

M: Then he'd be negating all the years when he told me I was fine. "Goodness, I must have all those broken veins like people that drink." He'd say, "You don't have any broken veins." And people would say to me, "Gee, those veins have cleared away." He was lying all those years. So he's in a bad situation.

TH: I think it's important now that you're not drinking to get some extra positive support.

M: I'm getting it from the person who is the most adversely affected by it—Mark. It didn't affect Smitty that much. So he isn't that excited about me not drinking. He isn't as excited; it doesn't affect him that way.

TH: That's not what I heard you say. You weren't saying it was a huge thing; but you liked the fact that you get to spend more time together. . . . I'm wondering if you could try something this week. I'm going to ask you guys to try a few things; at least for a week at a time and see what you think of them. I'd like you to try to give Mary some sort of positive feedback.

T: She'll know it's fake.

TH: I don't want you to make up things that aren't true.

T: Oh, alright.

TH: But say in the evening if . . .

T: Say what I'm thinking.

TH: Yeah. If in the evening Mary happens to look nice, you may want to tell her she looks nice.

T: She looks nice all the time.

TH: You may want to tell her that. I guess I'd like you to try it. See how it feels. It may seem ridiculous. You may feel that this isn't what you need. You may decide you feel foolish. But if you can each day try to think of something, a positive thing to say—if it's related to Mary's not drinking, all the better. Even if it was a quiet evening together and you say you enjoyed it. Or it was nice because you were up late together and it was enjoyable. Just sort of see how it feels to do that. If it just seems artificial and it doesn't seem supportive to you, then it would be something that you'd not continue to do. When you do that, could you just make a little notation on the back of your card? You can put two words—nice evening, or looks good, whatever; just somewhere kind of keep track of it. . . . I want you to be self-conscious of it. I want you to be very deliberate about it and when you fill out your card if you realize that the back is empty, that's good. 'Cause I want you to try something new.

This sequence was not atypical for alcoholic couples. The nonalcoholic spouse is often reluctant to provide reinforcement for abstinence. Some of the more common reasons offered include: (1) The client is doing what should have been done all along, so why should he or she be complimented? (2) If too much is said maybe he or she will stop trying. (3) He or she has to do this alone. (4) He or she does not like compliments. All of these kinds of objections can be addressed through discussions about the need for reinforcement for new behaviors, and the idea that abstinence is difficult and has to be worth all the effort in order to continue. With Tom, despite all of his objections, he did provide Mary with some compliments during the next week, including commenting on her appearance one day, and saying "that was fun" when they had watched a particularly funny movie on television during the week (something they never could do when Mary was drinking because she'd fall asleep too early). While they were willing to try this out as a homework assignment, Tom did not feel comfortable with the idea of compliments contingent on abstinence, did not agree that they were important, and did not continue them after the specific homework assignment.

In summary, Mary had made a firm commitment to stop drinking. In many situations, she made simple behavior changes and drank club soda. She had to develop somewhat more elaborate self-management strategies for some situations, but by the sixth session in treatment she still was not comfortable with being direct with people about her abstinence (this came after about 11 weeks of treatment). However, she was obtaining reinforcement from a close friend and from her youngest son, and she was feeling pleased with herself for managing to change her behavior. These external and internal reinforcers helped reinforce her abstinence, and the self-management strategies were making her day-to-day life relatively easy to sustain without drinking. However, she continued to have problems in the areas of assertion, her irrational expectations about her own behavior, and her difficulties in relaxing, and so treatment then began to focus on these areas more directly.

GENERAL COPING SKILLS (SIX SESSIONS)

A major problem area for Mary was having persistent, unrealistic expectations of herself. This was a problem area that was addressed repeatedly in the treatment. The initial strategy I selected to use was to challenge the rationality of these beliefs and to suggest alternative ways of thinking about herself. Even in the first session of treatment, when Mary talked about her desire to please her mother and her other relatives, I began to challenge that assumption, and suggest that she could not continue to take that assumption as true. This challenging of her assumptions continued through the self-management planning section of treatment and was an important component of her ability to make realistic plans for her holiday entertaining. After several sessions of informally addressing the cognitive restructuring issue, I formally introduced her to the idea that sometimes her unrealistic beliefs created problems and that she could consciously and deliberately change the way that she thought, developing patterns of thinking that would not lead her to feel so uncomfortable. After some further discussion, I suggested an exercise that would help her to learn how to do this. In the treatment session we took a recent example of a situation with her daughter about which she had felt guilty and unhappy. Her daughter had a 2-year-old child, for whom Mary and Tom enjoyed babysitting.

However, the previous weekend, her daughter and husband had gone to a party, leaving the baby with Mary and Tom. At 2:00 a.m. Stephanie called and said that they were still at the party and asked if it would be acceptable for them to pick the baby up in the morning. Mary agreed, but reminded her daughter that she and Tom were going to a brunch at 11:00, so they should get the baby before that. Stephanie did not come for the baby by 11:00, and in fact appeared at about 1:30, with no explanation or apology. Mary handled the situation quite assertively, telling Stephanie how angry she was, that she felt that she had been taken advantage of, and that she and Tom would not be willing to continue to do weekend evening babysitting if Stephanie did not stick to her agreements about when she was picking the baby up. Mary also emphasized how much she loved having the baby, but that they did have other things in their lives as well. After being appropriately assertive, Mary began to feel guilty. In the session we identified thoughts she was having that contributed to her guilt. These included, "If I had done a better job as a mother I wouldn't have to criticize her now," "I was grandstanding and made this more than it really was," "She stayed late to please her husband, and she's trying to be the same kind of wife as I was—this wouldn't have happened if I hadn't taught her to be that kind of wife." I then asked her if she could think of constructive ways of challenging each of these thoughts, by substituting more rational thoughts for her exaggerated self-blaming ones. We were able to develop several alternatives, including: "I didn't do anything to feel guilty for—it was legitimate anger," "I can only do so much, then it's up to Stephanie," "She created the problem—if she didn't want to stay later, then it was up to her to say something," "It was alright to grandstand, because I needed to make a statement about my needs and our needs," "I can't redo my life—there's nothing that I can do about it." Mary seemed to think that thoughts such as these would have been helpful in decreasing her sense of guilt about the confrontation. I then suggested that she identify two times during the coming week when she was feeling upset, articulate the irrational thoughts that were contributing to these feelings, and develop rational alternatives. I also suggested that she write down both the rational and irrational thoughts.

Fortuitously, two rather major situations arose during the week that related to this area. In the first she had agreed to hold a teachers' meeting at her house, and was expecting 12 people at the meeting. She had cleaned up the house, made some snacks, and generally put some effort into preparing for the meeting, (although fortunately by this time, she had not done major cooking for the group). The day of the meeting, all but three of the teachers had excuses for not coming. Mary was angry, but then started to think that it was wrong for her to be angry at all. Her irrational thoughts included: "I'm overreacting—what if I did do housework all weekend," "I'm self-indulgent to show my annoyance this way," "I'm not in control or I would not register my feelings," "I always try to keep to my plans, but maybe that's because I'm boring and don't do anything spontaneously." She was able to identify these thoughts and then come up with constructive alternatives, such as: "It wasn't silly to do housework when I knew 12 people were coming to my house," "There's nothing childish about letting them know that I disapproved of their changing their plans," "It's human to react and I'm human," "I keep plans because I respect other people; they should too; if not they should not be coddled and told that I don't mind."

The other situation was similar, and so the details will not be discussed. However, it was apparent from both of these situations, as well as from the example that we discussed in the previous treatment sessions, that some of Mary's negative thoughts had to do with believing that anger was an irrational, unacceptable emotion, and that she should never show her anger. I challenged this belief, suggesting that it may be leading to her unassertiveness. She agreed, saying that she also thought that if she expressed her opinions or contradicted others that they would no longer like her. We therefore began assertiveness training, focussing on the cognitive and skills components of assertiveness. I gave her some handouts on assertiveness, which described components of an assertive response (e.g., beginning with a statement of feelings rather than accusing the other person; describing what a person did that was upsetting rather than attacking them as a person, as in, "I feel angry when you leave your clothes on the floor," as opposed to, "You're a slob"). Then, as with the cognitive restructuring, we began to discuss several potential assertion situations and how she could apply these guidelines. We did some role playing, and she rehearsed these skills during the week. Several situations arose during the next 3 weeks, including a problem in the teachers' union, and a situation at a party. The latter was particularly interesting, because it was a minor situation that had a great deal of impact on Mary. She and Tom were at (yet another) dinner party, when one of the women there began to talk about a new book she had read. Mary had also read the book and was convinced that the woman was missing the point of the book. In the past she would have been quiet, and then made sarcastic comments to Tom on the way home. Instead, she decided to express her own opinions, and told the woman how she had interpreted the novel. Much to Mary's surprise the woman was not offended, but instead said "Do you really think so? I hadn't thought about it that way. Why did you interpret it that way?" Mary went on to talk about her opinion of the book, and the two of them had an enthusiastic discussion. She left the party excited, glad that she had said something because it made the conversation much more fun, and absolutely amazed that people had seemed to enjoy the fact that she had dived into the conversation. This experience served as a major one that helped her continue to be assertive with her family, fellow teachers, and children.

Once Mary was using the cognitive restructuring and assertion skills, we turned to the final problem area. I taught simple, progressive muscle relaxation to Mary and Tom. They each practiced several times during the week, achieving relaxation in the range of 5–15 Subjective Units of Discomfort (SUDs). The next week, Mary began to use the relaxation with her problem classroom, and Tom used it in a difficult corporate meeting. Both found the skill easy to learn and use and thought it was helpful.

At this point Mary and Tom had been in treatment for about 14 weeks, plus the assessment and screening sessions. Mary had not had anything to drink at all during treatment, and had not experienced any urges to drink since the 5th week of treatment. She had achieved a number of the things that I think are necessary for successful abstinence: Her commitment to not drinking remained high; she had developed ways of maintaining that commitment (primarily through contacts with Anne); she had developed a comfortable set of skills to avoid drinking in most routine situations; and had developed alternatives to drinking for coping with three major sources of stress—her unrealistic beliefs about herself, her lack of assertiveness, and her difficulties relaxing. She also was experiencing many naturally occurring reinforcers for her abstinence (feeling awake in the evenings, having more energy, feeling more competent and in control of her life), was receiving external reinforcement from her youngest son and from Anne, and was receiving support for her abstinence from her husband. At this point I thought that she was ready to discontinue treatment. The final concern was to plan long-term maintenance strategies. In maintenance planning I normally fade the frequency of the treatment session, and schedule follow-up sessions for several months after the completion of the initial part of treatment. At times, I may see clients for 2 years or more, once every few months, to review their current status, discuss problems that have come up, and continue to reinforce their successes. Continuing to have intermittent contact makes it easier for clients to increase the frequency of their contacts if they are having difficulties, and hopefully helps them to solve problems before their abstinence is threatened. However, since Mary and Tom were part of a clinical research project, we could not schedule booster sessions. They received monthly telephone follow-up interviews, so that they had continuing contact with the program and had to do a monthly review of Mary's drinking, drinking urges, and overall life functioning. Every 6 months they were scheduled for more extensive in-person research evaluations, so that they had a good deal of follow-up contact.

Maintenance Planning (One Session)

In planning for long-term maintenance, I find it helpful to review with the client what components of treatment were most helpful and to identify ways to continue to implement these new behaviors. In addition, it is important to help a couple to identify signs that they are beginning to have problems again and to have ways of responding to those problems quickly. In the last session with Mary and Tom, we covered a number of issues related to maintenance.

TH: What have you gotten out of all of this? What's been useful in this treatment for the two of you?

M: I think it gave me a chance to sit back and look at myself, having to listen to myself an hour and a half a week.

T: Terrible.

M: No, I really, I verbalized a lot of things that I realized were not valid, that I thought were valid until I had to listen to myself say them.

TH: What kinds of things?

M: Well like the things I told you, I couldn't change holidays and that certain things couldn't be done. I was so worried about other people's responses to me and my feeling, you know, being the good Samaritan all the time, Lady Bountiful and all of that. I realize that, that really . . . I was paying a high price to do all of those things. One of the prices was that I was consoling myself by drinking too much, because I was doing things that I didn't want to do a lot and I don't feel as though that makes any sense anymore. I listened to myself and thought, that woman sounds silly. You think she could figure out a better way to do it than that, and I think I have. And I don't feel any need anymore to be as passive as I was. I don't mean passive. I don't know if I was ever passive, but I almost would say hypocritical, just to make believe that I think something is acceptable and I don't think it is acceptable. I don't think I feel that way anymore. In other words, I'm not always trying to placate people and make them feel better. Sometimes I think it's better that they don't feel better. Especially if they're wrong. . . .

TH: Early on in treatment I did some things with you like having you list some of the pros and cons of drinking and not drinking and reviewing those lists.

M: Those were helpful when I did them. Yeah, I think they were helpful at the time.

TH: At this point do you think that's something you'd want to continue to look at or not?

M: I don't think I need to anymore, it's kind of become second . . . I don't mean that you don't need it, I'll probably always need to think about pros and cons. But I don't know if I need to think about it that much anymore.

TH: OK. The one other thing I wanted to ask you, Tom, was how you felt now about whether Mary had a drinking problem. Also, Mary, you weren't sure if you needed to stop and I said that I thought that at least through treatment I wanted you to stop. Then you'd really be able to evaluate how things are when you don't drink—it would help you make decisions for the long run. Where are you at on all that now?

M: Well, I think,—do you see now that I have a problem?

T: Yeah. There's no question about it. At least you're around during the evening hours now.

M: But you didn't admit that I had that much of a problem. You didn't even know why I wanted to come when I first told you. . . . If it's interfering in any of the quality of your life then it's a problem. I don't think a lot of people realize that.

TH: Right.

M: I was lucky because I had always read a lot about it and I'm not even sure why. It was long before I realized my mother had a problem with drinking because my mother's problem with drinking didn't happen until late middle age. I really don't know why I was interested or attracted to it. Then I remembered I was very influenced or impressed and saddened by the movie *Days of Wine and*

Roses. It was first on at Playhouse Ninety. I was in college, I think, when it first came out. And I remember thinking I liked the connection they made at that time, and I still think it's valid from all the things that I've been able to read. They made the connection then that she was compulsive about chocolate, so that her compulsive personality had carried over from one thing, she just transferred it to something else. And I thought that was interesting and the more I read the more I thought there was a connection in personality types more than it was a physical . . . The first drop of alcohol you become addicted. I realized that it was emotional and a personality type problem, early. Then I also realized, I didn't realize it at all in those days, then I started realizing later, and I look back on it, that I'm compulsive by nature. I was a compulsive housekeeper for years, compulsive mother—I had to do everything right. Then I also use to be compulsive about food. I used to eat a quart of ice cream for lunch every day. When I wasn't teaching school I use to reward myself for being a good girl and doing all my housework by eating a quart of ice cream. . . .

TH: What are your long-term thoughts about drinking for yourself at this point?

M: I think eventually, I think because I know now that I can handle my own feelings about myself, I might end up having a drink once in a while. I'm not sure that I'll spend the rest of may life without drinking at all. But I'll never again, as I told you once, ever again want to get drunk. That's never going to change, I don't think. I don't ever want to lose control. I'll never use it as a narcotic.

TH: Given that you think at some point you may have a drink occasionally, what kinds of things would tell you that you were getting into trouble?

M: Oh, I'd notice. I could tell that right away.

TH: OK, you're saying now you could, but I'm writing some of these things down. The reason I am is because nobody likes to admit they're out of control, that they're stepping backwards.

M: I know, but once you've admitted it once you've been able to do it once, I would think it would make it easier the second time.

TH: Sometimes it does.

T: I could tell her.

M: But I also think that I could tell. If I start going to sleep earlier at night than I want to—that's one thing that I really disliked, I told you that the last time. That's one of the reasons that I found I wasn't getting enough time out of the day. I wasn't able to read as much as I wanted to read. I was working and I was doing all the things that had to be done in my life, but I wasn't getting the things out of it that I wanted to get out of it, as far as hours of the day.

TH: What else would suggest . . .

M: Compulsiveness beginning again.

TH: What do you mean compulsiveness?

M: Compulsiveness about drinking . . .

TH: Anything else that would be a sign that it was a problem? What about ways in which you drink, or reasons for drinking?

M: I don't think that those are valid anymore. Even to myself I've proven that they're not valid.

TH: What kind of reasons for drinking do you think would be invalid?

M: Saying that it was because I had a bad day. Saying that it gives me courage, or I'm more sociable, or able to relate to people better socially. I don't think that's true. Those were a lot of handy reasons to give myself but I know they're not true.

TH: OK, but if you found yourself saying, "Well I think I'll have a drink, I had a really lousy day today. Those special-class kids just got under my skin." If you heard yourself saying that that would be a sign that you weren't handling it. How about quantities? Are there any quantities that you think would be excessive for you?

M: I don't know if I think quantities are that important, especially with someone like me who can't drink very much anyway. It's the effect. So, I don't think it would be safe for me to give myself a quantity. [I then wrote a summary for her, labeled it "warning signs," and gave it to her to keep.]

TH: Another thing that I think is helpful is reviewing things with Anne and talking with her. It is clear that the two of you give each other an incredible amount of support. Reading the handouts is helpful too, rereading them on occasion.

M: Yes it is, and I have got all of those too. Plus you know, I bought that book. I do like his book. That is a very readable book. Plus there is another book that Anne found and I read before I came here written by a doctor—Mid-Westerner. He uses the term alcohol troubled person. One of the first persons to put it into book form . . .

Commentary on Treatment

Mary and Tom's treatment was smooth and uneventful. As can be seen in Figure 5-3, Mary's urges to drink dropped off rapidly and she did not drink at all during treatment. She continued to do well over the 18 months of follow-up. She reported light drinking on 3 days, while her husband only reported that she drank on one occasion. However, treatment does not always go as smoothly as it did with this couple. There are a number of clinical problems that often arise during treatment. These will be addressed in the next section.

CLINICAL PROBLEMS

Noncompliance

A number of problems arise that impede the implementation of treatments. Two problems are related to noncompliance: dropping out of treatment and not completing homework assignments. As many as 50%–75% of persons presenting for outpatient alcoholism treatment do not complete the treatment (Baekeland

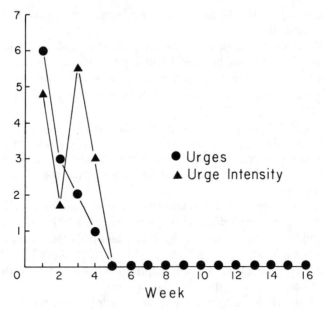

FIGURE 5-3. Urges and urge intensity during treatment.

& Lundwall, 1975). A number of approaches may be helpful in minimizing dropouts. First, it is essential to attempt to assess and meet the most pressing, immediate needs that the client presents (Chafetz *et al.*, 1962). Second, simple techniques may help, such as phone call midway between the first and second session, a follow-up phone call or letter if the client misses an appointment, or the early involvement of a significant other in the treatment. As a rule, aggressive outreach is important early in treatment, because of the ambivalence, shame, and embarrassment described earlier.

Noncompliance with homework assignments is another potential problem. The clinician should be certain that assignments are not too difficult, and that the client both understands and remembers the assignments. In the early weeks after stopping drinking, memory is poor, so that assignments should be written down. I find it helpful to supply a folder in which to put homework assignments and readings. Handouts and other reading are also helpful, because the client may not fully understand or recall information presented in treatment and may not understand the rationale for a homework assignment, leading to noncompliance. Strict limits must be set on chronic noncompliance (discussed previously). It may be necessary to cancel a session if the client does not complete a homework assignment (e.g., McCrady, 1982), or to even suspend treatment. While these may seem to be punitive measures, the success of treatment requires practice of skills being taught. Many alcoholics also have a history of not following through on verbal commitments because their drinking disrupted their behavior, and it is important that they begin to establish new patterns of behavior that will facilitate their longer term change.

Drinking during Treatment

Another problem is drinking during treatment. I ask clients to stop drinking at the beginning of treatment, for several reasons. First, it is easier to learn and retain new behaviors when abstinent than when drinking. Second, in order for abstinence to be reinforced it must occur. Third, many spouses cannot or will not become actively involved in treatment if the client continues to drink. Though abstinence is desirable, most clients do not have a vast repertoire of skills for maintaining abstinence. Therefore, drinking during treatment is common. The clinician's response to these episodes is crucial. First, the client's honesty must be reinforced. If it is not, the therapist may believe that all is well, when the client is drinking and lying about treatment successes at the same time. This kind of situation is not helpful, and eventually leads to dropping out of treatment.

Responses to drinking should involve four components: assessment of the need for emergency interventions, assessment of the circumstances around the drinking, development of alternative coping strategies for similar situations, and limit setting. Emergency issues include: does the person pose any immediate danger to himself or herself or others? Is detoxification needed? Did the client drive to the treatment session, and if so, is he or she fit to drive home? What is necessary to help the client regain abstinence? If the client is reporting drinking during the week, but currently is sober, the therapist can treat the drinking the same way that urges are treated—identifying the cues for the drinking, thoughts, and feelings that led to the drinking, and identifying both positive and negative consequences of the drinking episode. Then, alternative coping strategies can be discussed and tried as homework. Such a reaction to drinking reinforces the person for honestly reporting drinking and provides important infomation about the progress of treatment. At the same time, however, the therapist must develop a sense of when limit setting is necessary. The decision to set limits on drinking must be tailored to the individual case. However, some guidelines may be helpful. If a client has returned to a daily, addictive drinking pattern every effort should be made to help the person decrease and stop their drinking. If such efforts are unsuccessful on an outpatient or partial hospital basis, then the person must get more intensive help to stop drinking. Continuing to treat a client on an outpatient basis when he or she is involved in continuous heavy drinking is futile, as the person will not be able to learn or benefit from the treatment when intoxicated. Another circumstance for limit setting occurs when the client engages in repeated drinking, and the therapist assesses that the main reason for these behaviors is lack of interest in making changes in behavior. First, the therapist must explore all other possibilities such as cognitive deficits interfering with the learning process in treatment, homework assignments that are too difficult, a change in the client's "ambivalence" that could be influenced by the therapist, or the introduction of external factors that are reinforcing a return to drinking. If any of these other factors are present, limit setting would not be appropriate. If these are not present, then the therapist needs to restate expectations about the client's behavior in treatment, and specify consquences for continued noncompliance. Often, developing both the expectations and the consequences with the client is helpful in constructive limit setting.

Finally, the clinician can teach the client ways to minimize the intensity and duration of drinking episodes. Such skills as stopping after the first drink and waiting a half hour before drinking more, leaving the drinking environment, calling someone, reviewing a list of negative consequences of drinking, or calling the therapist may all be helpful (Marlatt & Gordon, 1985). It is important that clients learn how to manage drinking episodes, because many will drink after they complete treatment (Hunt, Barnett, & Branch, 1971), and if they can learn how to minimize these episodes they may have a better long-term outcome.

Drug Use

A third clinical problem is when the client uses other drugs during treatment. The clinician needs to periodically inquire about other drug use, and observe the client's behavior during treatment. If a client seems to be having comprehension difficulties, seems flat or agitated, or is noncompliant with treatment, drugs may be involved. If the clinician has such services available, a simple drug screen can be done, using either a blood or urine sample. Such a screen can provide valuable information and, like breath testing for alcohol, can be used to avoid guessing and the development of suspicion during treatment. If the clinician knows that the client is using other drugs, and if the client is clear that he or she will continue to use these drugs, then the clinician has another kind of dilemma to consider. First, the clinician must determine if the use of the other substance is interfering with the implementation of the treatment program for the person's drinking problem. Second, it should be assessed whether or not there is a functional relationship between the other drug use and drinking (e.g., is the person more likely to drink when smoking marijuana?). If the drug use is interfering with treatment, or if the drug use increases the probability of drinking, then a discussion of abstinence from the drug is appropriate. If the treatment is geared toward the development of a healthy alternative lifestyle, the drug use is probably in conflict with the treatment goals. And, if the client appears to be using the drug for the same functional reasons as the alcohol, then again the drug use becomes a problem and necessary to include in the treatment. While some clinicians in the field believe the alcoholics must abstain from the use of all drugs at all times, I think that this is an extreme view. Often, however, a period of complete abstinence is useful, and if the drug use is involved in any of the above described ways, then it needs to be discontinued.

CLINICAL PREDICTORS OF SUCCESS OR FAILURE

Most of the research on predicting treatment outcome has focussed on client characteristics. However, few client characteristics seem to consistently predict success across studies. The most stable predictors of positive outcomes are being married, having stable occupational functioning, and being of higher socioeconomic status. Longabaugh and Beattle (in press) have postulated that each of these characteristics suggests a high level of personal resources and involvement in social systems that could reinforce abstinence rather than alcoholic drinking.

While such predictors of success (or failure) that have been identified through controlled research are useful, the clinician is also faced with the dilemma of trying to determine whether or not a particular client will do well, and how to positively influence that process if the client appears to have a poor prognosis. As a clinician, I have observed a number of client patterns that seem to suggest a good prognosis for treatment. Mary and Tom illustrated many of these points. First, when a client can identify negative consequences of drinking, describe these, experience the affective impact, as well as have an intellectual understanding of these consequences it seems to bode well for treatment. At the same time, however, they must experience some rather immediate positive consequences of stopping drinking or starting treatment. These positive consequences may be experienced or created by the client, provided by the natural environment, or engineered by the therapist. However, if they do not occur, clients often discontinue treatment, because there is just not sufficient reinforcement for continuing to engage in the rather difficult set of behaviors required to remain abstinent. A third element that appears to be predictive of success is a combination of being able to decrease some of the personal self-blame and self-hatred about drinking, and maintain an acute awareness of what those feelings were. Many clients seem to achieve this by being able to laugh at themselves, and to tell their stories with a kind of self-aware humor. A fourth element that seems to be predictive of success is how the client handles with friends and acquaintances his or her decision to stop drinking. While I do not advocate that clients tell everyone they know that they have stopped drinking, it appears that being honest with friends and refusing drinks in a way that does not involve deception is a positive indicator of successful outcome. During treatment, usual client behaviors, such as compliance with homework assignments, coming to appointments and coming on time, and successfully staying abstinent during treatment itself are associated with success.

Many of the predictors of failure are the obvious converse of the qualities described above. When the client is unable to recognize and affectively experience the negative consequences of drinking, or when the person's environment reinforces continued drinking, and when neither factor is changed successfully by the treatment, then success is unlikely. In addition, I think that therapists can do a number of things that negatively affect the course of treatment. One of the greatest dangers with alcoholic clients is trying to move too quickly in treatment. Clients need a good deal of redundance in the beginning of treatment and often will be struggling over and over with whether or not they have a problem, need treatment, or want to change. If this is ignored, and the therapist plunges ahead with a structured behavioral intervention, then failure is likely. A corollary of this problem is that of the therapist getting into an adversarial relationship with the client. This often comes from trying to move too quickly and becoming frustrated and angry. It can also occur when the client has a number of relapses during the treatment. Therapists need to understand that alcoholism treatment is an extremely slow process, and that learning occurs gradually. Marlatt (1983) has nicely illustrated this point in looking at learning curves and recovery, and recent case studies by Nathan (1982) and P. Miller (1982) also demonstrate the patience that is often necessary.

CONCLUSIONS

Behavioral alcoholism treatment is more than the application of specific techniques. Alcoholism is a problem that requires a broad knowledge base in the physiological, psychological, and social spheres. Throughout the chapter I have emphasized the kind of decision making that the clinician must engage in in order to provide successful treatment. Treatment then requires both general clinical skills and the careful and systematic application of behavioral interventions. These usually include a skills-building component and a restructuring of the client's social network to assure that the individual changes will be positively reinforced.

I suggested at the beginning of the chapter that many clinicians do not like the treating alcoholics and alcohol abusers. The complexities of the treatment are evident, and many clients will not have successful outcomes. Some will drop out of treatment, drink, call the therapist at inconvenient times, and create all kinds of disruptions to an orderly clinical (or personal) life. However, the rewards of alcoholism treatment are powerful. Some clients will successfully stop drinking and create a new life for themselves and their families. Participating in this process as a therapist is exciting and special. Some clients will struggle, but will work with their therapist, somehow trusting that they will eventually "get it right." Working with a client who achieves a successful and abstinent life after 30 hospitalizations, jail, cirrhosis, and the unbelievable chaos of 24 years of drinking (as was true with one alcoholic whom I know) is time-consuming, often discouraging, but eventually worth it. Finally, any clinician who works with many alcoholics will eventually develop a group of "old friends." These may be clients who never achieve any kind of lasting abstinence, but who will turn to a therapist for help when they most need it, even if it is to get them into a hospital for detoxification and medical treatment before they begin drinking again. While working with this kind of client does not meet our usual notions of "treatment," providing a link to the health care system for such persons, and treating them as human beings who deserve respect is an important clinical service in its own right, no matter how far it may be from the notion of "behavioral alcoholism treatment."

References

Argeriou, M., & Manohar, V. (1978). Relative effectiveness of nonalcoholics and recovered alcoholics as counselors. *Journal of Studies on Alcohol, 39*, 793–799.

Azrin, N. H. (1976). Improvements in the community-reinforcement approach to alcoholism. *Behaviour Research and Therapy, 14*, 339–348.

Baekelund, F., & Lundwall, L. (1975). Dropping out of treatment: A critical review. *Psychological Bulletin, 82*, 738–783.

Blakey, R., & Baker, R. (1980). An exposure approach to alcohol abuse. *Behaviour Research and Therapy, 18*, 319–326.

Blum, E. M. (1966). Psychoanalytic views of alcoholism. *Quarterly Journal of Studies on Alcohol, 27*, 259–299.

Chafetz, M. E., Blane, H. T., Abram, H. S., Golner, J., Lacy, E., McCourt, W. F., Clark, E., & Meyers, W. (1962). Establishing treatment relations with alcoholics. *Journal of Nervous and Mental Diseases, 134*, 395–409.

Edwards, G., Orford, J., Egert, S., Guthrie, S., Hawker, A., Hensman, C., Mitcheson, M., Oppenheimer, E., & Taylor, C. (1977). Alcoholism: A controlled trial of "treatment" and "advice." *Journal of Studies on Alcohol, 38*, 1004–1031.

Emrick, C. D. (1975). A review of psychologically oriented treatment of alcoholism: II. The relative effectiveness of different treatment approaches and the effectiveness of treatment versus no treatment. *Journal of Studies on Alcohol, 36*(1), 88–108.

Emrick, C. D., & Hansen, J. (in press). Thoughts on treatment evaluation methodology. In B. S. McCrady, N. E. Noel, & T. Nirenberg (Eds.). *Future directions in alcohol abuse treatment research*. NIAAA Research Monograph No. 15.

Femino, J., & Lewis, D. C. (1980). *Clinical pharmacology and therapeutics of the alcohol withdrawal syndrome*. Brown University Program in Alcoholism and Drug Abuse, Medical Monograph No. 1.

Folstein M. F., Folstein, S. E., & McHugh, P. R. (1975). "Mini-mental state": A practical method for grading the cognitive state of patients for the clinician. *Journal of Psychiatric Research, 12*, 189–198.

Goldfried, M. R., & Sprafkin, J. N. (1974). *Behavioral personality assessment*. Morristown, NJ: General Learning Press.

Goldman, M. S. (1983). Cognitive impairment in chronic alcoholics: Some cause for optimism. *American Psychologist, 38*, 1045–1054.

Hay, W. M., Hay, L. R., & Nelson, R. O. (1977). The adaptation of covert modeling procedures to the treatment of chronic alcoholism and obsessive–compulsive behavior: Two case reports. *Behavior Therapy, 8*, 70–76.

Hay, W. M., & Nathan, P. E. (Eds.). (1982). *Clinical case studies in the behavioral treatment of alcoholism*. New York: Plenum.

Haynes, S. N. (1973). Contingency management in a municipally-administered Antabuse program for alcoholics. *Behavior Therapy and Experimental Psychiatry, 4*, 31–32.

Hedberg, A. G., & Campbell, L. (1974). A comparison of four behavioral treatments of alcoholism. *Journal of Behavior Therapy and Experimental Psychiatry, 5*, 251–256.

Hingson, R., McCrady, B. S., & Walsh, D. (1984). Adverse social consequences of alcohol use and alcoholism. In *Fifth special report to Congress on alcohol and health* (DHHS Publ. No. 84–1291). Washington, DC: U.S. Government Printing Office.

Hodgson, R. J., & Rankin, H. J. (1982). Cue exposure and relapse prevention. In W. M. Hay & P. E. Nathan (Eds.), *Clinical case studies in the behavioral treatment of alcoholism*. New York: Plenum.

Hore, B. D., & Plant, M. A. (Eds.). (1981). *Alcohol problems in employment*. London: Croom Helm.

Hunt, G. M., & Azrin, N. H. (1973). A community-reinforcement approach to alcoholism. *Behaviour Research and Therapy, 11*, 91–104.

Hunt, W. A., Barnett, L. W., & Branch, L. G. (1971). Relapse rates in addiction programs. *Journal of Clinical Psychology, 27*, 455–456.

Jellinek, E. M. (1951). Current notes: Phases of alcohol addiction. *Quarterly Journal of Studies on Alcohol, 12*, 673–684.

Johnson, V. *I'll quit tomorrow*. New York: Harper & Row, 1973.

Kaim, S. C., Klett, C. J., & Rothfeld, B. (1969). Treatment of the acute alcohol withdrawal state: A comparison of four drugs. *American Journal of Psychiatry, 125*(12), 1640–1646.

Kissin, B., & Hanson, M. (in press). Integration of biological and psychosocial interventions in the treatment of alcoholism. In B. S. McCrady, N. E. Noel, & T. Nirenberg (Eds.), *Future directions in alcohol abuse treatment research*. NIAAA Research Monograph No. 15.

Knox, W. J. (1971). Attitudes of psychiatrists and psychologists toward alcoholism. *American Journal of Psychiatry, 127*, 1675–1679.

Leach, B., & Norris, J. L. (1977). Factors in the development of Alcoholics Anonymous (A.A.). In B. Kissin & H. Begleiter (Eds.), *The biology of alcoholism* (Vol. 5, *Treatment and rehabilitation of the chronic alcoholic*). New York: Plenum.

Locke, H. J., & Wallace, K. M. (1959). Short marital adjustment and prediction tests: Their reliability and validity. *Marriage and Family Living, 21*, 251–255.

Longabaugh, R. L., & Beattie, M. (in press). The health care delivery systems. In B. S. McCrady, N. E. Noel, & T. Nirenberg (Eds.), Future directions in alcohol abuse treatment research. NIAAA Research Monograph No. 15.

Longabaugh, R. L., & Beattie, M. (in press). Optimizing the cost effectiveness of treatment for alcohol abusers. In B. S. McCrady, N. E. Noel, & T. Nirenberg (Eds.), *Future directions in alcohol abuse treatment research*. NIAAA Research Monograph No. 15.

Marlatt, G. A. (1983). The controlled-drinking controversy: A commentary. *American Psychologist, 38*, 1097–1110.

Marlatt, G. A., & Gordon, J. R. (Eds.). (1985). *Relapse prevention: Maintenance strategies in the treatment of addictive behaviors*. NY: Guilford.

McCrady, B. S. (1982). Conjoint behavioral treatment of an alcoholic and his spouse: The case of Mr. & Mrs. D. In W. H. Hay & P. E. Nathan (Eds.), *Clinical case studies in the behavioral treatment of alcoholism*. New York: Plenum.

McCrady, B. S. (1984). Women and alcoholism. In E. A. Blechman (Ed.), *Behavior modification with women*. NY: Guilford.

McCrady, B. S., Duclos, S. E., Dubreuil, E., Stout, R., & Fisher-Nelson, H. (in press). Stability of drinking prior to alcoholism treatment. *Addictive Behaviors*.

McCrady, B. S., & Hay, W. (1983). *Alcohol abuse: A behavioral-systems matrix*. Unpublished manuscript.

McCrady, B. S., Longabaugh, R., Fink, E., & Stout, R. (1983). Behavioral alcoholism treatment in the partial hospital. *International Journal of Partial Hospitalization, 2*, 83–95.

McCrady, B. S., Longabaugh, R., Fink, E., Stout, R., Beattie, M., Ruggieri-Authelet, A., & McNeill, D. (1983). *Cost effectiveness of alcoholism treatment in partial versus inpatient settings: Twelve month outcomes*. Unpublished manuscript.

McCrady, B. S. & Noel, N. E. (1982, November). *Assessing the optimal mode of spouse involvement in outpatient behavioral alcoholism treatment*. Paper presented at the 16th Annual Meeting of the Association for Advancement of Behavior Therapy, Los Angeles, CA.

McCrady, B. S., Paolino, T. J., Jr., & Longabaugh, R. (1978). Correspondence between reports of problem drinkers and spouses on drinking behavior and impairment. *Journal of Studies on Alcohol, 39*, 1252–1257.

McCrady, B. S., Paolino, T. J., Longabaugh, R. L., & Rossi, J. (1979). Effects on treatment outcome of joint admission and spouse involvement in treatment of hospitalized alcoholics. *Addictive Behaviors, 4*, 155–165.

McLachlan, J. F. C., & Stein, R. L. (1982). Evaluation of a day clinic for alcoholics. *Journal of Studies on Alcohol, 43*, 261–272.

Miller, P. M. (1972). The use of behavioral contracting in the treatment of alcoholism: A case report. *Behavior Therapy, 3*, 593–596.

Miller, P. M. (1982). Behavioral treatment of binge drinking. In W. M. Hay & P. E. Nathan (Eds.), *Clinical case studies in the behavioral treatment of alcoholism*. New York: Plenum.

Miller, W. R. (1978). Behavioral treatment of problem drinkers: A comparative outcome study of three controlled drinking therapies. *Journal of Consulting and Clinical Psychology, 46*, 74–86.

Miller, W. R., & Muñoz, R. F. (1976). *How to control your drinking.* Englewood Cliffs, NJ: Prentice-Hall.

Miller, W. R., Taylor, C. A., & West, J. C. (1980). Focused versus broad-spectrum behavior therapy for problem drinkers. *Journal of Consulting and Clinical Psychology, 48*, 590–601.

Mosher, V., Davis, J., Mulligan, D., & Iber, F. L. (1975). Comparison of outcome in a 9-day and 30-day alcoholism treatment program. *Journal of Studies on Alcohol, 36*, 1277–1281.

Nathan, P. E., (1982). Louise: The real and the ideal. In W. M. Hay & P. E. Nathan (Eds.), *Clinical case studies in the behavioral treatment of alcoholism.* New York: Plenum.

Nathan, P. E., & Briddell, D. W. (1977). Behavioral assessment and treatment of alcoholism. In B. Kissin & H. Begleiter (Eds.), *The biology of alcoholism* (Vol. 5, *Treatment and rehabilitation of the chronic alcoholic*). New York: Plenum.

Nathan, P. E., & Lipscomb, T. R. (1979). Behavior therapy and behavior modification in the treatment of alcoholism. In J. H. Mendelson & N. K. Mello (Eds.), *Diagnosis and treatment of alcoholism.* New York: McGraw-Hill.

O'Briant, R. G. (1974–1975, Winter). Social setting detoxification. *Alcohol Health and Research World*, 12–18.

O'Farrell, T. J., Cutter, H. S. G., & Fortgang, G. (1979, September). *Behavioral group therapy with hospitalized alcoholics.* Paper presented at the 87th Annual Convention of the American Psychological Association, New York.

Orford, J., Guthrie, S., Nicholls, P., Oppenheimer, E., Egert, S., Hensman, C. (1975). Self-reported coping behavior of wives of alcoholics and its association with drinking outcome. *Journal of Studies on Alcohol, 36*, 1254–1267.

Orford, J., Oppenheimer, E., & Edwards, G. (1976). Abstinence or control: The outcome for excessive drinkers two years after consultation. *Behaviour Research and Therapy, 14*, 409–418.

Page, R. D., & Schaub, L. H. (1979). Efficacy of a three- versus a five-week alcohol treatment program. *International Journal of the Addictions, 14*, 697–714.

Pattison, E. M. (in press). New directions in alcoholism treatment goals. In B. S. McCrady, N. E. Noel, & T. Nirenberg (Eds.), *Future directions in alcohol abuse treatment research.* NIAAAA Research Monograph No. 15.

Ritson, B. (1968). The prognosis of alcohol addicts treated by a specialized unit. *British Journal of Psychiatry, 114*, 1019–1029.

Rosenberg, C. M. (1982). The paraprofessionals in alcoholism treatment. In E. M. Pattison & E. Kaufman (Eds.), *Encyclopedic handbook of alcoholism.* New York: Gardner Press.

Sausser, G. J., Fishburne, S. B., & Everett, V. D. (1982). Outpatient detoxification of the alcoholic. *Journal of Family Practice, 14*, 863–867.

Selzer, M. L. (1971). The Michigan Alcoholism Screening Test: The quest for a new diagnostic instrument. *American Journal of Psychiatry, 127*, 1653–1658.

Sobell, L. C., & Sobell, M. B. (1975). Outpatient alcoholics give valid self-reports. *Journal of Nervous and Mental Disease, 161*, 32–42.

Sobell, M. B., Maisto, S. A., Sobell, L. C., Cooper, A. M., Cooper, T. C., & Sanders, B. (1980). Developing a prototype for evaluating alcohol treatment effectiveness. In L. C. Sobell, M. B. Sobell, & E. Ward (Eds..), *Evaluating alcohol and drug abuse treatment effectiveness: Recent advances.* New York: Pergamon.

Sobell, M. B., & Sobell, L. C. (1973). Alcoholics treated by individualized behavior therapy: One year treatment outcome. *Behaviour Research & Therapy, 11*, 599–618.

Sobell, M. B., & Sobell, L. C. (1976). Second year treatment outcome of alcoholics treated by individualized behavior therapy: results. *Behaviour Research and Therapy, 14*, 195–216.

Sobell, M. B., Sobell, L. C., & Samuels, F. H. (1974). The validity of self-reports of prior alcohol-related arrests by alcoholics. *Quarterly Journal of Studies on Alcohol, 35*, 276–280.

Sobell, M. B., Sobell, L. C., & VanderSpek, R. (1979). Relationships among clinical judgment, self-report, and breath-analysis measures of intoxication in alcoholics. *Journal of Consulting and Clinical Psychology, 47*, 204–206.

Stein, L. I., Newton, J. R., & Bowman, R. S. (1975). Duration of hospitalization for alcoholism. *Archives of General Psychiatry, 32*, 247–252.

Steinglass, P. (1976). Experimenting with family treatment approaches to alcoholism, 1950–1975: A review. *Family Process, 15*(1), 97–123.

Voegtlin, W. L. (1940). The treatment of alcoholism by establishing a conditioned reflex. *American Journal of Medical Science, 199*, 802–809.

Willems, P. J. A., Letemendia, F. J. J., & Arroyave, F. (1973). A two-year follow-up study comparing short with long stay in-patient treatment of alcoholics. *British Journal of Psychiatry, 122*, 637–48.

Wing, J. K., Cooper, J. E., & Sartorius, N. (1974). *Measurement and classification of psychiatric symptoms*. New York: Cambridge University Press.

Zitter, R., & McCrady, B. S. (1979). *The Drinking Patterns Questionnaire*. Unpublished questionnaire.

6

OBESITY

KELLY D. BROWNELL AND JOHN P. FOREYT

In this chapter two of the leading scientists in the area of obesity provide an authoritative account of the most up-to-date treatments for this extremely difficult but common problem. Behavior therapists may be surprised to learn that behavioral techniques alone are no longer considered the treatment of choice for the moderately or severely obese patient, but that a combination of these techniques with newly developed, very-low-calorie diets show considerable promise. Brownell and Foreyt also deal with some of the myths that have guided our treatment for some time, such as the theory that all obese people are controlled by external food cues, and present a more up-to-date biobehavioral model of obesity taking into account the latest scientific developments. But the most important part of this chapter for all clinicians confronted with this most difficult problem will be the presentation of how these therapists handle the inevitable problems of attrition, compliance, relapse, and methods for motivating increased exercise. Detailed transcripts make it clear that this is not always an easy task. Also important are the factors listed by Brownell and Foreyt that one must consider in deciding if an obese person should be treated or not and which approach to use if one decides to treat. For example, should one recommend a self-help group versus more formal treatment; a group approach versus an individual approach; or the inclusion of the spouse in treatment? In recommending the inclusion of the spouse, wherever possible, and detailing how this is done, the authors also subscribe to the importance of considering the patient's social system as necessary in promoting and maintaining change. There are few areas in which our thinking has changed of late as much as this one, and these changes are reflected in the treatment protocol described in this chapter.—D. H. B.

INTRODUCTION: EXTENT AND SEVERITY

Obesity is a serious problem that frustrates its victims and the professionals who seek its remedy. The problem afflicts a sizable portion of the population; estimates of the prevalence of obesity range from 15% to 50% of adult Americans (Bray, 1976; Van Itallie, 1977). The high prevalence would be less alarming if obesity did not have such serious consequences. With increasing body weight,

Kelly D. Brownell. Department of Psychiatry, University of Pennsylvania School of Medicine, Philadelphia, Pennsylvania.

John P. Foreyt. Diet Modification Clinic, Baylor College of Medicine, Houston, Texas.

a person is at greater risk for dangerous medical conditions (e.g., hypertension, diabetes, hyperlipidemia) and for disturbing social and psychological problems (Bray, 1976; Brownell, 1982; Stunkard, 1980).

The refractory nature of obesity is well known to professionals who deal with the problem and is even more salient for the patient who loses weight and gains it back countless times in the pursuit of thinness. In 1959 Stunkard and McLaren-Hume noted that only 5% of obese persons will lose a significant amount of weight and keep it off. In 1982 Brownell stated that the cure rate for obesity is lower than that for many forms of cancer.

This is sobering information. Viewing obesity from this perspective leads us to several conclusions. The first is that obesity is a complex problem that is not easily treated. Encouraging patients to lose weight is far more difficult than simply prescribing a diet or admonishing the person to eat less and exercise more. The second conclusion is that professionals cannot expect success in all patients. As obvious as this may seem, many professionals harbor unrealistic expectations when dealing with obese persons and are prone to be discouraged as experience increases.

The picture we just presented is a gloomy one, not because this reflects the state of the field—it does not. Rather, we wish to set the stage for the remainder of the chapter in which we will show how the problem needs to be taken seriously and treated aggressively. Working with patients on their weight problems can be very interesting and quite rewarding. There is good news ahead!

THE TORMENT OF OBESITY

To deal effectively with obese persons it is important to appreciate their suffering. This appreciation is crucial to establishing rapport with patients and to understanding aspects of their behavior that might otherwise seem puzzling. The torment surprises most professionals because they feel that obese persons are not truly disabled and that they should at the very least be able to set aside the problem and lead a normal life. The extent of this suffering is apparent from the following interaction, which occurred in a group meeting.

THERAPIST: Someone mentioned how troubling it is to be fat. How do you think it compares with other problems?

CLIENT 1: Sometimes I think it isn't so bad, but then other times I think I would rather have any other problem. I have one friend who is depressed but I get just as depressed about my weight.

CLIENT 2: I would rather be alcoholic or a drug addict than be fat. I think about it all the time and I hate myself for getting this way.

THERAPIST: Is that true Sally, you would rather be alcoholic than fat? That is a serious statement.

CLIENT 2: It seems at times that I cannot put up with another minute of hating myself. I would do anything to be rid of this fat body.

This self-doubt and even self-hatred is common among obese persons. It has many sources and is not easy to alleviate, even with intensive psychotherapy. Why does it occur?

Obesity as a Social Disability

There are many social disadvantages to being overweight. Thinking back to grade school days, most people can remember the fat children being teased, picked last for teams, and excluded from social groups. During adolescence, fat children date less and are less involved in school activities. Overweight high school students are less likely than their thin peers to be admitted to high-ranking colleges, even after receiving good grades and participating in extracurricular activities. Into adult life overweight individuals face employment discrimination and sometimes find it difficult to face social and sexual situations.

Most people in our society have negative feelings about obese persons. Some get angry at an obese person whom they may not even know. Most of our patients have been the target of derogatory comments in public places.

THERAPIST: Judy, you seem reluctant to be in public because of the things people might say.

CLIENT 1: You better believe it. Can't you see how embarrassing it is to have kids stare at you in the supermarket? One time a man came up to me downtown and told me I should lose some weight for my own good.

CLIENT 2: People always look to see what I put in my shopping cart or what I order to eat at restaurants. It puts pressure on me to know that I am always being judged. Most of the time I eat less than I want to in public even when I'm not dieting, because I don't want people talking about me.

THERAPIST: Do you think these people are mean or that they would like the best for you?

CLIENT 2: They are mean. You can tell by the way people say things.

CLIENT 3: Once in seventh grade I was absent from class because I had the flu. One boy told me the next day that the industrial arts teacher had taken attendance, and when he discovered I was absent, he said to the whole class, "Tom must have taken the day off to eat."

Research supports the feelings of these patients. There are pervasive negative feelings about obese persons. It is so ingrained in our culture that it is found in children as young as the age of 6 years. In one study children rated pictures of a normal child, an overweight child, and children with several serious physical handicaps (Staffieri, 1967). The children rated the obese child as less likeable than any other. Even the overweight children rated the fat child as less likeable! A recent study by Feldman (1982) examined the attitudes of 5- to 11-year-old children. These children felt that fat children were heavy because they ate excessively and that they could lose weight if they wanted to.

Internalizing Society's View

Overweight persons internalize society's dim view of obesity at a very early age. Obese persons may feel that they are inadequate and may feel the same about other overweight individuals (Stunkard, 1976; Stunkard & Mendelson, 1967). There is a growing movement to challenge society's emphasis on thinness, but this has influenced few people. It is the common pattern for obese persons to accept existing standards and to condemn themselves for not attaining the standard.

The two most common effects of this internalizing process are constant attention to weight and body image disparagement. Most obese persons fashion the enormous pressure to be thin into a persistent concern with dieting (Brownell, 1982; Stunkard, 1976). In addition, many overweight people have what Stunkard and Mendelson (1967) labeled "body image disparagement." This refers to a person perceiving his or her body to be detestable, unattractive, and repulsive to others. Stunkard (1976) has noted the persistence of these feelings, even when a person loses weight, especially among childhood-onset obese persons.

Obese persons suffer from a double disability of sorts. Their condition has troublesome social and psychological consequences, but it is the attribution of blame that may be more disabling. Most people, including the obese persons themselves, feel that personal failings are at the root of the excess weight. Individuals with other disabilities (e.g., blindness, paralysis) are not blamed for their condition, but obese people are. This generates the self-doubt that so torments the obese person.

A MODEL FOR ETIOLOGY AND TREATMENT

The complexity of obesity argues against a simple model for its etiology and treatment. We favor a biobehavioral model that considers the interaction of genetics, physiology, psychology, and cultural factors. The model forms the foundation of our current view of obesity. Treatment is guided by a knowledge of metabolic and nutritional factors, as well as a strong emphasis on behavior change. This focus on behavior is grounded in social learning theory.

The Biobehavioral Model

Physiological factors may contribute a great part of the variance in explaining why some people are fat, whether they can lose weight on conventional diets, and whether they are capable of sustaining weight loss once it occurs. For example, one study from Sweden reported that 81% of the variance in weight loss in obese women could be explained by a combination of fat cell size and resting metabolic rate (Krotkiewski et al., 1980).

We choose to discuss physiology for two reasons. First, one of the newest and most promising forms of treatment is the protein-sparing modified fast, also called the very-low-calorie diet. This diet has profound metabolic consequences. These consequences present both the promise and the danger of the diet and must be understood. Second, developments in the physiology area are happening very rapidly and may eventually provide new insight into etiology and treatment. Our knowledge of these factors helps us appreciate the complexity of the problem and some of the interindividual variability so common in clinical settings. This chapter is not, however, the forum for a detailed discussion of physiological aspects of obesity. We will present information on two popular theories that are useful for conceptualizing the contribution of physiological factors. The two theories are the set-point theory and the fat cell theory.

Set-Point Theory

Some scientists have hypothesized that all humans and animals regulate their body weight around a biological ideal (Keesey, 1980). The ideal may be different for different people. The implication of set-point theory is that weight loss below the ideal will set into motion a number of physical and psychological reactions, which will force the organism back to the set point. If some overweight persons have set points above society's standards, then weight loss can occur only at great physiological and psychological cost.

This theory has great appeal to several parties. Some patients believe the theory because they want desperately to lose weight, but they always regain the weight after a successful diet. Professionals like the theory because it provides some nonpsychological explanation for the failure of patients who have been given the best available treatment.

Set-point theory has not been proven, although some claim that the congruence of evidence from many studies gives the theory strong support (Bennett & Gurin, 1982). Currently, the theory influences our practice for a small subgroup of the patient population. These are the persons who fail to lose weight on very low calorie levels. One of us (Brownell) is working with a woman who loses no weight on a diet of 600 calories each day. These individuals are rare, but they do exist, perhaps because their bodies have adapted to prevent weight from going further below the set point. We sometimes advise these patients to curtail their efforts at dieting, but only after we are certain that the diet has been given an adequate trial.

Fat Cell Theory

The amount of fat on the body is determined by the number and size of the fat cells. A person who is hypertrophically obese has enlarged fat cells, while hyperplastically obese persons have an increased number of cells. Many people, particularly those with childhood-onset obesity, are both hyperplastic and hypertrophic.

The majority of fat cells develop by the end of adolescence. Thereafter, weight loss is thought to occur mainly by enlargement of the existing cells. When a person loses weight, the cells reduce in size but no cells are lost. The fat cell theory maintains that each adult has a specific number of fat cells and that weight loss can occur only until the cells have reached normal size. Beyond that point, the cells become depleted of lipid and may exert internal pressure for the person to replenish the energy stores.

This is where the set-point theory and the fat cell theory converge. The set point may be determined by the size of the fat cells, and the weight at which this occurs may depend on the number of cells. As an example, two women may each weigh 200 lb; however, one may have a normal number of fat cells, which are enlarged, while the other has an excessive number of fat cells, which are normal size. Weight loss and maintenance for the hypertrophically obese woman may be possible, because she can reduce the size of her fat cells and still maintain adequate lipid volume. The hyperplastically obese woman already has normal-sized fat cells, and the only path to weight loss is to deplete each cell to a level below normal. Even if she can overcome the set point because of extraordinary motivation, she would still be prone to regain the weight later.

It is apparent from the discussion above that the physiology studies provide an interesting perspective on the process of weight loss. The set-point and fat cell theories do not have many practical applications presently, but that may change in the near future.

Social Learning Theory

We have observed a great many treatment programs differing in location, educational background of the professionals, cost, and nature of the patient population. It is remarkable how similar behavioral programs have become. We will first present the techniques common to all programs, and then discuss social learning theory and how it has made the current generation of behavioral programs much more sophisticated.

Self-Monitoring

Patients are given diaries and instructed to write down all food and drink ingested during the entire treatment period. Along with what is eaten, the time, place, number of people present, and mood state are also recorded. All these items are written down immediately after the food is eaten. The diaries are brought to each treatment session where they are reviewed by the therapist who comments favorably on examples of good behavior and makes suggestions on how to deal with problem situations.

Body weight is also self-monitored. Patients are given charts with weights written in along the left-hand column and days of the month along the bottom row. The weight chart is then posted in some prominent place, usually above the bathroom scale or on the refrigerator door, and patients record their weights on a regular schedule, usually once a day or once a week.

Stimulus Control

Patients are instructed to limit their at-home eating to one place, either at the dining room table or kitchen table, sitting in a chair. No eating or drinking is allowed anywhere else in the home except at the table. Distractions are reduced during the meal. No watching television, listening to the radio, or reading newspapers, magazines, or books is permitted. Meals are scheduled at regular times with unplanned snacking not allowed. Other stimulus control strategies include instructions on how to shop (e.g., prepare lists ahead of time, do not buy problem items), store (e.g., reduce visibility of foods that may interfere with staying on the diet), and prepare food (e.g., do not taste foods while preparing them, wear a surgical mask if necessary; do not prepare too much food at any one time or leftovers will be a problem), along with suggestions for increasing daily activity (e.g., walk upstairs to your office rather than ride the elevator, park a distance from the supermarket).

Changing Eating Behavior

Patients are taught to eat more slowly. This is done by laying down utensils between bites, drinking lots of water during a meal, or taking short breaks between courses. The length of meals is increased to more than 20 min.

Contingency Contracts

Patients put up cash, agreeing to lose weight at a rate of 1–2 lb a week for a specific period of time. The money is refunded on a specific schedule as the weight is lost. Contracts are also written for specific behavioral changes such as keeping food diaries, agreeing to eat in one place, or slowing down the rate of eating.

These strategies, along with heavy doses of nutrition education, involving the weighing and measuring of food and counting calories or using a food exchange system, are presented in a specified number of sessions, usually 8, 10, 12, 16, or 20, usually in a group, and usually once a week. Group leaders vary, but in research settings leaders are most often dietitians, psychologists, or psychology graduate students. In clinical settings backgrounds and qualifications of group leaders vary widely.

Emphasis on one or more of the above strategies differs among treatment centers with idiosyncratic variations of group leaders, but by and large the overwhelming majority of treatment centers treat obese patients in surprisingly similar ways.

Why the great similarity in treatment programs? How did the "standard" behavioral treatment program evolve? Where is the field going? Although this chapter is not a theoretical one, a very brief description of the evolution of our treatment approach seems desirable if only to alert clinicians to the limitations of our basic treatment package.

The Past

Some early behavioral theorists (e.g., Ferster, Nurnberger, & Levitt, 1962) observed that certain environmental cues seemed to increase the probability of overeating in obese people. If this were so, then obese people ought to limit the cues associated with their inappropriate eating. Hence, the development of the stimulus control strategies which, as we mentioned above, quickly became the basis of behaviorally oriented treatment programs:

- Eat only at specific times and in specific locations (e.g., three times a day sitting at the dining room table).
- Eliminate all other activities (e.g., watching television, reading the newspaper, or listening to a radio) while eating.
- Keep tempting foods out of sight (e.g., do not allow them in the house or always keep them in opaque containers).

A second related observation, that obese people have a particular eating style, also has proved to be a popular concept. Some theoreticians believed that obese people ate more rapidly than normal-weight people, presumably leading to overeating. To correct this problem, strategies were developed to reduce the rate of eating:

- Placing food on utensils only after the food in the mouth has been thoroughly chewed and swallowed.
- Interrupting eating during the meal by drinking water.
- Laying down utensils between each bite of food.

The goal of these strategies was to teach obese people to eat like normal-weight people (who presumably ate slower) and thereby help them lose weight.

The rationale for including self-monitoring in obesity treatment programs grew out of the theoretical notion that feedback of relevant information is critical for lasting behavioral change.

These deceptively attractive ideas about how and why people become obese received support during the early 1970s, when Schachter and colleagues (Rodin, Herman, & Schachter, 1974; Schachter, 1971) conducted a number of very clever studies in which they found that obese individuals were indeed more responsive to environmental food cues than normal-weight individuals. They reported that obese people in general were hypersensitive to environmental cues. For example, obese people had lower tachistoscopic recognition threshholds, better short-term recall, and faster disjunctive reaction times (Rodin et al., 1974), all suggesting that the obese had a greater tendency to react to salient stimuli. Their studies led to an interesting theory, popular in the 1970s, called the "externality theory," which said that not only were obese individuals more externally responsive to food cues than normal-weight individuals, but also that they were less responsive to internal, physiological cues of hunger. These theoretical concepts led to considerable research and reinforced the treatment strategies aimed at limiting environmental food stimuli for obese clients.

To summarize, the basic underlying assumptions that have guided our originial behavioral treatment programs can be described succinctly as:

- Obese people are overeaters.
- Obese people have an eating style that differs from normal-weight people.
- Obese people are more influenced by external food cues than normal-weight people.
- Obese people who change their eating style to that of normal-weight people will lose weight.

The Present

Based on these simplistic notions, the specific behavioral techniques outlined above became standard treatment procedure. Unfortunately, accumulated research has now suggested that the above beliefs are not true for many obese people. The externality theory, for example, is a good example of a belief that has lost favor through careful research. Rodin (1978, 1981) has shown that obese and normal-weight individuals are *not* measureably different in their responsiveness to external and internal cues. External responses can certainly be a problem for some obese people, but may also be a problem for some normal-weight people.

As we will repeat time and again in this chapter, obesity is an extremely complex phenomenon for which simple causation theories, behavioral or otherwise, have little relevance. Simply assuming that obese people are obese because they overeat, that they overeat because they learned to eat that way, and that by teaching obese people to eat like normal-weight people they will lose weight are gross oversimplifications that have little relevance for the majority of obese people in our society. Unfortunately, these simplistic assumptions have produced a treatment methodology that is in wide use today. This methodology still attempts to teach obese people to change their patterns of behavior and specific environmental factors that are correlated with their "abnormal" eating habits. The use of these strategies has met with modest success at best, and their limitations have become embarrassingly apparent during the last few years (Foreyt, Goodrick, & Gotto, 1981; Wilson & Brownell, 1980).

In addition to the often incorrect assumptions, behavioral therapists tended to ignore the processes by which weight loss occurred or did not occur. The behavioral strategies used were often *presumed* to be effective because patients lost weight during treatment. Obese clients who did not lose weight were simply considered to be "poorly motivated" or "bad clients" who were not following the behavioral strategies. Unfortunately, some obese patients presumably did follow behavioral strategies exactly as instructed and still were unable to lose much weight because of physiological limitations at a specific level of caloric intake. Until we are better able to assess changes in energy balance, the efficacy of these current therapeutic strategies will not be clearly known. The research that has attempted to explore the relationship between compliance with therapeutic instructions and subsequent weight loss has been equivocal at best. The majority of studies have been confounded by the limitation that compliance with therapeutic instructions is almost always assessed through self-report information.

Our theoretical understanding of the causes, maintenance, and treatment of obesity has broadened in the last several years. Extremely modest treatment results and the growing recognition of the limitations of the behavioral strategies have tempered our early enthusiasm from our extremely narrow view that obesity was largely a function of maladaptive learning. Behavioral theorists have now incorporated into their models of obesity the influence of many factors including physiology, personality variables, social standards, cultural expectations, and cognitive structures. These factors function in a highly interactional manner with all of them having some influence upon body weight.

The Future

Social learning theory continues to serve as the unifying force for the development of behavioral treatment approaches. The theory assumes that behaviors are developed and maintained by three regulatory systems: classical conditioning, operant conditioning, and most important, cognitive mediational processes (Bandura, 1977). Cognitive–behavioral strategies in particular are becoming increasingly important in behavioral treatment programs (Foreyt & Goodrick, 1981; Mahoney & Mahoney, 1976). For example, we ask our clients to keep a "thoughts diary" in which they record their thoughts about food and eating behavior each evening.

A recent verbatim example of an evening's "thoughts" included the following by one of our clients, Marcella:

I have learned something very important tonight about my behavior and eating habits. I am not hungry and it is dinner time (7:15). I have eaten a large salad but I wanted to eat all the wrong foods or at least some of the foods that I normally would eat when I feel the way I do right now. I am *angry*—at myself, but most of all at my ex-husband. I have not felt like this since I started the program. I realize that ordinarily the only way I could get rid of the anger previously was by eating. I have always suspected that I ate because of anger and tonight I truly realized it. Only difference is that I will not eat. Nothing will make me go off the program. I have to deal with the anger but will have to find another way. I am feeling sorry for myself right now because of ongoing problems with children and my ex-husband and would have pacified myself with food in order to alleviate the feelings. This is the first time that I have ever analyzed my feelings and behavior *vis-à-vis* food and eating habits. Most reassuring to me is the knowledge that I will not cheat. Reaching my goal is the most important thing to me right now.

We review each diary with our clients and emphasize problem-solving strategies for each specific problem. We have found Mahoney's (1977) "Personal Science" procedure particularly helpful. Using the letters, "S-C-I-E-N-C-E," we teach the seven subskills needed for successful adjustment:

- Specify the general problem.
- Collect information on it.
- Identify the causes.
- Examine potential options.
- Narrow the options and try one of them.
- Compare the results.
- Extend the strategy, revise or replace it.

Eating problems are amenable to scientific reasoning and the skills needed to solve them parallel scientific research skills. The model is helpful for any dietary problem that might arise after our formal treatment program has ended. We have found it especially useful with bright, motivated clients; it is less helpful with semiliterate, poorly educated clients.

There is also a greater understanding and appreciation for the role of physiological factors in producing and maintaining obesity. Both fat cell theory and set-point theory are playing increasingly important roles in our understanding of the development and maintenance of the obese state. Likewise, the role of exercise and its influences on metabolic rate are also adding to our knowledge of obesity and a growing appreciation of its role in treatment.

The inadequacies of our present theoretical understanding of obesity and treatment have yet to be fully addressed. The development of an encompassing and adequate theory of obesity is an obvious need for the future. As our knowledge and our understanding of the obese state increases, better theories will certainly emerge.

WHO SHOULD BE TREATED?

An important issue arises when a professional makes the decision to assist a person with weight reduction. The issue has ethical, scientific, and practical implications. We suspect that the reader may be puzzled by this discussion. In most clinical settings the goal of weight loss for an overweight person is accepted by the professional. This may not be advisable in all cases. In some medical settings, weight reduction is recommended only for patients who have definable medical risks. We also feel this is not advisable in all cases. There are no established guidelines to follow for this issue, so we will share our approach, which is based partly on therapeutic experience with obese patients and partly on the literatures of medicine, epidemiology, and nutrition.

One perspective on this issue is that medical risk is the only justification for weight reduction, particularly when the treatment itself carries some risk, as with very-low-calorie diets or surgery. However, the weight at which risk occurs has been disputed for years. Starting in the early 1960s, the actuarial tables from the Metropolitan Life Insurance Company were used, and any weight above ideal was considered unhealthy. As the epidemiological evidence began to mount, the picture became more confusing. It is clear that persons who are more than 30% above their ideal weight are at increased risk, but people who are below this level may or may not be, depending on the faith one places in any particular study. Some experts argue that individuals below 30% overweight should not merit the attention of professionals unless they have accompanying risk factors like hypertension. We feel that the medical risk is only part of the picture.

The emphasis on medical risk ignores the reason why most patients seek treatment. They hate their bodies and feel that obesity is a great psychological and social disadvantage. Their logic is sound. Everything else being equal, their acceptance by society in general will probably be better if they are thin. In many cases the weight loss will produce improvements in self-esteem, social confidence, and other important aspects of coping with life. These benefits are important, so we feel that weight reduction may be advisable for social and psychological reasons, irrespective of medical risks.

This does not mean that any person who wishes to lose weight should be encouraged to do so. There are those, particularly young women, who harbor an obsessive concern with their weight. Bulimia and anorexia are the most pathological extremes of this obsession, but many individuals have the same concern to a lesser degree. Weight reduction may be indicated, but only after the weight obsession has been covered in therapy. Typically, these persons are only mildly overweight if at all, have a history of constant dieting, have negative feelings about their bodies, and report thinking about their weight in an obsessive fashion. This information can be gathered in an initial assessment.

There may also be individuals who are quite overweight who should be encouraged to accept their condition rather than suffer through the rigors of dieting. This position has been championed by the group National Association to Aid Fat Americans (NAAFA). The group is comprised mainly of very heavy women who challenge society's pressure to be thin. They fight for the rights of fat people in employment and other settings and support the view that a person should be judged on qualities other than body weight. The NAAFA stance of weight reduction, although not stated clearly, appears to be that the desire to be thin is a sign that a fat person shares society's incorrect view. The view should be changed, not the weight. In cases where there are important medical or psychological reasons to lose weight, attempts to reduce are appropriate, but once a person has tried and failed many times, the pressure should be relieved and acceptance is the goal.

This idea of acceptance rather than reduction is a wise course to follow for some patients. We have patients who have tried repeatedly to lose, and after we are confident that they have failed at the best available treatment, we will work with them on accepting their body size. These individuals may cope better this way than if they continue their history of failing at diets, using money that could be better spent, and incurring the negative feelings of family members and friends who are encouraged and then disappointed. The sensitive issue is who should fall into this category. It is not a decision to be taken lightly, because the task of helping a person accept the obesity can be very involved. We reserve this option for relatively few individuals and proceed with this course only when certain that weight loss is unlikely.

SETTING

There is no shortage of treatment techniques or treatment settings for an obese patient. Where is the obese patient to turn when the decision to lose weight is made? The answer to the question depends on several factors. How much weight does the patient have to lose? What has the patient previously done to lose weight? How much weight has been lost before? What strategies have been most successful?

Many obese people lose weight on their own and maintain that weight loss for many years. We both know a number of individuals who made a decision to lose weight, went on a diet on their own, lost significant amounts of weight, and are maintaining their losses reasonably well. We also know other people who have tried most everything and have been unable to lose or maintain any appreciative amount of weight.

Our feeling is that obese people should first try to do it on their own. They should choose a good well-balanced diet, gradually increase their amount of activity, and see whether they are successful by themselves. If they are not able to lose much weight, they have several options. If they live in a city with a college or university, they can often find an obesity clinic run by faculty members in the department of psychology. These clinics in educational settings are usually research-oriented and treatment is often free or quite inexpensive. Medical schools also commonly provide either a research or a service clinic, often at a nominal fee. We generally advise obese clients to seek out free or inexpensive treatment programs before signing up with commercial clinics.

Churches, YMCAs, YWCAs, and other community organizations often also offer relatively inexpensive treatment programs. Quality of programs varies greatly and patients should always ask about the credentials of the people running the programs before committing to them.

Over the past few years, there has been a huge number of commercial weight reduction clinics that have entered the market place. To expect an obese person to choose which clinic to go to is extremely difficult. Much of the advertising that some commercial clinics do is extremely misleading. Weight loss claims (e.g., lose 30 lb in 30 days) are often highly unrealistic and misleading. These claims are frequently supported by testimonials of successful but highly unrepresentative clients.

When choosing a commercial clinic, we advise patients to get the answers to several questions before joining. First, is treatment preceded by careful medical and behavioral assessments? Assessment of both eating and exercise behaviors are important since the obese state may be maintained more by lack of exercising than by overeating. Some commercial clinics only emphasize dietary changes and do not include recommendations for exercise. Second, does the clinic offer state-of-the-art therapy? Behaviorally oriented programs still are the treatment of choice for patients needing to lose less than 40 lb. Patients needing to lose more than that may require more drastic treatment approaches. Very-low-calorie diets, for example, are being offered at numerous clinics today. These diets are extremely powerful, potentially dangerous, and close medical supervision is essential. Third, is the program structured in such a way to encourage a therapist–patient relationship that lasts long enough for the obese individuals' changes in both eating and exercise to become part of a new lifestyle? These changes often require over a year to occur. Fourth, what is the clinic's success rate? Clinics should provide the prospective client with data regarding dropout rate over time, average posttreatment weight losses, and average weight losses at least 1-year posttreatment. Only from such information can the patient determine the probability of success.

Quality of treatment, likelihood of success, and cost, should all be considered before the patient decides to utilize the services of a commercial clinic.

SOCIAL AND FAMILY FACTORS

Social factors play an extremely important role in the etiology and treatment of many diseases (Cobb, 1976; Colletti & Brownell, 1982). These factors are thought to influence recovery from serious diseases like cancer and heart disease and appear to act as buffers against life stresses such as job loss or loss of a spouse. The Alameda County Study in California (Berkman & Syme, 1979), a 9-year prospective epidemiological evaluation of 7000 adults, found greater mortality in persons who lacked four social bonds (marriage, contact with close friends and neighbors, church affiliation, and formal and informal group associations).

Social support also appears to have an important role in understanding and treating obesity. There are three main issues relevant to clinical practice: family and spouse interactions; group versus individual treatment; and self-help and commercial programs.

Spouse Involvement

For most overweight persons the excess weight can be an important issue in the marriage. This has never been studied systematically, so we must rely on clinical experience. This experience indicates that marital factors may be the most important determinant of whether some persons will succeed in treatment. Obese persons enter treatment with a social network in the background. This system may help or may hinder, but one challenge for the professional is to bring the system into the foreground for examination.

There are a number of reasons why the spouse plays an important role for the obese person. First, the spouse may be the "gatekeeper" of food that enters the house. Second, the spouse may overtly or covertly encourage or discourage the patient to lose weight. Third, the marital relationship may change as the obese person loses weight. Fourth, the sexual relationship may change when body size changes. Fifth, weight loss in the obese person may trigger feelings about the weight of the spouse.

The Issue of Sabotage

Every clinician has seen examples of sabotage from the spouses of dieters. The dieter may not be aware of what is occurring, so the issue must be handled in a sensitive fashion. We will first list the most common reasons why spouses are threatened by weight loss in the dieters and then will discuss the methods we employ to alter this aspect of the social network.

There are a number of reasons why some spouses experience negative reactions when their husband or wife loses weight:

1. The dieter may become more physically appealing. This engenders the fear in some spouses that the person will leave them or will become the target of sexual advances from others.

2. Weight loss in the dieter is often accompanied by increased self-confidence and the desire to make changes in lifestyle. Some seek employment when they have not worked before, others will become involved in social organizations, and others may become very involved in exercise activities (joining a tennis league, etc.). This can threaten the spouse because of the time involved or the change these alterations bring to the marriage.

3. The increased self-confidence sometimes makes the dieter more assertive in asking for changes in the marital relationship. If the relationship was weak, the dieter may wish to leave. Some spouses are threatened by any behavior that suggests the relationship needs improvement.

4. Some spouses, particularly men, find their mates less physically appealing as they lose weight. These men are sexually attracted to very heavy women. The members of NAAFA call these men "fat admirers." These men may never have discussed this with their wives, and most professionals are not familiar with this phenomenon, so this issue is often not uncovered.

5. Some spouses may be threatened by the success of the dieter. The weight loss is a sign that the dieter is taking control of some aspect of life, and this mastery itself may make some spouses feel inadequate.

6. If the spouse is overweight, weight loss by the dieter may stimulate intense feelings of inadequacy.

There are a number of signs that can alert the professional to the possibility of a negative spouse. The following are some examples from our patients:

CLIENT 1: It is hard for me to get here on Wednesday nights because my husband seems to have things to do. I may have to stop the program.

THERAPIST: Tell me about some of the things your husband has to do.

C1: He says he has to stay late at work or he wants to go watch a ball game with some of his buddies.

T: Has he always done these things?

C1: Not really. He works late only a few times a year and he has always been happy to watch the games at home.

CLIENT 2: I can't take the criticism anymore. When I have a good day and eat nothing but salad, he makes fun of the food I eat. He tells me that I am wasting our money on this program and that I may as well get used to being fat.

T: Is your husband usually critical of the things you do?

C2: Sometimes, but it seems worse lately.

T: You told me about once before when you lost 50 pounds by going to Weight Watchers. How did you and your husband get along then?

C2: It was bad then, but it was just after his mother died, and I thought he was upset about that.

T: Can you remember other times when you lost weight? How did your husband react then?

C2: One time about 10 years ago I lost weight on drugs that my doctor gave me. My husband seemed upset then, but I thought it was because the drugs made me crazy.

CLIENT 3: My wife has started talking about affairs. I can't understand it because she never did this before. Maybe it's nothing to worry about because she only kids about it.

T: Tell me what she says.

C3: If she calls me at work and I am out to lunch, when I call back she asks if I have been out with my secretary. Last weekend I went to the mall to buy some smaller clothes. When I got home she laughed and said that I probably stopped off at a bar on the way home and met some woman.

T: Has your wife said anything about why she is making these comments? Do you have any ideas?

C3: She has said that I am so thin now that other women will like me. I tell her that I still love her and that I would never fool around, but the comments keep coming.

CLIENT 4: My husband complains when we are in bed. He says I am all skin and bones.

T: Didn't your husband want you to lose weight? Many husbands tease their wives about being fat and pressure them to go on diets.

C4: He was never like that. He says he likes me the way I am, at least until now. Now he says I have lost that soft and cuddly feeling.

CLIENT 5: It is hard for me to stick to the program. My family wants their regular meals and my husband needs to have his ice cream and pretzels to snack on.

T: Why does this make it hard on you?

C5: Being around my favorite foods is murder.

T: It also sounds like you feel guilty about disrupting the normal style of your family.

C5: That's right. At first I thought they could help me by changing themselves, but my husband reminded me that this was my problem and that they should not suffer.

T: How often does you husband eat the ice cream and pretzels?

C5: He usually eats them once in a while. A bag of pretzels would sit on the shelf for 3 weeks if I didn't eat them. But now he wants them every night and he always eats them just when I am hungriest.

These examples show several of the signs of overt or covert sabotage. The spouses often show a change in their normal behavior. The dieters sense that the marital relationship is changing but may attribute it to their own actions. The more direct acts by the spouse are apparent. These include offering food to the dieter, telling the dieter that "a little bit won't hurt," or suggesting that the diet is dangerous and that the program staff is not competent. The covert acts are more difficult to uncover, but can be revealed by questioning like that displayed above.

The best course to follow is to involve the spouse in treatment, but it is not always possible to elicit the cooperation of a threatened spouse. The issue is a delicate one, because the approach to the spouse is usually done through the dieter, so the dieter–spouse relationship must be considered. By the time the involvement of the spouse is considered necessary, the dieter may have sensed that the spouse may be acting in a counterproductive way. It is crucial that the dieter not confront the spouse with these speculative notions. Therefore, the dieter must be warned about confrontation and must be given the skills to approach the spouse in a positive way. Behavioral rehearsal is often useful in this regard.

It is useful to approach the spouse as an ally in the movement to aid the dieter. A phone call from the therapist to the spouse can convey to the spouse that he or she is an important person in the life of the dieter and that the therapist would benefit from the perspective of the person who knows the dieter best. This approach must be explained to the dieter so the spouse is receiving consistent messages. Once the spouse is involved, both the dieter and spouse can be trained in specific ways to deal with each other.

Group versus Individual Treatment

The issue of group versus individual therapy for obese persons has received relatively little attention in the scientific literature, despite its obvious importance. The two approaches have much different social effects on most individuals, so that the same treatment may benefit a person in one setting and be ineffective in the other.

The only study on this was done by Kingsley and Wilson (1977). Obese subjects were randomly assigned to conditions in which they received a behavioral program in small groups or in individual sessions with trained counselors. The two approaches did not differ at the end of an initial treatment phase, but the group meetings were superior during a follow-up period.

We feel that patients are the best judges of which form of treatment to pursue, but we feel that group treatment is the best option unless we can be convinced otherwise. This bias occurs for several reasons. Cost to the patient is less in group treatment. Even more importantly, however, the group can provide support and encouragement of a different nature than the therapist–client relationship provides. The patients often feel more at ease discussing their problems if they know others suffer similarly. The patients in a group will often generate creative solutions to specific problems. In addition, patients may sometimes accept advice better from another patient than from a professional.

There are a number of reasons why a person may be more appropriate for individual sessions. These are listed below:

1. The patient may have emotional difficulties that are not appropriate for a group or may require more attention than the group can provide.

2. The person may be very shy or reluctant to speak before others. These individuals can usually be identified after a few group meetings in which they are silent and give only short answers when called upon. There are some patients who are successful in group meetings despite the silence, but this behavior is a signal to investigate the possibility of individual treatment.

3. Some patients have been in group programs before, most likely Weight Watchers, and do not like the idea of speaking before others and having others know their weight status. These misgivings can be allayed in some cases by telling the patient that the groups run in clinical settings are much different from those in the commercial programs.

4. Patients who are destructive to the group process should be seen individually. This is done for the benefit of the remaining members of the group. One indication is psychopathic personality characteristics or a borderline personality. Another is a personal conflict with the therapist. The destructive nature of some patients cannot be determined until the group begins, but when identified, it is best for all concerned to investigate another form of treatment.

Group and individual treatment are not mutually exclusive. Some patients do well in groups if they receive periodic individual attention. Others may do well in groups and then require individual treatment during crisis periods. Some patients need individual attention initially to start the process of behavior change, but then can switch to a group. This requires ongoing assessment of the patient's status.

Self-Help and Commercial Groups

There are an array of self-help and commercial treatments available for obesity. They range from scandalous to safe. Many professionals do not look favorably on these groups and may discourage patients from joining. This is due in part to lack of knowledge about these groups, the absence of scientific evaluation of most groups, and a general distrust of money-making enterprises for weight reduction. In some cases this distruct is warranted, but in other cases it is not.

Self-help and commercial groups can be a very valuable resource for the professional. These groups are an important part of treating obesity from a public health perspective, because the vast majority of dieters use this approach. The groups are effective for some patients, sometimes in lieu of professional treatment and sometimes in conjunction with a professional program.

A detailed view of these groups will not be given here. We refer the reader to Stuart and Mitchell (1980), Stunkard and Brownell (1979), and Colletti and Brownell (1982). These reviews have shown that the major shortcoming of these groups is attrition. Between 50% and 80% of enrollees drop out of these groups within 6 weeks. The average person who joins Weight Watchers has joined three times before. For those who remain in the program, weight losses are usually moderate.

The high attrition from these groups is viewed by some as an indictment of the self-help and commercial approach. We feel differently. Many of the groups are offered at low cost, so people who are minimally motivated may join and then drop out. The issue is to decide which patients would profit from this approach.

The first step is to become acquainted with the details of the various programs. This can be done by calling or visiting the program, but the most valuable information can be obtained from the patients who have been in the groups. The groups are very different in their procedures and the way in which they approach obesity. For example, Overeaters Anonymous (OA) is modeled after Alcoholics Anonymous (AA). Its participants are called "compulsive overeaters" and are encouraged to call upon a higher power for strength and to use the assigned sponsors to cope with crises. Its members are never weighed. Weight Watchers, on the other hand, has no spiritual overtone, has a specific diet, and relies on the regular weigh-in for motivation.

The next step is to match patients with a possible group, if the professional and patient determine jointly that a self-help or commercial group would be appropriate. This can be done by discussing the details of the different approaches with the patient and by encouraging the patient to speak with others who have been in the programs. Patients often benefit from entering self-help groups after a professional program ends, as exemplified by this patient:

THERAPIST: Susan, it has now been 1 year since our program has ended. Tell me what has happened with your weight.

CLIENT: I regained about 10 pounds after I was here, and I really felt the control slipping away. I decided to join Overeaters Anonymous and I lost the weight. This makes me feel guilty because I thought after the program that I should be able to do it on my own.

T: What is most important is that you find what works best for you. If that solution is OA, fine. OA is really nice for some people.

C: Now that I think about it, your program taught me the procedures to follow to keep my weight under control, but what I need is the motivation to do it. OA helps me with it. But, don't you think I should be able to do it on my own?

T: You *are* doing in on your own. You have discovered the steps to keep the weight off, and you are following those steps. You get the credit for taking those steps, not the program which helps you. It is like playing the piano. If you take lessons and become a virtuoso, do the lessons get the credit for a fine performance or do you?

THERAPIST AND PATIENT VARIABLES

Linda lost 56 lb over a 4-month period on one of our very-low-calorie diets. She had been coming to weekly maintenance classes faithfully and was holding her losses nicely. She unexpectedly did not come to her class 1 week and then stopped coming entirely. When our dietitian, Gayle, called Linda to ask her why she had dropped out of the program, Linda replied that she had come to maintenance class 1 week when Gayle was on vacation and another dietitian, Lorie, had filled in for her. Lorie had reviewed Linda's chart, and among other things, said to her, "Is that all you have lost during maintenance?" Linda felt hurt and angered by Lorie's attitude, and abruptly quit our program.

Therapist Variables

Therapist variables are an integral part of treatment success. If you interview a hundred successful weight-loss patients and a hundred patients who failed at weight loss, you will invariably find that during your interview they will mention the therapist as an important influence in either their success or failure.

What are the qualities of an effective therapist for weight loss? Surprisingly little research has looked at the question. One study showed that experienced therapists produced greater weight losses than novice therapists (Jeffery, Wing, Stunkard, 1978); another that professional therapists had better results than lay therapists (Levitz & Stunkard, 1974). However, the area is one that needs considerable research. Presumably, the same characteristics that make for an effective therapist in any other field, including empathy, positive regard, respect, warmth, and genuineness, are required in obesity counseling. The most effective therapists we know in the field possess those characteristics along with the specific knowledge in nutrition, physiology, and psychology this counseling requires.

Patient Variables

What wonderful jobs we would all have if we could reliably predict with whom we would be successful and with whom we would fail. We could then limit our work to only those with whom we would succeed. Unfortunately, one of the biggest limitations of our field has been the almost total inability to identify predictors of treatment outcome. There have been countless research studies attempting to correlate age, sex, onset of obesity, and a variety of personality characteristics with outcome of treatment, with no consistent success. It is our clinical impression that males seem to lose more weight than females, but that may be because they are heavier than females, we see fewer of them, and the ones we do treat are highly motivated. People who are chronically obese seem to have a harder time of it than those who have not been obese as long, but when we try to substantiate our hunch, the data never come out the way we expect. To date, about the only helpful finding to emerge from the research is the fact that behavioral treatment programs are not very helpful with morbidly obese (weight over 300 lb) people.

THE PROBLEM OF ATTRITION

Attrition is a problem that plagues many treatments for obesity, yet the issue receives surprisingly little attention in the literature. Every clinician and researcher has struggled with patients who drop out of treatment, despite heroic efforts to aid them. One of the greatest challenges in treating obese patients is keeping them involved in treatment:

Attrition is one of the most important and often overlooked issues in the treatment of obesity. The usefulness of any program depends in part on the number of persons it attracts and the number of persons it graduates. Large weight losses become less impressive if the program appeals to few or if most of the participants drop out. (Wilson & Brownell, 1980, p. 58)

Attrition for general medical treatments can be as high as 80%, and the dropout rate from the self-help and commercial groups is in the range of 50%–80% (Stunkard, 1975; Wilson & Brownell, 1980). In contrast, attrition in behavior therapy programs is far lower. Wilson and Brownell (1980) reviewed 17 studies with follow-up periods of greater than 6 months. The dropout rates ranged from 0% to 26%, with mean attrition of 13.5%. This is a major accomplishment and is one of behavior therapy's greatest strengths. An examination of this issue from a behavioral perspective may provide some insight into methods for encouraging patients to remain in treatment.

Methods for Reducing Attrition

The problem of attrition can be approached in one of two ways. The first is the most obvious—to manipulate aspects of the program itself. The second, which may be as important, is to screen the individuals who are allowed in the program. We feel attrition can be minimized by emphasizing both areas.

The Screening Process

Within the past 3 years, we have instituted a screening phase for our treatment programs, irrespective of the type of treatment being used or the degree of obesity in the patients. To qualify for the program, patients must satisfy two requirements. They must lose at least 1 lb for each of 2 weeks in the screening phase, and they must complete a daily self-monitoring record of food intake. Patients who do not satisfy the requirements are allowed a 1-week "grace" period in which to comply, and otherwise are not permitted in the program.

There are several virtues to this approach. First, it gives the program a reputation for being "tough" even though the screening requirements are not rigorous. This discourages some persons who are not committed from attempting to join. Second, it provides a concrete behavioral index for the professional to make an initial assessment of motivation.

Our screening procedure has been criticized, particularly by the few patients who are barred from the program, on the grounds that we are not administering treatment to those in need. This argument assumes that the screening process yields false-negatives; that is, there are persons screened out who would otherwise go on to do well. We feel that this phenomenon is exceedingly rare. The usual approach, which does not employ a screening phase, yields false positives (individuals qualify and then do poorly).

The false positives create problems. Patients' lack of progress discourages the staff and certainly promotes a negative emotional experience for the patient. In addition, nonmotivated patients can damage the morale of other patients in the clinic, a problem which is most severe if the patients participate in group meetings. Therefore, we feel that the benefits of screening far outweigh the hazards. In practice the major function of the screening is to produce a motivated group to begin treatment, because most patients satisfy the screening requirements once they begin.

The Deposit–Refund System

In our programs at the University of Pennsylvania and the Baylor College of Medicine, deposit–refund systems are a standard part of the treatment protocol. The system requires the patient to make a financial deposit in addition to any charge for treatment. The deposit is then refunded for attendance, weight loss, completion of records, or any behavioral requirement established by the clinic staff.

The amount of the deposit is usually determined by the cost of the program itself and by the financial status of the patients. A typical deposit–refund system might require a patient to deposit $100 in addition to a treatment fee of $200. Half of the deposit would be returned if the patient attends 80% of the meetings in the initial treatment phase and the remaining $50 would be returned for attendance at 80% of the follow-up meetings.

Our clinical experience with the deposit–refund system has been positive. In addition, evidence from the literature supports its use. In the review by Wilson and Brownell (1980), average attrition was 19.3% in studies not using a deposit and 9.5% in studies with a deposit. Hagen, Foreyt, and Durham (1976) carried out the only controlled test of the deposit–refund system. Attrition was measured during a 6-week program of 12 sessions for subjects having no deposit, a $5 deposit, or a $20 deposit. Subjects with the $20 deposit had significantly lower attrition than subjects in the other two conditions, which did not differ significantly from each other. The deposit–refund appears to work both by discouraging nonmotivated persons from joining a program and by encouraging patients to remain in the program once it begins.

THE IMPORTANCE OF EXERCISE: A CLINICAL VIEW

Early in the treatment of obesity, exercise was ignored completely. Several factors were responsible. First, exercise is not popular among obese persons, for obvious reasons. Second, little was known about the physiology of physical activity, particularly in the area of body weight regulation and appetite control. Third, the prevailing attitude was that overeating was at the root of obesity. Fourth, both patients and professionals tended to be discouraged by the seemingly small effect of exercise on energy expenditure. For instance, a jumbo hamburger, small order of french fries, and a small soda at a typical fast food restaurant totals approximately 1100 calories. To "burn" this off via exercise would require jogging approximately 11 miles! This is a heroic amount of exercise to expend the calories in only a portion of the day's eating.

The tide has now turned. Exercise has become a very popular endeavor to promote. All obesity programs tout the importance of exercise, but there is great variability in how the focus on exercise is applied. Some programs simply talk about exercise in a positive fashion, others give patients guidelines for types and amounts of exercise, some do a functional analysis of exercise and prescribe behavioral procedures to increase adherence, and still others have exercise instructors who supervise a physical activity program.

There are many reasons for this turn in attitude. There is tremendous enthusiasm in the general society for exercise, at least compared to 10 years ago. Exercise physiologists and psychologists have discovered many of the benefits of physical activity, and these are becoming more widely recognized. In addition, many overweight people are feeling less timid about physical activity.

This is a very positive move for the obesity field to take. There are many indications in the literature and in our clinical experience to suggest that exercise is important. Yet, there emerges a difficult clinical challenge to encourage overweight persons to be physically active.

The Psychological Benefits of Exercise

The psychological, cognitive, perceptual, and social benefits of physical activity have been studied in earnest only within the past decade. Many of the benefits relate to general quality of life, which is an important issue for a person undergoing the rigors of dieting. A comprehensive review of this area has been written by Folkins and Sime (1981).

In addition to these general benefits, there are specific benefits for the obese person (Brownell & Stunkard, 1980). Recent studies have indicated that exercise is one of the few factors that is associated consistently with long-term success at weight reduction (e.g., Dahlkoetter, Callahan, & Linton, 1979). There appear to be psychological correlates of this phenomenon.

Physical activity seems to have a general effect on a person's ability to adhere to a dietary program. This could be a physiological effect (see following discussion), but it appears to have psychological roots as well. In our experience, exercise serves as a specific cue to eat less and to remain faithful to a program and serves as a general cue that self-improvement is occurring. This can be very important in the long-term picture. Motivation fades as time passes and the general sense of well-being that comes with exercise can be quite helpful.

The Physiological Benefits of Exercise

There are very compelling physiological reasons to be physically active. Some of these reasons relate specifically to overweight people, as there are more general benefits (McArdle, Katch, & Katch, 1981). These will be discussed only briefly here because the area has been reviewed elsewhere (Brownell & Stunkard, 1980; Thompson, Jarvie, Lahey, & Cureton, 1982).

Exercise *does* burn calories, but the acute effects are not impressive. Its main benefit in this regard may lie in its chronic use. For instance, substituting going up and down two flights of stairs each day for using an elevator amounts to 6–12 lb of calories in 1 year. Therefore, prescribing low levels of activity that can be worked into the daily routine may be helpful.

Exercise may help suppress appetite. This is a complex issue that has not been addressed adequately in the human literature. Even the evidence in animals is conflicting. However, there are no reports that exercise in modest amounts increases appetite in obese persons, so activity seems to have positive or neutral effects on appetite (Brownell & Stunkard, 1980; Thompson *et al.*, 1982).

Physical activity can help prevent the loss of lean body mass during dieting. This is a difficult concept to explain to patients, but it can be very motivating if the important points can be conveyed. What follows is the rationale we give patients:

When you eat fewer calories than your body needs to function, the energy must be obtained somewhere. Much of the energy comes from fat (which is just what you want), but some also comes from your body's stores of muscle. This muscle is also called "lean body mass." You can reduce the loss of muscle by having adequate protein, carbohydrate, vitamins, and minerals in the diet, but some muscle is almost always lost.

It is unhealthy to lose muscle, and our goal in this program is to help you lose as much fat as possible. This is where exercise is important.

When most people regain after they lose weight, they regain more rapidly than their body can replace the muscle that was lost. This means that the body becomes more fat and less muscle, even if weight does not change.

Let's take an example. Tara is a hypothetical patient. She weighs 170 lb and loses to

150 lb. Of the 20-lb loss, 18 lb are fat and 2 lb are muscle. If Tara regains weight rapidly, she might be able to replace only 1 lb of the 2 lb of lost muscle. If she regains back to 170 lb, she has added 19 lb of fat while she lost only 18 lb on the way down.

Tara is at a real disadvantage now. She weighs exactly the same as when she started, but she has more fat and less muscle. The muscle is more metabolically active than fat, so she lost a pound's worth of opportunity to expend more energy.

Exercise can help minimize the loss of muscle when you are reducing and can increase the amount of muscle you add if you regain. This is important for the long-term picture, because many people gain and lose many times.

The final, and perhaps most important reason for overweight people to exercise is that it may help offset the decline in basal metabolic rate that occurs with dieting. This decline occurs almost immediately upon the onset of dieting and can reach as much as 20% in 2 weeks (Bray, 1976). Since basal energy requirements account for some two thirds of all energy expenditure, a 20% reduction is significant. What this means to the patients is that as they lose weight it becomes harder to lose. Exercise has been shown to increase metabolic rate for an undetermined time after the actual exercise (McArdle et al., 1981). Some obesity researchers have suggested that exercise in obese persons will help offset this troublesome decline in basal metabolic rate (Stern, 1984).

Psychological Barriers to Exercise

It is clear that most overweight people would rather not exercise. Some professionals attribute this to lack of compliance or even to laziness. The problem is much more complex than such views imply. Treatment can often be facilitated when the professional shows some appreciation for the psychological obstacles to exercise.

One reason exercise is unpleasant for obese persons is the simple mechanical burden of carrying excess weight. This makes the exercise itself more difficult and increases the residual pain. In addition, the excess weight usually inhibits performance, so the overweight person may have difficulty doing as well at an activity as a thin friend or family member.

Most overweight persons are embarrassed about their bodies. As mentioned earlier, body image disparagement is one of the major psychological perils of obesity (Stunkard, 1976). As a consequence, many dieters are reluctant to shop for exercise clothing, to be seen jogging, to compete with peers in sports, or to appear in revealing sports apparel like swimsuits. This limits the range of activities that most overweight people will undertake and eliminates some of the most enjoyable methods of increasing activity.

Psychological resistance to exercise is especially strong in childhood-onset obese persons. Many avoided sports and games and never developed a cognitive sense that they could be physically active, much less enjoy it. There is also a legacy of negative associations that must be overcome. Overweight children are often teased by their peers, picked last for teams, and shamed by their poor performance. Some beg their parents for excuses to avoid gym class.

It is important to discuss these issues with the patients. This helps an overweight person understand and counter the negative associations they have with exercise and can enhance the credibility of the professional to show this understanding.

Methods of Encouraging Physical Activity

Helping overweight people change their exercise habits requires much more than a simple pat on the back and exhortation to "get more exercise." The issue must be taken seriously and treated aggressively.

These are the main points we emphasize in general clinical treatment of the obese patient:

1. Do a Functional Analysis. Self-monitoring records can be helpful in determining the psychological, environmental, and social determinants of activity patterns.

2. Start with Modest Amounts. A certain path to failure is to require too much too soon. We begin with most patients by requiring no more than 10–15 min of walking. This is then increased in a stepwise fashion to the point where patients are doing more rigorous activity.

3. Emphasize Lifestyle Activity. Certainly before, but even after patients are exercising vigorously, it is important to increase lifestyle activities. These are the activities that are part of the day-to-day routine. We ask patients to use stairs in lieu of elevators and escalators, park some distance from a destination, move about whenever possible, and so forth.

4. Use Behavioral Principles. The same principles that can be applied to eating can be used for exercise. These include self-monitoring for feedback and reinforcement, stimulus control to increase the environmental cues for exercise, reinforcement, and cognitive restructuring to counter self-defeating thoughts.

5. Emphasize Social Activities. Exercise can be more enjoyable for some people when they have company. The best outcome of this suggestion is when a patient contracts (formally or informally) with a friend or family member to exercise together. This makes the activity more pleasant and also increases motivation and accountability.

6. Encourage Formal Exercise Programs. Many patients profit from joining fitness clubs, spas, the YMCA or YWCA, and the like. Having a special exercise program and facility can be helpful. The problem with this approach is that long-term adherence to these programs is generally poor, so it should not be the sole source of exercise. In addition, not all patients like the idea of exercising in public, so this should be prescribed selectively.

A CLASSIFICATION SCHEME

Most researchers and clinicians have been frustrated in the search for a single treatment approach that will work for all obese persons. Yet, studies continue to appear in the literature in which one treatment is compared to another, as if a contest between approaches could yield an ultimate answer.

These studies usually provide little descriptive information about the patients being treated. Crucial variables, which could potentially explain the great intersubject variability in treatment studies, are not described. These include age at onset, degree of obesity, weight history, reasons for reducing, social support, and so on. The field is not yet advanced to the point where we could even list which variables should be described. However, there is increasing appreciation that not all obese patients are alike and not all should be treated similarly.

Interestingly, the desire to "classify" obese persons has its impetus in the medical field, even though psychologists emphasize individual differences. In 1981 the National Institutes of Health sponsored a consultant conference at Vassar College on the classification of obesity. The meeting was cochaired by Dr. M. R. C. Greenwood, a biologist and physiologist, and Dr. Wayne Calloway, a physician.

The purpose of the meeting was to assemble basic and applied researchers from many disciplines, and to develop guidelines for classifying obese persons. It was apparent from discussions at the meeting that assessment was the key to classification, and methods were covered on assessment for treatment, basic research, and applied research. The guidelines should be published in 1985 in the *International Journal of Obesity*.

Categorizing Obese Patients

The most advanced work on classification has been done by two physicians, one in England (Dr. John Garrow) and one in the United States (Dr. Albert Stunkard). Both have proposed that obese persons be categorized according to their degree of obesity (Garrow, 1978, 1981; Stunkard, 1984). Garrow (1981) lists "grades" of obesity and discusses how obesity in each grade should be treated. Stunkard proposes three levels of severity of obesity, each with different implications for treatment.

These classification schemes arose from the realization that obese patients differed in their response to treatment, cellular pathology, risk for disease, and long-term prognosis. We will present here an adaptation of Stunkard's (1984) scheme, although many of the ideas are similar to those of Garrow (1978, 1981).

Mild Obesity

Patients are considered "mildly" obese in this classification scheme if they are less than 30%–40% overweight. These patients are generally hypertrophically obese and do not have increased fat cell number. Their risks for chronic disease are uncertain.

Mildly overweight persons are ideal for a program of behavior modification. The average weight losses in the current generation of behavioral programs are 20–25 lb. This is about the weight that mildly overweight persons have to lose, and the behavioral approach offers the greatest chance for long-term maintenance of weight loss. This does not imply that the behavioral program is effective for all patients in this category, but it is the treatment of choice. More dramatic approaches may not be justified, because their risk may exceed the risk for the mild degree of obesity.

Moderate Obesity

Moderate obesity is considered 40%–100% overweight. These persons are at "conditional" risk for disease; that is, their risk depends on whether other conditions are present, such as hypertension, diabetes, hyperlipidemia, and so forth. Many epidemiologists feel that obesity in this range is an independent risk factor for heart disease, but some disagree. Persons in this category are all hypertrophicaly obese, and many, but not all, are hyperplastically obese.

The treatment for choice for these patients is a combination of a very-low-calorie diet (discussed in the following section) and behavior modification. The diet produces large and rapid losses, and the behavior modification is used to sustain the losses. Behavior modification alone is the most commonly used treatment for this group, but the losses are not great enough for the majority of patients.

Severe Obesity

Patients are considered severely obese if they are greater than 100% overweight. These patients are relatively rare, but we see them in our clinics frequently. They are at greatly increased risk for chronic disease and premature death. They are uniform in their pathology to the extent that all are both hypertrophically and hyperplastically obese.

Treatment of these patients is most difficult. As a rule, these patients have tried and failed at dozens of programs. It is an unusual patient in this category who has not lost many pounds, sometimes as much as 50–100 lb, and then regained the weight. Patients and professionals become discouraged because even significant weight losses make no difference in appearance and in self-concept.

Gastric bypass surgery is the treatment of choice for many severely obese patients, but only after less dramatic forms of treatment have failed. We use a combination of the very-low-calorie diet and behavior modification with these patients. Some respond very well, but others do not. The choice then is either surgery or helping the patient adapt socially and psychologically to being overweight.

This classification scheme is only a preliminary conceptual plan for viewing obesity. The numbers listed for the categories are not exact, and the scheme will almost certainly misclassify some individuals who, by nature of their physiological pathology or their behavioral response to treatment, should be in a different category. The scheme does stimulate us to view obese people according to their own specific characteristics and may lead to further refinements in assessment and treatment.

VERY-LOW-CALORIE DIETS: AN IMPORTANT ADVANCE

One complaint about most diets is that patients lose too little weight and they lose it too slowly. More aggressive diets are available, but have been limited in their use because of concerns over safety and high rates of relapse. The picture is changing, because of new advances with very-low-calorie diets.

The most rapid way to lose weight is to starve. Since the early 1900s, hospital programs have tested fasting for obese persons. Weight losses are large and rapid, but these approaches produce almost 100% relapse. In addition, starvation is associated with many serious metabolic effects, even in obese people who have much weight to lose before hitting ideal weight. Physiologists and medical researchers began experimenting with supplemented fasts, which might prevent the metabolic disturbances while offering the large losses.

One of the most dangerous consequences of fasting is the loss of lean body mass (protein). This led some researchers to supplement a fast with protein, in hopes that the body would draw its energy only from fat. Research was progressing nicely on this diet in the 1970s, but there were many unanswered questions when the diet hit the public.

In 1976 Robert Linn, an osteopath from Philadelphia, published a book called *The Last Chance Diet* and in the process, popularized his own brand of liquid protein. The diet was associated with at least 60 deaths. The reasons typically evoked for the deaths were the use of low-quality protein, absence of medical supervision, inadequate mineral supplementation, and the failure to have preexisting coronary disease monitored. In the meantime, research in several laboratories continued in a carefully controlled manner.

Very-Low-Calorie Diets plus Behavior Modification

Very-low-calorie diets, also known as the protein-sparing modified fast, are making a comeback. The use of these diets has been discussed in detail by Wadden, Stunkard, and Brownell (1983) and by Bistrian (1978). We will discuss their use only briefly here.

The diet is basically a fast that is supplemented by small amounts of lean meat, fish, or fowl as sources of protein. Some programs use powdered supplements for protein in place of the real foods, the most thoroughly studied of which is Optifast® (Delmark; Minneapolis, MN). Patients are also given vitamin and mineral supplements, and some programs include small amounts of carbohydrate to prevent severe ketosis. Patients are seen by a physician for a thorough examination (with ECG and blood work) and then are monitored at least every other week by the physician during the program.

We favor the use of these diets with patients who are at least 40 lb overweight. It is this group of patients for whom the slight risk of the diet is justified. The diet and its supervision are administered under very carefully controlled circumstances by trained professionals. The diet is not to be used by mildly overweight persons and is not to be used by the general public without this supervision.

The diet has impressive effects. Patients lose weight rapidly, as much as 8–10 lb the first week for some. Average weight losses in our clinics, where the diet is used for no longer than 2–3 months, is in the range of 40–50 lb. Many patients report absence of hunger while on the diet and are grateful that they are not forced to make decisions about eating. The weight loss, of course, is very gratifying.

Assuming that the diet is administered safely, that the patient adheres, and that the weight loss is large, the important issue of maintenance still exists. Intuitively one would expect high rates of relapse in people who underwent a program depending so much on an external method for promoting loss. In fact, the few studies that have examined long-term results show high relapse rates (Wadden *et al.*, 1983).

The most promising results in the area have come from a combination of very-low-calorie diets and behavior modification. Two uncontrolled reports have shown impressive losses and good maintenance of loss with this combination of approaches (Lindner & Blackburn, 1976; Wadden, Stunkard, Brownell, & Dey, 1984). It is possible that this marriage of medical and behavioral techniques will elicit the best of both, namely the large losses with the diet and the long-term maintenance with the behavior modification.

A TREATMENT PROTOCOL

Most behavioral programs use slightly different protocols even when administering essentially the same techniques. The programs differ in the sequence in which techniques are covered and also in the relative emphasis on specific components. For instance, our programs at the University of Pennsylvania and the Baylor College of Medicine emphasize specific skills in the area of social support, but other programs may not include this topic. Other programs use relaxation training; we do not.

When we discuss these differences with each other, we find ourselves referring to the "old-time" behavioral program, which consists of self-monitoring, stimulus control, and a few additional techniques. The new programs, which include these techniques along with social support, cognitive restructuring, and exercise, have been producing greater weight losses, as discussed earlier. We feel the protocol presented in Figure 6-1 is fairly representative of the new generation of behavioral programs.

FIGURE 6-1. Table of Contents from the Behavioral Treatment Manual (Brownell, 1979).

- Introduction
  - The Behavioral Approach
  - Program Description
- Section 1: Energy Balance, Calories, Record Keeping
  - Explanations of Overweight
  - The Energy Balance Model
  - What Is a Calorie?
  - Record Keeping (Diet Diary)
- Section 2: Interpreting Records, Calorie Levels, Daily Log
  - What Your Diary Means
  - Extending Your Diary
  - How Many Calories Should You Have?
  - Explanation of the Daily Log
  - Daily Log—Section 2
- Section 3: Interpreting Records, Nutrition, Slowing Eating
  - Interpreting Your Diary
  - Nutrition and Your Diet
  - Slowing the Rate of Eating
  - Daily Log—Section 3
- Section 4: Signals to Eat, ABCs of Behavior, Cue Control, Shaping
  - Eating, Hunger, and Signals to Eat
  - The ABCs of Behavior
  - Cue Control
  - Shaping New Behaviors
  - Daily Log—Section 4
- Section 5: Review, Diet and Nutrition Myths
  - Taking a Break
  - Myths about Dieting and Nutrition
    - Dieting and Your Body
    - Other Popular Myths
  - Review of Early Material
  - Daily Log—Section 5
- Section 6: Review, More Diet and Nutrition Myths
  - What Did You Learn?
  - More Myths on Dieting and Nutrition
    - Eating the Right Foods
    - Health Foods
  - Further Review of Earlier Material
  - Daily Log—Section 6
- Section 7: Cue Quiz, Situational Control
  - More about Dieting and Cues to Eat
  - Quiz on Signals to Eat
  - Controlling Time, Place, and Activities
  - Daily Log—Section 7
- Section 8: Rate of Progress, Visual Signals, Preparing Foods
  - Your Rate of Progress
  - Visual Signals—Out of Sight, Out of Mouth
  - Hints for Preparing Meals
  - Daily Log—Section 8
- Section 9: Cognitive Changes
  - The Psychology of Fat People Who Stay Thin
  - Goal Setting
  - How to Banish an Imperative
  - How to Change Your Thoughts
  - Daily Log—Section 9

(continued)

FIGURE 6-1. (*Continued*)

Section 10: Eating at Home
  Eating Sensibly at Home
  Daily Log—Section 10
Section 11: Behavioral Chains, Shopping for Food
  Behavioral Chains and Your Eating
  Shopping for Food
  Daily Log—Section 11
Section 12: Exercise
  Exercise, Activity, and Your Weight
  Why Exercise?
  Modest Exercise and Weight Loss
  Programmed Exercise
  Routine Exercise
  The Stairs and Escalator Study
  Myths about Exercise
  Calorie Values of Exercise
  Daily Log—Section 12
Section 13: Social Support from Family and Friends
  The Importance of Social Support
  Support from the Family
  How to Discuss This Program with Your Family
  Behaviors for the Family
  Social Support from Friends
  Daily Log—Section 13
Section 14: Alternative Behaviors, Premeal Recording
  Using Incompatible (Alternate) Behaviors
  Premeal Recording
  Daily Log—Section 14
Section 15: Eating Away from Home, Review
  The Challenge of Eating Away from Home
  Review of Recent Material
  Daily Log—Section 15
Section 16: Special Events, Concluding the Program
  Dealing with Special Events and Holidays
  Anti-Orgy Techniques
    Cocktail Parties
    Office Parties
    Your Own Parties
  Concluding the Program: Becoming a Weight Control Expert
  Master Daily Log
  Master List of Program Behaviors

This protocol is taken from a 100-page treatment manual by one of us (Brownell, 1979).[1] The manual provides a step-by-step description of our behavioral program and is used both to train professionals in administering the program and to serve as a clinical guide to patients during the program. Our behavioral program is 16 weeks in duration. Accordingly, the contents of the manual are divided into 16 sections, after a general introduction.

1. For information on obtaining the manual, write to Kelly D. Brownell, Department of Psychiatry, University of Pennsylvania, 133 South 36th Street, Philadelphia, PA 19104.

We use this protocol in work with patients at all levels of obesity. With mildly obese subjects, this program, delivered in a group context, is the sole form of treatment. With moderately overweight patients, the protocol is used in conjunction with the very-low-calorie diet (VLCD). Patients in the severe obesity category also receive this approach, usually in combination with another method of weight loss (either surgery or a VLCD).

The case study that begins in the following section describes some of the key points in the progression through this program. The patient described, Sarah, received our program, which combines the VLCD with behavior therapy. With this approach the behavioral protocol is superimposed on the management of the diet.

In use with the VLCD, the timing of the behavioral program is an important issue. For example, patients cannot practice eating slowly if they are not eating. Shopping for food is not an issue when people are on a modified fast. Therefore, the programs are staggered so that during the time on the VLCD the sections on self-monitoring are covered, along with introduction of the materials on exercise and cognitive restructuring. As the diet ends and patients enter the "refeeding" stage, the behavioral program begins in earnest and the protocol shown below is followed. The material introduced earlier (on exercise, attitudes, etc.) is covered in great detail during this period.

CASE STUDY

We will present a case of a patient, Sarah, to give clinical examples of the approach we take in treatment. Sarah presented a very challenging case, for she had failed at many forms of treatment. Her case illustrates many of the most difficult clinical problems in the clinical treatment of obesity.

Case Description

Sarah is a 48-year-old female employed as an administrative assistant in a bank. She is married to Larry, a 53-year-old real estate executive. They have two children, a married daughter (aged 24), who is a nurse, and a single son (aged 22), who is an accountant. Both children live away from the home.

When Sarah entered treatment, she weighed 186 lb and stood 5′ 4″ tall. She was overweight from the age of 8 years and had lost weight and gained it back "at least 15 times." On one occasion, she reduced her weight from 155 lb to 128 lb and was "euphoric," but then regained the weight. She gained approximately 10 lb after each pregnancy. Each time she dieted and regained, she seemed to add a few more pounds above her baseline weight.

Sarah began treatment right after New Year's Day. She recounted feeling terrible over the holidays because she was around several relatives she had not seen in years, and she felt they were avoiding her because of her weight. In addition, her son was going to be married in March and Sarah wanted to look good for the wedding.

Larry was "supportive" of Sarah's attempts to reduce, to the extent that he rarely complained about her weight or about the money she spent on diet programs. Sarah felt that Larry was somehow upset when she was able to lose weight, even though he said he wanted her to be slimmer.

Before our program Sarah had been on countless diets and had been in many formal programs. Weight Watchers worked for a month or so, but then she dropped out. She tried joining exercise centers several times, but found the workouts so boring and painful that she could not continue. Approximately 2 years before joining our program, she took part in a behavior modification program run by a dietitian and a physical therapist at a local hospital. She lost weight very slowly and found the procedures like putting the fork down between bites demeaning.

Assessment

Assessment of the obese patient is a complex and important issue. The assessment must include social and psychological factors, eating and exercise behaviors, weight history, medical problems, and many intangible factors like reasons for losing weight, body image, and relationship factors. A detailed plan for assessment has been described elsewhere (Brownell, 1981). We will cover several of the intangible factors that are rarely discussed.

Several aspects of Sarah's background indicated specific issues for assessment. One issue was her failure in a program that employed behavior modification.

THERAPIST: Sarah, you seem unhappy with your experience in the behavioral program at the hospital. Tell me more about your experiences there.

SARAH: The group leaders didn't know what they were doing. They told us to do silly things like eat in one place, but never told us why this would help. Even when I did these things, it didn't help me lose weight because I was as hungry as ever.

T: I have told you that this program is primarily behavioral in nature. How does that strike you?

S: I guess it's OK. Maybe you people know what you are doing. After all, you are supposed to be the experts.

T: You will just have to wait to see whether our program is better than the ones you have tried in the past. One thing is certain, however. If you are half-hearted about the program because of this past experience, I suggest you not join. The program requires a tremendous effort on your part, and if you do not practice the behaviors we discuss, you will have no chance for success.

S: I promise to try hard. This is my last chance.

T: Fine, we will do whatever we can to help you through the program. It will be important that you alert us if you feel your motivation slipping. There are a number of things that we can do to help if this happens.

Another key aspect of the assessment with Sarah was to evaluate whether she had psychological and environmental obstacles to success. One obstacle was her desire to look better for her son's wedding.

THERAPIST: You mentioned your son's wedding. How far off is it?

SARAH: The wedding is in March, so it is about 10 weeks away.

T: How much weight can you lose in that time? How would you like to look?

S: I know I won't be skinny, but I want to be at least as thin as when my daughter was married?

T: How much did you weigh then?

S: I weighed about 145.

T: A red flag just went up in my mind. It is nice that you want to look good for you son's wedding, but your expectations are unrealistic.

S: What do you mean? I lost that much weight once before.

T: To lose 40 pounds in 10 weeks is an average of 4 pounds a week. You would not lose this much if you starved completely. You would do very well to lose 20 pounds in that time.

S: I guess that's true, so we might as well get on with it.

T: Just a minute, Sarah. You are primed for trouble. You could lose 6 pounds in the next 3 weeks, which is very good progress, but still be discouraged because the image in your mind is of being thin for the wedding. The best thing to do is to forget the wedding and take a view that extends further into the future.

S: But the wedding is one of the reasons I joined this program.

T: The wedding is not a good reason. What happens after the wedding? Then is it OK to regain all the weight?

S: Of course not. I want to be thin anyway.

T: It is sad that you do not have time to get thin before the wedding, but it is a fact of life. You must decide that you want to lose the weight for *you*.

These are several of the issues to be covered in the assessment. These are special clinical issues that can interfere with treatment, so they were described in detail. It is also important to evaluate eating behavior, physical activity, and other psychological and behavioral factors (Brownell, 1981).

Screening

Screening is an important aspect of treatment because it provides a behavioral test of a person's motivation. Since Sarah was skeptical about the program and since she had unrealistic expectations about weight loss, there was reason to believe that Sarah might not be sufficiently motivated to follow a very involved protocol.

As mentioned earlier, our screening phase lasts 2 weeks and requires a person to lose 1 lb each week and to complete the self-monitoring records in a satisfactory manner. Sarah lost weight the first week (2 lb), but had completed the records only the first 2 days.

THERAPIST: Do you recall what rules apply during the screening phase?

SARAH: Yes. If I do not complete the records and lose weight, I can't be in the program.

T: Do you think you should go on with the program?

S: I don't know. You don't seem to think I can do it?

T: Why do you think you resisted keeping the records?

S: I didn't see what good it was going to do me.

T: Let me show you what type of information we can get from the records, and then maybe you will see more utility to our request that they be completed every day.

I can see from your records that you do not eat breakfast, that you have very little for lunch, and that you do most of your eating between 6:00 and 10:00 in the evening. Is that correct?

S: That's right.

T: There is much to be learned from this. You have a much different pattern than someone who snacks all day long, and we will be advising you accordingly.

S: That's pretty good. The people in the other modification program never learned that much about me.

T: We still have the issue about whether you are motivated.

S: I really think I am. I'll try to be more cooperative. I'm more convinced that these things can help me.

Sarah lost weight the next week and was able to keep the records. The screening phase has served its purpose in her case because it caused both her and the therapist to evaluate the reasons behind her uncertainty.

At this point, Sarah had qualified for treatment. She needed to lose more than 50 lb, her motivation was somewhat suspect, and she had not been happy with the slow weight loss of a previous behavioral program. She was a good candidate for our program, which combines the VLCD with behavior modification.

One remaining issue was whether Sarah would be appropriate for group treatment. She had made it through the screening program, but not without difficulty. Her skepticism about the program and her controlling nature were possible warning signs that she could disrupt the group process, but she began in the group setting in hopes that she would profit from the motivation of the other group members.

Initial Treatment

Attribution for Change

There is a tendency for many patients to ascribe magical properties to a diet, an appetite suppressant, or to any specific qualities of a program or a therapist. This actually facilitates compliance early in the course of treatment, but can be disastrous later. If patients attribute their weight change to something external instead of to their own efforts, the chances of relapse are greater once the "magic" ends. With some patients this can be predicted in advance, because they appear frightened by the prospect the diet will end.

This was a problem with Sarah because she wanted to believe that there was magic available for her. She had been in many programs before, and in her mind, she needed something very special.

THERAPIST: What do you think about the very-low-calorie diet we are using?

SARAH: I think it is my only hope. I sure hope it takes away my hunger and helps me stick to the program.

T: You mean that the diet might be just the trick you need to lose weight?

S: Right, but I hope it is different from the other things I have been on.

T: Sarah, it seems that you are looking for *us* to supply *your* answer. The diet can help, but it is *you* who decides whether or not to follow the diet.

S: But I haven't been able to follow other diets.

T: Whether you follow this one depends on your motivation. It must be high, and it must come from inside you, or it is best to put off a diet until that motivation occurs. Remember, if you do poorly on the program, you will probably blame yourself. There is another side to that coin. If you do well, you deserve the credit, not the diet.

This tendency to ascribe progress to the VLCD is manifested in the fear of what will happen when the diet ends. Some patients talk about this from the very beginning of the diet, whereas others do not express these concerns until the end of the diet is imminent. In Sarah's case, the concern came early.

THERAPIST: Sarah, you have only been on the diet for 2 weeks and you seem worried about when it might end. Why this feeling?

SARAH: Even when I don't cheat on this diet, I feel like it lots of times. It is only this diet that keeps me going. What do you think will happen when it ends?

T: What do you think will happen?

S: I think I will fall apart. I will go right back to same old stuff and I will overeat every night.

T: Perhaps you can take more credit for what happens on the diet. After all, not everybody sticks to the diet—you have trouble yourself. If you stick to the diet, it is because you have made the commitment to yourself to lose weight.

If you stick to the diet, it is because of your efforts, not the diet. These same efforts can be used to learn our behavioral procedures to help you keep the weight off.

S: That all sounds fine, but why do I have so much trouble sticking to the diet when others in the group have no trouble at all?

T: The others probably have more trouble than you think, but even if they don't, you knew all along that it wouldn't be easy. You can't look to a diet to make a hard task easy. The fact is, losing weight is a difficult endeavor for you and you must decide whether the benefits are worth the sacrifices.

Compliance

As patients begin the VLCD, compliance is the major issue. The VLCD demands strict adherence, because the risk of dangerous complications increases if patients eat proscribed foods and/or fail to take necessary supplements (Bistrian, 1978; Wadden et al., 1983). The major problem with supplements comes, surprisingly, from patients who are so motivated that they ingest less protein than prescribed to save calories. These patients are less common than those who "cheat" by breaking the fast and eating foods other than the supplements.

Small slips in compliance may or may not be dangerous medically, but they often signal more slips with more food. This puts the patient at risk not only for the complications, but for the behavioral problem of abandoning the diet completely.

THERAPIST: Sarah, I see from your food records that you had a donut on Wednesday and that yesterday you had some potato chips during the evening.

SARAH: After what you told us, I thought I would die if I did this. Looks like it's not so bad after all.

T: I am completely serious about adherence to the diet. This is not a diet to be taken lightly. That is why we have you seen by a physician so often. It is true that you may cheat and get away with it, but it is also true that you may suffer serious complications. You must decide whether it is worth the risk.

Sarah's initial cheating was indeed a prelude to more and more transgressions. At this point her inability to adhere to the diet was disturbing the morale of other group members. This issue of group morale will be discussed below, but the issue of Sarah's cheating needed to be confronted in depth. This was handled by scheduling an individual session.

THERAPIST: Sarah, I wanted to meet with you individually so we could talk in more detail about several issues. Your food records and our physiological tests show that you have been slipping from the diet more and more. What do you think is happening?

SARAH: I don't think this program has the answers. I think I need more help than you can give me.

T: Perhaps you're right. What type of help do you think you need?

S: I don't know exactly, but one thing is for sure. You haven't given me anything I didn't know already.

T: I see two points from what you just said. The first is a positive one. We still may teach you some new things, but I think you are a smart and savvy woman. You know this area and could probably teach a course yourself. The answer lies less in "knowing" something than in applying what you know already.

S: But what I know already hasn't helped.

T: That is the second point I wanted to raise. Since other diets haven't worked for you, at least over the long run, you want something new. The only new things you will find are miracle diets offered by people wanting your money. It will be an important emotional point in your attempts to diet when you stop looking for a special answer and get down to the task of doing what has to be done.

S: I hadn't really looked at it that way before. Give me another chance on the diet, and I'll do better.

T: As I mentioned, I am concerned about the safety of the diet if you aren't able to adhere better. Let's go week by week. At the point I feel you are cheating too much, I will discontinue the diet.

Group Factors

Some patients profit a great deal from group treatment. The reasons for this were mentioned earlier in this chapter. For patients who do not do well in groups, it is important to recognize the symptoms and to make alternative arrangements for treatment.

Sarah was negative and controlling at some group meetings. This was manifested in sarcastic comments to other patients and to the group leader, and in doubts about the program.

THERAPIST: Let's discuss in the group today how you did with the food records for this 3rd week on the diet.

JACKIE: The records helped me because it showed me what situations make me hungry.

SARAH: We all know this anyway. It seems to me like keeping the records is just a lot of paperwork. I don't see why they are necessary.

T: How helpful do the rest of you find the records?

KATHY: Sometimes they help me, but sometimes I feel like Sarah and it seems like lots of work.

This is an example of how "negative contagion" can occur in a group. The tone of the discussion started out to be positive, but then turned the other way because of a negative patient. Professionals skilled with group process can deflect these comments, can have positive members of the group help the negative members, and can reflect to the group how there is a tendency to let negative attitudes interfere with the diet process at the least provocation. However, there are times when it is best to have a person leave the group setting.

Such was the case with Sarah. She was having a negative influence on other members of the group. She was in a battle for control with the therapist and was using her own lack of progress as a sign that the therapist was failing. On a number of occasions, she criticized the therapist for not giving her the "answer" to her problems.

Sarah was treated individually from this point on. The decision was explained to her as the need to better understand her situation and to tailor treatment strategies to her environment. For clinical reasons she was not told that she was destructive to the group. In addition, she was more likely to respond to treatment if the therapist–client issues could be handled in the absence of an audience (the other group members).

At this point Sarah and her husband were seen together. His resistance to her weight loss was a focus of several meetings. As he became more of an ally in the process, after he was convinced that she would still be committed to him if she became more attractive, Sarah's problems with compliance began to improve. She still struggled, but was able to get back to the right path with less trouble.

Sarah began to adhere to the VLCD and was able to lose 47 lb, so her weight was 139 lb. A key change in her attitude came as the control issue with the therapist was discussed and as Sarah began to see that a partnership with the therapist was the only way for her to succeed. The attitude confrontation that had been occurring throughout treatment had finally had its effect, and Sarah was able to see that she could lose weight only by following what she knew was a sound program, rather than searching for a miracle program. The main issue then became that of maintenance.

The Maintenance Part of Treatment

Long before treatment ends, the emphasis shifts from weight loss to the maintenance of loss. This change in emphasis raises a number of clinical issues. There are the general psychotherapeutic issues of termination. There are issues about programming support into the patient's day-to-day environment. These are only examples of the factors that need attention during maintenance. These have been covered in earlier sections of this chapter and have been discussed in detail elsewhere (Brownell, 1982; Foreyt & Goodrick, 1981; Stunkard, 1976; Wilson & Brownell, 1980). We will discuss a few of the less frequently mentioned issues here.

Need for Further Contact

Most patients get worried as the time for a treatment program draws to an end. This seems to occur even if the program has gone on for many months. Our programs involve regular contact with patients for well over a year, and there is a chorus of complaints as a group of people prepares to "graduate." The patients feel that the support of the group has been their salvation and that they will have great difficulty if they are no longer accountable to the professional or other group members. The usual request from the patients is for more meetings.

We have experimented with more meetings. Some clinicians believe that patients must have the structure of treatment indefinitely. This does not seem to be the case. Even though most patients request more meetings after treatment, few attend when such meetings are offered. Those who do attend seem to do no better than those who do not.

This does not rule out the possibility that continued treatment over several years will have a positive effect. Only controlled research will show this. It is our impression that there comes a time for a patient to leave a program, and that the major challenge of the last months of a program is to instill in the patients that they have the skills to succeed on their own.

THERAPIST: We have six more meetings left, Sarah. Have you given much thought to this time in the program?

SARAH: I am scared. Actually, I am terrified. I am down to less than 140 and I hope to God I never go back up. But I just don't know if I can do it. Being on this program has helped me and I don't know what will happen when I can't come in.

T: You have always gained the weight back in the past. Will this time be any different?

S: I think so. My husband is helping me now and before he only made things worse. Also, you have been telling me that I am responsible for the progress I made.

T: You have heard what I have been saying but I am not certain you believe it.

S: I guess that's true.

T: There *are* some aspects of this program and our meetings which are undoubtedly important to you. You can improve your chances of long-term success by deciding what those aspects are and by duplicating them at home.

Detailed discussions were held with Sarah in the subsequent weeks about what she could do to use her own resources and to develop resources available outside of our program. More meetings with her husband were held so that he could provide some of the support that was coming from the regular meetings with the therapist.

Sarah also concluded that accountability to the staff in our clinic was central to her success. She reported feeling that she controlled her eating sometimes because she knew she was going to be seeing people she knew. We discussed ways to program this into her environment. One possibility was to enlist the aid of a friend who also wanted to reduce or to keep weight down. They could have periodic weigh-ins. These are examples of the problem-solving approach that occurs in planning for maintenance.

Relapse

Even the most successful patient will violate the self-imposed rules for what constitutes acceptable behavior. Many times these rules are unrealistic, as patients make vows like, "I will never eat ice cream again," or "I will exercise every single day." The cognitive restructuring techniques described earlier are useful in countering this problem in standard setting.

Inevitably, a patient must slip. All will eat foods they feel they should avoid, all will want to give up at some point, and all will gain some weight sometime. In most cases the event or slip itself is much less important than the feeling it produces.

As an example of this process, a patient who "slips" by overeating at a wedding is at risk for relapse. If the patient consumes a great deal at the wedding, say 3500 calories (a convenient number!), the resulting influence (a 1-lb gain) is trivial, especially compared to the many pounds lost in a long and arduous diet. However, the patient may feel that this slip is a signal that more slips will occur. This weakens restraint and increases the likelihood of further eating, which weakens restraint even more, and so on.

This is a very common phenomenon among dieters. It *must* be covered in therapy, or a person is tempting the forces that have caused great trouble in the past. This can be done by helping each patient develop a list of high-risk situations, so the determinants of relapse can be identified. Specific behavioral techniques, particularly stimulus control, can be used to avoid the relapse traps. This is the place where the patients may succeed or fail at applying what they have learned during a program.

At least as important as restructuring the environment is restructuring thoughts. Patients can learn to anticipate these troublesome feelings and to counter them with more positive thoughts. For example, a common thought when overeating occurs is, "This shows I have no control." This could be countered with, "It is true that I am not perfect, but I am doing much better than before." Another possible counter would be, "This overeating is not the end of the world. I will eat less at dinner tonight and will go jogging in the morning." There are dozens of countering statements, and they must be matched to a patient's needs. The key is to have patients prepared for the slips by rehearsing the negative statements and the positive counterstatements.

CONCLUDING COMMENTS

It is impossible, even in a chapter of this length, to cover the multitude of factors that must be considered in giving good clinical care to obese persons. Much of what we have said has not been written before, which is testimony to the lack of clinically oriented material in this important area. This is an unfortunate phenomenon because only a portion of what occurs in treatment can be obtained from reports of research projects.

It is clear that the treatment of obesity is more complex than applying the common behavioral techniques like putting the fork down between bites. There are different categories of obese persons; each category has special implications for treatment. The complicated nature of the disorder, its multiple etiologies, and its highly refractory nature, make obesity a puzzling and challenging public health problem.

Our purpose in writing this chapter is to share some of our experience, which is borne both from research and from clinical practice. We recognize the need for more efforts of this nature. It is our hope, therefore, that this chapter is just the first of many steps in the direction of developing a better clinical understanding of obesity.

References

Bandura, A. (1977). *Social learning theory*. Englewood Cliffs, NJ: Prentice-Hall.

Bennett, W., & Gurin, J. (1982). *The dieter's dilemma: Eating less and weighing more*. New York: Basic Books.

Berkman, L. F., & Syme, S. L. (1979). Social networks, host resistance, and mortality: A nine-year follow-up of Alameda County residents. *American Journal of Epidemiology, 109*, 186–204.

Bistrian, B. R. (1978). Clinical use of a protein-sparing modified fast. *Journal of the American Medical Association, 21*, 2299–2302.

Bray, G. A. (1976). *The obese patient*. Philadelphia: Saunders.

Brownell, K. D. (1979). *Behavior therapy for obesity: A treatment manual*. Unpublished manuscript, University of Pennsylvania.

Brownell, K. D. (1981). Assessment of eating disorders, In D. H. Barlow (Ed.), *Behavioral assessment of adult disorders*. New York: Guilford.

Brownell, K. D. (1982). Obesity: Understanding and treating a serious, prevalent, and refractory disorder. *Journal of Consulting and Clinical Psychology, 50*, 820–840.

Brownell, K. D., & Stunkard, A. J. (1980). Exercise in the development and control of obesity. In A. J. Stunkard (Ed.), *Obesity*. Philadelphia: Saunders.

Cobb, S. (1976). Social support as a mediator of life stress. *Psychosomatic Medicine, 38*, 300–314.

Colletti, G., & Brownell, K. D. (1982). The physical and emotional benefits of social support: Applications to obesity, smoking, and alcoholism. In M. Hersen, R. M. Eisler, & P. M. Miller (Eds.), *Progress in behavior modification* (Vol. 13). New York: Academic Press.

Dahlkoetter, J., Callahan, E. J., & Linton, J. (1979). Obesity and the unbalanced energy equation: Exercise versus eating habit change. *Journal of Consulting and Clinical Psychology, 47*, 898–905.

Feldman, B. (1982). Developmental differences in the conceptualization of obesity. *Journal of the American Dietetic Association, 80*, 122–126.

Ferster, C. B., Nurnberger, J. I., & Levitt, E. B. (1962). The control of eating. *Journal of Mathetics, 1*, 87–109.

Folkins, C. H., & Sime, W. E. (1981). Physical fitness training and mental health. *American Psychologist, 36*, 373–389.

Foreyt, J. P., & Goodrick, G. K. (1981). Cognitive behavior therapy. In R. Corsini (Ed.), *Handbook of innovative psychotherapies*. New York: Wiley.

Foreyt, J. P., Goodrick, G. K., & Gotto, A. M. (1981). Limitations of behavioral treatment of obesity: Review and analysis. *Journal of Behavioral Medicine, 4*, 159–174.

Garrow, J. S. (1978). *Energy balance and obesity in man* (2nd ed.). Amsterdam: Elsevier.

Garrow, J. S. (1981). *Treat obesity seriously: A clinical manual*. London: Churchill Livingstone.

Hagen, R. L., Foreyt, J. P., & Durham, T. W. (1976). The dropout problem: Reducing attrition in obesity research. *Behavior Therapy, 7,* 463–471.

Jeffery, R. W., Wing, R. R., & Stunkard, A. J. (1978). Behavioral treatment of obesity: The state of the art in 1976. *Behavior Therapy, 6,* 189–199.

Keesey, R. E. (1980). A set-point analysis of the regulation of body weight. In A. J. Stunkard (Ed.), *Obesity.* Philadelphia: Saunders.

Kingsley, R. G., & Wilson, G. T. (1977). Behavior therapy for obesity: A comparative investigation of long-term efficacy. *Journal of Consulting and Clinical Psychology, 45,* 288–298.

Krotkiewski, M., Garellick, G., Sjostrom, L., Perrson, G., Bjuro, T., & Sullivan, L. (1980). Fat cell number, resting metabolic rate, and insulin elevation while seeing and smelling food as predictors of slimming. *Metabolism, 29,* 1003–1012.

Levitz, L. S., & Stunkard, A. J. (1974). A therapeutic coalition for obesity: Behavior modification and patient self-help. *American Journal of Psychiatry, 131,* 423–427.

Lindner, P. G., & Blackburn, G. L. (1976). An interdisciplinary approach to obesity using fasting modified by protein-sparing therapy. *Obesity/Bariatric Medicine, 5,* 198–216.

Linn, R. (1976). *The last chance diet.* Secaucus, NJ: Lyle Stuart.

Mahoney, M. J. (1977). Personal science: A cognitive learning therapy. In A. Ellis & A. Grieger (Eds.), *Handbook of rational emotive therapy.* New York: Springer.

Mahoney, M. J., & Mahoney, B. K. (1976). *Permanent weight control: A total solution to the dieter's dilemma.* New York: Norton.

McArdle, W. D., Katch, F. I., & Katch, V. L. (1981). *Exercise physiology: Energy, nutrition, and weight control.* Philadelphia: Lea & Febiger.

Rodin, J. (1978). Environmental factors in obesity. *Psychiatric Clinics of North America, 1,* 581–592.

Rodin, J. (1981). Current status of the internal–external hypothesis for obesity: What went wrong? *American Psychologist, 36,* 361–372.

Rodin, J., Herman, C. P., & Schachter, S. (1974). Obesity and various tests of external sensitivity. In S. Schachter & J. Rodin (Eds.), *Obese humans and rats.* Potomac, MD: Erlbaum.

Schachter, S. (1971). Some extraordinary facts about obese humans and rats. *American Psychologist. 26,* 129–144.

Staffieri, J. R. (1967). A study of social stereotype of body image in children. *Journal of Personality and Social Psychology, 7,* 101–104.

Stern, J. S. (1984). Is obesity a disease of inactivity? In A. J. Stunkard & E. Stellar (Eds.), *Eating and its disorders.* New York: Raven.

Stuart, R. B., & Mitchell, C. (1980). Self-help groups in the control of body weight. In A. J. Stunkard (Ed.), *Obesity.* Philadelphia: Saunders.

Stunkard, A. J. (1975). From explanation to action in psychosomatic medicine: The case of obesity. *Psychosomatic Medicine, 37,* 195–236.

Stunkard, A. J. (1976). *The pain of obesity.* Palo Alto, CA: Bull.

Stunkard, A. J. (Ed.). (1980). *Obesity.* Philadelphia: Saunders.

Stunkard, A. J. (1984). The current status of treatment of obesity in adults. In A. J. Stunkard & E. Stellar (Eds.), *Eating and its disorders.* New York: Raven.

Stunkard, A. J., & Brownell, K. D. (1979). Behavior therapy and self-help programs for obesity. In J. F. Munro (Ed.), *The treatment of obesity.* London: MTP Press.

Stunkard, A. J., & McLaren-Hume, M. (1959). The results of treatment for obesity. *Archives of Internal Medicine, 103,* 79–85.

Stunkard, A. J., & Mendelson, M. (1967). Obesity and body image: I. Characteristics of disturbances in the body image of some obese persons. *American Journal of Psychiatry, 123,* 1296–1300.

Thompson, J. K., Jarvie, G. J., Lahey, B. B., & Cureton, K. J. (1982). Exercise and obesity: Etiology, physiology, and intervention. *Psychological Bulletin, 91,* 55–79.

Van Itallie, T. B. (1979). Obesity: Adverse effects on health and longevity. *American Journal of Clinical Nutrition, 32,* 2723–2733.

Wadden, T. A., Stunkard, A. J., & Brownell, K. D. (1983). Very low calorie diets: Their efficacy, safety, and future. *Annals of Internal Medicine, 99*, 675–684.

Wadden, T. A., Stunkard, A. J., Brownell, K. D., & Dey, S. C. (1984). The treatment of moderate obesity by behavior modification and very-low-calorie diets. *Journal of Consulting and Clinical Psychology, 52*, 692–694.

Wilson, G. T., & Brownell, K. D. (1980). Behavior therapy for obesity: An evaluation of treatment outcome. *Advances in Behaviour Research and Therapy. 3*, 49–86.

7

MARITAL DISTRESS

LISA F. WOOD AND NEIL S. JACOBSON

Any clinician who has worked with severe marital distress has learned that simply managing a treatment session, let alone facilitating improvement, often requires all of the art and science one can muster. Because of this challenge, effective marital therapy in the past required considerable clinical talent, and some of our best clinicians, from the point of view of interpersonal skills, were to be found in this area. During the last 10 years, however, a technology that is direct and programmatic and with proven effectiveness has evolved that can be utilized by any well-trained clinician. Based on over 10 years of experience in working with distressed couples, as well as a major role in the origination of much of this technology on the part of Jacobson, the authors discuss in great detail the actual application of this technology to distressed couples presenting for treatment. As Wood and Jacobson point out:

Treatment is homework-based and focuses on the instigation of mutually pleasing interactions in the couples' own environment. In addition, couples learn to communicate effectively about problems, to reduce conflict as it occurs, and to implement viable solutions in a consistent fashion. The content of treatment . . . usually emphasizes the acquisition of relationship-enhancing skills such as problem solving and skills relating to improving the quality of companionship. The treatment process works to release the rigid cognitive biases by training couples to observe their relationship more closely and to balance negative and positive perceptions of their own and their spouses' behavior.

The value of this chapter to the clinician is far more than a description of the latest and most up-to-date technology for treating marital distress. More important are detailed descriptions of the process, and thereby the art, of applying marital therapy. Every step of this treatment program is not only described, but its application is illustrated in numerous transcripts with a variety of different cases. Such issues as how the therapist should ask questions in order to avoid eliciting streams of negativism and accusations during both the conjoint first session, as well as the second session where spouses are seen individually, will be extremely valuable to clinicians. How therapists can keep an emphasis on positive aspects of the relationship, and how major arguments or conflicts during the course of therapy can be turned into a therapeutic advantage through the use of "troubleshooting" technology will also be useful. Perhaps one of the more important sections will be the detailed description of the application of strategies to promote further change and prevent relapse, as well as a very clear set of therapeutic approaches for dealing with noncompliance or "resistance," so commonly encountered in one or both spouses. This chapter illustrates, as well as any other, the importance of combining art and technology in therapy—D. H. B.

Lisa F. Wood and Neil S. Jacobson. Department of Psychology, University of Washington, Seattle, Washington.

INTRODUCTION

Behavioral marital therapy (BMT) is an intensive short-term approach to the amelioration of marital distress. It has evolved in the past 15 years from a purely operant approach (Liberman, 1970; Patterson & Hops, 1972; Stuart, 1969) to one including communication and problem-solving training as well as cognitive interventions (Jacobson, 1984). While BMT continues to develop and change as a direct result of research investigating its effectiveness (Jacobson, 1977, 1978a, 1978b, 1979; Liberman, Levine, Wheeler, Sanders, & Wallace, 1976; Turkewitz & O'Leary, 1981), continuity is retained in the idiographic emphasis and the direct instigative approach to evaluation and treatment.

The basic social learning hypothesis of marital distress proposes that the relative rates of pleasant and unpleasant interactions determine the subjective quality of the relationship, (Jacobson & Moore, 1981; Stuart, 1969; Weiss, Hops, & Patterson, 1973). Happy couples report higher frequencies of positive exchanges than their distressed counterparts, while the latter report higher frequencies of negative or unsatisfying exchanges. In addition, distressed spouses are highly reactive to immediate or recent events in their relationship, while happy couples tend to maintain their satisfaction independently of recent events (Jacobson, Waldron, & Moore, 1980; Margolin, 1981). Distressed spouses seem to operate on the basis of immediate rather than long-term contingencies, whether they be positive or negative, with rapidly fluctuating and unstable satisfaction (Jacobson, Follette, & McDonald, 1982). They are also more likely to reciprocate negative or punishing behaviors initiated by their partner (Billings, 1979; Gottman, 1979; Margolin & Wampold, 1981). In contrast, nondistressed marriages are relatively resilient, even in the face of unpleasant events, and less vulnerable to the impact of negative interchange. While happy couples also respond to variability in the quality of day-to-day interactions, their degree of affective reactivity is much lower than that of distressed couples.

Based in part on the results of these studies, BMT focuses on increasing the rate of positive interactions and decreasing the reactivity of spouses to negative events. Techniques that aid in the instigation of rewarding exchanges are utilized in conjunction with cognitive interventions that mitigate against selective attention to negative aspects of the relationship. Conflict reduction and problem-solving skills are taught so that distressed couples may learn to interrupt patterns of negative reciprocity, substituting effective problem resolution for conflict and escalation. These latter techniques also follow from the research on couple's communication and skills training models of therapy, which indicates that deficits in conflict resolution or communication skills discriminate between distressed and nondistressed couples (Billings, 1979; Birchler, Weiss, & Vincent, 1975; Gottman, 1979; Jacobson et al., 1980; Markman, 1979; Vincent, Weiss, & Birchler, 1975).

Consistent with the social learning model of marital distress and research on couple's communication, the working assumptions of BMT integrate clinical observations with empirical models and facilitate the development and implementation of treatment strategies. These assumptions are as follows:

1. First and foremost, we assume that couples entering therapy genuinely desire positive changes in their marriage. In those instances where one or both spouses are seeking a divorce, treatment strategies shift dramatically, and the approach outlined in this chapter is not utilized. However, in most instances, even while ambivalence about the relationship may be high, we assume that spouses want to work toward improvement, and proceed accordingly.

2. We also assume that couples experiencing difficulties in their relationship are uncertain about how to deal with an unsatisfactory marriage. They enter therapy as adversaries rather than partners, and one or both spouses may feel depressed, frightened, angry, or demoralized by their inability to resolve their problems independently.

3. Couples in distress generally lack skills necessary for resolving conflicts and for changing their behavior. Such skill deficits may exist in the areas of communication, life management, negotiation, or other aspects of their relationship. As a result, spouses often enter therapy in a high state of conflict with one another, conflict that may assume crisis proportions.

4. We assume that positive changes cannot be secured within therapy sessions alone. Couples must work together at home if transfer and generalization of therapeutic gains are to occur. Homework is thus integral to the therapeutic process.

5. Progress in therapy remains contingent upon a bilateral commitment to intensive work on the marriage. This translates into a commitment to carry out homework as assigned and to work collaboratively during sessions.

6. For a variety of reasons, couples do not always complete homework as assigned, nor do they behave collaboratively at all times during therapy sessions. Noncompliance must be addressed directly and effectively if therapy is to be successful.

7. It is likely that relapses will occur during the course of therapy as well as after its completion. Anticipation of and preparation for such setbacks remain critical to a positive treatment outcome and long-term maintenance.

8. Spouses tend to be inaccurate observers of their relationship and underestimate their own individual contributions to problems. Their perceptions of the relationship tend to be colored by the quality of recent events rather than long-term trends. Their biases lean toward a negative and hopeless outlook on improving their relationship. (Jacobson *et al.*, 1982). In spite of these perceptual biases, it is assumed that couples already know how to please one another in some areas of their relationship. We assume that couples can be taught to improve their perceptual skills and to elaborate on the functional aspects of their relationship by adding to their repertoires of pleasing behaviors. In other words, they can learn how to be nicer to one another while they learn to resolve problems and restore a more positive view of the relationship.

9. As an outgrowth of the perceptual biases, it is frequently the case that spouses no longer express appreciation to one another for pleasing behaviors and positive interactions. This paucity of mutual appreciation contributes to lowered self-esteem as well as feelings of resentment and a recalcitrance regarding the initiation of positive changes. The refrain, "Why should I change, he [or she] won't appreciate it anyway," is most familiar to marital therapists. In spite of this factor, distressed couples can be taught to demonstrate greater appreciation to one another, although this task remains one of the most challenging to both therapist and clients.

10. Couples can learn viable modes of communication, which will lead to conflict resolution and the successful implementation of change in the marriage.

Treatment Strategies

The treatment strategies described in this chapter follow directly from the above assumptions and research findings. Treatment is homework-based and focuses on the instigation of mutually pleasing interactions in the couples' own environment. In addition, couples learn to communicate effectively about problems, to reduce conflict as it occurs, and to implement viable solutions in a consistent fashion. The content of treatment may vary depending on presenting concerns, but it usually emphasizes the acquisition of relationship-enhancing skills such as problem solving and skills related to improving the quality of companionship. The treatment process works to release the rigid cognitive biases by training couples to observe their relationship more closely and to balance negative and positive perceptions of their own and their spouses' behavior.

As a skill training package, BMT emphasizes the overlearning of targeted behaviors. In sessions couples are asked to rehearse problem-solving and conflict-reduction skills and are further instructed to practice such behaviors at home. In subsequent sessions homework is reviewed and problems are discussed as necessary. The content and pacing of homework assignments are tailored to the needs and abilities of each couple so that the likelihood of success is maximized. Therapy thus progresses incrementally and progress is determined on a relative, rather than an absolute basis.

Behavioral marital therapy usually encompasses 12–16 therapy sessions lasting 60–90 min. Sessions tend to be highly structured, with the therapist setting the agenda at the outset of each meeting. A typical session includes the following: (1) setting the agenda, with input from the couple; (2) reviewing the previous homework assignment; (3) troubleshooting problems with the homework or general issues that have arisen during the week; (4) new material, for example, the presentation and practice of skills to be practiced at home during the week; and (5) assignment of homework and answering questions. While there exists some variability from session to session, most will include these elements. However, troubleshooting may be optional in some sessions depending on the couple's success with the homework and their level of conflict during the week.

Typically, the first few sessions of BMT focus on the instigation of positive exchanges in the relationship. Latter sessions emphasize communication and problem-solving training. The final sessions emphasize the generalization and transfer of treatment gains and may be extended over the course of several weeks in a pattern known as fading. These time delineations remain somewhat flexible and are dependent on each couple's rate of improvement and level of distress. Therapy sessions are usually but not always conjoint and may be conducted in any standard treatment setting.

Therapist Characteristics

Successful implementation of BMT hinges upon the therapist's ability to adopt a number of roles with flexibility and effectiveness. The balancing of didactic presentations with the communication of emotional support represents a constant challenge as does the balancing of alliances with each spouse. When teaching couples how to improve their relationship, effective communication of a rationale for treatment strategies, overt modeling of the desired behaviors, and instigation of collaborative behavior change both within and outside of sessions remain essential. The therapist directs and paces the flow of therapy, integrating the content of each meeting with homework assignments. Careful and consistent follow-up on homework in subsequent sessions contributes to a sense of continuity as well.

The successful therapist remains sensitive to the needs of each spouse and to the dynamics of the couple's relationship while simultaneously providing reassurance and encouragement to each individual. The therapist serves as a director, sympathizer, teacher, model, evaluator, instigator, and a juggler balancing these roles while providing perspective and insight as necessary. The tasks of the BMT practitioner are taxing and difficult to master without much practice and adequate supervision. Following are descriptions of some specific therapeutic skills necessary for the implementation of BMT.

Teaching Skills

Behavioral marital therapy is highly structured and frequently didactic in its approach to the amelioration of marital problems. Thus, the BMT therapist often plays the role of teacher, explaining the rationale for homework as well as the skills that will be taught within sessions. Not only must the therapist provide a cogent rationale for the procedures of BMT, but he or she must be able to model the skills that will be taught as well as coach the couple as they practice them. Clarity and simplicity of explanation, the avoidance of jargon, and the use of appropriate examples when necessary represent the verbal tactics that are essential to the teaching process. The therapist must also be capable of enforcing the rules of BMT, by interrupting inappropriate behaviors and shaping more appropriate responses. This requires that the therapist maintain control of the sessions and that he or she gain credibility as an expert in marital therapy.

Instigative Skills

Not only must the therapist motivate couples to comply with homework assignments and the tasks of each therapy session, but he or she must instigate their collaboration, that is, get couples to work together on learning new behaviors. The practitioner who is capable of expressing optimism, while simultaneously promoting an ethic of hard work, is likely to be successful at these tasks. Firmness, consistency, and tenacity are characteristics which in and of themselves contradict the ambivalence and confusion inherent to the dilemma of distressed couples. Thus, the demeanor and outlook of the therapist remain critical to the provision of support and motivation. It is hoped that couples will adopt an experimental attitude toward their relationship, trying out new behaviors and modes of interaction without excessive fear of failure.

Pacing Skills

Because BMT is by nature a short-term mode of therapy, the pacing of sessions and homework is critical to its successful implementation. The therapist is responsible for setting the agenda of each session and sticking to it. Couples in distress become masters at sidetracking and the therapist must often intervene so that the tasks of each session are completed. Further, homework assignments need to be paced so that couples meet challenges with a high probability of success. Careful consideration and planning is necessary so that the assignments serve as challenging opportunities for growth without arousing undue frustration. Finally, the therapist maintains a perspective on the therapeutic process as a whole so that the appropriate amount of time is spent on each task or problem. Although it is not always possible to predict how long it will take to work with a couple on a given problem, it is possible to set reasonable goals for therapy and assess the amount of progress made as treatment proceeds. If it appears that the initial goals of treatment may not be met in a reasonable time period, then it may be useful to reassess with the couple what goals will be reached during the time of treatment, or to contract for further sessions.

Relating to the Couple: Dyadically and Individually

The therapist is necessarily participating in three relationships during conjoint marital therapy, one with each spouse individually, and one with them as a couple. Within each of these relationships, both the provision of emotional support and guidance for behavioral change are essential. Of course it remains difficult to serve these functions in all three relationships simultaneously. Thus, over the course of treatment, the therapist must balance his or her alliances and interventions with each spouse and the marital dyad, such that both spouses feel supported and share the responsibility for improving the relationship. At any given time the therapist may provide more support to one or the other spouse as needed. Similarly, in some sessions, greater attention may be given to the behavioral or cognitive changes required for one spouse. Over the course of therapy, these temporary imbalances may be useful, as long as they are counterbalanced between sessions in the long run.

It is necessary from time to time to assess spouses' response to therapy as a means of providing them support and for bringing to the surface any reservations they may have about treatment. This type of inquiry provides the therapist with information and also encourages spouses to be open about their feelings with the therapist and with each other. Behavioral marital therapy ought not be reduced to a package of didactic presentations and exercises. The therapist's ability to convey his or her understanding and recognition of each spouse's feelings and uniqueness is integral to the therapeutic process.

Although BMT is a relatively structured approach to the treatment of marital discord, there is much room for creativity in the course of implementation. Each couple provides unique challenges to the therapist, as they present with different issues and a wide variety of abilities and areas of deficit. Further, as therapy unfolds, the couples' response to homework assignments and their behavior in sessions provide opportunities for assessing interaction patterns and designing appropriate interventions. Thus, the challenge to the therapist in implementing BMT rests in its adaptation to the needs of each couple individually.

Client Characteristics

Couples entering therapy present with a wide variety of concerns and vary considerably in their ability to resolve conflicts successfully. It is most common for couples to describe their problems in terms of communication deficits or simply a lack of satisfaction in the way they interact. Issues around trust, distribution of responsibility, and decision making are also frequent presenting problems as are general feelings of inadequacy and a sense of being unappreciated by the partner. Many couples report that they are less affectionate with one another than earlier in their relationship and that the quality of their sexual interaction has decreased. Thus, the most common complaints center on a decrease in satisfaction with companionship and an increase in conflict around one or more issues. Couples with children will often express conflict around child-management issues, while those experiencing acute environmental stressors, such as the loss of a job, will express conflict about those concerns. Regardless of content, however, the pattern of decreased satisfaction and increased conflict holds.

In addition to this general malaise in the relationship, marital distress is often accompanied by severe emotional or behavioral problems in one spouse. Acute psychosis, clinical depression, addictive disorders, psychogenic illnesses, and anxiety disorders, particularly agoraphobia, are often presented by couples as problems interfering with their relationship satisfaction. In such cases it is not always clear that BMT would be the treatment of choice. However, BMT may be utilized as an adjunct to therapy that directly addresses the individual spouse's problems. In such instances treatment may be modified so that marital therapy complements and supports interventions designed to help the spouse with the above problems. Such modifications, however, will not be addressed in this chapter.

Another category of couples frequently seen in marital therapy are those who possess little or no reinforcement value for one another and who seem to be mutually disengaged. Such couples may have entered the relationship and chosen to marry, even though there was little gratification in doing so. Economic circumstances, unexpected pregnancies, and personal insecurity all serve as motivation for the formation of such relationships. Couples may also have simply grown apart, having come together at a time in their lives when they held much in common, and having developed individually in divergent directions so that they no longer find gratification in each other's company. They may have already developed separate lives in terms of activities, friends, and work, but maintain their relationship out of a sense of duty or a fear of repudiation, should they separate. In these cases treatment becomes markedly difficult, as the resources, insubstantial to begin with, have been depleted either through neglect or consistently high levels of conflict. In such instances the goal of therapy may be to work toward amicable separation, rather than a continued suppression of satisfaction. However, it is useful for even the most disengaged couple to work toward relationship enrichment over a limited time period, as a means of making such a determination.

In summary, couples present with wide-ranging concerns, many of which center upon issues of compatibility and difficulties with conflict reduction and problem solving. The variability in styles of interaction, individual personalities, and mutual reinforcement value calls for flexibility in therapeutic interventions and in the establishment of treatment goals. While BMT provides a framework for addressing general skills deficits, a paucity of reinforcing exchanges, and cognitive distortions, it remains adaptable to the range of problems and issues that inform these patterns of behavior and interaction. Thus, the emphasis in this chapter will be on the ways in which particular therapeutic techniques may be adapted to the needs and issues of individual couples. We have chosen to document a number of cases so that the flexibility of BMT may be highlighted along with the variability in each couple's responsiveness to BMT interventions. The couples featured in the chapter vary in age, economic status, educational level, and presenting concerns.

The approach to be discussed in the paragraphs below describes one version of BMT. It is based on previous work by Jacobson and his associates (cf. Jacobson, 1981, 1984, in press; Jacobson, Berley, Melman, Elwood, & Phelps, 1985; Jacobson & Margolin, 1979). It is also derived from the pioneering work of Richard B. Stuart (1969), Gerald R. Patterson (Patterson & Hops, 1972), and Robert L. Weiss (Weiss, Hops, & Patterson, 1973). For other contemporary versions of BMT, the reader may consult Stuart (1980), Weiss (1980), Liberman, Wheeler, deVisser, Kuehnel, and Kuehnel (1980), and O'Leary and Turkewitz (1978).

ASSESSMENT AND THERAPY: A FALSE DICHOTOMY

We typically devote two or three sessions to the task of assessment, sessions which also lay the groundwork for subsequent therapeutic interventions. Therefore, in theoretical terms, the distinction between assessment and treatment sessions is not always clear cut. Nevertheless, in practice, we label these early sessions as "assessment" and tell clients not to expect any changes to occur during the assessment period. This labeling serves an important function, that of averting the spouses' disappointment, should their relationship not immediately improve. Although the distinction between assessment and therapy seems clear to a mental health professional, such a distinction remains patently obscure to most clients. Couples often expect the relationship to improve immediately and are disappointed when these benefits are not forthcoming, despite the therapist's explicit delineation of the distinction. Thus, in BMT, couples are reminded throughout the course of assessment sessions that no immediate change is to be expected in their relationship.

Paradoxically, while we emphasize the distinction between assessment and therapy to clients and caution them against expecting immediate changes, we actually structure the evaluation process so that the likelihood of improvement is maximized. By describing the assessment procedures as if they contain no therapeutic goals, the therapist sets appropriate expectations for the evaluation phase without precluding the possibility of positive changes. Although no change is expected by clients, if it occurs, so much the better. On the other hand, if no rapid improvement is apparent, treatment credibility remains uncompromised.

Couples are often relieved when told that treatment will not begin until a thorough assessment is completed. In fact, during the initial contact with a therapist, one or both spouses often appear tentative or ambivalent about the idea of therapy. The therapist, in effect, supports this tentativeness by announcing that therapy will be postponed for a few sessions. By following this announcement with a brief description of the assessment process, therapist credibility is enhanced, and the couple's initial anxiety about treatment is reduced; the former follows from the careful and thorough evaluation, the latter from the opportunity to postpone the commitment to therapy. In summary then, the overt separation of assessment and treatment serves to enhance positive expectancies regarding therapy by alleviating anxiety, promoting appropriate expectations regarding improvement, and emphasizing the need for a thorough evaluation. The following techniques are utilized during assessment interviews to facilitate the gathering of information and to counter feelings of helplessness and frustration.

Structuring and Focusing the Interview

Couples enter marital therapy with a mutual sense of helplessness and lowered self-esteem. The skillfull therapist will recognize this and offer as much support and encouragement as possible, even while acknowledging the existence of problems in the relationship. One way to promote hope is by delimiting the scope of problem presentation. For example, our initial inquiry about reasons for seeking therapy focuses on precipitating factors rather than the entire history of existing problems. A general question such as, "What's wrong?" is likely to elicit a range of responses, many of which will involve cross-blaming or negative descriptions of the relationship. On the other hand, a question that taps into recent precipitants for seeking therapy is likely to yield more specific information. Further, when the focus of inquiry is narrowed, couples have an opportunity to assess factors contributing to their recent distress and are less prone to catastrophize about their marriage.

The therapist sets the tone for therapy from the outset by conveying that the information of interest is that which will lead to successful solutions and positive changes. One goal then is to gain a solid understanding of those issues that are most critical to each spouse, without becoming mired in details, nor in a myriad of side issues. The use of highly focused questions and the inhibition of negative dialogue about the marriage serve to counter despair and hopelessness about the relationship.

Eliciting Positives

As part of this structuring process, we extract a balance of positive and negative information about the couple's functioning, a strategy which contradicts the couple's beliefs that their marriage is fraught with problems and devoid of assets. One effective means of balancing negative with positive is to discuss the early history of the relationship. This line of inquiry yields vital information about the couple's prior level of satisfaction in the marriage, as well as their capacity for mutual reinforcement. The exploration of positive memories provides a welcome opportunity for laughter, and for recognizing that the relationship has not always been problem laden. In cases where the history reflects distress from the outset, one can comment on the couple's tenacity and strength in dealing with long-term difficulties. However, discussion usually turns to pleasant memories, coupled with sadness over the decline of marital satisfaction. Some specific questions that elicit positive memories include: (1) How and when did you meet? (2) What attracted you to each other? (3) How did your courtship proceed? (4) When and how did you decide to marry? (5) What was your wedding like?

As part of our discussion of early relationship experiences, we also inquire about early signs of conflict. Couples usually respond to this inquiry with highly specific recollections of problems early in their relationship or with memories of a relatively harmonious period. Regardless of content, a productive and positive tone should be fostered. Distressed couples are highly cognizant of the weaknesses in their relationship and will tend to reiterate them to the therapist, regardless of the stated topic of inquiry. Thus, it remains essential that the therapist limit the time spent discussing problems and guide the discussion so that strengths and weaknesses are balanced as much as is possible. Should one spouse reflect on current problems when describing strengths in the relationship, it is the therapist's responsibility to reorient the discussion gently and firmly. For example, a spouse might be describing how thoughtful his or her partner was during courtship, adding that such consideration has been replaced with hostility and insensitivity. Such a comment will inevitably shift the focus of discussion to the negative aspects of the marriage and may even instigate an argument. If the therapist interrupts the speaker, reminding him or her to focus on the positive aspects of the spouse's behavior, a more optimistic outlook may be fostered.

The primary goal, then, is to emphasize pleasant memories and to underscore past and present strengths in the relationship. The therapist teaches couples to balance their perceptions of the marriage by championing the functional aspects of the relationship. Thus, the experience of self-disclosure is coupled with pleasant memories and feelings of competency. As a result, the couple may feel safer when discussing problem areas during subsequent sessions.

Another technique that serves to highlight strengths in the marriage is to have couples describe their previous efforts to solve problems. It is generally the case that couples have individually and collectively made some attempt to resolve issues prior to entering therapy. A brief discussion of such efforts yields important diagnostic information about the couple's functioning and also provides an opportunity to support and reinforce their attempts to improve the relationship. Any prior efforts, effective or not, may be framed as signs of commitment to the marriage and as evidence that the couple already has some skills in working together on their relationship. Strategies that enhance feelings of competency and effectiveness in the couple are appropriate and desirable, as are measures to provide empathy for the frustration and demoralization many people feel at the beginning of therapy.

Normalizing Problems

Distressed couples often perceive their problems as unique. They express embarrassment when describing their difficulties, noting their feelings of failure and inadequacy. Thus, during the initial sessions, we provide encouragement by placing their concerns in perspective and thereby normalizing them. This involves two techniques, one of which is to suggest that the couple's concerns are justified, but not unusual in our experience as experts in this area. One can also identify environmental stressors, which may have prevented the couple from finding ready solutions to their problems. This added perspective helps couples to redistribute the weight of responsibility for their difficulties. They may begin to see themselves as normal respondents to complex challenges, rather than as helpless victims of their inability to cope with each other and with life. By acknowledging the couple's concerns and by framing them as difficult yet manageable challenges, the therapist provides both empathy and encouragement. This strategy, in particular, seems to enhance expectations for a successful outcome from therapy.

Thus, structured interviewing, the elicitation of relationship strengths, and normalization of problems represent overlapping techniques, all of which mitigate against the unbridled negativism that characterizes most distressed couples' view of themselves and their relationship. The use of the singular "view" is intentional here, because distressed couples often share common beliefs about their relationship, many of which reflect feelings of hopelessness about the possibility of achieving greater satisfaction. It is therefore paramount that the couple leave the first session with greater optimism about possibilities for improvement. This goal supercedes that of evaluation *per se*. Because several sessions will be devoted to assessment, the therapist may focus on clinically desirable outcomes even at the expense of assessment information.

The following transcripts illustrate techniques utilized during a preliminary interview. Alan and Carol, both in their mid-30s, had been married for 6 years, with a daughter, aged 3, named Lauren. Alan worked as an advertising salesman, while Carol worked part-time at home as a seamstress and homemaker.

THERAPIST: What I'd like to do now is find out from you what it is that's happening currently in your relationship or in your lives that has led you to come in for counseling. In other words, not all of your problems, but what is it *right now* that has made you decide to get some help?

ALAN: Well for me, I think it's uh, feeling that there's a lack of mutual trust or respect that we have with each other. And I'd like to see that be improved.

T: Umm hmm. Is that something you've thought more about recently, or is that a longstanding issue in your relationship?

A: Well, that's been in my mind for a long time, but I think that it's uh, more or less not immediately recently, but say, the last 3 or 4 months it's something that I've been able to connect with the type of arguments that we have I guess, and uh, in making that connection it seemed practical to find a solution.

T: Umm hmm. So, in evaluating or thinking about arguments you and Carol have been having over the past few months, you've decided that there's an issue of trust?

A: Well I've felt that there was an issue of trust for a long time. But I didn't know how that was expressed. And so when we were having some arguments, I thought, well, this seems to be related to that.

T: Can you give me an example of what you mean by trust?

A: I would say that it would be trust in the sense of trusting that we're gonna be together, and trusting that uh, and then the idea of just respect, you know. And I think that that's mutual. We each have problems in that area from time to time. I don't trust Carol to be what I think she oughta be, or that she's gonna fulfill things the way I want them fulfilled. And then I feel not trusted a lot of times myself, in that same way.

T: I think that's clearer. So trust about whether or not you're gonna stay together, and about whether or not each of you will fulfill expectations in your relationship?

A: Uh huh, yeah.

T: And so feeling not trusted or believed in . . .

A: Yeah, yeah.

T: What about for you, Carol?

CAROL: Well, um, I find for me a lot of what brings it up is issues with our daughter. And, um, uh, that does revolve around trust because some of the ways I see Alan dealing with our daughter, I get really angry at. And uh, there's a few instances where I feel like he's, like I've trusted him and he's broken the trust. And I have resentment about that.

T: Umm hmm. Yeah. Has this been a more recent issue?

C: Well, actually, for the last 6 weeks or month, we've gotten along really well. The time that came to a head the most was I guess 6 weeks ago now. For a period of a month or so.

T: Umm hmm. What happened at that time?

C: Well um, what happened at that time was uh, that, you know our little girl was sick and you know she was waking up some at night. And um, I had to go to work, I mean a lot of things were happening but this is the time I remember most vividly. I had to go to work the next day. Well I went in to take care of her some, and when I came back to the room, Alan was furious because I'd gone into her room during the night to help her, and he wanted to maintain a strict rule of never going in, that I should never go in at night. I felt since she was sick it was an exception, and um, when I came back he was furious, and he wouldn't speak to me, and he went in to the other room to sleep. And the next morning when I tried to talk to him about it he just yelled at me furiously to get out of the room (*crying*) in such a way that it really frightened me. I didn't realize how much feeling I still have over this. I haven't talked about it or thought about it for a while. So anyway, Alan promised to take care of Lauren while I worked the next day, because she was sick and I couldn't take her to day-care. And the next morning, just before I was supposed to go, he shut himself in his room and wouldn't come out, and he refused to take care of the baby. And so 10 minutes before I was supposed to be someplace I was stuck. And you know, I just felt like something was really wrong, and I felt like I really wanted to get help. That's what I decided.

T: So, for you, issues around child care tend to bring up the larger issue of trust in your relationship with Alan.

C: Yeah, often that's a problem.

T: The situation you described sounded really difficult, and I'm wondering what you did do to try to make things better? It's been 6 weeks and you said things have been going a lot more smoothly. What did you do to try to resolve things, or set things right between the two of you over that particular set of events?

C: Yeah. Um, I just remember I came back in and I said, "Look, I feel really strongly about this, that we've got to, I don't know what to do, I don't know what the answers are, but we've got to do something." And Alan, he didn't want to get help from anyone at that time. But I think after I said it, then an hour later or so he came back and said (*to Alan*) you had decided that you wanted to too. Is that right?

A: Umm hmm.

C: You said that you wanted to get some counseling with us together and that you wanted to get some individual counseling. But at that time, I thought I'd like to get some individual counseling too, although I wasn't sure. But we both agreed to get some help with our marriage. (*To Alan.*) What else have we done besides decide about counseling?

A: Well, um, I think that uh, in deciding that was something we were going to try and do, uh that coming to an agreement about that was healthy for us in some way. (*Laughs.*) And uh, that uh, maybe that we've treated each other with a little more respect in the meantime, because of that. Or maybe because of knowing that we would get help that we didn't need to try and solve it by making the other person feel the pain that we have inside, or something like that.

C: We haven't talked about the things that happened and we have tried to work on the various routines and all that happen in the morning to make them go smoothly. Like with the transitions with Lauren and all. We've worked on that, and it's gone better. And uh, we worked on the things that improve our feelings toward each other, like getting out together without Lauren and going out with friends.

T: Well it does sound like you've made quite a few steps that are working for you. You decided to get some help; you've made some decisions about how morning routines should run—that's usually a hard time for people who work and have a child—and you've been trying to make time together without Lauren, time alone. All of those things sound really good.

A: They've helped a lot.

T: It does seem that you've set the trust issue aside, to work on in here.

C: That's something I think we'd both like to improve.

A: Umm, hmm. And getting together on child-care issues in general.

T: Yeah. That sounds good. Let's talk very briefly about other areas in your relationship in which you'd like to see some change.

In this short excerpt techniques of balancing positive strengths with problem areas are exemplified. The therapist shuttles back and forth between specific descriptions of problem areas and identification of productive efforts at problem solving. In general the discussion of problems during the first session tends to be fairly cursory. The utilization of self-report questionnaires, described later in this section, provides the therapist with substantial information about the couple's functioning and areas where change is desired.

With Alan and Carol it was easy to extract positive elements of the marriage; they were cooperative and in agreement about their reasons for entering therapy. Couples do not always present themselves in such a manner. There may be disagreements about the precipitants for seeking therapy and about problematic areas in the relationship. Spouses frequently portray their partners as perpetrators, while describing themselves as innocent victims. Also, the stated goals of each partner may be diverse and conflicting. Thus, while the goal for the first session remains consistent with the rationale above, the strategies of implementation may vary, depending upon the presenting issues and communication style of each couple. Alan and Carol exemplify couples who have well-developed communication skills and are willing to take responsibility, on an individual basis, for the problems in their marriage. While they acknowledged significant difficulties, they also recognized strengths and openly expressed a mutual desire to improve their relationship.

The following transcript illustrates the initial interview techniques, utilized with a highly distressed couple. Pearl and Morrie, both in their 60s had been married for 7 years. While their courtship had been a satisfying time for both of them, and while they continued to have numerous common interests, they bickered constantly and expressed great frustration with their relationship. Hence, during the initial interview, the balancing of positive and negative attributes in the marriage, as well as the focusing of discussion, were difficult and challenging tasks for the therapist.

THERAPIST: First of all, I'd like to know what has brought you in for counseling right now. What, if anything, has precipitated your decision to seek help?

PEARL: Well, we've been married, well it'll be 7 years in March, and it really has never really been a real good relationship. And Morrie retired at the last of October. A lot of people our age have problems adjusting to retirement, which has really been hard. It's hard for us to communicate. We really don't have much going for us together. And when this was recommended, I mean, I'll admit, I was ready for a separation, because I figured in my older age I want to be happy; I want to enjoy myself, you know, doing the things that make me happy. And I thought, well since we can't make it together, I've gone in for counseling, we've gone twice together, nothing's come of it, and when this was suggested I thought, I'm personally talking for myself, I'll give it another try, and see what comes of it. If it doesn't work, well then there's nothing left to do but separate. So that's the way I feel about it.

T: So, you sort of see the retirement last October as having made things much harder, even though they were difficult before.

P: Yes, definitely.

T: What about you Morrie, why do you think the two of you are coming to counseling right now?

MORRIE: Well, the same reason, I'm trying to make a go of our marriage, and uh, it's been unsuccessful so far. Like she says, we went to two different counselors together, and then this last one, she went by herself. She said she wanted to go by herself, so she went by herself. And uh, like I say, uh, there are things we just can't communicate about. And why, I don't know, it always ends up in an argument, even the least little thing we talk about. So it's a matter of communication mainly. And I don't know if this will help, maybe it will and maybe it won't. And I'm willing to try anything. So that's why I'm here.

T: Umm hmm.

M: I think communication is the main thing in our case.

T: Do you think that communication has become more difficult since your retirement?

M: Yes I do, because she didn't want me to retire and I waited until past the age of retirement. I waited 8–10 months past the time, so she shouldn't complain at all, because I waited.

P: Well, I think the reason I didn't want Morrie to retire, I raised six children, I was in business for 19 years selling real estate, and when I married Morrie, I wanted to make a home for him. So I quit working, I gave up my job. But now I'm doing more than I ever did before, with a big house and a big yard. And besides that, we can't even sit down and talk anything out without an argument. And then we close up, we don't talk; we go our separate ways. And we argue more than we get along. This is the reason I didn't want him to retire, because I knew I'd have less privacy at home, you know my little time for myself; I like to keep my house neat and spend time in doing outside activities, going to church; I like to be active, whereas Morrie likes to stay home and you know, read, or watch the television.

T: Well let me see if I'm understanding all of what the two of you are saying. It seems like your retirement has meant that the two of you are home together most of the time, and that's a big change from before, when Morrie was working. And then, on top of spending lots of time together at home, you've been having trouble communicating and tend to argue a lot.

M: Arguments! That's what it is . . . over petty little things that don't mean a hill of beans!

P: It's true, we do argue a lot, and mostly about housework.

M: Well, there again, see I got to say something in rebuttal. When I was working she did what she wanted to do, all the time. But now that I'm home, I do a lot of work. I wash clothes, I do the dishes, I vacuum. And if she doesn't think I do that, it's not true. She insists on doing everything right then and there. And I don't work that way, especially now that I'm retired. You know, you take orders in a factory, you work for a supervisor and you do what they tell you. We're at the point where we can do things at our own pace. Why do I have to do the dishes immediately after I eat? And I tell her, leave it, I'll do it. If you don't want to do it I'll do it, but she can't wait, and then she complains.

T: It sounds like you and Pearl have different styles and different paces at which you like to do things and that these differences are making it hard for the two of you to get along.

P: Well I need to say something here, because we're two different people. I'm an organized person. And Morrie doesn't do the things he says he does. He doesn't. And when I ask him to do things for me once in a while, he resents me telling him what to do around the house. He says that's a woman's job, not a man's, or that he's retired. According to Morrie, my work is housework, and he looks at a lot of TV, and I resent the fact that his retirement is spent doing what he wants to do, and I *have* to do all these other things.

M: Oh no . . . see . . .

P: Well there is . . .

(*Both talk at the same time.*)

T: OK, let me stop both of you for a minute so I can make some comments. . . . Something you said, Pearl, at the very beginning really struck me . . . and that is that many people have a hard time adjusting to retirement. And I think that's probably true. What you're each describing are the problems you are having in adjusting to major changes in your day-to-day routines of living. You're talking about how you spend your time, who takes responsibility for various chores, things which are bound to be different, now that Morrie's retired. And it also seems that you have your own ways of doing things, and those ways aren't always compatible. So it makes a lot of sense to me that you'd be arguing more often now.

P: It's two different worlds. Yeah.

M: And there's no need for it. That's what I claim.

T: Well, I know you're both feeling very frustrated right now, but I want you to know that the kinds of issues you're describing are things we definitely can work on in here. And I'm beginning to get a clear idea of the difficulties you both are experiencing. I'm going to ask you more about those issues later, particularly next session. So, I want to switch gears for a few minutes and talk about how you met and what the early part of your relationship was like.

M: Well, we met at a dance. It was a single's club, a Methodist single's club, and uh, we had a dance at a nice restaurant in Westbridge, no Eastbridge. And uh . . .

P: I came with some mutual friends of ours. . . .

M: She went with some friends, right, and uh, she noticed my steak, it was bloody rare, which I didn't want actually, I wanted medium, but they gave it to me. I don't know what she said to herself, but she said she abhors steak that is rare, that she likes hers well done. There again we were different. I want mine medium . . .

T: OK, but go ahead.

M: But anyway, I asked her to dance, and to make a long story short, we got along real good in dancing, she liked my dancing, I liked her dancing, and that was the start of it. We started going together, and we were going to dances all the time. We still love dancing, but it's going, fading away because of our bickering and communication and so on. . . . So, that's how we met.

T: So, you met at a dance, and you really liked each other's dancing.

M: Dancing, yeah.

P: Well that's it, we both loved to dance. And then later, he lived not far from me, and his children went to the same school as mine. And we had so much in common. We'd get together for Thanksgiving and Christmas. We went together for 3 years, just going out and going out to dinner.

T: So you've really known each other for 10 years.

P: Yes, yes.

M: And besides, we both had daughters named Katherine.

P: And, you know really, I used to get a thrill when Morrie would call me and we'd talk on the phone. He'd call me, and I'd be ready to call him, we had so much in common.

M: So *much* in common.

P: And then goodnight, I went my way, and he went his way, and we didn't live together. And our problems started when we got married.

M: Yeah, she followed me. She never objected to anything. Now, it's objections to a lot of things that we were doing before we got married. . . .

T: OK, let me stop you for a second. What I'd like you to do is stick with the memories of how you got together. You've told me how you loved to dance and how much you had in common.

P: Well I'll continue now for a while. . . .

It is not without continual prodding that the therapist kept Pearl and Morrie on task. They were each ready to initiate an argument at the slightest instigation and tended to portray their problems as irreconcilable. In later sessions the therapist needed to repeatedly normalize their concerns and interrupt their negative tracking. Again, with this couple the analysis of problems in the first session was brief and cursory. The strongest emphasis was on the functional and positive aspects of their relationship. It was encouraging that they were able to agree about the pleasure each felt during the early stages of their relationship. In spite of their discord, there was reason to be optimistic about their marriage given this information. However, improvement would require considerable effort by each of them, as well as from the therapist.

Interviews with Individual Spouses

The second assessment session provides an appropriate opportunity to delve more deeply into issues and problems in the relationship. At this time we typically spend approximately 1 hr with each spouse separately, during which time individual histories are taken and issues that were discussed in the first session are explored further. Depending on the presenting issues, detailed interviews may be conducted concerning sexual history, prior relationships, family of origin, and problem behaviors such as addictions or depression. The agenda for this interview may be adapted for each spouse in terms of individual as well as marital functioning. In addition to the aforementioned areas, the therapist can assess each partner's expectations and hopes regarding the outcome of therapy, their sense of self-esteem, and their willingness to take responsibility for issues in the relationship. One can note whether or not spouses are protective of one another when discussing the marriage, or whether they tend to complain more freely when interviewed alone. In addition, areas of agreement and disagreement about the relationship seem clearer when spouses are interviewed separately.

The second assessment interview is particularly significant because it represents one of the few (if not the only) opportunities for individual contact with each spouse. The primary goals of this assessment are to obtain detailed information and to build rapport. As with the initial session, it is the therapist's job to structure and pace the interview so that each spouse feels supported in his or her views, as well as optimistic about therapy and the opportunity to make desired changes. Should the therapist require more time for detailed assessment, the individual interviews may be carried over to the next session.

Other Assessment Tools

In conjunction with the two interview sessions described above, couples also complete a number of written assessment forms prior to the first interview. They are also asked to discuss a topic in their relationship while being observed and videotaped as a means of assessing their communication skills. Procedures for the communication assessment and a brief description of written assessment tools follows. More detailed information is available in other recent publications (Jacobson, Elwood, & Dallas, 1981; Jacobson & Margolin, 1979).

Self-Report Questionnaires

Self-report questionnaires aid in the structuring of interview sessions and provide behavioral analyses of relationship functioning, for example, descriptions of those discrete behaviors that are considered problematic by spouses. These measures elicit phenomenological information from each spouse as well and thus allow for the comparison of spouses' perceptions of the relationship. The questionnaires provide general information about the couple's satisfaction with their marriage and the structure of their interactions, that is, when and how they spend time together. Additionally, some of the measures described below are utilized to document progress in the relationship and are administered subsequent to the completion of therapy.

The *Areas of Change Questionnaire* (A-C), developed by Weiss and his associates (Patterson, 1976; Weiss et al., 1973), provides information about behaviors in which change is desired. The quantity of change is specified on a Likert scale, and areas of major concern are noted. The A-C is particularly useful in pinpointing specific behaviors where change is desired by each spouse and thus has great clinical utility.

The *Marital Status Inventory* (Weiss & Cerreto, 1980) measures each spouse's behavioral proximity to legal termination of the marriage. The 14-item checklist assesses each partner's desire for divorce, as measured by the number of actual behaviors that have been undertaken as steps toward separation and divorce.

The *Dyadic Adjustment Scale* (Spanier, 1976) Provides a global measure of marital satisfaction and distress. It offers a reliable score that places each spouse along a standardized continuum of marital satisfaction. It also provides information concerning those areas of the relationship in which conflict and disagreement tend to be high.

The *Marital Precounseling Inventory* (MPCI; Stuart & Stuart, 1972) provides a comprehensive self-report package, consisting of nine separate questionnaires. We currently utilize the subscale, which evaluates the rules for decision making in the relationship. The scale also assesses the level of satisfaction experienced by each spouse, with regard to the distribution of authoritative roles in the marriage.

The *Marital Activities Inventory* (Weiss *et al.*, 1973) assesses the distribution of time spent in activities together and separately. It also elicits information regarding changes each spouse would like in terms of these time distributions.

The *Sexual Interaction Inventory* (LoPiccolo & Steger, 1974) provides information about the quality of a couple's sex life, as well as their preferences and satisfaction with regard to specific sexual behaviors. In addition, spouses perceptions of each other's level of satisfaction is recorded.

Spouses generally complete these questionnaires independently and confidentially. By comparing spouses' responses on the self-report measures with the content of the first interview, the therapist can informally assess their willingness to be open with one another regarding problems in their relationship. Often, spouses present only a small fraction of the issues concerning them during the first interview. Thus, the therapist may rely heavily on questionnaire data when interviewing spouses individually and when formulating a treatment plan.

Assessment of Communication Skills

A number of investigators have developed formal procedures for the study of communication patterns in couples (Gottman, 1979; Gottman & Porterfield, 1981; Harper, Wiens, & Matarazzo, 1978). Because such procedures have been designed for use in empirical research, rather than clinical practice, they tend to be cumbersome and require the use of videotape equipment, which is not always available to clinicians. Therefore, what follows are procedures for the informal assessment of couples' problem-solving skills, methods easily adapted to any treatment setting.

Couples are asked to discuss an issue in their relationship for a maximum of 10 min, during which time they are to work towards an agreement. The topic for discussion is usually selected from the A-C questionnaire and relates to an area in which both spouses have indicated a desire for change. Topics may also be selected from the content of interviews.

A number of specific skills seem to contribute to the effective negotiation and resolution of problems. Spouses who listen to one another and who validate each others' ideas tend to be more satisfied with their relationships and to be more successful at resolving conflicts (Gottman, 1979). Further, the skills of focusing on a topic and the sharing of feelings tend to enhance this interactive process. By contrast, a number of behaviors tend to undermine the problem-solving process, including sidetracking, and cross-complaining. The therapist can observe these behaviors in a brief assessment such as this. In addition, he or she can note the relative contributions made by each spouse to the conversation, that is, who if anyone, seems to be leading, or whether or not the collaboration seems to be balanced. Even in a brief assessment such as this, idiosyncratic qualities in each couple's communication may be recognizable—characteristics which may either impede or foster mutual cooperation. Thus, careful observation of such patterns aids in the anticipation of communication problems that may undermine the process of therapy. Communication and problem-solving training may be tailored to counteract any deficits unique to a particular couple.

Because this assessment of communication involves an element of artifice, as in role playing, one tries to determine its relevance to the couple's typical interactions at home. We simply ask couples at the end of the conversation whether or not their attempts to solve problems at home bear any resemblance to the previous interaction. The discussion of how the couple usually handles problems at home provides information that is vital to the development of appropriate goals as well as for the pacing of treatment and homework. For example, many couples report that they never actually sit down to discuss a problem with the goal of resolving it. For such couples, one aspect of communication training will involve the discussion of setting characteristics that foster productive conversation and problem solving. Couples also report that while they frequently engage in conversations leading to agreements, they rarely follow through with their verbal contracts. In such cases, greater emphasis may be placed on the behaviors and attitudes that enhance the successful implementation of change agreements. Thus, treatment strategies may be applied flexibly in response to the needs of each couple.

Spouse Observations

Throughout the course of therapy, couples are asked to rate their daily satisfaction with their marriage and with themselves on a Likert scale ranging from 1 to 7, where 1 is abysmal and 7 ecstatic. In addition, they complete a comprehensive checklist every day, usually during the evening, noting those pleasing and displeasing exchanges that occur in their marriage. A revised version of the Spouse Observation Checklist (SOC; Patterson, 1976; Weiss & Perry, 1979), described elsewhere (Jacobson et al., 1980; Jacobson & Moore, 1981), is utilized to gather this information. The checklist consists of 409 items, including both joint activities and partner initiated behaviors, and spans 12 content areas (companionship, affection, consideration, sex, communication, couple activities, child care and parenting, household responsibilities, financial decision making, employment and education, personal habits and appearance, self- and spouse independence). Each spouse independently marks partner behaviors and joint activities that have occurred during the preceding 24 hr, rating the valence of each event as positive, neutral, or negative in its impact upon the receiver.

The SOC serves a number of purposes, both evaluative and therapeutic. It provides empirically derived information about the reinforcing or punishing value of particular behaviors. Secondly, the SOC indicates the degree to which spouses share the same perceptions regarding the occurrence of given behaviors and activities, that is, the extent to which spouses agree on what has happened each day. Third, highly specific information is derived from the SOC regarding the behaviors that occur in the marriage. Finally, the SOC provides ongoing data on the state of the marriage and the effectiveness of therapy in terms of global satisfaction and the relative frequencies of pleasing and displeasing exchanges. The SOC also provides a stimulus for spouses regarding possible avenues for improving their relationship. For example, it is not unusual for couples to experiment spontaneously with new activities and behaviors upon filling out the checklist for the first time.

Couples' SOC data may be plotted and utilized to illustrate trends in marital interactions, the effectiveness of therapeutic interventions, and the covariance of spouses' satisfaction with their relationship. This visual representation of progress in therapy promotes subsequent commitment, as it clearly illustrates the positive effects of treatment thus far. Further any relapses or recurring trends in satisfaction with the marriage are made apparent. This ongoing evaluation and illustration of relationship trends counteracts the ready negativism that distressed spouses express when relapses occur. Utilizing the graphs the therapist is able to emphasize the fact that things were in fact better 1 week previously, for example, and can then enumerate the activities and behaviors that contributed to the higher level of satisfaction. Thus, with the graphs the SOC functions as a measure of both microbehaviors and the larger patterns within a relationship. It simultaneously counteracts overgeneralization of negative events and underestimation or disregard of the positive. While the SOC tends to be cumbersome and unpleasant for many couples, the advantages it affords therapist and client far outweigh the inconvenience that may be incurred. Issues concerning compliance with this measure as well as other assignments during the treatment process are discussed in detail beginning on page 405.

Promoting a Collaborative Set

When the therapist has completed the collection of pretreatment assessment information, he or she meets with the couple and presents them with the results. This "roundtable" discussion includes a presentation of the relationship strengths, an analysis of their difficulties, and a proposed treatment plan. The decision as to whether or not to embark on a course of BMT is put forth as the goal of this roundtable discussion.

Several facets characterize the roundtable session. First, although the therapist comes prepared to present the assessment results and propose a treatment plan, clients are given ample opportunity to add their input and to react to the therapist's feedback. Second, in describing the treatment plan, the therapist is as explicit as possible regarding what will be expected during the course of therapy. The couple must grant an "informed consent" before the actual treatment program begins. Thus, a commitment to therapy means an agreement to perform the tasks required for a successful outcome. Finally, the therapist utilizes this session to promote a stance toward therapy that remains critical to the achievement of a more satisfying relationship, that is, the adoption of a collaborative set by both spouses.

The "collaborative set" refers to those attitudes and behaviors that foster a cooperative effort toward building a better relationship. The adoption of such a set entails that spouses acknowledge reciprocal responsibility for the problems in their relationship and commit themselves to working together in order to improve it. Two basic strategies are employed during the roundtable to encourage the adoption of a collaborative set. First, the therapist presents an analysis of the relationship problems that emphasizes reciprocal responsibility. Second, the therapist elicits a verbal and written commitment from each spouse to proceed on the assumption that the therapist's model is accurate. This means that each spouse offers a unilateral yet parallel commitment to change his or her own behavior in ways that will foster relationship improvement.

The presentation of a plausible dyadic model of problems in the relationship counters spouses' tendencies to view themselves as innocent victims of the other's oppression. Since spouses typically enter therapy holding the other responsible for relationship disintegration, the therapist must address such counterproductive theories directly in order to justify the expectation that spouses behave collaboratively. Further, by presenting an alternative theory emphasizing mutual responsibility and reciprocal causality, the therapist lets each spouse know what the working assumptions of therapy will be. Let us take Carol and Alan, introduced earlier in the chapter, as an example. Among their presenting concerns is the issue of trust or mutual respect. At the roundtable, the therapist discusses this concern by acknowledging their terminology and perspective, while simultaneously emphasizing the specific behaviors or absence thereof, which inform the problem. Additionally, the dyadic nature of trust issues is highlighted as is the mutual responsibility for their resolution. Such a presentation would follow a detailed description of the strengths in the relationship and might be delivered as follows:

One of the issues both of your raised during our first talk was that of "trust," that is, the difficulty each of you has in trusting the other. Now, trust is a fairly broad concept and we are going to need to break it down into smaller parts in order to work on it. We need to identify those behaviors, either words or deeds, that promote trust in your relationship and also those that lead to feelings of mutual distrust. From what you have told me so far, it sounds as though child care is an area in which you each have difficulty trusting the other. There may be other areas, but let's just talk about childrearing activities as one example. Here is an area where each of you wants to do the best job possible, right? . . . And yet, you have different ideas about how that is to be done. Well, it strikes me that one aspect of this trust issue is an absence of clear communication about how you would each like to raise Lauren. Instead of discussing your similarities and differences, you each continue to act on your individual philosophies of childrearing and that leads to misunderstandings and conflict. So, one of the things we will be working on in here is communicating and problem solving about childrearing. In a sense, I am redefining trust as a communication issue, at least for the time being. Because without clear communication, it is very hard to predict each other's reactions and behavior and even harder to express your own needs and desires when a conflict arises. How does what I have said so far sound to you?

In this presentation, the therapist translates a global construct, "trust," into concrete behavioral terms. Of course, this is only the beginning of such a redefinition process. With the couple's help, the therapist continues to identify situations, behaviors, and attitudes that play a role in any given problem. Although the overall format is one of the therapist presenting his or her formulations, in actuality there is continuous interchange between therapist and clients, both to induce collaboration and to secure the best possible fit between therapist formulations and to couple's current perspective on their issues.

Our experience is that spouses who view themselves merely as victims will relax their positions a bit in response to an alternative model presented by an expert. If the rigidity of their position is loosened, collaborative behavior is more likely. Whether or not the therapist's model is accepted, however, spouses must commit themselves to the behaviors that follow from this model, if therapy is to proceed. Such collaborative behaviors include obeying the rules, adhering to the agenda of each therapy session, complying with homework assignments, and focusing on changing one's own behavior. If the therapist insists upon this commitment from each spouse as a precondition to therapy, couples will almost always agree to it. More importantly, an explicit commitment to behave collaboratively greatly reduces the likelihood of subsequent noncompliance.

The therapist must not force this commitment on couples who are ambivalent. If anything, the typical posture should be one of playing devil's advocate, using statements such as the following:

I want you both to carefully consider this decision. Frankly, I have some doubts to whether you are capable of a collaborative effort. This treatment program will be a waste of time unless each of you focus on what you can do to improve the relationship. Do not agree to it unless you are sure you can follow through.

Thus, the therapist is explicit about exactly what a commitment to therapy entails. Couples are informed that therapy is likely to improve the relationship but that ultimately it is up to them. Expressing optimism regarding the ultimate outcome of therapy, while at the same time emphasizing the hard work and collaborative effort that will be necessary, represents a proper balance between positive expectancies and a sober appraisal of the process. The commitment is symbolically sealed with a written contract that specifies the mutual expectations of therapist and clients.

THERAPY: INCREASING POSITIVE EXCHANGES

During the first four to five sessions of therapy, the primary goal is for couples to increase the quantity of pleasing interactions in their relationship. Each spouse is asked to increase those behaviors that are already in their repertoire, low-cost, and pleasing to their spouse. The SOC is instrumental in the discovery of these behaviors. Spouses are encouraged to study each other's checklists as a means of identifying potential reinforcing behaviors.

The emphasis at the outset of therapy is on enhancing positive aspects of the relationship. This selective focus serves a number of purposes. First, it fosters optimism about the possibility for change by highlighting those functional aspects of the marriage that can be considered strengths. Second, the acceleration of positive behaviors counters spouses' helpless outlook on the marriage, providing them with a structured task that gives them some positive control over their partners' satisfaction. In other words, the opportunity to please and be pleased renews energy for working on the marriage and encourages clients to stick with their relationship, even while working on difficult problems. In cases where a crisis is presented at the beginning of therapy, the use of this intervention would be postponed until the presenting issue has been addressed. In the majority of cases, however, the initial emphasis on positive exchanges serves to improve the relationship, regardless of the level of marital distress.

At the beginning of therapy, spouses are often at an impasse, where neither has made much of an effort to improve the relationship for months or in some cases years. Each partner is waiting for the other to change first. Thus, by initiating mutual positive exchanges, the therapist helps the couple to transcend this impasse, and to begin collaborating. The initial goal is to foster each spouse's voluntary efforts to change his or her own behavior. Successful implementation of positive behavior acceleration hinges on the therapist's ability to inhibit blaming and negative tracking. Further, the therapist must artfully facilitate each partner's discovery and specification of low-cost behaviors. Thus, the two primary skills inherent to successful behavior exchanges are those of pinpointing low-cost behaviors and focusing on oneself.

Pinpointing

Specifying or pinpointing target behaviors is a prerequisite to the successful implementation of behavior exchange procedures. The goal is for couples to actively consider what behaviors please their spouse and to specify both the topography of reinforcing behaviors and the conditions under which their reinforcing impact is likely to be maximized.

With the initial homework assignment, each spouse might be asked to peruse the partner's SOC and identify behaviors that seem to please the other. This can be accomplished in a number of ways. For example, each spouse may be asked to list all behaviors that were marked as positive by their partner.

Alternatively, spouses may identify reinforcing behaviors in their repertoire by listing those events that occur on days when the partner's overall satisfaction with the relationship is high (as indicated by the Daily Satisfaction Ratings [DSRs] on the SOC). Then these lists are discussed during a subsequent treatment session. During these discussions the therapist helps each partner to consider what made the behavior positive. If, for example, the husband writes down "Spouse complimented me" as one behavior for which he received a plus from his wife, the therapist and the husband can pinpoint specific features of that compliment that made it reinforcing. The following questions might be asked: (1) What was said? (2) How was it stated? (3) When was it said? (4) Why does he think that was pleasing to his spouse? (5) Are there other times when such a compliment would be especially positive for the wife? In other words, a behavioral analysis focuses on the specific aspects of the interaction that made it pleasant. The extrapolation of general features or principles increases the likelihood that the pleasing behavior will occur in similar situations.

Focusing on Oneself

Generally, when spouses are assigned the task of pinpointing behaviors in their repertoire that would be pleasing to their partner, each is asked to work independently without verbal input from their partner. At first glance, this may seem counterintuitive. It might seem more reasonable to simply ask each recipient to generate lists of behaviors that they would like to "get" from their partners. Indeed, this latter type of request from the receiving spouse does correspond to the standard mode of implementation described in the behavioral marital therapy literature. However, we have moved away from this procedure in the past few years, and we now add input from the recipient only after each spouse has independently identified potentially pleasing behaviors in his or her own repertoire. By asking each spouse to focus on his or her own capacity to "please" the partner, that is, on what each can do to enhance the quality of the relationship for the other, a collaborative set is promoted. Moreover, if positive changes can be generated without specific requests from the receiving spouse, their impact will be more powerful and both partners are likely to perceive themselves as having *chosen* to enact the positive behaviors (cf. Jacobson, 1984, in press).

Thus, homework assignments during the first few therapy sessions are characterized by the requirement that each spouse focus on himself or herself. This attention to individual behavior is maintained during the therapy sessions as well. During discussions or debriefings of the early homework assignments, both spouses are asked to critique their own performance during the week and avoid evaluating the partner's performance. When this rule is violated, the therapist immediately interrupts the spouse who has violated the rule and redirects him or her back toward the task of self-monitoring. Consistent adherence to this rule maximizes the likelihood that collaborative behavior will occur during early treatment sessions.

The therapist is likely to encounter stiff resistance to this insistence on self-focus at first. The inclination to focus on the partner, and what the partner is doing for them, is natural in a distressed relationship. Spouses may feel arbitrarily discounted and cut off if the therapist simply interferes with these tendencies. It is extremely important, therefore, that the therapist repetitively teach the rationale for this rule while enforcing it consistently. For example, when a spouse is interrupted for deviating from the self-focus, the therapist must explain the basis for the interruption. Or, better yet, the therapist might ask the spouse to come up with the rationale, by asking, "Why am I stopping you?" By being asked to critique their own deviations from self-focus, spouses learn to regulate their own behavior so that less time needs to be devoted to such digressions in subsequent sessions. Self-regulation in the therapy sessions is certainly a necessary if not a sufficient precursor to the maintenance of a self-focus at home.

Specific Procedures for Instigating Behavior Exchange

As stated previously, a first homework assignment during behavior exchange might be for couples to simply exchange their checklists. Prior to this time they may have completed them privately as part of the pretreatment assessment procedures. While couples are not encouraged to discuss their reactions to the other's checklist, they may be asked to make a list of all the behaviors for which they received pluses each day. This assignment serves to emphasize the behaviors that were pleasing and helps partners to begin the task of pinpointing reinforcing events.

When spouses first exchange SOCs, they may have a variety of reactions to their partner's record of their behavior. They may report that it is easier to receive feedback about displeasing behaviors when it appears on a checklist. Often, minor irritating behaviors are eliminated immediately. All too frequently, however, spouses react adversely to the negatives and all but ignore those behaviors that pleased their spouse. Thus, the emphasis on positive behaviors may be difficult to maintain. Yet it remains essential that the therapist not be dissuaded from this task. The following transcripts illustrate both the procedures of behavior exchange and the techniques for highlighting positive exchanges.

Jack and Anita, a couple in their early 30s, had been married for 6 years and had one child, aged 3. Their presenting concerns revolved around differences in expectations regarding roles, conflicts over how to spend leisure time, and not spending enough time together. In terms of individual problems, Jack had a history of depression, while Anita had been treated for acute anxiety reactions. They were both articulate and voluable. Jack worked as an accountant and Anita assumed primary responsibility for childcare and household maintenance.

During this first discussion of the checklists, both Jack and Anita attended selectively to negative behaviors noted by the other. This first conversation illustrated one way of reorienting their attention to positive behaviors.

THERAPIST: I want to spend most of our session on the checklist and also, if anything came up this week which was a problem, we can talk about that as well. Do either of you want to add anything to that agenda?

JACK: That sounds reasonable.

ANITA: That's fine. I'd like to talk about these things.

T: OK, then let me find out for starters, what it was like for each of you to read each other's checklist?

J: I'd say in my case, and I think I mentioned this to you one time before, that I don't think Anita put a minus on the whole thing. And that doesn't seem very realistic to me. So now, if she puts a check, I think of that as a minus.

A: No, that's not what I mean.

J: But anyway, the thing that stood out for me, was first of all, that in some areas we were remarkably similar. It wasn't exact. But then in other areas I could see that she looked at things a little bit differently than I did. For example, we differ a little bit on what was companionship, or what was consideration and so forth. So, that part was interesting. But I still sorta feel that she's sort of glossing over some things that come out if we really have a confrontation.

A: I'm not.

T: (*To Jack.*) Would you like to get more feedback on things that you do which pose problems for Anita?

J: Yeah, that's the point I think. I mean, I don't hold back when I fill mine out and I just figure, well it was a little weird knowing she was going to look at it. Before, I knew she wasn't so I didn't talk about it with her and we didn't really talk about it this time. But I knew she was going to look at it.

A: Except I said, "How come you give me so many minuses?"

J: Well I tell her I'm not giving her a minus, I'm just saying that this particular thing is negative for me and maybe it shouldn't be negative for me, it doesn't mean that it's like a grade.

T: It's just how you're experiencing it.

J: Yeah. So, I mean if there are really no things that I'm doing that are negative things to her, that's one thing. But it just seems like there must be because they come out at other times.

T: Well, one of the things I usually do at the beginning of therapy is look at the positive aspects of a marriage, and at the pluses on the checklist. So, in a way, it's not critical that Anita be putting down negatives. It's also possible that things are fairly positive for her, and you may have to accept that for now.

J: I always focus on the negative in life.

A: Well, I'm not really saying everything is so wonderful, but a lot of times things bother me if they're not occurring and it would be nice if they would. So it's not that Jack does things wrong, it's just that he doesn't do some things I would like him to do.

T: That's a really good point Anita. What Jack may need to focus on when he reads your checklist is doing more of the things which please you. Right now, (*to Jack*) you can focus on adding to what you're doing and you don't need to worry about discontinuing anything right now.

A: Yeah, cause the stuff he does is fine. He doesn't complain a lot, like he has marks in there that I complained and stuff, he's not the type of person you complain about.

T: But you are talking about adding things.

A: Yeah.

T: (*To Anita.*) Are there other things you want to say just in general about how it was for you to read Jack's checklist?

A: Well, I thought I sounded awful. I thought when you read that you're gonna think, goll, she's terrible.

T: Umm hmm. So you were concerned about what I would think of you.

A: Well, or if that's what I'm like. I mean, that concerns me if that's what I'm like.

T: So you were uncomfortable with what the checklist might imply about you?

A: Well, I had to mention a couple of things to him, like he checked that I opened his personal mail. The only thing I opened with his name on it he said I could. It was some bill thing and I said, can I open this, it's from such and such. I don't open stuff that has his name on it unless it has my name on it too. And so, things like that, I thought, man, if you're looking at this you're gonna think, gosh, she opens his mail, she complains, she does this and it sounds awful. Or for myself to read it, I thought, this person doesn't sound like a very wonderful person.

T: OK, so you are concerned a little bit about how you come across.

A: Well, yeah, if I'm really like that. I mean, I'm sure I am. I can't argue with a lot of the things on there, but I think a few of them, like opening his personal mail wasn't accurate.

T: So a couple of things didn't fit for you.

A: Yeah, just a couple.

T: In general, it's hard for you to think that I'm going to be looking at all the things you do or don't do. You feel embarrassed about that.

A: Well, yeah. I mean it sounds awful when you look and see that "Spouse complained," "Spouse wanted to know what I spend money on," stuff like that. It sounds like this shrew waiting with a rolling pin when the husband comes in the door.

T: I'm not nearly as critical as you would imagine.

A: Well, even for me, not just for you reading it, but for me. Sounds like an awful person.

T: Well, I can understand your feelings, but I want to emphasize that what I'm most concerned with are the positives, the pluses. And it looks like Jack gave you a lot of those. So for now, I'm not going to even look at the checks or negatives. We won't address those at all for a few weeks. And since you've put down lots of pluses for Jack, we have more than enough to work with. OK?

A: That's a relief.

J: Fine.

T: Let's go through each of your checklists and identify those activities or actions which pleased each of you. We're going to make some lists now of those things you already know how to do to please each other. Then we'll look at some of the things you can add to your lists that you might want to try out, as a way of pleasing each other. Let's start with yours, Jack.

After behaviors that are hypothesized to be reinforcers are pinpointed, the therapist begins to direct spouses toward increasing their frequency. We recommend a homework assignment such as the following:

For next week, I would like each of you to pick some of the items on your lists and increase their frequency. You both have long lists of items, and you should not try to increase everything on your lists. But pick a subset of them, stick to those that will be relatively easy for you to implement. The goal is to increase the other's daily satisfaction with the marriage. Make a list of the things that you try to do more often during the course of the week, and specify when and how often you tried them.

The purpose of this assignment is to demonstrate that the relationship can be improved by providing low-cost pleasing behaviors on a day-to-day basis. The key to its success is the maximum amount of choice and latitude given to each spouse regarding what to increase. They are not being directed to change any specific behavior. Nor are they responding to a request for change from the receiving spouse. Moreover, they are specifically discouraged from making major changes. The effect is usually to produce positive changes that have an enhancing impact on each spouse at minimal cost to the provider. Each, simultaneously playing the roles of giver and receiver, benefits from the maximal freedom of choice inherent in the task. As providers of benefits, their options for fulfilling the assignment are maximized; when combined with the fact that they are enjoined from providing high-cost behaviors, the likelihood of compliance is greatly enhanced. As receivers, each knows that the other *chose* which behaviors to provide, and therefore whatever behaviors are delivered are likely to be attributed to the other's spontaneous desire to improve the relationship. From this task each learns that the relationship can benefit considerably from daily attention directed toward enhancing the other's satisfaction.

The following transcript illustrates the questions typically raised by couples when this assignment is presented. It is not unusual for one or both partners to be put off by the artificial emphasis on pleasing one another. Couples are particularly hesitant to instigate affectionate behaviors at the therapist's suggestion. By normalizing these concerns and emphasizing the element of choice available to each spouse, the therapist can successfully motivate couples to give this approach a try.

THERAPIST: What I want you to do with these lists is try to implement some of these ideas. Try to increase three things you're already doing to please each other. And try out three new things which you think might raise each other's daily satisfaction. You have long lists to choose from and I don't care which ones you choose, as long as they're not too difficult or costly in terms of time or energy. And then, when you come in next week, I will have graphed your daily satisfaction ratings [DSRs] and the average number of pluses in each category. Hopefully, your DSRs will go up and you'll have more pluses in areas which you work on. A lot of change can happen, just when you pay attention to the positives. Is that clear?

JACK: I think that makes a lot of sense.

ANITA: Well, isn't it hard for people to do this? I mean, I don't want Jack to come home and think he has to walk in the door and give me a big hug and kiss because he wants to make my DSR higher. I mean, if it's just an exercise like that, maybe the person doesn't feel like doing it or something. I mean, do they have to do that even if they don't want to? What if they're not like that?

T: I'm glad you raised that question, because it's something couples often ask when they first begin this process. And what I usually say is that it's really up to each of you to choose what you want to work on, what you want to try. You've made long lists and you can decide yourselves which activities are most meaningful and natural for you to carry out. Having a choice really seems to help people get started with this. And once you're into the swing of it, trying to please each other will feel natural to you, even when you try out new things.

A: Umm hmm. I just, you know, do you know what I mean? If a person isn't a naturally warm affectionate person, if they start doing that every day because that's what they're supposed to do and they've got it on their list—it just doesn't seem like it's natural.

T: Well, this is a learning process, and sometimes when you're learning a new skill, there's some awkwardness . . . like when you learn to ride a bicycle. You might use training wheels at first, and when you take them off, you might wobble a lot and fall. But that's part of learning a new skill. And I'm asking you both to learn some new skills. I'm asking you to focus on yourself, look carefully at what you're already doing to make your marriage strong, and do more of those things. Also, I'm asking you to try out some new activities and ways of relating to one another. When you first establish a relationship, like when you were courting, you try to do things to please your partner. And you try to find out what he or she likes. Right? And it doesn't seem artificial because most people expect to be pleased then. And there's no reason for you, Anita, not to expect to be pleased now. Is there?

A: No, I guess not. I guess there's no reason to worry about getting too much affection is there? (*Laughs.*)

J: I can see the potential for it. It's the kind of thing that you know in the back of your mind. I mean if I had sat down and put something like this together, it would have occurred to me that this is the right way to get something done. If you write down all of these things and then have some specific areas you're working on, and just a few at a time, that's always the way you make anything better. You single out three or four things and you work on those and then you move on to something else. It never happens all of a sudden. So, I think that's good. I even think we're already doing some of this, because of the list. I think I know if I did this, I'd probably get a plus.

A: I'm doing that too.

T: Well you're both naturally motivated to improve your marriage. I can see that in lots of ways, by the way you complete all your forms, the kinds of questions you ask, and in the way you're both trying already to add positives whenever you can. The most important thing you're doing is following through on your commitment to each other and to me. And that may be much more important than what I ask you to do for homework. But these are tools to help you improve your relationship. They aren't magic formulas; they're just tools. But they're tools that work. That's the critical thing. They do work. And you can be as creative as you want with this homework assignment. I'm not asking you to be stilted or to do just what's in the checklist. Be creative. Have a good time with it, OK?

A: I always wanted to check, "Spouse wore curlers when I was home," just for your benefit, just so you could read that and go, "What? Jack's wearing curlers?"

J: No chance of that.

The preceding transcript embodies a number of important ingredients in the effective presentation of the task. In particular, it suggests strategies for countering typical reservations spouses have regarding behavior exchange assignments. The concern regarding artificiality is dealt with using the analogy of learning a new skill. The referral to courtship is also worth noting. Although it is rare that assignments such as this one reproduce the passion and excitement of courtship, in many ways we *are* asking couples to return to a phase in their relationship when they are offering positives in an essentially noncontingent manner. They are reminded that noncontingent exchange was once a norm in their relationship, and indeed the unconditional giving was associated with happier times.

From this initial assignment, behavior exchange procedures can move in a number of directions. Most commonly, the process evolves toward more demanding tasks involving the added input from the receiver, direct requests from the receiver, and negotiation around major problem areas in the relationship. In part, the progression to each subsequent step requires mastery of the previous step. Therapy sessions are structured so that the previous week's homework is debriefed, and any problems that occurred are discussed and hopefully resolved. Sessions also involve some sort of cumulative evaluation of progress. During the middle and latter phases of each treatment session, the next step in the treatment program is discussed and implemented. The following transcript embodies procedures for reviewing the initial assignment to increase positive behaviors. The emphasis during this first review is on those behaviors that were well received. The therapist emphasizes the need to show appreciation for positive events and interchanges.

THERAPIST: Let's start with what you did try to do to please each other and raise each other's DSRs. What do you think went well?

JACK: Well, you know the problem with this is, that I tried them but not for very long. There were a few days when I was paying attention to pleasing Anita, and a few days where things weren't going so well.

T: Umm hmm. Let's just talk about what went well, even if you just tried it one time, that's OK, that's fine.

J: I think I must have tried everything on this list at least once. Or more. I put down here that I wanted to try and be a little bit more responsive when Anita asks about what's going on with my work. And I can remember 2 or 3 days when I thought about that in a specific way, and when she asked I tried to do that.

T: How do you think she responded to your willingness to talk about your work?

J: Well the one or two times I talked about work, Anita responded fine. I think we had some kind of a conversation about whatever project it was that I was working on.

T: Good. Let me ask you Anita, did you notice that Jack made an effort to share his work with you in that way?

ANITA: Yeah, I noticed those times.

T: How was that for you?

A: I always appreciate it, I like talking about things. Sometimes I don't think he talks to me enough, about things, and so when he does I appreciate it.

T: So you noticed his efforts and appreciated the conversation, and I'm wondering if you let him know in any way that you noticed and appreciated what was happening?

A: Well for me, to show I like it, is just to talk back to him.

T: OK, so responding and talking is one way for you to show appreciation. Good. Can you think of any way that would be especially nice for Jack?

A: We've never really discussed what we want from each other, as far as appreciating goes, and I don't really know what he would like, except for me to leave him alone when he's reading.

J: Well it's not really to leave me alone. And I can't think of any big positive thing that she could do that I would be looking for. All I would want would be just sort of a balance, so that if I did bring up a discussion of work, Anita wouldn't automatically expect a whole lot more. Just some sign that she understood that for me to talk about what goes on during the day required my setting aside what I wanted to be doing, which is anything but talk about work, and just being reasonable in her desire to talk about that I guess, really. Like if something happened during the day that I thought would be interesting to Anita, the ideal thing would be if I was thoughtful enough to say something did happen of interest and tell her about it. And then if nothing did happen that seems to me to be of interest, I wouldn't have to rehash stuff that just seems like a waste of time.

A: So you just want to feel that I trust your judgment and won't resent it if you don't want to rehash boring events during the day?

J: Right. And that would feel like a reward for the times that I do talk with you about my job.

T: OK, good. Let's move on to something (*to Anita*) you've tried out as a way of increasing Jack's satisfaction and raising his DSR.

A: Well, I've been supporting his independent activities.

T: How have you done that?

A: Oh, I just say, "Have fun" or something, or ask him what it was like when he gets home. I mean I try to make him not feel guilty for going. One night he said he felt guilty because it was an extra night during the week and I was sick and couldn't go. I just said go, and he said he hated to go, and I said go 'cause I really wanted him to.

T: So you gave him a lot of encouragement. Do you think he appreciated that?

A: Sure, I hope so.

T: So you're not really sure of his reaction.

A: Well, he acted like he did. Because I've done the thing before when I know he's going—I'm sure I'm not the only one who does this either—but I kind of made him feel guilty. . . .

T: OK, try to stick with the positive, with what you've done well, rather than the negative thing you're not doing. Here you've been cheerful, you're saying have a good time, asking Jack about how things went. In sum, you're doing things that make him feel positive about leaving for the evening. And you can tell he appreciates that by the way he acts. Let me ask you, Jack, did you notice and appreciate Anita's efforts to be supportive of your independent activities?

J: Oh yeah, I did. And her enthusiasm made it easier to feel good about leaving and doing what I wanted to do. Yeah.

T: Somehow she got the message that you appreciated that, and there probably are some other ways for you to let her know that you like it when she does that.

A: I've got a couple more. I've been trying to make foods he likes. I have been, you know, making bread and we had people over for dinner Friday, Saturday, and Sunday, so I've been trying to cook good things. And the other ones . . .

T: Wait. Do you think Jack noticed that you were cooking foods he likes?

A: I don't know, 'cause he didn't say anything.

T: OK, let's stop for a second. (*To Jack.*) Did you notice that she did . . .

A: I was really hoping that you'd say something sometime about . . .

T: Wait Anita, I'm asking Jack if he noticed your cooking.

J: Are you talking about Sunday in particular?

A: Not in particular . . .

J: Uh, I'm trying to . . .

A: One day you said, "Oh, you made bread" and I thought you'd say something like, "Oh, it's good" or "Thank you" or something, but you didn't.

T: OK, wait Anita. I'm asking Jack.

J: Uh, I guess the thing about that is that it's not particularly out of the ordinary. The way Anita cooks has never been a complaint because I think she does a good job. So again, that's a question of not saying something positive to encourage her.

T: So, it wasn't that you didn't appreciate Anita's cooking, but more that you didn't consider it an extra special issue, so you didn't bother.

J: Um, well yes. Plus, there's sort of a built-in problem with that too. You probably don't want to get into that right now.

T: Right. I don't want to get into that now, and I appreciate your stopping yourself. What I want to emphasize though, is that couples often take each other's efforts for granted. What I want you to do, is to think about how you can pay more attention to the efforts Anita makes to please you. She shouldn't have to perform extraordinary feats to receive attention and appreciation for the efforts. Also, I have a sense that Anita's someone who just really responds to your positive attention, and it wouldn't take much on your part to have an effect. Do you understand what I'm getting at?

J: Yeah, it's definitely something I need to work on.

T: Good. (*To Anita.*) What was the other one you were going to mention?

A: Oh, I've been picking up my clothes, haven't I?

J: Yeah, that's another case where I marked it down every night on my SOC, but just didn't say anything.

T: Did you appreciate her doing that?

J: Sure.

T: Great. Then, that's something you need to let her know, maybe not everyday but once in a while.

J: OK, see uh, it takes a certain amount of tact to even compliment Anita, because in a way it's like rubbing salt in a wound if I come on too strong, you know, "I'm glad you're picking up your clothes now," instead of saying, "Before you were such a slob."

A: Yeah, so I don't really care if he says anything.

J: It's almost by not saying anything about the clothes being out, that's like a compliment. But I would like to think I'm creative enough to come up with a way of complimenting Anita that's not negative.

T: So the main emphasis of this session is really how you two exchange appreciation of each other. And what I see is that you're setting up ways where you're not noticing each other's efforts or you're not clear on effective ways to show appreciation. And you need some practice with those skills. It's just a matter of taking the time to change your patterns. I feel confident that you'll be able to do that. Right now, you're just becoming aware of this issue. (*To Jack.*) Let's spend a few more minutes on things you did to please Anita, and then we'll move on.

It is not uncommon for spouses to need instruction and encouragement when it comes to overt expressions of appreciation. For Jack and Anita the assignment had been relatively successful. At times this initial assignment does not succeed as planned, and in these instances the therapist must find out what went wrong. Generally speaking, there are three basic causes of the assignment failing. First, one or both spouses may not have complied with the task. Techniques for dealing with noncompliance will be discussed in a later section.

Second, the behaviors that one or both spouses increase fail to have a reinforcing impact on the receiver. Attention must then be directed to either finding alternative behaviors that may be more effective, or working with the receiver to explore cognitive factors that may be interfering. At this stage input from the receiver is required to make the assignment work. The third possibility is that the assignment was implemented and it had a reinforcing impact on both spouses, but for some reason one or both are withholding the positive feedback. This rarely occurs; when the efforts are made, spouses are usually both delighted and relieved, and the impact is obvious. However, when it does occur, it is a bad sign. It usually means that either a major issue is assuming so much importance that day-to-day improvements cannot have much of an impact, or that a spouse has an active investment in not providing the partner with positive feedback.

Behavior exchange instigations play greater or lesser roles in the therapy process, depending on the idiosyncratic concerns of a particular couple. For some couples the instigation of such exchanges plays a primary role in therapy. For others such an emphasis may not be relevant. Moreover, this initial assignment constitutes merely one example of a behavior exchange instigation. Many other examples are described in the literature (Jacobson & Margolin, 1979; Liberman *et al.*, 1980; Stuart, 1980; Weiss *et al.*, 1973). Space does not permit us to describe all of them. We have chosen to focus on these early interventions because the groundwork for change often hinges on a rapid reversal of distressed interaction patterns. Without immediate change a collaborative set will not be maintained; with immediate change the momentum can often be self-perpetuating. We are duly impressed by the impact of the early interventions described in this section; they are highly recommended.

Troubleshooting

It is not uncommon for one major argument over the span of a week to undermine all of the positive events that took place. Frequently, these arguments involve escalating coercive exchanges in which each spouse perceives himself or herself as helpless and unable to reverse the tide. The therapist must be able to help couples overcome the hostility and helplessness engendered by such experiences, and, if possible, turn them into constructive opportunities for growth and learning. *Troubleshooting* is a technique that can accomplish both of these ends.

Troubleshooting can be defined as a detailed evaluation and reconstruction of an event or interaction that posed problems for the couple during the week. Any type of problem may be tackled with troubleshooting, as long as both spouses were involved. The troubleshooting process requires that the therapist serve as both mediator and interviewer, guiding and controlling the process. Three basic steps are included: (1) reconstruction of the event, a kind of play-by-play description of each spouse's behavior; (2) the generation of alternative interpretations and behaviors that might have led to a different outcome; and (3) the extrapolation of general principles regarding this and similar situations that are likely to arise. A further step is sometimes added: a reenactment of the entire event, using the alternative strategies generated during the therapy session. Often, a change agreement is written at the end of the exercise that embodies these basic principles. Thus, troubleshooting serves directly as a tool for conflict resolution and provides an opportunity for changing problematic patterns of interaction in the marriage.

During the first phase of trouble shooting, either spouse may begin to describe the event or interaction briefly. The primary purpose here is for the therapist to gain relevant information. After hearing one spouse's view, the therapist may then solicit the partner's perceptions of the same event. Only relevant information is essential to the process, and extensive blaming or sidetracking must be discouraged. Once the basic scenario has been described, the therapist summarizes the event, reducing it to a brief synopsis, one embodying both partners' views of the situation. Then, taking each step in turn, the therapist solicits alternative possibilities for behavior from each spouse, asking "What could you have done differently that might have led to a better outcome?" Each spouse is asked to focus on his or her contribution to the interaction, both in terms of cognitive processes and overt behavior. The therapist must insist that each examine his or her own contribution before considering the partner's behavior.

After each spouse has been given an opportunity to generate alternative behaviors that they might have adopted, suggestions are solicited from the partner. For example, the partner might be asked, "Can *you* think of anything your partner might have done at that point that would have eased the situation?"

Finally, the therapist contributes a suggestion if the couple's ideas have not adequately addressed possible alternatives. All suggestions may be written down as they are summarized. The therapist then states that although a number of alternatives existed, the couple in fact chose another path, which led to the next stage in the interaction. This is followed by an analysis of the next phase (which usually involves the partner's response) in terms of alternatives that might have averted conflict. The same procedure is followed as above, with the therapist summarizing alternative behaviors or interpretations and pressing on to the next stage in the interaction. Each step is taken sequentially and analyzed until each spouse has identified a number of alternative responses he or she might have emitted and which would have diffused the conflict. At each stage the therapist must ensure that both spouses focus on their own behavior except when suggestions for input are directly solicited from the therapist. This self-focus safeguards the cooperative spirit of such an analysis and averts further arguing. The message is that at each stage of the interaction both had the opportunity to deescalate the conflict.

Frequently, when troubleshooting is initiated by the therapist, spouses continue to feel angry and frustrated about the event at hand. One or both partners may be unwilling or unable to identify alternative behaviors. The therapist can provide empathy and support while still adhering to the task. It is explained that the search for a winner will yield fewer benefits than the quest for alternate means of coping with similar situations. Further, spouses often assume that their behavior is automatically elicited by powerful affective reactions. The troubleshooting analysis teaches that behavioral control can be exerted at any time, regardless of one's feelings. Partners are often surprised to learn that they can stop and think before acting, and that their behavior can be modified to achieve their goal of greater marital satisfaction.

Cognitive interventions play a major role in troubleshooting, especially when spouses are learning to stop and assess a situation prior to choosing a plan of action. The therapist may suggest that, at each stage of the escalation process, spouses stop and evaluate the situation. Often, misguided assumptions about the motivation of the partner's behavior and/or misinterpretation of the situation itself lead to conflict. Slowing down the assessment process usually helps spouses to correct their errors. A time-out period affords each spouse an opportunity to generate another behavior besides the overlearned coercive responses usually elicited in similar situations. The skills involved in reevaluating an interaction or in taking a "time-out" are difficult to acquire. By identifying relevant cues that help couples to appropriately label their own unproductive responses, the therapist fosters the acquisition of these skills. For some couples these cues are readily apparent, while for others, the signs of impending conflict are usually obscured. Thus, the first skills to be acquired for many couples are those of identification and labeling; couples need to identify unproductive patterns before they can change them. The following cues often help partners to identify the onset as well as the course of their escalation patterns.

1. Signs of emotional arousal. Spouses are often unaware when either they or their partners are feeling upset. While signs of anger may be apparent once arguing commences, the signals preceding a fight may be difficult for many people to detect. Thus, couples are instructed to notice the physiological state that accompanies their own feelings of hurt, rejection, anger, elation, and so on. In addition, each partner is asked to pay particular attention to his or her spouse's physiological changes during a discussion. Signs such as flushed cheeks, watery eyes, and/or fast breathing may be reliable indicators that conflict is brewing. At these times either member of the couple may suggest a 5-min time-out period, or may immediately instigate an alternate plan for dealing with whatever issue is at hand. At this time either partner may also label the interaction if it falls into a typical pattern of escalation. It is the therapist's role to help in identifying repetitive and unproductive interaction patterns.

2. After a situation has been identified as problematic, both partners have an obligation to reduce the intensity of the conflict and to offer other avenues for interacting. Some internal cues of self-statements are offered as models for stimulating this kind of a reversal. Spouses can ask themselves one or more of the following questions: (a) Am I doing the best I can do here? (b) How can I help my spouse to cool down? (c) What seems to be the central issue at this time? (d) What else could be adding to the problem here? Clearly any self-motivated question producing a reevaluation of the situation and enlisting alternative behaviors will be helpful. The therapist may solicit cues that will serve as discriminative stimuli for deescalating the argument. Such cognitive cues are essential for successful transfer and generalization of skills acquired during troubleshooting sessions.

What seems most critical to successful troubleshooting is the reframing of problems as opportunities for greater marital collaboration. We encourage couples to take risks at this time during sessions, to express thoughts and feelings. The careful mediation of the therapist serves to reduce the anxiety associated with problem solving. As such, troubleshooting functions as a prelude to the formal problem-solving training that follows in later sessions.

The next step in troubleshooting involves the extrapolation of general rules or principles from a specific example or incident. The usefulness of this procedure will be diminished if couples cannot generalize from one situation to analogous events. It is the therapist's responsibility to highlight the structural features of each behavioral sequence and solicit general principles from each spouse. This process of solicitation facilitates an evaluation of how the couple has processed and assimilated the feedback received during the session. At this time the therapist may correct misapprehensions and make further suggestions about applying suggestions and rules in future situations. A contract may then be written, embodying whatever principles seem most useful. As with any behavioral contract, couples agree to carry out the cognitive and behavioral changes. In future sessions this contract may be reviewed and revised as necessary.

The following example, again featuring Alan and Carol, provide an illustration of the troubleshooting process.

THERAPIST: Let's spend some time with what came up yesterday. Who would like to give me a description of the scenario?

ALAN: Well, uh, I came home last night, and Carol was there taking care of a couple of kids, Lauren and one other kid. Everything seemed to be pretty mellow when I walked in the door, but then fairly soon after I had come home the kids started becoming real provocative, I guess that would be the way I would describe it . . . you know, doing things specifically to be irritating, to each other primarily. And, uh, I attempted to discipline them in that situation and didn't really follow through on it because Carol was there and had another perception of what was going on, and seemed to want to stay in control of it. So, I went about my business and the kids seemed to be becoming worse and it ended up that Lauren peed in her pot and then turned it upside down on the living room rug. And so I got upset about that and told her to take it in the bathroom and she didn't do it and so I told her again and then she threw her pot across the room. So I told her to go to her room and she didn't, so then I reached over and pushed her in the direction of her room and she fell down and hit her head. And she went to her room and I went back and talked to her and it was OK. But Carol was upset that I had gotten as mad as I did and that Lauren had fallen down and hit her head. And so, we talked about it this morning.

T: Umm hmm. (*To Carol.*) What's your perception of the event?

CAROL: Well, Alan thought Lauren had peed in her pot, and she really hadn't. And when she turned it upside down, all that came out was a few drops of water from when I had rinsed it out. That's one misconception that happened. And after that, well, I felt that things escalated between the two little girls because I was there and Alan was there, and we were both watching, and they'll tend to do things like that when there's a lot of attention on what they're doing. And so I somehow felt uncomfortable with that. I knew Alan was in the middle of cooking his dinner, and he wasn't willing to take over, and yet he was sort of standing there and disciplining each of them when they took something away from the other one. So I didn't feel I ought to leave; it was just something I felt uncomfortable with. After that, the thing that got me furious was the time when Alan yelled at Lauren for just turning the pot upside down, which had nothing in it, and then grabbing her and hitting her head. And I was really upset that it happened. We needed to talk about it last night, only it wasn't appropriate to have a discussion with the two children there, and so we waited. And Alan went in his room and closed the door and I thought he was waiting to talk to me. But then I got involved with a phone call and by the time that was over, Alan had turned the light out and I thought it wasn't the time to try to talk to him, so I waited until this morning.

T: OK, let me see if I understand what happened. OK, Alan, you were cooking your dinner, and Carol, you were taking care of the children . . .

C: Yeah, I was in the back room with them at first.

T: And they were playing and started to get sort of rambunctious, teasing one another, and probably getting louder . . .

C: Yeah, no big deal though really.

T: I'm trying to mix the two perspectives, but they were playing more roughly. And my guess is that it was irritating to you, Alan.

A: Yeah, it was. At first they were in the back, and when I came home I went in there to say hi, and when I saw what they were doing I got irritated and so I left the room. I picked up that Carol really didn't feel that what I was doing was effective, and I could see that it really wasn't, so I left. And then the whole crowd just followed me out there, and it started happening again.

T: So you went in to say hi, and you got involved in the child-care process, but felt that Carol maybe was not appreciating your involvement and that what you were doing wasn't very effective, and so you left. Then everyone came out into the front room, continuing to play roughly and the incident with the toilet bowl happened. And then you shoved Lauren in the direction of her room, and she hit her head, and that's sort of the basic scenario. And then you two didn't talk about it until this morning, and you were both very angry. That's a short summary, but does it cover most of the main events?

C: There were some other things going on, but that's the most important part of what happened.

A: Yeah, that covers the main things which were a problem.

T: OK, let's take it step by step. The first step, in my mind, is you Alan, coming back into the playroom and seeing something that's irritating to you and trying to make some interventions with the girls. Let me start with you then by asking what you might have done differently at that point which might have helped to avoid a problem.

A: Well, I think to do what I did basically, just to leave.

T: And so leaving was one way to slow things down and keep things from escalating. Do you have any other ideas?

A: I can't really think of anything else right now.

T: OK, (to Carol) do you have any ideas about things Alan might have done differently that would have helped, other than leaving?

C: Well, one thing I would have liked to have seen you do would have been to tell me when you came home whether you're working or not working . . . and um, you know, how long you were gonna be with us.

T: How would that have helped?

C: Well, I would have known whether you were just gonna put in your two cent's worth and then leave, or else whether you were really gonna be involved.

T: You were reacting to the feeling that Alan was just coming in for a minute, putting in his opinion, and not committing himself to being with you and the girls. And how did that affect your reaction to Alan at that point?

C: Well, it made me a lot less willing to relinquish control in that situation, you know, to share the situation. It made me less accepting of what he was doing with them.

T: OK, so now that you know that that's an issue for you, what could you do differently that might help in that situation?

C: I could say um, I could just say, what's on your agenda tonight? I could have said well, are you gonna join us, or I could have said are you gonna join us or are you doing something else now?

T: Supposing Alan had said, yeah, I do have some time, I'd like to be involved here. Would that have changed anything?

C: Yeah, I think so.

T: Alan, would that have helped?

A: Well I don't think so, because I really didn't want to come in. Well, I mean, I wanted to come in and say hi, and make my dinner, you know. And in being there I saw things happening that I felt compelled to moderate, and I guess what I should have done would have been just to say hi, and then to go and make my dinner instead of getting involved on any level at all. So, if Carol had asked me, it might actually have helped me to remember what I was actually involved in myself, so, yeah, that would have helped.

T: OK, let's digress for a minute and just say (to Carol) that you did invite Alan in, and Alan did have the time and decided to participate. And the same problem arose, where there's a different in parenting styles, which happens for you both . . .

A: Yeah, that's an important thing . . .

T: What could you do differently, each of you, given those elements, which might have made it more workable to share the childcare experience?

A: I think that's a problem we have that we don't how the answer to.

C: Well, I've some ideas. I think maybe you know, if Alan was really gonna be there, we could have, rather than sitting and watching the girls and waiting for a chance to tell them they were doing something wrong, maybe I could have drawn us in, I could have said, Let's do something, you know, let's play ring around the rosey or something like that.

T: So you could have initiated another game, including Alan, that would have shifted away from the hassles. How do you think that would have worked, Alan?

A: I think that would have worked pretty well.

T: Good. OK, we have two ideas of things you could have tried. One is related to defining whether or not Alan is coming or going or staying for a while. The other really pertains in general to your collaboration as parents. I've got those written down, so that we can make up a contract later. Let's go ahead with it. Let's assume that you didn't do these things, which you didn't. And Alan, you left the room and the kids came out into the living room and got into hasseling each other again. What could have happened here, what could you each have done differently that might have helped to reduce the level of conflict and avoid an argument?

A: Well I could have told Carol more of what I wanted, which was some quiet while I ate, and for the girls to calm down, and she could have taken care of that, since she was doing the babysitting at that time anyway.

T: OK, so you could have asked Carol to handle the situation with the girls and let her know what you were irritated about. Carol, how do you think that would have worked?

C: Well, if it was made clear that I was responsible for the children, I mean, basically most of the time I feel that I'm responsible for doing the work, but I'm not in charge . . . so if Alan had let me know what he wanted and that I was in charge, I think I could have taken care of the situation, maybe by coaxing the girls back into the playroom or something like that.

A: You know, I think that my reluctance, I mean I think that it was my ambivalence in the situation that caused a problem. And I thought that Carol wished she wasn't babysitting anymore and that I was, since I was home and done working. And uh, I think that rather than talking about it I was just sort of maintaining this idea that I would do what I wanted, but I felt guilty about not helping, because I knew that she wanted me to do it.

C: Well, you know, I didn't wish that I wasn't doing child care anymore. I was having a good time with the girls.

A: Well, I should have tried to talk to you about it so that it would have been clear to me and so I wouldn't have felt so guilty.

T: OK, let me stop you here for a second.

The preceding transcript illustrates the effectiveness and potential flexibility of troubleshooting, particularly when implemented with a collaborative couple such as Alan and Carol. What is noteworthy is their ability to acknowledge their mutual failure to communicate and their willingness to accept responsibility for their behavior. This transcript includes some deviations from a strict troubleshooting format, especially when considering the hypothetical situation that did not occur. It is possible with a cooperative couple to flexibly explore issues surrounding an event or specific incident. In this case the general concerns of child care represented a major area of conflict for this couple and warranted a good deal of attention.

After considering each segment of this interaction, Carol and Alan, with the therapist's assistance, formulated a contract designed to ameliorate general issues surrounding child care. The contract read as follows:

1. Alan and Carol will schedule one 2-hr period each week, during which time they will work together as caretakers for Lauren. During this time Alan will not work on other projects. After the first 2 weeks another child may participate in these sessions.
2. On other occasions, Alan will try to communicate clearly how much time he has to spend with Carol and Lauren when he arrives home from work. If he forgets to do this, Carol will ask him how much time he plans to spend with the family.
3. If Carol is tired or frustrated with child-care duties, she will take responsibility for communicating that to Alan. If Alan is concerned about Carol's willingness to do child-care, or her fatigue, he can ask her about how she is feeling.
4. Rather than giving commands regarding child-care strategies, both Alan and Carol will phrase ideas in terms of suggestions, that is, how you might do it.
5. Alan and Carol will try to support each other's child-care strategies. For example, Carol will encourage Lauren to deal directly with Alan, and Alan will not intervene directly when Carol is interacting with Lauren.
6. Things both Carol and Alan can do when there is a disagreement over child-care strategies:
   a. Set a time limit for current strategy to work, then agree on what to try next.
   b. Discuss disagreements after child is put to bed.
   c. Offer suggestions (probably one only) in a supportive tone of voice.
7. Alan and Carol will try to learn from each other by observing and saving comments for later.
8. Carol and Alan will compliment each other on what works, while it is happening and afterward.

Therapist	Carol	Alan

During the subsequent therapy session, this contract was reviewed. Alan and Carol had successfully implemented most of the contract and were pleased with their progress in this area. However, they had found some part of the 2-hour joint child-care session very difficult. After some discussion it became clear that a brief planning session prior to the actual babysitting would be helpful in avoiding conflicts over procedures. This feature was added to the contract, and an agreement was made to review the effectiveness of the contract during the following session. This process of refinement and renegotiation is essential for the successful utilization of change agreements.

Problem-Solving Training

Problem-solving training proceeds logically from troubleshooting, and provides couples with the skills to ameliorate marital difficulties of both a chronic and acute nature. These techniques for effective communication are utilized both in the home and during therapy sessions. As with troubleshooting, the therapist teaches and models appropriate communication skills during the session. Emphasis is placed on the generalization of these skills, specifically those that will aid in the definition of problems, and the discovery as well as implementation of appropriate solutions. Thus, couples are asked to practice those behaviors that lead to productive and collaborative problem solving. They are then required to practice these techniques in formal problem-solving sessions at home. Progress is assessed in each subsequent therapy session. After they have acquired the specific skills necessary to solving a problem, they apply these skills to problem areas in their relationship, starting with minor problems and moving gradually toward a focus on major issues. Once couples are able to utilize effectively problem-solving techniques, troubleshooting is replaced with direct problem-solving communication, requiring little or no mediation by the therapist.

Problem-solving strategies represent a type of communication specifically suited to conflict resolution or reduction. The rules are not intended as substitutes for other forms of conversation, nor are couples expected to utilize these formal procedures every day. Rather, problem-solving strategies can be summoned whenever difficult issues arise. However, couples must practice these skills on a regular basis if they are to gain facility with them. Along with training, couples must be taught when and how to engage these skills. The major goals of problem-solving training are as follows:

1. To identify specific areas or behaviors that are of concern to one or both spouses.
2. For each spouse to understand or at least perceive the other's point of view.
3. To develop and implement reasonable problem solutions, ones that may include compromises in expectations, behavior changes, and the restructuring of situations.
4. For each spouse to acknowledge his or her contribution to the problems that are discussed and to take responsibility for changing his or her behavior as necessary (the enhancement of collaboration).

Problem-Definition Phase

Problem solving involves two distinct phases, defining the problem and finding a solution. The initial phase of problem solving involves the definition of the problem. The definition is arrived at by a process involving (1) an expression of appreciation delivered by the spouse who is upset; (2) a specific behavioral description of the problem; (3) expressing feelings; (4) mutual acceptance of responsibility; and (5) the use of paraphrasing each step along the way by both spouses.

EXPRESSION OF APPRECIATION
The "expression of appreciation" is justified as a means of placing a problem in perspective. Clearly, it is easier to accept a compliment than a

criticism, and it is easier to accept criticism when framed with an expression of appreciation. Consider the difference between the following phrases: "Lately you haven't been washing the car"; or "Generally, you are very fastidious and that's something I really appreciate about you, but lately you haven't been washing the car." Most people would agree that the latter phrase would be easier to accept than the former. The compliment should be specific and should reflect a genuine expression of appreciation rather than a perfunctory preface to a critical statement. Also, any compliment must relate in some way to the problem area. With some careful consideration, partners can identify an area of strength in their spouse that relates to the particular problem at hand. The balancing of appreciation and problem identification provides a perspective usually lost when problems are pinpointed in isolation.

SPECIFYING THE PROBLEM

Couples frequently describe problems in terms of their impact rather than the behaviors or situations that evoke them. Couples utilize global terminology, such as personality traits, to summarize a cluster of behaviors, each of which may have particular determinants. Thus, spouses must be educated and encouraged to be as specific as possible when presenting an issue during problem solving. While behavior exchange procedures may afford spouses some insight into the situational and temporal determinants of behavior, further discussion is generally warranted during this phase of therapy, if the skills of pinpointing are to be internalized. One way for spouses to develop such skills is to begin by practicing on hypothetical problems that are irrelevant to their own presenting concerns. The therapist can encourage cooperation and collaboration by taking each scenario and having the couple work together to develop a variety of viable and specific problem definitions.

One example might be a scenario in which an imaginary couple attends a party. One spouse is unfamiliar with the other guests, and sits alone, sipping a drink. At the same time, the partner converses with ease and aplomb, spending most of the party with members of the opposite sex. The therapist can describe the typical kinds of responses each spouse might have, and the corresponding problem definitions that might be formulated. The gregarious spouse might accuse the partner, saying "You're no fun at parties and you don't like any of my friends. What, are you too good for them?" The spouse might respond with a statement such as, "Well if you weren't such an inconsiderate flirt, I might have enjoyed myself." Such a description illustrates the problem with overgeneralized definitions, that is, they usually promote defensiveness and almost inevitably lead to arguments. Couples may formulate alternative descriptions of the hypothetical problem, ones that specify the behavior and the relevant situational determinants. Utilizing the example above, one useful definition, from the standpoint of the spouse who sat alone, might include a description of the situation, for example, "parties where I know few of the other guests," and a specific description of the spouse's *behavior*, such as, "when you talk with other guests, particularly those of the opposite sex, and don't check to see how I'm doing." Effective pinpointing might also include a temporal description such as, "on days when I work long hours, especially toward the end of the week," or "when we first arrive at parties."

When couples develop definitions for their own problems, as opposed to defining hypothetical issues, they may have difficulty centering in on specific behaviors relevant to the problem. It is often helpful, in such circumstances, if the spouse envisions a particular example in his or her own mind, and then tries to focus on the exact behaviors that have caused him or her difficulty. Specific and direct questioning by the therapist may help in describing situational and temporal determinants. Further, it is not essential to address the entire problem in one sitting. In fact, the goals of problem solving are better served if the problem is divided into manageable chunks. Thus, some problems may be subdivided and addressed as a cluster of issues to be resolved over time.

EXPRESSION OF FEELING

When one or both spouses pinpoint problem behaviors in the other, they are encouraged to make explicit the affect associated with the behavior. For example, "When we're at parties with your co-workers and you spend most of the time talking to other people, I feel angry and hurt." Direct expression of feelings is often not included in couples' habitual pretherapy conflict-resolution repertoire. People have a difficult time disclosing such feelings to their partners because they become vulnerable as a result. Disclosure also tends to be disarming; it reduces defensiveness in the receiver and thereby promotes collaboration. Many clients do not know the difference between thoughts and feelings and will be inclined to provide the former when asked to express the latter. Feeling checklists, along with practice at distinguishing between cognition and affect, are both useful devices to counteract these tendencies.

VALIDATION, ACKNOWLEDGMENT OF ONE'S ROLE, AND ACCEPTANCE OF RESPONSIBILITY

The collaborative set receives one of its sternest tests following the initial statement of a problem by one spouse. In many distressed spouses the habitual response to a complaint is to defend oneself through denials, cross-complaints, excuses, or justifications. This is where conflict-resolution discussions most often break down. The problem-solving format precludes such responses, and substitutes one of many possible collaborative responses: empathy, admissions, apologies, and recognition of the other's feelings are possible alternatives. Spouses put up great resistance to this dramatic change from their normal strategy. They fear that any collaborative response at this point in the discussion would be tantamount to "losing" or admitting that the partner is correct and justified in his or her complaint. To acquire compliance with this rule the therapist must explain that compliance does not mean accepting blame; rather it is simply a way of ensuring that the partner's point of view is understood.

In the same way spouses who are pinpointing problems in their partner are expected to acknowledge whatever role they play in either creating, maintaining, or exacerbating the problem. Like expressions of appreciation and feelings, such acknowledgments tend to reduce defensiveness in the partner; a collaborative response is more likely if the dissatisfied spouse acknowledges the dyadic or reciprocal nature of the problem.

THE USE OF PARAPHRASING DURING PROBLEM SOLVING

Paraphrasing plays a major role during the problem-definition phase. Paraphrasing is used to ensure that each spouse listens and demonstrates that he or she understands the other's comments.

Distressed couples are not naturally inclined to paraphrase their partners' problem statements. The first impulse is to argue with the formulation or to make excuses for themselves. The skill can be more easily learned if practice begins with hypothetical conflicts experienced by fictional couples, where each spouse role plays the same-sex counterpart in the fictional scene. Because the "content" of the discussion is irrelevant to the clients' own relationship, they can more effectively focus on the process skills being taught.

The following transcript illustrates some of the difficulties that arise even when couples work on hypothetical problems. Abe and Janet had been working on developing problem definitions using hypothetical problems that the therapist provided. They had just worked on definitions at home for the first time, and they rehearsed them again in session.

THERAPIST: OK, Abe why don't you start with one of the problems you defined.

ABE: OK, I'll read the problem first. Bill and Louise have been married for 10 years. They have recently moved to a different city because Bill obtained a new job. Bill feels that since they have moved, his wife has been spending too much money on telephone calls to her friends in their previous neighborhood. Louise feels that it is difficult for her to make friends in their new location and that she needs to talk to her old friends to fight off her loneliness. She opposed their move and feels that since she finally did agree, Bill should allow her to talk to her friends until she feels more settled. However, Bill feels that Louise's conversations are excessively long and that she could cut down on the bills if she tried. Louise thinks that Bill does not understand her need for her old friends. Here's my definition. I really appreciate you're a very frugal person and you've stretched our dollar; you've been very good with that. However, I'm very concerned and a little upset that you are spending too much time and too much money on the telephone talking to your old friends in Oshkosh.

JANET: I see you're concerned that I'm spending too much time on the telephone and it's costing too much money. I realize that I have been doing that, and I know it's a drain on our budget.

A: I understand that I'm part of the reason that you're lonely and that you need your pals. I dragged you away from Oshkosh and I understand that it's hard for you to make pals and I don't mind you making some phone calls, but it's still become a little burdensome . . .

T: Wait a second. Do you know why I'm stopping you?

A: I know, I got away from it.

T: Just take some responsibility.

J: Without attacking.

A: I didn't attack.

J: I consider it an attack.

T: Hold it. Where were we?

A: I was going to try taking responsibility again.

T: OK, go ahead.

A: Well, I can understand that some of this is my fault for having taken you all the way away from your pals and stuff; I appreciate your having come with me. I know that I am some of the problem as well.

T: Good. Very nice.

On the whole, this transcript represents a successful utilization of problem-definition techniques. Abe's initial statement of the problem included an appropriate compliment, a statement of feeling, and a specific description of the problem itself. Janet's use of paraphrase was clear and succinct. She took responsibility for her behavior and acknowledged the costs involved. When Abe took responsibility for his contribution to the problem, he embarked on what looked to be a reiteration of the problem. Although this was a hypothetical issue, one bearing no relation to Abe and Janet's presenting concerns, difficulty in accepting responsibility arose, as it often does when couples work on their own issues. The acceptance of responsibility is often resisted by the partner who raises the issue to begin with, and defensiveness on the part of the receiver is also common. It is helpful to anticipate this sort of difficulty, warning the couple in advance, and intervening as necessary.

Problem-Solution Phase

BRAINSTORMING

Once the problem has been defined, the remainder of the problem-solving process is focused exclusively on the generation of a viable solution. The first step in this process involves *brainstorming*. "Brainstorming" is a procedure designed to generate a list of potential solutions to a problem. Its specific procedures are as follows: (1) Solutions are suggested by each spouse and recorded in writing by the partner who has presented the problem; (2) no evaluative comments are allowed while the list is being generated; (3) spouses are instructed to suggest anything that enters their minds, without censoring ideas, no matter how silly or absurd they might seem.

The directive to generate a long list of potential solutions without editorial commentary is designed to liberate couples from the censorship that often accompanies conflict discussions. We have found that quantity leads to quality: that is, if large numbers of solutions are generated, among that list will be some that are viable. Couples are encouraged to consider a number of perspectives when developing their list of possible solutions. They are encouraged to make solutions dyadic, so that each contributes in some way to the amelioration of difficulties. Without such encouragement, spouses will frequently suggest solutions involving changes in only one spouse's behavior. Solutions should also consider the role of unrealistic expectations in marital problems, as well as the necessity of reinforcing changes.

Some education about the nature of marital problems seems useful to couples at this point, as it aids them in the development of viable solutions. Utilizing a hypothetical scenario or problem, the therapist can point out the various elements contributing to a problem. Elements such as behavioral deficits and excesses, perceptual difficulties, divergent expectations, and situational constraints may be highlighted. Couples may then be encouraged to analyze the different components of hypothetical problems. While problems may assume a variety of forms, they usually may be characterized by one or more of the following:

1. A behavioral excess
2. A behavioral deficit
3. A poor fit between expectations and behaviors
4. A low rate of reward for costly behaviors
5. Situational variables that contribute to the problem, involving time, place, rate, and/or structure

It is important to note that a given problem may be characterized by any or all of these aspects. Therefore, solutions may address behaviors, cognitive variables, and situational factors. Utilizing the hypothetical scenario of the party, described previously, solutions might address the following factors:

1. One spouse's tendency to converse too much and too often with party-goers other than his or her partner. (Excess.)
2. The same spouse not initiating conversations with his or her partner. (Deficit.)
3. The couple not discussing the party before going, that is, reviewing who would be there and what kind of party it would be. Hence spouses arrived with divergent expectations of the event and one another. (Poor fit between expectations and behavior.)
4. When one spouse did initiate conversation with the other, he or she was rebuffed or ignored. At the same time other guests were eager to engage in conversation. (Low rate of reward for behavior, with competing reinforcement from elsewhere.)
5. The party started late and one spouse was tired. It was held in a place where it was difficult to move around; hence mingling was a major task. The couple had not attended parties together for years and were out of practice with each other in terms of socializing. (Situational variables contributing to behavior and responses.)

It seems clear from this analysis that a number of solutions might be generated that would address the problem at multiple levels simultaneously. The above analysis addresses the concerns of only one spouse; note particularly that items 1 and 2 describe unilateral, rather than interactive processes. In this instance either partner may have been targeted in terms of behavioral excesses or deficits. To offer the alternative approach, the spouse who sat alone could have been characterized as having emitted an excessive number of messages that were interpreted as rejection by the spouse, for example, sitting alone, actively ignoring overtures by the partner, staring into space, and so on. In terms of deficits this same spouse may have been portrayed as having failed to communicate his or her needs and desires along with the aforementioned lack of socializing behaviors (e.g., not making eye contact with anyone). Thus, either spouse may have been viewed as responsible for at least part of the problem. These interpretations are complementary rather than conflicting. If spouses learn to identify a number of possible interpretations of a problem, they will also be better equipped to solve it. While either spouse might choose to define the problem using only one perspective, the generation of solutions may encompass numerous perspectives. Similarly, while the problem may be framed as unilateral in nature (one spouse's excessive or deficient behavior), solutions may be dyadic. The most collaborative approach seems to be the latter.

The following transcript features Abe and Janet during a brainstorming sequence. This was the second time they had tried this procedure, and they both had some difficulty sticking with the format. They were working on the hypothetical problem concerning Janet's phone calls to her friends back home.

THERAPIST: Now, whoever has presented the problem—in this case it's you, Abe—turns to the partner and suggests that brainstorming begin. And you're also in charge of recording all proposed solutions. Before you start, I want to remind you again about the rules of brainstorming. No smiles, or grimaces, or sighs. Also, remember that you'll have ample time to discuss these ideas during the cost–benefit phase. And one more thing, remember to start with something absurd. Go ahead and begin.

ABE: OK, why don't we go ahead and brainstorm this problem.

JANET: Fine.

A: Let's buy the phone company.

J: We could get a Watt's you know.

A: That's a good one, I like that one.

T: OK, you're not supposed to comment.

A: It's my turn again. Let's call on low-budget hours.

T: You don't really have to take turns here, as long as you're both contributing.

J: Why don't I get a part-time job? So we can pay more phone bills so I can make more phone calls?

A: What about the children?

T: OK, let's stop. Do either of you know why I'm stopping you?

394 WOOD AND JACOBSON

A: Because we're misbehaving, we're talking out of turn.

T: No. That's not why I'm stopping you. What do you think Janet?

J: Well, I know I was giving a lot of reasons, sort of discussing the issues when maybe I just should have given the idea.

T: Good. That's definitely part of the reason I stopped you. Also because you were beginning to discuss this issue together and you need to save that for the cost–benefit section. Also, your tone of voice, the use of a question implies that you want Abe's approval of your idea; you're in a sense soliciting a comment from him. Understand?

A: Yeah. Let's try it again, no editorials. Let's make a phone schedule to your mates in Oshkosh, every week you may call one during budget hours.

J: I would like to take a night class. You could agree to give up your bowling night and I could go out.

A: What does that have to do with the phone?

J: Because it's the idea of making friends. Loneliness is at the issue.

T: Try to save your comments for later.

A: Go bowling one night (*writing this down*).

J: No, you give up your bowling so I can go out one night.

A: OK, got it now. How many of these things do we do?

T: As many as you each can thing of. But if you've run out of ideas, then you can just say so and ask if your partner has any more. You should shoot for about 10 ideas altogether.

A: OK, I'm sort of out of ideas, how about you Janet?

J: I can't think of any either.

T: I have one idea to add. Janet agrees to set a timer when she's talking long distance and phone calls will not exceed 15 minutes.

A: OK, let me write that down.

T: Good work. You're both starting to get the hang of this. You've come up with a number of solutions, some of which are absurd, and some of which look to be viable solutions. What was it like for you to do this?

A: Very interesting. We usually don't come up with that many ideas at one time.

J: I think it's kind of fun. We seem to be very good with absurd ideas, which is no surprise, really.

T: Well you're both very creative and witty, which will help a lot during this process. The only thing you really need to watch is the commenting and discussion . . . but that's just a matter of practice, and we can work on it in here.

Once again, the use of a hypothetical problem seemed to promote a relaxed and cooperative spirit during brainstorming. Nevertheless, Abe and Janet had trouble with adherence to the nonevaluative format. Because their attitude was positive and they were working together, the therapist did not interrupt them to highlight each rule violation. However, consistent prodding and reminding is necessary if couples are to internalize the rules. One needs to strike a balance between the enhancement of a collaborative spirit and the need for strict adherence to procedures. Further, the therapist needs to set appropriate expectations for the first few trials of any new skill. By reinforcing successful approximations of the desired behaviors, couples usually master these skills within a few sessions.

After partners have developed a list of at least 8–10 possible solutions, they are asked to review the list together, and to eliminate all absurd solutions. They then review the list a second time and eliminate those solutions that do not address the problem. If either spouse perceives that a solution *does* address the problem, it is kept. The therapist does not allow couples to eliminate solutions simply because they do not like them, or perceive them as too costly. At this point in the process, only those proposed solutions that are patently absurd or off the topic would be eliminated.

THE PROCESS OF DERIVING A CHANGE AGREEMENT

The spouse who has defined the problem leads the discussion and writes down all information. Each proposed solution is considered in terms of its merits and costs. Spouses are asked to paraphrase each others' comments, since this is a critical time for understanding the partner's concerns. After pros and cons are listed for a solution, spouses may decide to eliminate a solution because it is too costly. They may also leave it for further consideration or approve it as one part of the final solution. During this decision-making process, solutions may be refined or modified as long as both spouses approve of the changes. Collaboration and flexibility are essential ingredients for success here. If spouses enter into an argument or noncollaborative discussion, the therapist must provide appropriate guidance.

Now back to Abe and Janet who moved on to problem solving with their own issue. They practiced contracting with hypotheticals and brainstormed one of their own problems at home. During the session we worked as a team to analyze the costs and benefits of each proposed solution and to formulate a contract. The following transcript embodies the highlights of that session.

THERAPIST: OK, you worked on one of your low-cost problems at home and completed brainstorming, right?

JANET: We did.

T: Who presented the problem?

ABE: It was my issue, the one we defined in here last week about the pots and pans.

T: (*To Abe.*) Let's start with you rereading the definition and listing the proposed solutions which you and Janet developed at home.

A: Here's the definition: Janet, you've been a great helpmate to me, keeping the house clean and sharing in cooking responsibilities. Lately, when it's been my turn to cook and your turn to do dishes, you've forgotten to wash the cooking kettles and this has made cooking the next day very hard and I've felt annoyed. These are the solutions we came up with during brainstorming: (1) Get disposable pots. (2) Always have TV dinners. (3) Buy several sets of pots. (4)

Abe will bus his pots to the sink and then Janet will wash them. (5) Children will wash pots. (6) Abe will wash pots. (7) Anyone who burns a pot, washes it. (8) Abe reminds Janet to wash pots. (9) Abe will limit the number of pots used during cooking to three; anything over three he will wash. (10) Ask neighbors to wash pots. (11) Ask Charlie to wash pots.

T: That's quite an impressive list. Did you have any difficulty brainstorming these on your own?

J: Actually, I think we did very well, (*to Abe*) don't you? I mean we did have some trouble not laughing at times, but overall we didn't talk about them or comment.

T: That's great news. How did it go from your point of view, Abe?

A: We definitely behaved ourselves this time, no problems at all.

T: Very good. I'm pleased. Let's move ahead then, and start by eliminating the absurd ones and the ones which don't address the problem.

A: OK. Ask Charlie to wash the pots.

T: Is that your dog?

J: It's a friend who comes over.

A: He should be here; he just got a divorce. He has nothing to do but come by and drink beer, watch my television. Feed him. Makes thirty thousand dollars a year and has nothing to do in his evenings. It's absurd to ask him to do dishes.

J: I agree.

A: Disposable pots, out.

T: Make sure Janet agrees.

A: I think it's absurd, what do you think?

J: I agree. Same with the TV dinners.

A: Yeah, out.

J: Do you agree it's absurd to ask the neighbors to do the dishes?

A: Out.

J: We had trouble not making faces over these. I'm going to read the ones we have left (*to Abe*), and you tell me whether you think they're absurd or not. Buying several sets of pots.

A: Out. Absurd.

J: I don't think so. What do we do now?

T: If one of you thinks it's not absurd, then it stays in.

J: Abe busses pots to sink.

A: I don't think that's absurd.

J: Agreed. Abe washes the pots.

A: That's absurd.

J: I think that has real merit to it.

A: *I* wash the pots, when it's your turn to wash dishes?

J: Exactly. When you cook . . .

T: Hold it. Stop. All you're supposed to do the first time through it decide whether they're absurd or not. Right? You're not going to do the costs and benefits just yet.

A: Well I thought that was absurd.

T: For one thing, if Janet thinks it's not absurd, it stays. Secondly, I don't want you to eliminate solutions just because you don't like them or you disagree. It's important to discuss disagreement in the context of costs and benefits.

J: OK. you burn the pots, you wash the pots. Do you think that's absurd, Abe?

A: Out. Absurd.

J: I think it has merit. It's not absurd.

A: OK, let's save it.

After reviewing the list and eliminating those solutions that both agreed were absurd, a second review of the list was made to eliminate any ideas that did not address the problem. The following segment covers the discussion of costs and benefits for the same problem.

JANET: OK, so that leaves us with several solutions which we're going to do costs and benefits on. So let's start with buying several sets of pots. What could the costs of that be?

ABE: Too much money to buy pots.

J: So you think it would cost too much money.

THERAPIST: Great paraphrasing, and I'm pleased to see that you remembered.

A: Another cost is you have no place to put them. We have enough pots and kettles and what not to feed the Russian army.

J: So there isn't any more room to store several sets of pots. Can you think of any more costs?

A: Not really, not now.

J: OK, what about benefits?

A: Well, you wouldn't have to wash pots for a week, you could just stack them up to the ceiling.

J: Wouldn't have to wash any pots for a week. Any other benefits?

A: No, I think that's about it. What about your point of view? What costs and benefits do you see to having several sets of pots?

J: I agree with you on all the costs you mentioned. One other benefit would be that you would always have a pot for your cooking.

A: Not necessarily. Not unless they were clean.

T: Wait a second. Do you know why I'm stopping you?

A: I forgot to paraphrase her statement didn't I?

T: That's right. Also, you were beginning to argue with Janet's point of view, which you should try to avoid at this time. Just paraphrase.

A: Alright, so I'd always have a pot to cook in and that would be a benefit.

J: Yeah. I can't really think of any more costs and benefits for this solution. Can you?

A: No, not really. Do you think the costs outweigh the benefits, or vice versa?

J: I think it's too costly and should be eliminated.

A: I agree. Out. Let's go on to the next solution.

J: That's, cook busses pots to sink.

T: This time Abe should take a turn writing down the costs and benefits and you should go first stating your ideas.

Abe and Janet took each solution in turn, listing its potential costs and benefits. They then eliminated all solutions that were too costly to implement.

Change Agreements

The final step in the problem-solving process involves the formulation of a written change agreement specifying what is to be done to resolve the issue. All solutions that have been maintained from the original brainstorming list are read aloud by the spouse who has presented the problem. Any solutions that remain questionable may once again be reviewed in light of their costs and benefits. After modification or elimination of these solutions, those remaining are synthesized and recorded in the form of a contract.

The next stage involves consideration of those factors that might interfere with the successful implementation of the agreement. Reinforcers for successful behavior change, as well as stimulus control strategies, can be added to the contract. A date for reviewing the agreement is established, and both spouses sign. The couple is encouraged to post the contract visibly in their home or wherever appropriate. Compliance with the contract is then reviewed briefly during each therapy session. Revisions may be made as necessary, as long as both parties are in agreement about these changes.

Abe and Janet completed the cost–benefit analysis of each solution as above, eliminating those suggestions that seemed too costly and preserving those whose benefits outweighed possible liabilities. The following contract was formulated:

Abe and Janet agree that during the next month the following procedures will be followed so that pots and pans will be cleaned in a timely fashion: (1) Whoever cooks will bus pots to sink from other parts of the kitchen. (2) The cook will wash any badly burned pots. (3) Whoever cooks will limit the number of pots and pans to three and will wash any that exceed that limit. Abe and Janet agreed that if the cook forgets to clear the pots over to the sink, the dishwasher is only obliged to clear once and remind the cook of his or her responsibility. If, after that, the cook still forgets to bus his or her pots, the dishwasher has the option of not washing them.

Abe and Janet agreed to post a copy of the contract on the side of the stove, where it would be visible during meal preparation. They set a date to review the contract (2 weeks later) and decided that upon successful implementation of all phases for a 2-week period, they would plan a special dinner out together as a reward and celebration. As with any contract formulated during therapy, all parties, including the therapist, signed.

The preceding transcripts are illustrative of procedural details as well as typical problems that arise during training sessions. It is not unusual for couples to find the rules and procedures difficult to follow. They often find the continuous use of paraphrasing to be artificial and difficult to implement. However, while the therapist wants to encourage any and all cooperative forms of communication, the successful acquisition of problem-solving skills hinges on over-learning and repeated practice. As a secondary gain, couples learn to monitor their statements more closely when they must attend to specific guidelines and goals. This self-monitoring skill may in fact facilitate the generalization of problem-solving skills, because it perhaps increases the likelihood that couples will observe and evaluate the quality of their communication in other settings.

The preceding transcript captures the beginning stages of problem-solving training, which are most taxing for couples at the procedural level and least taxing in terms of content and complexity of the problem at hand. As couples begin working on the distressing areas of their relationship, they are more likely to deviate from these procedures. Therefore, it is essential that the therapist acknowledge the occasional artificiality of the format while insisting that couples continue to work within the guidelines. Table 7-1 provides a cue sheet that may be utilized during problem-solving sessions as a reminder of the correct procedures.

GENERALIZATION AND TRANSFER OF TRAINING

Throughout the course of therapy, attention must be paid to issues of generalization and transfer so that maximum therapeutic benefits may be attained. It is not sufficient that couples be able to demonstrate competent problem-solving, pinpointing, and collaborative behaviors in session. The ultimate goal of therapy is for couples to utilize these skills as necessary, at home and in other settings outside the therapist's office. It is also paramount that couples be able to apply what they have learned to problems and situations that may not have been dealt with during therapy.

When formulating agreements and contracts, we ask couples to consider those factors that will increase the likelihood that the contract will be honored. Further, we ask them to imagine any situations or circumstances that would interfere with the successful implementation of the agreement. Consequences and rewards are then stipulated to aid in the maintenance of change. Specific cues are developed that will remind couples of their agreements, and dates are set for the review and possible revision of any contract. In addition to these preventative measures, the analysis of any relapse provides immediate and direct information about those circumstances and behaviors that are likely to trigger future problems. Any difficulties arising during the course of therapy are utilized in the formulation of preventative measures. Thus, as in the troubleshooting section above, we emphasize the need to extrapolate general principles from the evaluation of a specific incident.

TABLE 7-1. Problem-Solving Cue Sheet

I. Partner presenting problem	Partner receiving problem
1. a. Starts with a relevant compliment to the receiver.	2. a. Listens to compliment, may paraphrase it as well.
b. Specific behavioral description of problem. (This can be an excess or deficit and situation can be described briefly as well.)	b. Listens to problem description, paraphrases, and checks to see if he or she heard the description accurately.
c. States the consequences that result from the problem behavior, focusing on feelings.	c. Listens and paraphrases statements of feelings.
4. Paraphrases partner and accepts responsibility for his or her contribution to the problem at hand.	3. Accepts responsibility for some contribution to the problem for the partner.
	5. Paraphrases partner's acceptance of responsibility.

II. Brainstorming procedures
  1. Be sure to write down every idea.
  2. Avoid all comments regarding quality of suggestions.
  3. Start with an absurd idea.
  4. Be creative in your thinking.
  5. Think of as many ideas as you can.
  6. Do not censor ideas, even if they have already been suggested.

III. Reviewing costs and benefits
  1. Eliminate absurd solutions. (Make sure they're really absurd.)
  2. Eliminate solutions that do not address the problem.
  3. Take each remaining solution and write down the costs and benefits of each one. Remember to *paraphrase* each idea presented by your partner.
  4. After all costs and benefits have been listed, ask yourself whether or not the costs outweigh the benefits, or vice versa. Either eliminate the solution, save it for further consideration, or consider it a definite part of the solution. Solutions can be modified at this point, with the consent of both partners.

  Remember: In all of the elimination procedures, if one partner wants to keep the idea in for further consideration, it stays.

IV. Contracting
  1. Final agreements should be specific and clear. Specific dates, times, and statements of "how often" should be included as necessary.
  2. Agreements should include how each partner will be reminded to carry out his or her part of the agreement.
  3. Agreements should include what will happen if the agreement is not met, and how the agreement will be reestablished.
  4. Agreements should be time limited and should include a review date.

Note. The authors wish to thank Robert Berley for his contributions in the development of this cue sheet.

Self-Initiated Evaluations

The long-term maintenance of positive change in the marriage depends on spouses' ability to monitor the current status of the relationship. Couples must learn to identify cues signaling that the marriage needs attention. We often ask couples to generate a list of critical signs that would indicate that a possible relapse is brewing. If the couple has difficulty generating such a list, it is up to the therapist to provide some cues. The following general signs may be mentioned:

1. *Feelings of anxiety, anger, or depression.* Some efforts to define these states may be necessary, and the solicitation of specific examples from each spouse is helpful. Further, spouses must learn to identify the signs of depression and frustration in one another.
2. *Avoidance of an issue or problem for one day.* While it is typical, though not preferable, for couples to avoid discussion of affect-laden issues, more than one day's delay should signal spouses to make a date for a problem solving session. If more than one day passes, spouses are usually setting themselves up for a relapse.
3. *Lack of follow-through on agreements made in therapy.* This includes not reviewing contracts, or posting cues.
4. *Giving or receiving criticism without setting a time to talk.*

After generating such a list of signals, couples are asked to formualte a list of strategies for turning the tide and getting back on course. It is useful, especially in service of generalization, for the therapist to prod each partner, until each offers at least one idea. Then, the therapist may offer one or more of the following alternatives as possible interventions:

1. The couple may hold a monthly evaluation meeting, where contracts will be reviewed and the relationship will be evaluated in general (start with positives).
2. If any of the previously listed signs appear, each spouse has the obligation to initiate a problem-solving session. It seems that some behavioral rehearsal of initiation is essential here.
3. Couples may reinstate positive behavior exchange procedures, as with the beginning of therapy, that is, each spouse focuses on his or her behavior and works to raise his or her partner's satisfaction.
4. Couples may schedule a therapy "booster" session.

Generalization of Problem-Solving Skills

Clients often wonder whether or not they are expected to have problem-solving sessions every week for the rest of their lives. We generally encourage couples to utilize problem-solving procedures as they have been taught in therapy, particularly when informal discussion of an issue is leading to conflict rather than productive solutions. We emphasize that ongoing communication about the quality of the marriage remains essential, whether or not a formal problem-solving format is utilized.

We suggest that if couples are going to talk informally about problems that they utilize the significant features of problem-solving training. Further, couples should return to a structured format if they find themselves arguing during their informal discussions. We suggest the following criteria for successful discussion:

1. Carry on a discussion only when both spouses agree to do so.
2. Distractions such as televisions, telephones, music, and so on should be minimized or eliminated.
3. A time limit for the discussion should be set (with a chance for negotiating another time to talk, should time run out before discussion is completed).
4. The scope of the discussion should be narrowed so that the topic may be covered within the time limit. If the area seems too expansive, several topics may be enumerated, and one selected for discussion at that time.
5. Paper, pen, and calendars are essential for planning discussions. Ideas, suggestions and dates for implementation should be recorded and kept in a notebook.
6. Couples should ensure adequate privacy; for example, discussions in restaurants are often interrupted and the public atmosphere can be inhibiting.
7. Taking turns talking, utilizing good listening skills, and occasional paraphrasing are essential for successful communication.

While these guidelines are also included in the problem solving as it has been taught during therapy, the strict procedures for defining a problem and finding solutions have been eliminated from these latter instructions. Although it is advisable for couples to continue to utilize brainstorming and the format for problem definition, some couples find the structure stultifying and prefer these latter guidelines.

Couples often seem to have trouble instigating a problem-solving session when it seems necessary. If they have stopped having weekly sessions and the need arises for conflict resolution, the skills for initiating a problem-solving session are essential. Therefore, some behavioral rehearsal seems useful here. By having couples role play an argument, each may take turns trying to call a time out and initiate a problem-solving session. Each spouse may serve in turn as the resistant partner who refuses to deescalate the conflict. This technique serves to anticipate and thereby prevent the resistance to problem solving that often occurs after the termination of therapy. Most importantly, each spouse learns to be tenacious in his or her efforts to diffuse a conflict.

Fading and Termination

Fading is a technique for fostering generalization and transfer of skills. It refers to widening the intervals between therapy sessions. By meeting every 2nd or 3rd week instead of every week, the therapist begins to play a lesser role in the process of change. Couples are encouraged to rely on their own resources and skills for maintaining and instigating positive change in the relationship. Therapy sessions are devoted to trouble shooting and the extrapolation of general principles for positive changes. In these sessions, the therapist plays a facilitative as well as didactic role, but consistently encourages the couple to take full responsibility for the continued improvement of their marriage.

We ask couples to meet with each other during the weeks when they do not attend therapy sesions. These "state-of-the-relationship" meetings are formal encounters during which time couples assess the quality of their interactions, solve problems as necessary, and set goals for the coming week. Our purpose in assigning these sessions is to ensure that our clients actuate the skills they have learned in therapy without the direct stimulus control of the therapist. This task compels couples to continue working on their relationship regardless of therapist involvement; their success in this endeavor seems essential to the overall achievement and maintenance of therapeutic gains, and provides a measure of their readiness for fading and termination.

During our final sessions the focus rests on the review of positive gains made in therapy, as well as the setting of future goals for the relationship. The therapist needs to solicit from each spouse his or her impressions of the improvements in each relevant area of the marriage. After sufficient attention has been paid to positives, the therapist may outline, with the couple's help, those areas still needing attention. The overall tone of discussion should be positive. The therapist may set expectations for future improvement, although relapses should be anticipated and the emphasis should be placed on slow improvement rather than overnight transformation. After reviewing those areas that may be problematic, that is, those situations that may instigate relapse, a change agreement may be written outlining preventative measures and the mutual commitment to continue working on the marriage. Finally, the therapist may leave the option open for the couple to return to therapy in several months for a booster session or for an assessment of their progress. In some cases, a 1-year follow-up session will suffice. The therapist's discretion is important here, for the goal is to provide support and an open door, without implying any prediction of failure. At times, couples will work harder when they know the support of the therapist is no longer provided. Yet, an opportunity for evaluating progress can also provide added motivation to work hard, and serves as a kind of insurance policy. The following transcript illustrates these procedures.

Gary and Beth, in their mid-20s, had been married 5 years and had attended therapy for 3½ months at the time of this transcript. Their presenting issues centered around communication problems and low satisfaction with companionship activities. Progress in therapy had been slow during the 1st month of treatment, but had accelerated rapidly during the 2nd month, at which time both Gary and Beth reported increased satisfaction with their marriage. During the final 6 weeks of therapy, progress slowed again in response to environmental stressors, most notably Gary's loss of his job. The focus of treatment then shifted to the new development of effective coping strategies, both individual and dyadic, and the maintenance of positive changes in their relationship. At the close of treatment, Gary and Beth had made a number of specific improvements in their mode of interaction and were feeling more satisfied with their marriage overall. However, as with many couples, a number of areas remained open to further improvement. This transcript exemplifies some techniques utilized at termination to increase the likelihood that further improvement will occur subsequent to therapy.

THERAPIST: This is our 15th session and we have one more after this. What I'd like to talk about then, is what you've learned here that's helped to improve your relationship, and how you can use those skills on your own. Obviously in a few months, we haven't covered everything. What do you think?

GARY: I think I'm more patient.

T: Umm hmm. Can you be more specific?

G: Not really (*laughs*) no I . . .

BETH: Understanding.

G: Maybe that's it, understanding or trying to be. It's always been hard for me to understand how Beth feels and how I'm supposed to react. But now I think I find myself just waiting a second and thinking about it before I say anything.

B: I can see that. I could see that in Gary even last night. He was out and I was home feeling really sorry for myself. And he called and I sounded really depressed on the phone, you know. Then I started feeling really sorry for myself and so I forced myself to go to an exercise class. I felt better after that, but once I got home I started feeling bad and acted really cold to Gary when he got home. Now usually, Gary would just get impatient and say, "What's your problem?" Buy this time he kept urging me to talk and asking me what was on my mind and just being nice. And that really helped me to quit feeling sorry for myself.

T: It's great to see that you are able to compliment Gary on the changes he's made. In fact that's something I've noticed each of you doing more of, and it seems very positive.

G: Well, just bearing in mind that this is the next to the last week, I've been finding myself really trying to put these things to use. I've been asking myself what we've done or what we've learned, and trying to use those things, even if it's something real tiny like trying to cool off instead of arguing. I've found myself doing things differently, like calling Beth and asking her about her day when I get home. These are just things I've noticed, 'cause I hate to think we've gone all this way and not gotten anything out of it.

T: So in other words, you've been trying not to let things slide. You're really making an effort to do the things which you know will help.

G: Yeah.

T: What are some other things you've learned here that you'd like to keep working on?

B: Taking time out. I think one of the most important things is just taking time out to share what's been going on. And I think it's something that we're gonna have to force ourselves to do. Even if we don't feel like it. Because it seems that when we haven't been in touch with each other, things start to go wrong.

T: So one thing you know helps you to feel satisfied and happy with each other is taking some time each day to talk. What are some other things.

G: Having our planning meetings, you know, where we schedule our time together for the week. That seems to remove a lot of tension about when we're going to see each other; then I feel more relaxed in general.

B: Yeah, and along with that, if I know when Gary's working, then I can plan to do some things on my own, like exercising, so I don't get lonely, and start feeling sorry for myself.

T: So you know that planning time together helps you to feel more comfortable with each other and allows you to coordinate your schedules. Good. You've pointed out a number of things you're already doing that help.

B: Just keeping up our contracts make a big difference.

T: Well, what are some things we haven't worked on, which are still issues for you and you'd like to work on?

G: Well, I think just being able to talk freely with each other would be something I'd like to see us do more of. Any maybe have a better sex life. I mean we started to work on that, and there's been some improvement, but we could be doing more in that area.

B: Well, yeah, the communication thing is still a problem, and that seems to get tied up with sex for some reason. So, if we can keep working on talking with each other, I think a lot of the issues around sex and stuff will improve. Don't you?

G: Well the bottom line is putting this stuff in action and seeing what happens.

T: Well, let's talk more specifically about the changes you'd like to see in these areas.

In this brief excerpt the therapist helped Gary and Beth to summarize their experience in treatment, underscoring their achievements and normalizing the fact that there is work ahead. The therapist facilitated the identification of areas in their relationship that will continue to require attention and aids in the development of realistic goals. As with the interventions previously described, the therapist encouraged Gary and Beth to think carefully about their marriage, guiding them without providing answers. This strategy seems particularly important at the time of fading and termination because the couple must then assume primary responsibility for the instigation and maintenance of positive changes in the marriage.

TYPICAL PROBLEMS THAT ARISE DURING TREATMENT

Noncompliance

If we were to judge on the basis of the questions posed to us at clinical workshops, noncompliance appears to be the most vexing problem for the community of marital therapists. Indeed, it is often puzzling and frustrating for therapists to deal with spouses who appear to be acting in ways that contradict their stated reasons for being in therapy. Noncompliance as well as other similar instances of self-defeating behavior have lead psychodynamic and systems theorists to posit constructs such as "resistance" to explain the obstructionist behavior.

Of course, noncompliance is a problem, and one that occurs at a fairly high rate. However, over the years we have become much more successful at preventing it. We have treated noncompliance the same way we would any other clinical problem and have attempted to refine our technology in order to reduce its incidence. Although we have no data to support our argument at this point, our clinical impression is that the problem occurs much less frequently than it used to.

Our basic assumption is that noncompliance can almost always be explained with greater parsimony than concepts such as "resistance" would allow. As Jacobson (1981) has argued, the aversive consequences associated with changing one's behavior are immediate, whereas the benefits to be derived (e.g., an improved relationship) are delayed. Homework assignments are aversive because they require effort, time, and the willingness to take risks.

In other instances noncompliance is a simple function of forgetting, misunderstanding the assignment, or underestimating the importance of the task. If strategies are designed to deal with all of these potential causes of noncompliance, the problem will be greatly minimized if not virtually eliminated. We divide our strategies for dealing with noncompliance into two categories: stimulus control and response control strategies.

Stimulus Control Strategies

We place much greater importance on this category than we do on the response control category. Stimulus control techniques constitute prevention; they are designed to prevent noncompliance before the fact. In our experience it is highly desirable to prevent noncompliance from occurring, rather than having to rely on the aversive control procedures necessary to stamp it out once it occurs. The general characteristic of all stimulus control strategies is their emphasis on the salience of homework. Beginning therapists often present homework assignments tentatively and almost apologetically, suggesting in a myriad of subtle ways that it is not important. Strategies routinely utilized to maximize salience include the following: verbally explicating the rationale for the assignment, and in the process emphasizing its importance; eliciting from the spouses a verbal or written commitment to comply with the assignment; anticipating in advance possible excuses for noncompliance and repudiating them before the fact; exaggerating the aversiveness of the task so that, if anything, the couple will be pleasantly surprised when they discover that implementation is not as aversive as they had anticipated; making sure that the clients understand the task by having them repeat the assignment back to us prior to leaving the office; providing written descriptions of the assignment for spouses to take home to ensure that they will not forget; and on occasion, telephone reminders. If the therapist routinely practices all of these strategies, noncompliance will be rare.

Of all of the specific strategies mentioned above, the three most important things to remember are: emphasize the importance of the task; gain a public commitment from both spouses to implement the assignment; and repudiate all potential excuses in advance. There is no reason to expect compliance from spouses unless they understand how the task relates to expediting their treatment goals. Commitment to compliance in advance is a very powerful way to ensure that compliance will occur. Moreover, the public commitment provides the therapist with a useful way of dealing with noncompliance if it occurs, by allowing him or her the leverage of referring back to the prior commitment. Finally, the anticipation and repudiation of excuses are ways of counteracting justifications that might be used as palliatives by spouses during the week when the temptation not to comply is at its peak. Over the years we have compiled a long list of commonly used excuses, and we routinely discuss each of these items with spouses and make sure that they understand that all constitute invalid excuses. The most common excuses used by couples in the wake of noncompliance are as follows:

1. I didn't have time.
2. I forgot.
3. Spouse didn't do his [or hers], so I didn't do mine.
4. We hardly saw each other all week.
5. Things were going so well that it didn't seem necessary to do the homework.
6. We had a fight and I didn't want to do the homework.
7. I was feeling discouraged about therapy.
8. I was mad at you [the therapist].

Response Control Strategies

The general principle underlying all response control strategies is that noncompliance is "not OK." If the therapist is overly supportive or sympathetic to the spouses' explanations for their noncompliance, it is likely that noncompliance will be reinforced. Moreover, if therapy becomes "business as usual" following an episode of noncompliance, spouses get the message that noncompliance does not matter. If therapy can procede in the same way whether homework is completed or not, then the only logical conclusion is that homework plays a peripheral role in therapy. Therefore, the typical response to noncompliance is to announce that the agenda for today's session will have to be eliminated, because the homework was to provide the basis for that agenda. In our work this is a true statement, because our therapy sessions begin and procede on the basis of the feedback provided by the homework. The new agenda is a focused discussion on the problem of noncompliance and how to deal with it. The session may be 10 min long if noncompliance discussions only require 10 min, or the session might take 1 hr if the solution to the problem of noncompliance requires 1 hr. Once the therapist suspends the treatment program to deal with the noncompliance, and it is absolutely clear that compliance is a ticket to the next step in treatment program, the problem rarely recurs. And by the way, couples are charged for the session.

It is also important that compliance is reinforced. Clients should be praised for doing the homework; the therapist should never take it for granted. Moreover, the homework must be used in the therapy session. If homework is not discussed then the unmistakable message is that compliance is unimportant.

In cases where only one spouse has completed the homework assignment, cancellation of the session may serve to exacerbate whatever issues are currently inhibiting the compliance of one spouse. Therefore, while the focus of the session may still rest with issues of collaboration and compliance, the stigmatization of one spouse is avoided. However, the difference in compliance often leads to an overall reduction in the previously cooperative spouse's motivation. Thus, some intervention is necessary so that *both* spouses will comply with future assignments. Further, the compliant spouse's frustration and anger must in some way be addressed and diffused so that collaboration is once again instilled in both partners.

First, noncompliance should be labeled as a problem, not only because it inhibits progress, but because one spouse has complied and the other has not. Both spouses are aware of the fact, and the therapist who ignores it compromises his or her credibility in the eyes of both partners. Second, some normalization of this divergence affords the therapist an opportunity to ally with both spouses while still promoting future compliance. It is in fact true that spouses frequently differ in their degree of compliance with homework assignments. By mentioning this fact, the therapist inhibits any unwarranted conclusions that either spouse might draw from his or her own or the spouse's behavior. The therapist may insist that noncompliance neither represents failure, nor implies that one spouse cares and the other does not. At the same time the therapist must acknowledge the frustration felt by the compliant spouse.

One way to promote compliance is by anticipating and verbalizing potential hazards that lie ahead. For example, it is likely that the compliant spouse, if sufficiently frustrated, will be tempted not to comply as fully with the homework, and will begin to question the effectiveness of therapy. The question, "Why should I try, if he or she won't?" is often raised subsequent to one spouse's noncompliant behavior. By predicting this response, the therapist both acknowledges and normalizes these feelings while communicating an explicit appeal for continued work on the relationship. Moreover, an exploration of the ways in which compliance can be increased in the hesitant or ambivalent spouse usually provides information about what has contributed to the problem and yields ideas for making effective changes. Thus, the focus shifts from normalization to a serious and direct discussion of the importance of collaboration and compliance. The therapist must throw the ball into the clients' court with questions such as, "What do you want to do about this problem?" and "How can I be of help to you?" The therapist can offer to make phone calls that will serve as reminders, or can schedule times when the spouse will call and report to the therapist. The posture of the therapist must be at once supportive and challenging.

In most cases the above procedures help couples to increase their level of collaboration and mutual compliance with homework. In the event that noncompliance continues beyond one session, the therapist can ask the couple to do the homework during the session. A simple reiteration of the issues discussed previously should suffice at this point, with the acknowledgement that progress is delayed when homework is carried out during sessions. In our experience couples rarely come unprepared more than once when all of these measures are employed.

Failure to Acknowledge Change

Another common problem is the hesitancy of one or both spouses to acknowledge the positive changes made by their partner. There are a number of reasons for this reticence. To begin with it is common for spouses to consider praise and appreciation unnecessary when everyday tasks such as cooking, cleaning, and repairs are completed. Thus, even though a request has been made for changes in such behaviors, no appreciation is shown when appropriate efforts have been made. Couples also fail to acknowledge positive changes in their partners' behavior because they attribute these improvements to the therapist, who may have facilitated or instigated the change. Another common reason that spouses appear to deemphasize the other's efforts has to do with selective tracking. Distressed couples tend to attend selectively to the negative interchanges of their relationship, as well as to the deficits and feelings of dissatisfaction. Therefore, one or both spouses may not notice change in his or her spouse.

Another factor that can sustain negative views of the relationship is the possibility that positive changes will be perceived as a threat. Although both spouses have expressed a desire for changes in their marriage, as positive changes occur, two questions arise: (1) For the receiver, "Is this satisfying enough for me to justify staying in this relationship?" and (2) For the giver, "Is this going to be enough, or is my spouse going to demand more than I can give?" Because each spouse has the dual role of giver and receiver, the level of ambivalence when the relationship starts to improve is usually high for both spouses. It is therefore quite common for spouses to have a relapse just as things begin to improve.

Several interventions seem useful when acknowledgment of change is low or when changes seem most threatening. The use of graphs, as stated earlier in the chapter, captures the positive gains in a visual mode, one which is easily interpreted by spouses as evidence for improvement. The therapist may also make a direct pitch for verbal acknowledgment of day-to-day contributions to the couple's lifestyle and well-being. It is not unusual for spouse's to take the other's contributions for granted. For example, the person who works outside the home is expected to do so without praise or appreciation, just as the spouse working in the home is perceived as simply doing his or her duty. Highlighting these tendencies is often sufficient to stimulate a change in perception about what warrants attention and praise. In cases where such interventions are less than successful, the therapist may structure a specific homework assignment requiring each spouse to notice and comment on the quotidian behaviors usually ignored.

When spouses are having difficulty acknowledging the other's efforts, the therapist's enthusiasm, optimism, and ability to elicit positive statements serve as powerful interventions in and of themselves. Further, by predicting relapses and normalizing the tendency to feel discouraged, a therapist can help couples to weather the storms that inevitably occur in a relationship. The following transcript illustrates the nature of these interventions. Again, we are looking at Pearl and Morrie, who were featured earlier in the chapter. The progress of therapy had been slow, both because of the couple's tendency to argue excessively and due to Morrie's propensity for arguing with the therapist over the usefulness of therapy. Typically, in sessions, Morrie would question the therapist about the necessity for carrying out a given task, or would refuse to stop arguing and blaming Pearl for a given problem. Pearl often stated that she felt left out at these times and that the therapist was paying too much attention to Morrie. During Session 5, Morrie had failed to comply with part of a contract he and Pearl had formulated. While the therapist was working with him to avoid future noncompliance, Pearl began to cry, stating that Morrie got all the attention, and that the therapist was always on his side. The following segment embodies the first few minutes of the subsequent session.

THERAPIST: What I'd like to do for the first few minutes today is talk about how you think therapy is going in general?

PEARL: Well, I think things have been, they've been better. But there's still the bad times too you know. I think there's been some improvement, although I have my times when I wonder.

T: Umm hmm. So there are days you feel discouraged.

P: Umm hmm, very, yeah.

T: That's real natural.

P: I think it is too. But um, the other night we had just a kind of a talking session, and we used a timer and the bell, and that worked pretty good, you know. And I really thought that worked pretty good. So, Morrie can tell you what he feels about it.

T: I always like that you're able to express positive things; I think that's a really wonderful quality.

P: Well, I think that's good that we can, because really, there's so many negative things, you have to think positive too, you know. 'Cause you're a positive person yourself though.

T: Yeah. But you're, you seem to be really good at that.

P: Thank you.

MORRIE: Well, that's what I say, there was some improvement, and then again we'll lapse back into the old habit and that kind of nullifies some of the improvement. And again it's over minor little things that actually don't mean a hill of beans. But that's part of life I guess, you have to accept it. So, I feel we've improved some, uh at least we're thinking the right way towards the same goal I hope, and uh, maybe at the end of this therapy, maybe we will have corrected most of our faults and so on. Yeah, that's about the only thing I have to say, like I say the conversation has been improved by the method that we use and you suggested, and uh, we still in some instances over-talk each other. We still have to be patient and wait until one person finishes talking. But like I say, it's improving.

T: Umm hmm. Well, I think you pointed out some real good things, Morrie, particularly the idea that you have to practice and that it takes time to change. You said that even with some amount of improvement, there's still more work to do, and that requires patience. I agree with all that.

P: Don't you think maybe there's a chance too that some of the things we may never be able to improve on, but maybe we can learn to handle them a little differently?

T: That's a really good point. You can't have the expectation that everything is going to change.

P: 'Cause we can't become perfect you know.

T: Right. I think if you can learn as you have already to be more accepting of one another, and to listen to each other more, that would be great for your marriage. And I can tell, just from the way you two are talking now, that there's some real changes.

P: That's good to hear too.

T: Just the way you're talking now is very encouraging to me. And the main thing is not to get too discouraged when you fall back into the old patterns, because old habits are hard to change.

M: Yeah, well, that's what I've been saying all along. It's just a matter of acceptance, regardless of what it is, and accept each other the way we are. Then we'll have most of the problems whipped. That's all there is to it. That's the way I feel about it anyway.

T: Yeah, well one thing I appreciate about you Morrie, is that you have so much optimism about your ability to solve these problems and to really learn to do things differently. And that's gonna help. It is helping.

M: I know I've got a short fuse; I know that much. But, uh, I'm conscious of it I guess a little more than I have been, and I still take off when it rubs me the wrong way and uh, I speak my mind. But, uh, I think I got it a little more under control than I had before.

T: Well you certainly are more aware of it. I can tell.

P: Well, I'd like to say this, that I've noticed in Morrie, I don't know what he sees in me, but I noticed in him that he is aware of some of the things that I didn't think he was ever aware of before. And that's important isn't it, for us to see these things by ourselves, you know.

T: Sure. You can't always change it just 'cause you see it, but at least you have the opportunity to be aware of it and that will lead you to being able to change it. If you don't know it's there, you sure can't do anything about it.

P: No, that's true. How can you do anything to help yourself if you can't see these things, you know? We can give you the credit for a lot of this you know, because you've really helped us to see a lot of things, that maybe we didn't want to see either.

T: That's good to hear. That's what we're all working towards. One thing I think I need to work on, well actually there are different things with each of you. One thing I need to try not to do, is get in arguments with Morrie during the sessions.

M: You get in arguments with me?

T: Well, we battle over issues.

M: Oh, yeah, well naturally, I object to something that rubs me the wrong way anyway. I do that to just about anybody and everybody I guess. I mean, I don't go along with every statement that's made by another party.

T: Sure. Right. Well, so I need to work on making our time as productive as possible, and not getting into too much of a struggle with Morrie when he has a difference of opinion with me. (*To Morrie.*) And you are opinionated; you have your own point of view; and that's as it should be. And as far as working with Pearl, (*to Pearl*) I need to remember to be real supportive of you.

P: And I do appreciate your support.

T: Yeah. Well, I need to remember that that's something you *do* appreciate and that is helpful to you in sticking with things and in feeling encouraged. Sometimes I get involved in, you know, working with Morrie on something and I forget.

P: I know; I understand that too. I think you're, it must be pretty hard for you, because we're both completely different people, to try to go this way and then to go this way, without kind of mixing up a little bit in the middle, you know.

T: Right. I get too involved in one thing and forget about the other. So, I'm going to try to work on that. . . . OK, well let's try and move ahead. I think you both realize that we're working well together and that we are making progress, though it does take time and patience. There's no doubt about it.

P: True.

T: So, let's try to make our sessions as productive as possible, and if you can keep up your end as well as you have up until now, by filling out the SOCs, doing homework, writing up contracts . . . all those things which you're doing at home, trying to improve your conservations . . . all of that really helps.

P: I think so.

T: Every single one of them, all of the effort counts. And we can add to that by making our time in here as productive as possible. If we can do all that, we're gonna be very far along in just a matter of a few weeks. Let's shoot for that.

Pearl and Morrie were at high risk for dropping out of therapy at this point. While they were complying with all homework assignments, they were each expressing a great deal of frustration during therapy sessions. At the outset of the session, the therapist tried to normalize their feelings of frustration with each other and with their progress in therapy. In addition she tried to model appropriate listening skills by acknowledging the validity of what both Pearl and Morrie had to say. Further, through eye contact, the therapist made sure to cue Pearl that she could speak first. This was particularly important because it was more likely that Pearl would be positive about therapy, and because she had been feeling that Morrie was garnering more of the therapist's attention.

As a direct intervention, the therapist accepted responsibility for the interpersonal difficulties that had arisen during sessions. Morrie reciprocated with some acceptance of responsibility for the problem. Similarly, Pearl accepted some responsibility for the issues that arose with her when the therapist initiated this process. Thus, both had been cued as to appropriate behaviors during therapy sessions, even though the overt message was one of support and empathy.

Finally, the therapist summarized and praised the successful efforts made by the couple, reorienting them to the positive aspects of their relationship. Her tone was upbeat and she infused optimism into the discussion. The remainder of the session was very productive and the couple exhibited more collaborative discussion than they had during any previous session.

Another problem that arises with considerable frequency in distressed relationships, as with Pearl and Morrie, is that of excessive bickering and arguing. These behaviors may inhibit the therapeutic process, particularly during problem-solving training, when couples are expected to conduct problem-solving sessions on their own at home. Specific interventions, designed to restrict arguing may be necessary for couples incapable of carrying out problem-solving homework. Asking them to record their problem-solving sessions will often serve as a cue for more collaborative behavior. Another strategy for home use is that of the timer and ball technique. Couples arrange to have conversation times during the week. They set a timer for 2 min, which represents the maximum length of time one person may talk. A ball, or other suitable object is passed back and forth as a reminder of who has the floor and to concretize the process of taking turns. We encourage couples to use a playful object as a reminder that they are not to take the conversation too seriously. An additional strategy for promoting more collaborative discussion is the use of paraphrase and paraconversation as mentioned earlier.

CONCLUSION

We have presented an overview of the version of BMT used in our clinical research program. The treatment program is in a perpetual process of development and evolution, as the results of our research continue to modify specific procedures. The results of BMT, both our version and that of others, appear to be promising (Jacobson, Follette, & Elwood, 1984), although it is also clear that a substantial minority of couples seeking our assistance fail to improve during the course of BMT. Thus, there have been rapid technological advances over the past decade, but marital distress remains a frustrating and challenging target for behavioral clinicians.

The steps toward building an even more effective marital therapy program involve a variety of considerations. In addition to designing more effective treatment procedures, improving our training programs for student therapist, and continuing to strive for rigorous research, client screening and diagnostic procedures will continue to play an important role. Marital distress is a heterogeneous category, and the treatment goals as well as the means utilized to achieve those goals will vary depending upon the idiosyncratic concerns expressed by a particular couple. Even the criteria for success and failure will vary from couple to couple. It is here where marital therapy is perhaps unique. For some couples, success means building a more intimate relationship. For others it means an amicable separation. For still others, one spouse wants to work for separation while the other wants to work for intimacy. At present, our monolithic outcome criteria oversimplify this diversity.

References

Billings, A. (1979). Conflict resolution in distressed and nondistressed married couples. *Journal of Consulting and Clinical Psychology, 47,* 368–376.

Birchler, G. R., Weiss, R. L., & Vincent, J. P. (1975). A multidimensional analysis at social reinforcement exchange between maritally distressed and nondistressed spouse and stranger dyads. *Journal of Personality and Social Psychology, 31,* 349–360.

Gottman, J. M. (1979). *Marital interaction: Experimental investigations.* New York: Academic Press.

Gottman, J. M., & Porterfield, A. L. (1981). Communicative competence in the nonverbal behavior of married couples. *Journal of Marriage and the Family, 43,* 817–824.

Harper, R. G., Wiens, A. N., & Matarazzo, J. G. (1978). *Nonverbal communication: The state of the art.* New York: Wiley.

Jacobson, N. S. (1977). Problem solving and contingency contracting in the treatment of marital discord. *Journal of Consulting and Clinical Psychology, 45,* 92–100.

Jacobson, N. S. (1978a). A review of the research on the effectiveness of marital therapy. In T. J. Paolino & B. S. McCrady (Eds.), *Marriage and marital therapy: Psychoanalytic, behavioral, and systems theory perspectives.* New York: Brunner/Mazel.

Jacobson, N. S. (1978b). Specific and nonspecific factors in the effectiveness of a behavioral approach to the treatment of marital discord. *Journal of Consulting and Clinical Psychology, 46,* 442–452.

Jacobson, N. S. (1979). Increasing positive behavior in severely distressed adult relationships. *Behavior Therapy, 10,* 311–326.

Jacobson, N. S. (1981). Behavioral marital therapy. In A. S. Gurman & D. P. Kniskern (Eds.), *Handbook of family therapy.* New York: Brunner/Mazel.

Jacobson, N. S. (1984). The modification of cognitive processes in behavioral marital therapy: Integrating cognitive and behavioral intervention strategies. In K. Hahlweg & N. S. Jacobson (Eds.), *Marital interaction: Analysis and modification.* New York: Guilford.

Jacobson, N. S. (in press). Clinical innovations in behavioral marital therapy. In K. Craig (Ed.), *Clinical behavior therapy.* New York: Brunner/Mazel.

Jacobson, N. S., Berley, R., Melman, K. N., Elwood, R. W., & Phelps, C. (1985). Failure in behavioral marital therapy. In S. Coleman (Ed.), *Failures in family therapy.* New York: Guilford.

Jacobson, N. S., Elwood, R. W., & Dallas, M. (1981). Assessment of marital dysfunction. In D. H. Barlow (Ed.), *Behavioral assessment of adult disorders*. New York, Guilford.

Jacobson, N. S., Follette, W. C., & Elwood, R. W. (1984). Outcome research in behavioral marital therapy: A methodological and conceptual reappraisal. In K. Hahlweg & N. S. Jacobson (Eds.), *Marital interaction: Analysis and modification*. New York: Guilford.

Jacobson, N. S., Follette, W. C., & McDonald, D. W. (1982). Reactivity to positive and negative behavior in distressed and non-distressed married couples. *Journal of Consulting and Clinical Psychology, 50*, 706–714.

Jacobson, N. S., & Margolin, G. (1979). *Marital therapy: Strategies based on social learning and behavior exchange principles*. New York: Brunner/Mazel.

Jacobson, N. S., & Moore, D. (1981). Spouses as observers of the events in their relationship. *Journal of Consulting and Clinical Psychology, 49*, 269–277.

Jacobson, N. S., Waldron, H., & Moore, D. (1980). Toward a behavioral profile of marital distress. *Journal of Consulting and Clinical Psychology, 48*, 696–703.

Liberman, R. P. (1970). Behavioral approaches to family and couple therapy. *American Journal of Orthopsychiatry, 40*, 106–118.

Liberman, R. P., Levine, J., Wheeler, F., Sanders, N., & Wallace, C. (1976). Experimental evaluation of marital group therapy: Behavioral vs. interaction–insight formats. *Acta Psychiatrica Scandinavica Supplementum, 266*, 3–34.

Liberman, R. P., Wheeler, E. G., deVisser, L. A. J. M., Kuehnel, J., & Kuehnel, T. (1980). *Handbook of marital therapy: A positive approach to helping troubled relationships*. New York: Plenum.

LoPiccolo, J., & Steger, J. C. (1974). The sexual interaction inventory: A new instrument of assessment of sexual dysfunction. *Archives of Sexual Behavior, 3*, 585–595.

Margolin, G. (1981). Behavior exchange in happy and unhappy marriages: A family cycle perspective. *Behavior Therapy, 12*, 329–343.

Margolin, G., & Wampold, B. E. (1981). Sequential analysis of conflict and accord in distressed and non-distressed marital partners. *Journal of Consulting and Clinical Psychology, 49*, 554–567.

Markman, H. J. (1979). The application of a behavioral model of marriage in predicting relationship satisfaction of couples planning marriage. *Journal of Consulting and Clinical Psychology, 4*, 743–749.

O'Leary, K. D., & Turkewitz, H. (1978). The treatment of marital disorders from a behavioral perspective. In T. J. Paolino & B. S. McCrady (Eds.), *Marriage and marital therapy: Psychoanalytic, behavioral, and systems theory perspectives*. New York: Brunner/Mazel.

Patterson, G. R. (1976). Some procedures for assessing changes in marital interaction patterns. *Oregon Research Institute Bulletin, 16*(7).

Patterson, G. R., & Hops, H. (1972). Coercion, a game for two: Intervention techniques for marital conflict. In R. E. Ulrich & P. Mounjoy (Eds.), *The experimental analysis of social behavior*. New York: Appleton-Century-Crofts.

Spanier, G. B. (1976). Measuring dyadic adjustment: New scales for assessing the quality of marriage and similar dyads. *Journal of Marriage and the Family, 38*, 15–28.

Stuart, R. B. (1969). Operant-interpersonal treatment of marital discord. *Journal of Consulting and Clinical Psychology, 33*, 675–682.

Stuart, R. B. (1980). *Helping couples change: A social learning approach to marital therapy*. New York: Guilford.

Stuart, R. B. & Stuart F. (1972). *Marital precounseling inventory*. Champaign, IL: Research Press.

Turkewitz, H., & O'Leary, K. D. (1981). A comparative outcome study of behavioral marital therapy and communication therapy. *Journal of Marital and Family Therapy, 7*, 159–170.

Vincent, J. P., Weiss, R. L., & Birchler, G. R. (1975). A behavioral analysis of problem solving in distressed and nondistressed married and stranger dyads. *Behavior Therapy, 6*, 475–487.

Weiss, R. L. (1980). Strategic behavioral marital therapy: Toward a model for assessment and intervention. In J. P. Vincent (Ed.), *Advances in family intervention, assessment and theory* (Vol. 1). Greenwich, CT: JAI Press.

Weiss, R. L., & Cerreto, M. C. (1980). The marital status inventory: Development of a measure of dissolution potential. *American Journal of Family Therapy, 8,* 80–85.

Weiss, R. L., Hops, H., & Patterson, G. R. (1973). A framework for conceptualizing marital conflict, technology for altering it, some data for evaluating it. In L. A. Hamerlynck, L. C. Handy, & E. J. Mash (Eds.), *Behavior change: Methodology, concepts and practice.* Champaign, IL: Research Press.

Weiss, R. L., & Perry, B. A. (1979). *Assessment and treatment of marital dysfunction.* Unpublished manuscript, University of Oregon, Department of Psychology, Oregon Marital Studies Program, Eugene, OR. (Address correspondence to Robert L. Weiss, Department of Psychology, University of Oregon, Eugene, OR 97403.)

8

SEXUAL DYSFUNCTION: LOW SEXUAL DESIRE
JERRY M. FRIEDMAN AND DOUGLAS R. HOGAN

Friedman and Hogan, both experienced sex therapists who have worked in one of the most sophisticated sex therapy centers in the country, point out that the typical case seen by sex therapists today is not the classic or pure sexual dysfunction problem with which everyone is so familiar. Rather, the cases are more complex and often beset by marital and motivational difficulties as well as a range of psychopathology in addition to the specific presenting sexual problem. Perhaps for these reasons, among others, our estimates of initial success with behavioral treatments has dropped considerably despite the fact that behavioral approaches are still far and away the treatment of choice, based on the evidence. Furthermore, our documentation of relapses has also increased. It is to this type of complex case that Friedman and Hogan turn their expert attention.

Within the context of increasingly complex cases, has emerged recently the seemingly ubiquitous problem of low sexual desire. Friedman and Hogan are certainly among the most knowledgeable in the world regarding this problem, which has come to be recognized by sex therapists as one of the most common and yet difficult disorders. Their comprehensive and extremely knowledgeable discussion of the conceptualization, assessment, and treatment of this problem provides a state-of-the-art account of current thinking and practice. And yet, despite the complexities of the case and the difficulties inherent in treating low sexual desire, all clinicians will recognize their own sexually dysfunctional patients in this chapter and can only benefit from increased familiarity with the most advanced treatment approaches.

Many different specific techniques are described in this chapter that have been gleaned from different sources. While the basic Masters and Johnson procedures remain, a description of the variety of additional innovative and seemingly effective procedures is a highlight of the chapter. Friedman and Hogan describe the integration of these techniques into treatment. In addition, some basic essentials of systems theory are integrated into behavioral treatment in yet another manifestation of the importance of involving the patient's social system in the therapeutic effort. But the sex therapists, with their necessary emphasis on the marital unit, have been doing this as long as anybody, and Friedman and Hogan are on the cutting edge of this development.—D. H. B.

Jerry M. Friedman. Department of Psychology, State University of New York at Stony Brook, Stony Brook, New York.

Douglas R. Hogan. Private practice, Garden City Park, New York.

INTRODUCTION

In the late 1950s Joseph Wolpe and James Semans initiated the behavioral treatment of sexual dysfunctions. Wolpe's (1958) *Psychotherapy by Reciprocal Inhibition* described the successful application of classical conditioning procedures to anxiety-based sexual disorders, and Semans's (1956) article described the "stop–start" method for treating premature ejaculation. In the next two decades, these works were followed by a number of creative and innovative behavioral, cognitive–behavioral, and quasi-behavioral approaches to the treatment of sexual problems, including Albert Ellis's (1962, 1971) rational–emotive therapy, Masters and Johnson's (1970) conjoint sex therapy, Arnold Lazarus's (1971a, 1971b, 1974) multimodal behavior therapy, and Joseph LoPiccolo's (1978) direct treatment of sexual dysfunctions. Although not all of these approaches were explicitly derived from behavioral principles or from laboratory experiments, they have in common a direct approach to the modification of sexual behavior rather than a treatment focus on hypothesized underlying dynamics and an emphasis on empirical validation of treatment techniques.

A number of studies found these approaches to be effective (Heiman & LoPiccolo, 1983; Hogan, 1978; Husted, 1972; Kockett, Dittmar, & Nusselt, 1978; Kohlenberg, 1974; Laughren & Kass, 1975; LoPiccolo & Hogan, 1979; Masters & Johnson, 1970; Mathews *et al.*, 1976; Munjack *et al.*, 1976; Obler, 1973), and by the late 1970s behavioral sex therapy had replaced the earlier psychodynamic approach as the treatment of choice for sexual dysfunctions.

Paradoxically, at the same time that behavioral approaches to sexual dysfunction have become the treatment of choice, several investigators have begun to question the extent of their current effectiveness. Three factors have prompted this questioning:

1. Recent experimental studies of the effectiveness of behavioral sex therapy, in which quantitative outcome measures and follow-up assessments were employed, found that, although these techniques were effective in treating sexual dysfunctions, they did not consistently result in the dramatic success rates claimed in earlier studies, and there was a significant relapse rate at long-term follow-up (DeAmicis, Goldberg, LoPiccolo, Friedman, & Davies, 1984, 1985; Heiman & LoPiccolo, 1983; J. LoPiccolo, Heiman, Hogan, & Roberts, in press).

2. Zilbergeld and Evans (1980) reevaluated the methodology of Masters and Johnson's (1970) study and concluded that the direct, quasi-behavioral techniques might not have been as successful as their proponents claimed.

3. There has been a noticeable change in the nature of the sexual problems that are presented to sex therapists. Cases seem to be much more complex than the ones seen years ago, with multiple dysfunctions being presented, and severe individual and relationship problems present, in addition to sexual problems. One reason that cases of "pure" sexual dysfunction are becoming increasingly rare, is that many people are taking advantage of self-help books and information available in the public press to help themselves. The cases that actually enter therapy often do not respond to an approach that focuses exclusively on reducing anxiety and providing education. Thus, a significant number of dysfunctional clients fail to respond to straightforward behavioral procedures (Kaplan, 1977; Zilbergeld & Evans, 1980).

Treatment failures seem to differ from earlier successful cases in a number of ways. They tend to exhibit more individual psychopathology, their marriages are more distressed, and they are less motivated to change.

One of the most striking changes in the nature of the problems presented for sex therapy is a marked increase in the incidence of low sexual desire, both alone and in conjunction with other dysfunctions (Kaplan, 1979; L. LoPiccolo, 1980). This is especially interesting, since low desire was not even identified as a discrete sexual problem by Masters and Johnson (1970) nor by Kaplan in her earlier work (1974). While there has been some mention in the literature of disinterest in sex for females, it is certainly the case that males presenting with low sexual desires were virtually unknown until the middle to late 1970s. Kaplan (1979) found that many of the treatment failures involved low sexual desire. She indicates that the prognosis for disorders of desire is substantially poorer than for excitement and orgasm dysfunctions. Even when low desire is successfully treated, the course of treatment tends to be longer, stormier, and more complex. Kaplan estimates that only 10%–15% of clients with inhibited sexual desire are "cured" within the average 15 sessions of sex therapy.

In response to these three factors and the consequent questioning of the effectiveness of the behavioral treatment of sexual dysfunctions, a number of clinicians have proposed treatment models integrating behavior therapy with other therapeutic approaches, particularly for complex cases involving inhibited sexual desire. Heiman, LoPiccolo, and LoPiccolo (1981) and J. LoPiccolo and Friedman (1985) have integrated behavioral techniques with a systems theory perspective; Kaplan (1979) has developed what she calls "psychosexual therapy," combining behavioral and psychodynamic techniques for cases of inhibited sexual desire; and L. LoPiccolo (1980) has proposed a multicomponent approach involving hormonal treatment, medication, cognitive and behavioral techniques, sensory awareness training, marital therapy, and psychodynamic techniques. This integration of behavioral techniques with other therapeutic approaches appears to be part of a general movement in this direction in the field of psychotherapy (Goldfried, 1980).

Over the past few years, a multidimensional behavioral treatment model for inhibited sexual desire has been developed. This model integrates four therapeutic components that have been found to be particularly effective for such cases (Friedman, 1983).

1. Experiential/sensory awareness exercises. Many clients presenting with inhibited sexual desire are unable to verbalize their feelings and are often unaware of their affective responses to situations involving sexual cues and sexual stimulation. In the course of therapy, it becomes apparent that these clients are experiencing strong feelings, such as anxiety, anger, or disgust, but they are at best only vaguely aware of these feelings. Experiential/sensory awareness exercises are used to help these clients become aware of these unacknowledged feelings.

2. *Insight.* Clients presenting with inhibited sexual desire routinely have misconceptions and self-defeating attributions as to the cause of their problems. For example, a man who is extremely enraged at his wife will attribute his lack of sexual desire for her to his increasing age or to an as yet undiagnosed physiological disorder. In the insight component of therapy, a client is helped to reformulate his or her attributions about the cause of the problem. The new insight or attribution does not have to be a complete description of all of the etiological components in the case under consideration (as Kaplan, 1979, points out, most cases of inhibited desire have multiple causes), but it must be a plausible and essentially accurate explanation. There is also an attempt to reformulate the problem in a way that is conducive to therapeutic change. For example, if a sexually anxious and inhibited man attributes his lack of desire to the fact that "That's just the way I am" (i.e., "I can't change"), he would be helped to see that his anxiety about sex (a factor that is potentially susceptible to therapeutic intervention) is lowering his sexual desire.

3. *Cognitive restructuring.* The cognitive restructuring component is aimed at altering irrational thoughts that inhibit the client's sexual desire. (These thoughts are more specific and immediate than the more general attributions and insights discussed above.) For example, if a client thinks that a man should always be able to get an erection with a woman, even if his partner provides no direct tactile stimulation, he might lose his sexual desire as a result of repeated failures at attempting to achieve an erection. In this phase of therapy, an attempt is made to replace such a cognition with more adaptive thoughts concerning sexual stimulation, arousal, and desire (e.g., "It's perfectly normal for a middle-aged man to require some physical stimulation to become aroused.").

4. *Behavioral interventions.* The final component of this model consists of direct behavioral assignments. Such assignments include the basic sex therapy and *in vivo* desensitization procedures developed by Wolpe (1958), Masters and Johnson (1970), and J. LoPiccolo (1978). In addition, nonsexual behavioral procedures (e.g., Bandura, 1969; Rimm & Masters, 1974) are utilized when indicated. Specific behavioral assignments are given that complement and potentiate the other three components. For example, a woman with inhibited desire might be assigned to do something pleasurable (but nonsexual) for herself between therapy sessions. If the woman feels guilty about doing almost *anything* that gives her pleasure (as is sometimes the case), the behavioral assignment will dramatically highlight this pleasure inhibition, and pave the way for a verbal intervention aimed at insight into one of the causes of her inhibited desire (e.g., "Perhaps your feelings of guilt over doing anything pleasurable for yourself are inhibiting you from experiencing pleasure in sex.").

These four components are employed in an integrated fashion throughout the course of treatment. Although one or two of the components might predominate in any particular case, most cases of inhibited sexual desire require at least some focus on each of the four components.

In this chapter the definition, diagnosis, assessment, and etiology of inhibited sexual desire will be discussed. The four treatment components will be described in greater detail and a case study of male inhibited sexual desire treated according to this model will be presented.

DEFINITION AND DIAGNOSIS

In 1974 Kaplan introduced a biphasic diagnostic system for sexual dysfunction. The dysfunctions were divided into "excitement phase" (erectile dysfunctions in men and general sexual dysfunction in women) and "orgasm phase" (premature ejaculation and retarded ejaculation in men and orgasmic dysfunction in women). Kaplan also included several dysfunctions that did not fit neatly into the biphasic system: vaginismus, dyspareunia, and sexual phobias. At this time, there was still no mention of desire problems. However, in 1979 Kaplan expanded her model to a triphasic one, adding desire phase dysfunctions to her classification system. Kaplan subdivided desire phase disorders into (1) "inhibited sexual desire," in which psychological factors have inhibited a person's sexual desire; (2) "hypoactive sexual desire," in which the etiology is undetermined; and (3) "hyperactive sexual desire," in which sexual desire is higher than normal.

In 1982 Schover, Friedman, Weiler, Heiman, and LoPiccolo developed a comprehensive, multiaxial, problem-oriented diagnostic system for sexual dysfunctions. This system incorporates features from Kaplan's system, but also contains a number of innovative features. Schover et al.'s system classifies sexual dysfunctions along six independent axes: (1) desire phase, (2) arousal phase, (3) orgasm phase, (4) coital pain, (5) dissatisfaction with frequency of sexual activity, and (6) qualifying information. Each of the first five axes is broken down into various subtypes of dysfunctions. (The two desire phase diagnoses are low sexual desire and aversion to sex.) Diagnoses on the first five axes are further categorized along three dimensions. The first dimension is lifelong versus not lifelong. Problems are labeled "lifelong" if there has never been an occasion of normal functioning. Problems are categorized as "not lifelong" when there has been a period of normal sexual functioning. The second dimension is global versus situational. A "global dysfunction" is one that occurs in all activities engaged in (masturbation, manual or oral stimulation, intercourse) and across partners. "Situational dysfunctions" occur only in some activities or with some partners. The third dimension indicates whether the problem was a presenting complaint of the client, or if the therapist determined that the problem was present. The sixth axis, qualifying information, enables the diagnostician to include in the diagnosis information on marital distress, psychopathology, substance abuse, sexual variations, medical illness, and other variables possibly affecting the client's sexual activity. With each individual potentially having a diagnosis in each of the six axes, this system allows for a precise description of sexual dysfunction and for the recognition of multiple dysfunctions. The use of such a multiaxial diagnostic system reduces the chance that problems of desire will be obscured by another dysfunction.

Although low sexual desire is a topic of current concern for sex therapists, there seems to be little agreement as to what this "syndrome" is, and particularly, how to operationally define it.

As a number of writers have pointed out, "normal" and "abnormal" sexual functioning are difficult terms to define, and the definitions depend upon the sexual attitudes, values, and behaviors of a particular society within a specific historical period, in addition to the values, beliefs, and behaviors of the person who is proposing the definition. Because of these factors, definitions of normal and abnormal sexual functioning are quite varied and change rapidly over time (J. LoPiccolo & Hogan, 1979; L. LoPiccolo & Heiman, 1978; Strupp & Hadley, 1977). These points are particularly relevant in attempting to define a "low desire" sexual dysfunction (Friedman, 1983; Kaplan, 1979; Zilbergeld & Ellison, 1980). Theoretically, if one knew the statistical distribution of the frequency of sexual desire within the general population, one could set a cut-off point for low desire at a certain number of standard deviations from the mean. However, we do not know the statistical distribution of the frequency of sexual desire, and even if we did, the cut-off point would still be highly arbitrary.

Another major difficulty in defining low desire involves the decision as to whether or not (and for whom) it is a problem. Inhibited sexual desire has achieved the status of a mental disorder as a result of its inclusion in DSM-III (American Psychiatric Association, 1980); therefore, by logical implication, a person with inhibited sexual desire is suffering from a mental or emotional disorder. But clinical reality complicates this issue. Friedman (1983) has pointed out that low desire should be defined within the context of a specific relationship. Often, it is the sexual partner of the client with low desire who defines it as a problem. The person with low desire is often perfectly content with his or her own level of desire, and comes to therapy because of pressure from his or her partner. This relationship aspect creates a number of interesting paradoxes in defining low desire, which have been discussed by Zilbergeld and Ellison (1980). Is a person who desires and obtains sex once every other month, who is content with this frequency, and who is not in a steady relationship, suffering from a dysfunction or a mental disorder? What about a person, A, who desires sex once a week, but is in a relationship with a person, B, who desires sex once a day? Suppose we label person A as suffering from low desire. Then A gets a new partner, C, who wants sex once every 2 weeks. Do we now change A's diagnosis to high desire? To complicate things even more, there are some couples in which both partners have low desire, and state that they are fairly content with their sexual frequency. However, they learn from their friends or the mass media that their sexual frequency is "too low", and then seek help because of a vague discontent or a desire to be more normal.

As scientists, we are sometimes tempted to obviate the problem by eliminating the diagnosis of low desire. Zilbergeld and Ellison (1980) have taken the view that the therapist should think in terms of a *desire discrepancy* within the couple, rather than diagnosing low desire in one partner. In some cases (e.g., the wife wants sex three times a week while the husband wants sex once a week) it is, in fact, more appropriate to think in terms of a desire discrepancy in the couple rather than low desire in an individual. However, there are other cases in which the identified low desire client appears to have a pathologically inhibited sex drive, and his or her low desire is creating serious marital distress. These are the global (and sometimes lifelong) low desire cases. Because of the existence of such cases, we must at least formulate a practical, clinical definition of low desire (cf. Zilbergeld & Ellison, 1980).

Friedman (1983) has pointed out that low desire is not a unidimensional phenomenon. A person who desires sexual activity (with any potential partner) only once a month is different from a person who desires sex with his or her spouse once a month, but who desires sex with a lover twice a week. Similarly, a person who once desired sex frequently, but following a period of stress only desires sex once a month, is clearly different from a person who has never desired sex more than once a month. Finally, the person who desires sex (from any and all sources of stimulation) less than once a month is different from a person who masturbates once a day but desires intercourse with her or his spouse only once a month. The modifiers in Schover *et al.*'s (1982) multiaxial diagnostic system (lifelong vs. not lifelong; global vs. situational) are used to highlight these clinical distinctions.

Another distinction made in this diagnostic system is between low desire and aversion toward sex. Some clients have no sexual desire, but experience pleasure and arousal once sex is initiated by their partners. Other clients with low desire find sexual activity repugnant or disgusting, and are therefore given the diagnosis of sexual aversion.

Finally, the multiaxial system highlights the fact that desire phase disorders can occur in isolation or in combination with other dysfunctions (in either the low desire client or in that client's spouse). The multiaxial system is a *descriptive system* and does not make any assumptions about etiology (e.g., whether an erectile dysfunction has caused the low desire or vice versa). However, the multiaxial diagnosis does give a clear picture of the topography (in Skinner's [1953] use of the term) of the desire phase dysfunction under consideration.

The lack of any unique behavioral referent that adequately defines low desire as a dysfunction, and the subjective nature of sexual desire, require the inclusion of subjective criteria in any comprehensive definition. Because of these complexities, the diagnosis of low sexual desire in our research is made on the basis of behavioral, subjective, and clinical criteria. An individual is *arbitrarily* diagnosed as global low desire if individual or partner sexual experiences (including oral, manual, or penile or vaginal stimulation) occur every 2 weeks or less *and* there is evidence of lack of subjective desire for sexual activity (including sex with mate, sex with other partners, masturbation, sexual dreams), lack of fantasies, and an absence of sexual reactions to attractive people of the opposite or same sex. If low frequency and low subjective desire are partner specific, situational low sexure desire is diagnosed.

MEASUREMENT AND ASSESSMENT OF LOW DESIRE

Low desire is as difficult to measure and assess as it is to define. This is largely due to the fact that there is no single behavioral referent for sexual desire. Sexual activity can occur at a "normal" frequency in a low desire individual who is pressured by his or her partner; conversely, low frequency of sexual activity can occur in an individual with "normal" desire as a result of another dysfunction or a partner's refusal of sex. It is even difficult to discover clear cognitive or verbal referents for low desire. There are clients with low desire who, when asked, "How often would you like to have sex?" or "How often do you think about having sex?" answer, "Two or three times a week." These clients, in the abstract, *would like to have* sex two or three times a week, but they do not actually *feel an urge of sexual desire* more than once every 2 weeks. Even a questionnaire item developed specifically to measure low desire ("How frequently do you feel sexual *desire*? This feeling may include wanting to have sex, planning to have sex, feeling frustrated due to a lack of sex, etc. . . ." with multiple choice answers ranging from "more than once a day" to "not at all") did not discriminate men diagnosed as low desire from non-low desire male clients.

J. LoPiccolo and his colleagues have developed a four-stage strategy for assessing couples with sexual dysfunctions. The four stages consist of: (1) questionnaires, (2) an initial intake interview with the couple, (3) medical and hormonal assessment, and (4) separate sexual history interviews with both members of the couple. This assessment strategy has been discussed thoroughly in previous publications (Lobitz & Lobitz, 1978; J. LoPiccolo & Hogan, 1979; L. LoPiccolo & Heiman, 1978; Nowinski & LoPiccolo, 1979), so only the highlights of the process will be presented here.

Each couple is given an extensive battery of questionnaires that assess individual and couple functioning in a number of sexual and nonsexual areas. The battery includes the Sexual Interaction Inventory (J. LoPiccolo & Steger, 1974) and the Sexual History Form (Schover et al., 1982), which assess a variety of dimensions of sexual functioning and sexual dysfunction; the Locke–Wallace Marital Adjustment Test (MAT), which is a measure of general marital satisfaction (Kimmel & Van derVeen, 1974); a Fantasy Scale, which assesses the clients' sexual fantasies; the Brief Symptom Inventory (Derogatis, Lipman, & Covi, 1973), which measures psychological disturbance; the Zung Scale (Zung, 1973), a measure of depression; goal sheets, which ask the clients to write down their goals for therapy; and a Medical Form, which asks questions about the clients' medical history, current medical status, medications, and drugs. These questionnaires provide a detailed picture of the clients' sexual, marital, and psychological status, and are very useful as aids in screening out cases for whom sex therapy would not be appropriate (particularly the Locke–Wallace MAT), for planning treatment (the Sexual Interaction Inventory and the Sexual History Form), and for research.

Questionnaires are highly cost effective (in terms of therapist time) for obtaining information: It would be extremely time consuming to gather this amount of information via interviews. However, clients often react negatively to such extensive batteries, and some clients even decline treatment rather than fill out the questionnaires. This is particularly true of low desire clients, who often resent being in therapy to begin with. Therefore, the practicing clinician should use his or her judgment as to whether or not any particular client should be asked to fill out a questionnaire or a battery of questionnaires. (For a contrasting view, and for more detailed information on these questionnaires, see Nowinski & LoPiccolo, 1979.)

The clinical interview remains the most successful method of diagnosing and assessing low sexual desire. The interview should include questions concerning desired and actual frequency of sex with the person's regular partner and with other partners and potential partners (including information on intercourse and on manual, oral, and anal stimulation), masturbation, the person's subjective feelings in reaction to these sexual activities, fantasies, dreams, reactions to attractive people, frequency of viewing or reading erotic material, and subjective reaction to such material. It is particularly important to interview the partner of the low desire client, who often will provide more accurate information on some aspects of the desire problem. It is not uncommon to encounter couples in which a low desire client says that he or she has not had intercourse for about 6 months, while the partner says that they have not had intercourse for 3 years (and then names the specific date on which they last had sex). Some partners of low desire clients even mark their calendars on the rare occasions when they do have sex.

At the first intake interview, both partners are jointly interviewed by the therapist. The goals of this interview are: (1) to obtain a clear picture of the clients, including their sexual functioning, psychological functioning, and their relationship; (2) to obtain enough information about the clients' problems to diagnose them according to Schover et al.'s (1982) system; (3) to formulate an initial hypothesis as to the etiological factors in the case; and (4) to determine whether sex therapy is appropriate for the couple, or whether the clients would be better served by a different type of treatment (e.g., marital therapy, individual psychotherapy, medical or surgical treatment). Other therapy modes are indicated for couples whose marital problems are so severe that a treatment focus on the sexual problem would be impossible or totally inappropriate; for couples in which one partner is currently having an affair and refuses to terminate the affair; for couples in which one partner is clearly not committed to the relationship; for individuals who are acutely psychotic or severely depressed; for active alcoholics who refuse to stop drinking; and for clients in whom the sexual problem is clearly secondary to a medical problem, and who should receive medical treatment prior to or instead of sex therapy.

The intake interview complements the questionnaires in several ways. While questionnaires are useful and efficient for quickly collecting a large amount of detailed, highly specific information, the interview is superior for obtaining more global, intuitive information about the couple. For example, information is obtained about how each of the clients views the problem; what the problem means for each of them; how the couple interacts verbally and nonverbally during the interview (e.g., to what extent and in what ways do the clients fight or show affection during the interview); how we (as therapists and as people) respond to each of the clients; how attractive, empathic, verbal, intelligent, and motivated the clients are; whether or not they appear psychotic or clinically depressed; and whether or not the couple would be able to engage constructively in sex therapy.

The intake interview is also useful for clarifying clients' questionnaire responses, for having them elaborate on their questionnaire responses, and for gaining an understanding of the frequent contradictions that appear in the questionnaire responses.

In conducting the interview, it is important to start with nonthreatening questions, such as "How did the two of you first meet?" and "What originally attracted you to each other?" Next come open ended questions about the problem (e.g., "Now I'd like each of you in turn to describe the problem or problems that brought you here"). Following that come direct questions about: (1) possible dysfunctions in each phase of the sexual process (desire, arousal, orgasm, coital pain); (2) onset, history, frequency, and severity of the problems; and (3) the situations in which the problem occurs and does not occur. Both global and specific questions should be asked about all phases of the couple's sexual functioning (e.g., "Now I'd like you to give me a detailed picture of what happens when the two of you get together sexually. Who usually initiates sex? How do you initiate sex? What types of foreplay do you engage in? How long does intercourse last?"). Clients are requested to give a general description of their marriage, including any serious problems (specifically ask about possible spouse abuse); a description of severe current and past stresses (family, in-laws, work); information on rape or sexual abuse; information on any psychiatric problems and medical problems (including medications); and whether or not they are currently in therapy or have been in therapy in the past.

Following the joint interview, each partner should be interviewed separately. During the individual interview, global questions (e.g., "Is there anything you'd like to tell me now that hasn't come up already?"), and questions concerning masturbation, sexual fantasies, sexual variations, and affairs are asked. If one partner is currently having an affair, the clinician should only accept the couple for sex therapy if the partner having the affair is willing to terminate it. This is required because a serious commitment to therapy and to the relationship is necessary if the therapy is to succeed. Finally, it is useful to ask an open-ended question about any unusual or traumatic events in the person's life. (See Lobitz & Lobitz, 1978, for a more detailed description of the initial intake evaluation.)

The third stage of the assessment process is the medical and hormonal evaluation. Preliminary medical information is obtained on the Medical Form and during the intake interview. This information should be supplemented by a medical history, review of systems, and a physical exam performed by a physician. When possible, male clients should be sent for a series of hormonal analyses including analysis of total testosterone, free testosterone, estradiol, and prolactin.

Following the first three stages of assessment, a decision can be made as to whether sex therapy is appropriate or whether the client(s) should be referred to a more appropriate treatment prior to or instead of sex therapy. If therapy is to continue, the next assessment stage is the sexual history interview.

In order to obtain an adequate sex history, each client should be interviewed individually. The goals of the history interview are to obtain a fairly complete understanding of the clients' sexual development and of the origin and development of the sexual problems, and to obtain a history of the couple's martial relationship. Following the history interview, it is possible to construct a more accurate formulation of the etiological and maintaining factors of the sexual, marital, and psychological problems experienced by the clients.

The history interview covers areas such as family background, childhood sexuality, religious influences, attitudes towards sex held by the family of origin, adolescence, sex education (formal and informal), dating, petting, coital experiences, hetero- and homosexual relationships, current sexual behavior, and current sexual attitudes. Lobitz and Lobitz (1978) discuss in detail the factors that should be covered in the sexual history interview, and L. LoPiccolo and Heiman (1978) have published a complete outline of the questions and areas to be covered in the interview. The most important factors in taking a history are: (1) the clinician should be comfortable asking direct questions about the client's sexual experiences; and (2) the clinician should help the client relax during the interview and should not come across as an inquisitor.

Friedman (1983) has listed additional categories of information that should be obtained when taking a sex history from a low desire client, including: (1) a description of the client's family of origin and of the client's (past and current) relationship with his or her parents; (2) the client's view of himself or herself and the world (e.g., is it a place for him or her to obtain pleasure, to suffer, to achieve?); (3) a history of the client's sexual desire; (4) gender identity issues; (5) preferred gender of sexual objects; and (6) relationship factors (communication, conflict resolution skills, decision making, sharing of responsibilities, affection, sexual satisfaction or dissatisfaction, love and attraction, expression of anger, power balance and power conflict, future relationship goals, and relationships with his or her children).

When interviewing the low desire client, the clinician should determine (1) whether or not the problem is lifelong, (2) whether the onset of the problem was associated with any particular event, (3) whether or not the problem was present in other intimate relationships, and (4) whether or not the problem is limited to certain sexual activities. It is critical to ask *both* partners all of the important questions. The role of the nonsymptomatic partner should not be ignored. Table 8-1 summarizes issues that need to be covered in the sexual history of clients with low sexual desires.

TABLE 8-1.   Issues to Be Covered in the Sexual History Interview

---

Individual history and assessment

Two generations—family structure
Assess for psychopathology
Interactive style
  (how communicative, assertive; how the individual goes about getting needs met)
Ethics, morals, religious beliefs
Individual life goals
Level of anxiety
  (both sexual and otherwise)
Extramarital relationships
Love for partner
"Filters"
  (how the individual views the world—is it a place to get pleasure? to suffer? to achieve? etc.)

Individual sexual history

Early sexual learning
Early sexual experience
History of frequency and desire
Masturbation
  (history and current behavior)
Sexual attitudes
Fantasies
Gender preference

Relationship history and status

Conflict resolution
Communication skills
Decision making and responsibility sharing
Affection
Sexual satisfaction
  (or dissatisfaction and how it is expressed)
Relationship with children and parents
Expression of anger
  (how? over what?)
Love and attraction
Power
Future relationship goals

Etiology of Low Sexual Desire

At this time, there is very little sound, empirical knowledge concerning the etiology of low sexual desire. However, clinicians have noted many possible causal factors of these variables, including biochemical, constitutional, hereditary, and environmental factors (L. LoPiccolo, 1980).

In a quasi-empirical study, L. LoPiccolo (1980) reviewed case reports of low desire at the Sex Therapy Center at Stony Brook, and found seven factors to be associated with low desire: depression, Catholicism, another sexual dysfunction, aversion to oral–genital contact, aversion to female genitals (in both male and female low desire patients), absence of masturbation, and marital problems denied by the couple. Kaplan (1977) has focused on fear of romantic success and fear of intimacy as major factors in the etiology of inhibited desire.

Although we have seen virtually all of these factors in at least some of the low desire cases that we have treated, it must be emphasized that at least some of these factors are probably artifacts of the uncontrolled nature of the clinical observation, and definitive statements concerning the actual causal pathways involved in the etiology of low desire cannot be made. For example, Kaplan (1974) has pointed out that many people with "unresolved Oedipal conflicts" do not have sexual dysfunctions, while some people who exhibit no evidence of "unresolved Oedipal conflicts" do have dysfunctions. Similarly, two of the factors (Catholicism and other sexual dysfunctions) found by L. LoPiccolo in her case review may be, in part, artifacts of the source of her sample: a sex therapy center on (predominantly Catholic) Long Island.

Kaplan (1974, 1977) and L. LoPiccolo (1980) have made three points about the etiology of low sexual desire that are of particular importance in attempting to understand this complex phenomenon: (1) the list of factors that can contribute to the etiology of low sexual desire is long and highly varied; (2) in any particular case a number of these factors may be involved; and (3) these factors can interact with one another and with low desire through complex constellations of feedback loops.

The authors' clinical experience over the past several years has led to a focus on a series of factors that appear to play a particularly strong role in the etiology of low desire. This series of factors includes variables operating at both the individual and relationship levels.

Individual-Based Factors

1. Performance anxiety. The same performance anxiety that may manifest itself in other cases in arousal and orgasm dysfunction can also contribute to low desire.

2. Stress. This refers to any life stress and anxiety other than sexual performance anxiety that may be inhibiting sexual desire. Probably any aversive event, if it occurs at a sufficiently high intensity and/or a sufficiently high frequency, can lead to low desire.

3. Depression. Clinical and subclinical levels of depression may be strong contributors to low sexual desire.

4. Deficient sexual learning history. This includes lack of information, deficient learning of sexual techniques, inappropriate role models, and deficits in the ability to sexually fantasize or to attend to sexual cues.

5. Absence of sexually arousing stimuli and/or the presence of aversive stimuli in the sexual situation. This can include individual- or couple-level avoidance of potentially sexually stimulating cues and not placing oneself in situations that would elicit sexual thoughts and feelings.

6. Antipleasure, antisex bias. This is an aspect of what is commonly called "the Puritan ethic," in which sex is viewed as frivolous and a waste of time. The individual just does not view himself or herself as a sexual person. Negative parental attitudes toward sex are important in the development of this outlook.

7. Idealized sexual expectations. If an individual has unrealistically high expectations about what a sexual experience "should" be like, he or she will consistently be disappointed, frustrated, and resentful. Such expectations can be based on portrayals of sex in Hollywood films, romantic or erotic novels, and on what the clients' friends say about their own sex lives.

8. Other sexual dysfunctions. Low desire often appears to be secondary to arousal dysfunctions, orgasmic dysfunctions, or to dyspareunia.

9. Religious prohibitions and guilt. Many low desire clients learned as children that sex is bad or sinful. Even though these clients, in adulthood, may not consciously believe that sex is sinful, they react to sexual activity, desire, and pleasure with feelings of guilt.

10. Displaced affect. Many clients have very disturbed relationships with their parents, particularly with the parent of the opposite sex. There is no single pattern that describes all of these parent–child relationships; rather, the disturbances take a number of different forms. In some cases the opposite-sex parent was overtly seductive, or the parent and child had an overtly incestuous relationship. In some cases an opposite-sex parent was extremely domineering and controlling. In other cases, female clients were overly involved with their mothers. As a result of these disturbed relationships, the clients experienced strong negative feelings (e.g., anger, rage) and/or sexual arousal and desire for a parent. Sometimes, the clients are aware that they had these feelings for their parents, while in other cases, the clients clearly describe the disturbed relationship in an interview, and we infer the affect.

When these clients marry they often feel similar negative feelings or combined negative and sexual feelings for their spouses. Usually, they are not conscious of these angry feelings toward their spouses (who often turn out to be as domineering, controlling, or seductive as the parents were), and the clients often strongly deny such feelings. The feelings are usually revealed by verbal implications, through outright verbal attacks on the partner, and through nonverbal cues (e.g., vocal tone, inflection, and volume; gestures; and posture).

Psychoanalytic constructs provide the most concise description of these patterns: These clients appear to have unresolved Oedipal conflicts, and consequently displace affect originally felt toward a parent into the spouse.

11. Conflict over sexual object choice. Some low desire clients may prefer same-sex partners. The existence of this homosexual desire may be: (1) admitted to the therapist, but not to the spouse; (2) not admitted to either the therapist or the spouse; or even (3) denied by the client to himself or herself. An example of the first category was a case in which the male low desire client admitted to the therapist that he had always had gender identity conflicts, often masturbated while cross-dressed, and would fantasize that he was a woman making love to a man while cross-dressing and masturbating. The wife was unaware of this.

A case in the third category (latent homosexuality), involved a low desire male client whose wife told the initial intake interviewer about a fantasy that her husband employed during intercourse. He would fantasize that his penis belonged to his wife, and that he was being penetrated by her penis. When the couple's therapists asked the male client about this, he denied ever having had such a fantasy. Later in therapy he admitted using the fantasy during intercourse, but quickly added that he only did so to arouse his wife. She, however, said that she had always found her husband's fantasy unpleasant. During all of these discussions, the male client's affect, as expressed through nonverbal cues, suggested extreme psychological conflict around this area.

Relationship-Based Factors

1. Lack of attraction to the partner, often accompanied by attraction to and affairs with other lovers. This produces the classic situational low desire pattern, but may result in global low desire as well, if guilt is also present.

2. Sexual communication deficit or inhibition. This involves the inability of clients to ask their partners to provide the types of sexual stimulation that would produce arousal. Consequently, these clients do not receive arousing sexual stimulation, and eventually lose interest in sex.

3. Inability to express anger directly. Many low desire clients would be diagnosed as having passive–aggressive or dependent personalities. These clients are unable to directly express anger toward their partners. Consequently, they lose desire as a result of the unexpressed anger, or else withhold sex as a passive–aggressive act.

4. Avoidance or fear of intimacy. In many cases the sexual relationship is satisfactory prior to marriage; however, once the marriage commitment is made, one partner loses desire as a way to maintain distance in the relationship. Kaplan (1979) and Zilbergeld and Ellison (1980) have discussed this pattern in depth.

5. Fear of vulnerability. This involves lack of trust for the partner, fear of being taken advantage of if one desires sex, fear of letting go, or fear of loss of control over oneself.

6. Sex-role issues and sex-role conflicts. In the past few decades, dramatic changes have taken place in our societal attitudes concerning sex-role behavior. These changes have led to ambivalent and confused feelings on the part of many clients in regard to their own and their partners' masculinity or femininity.

7. *Power and control conflicts.* Withholding sex is one way of maintaining control in a relationship in which an individual has few other ways of maintaining control. Although the overt conflict is over sex, the underlying dynamic is a power conflict.

8. *Conflicts concerning pregnancy and childbirth.* Fear of pregnancy or childbirth, particularly in a person who has strong religious beliefs against the use of artificial contraception methods, or whose spouse strongly desires children, can inhibit sexual desire.

9. *Love versus sex.* Frequently, male clients with situational low desire feel sexual desire toward attractive, sexy women. However, these men are unable to feel desire toward their more conservative, sexually restrained wives, whom they love. They wish to see their partners as good wives and mothers, and not as sexual beings.

It would be esthetically pleasing to be able to report that the above factors tend to cluster in predictable patterns, that a specific type of personality subjected to a specific type of stress will develop low desire, or that the different subtypes of low desire are usually associated with specific etiological factors. However, this is not the case. These etiological factors can combine in kaleidoscopic fashion and can interact in complex ways to produce different patterns of low desire. It is this extreme variability and lack of predictability that necessitates a multistage, individualized assessment strategy and a multicomponent, highly individualized approach to the treatment of low sexual desire.

TREATMENT OF LOW SEXUAL DESIRE

Setting, Client, and Therapist Variables

The treatment model for low sexual desire is flexible and readily adaptable to a variety of clinical settings. The model was developed and first implemented by the authors at the State University of New York at Stony Brook. The treatment model has also been used in private practice settings with only minor adaptations (e.g., increased flexibility in terms of number of sessions). The treatment model can be used in general psychotherapy or marital therapy clinics, hospital psychiatry outpatient clinics, clinics in psychology or social work departments at universities, and psychotherapy training institutes.

There are two factors that could impede the implementation of this model in certain clinical settings: (1) The model requires a high level of skill, knowledge, and sophistication on the part of the therapist. Advanced graduate students in clinical psychology have been trained to use this treatment model, but only under close supervision, involving the supervisor's viewing of videotapes of therapy sessions and observation of therapy sessions from behind a one-way mirror. Neophyte therapists who are not specifically trained in sex therapy, not adept at both psychotherapy and marital therapy, and not closely supervised by an experienced sex therapist will have difficulty mastering this model. (2) The model requires an eclectic mental set on the part of the therapist. Therefore, a clinical setting in which any one theoretical approach is rigidly adhered to in a doctrinaire manner will not be an appropriate setting for this treatment model.

An important treatment variable is the participation of both sexual partners in the treatment process. The treatment of low sexual desire in clients without partners is extremely problematic: Relationship factors cannot be addressed in such a situation, and many of the sexual homework assignments require the participation of two people. In addition, even when one focuses exclusively on the individual-level factors involved in such a case, therapy can take on a somewhat abstract quality when there is no current partner.

However, the sex therapist is frequently confronted with cases in which single individuals, usually male, seek help for low sexual desire (often in conjunction with erectile dysfunction). A modified version of the model is used in such cases. If the person presents with global low sexual desire, the first three phases of the program (experimental/sensory awareness, insight, and cognitive restructuring) can be employed as usual, as can those behavioral assignments that do not require a partner. (Individuals with situational low desire are unlikely to seek therapy individually with low desire as the presenting complaint. If such a client did seek therapy, an extremely careful assessment would be required.) In addition to these components of therapy, it is imperative that the therapist focuses on those variables that, in addition to low desire, prevent the client from obtaining a partner or maintaining a stable relationship (e.g., interpersonal anxiety, social skills inhibitions or deficits). The therapist also directly encourages the client to attempt to form a relationship (or relationships). Once the client enters into a relationship, more information regarding the etiology and maintenance of the desire disorder will be obtained, and it may be possible to give behavioral assignments that involve the partner.

It is even more difficult to treat individuals who have partners, but whose partners refuse to enter therapy with them. This refusal usually indicates (1) that the partner blames the dysfunctional individual for the problem and is refusing to share any responsibility and/or (2) that serious marital problems exist. In either case direct treatment of the low desire is virtually impossible. If the therapist attempts to give the dysfunctional individual behavioral assignments to do with the partner at home, the partner (or the dysfunctional individual) will usually sabotage therapy. In such cases the focus should not be directly on the low desire, but rather on the client's attitudes and feelings toward himself or herself, toward the partner, and toward the relationship. Other client variables that contraindicate the application of this treatment model are: (1) low desire with a totally organic etiology; (2) severe marital problems; (3) lack of commitment of one partner to the relationship; (4) acute psychosis; (5) severe depression; or (6) current alcoholism or drug abuse.

Client variables that appear to be associated with a successful outcome include: (1) strong commitment to the relationship on the part of both partners;

(2) a feeling of love on the part of each partner toward the other; (3) motivation for change on the part of each partner; (4) lack of defensiveness; (5) good health; (6) the absence of current severe stress; and (7) a positive working relationship between the client couple and the therapist.

There are no empirical studies available on therapist variables that influence therapy outcome in the treatment of low sexual desire. Presumably, the therapist variables that influence outcome in psychotherapy and marital therapy in general are also important in sex therapy with low desire patients. Such factors as therapist warmth, empathy, lack of significant intrapsychic conflict around sexual issues and sex role issues, the ability to discuss sexual issues in a direct and relaxed manner, and knowledge about human sexuality and sex therapy are all important for successful outcome. The therapist must also be skilled in a number of therapeutic modalities to implement this treatment approach effectively. Low desire is the most difficult of the dysfunctions to treat, and the therapist must be at least moderately skilled and knowledgable about cognitive-behavior therapy, communication-systems theory, and marital and sex therapy. In addition, some knowledge of psychodynamic, Gestalt, and transactional analysis techniques and concepts is helpful.

Preparation for Therapy

The following is a description of how low desire clients may be prepared for treatment. Some of the elements described are relevant to all clinical settings, while others are relevant only to clinical research or training centers.

At the intake interview the therapist provides the clients with a description of the following: (1) procedures at the clinical setting as applicable, including the time-limited nature of the therapy (15–25 sessions), videotaping of therapy sessions (for training and supervision), observation of sessions by staff members through a one-way mirror, and the clients' participation in the research program; (2) the patients' responsibilities (e.g., regular attendance of therapy sessions on the part of both partners, fees, filling out questionnaires); and (3) the treatment program. Due to reports about sex therapy in the mass media, patients often have the fear or fantasy that they will be required to engage in sexual activity at the clinical setting. They are directly informed at the intake interview that no sexual activities take place during therapy sessions, that the therapy sessions involve only verbal, and not sexual, behavior; and that all sexual activity will take place in the privacy of their homes.

The importance of mutual responsibility of the couple for solving the problem is emphasized, as is the concept of the sexual problem being a problem of the couple, and not just a problem of one of the partners. Because of the necessity of both partners being totally involved in the treatment process, it is explained to each partner (individually) that any current extramarital affairs must be terminated.

The therapist tells the clients that the core of the therapy process is a series of homework assignments that will be individually tailored for them and that these assignments will require a strong motivation on both their parts and a considerable commitment in terms of time and effort. The therapist briefly outlines the type of assignments (e.g., sensual massage, a temporary ban on intercourse, masturbation if indicated, and a gradual progression of assignments). The clients are informed that the therapy sessions will usually include both partners and will focus on their reactions to the behavioral assignments and on learning to change and improve their sexual functioning. They are told that they may be asked to purchase one or more books on sexual topics (e.g., Heiman, LoPiccolo, & LoPiccolo's [1976] *Becoming Orgasmic* or Zilbergeld's [1978] *Male Sexuality*, and that they may be shown educational films with explicit sexual content. Finally, the clients are given the opportunity to ask questions concerning the treatment program.

The preparation of the clients is completed following the first session of therapy. Following the sexual history interviews, the therapist gives the couple feedback about his or her formulation and the rationale for the treatment program.

The Therapeutic Program

The program is based on the following therapeutic assumptions:

1. Many clients with low desire are not aware of their affective responses to sexual stimuli. They frequently state that sex is a neutral experience, yet behave as if engaging in sexual activity were negative, or as if they derived some positive gains from not engaging in sexual activity. Therefore, one goal of therapy is to help clients become aware of their physical responses associated with their affective response under the assumption that these responses can provide important informational feedback.

2. It is clinically useful for clients to have some idea *why* they have low desire. Being able to attribute their desire difficulties to something concrete and understandable allows them to adopt a solution-oriented cognitive set.

3. There is no evidence for a qualitative difference between inhibition of sexual desire and aversion to sex. Those who complain of aversion to sex have a much stronger active negative emotional response to sex and are consciously aware of this negative response. The treatment concept remains the same for both low sexual desire and aversion to sex, while the content and focus may vary.

4. It is important for the *couple* to be involved in the therapy, although some therapy time may be spent with each partner alone. This is based on the clinical observation that the higher desire partner is often a contributor to the maintenance, if not the cause, of the problem.

5. The use of a graded series of sexual tasks beginning with mutual sensual pleasuring, and leading eventually to intercourse (Masters & Johnson, 1970) remains a part of the treatment program. These tasks serve two functions in the current program; (a) to elicit emotional responses during the course of therapy, and (b) to provide a set of behaviors in which the clients can use self-help skills gained during therapy.

Four major overlapping elements provide the conceptual framework for treating couples with low sexual desire or aversion to sex. These elements are drawn from different theoretical orientations, and within the context of this therapy format, provide a comprehensive, integrative method for treating low desire within a brief therapy framework of 15–25 sessions. A special emphasis of this program is on maintenance and generalization of the therapeutic gains. The four elements are experiential therapy and sensory awareness, insight, cognitive restructuring, and behavioral assignments. These are described briefly below. The case study material will demonstrate how each phase is implemented.

Experiential/Sensory Awareness

It is assumed that sexually related anxiety underlies most cases of low sexual desire, even though many low desire clients may claim complete neutrality about sex. Such a client may acknowledge that when sex is engaged in it is somewhat enjoyable, but report that he or she could go on indefinitely without sex if the partner did not initiate. Usually, in these cases, the couple presents for therapy at the insistence of the extremely distressed, higher desire partner who may have threatened leaving the relationship if the difficulty is not resolved. The low desire partner often agrees to come for therapy, not because of a motivation to change the sexual appetite, but to "save" the relationship. One cannot help but wonder why, if sex is truly a neutral experience, the low desire client does not engage in it simply to satisfy the partner and eliminate the relationship distress that results from not engaging in sex. Clearly, sex is not a neutral experience, but one that is being actively avoided. In some cases there may be other affective reactions, besides anxiety, operating. For example, in a relationship where the only power an individual has is to withhold sex, this "punishment" of a partner can produce feelings such as satisfaction or even pleasure.

The experiential phase of therapy is an attempt to get clients to recognize, using bodily cues, when they are experiencing anxiety, fear, satisfaction, pleasure, anger, digust, and other negative reactions. While some clients deny any feelings about sex, labeling it a neutral experience, others do recognize a generalized negative response but cannot identify or label the feeling. Still others can only recognize feelings after the feelings have become intense, but do not recognize the early stages and progressive nature of these feelings. The experiential phase of this program helps clients attend to bodily cues and thereby recognize the early stages of their affective response and also helps them to identify these feelings. For example, some clients may attribute their lack of sexual desire to a feeling of anger toward their spouse. However, anger is often an "umbrella" feeling, covering other feelings such as fear of rejection, fear of intimacy, frustration, or hurt. This phase of therapy can help clients make these differentiations. Most clients who experience difficulty with recognizing and labeling their feelings do so not only in the sexual area, but in other areas of their life as well. Body awareness training and other interventions derived from the Gestalt tradition (Fagan & Shepherd, 1970; Perls, 1960; Stevens, 1971; Zinker, 1977) are used extensively in this phase of the therapy.

Clients are frequently asked questions such as "How do you feel about. . . ?" and helped to differentiate responses that reflect their cognitive rather than their affective states. Clients are encouraged to identify and describe the cues that mediate their feelings and may also be asked such questions as, "How do you know that you are feeling happy (sad, etc.)? Describe the feelings in your body." Homework and in-session assignments that include sensate focus, fantasy training, and body awareness exercise are quite useful. After clients have learned to fantasize, a typical assignment might be to spend 10 min fantasizing a pleasurable scene and identifying bodily responses and then fantasizing an anxiety-provoking scene and identifying bodily responses. Frequently, it may be necessary to elicit emotional responses in-session from clients who deny their feelings. This can be done through encouragement, by provocation, by giving permission to be angry, sad, happy, and so on, and by use of such Gestalt techniques as the "empty chair" or imaginal recreation of an earlier traumatic experience. The amount of time spent in this phase of therapy will depend on how much difficulty the client has in acknowledging, identifying, and labeling feelings. The insight phase of therapy may be done concurrently with the experiential phase. However, if the client demonstrates strong resistance to the experiential exercises, or is unable to engage in these exercises, the insight phase is implemented first.

Insight

In the insight phase of therapy, the therapist helps the clients gain insight into the factors that cause and maintain the low sexual desire. While insight, even when combined with standard behavioral sex therapy, may not be sufficient to induce significant clinical changes in a reasonable amount of time for most low desire couples, it is often a necessary part of the change process, because it enables the clients to begin to understand and take responsibility for their own behavior and recognize that change is under their control. In general, when individuals have an explanation for why they behave in a particular way, their anxiety tends to decrease. Insight can also serve to diffuse anger. For example, if a wife learns that her husband has low desire for her because he has difficulty having sex with someone he loves rather than because he does not love her, her feelings of rejection may dissipate, leaving her with fewer angry feelings and a greater willingness to cooperate in therapy. Insight into the factors that cause and maintain the low desire can help provide a cognitive map for the clients, which along with the other elements of this program, can facilitate change. Insight sets the stage for the cognitive and behavioral interventions to follow and provides a rationale for proceeding with these interventions.

The insights are based on material derived from the pretherapy assessment battery, the intake interview, and the individual psychosexual history interviews. Additional information is gathered and processed with each therapy session as each partner's individual personality and the couple's interactive dynamics become more familiar to the therapist. Early sexual assignments provide additional information on how each individual reacts to sexual contact when it is prescribed by the therapist.

The therapist utilizes a number of techniques to help the clients gain insight into their problems. These techniques include interpretation, reframing, empathic reflection, response demand (e.g., "Give me three reasons why intimacy may be frightening to you. You have to come up with three reasons even if you make them up."), and helping the clients to conceptualize family of origin issues within a learning framework (e.g., "Where did you learn that it is uncomfortable to get too close to someone you love?"). During this phase of therapy, the therapist also helps the higher desire partner gain insight into how he or she is contributing to the maintenance of the problem and possibly even to its cause.

The insight phase of the program can vary greatly, both in terms of time and focus, depending upon the particular factors involved. Helping clients recognize that the problem may be due to severe marital distress takes a much shorter time than helping them realize that they are dealing with displacement of anger at an opposite-sex parent.

Cognitive Restructuring

The cognitive phase of therapy helps clients identify self-statements that interfere with sexual functioning. Systematic rational restructuring (Goldfried & Davison, 1976; Goldfried, Decenteceo, & Weinberg, 1974), a structured social learning adaptation of rational–emotive therapy (Ellis, 1962), is employed. The procedure involves helping clients to recognize that self-statements mediate emotional arousal and to accept the general assumption that their emotional reactions can be directly influenced by expectations, labels, and self-statements. They are taught that irrational or unrealistic beliefs may mediate their own emotions, and that practice in changing these unrealistic self-statements can help them reevaluate specific situations more realistically. Individualized coping self-statements are developed to help the client cope with rather than avoid emotional reactions to particular situations. This procedure has been found to be effective in dealing with various problems, including test anxiety, unassertiveness (Linehan, Goldfried, & Goldfried, 1979), interpersonal anxiety (Kanter & Goldfried, 1979), and marital distress (Broderick, Friedman, & Carr, 1981).

Once the clients have accepted the explanation(s) for the low sexual desire and are making good progress toward recognizing bodily cues and identifying feelings, the rational restructuring phase of therapy can begin. One effective technique for introducing this intervention is the use of a "devil's advocate" procedure (Goldfried & Davison, 1976), in which the therapist argues for an irrational belief and the client is instructed to convince the therapist that the belief is indeed irrational. Clients are also made aware of the dysfunctional use of the word "should," and are taught to replace such internal statements as, "You should behave in a certain way" with, "I would like it better if you behaved in a certain way." In addition, clients are helped to generate coping statements to cope with dysfunctional feelings (cued by bodily responses) that may be keeping them from engaging in sexual activity. Such coping statements might include, "Just because I engage in sex does not mean that I'm a bad person," or "I know that when I was younger, I learned to feel guilty about engaging in sex, and I don't want to, nor do I have to, feel that way anymore." Another useful cognitive intervention is to help clients identify and reevaluate their worst fears concerning change in their sexual functioning. For example, the therapist may ask: "What is the worst thing that can happen if you (or your mate) becomes a very sexual person?" Clients are taught that their behavior is, for the most part, under their own control, that they can take responsibility for what they currently do, and that it is within their power to change their own behavior.

A modified transactional analysis framework (Berne, 1964; Steiner, 1974) is utilized to help clients recognize their own power and to help them bridge the gap between feelings and cognition. Clients are told that they have a two-sided "parent" tape (one the judgmental parent, the other the nurturing parent) as well as a two-sided "child" tape (one the frightened or acting-out child, the other the playful child). They are also told that they have an adult processor, which takes input from the environment and from the parent and child tapes and helps them make rational decisions. All feeling responses come from the child, while attitude and opinions come from the parent. Helping the client label feelings, thoughts, and behaviors as coming from the "frightened child" or "scolding parent" can make them more aware of their own responses. They are encouraged to develop their "playful child" and their "nurturing parent." Giving them permission to let their "playful child" out to play often has a direct result in changing sexual behavior.

Behavioral Interventions

The fourth major elements of the program is the behavioral component. Behavioral techniques are used throughout the therapy process for four purposes. First, behavioral interventions are used early in therapy to help induce feelings that clients can then process in the experiential/sensory awareness exercises. These behavioral interventions include progressive sensate focus exercises, behavioral rehearsal, role playing other characters or personality types, and role reversal.

The second purpose of behavioral interventions is to help clients develop alternative methods for interacting with each other and their environment. The goal here is to help resolve some of the issues that may be contributing to the cause and maintenance of the sexual difficulty. The particular interventions selected will depend on what hypotheses the therapist has generated during the insight phase of therapy. Particular interventions that are useful for this purpose include assertion training, behavioral training in communication and negotiation, the use of caring days (Broderick, Friedman, & Carr, 1981), problem solving (Goldfried & Davison, 1976), contact with sympathetic clergy, and stress reduction interventions.

The third major purpose of behavioral interventions is to develop new behavioral skills to help clients function more effectively once therapeutic gains allow for this opportunity. Interventions in this category include bibliotherapy, the use of films about human sexuality and sexual techniques, and training in initiation and refusal.

Lastly, behavioral intervention can be used to "prime the pump," that is, help make sex more salient. "Pump-priming" involves exposure to sexual stimuli both imaginally and *in vivo*. The use of a desire checklist or desire diary can be quite useful. The client is asked to keep a diary of any sexual thoughts or feelings occurring during the day. This helps focus attention on any feelings or thoughts about sex that are present, as well as encourage such feelings or thoughts. The assignment of "fantasy breaks" in which the client is asked to spend several minutes each day consciously having a sexual fantasy is another example of a pump-priming exercise.

Thus, the basic clinical procedure in the treatment of low desire is to help clients to recognize *why* they are not interested in sex, to attend to their bodies for cues to the feelings that usually result in disinterest or avoidance of sex, and to make cognitive coping statements that can lead to alternative responses. They also need to practice alternative responses as well as to practice being sexual. In its most general form, the sequence of internal dialogue is: "I am feeling . . . (awareness). That must be because . . . (insight). Now what can I say to myself that will allow me to respond in a different way in spite of these feelings, or can I accept these feelings and behave differently anyway? (cognitive restructuring)." Behaviorally, the client can now try alternative responses and learn ways to make sex more salient. If the client can become aware of bodily cues identified with a particular affect, and if the feeling can be automatically linked to a cognition that recognizes and copes with the feeling, then it would be extremely difficult for the individual to return to the old way of responding (maintenance). In addition, affective responses to other situations could "trigger" a cognitive reevaluation as well (generalization). This program allows therapists to try a wide variety of interventions geared to a particular case and still have the "security" of operating from within a framework which can tie these interventions together.

CASE STUDY: ANN AND BOB

Ann and Bob, both 30 years old, had been married 4 years at the time of intake. Bob reported that for the past year, he had not been able to get an erection in any way with Ann, and he had experienced no spontaneous sexual desire for her. In the last 6 months, Ann and Bob had completely discontinued any attempts at sexual activity. Bob's desire to masturbate had disappeared as well, and his low desire was global. According to Ann and Bob, the onset of the erectile dysfunction occurred simultaneously with the onset of low desire.

Ann works as a medical assistant and Bob is a salesman. They have no children. Ann is quite committed to having children, while Bob claimed to be ambivalent.

Background: Bob

Bob's parents married late in life and were in their middle 30s when he was born. He had two younger siblings. Bob described his parents' marriage as poor. He described his father as a straight-laced, career-oriented person without much humor, and his mother as a more humanistic "bohemian'" artist. He did not see much of his father as he was growing up and did not feel very close to him. He was somewhat closer to his father at the time of intake and was making an effort to improve the relationship. He did not feel terribly loved as a child, and affection and caring were not shown very much at home. Bob's parents were atheists and taught Bob to be an atheist as well. He described himself as an agnostic. Bob believed his mother held most of the power in the family. His parents had separate bedrooms and he did not think they were very sexually compatible. He thought his mother was probably more sexual than his father. Sex was not discussed in the home and Bob never felt comfortable asking questions concerning sex.

Bob started experimenting with masturbation around the age of 12 or 13 years, at the onset of puberty, and continued to masturbate several times a week. He learned the facts of life from an educational pamphlet that his parents gave him and from his circle of male friends. He described himself as quite shy and not part of the "in" group through most of high school. Bob saw himself both then and as an adult as basically unassertive, someone who wanted to keep things pleasant and "not make waves." As an adolescent, he did have several friends, mostly other "non-mainstream" boys. He began dating at the age of 13 years, and he estimates that he dated approximately eight people before meeting his wife. His early petting experiences were never totally enjoyable because they never occurred in safe places and he could never be completely relaxed. He never attempted intercourse with anyone prior to Ann and always felt some anxiety at the prospect of intercourse. Masturbation fantasies never included intercourse although they were always heterosexual.

Backgound: Ann

Ann's father was an alcoholic. Raging arguments frequently occurred in her home, and her neighbors would call the police to quiet them down. Sometimes Ann's father would hit his wife and children. When Ann was 14 years old, her parents separated. She has three older siblings, all of whom were out of the house and on their own before the separation took place. Ann, however, continued living with her mother. Subsequently, her parents reconciled and her father stopped his drinking.

Ann was raised as a Roman Catholic and remained fairly religious until the age of 17 or 18 years when she claimed to have given up some of her religious beliefs. She met Bob when she was 19 years old and his agnostic views helped her move away from her religion. Ann did not feel terribly close to either of her parents, and she would not have felt comfortable discussing sex with them. She was aware that her parents had sexual problems and believed that this might have contributed to her father's abuse of her mother and the children. Ann's mother suffered from some form of emotional problem and would occasionally "go into a trance" and have to be taken to a hospital emergency room. In more recent years Ann had made an effort to reestablish contact with her father and claimed she was closer to her parents than ever.

When Ann was growing up, her parents were very strict with her, and she was not even permitted to talk to boys until she was in high school. When she did start dating, her parents monitored her time and activities very closely. Ann did not recall how she learned the facts of life, but believed it was probably from her friends. She started to menstruate at the age of 12 years and was not prepared for this. Her older sister calmed her fears and explained the process. Ann dated three boys seriously before meeting Bob and had intercourse with two of them. The first experience was not very enjoyable, but with the second, she became much more aroused and responsive. Ann had never masturbated and claimed that the only reason for not doing so was that it had never occurred to her.

Backgound: Ann and Bob

When Bob and Ann first met, they both felt very attracted to each other. Bob described their first intercourse experience (his first with anyone) as quick and fumbling. The couple continued to see each other for approximately 7 years with one break in the relationship. For the most part, Bob maintained his interest in sex during this time, but found that he always had a certain degree of nervousness during his sexual encounters with Ann. He recalled that he completely let go with her during sex only once or twice. Premature ejaculation occurred during most of these encounters, although neither Bob nor Ann viewed this as a serious problem. Bob described himself as very inhibited about sex, and said that his inhibition prevented him from asking for what he wanted within the sexual relationship. Although Ann was a responsive sexual partner who frequently had orgasms, she found it difficult to completely involve herself sexually and was always somewhat self-conscious and inhibited.

As time went by Bob found himself less attracted to Ann. During the 7-year period that they were dating, Bob had one episode of erectile failure and subsequently decided to break off his relationship with Ann. During the time they were apart, he had a single sexual experience with another woman that did not include intercourse. He decided that he loved Ann and went back to her.

At the start of therapy, Bob and Ann stated that they felt very comfortable together and that they had an excellent relationship and equal partnership. Except for the one experience mentioned above, neither Bob nor Ann had any other sexual or romantic relationships since marrying.

Bob stated that more recently his nervousness and pressure to perform sexually had increased. Bob began having erectile difficulties approximately 1 year before the intake interview. For the first several months after the difficulties began, the couple attempted intercourse two or three times each week. During these attempts, Ann would stimulate Bob's penis manually and, occasionally, orally. However, he did not get any erections at all. They described these encounters as Bob lying rigidly, covered with cold sweat, trying his best to get an erection, while Ann would become very upset and eventually cry at his failure to do so. Ann's distress came mainly from a fear that if Bob did not get an erection, he would leave her, as he had in the past. In the 6 months prior to intake, Ann and Bob had discontinued any attempt at sexual activity at all. Until 2 months prior to intake, Bob masturbated several times each week and did not have any difficulty attaining an erection during masturbation. However, his desire to masturbate had disappeared along with his desire for partner sex, and at the time of intake his low desire was global in nature.

Bob's goals for treatment were to enjoy sex more, to become less inhibited, and to get his erection back. Ann's goals for treatment were to have a better sex life, including intercourse, to communicate more sexually, and to be more relaxed and a better lover.

Ann and Bob reported no significant medical or health problems. At the time of intake, they were not using any method of contraception. Although Ann and Bob reported that their overall communication skills were excellent, they seemed inhibited in the direct expression of anger. Furthermore, even though Bob was very unassertive, Ann yielded to what she perceived to be his wishes in order to avoid a break-up of the relationship. (For results of pretherapy assessment, see section entitled "Assessment Data," later in chapter and including Table 8-3.)

Initial Hypotheses

The intake and history interviews, in combination with the assessment data, yielded the following hypotheses about the etiology and maintenance of Bob's low sexual desire and erectile dysfunction:

1. *Performance anxiety.* Bob's strong concerns about being a good lover and his anxiety over attaining an erection may have inhibited him from obtaining an erection and may have inhibited his sexual desire.

2. *Communication dysfunction.* Both Bob and Ann were uncomfortable, anxious, and inhibited in regard to communicating about sexual issues, particu-

larly in regard to letting one another know what types of sexual stimulation they would have liked to receive. Consequently, it was hypothesized that they were unable to provide one another with pleasurable and arousing sexual stimulation. This further reduced Bob's erectile ability and his sexual desire.

3. Pregnancy and childbirth issues. Ann wanted to have children, while Bob was ambivalent about this. It was hypothesized that Bob's concerns about Ann becoming pregnant inhibited both his sexual desire and his erectile functioning.

4. Other sexual dysfunctions. Bob's history of premature ejaculation and Ann's inhibited sexual response led to repeated negative sexual interactions. This history of negative sexual experiences may have reduced Bob's desire. In addition, although Bob reported that his erectile dysfunction and low desire originated at the same time, it has frequently been observed in other cases that a few incidents of erectile dysfunction can inhibit a man's desire. It was therefore hypothesized that Bob's erectile dysfunction may have been a contributing factor in the etiology and/or maintenance of his low desire.

5. Guilt. Bob indicated in his history interview a good deal of discomfort about engaging in intercourse both in fact and fantasy. Therefore, the hypothesis was developed that he might have some ambivalence about the appropriateness of being a "sexual person." Ann similarly might have had inhibitions about "letting go."

6. Lack of sexual attraction to Ann. Bob reported that he did not find Ann very sexually attractive. It was hypothesized that this lack of attraction further reduced his sexual desire for her.

Table 8-2 contains a session-by-session outline of the specific in-session therapeutic procedures, as well as the homework assignments for Ann and Bob.

Hypothesis 1: Performance Anxiety

The experiential phase of the program was introduced early in therapy. Ann and Bob were both taught to notice their bodily reactions to stressful situations. Bob was able to describe a tightening across the back of his neck and shoulders when feeling anxious or threatened. Ann identified her stomach as a place of discomfort when feeling anxious or frightened. Both Ann and Bob were taught to locate these areas by closing their eyes, fantasizing about an anxiety-provoking situation, and focusing on various parts of their bodies to see where the reaction was taking place.

Behaviorally, the couple was introduced to "sensate focus." They were asked to have two sensual massage sessions that excluded stimulation of breasts and genitals, orgasms, and intercourse. Each was asked to initiate one session and to make it as romantic as possible by utilizing enhancers such as candlelight, wine, music, and scented oils. In addition, each individual was asked to spend approximately 10 min on a body inventory—that is, examining his or her body in a full-length mirror and writing down the things he or she liked best and also those things he or she would like to improve. They were told to notice their reactions to this exercise, that is, did they experience any of the bodily cues they

TABLE 8-2. Session-by-Session Outline of Thearpy

Session 1

A. Within session

Ann and Bob: Individual psychosexual history interviews.

B. Homework assignment

Couple assignment: Do something sexual together, and keep records of what they did.

Session 2

A. Within session

1. Explored possible reasons for low desire. (1) (2) (3) (4) (5) (6)
2. Discussed how to notice bodily reactions to stressful situations. (1)
3. Introduced sensate focus. (1) (2) (4)

B. Homework assignment

Ann: 1. Spend 10 min looking at own body; write a list of likes and dislikes. (1)
       2. Tune into bodily cues for anxiety. (1)
       3. Explore body by touch, and pay attention to bodily cues. (1)

Bob: Same assignment as for Ann. (1)

Couple: Two sensate focus sessions, with nongenital pleasuring, no touching of breasts, no orgasms, no intercourse. (1) (2) (4)

Session 3

A. Within session

1. Showed sexually explicit film (*Sharing Orgasm*) in the context of recognizing sensations associated with anxiety and tuning into bodily responses. (1) (2)
2. Bob and Ann practiced self-disclosure of information regarding their own masturbation patterns to each other. (2)
3. Helped Ann achieve insight into her pattern of assuming responsibility for Bob's erectile problem. (2)
4. Helped Ann to ask Bob for what she wanted sexually. (2) (5)
5. Exploring cognition behind anxiety. (1)

B. Homework assignment

Ann: 1. Look at genitals with hand mirror. (1) (4)
       2. Explore genitals tactually for sensation. (1) (4)
       3. Write down three things to say to herself to make her feel better when taking responsibility for Bob's erectile problem. (1) (5)

Bob: 1. Pause and squeeze techniques (during masturbation). (4)
       2. Write down three things to say to himself in order to feel better when he gets anxious in a sexual context with Ann. (1)

Couple: 1. Two sensate focus sessions, with the focus on giving and receiving feedback. (1) (2) (4)
       2. Read first chapter of Zilbergeld's *Male Sexuality*. (1)

Session 4

A. Within session

1. Explored fears of intimacy. (5)
2. Exercise on tuning in to physical response to anxiety. (1)
3. Cognitive phase formally introduced with a discussion of cognitive coping statements, rational restructuring, and automatic thoughts. (1) (4) (5)
4. Discussed fear of pregnancy. (3)

B. Homework assignment

Ann: 1. Tactually explore body (including genitals) for sensation, learn which parts are the most pleasurable. (1) (4)

Bob: 1. Practice pause and squeeze techniques in masturbation. (4)

Couple: 1. Read Chapters 2 and 3 in *Male Sexuality*. (1)
       2. Sensate focus, including touching breasts. (1) (2) (4)
          a. with focus on noticing bodily cues associated with anxiety, and
          b. identify automatic thought leading to anxiety.

(*Continued*)

TABLE 8-2. (*Continued*)

Session 5

A. Within session

Discussed how they learned and formulated their attitudes regarding male and female sex roles. (5)

Discussed the development of their irrational automatic belief systems. (5)

Introduced transactional analysis concepts. (5)

Worked on communication training. (2)

B. Homework assignment

Ann: 1. Explore body, tactually, for pleasure. (1) (4)

2. Begin reading Heiman, LoPiccolo, and LoPiccolo's *Becoming Orgasmic*. (4)

Couple: Continue sensate focus, including breast stimulation. (1) (2) (4)

Session 6

A. Within session

1. Continued cognitive restructuring and tuning into bodily responses. (1)

2. Practiced communicating about sexual issues. (2)

3. Discussed Zilbergeld's myths about male sexuality; discussed which of these Bob believed. (1) (2)

B. Homework assignment

Ann: *Becoming Orgasmic* exercise on learning how to focus and using fantasy. (4)

Couple: 1. Read through Chapter 9 in *Male Sexuality*. (4)

2. Sensate focus, including genital stimulation. Orgasm optimal for both partners, but for Bob only if he has an erection. Orgasm should not be the last thing they do in the sensate focus session. (1) (2) (4)

Session 7

A. Within session

1. Discussed Ann taking more initiative in their sex life. (4) (5)

2. Explored Bob's responding to feeling threatened when Ann is "too sexual." (5)

3. Discussed cognitive self-statements about giving themselves permission to be more sexual. (5)

4. Focused on ways Bob could increase his sexual desire with fantasy and cognitive self-statements. (1) (5)

B. Homework assignment

Ann: 1. Think of a sexual fantasy she might like to try, and write it down. (2)

2. Focus on self-pleasuring. (4)

3. Kegel's exercises. (4)

Bob: 1. Think of a sexual fantasy he might like to try, and write it down. (2)

2. Daily 5-min fantasy breaks, with one half of the fantasies being about Ann. (5)

3. Kegel's exercises. (4)

Couple: Two sensate focus sessions, orgasms optional (still no intercourse), (1) (2) (4)

Session 8

A. Within session

1. Showed a second sexually explicit film. (1) (4) (5)

2. Ann and Bob shared their fantasy outlines with each other. (2) (5)

3. Transactional analysis work on letting the "child" out to play, letting go sexually, having fun with sex. (5)

4. Communication training continued. (2)

B. Homework assignment

Ann: 1. Focus on self-pleasuring. (4)

2. Kegel's exercises. (4)

Bob: 1. Fantasy breaks. (5)

2. Kegel's exercises. (4)

TABLE 8-2. (*Continued*)

Couple: 1. Act out Ann's sexual fantasy. (5)
      2. Act out Bob's sexual fantasy. (5)
      3. Each to role-play being sexually aroused in an exaggerated fashion, and role-play exaggerated orgasm. (1) (5)

Session 9
A. Within session
   1. Showed sexually explicit film (*Heterosexual Intercourse*). (2) (5)
   2. Worked on intimacy issue; what it would mean if they got closer to one another and enjoyed sex. (5)
   3. Worked on issue of letting go sexually, letting the "child" out to play. (5)
   4. Discomfort about intercourse. (5)
B. Homework assignment
Ann: 1. Individual masturbation session with the focus on pleasure. (4)
Couple: 1. Act out Ann's sexual fantasy (they had not done so previously). (5)
      2. One sexual session, with both of them exaggerating the behaviors and sounds of high levels of arousal (letting go). (1) (4) (5)
      3. One couple session, doing anything they want, with the following restriction: If Bob gets an erection, they can have 1–2 min of penetration, with no orgasm, and they should resume the pleasuring session following the penetration. (4)

Session 10
A. Within session
   1. Discussed initiating and refusing sex. (2)
     a. Bob saying "no" to Ann's overtures.
     b. Ann learning how to ask for what she wanted sexually without turning Bob away.
     c. Learning to trust each other within the context of initiating and refusing sex.
B. Homework assignment
Ann: 1. Read the chapter in *Becoming Orgasmic* on orgasm triggers and use triggers in an individual session. (4)
Couple: 1. Do whatever they want sexually but ask for what they want. (2)
      2. Exaggerate their arousal levels. (1)

Session 11
A. Within session
   1. Explored the issue of assertiveness, including her repressed anger, her feeling of "walking on eggshells," and his turning off to her (and not speaking up) when annoyed at her. (2)
   2. Explored his discomfort at her reaching orgasm during masturbation. (2)
   3. Transactional analysis: Ann learned to generate coping statements to use if Bob turned off to her when she was assertive.
B. Homework assignment
Ann: One individual session. (4)
Couple: 1. do whatever they want sexually, but make it as new, interesting, and exciting as possible. (1) (2) (4)
      2. Ann "pressure" Bob for sex. Bob go along, or be assertive and refuse. (1) (2)

Session 12
A. Within session
   1. Gestalt exercise: Bob had a conversation between his sexual self and nonsexual self, with the goal of integrating the two. (5)
   2. Reevaluation of performance anxiety hypothesis. (1)
B. Homework assignment
Couple: 1. Do whatever they want sexually.
      2. Sensation training continued. (1) (5)

(Continued)

TABLE 8-2. (*Continued*)

Session 13

A. Within session

Reviewed family histories, and related their backgrounds to their current sexuality. (5)

B. Homework assignment.

Couple: Do whatever they want sexually.

Session 14

A. Within session

1. Empty chair exercise: Bob talking to his father. (5)

2. Explored how Bob's father and mother had influenced his comfort with intimacy and letting go. (5)

B. Homework assignment

Couple: 1. Do whatever they want sexually.

2. Write up lists of future goals and ways to maintain progress.

Session 15

A. Within session

1. Worked on maintenance lists.

2. Closure, termination.

Note. Numbers in parentheses refer to hypotheses; see text.

had previously described? They were also asked to spend 15–20 min each, in privacy, exploring their bodies, trying different styles of strokes and pressures, and writing down any discoveries and reactions they might have to this exercise.

During the third therapy session, Bob and Ann were shown an explicit film, called *Sharing Orgasm* (1977), and were asked to be aware of their own bodily reactions to the film. Both indicated that they were extremely uncomfortable and quite anxious during the showing of the film and were very aware of their characteristic physiological responses; that is the tightening of the neck and shoulders for Bob and the tightening of the stomach muscles for Ann.

The cognitive phase was begun by asking Bob and Ann to express what thoughts they believed to be behind the feelings of anxiety and discomfort. When they claimed they did not know, they were requested to come up with at least one possible thought even if they had to make it up. Both agreed that the discomfort probably stemmed from the fact that they feared that the other person would think they were inadequate in bed after watching the couple in the film.

Review of the couple's homework indicated that both Ann and Bob had moderately realistic and positive feelings about their own bodies, with Ann somewhat less positive than Bob. Both found their sensual sessions together to be very pleasing. Bob believed that Ann enjoyed the sessions much less than she actually did. Many of his comments on the homework write-up were phrased in terms of her response rather than his own, and it was quite clear that he was very aware of her reaction throughout.

Sensual sessions were again assigned. The couple was asked to be aware of any anxiety reactions to these sessions. Bob was also asked to write three things that he could think to himself that would make him feel better, if and when he felt sexually anxious with Ann. Bibliotherapy was initiated by the assigning of the first chapter of *Male Sexuality* (Zilbergeld, 1978), a book that helps men deal with the myths about their sexuality and helps them modify their unrealistic expectations for themselves.

At the fourth session Bob and Ann reported that they enjoyed their couple sensual massage and were successful in recognizing their own sensual feelings. Bob stated, "I found the whole experience very relaxing, especially when my back was rubbed, and more sensual when my stomach and upper legs were rubbed."

During this session further work was done in the experiential phase of the program and the couple was given more practice in focusing on their own bodies and recognizing the physical symptoms that frequently accompanied anxiety. This was done by having them attend to and report bodily responses as issues of varying anxiety potential were discussed in-session. In addition, the rationale behind cognitive restructuring was explained to them. They were told that some of their maladaptive emotional reactions were probably mediated by internal sentences or irrational beliefs that had become automatic. Examples were offered of how feelings can be affected by what we tell ourselves. The couple was asked to think about what kinds of cognitive coping statements they could make when they recognized the physical symptoms of anxiety.

During subsequent sessions behavioral assignments of an increasingly sexual nature were assigned. Breasts and then genitals were included as part of the sensate focus exercises, basically as described by Masters and Johnson (1970).

Throughout, Ann and Bob were reminded that performance anxiety could play a very large role and could be at least partially responsible for Bob's low desire (insight), and that by doing these exercises (behavioral), tuning into any physiological symptoms of anxiety (experiential), and making cognitive coping statements to help reduce this anxiety (cognitive) the problem could be overcome.

By session 6, both Ann and Bob reported feeling totally relaxed and sensual during the couple sessions. The couple used candlelight, incense, and soft music to help create a romantic setting and mood. Ann reported, "I was able to tune into my bodily sensations and felt totally relaxed. Bob also enjoyed this session and had an erection. He seemed really happy." Bob reported, "I was aroused for nearly the entire time period. Only once during the session I felt a twinge of a tightening in my shoulder." When questioned further Bob reported that he tried to identify the thoughts he was having during this moment of anxiety: They involved the desire to proceed to further sexual activity and a concern that he would lose his erection. He was able to "shrug this off" and continue with the pleasurable feelings.

By session 7 the couple reported no negative reactions at all. Bob had an erection virtually the entire time the couple was together. At session 8 Bob was able to reach orgasm through Ann's manual stimulation and achieved full erections. By session 10 the couple was encouraged to continue to reduce performance anxiety by exaggerating the reactions and sounds they made during lovemaking. They were both extremely aroused by this and had intercourse two times, with Bob having an orgasm intravaginally.

At session 12 the performance anxiety hypothesis was reexamined. Bob indicated that he felt very relaxed and was enjoying his sexual experiences with Ann tremendously. However, he felt that he still was not totally involved with the sexual experience. That is, to some extent he continued to observe himself as a spectator of his own sexual performance. Part of him was still uncomfortable about being very sexual and particularly about having intercourse.

Hypothesis 2: Communication Dysfunction

It was suggested to Bob and Ann that difficulty with sexual communication might play a role in Bob's low sexual desire. Although the couple claimed to have good general communication skills, it was pointed out that frequently couples have difficulty asking for what they want in a sexual situation. During the third session Ann and Bob were shown an explicit film, *Sharing Orgasm* (1977), that demonstrated good sexual communication. Later in the same session, Bob was encouraged to share with Ann the fact that he did occasionally masturbate, information which he had not previously shared. This conversation concerning masturbation occurred during the session with both Ann and Bob encouraged to monitor their affective responses. The couple had already been trained to recognize the physical responses that usually accompanied anxiety. Bob described having these feelings of tension in the back of his neck as he was telling Ann about his occasional masturbation. He clearly had a sense of being ashamed, and believed that the sexual activity was wrong and that Ann would think less of him for masturbating. Ann, on the other hand, seemed somewhat upset when she found out that he did not have erectile difficulties when he masturbated. She blamed herself. She was helped to see that she chose to interpret these actions as a statement about her, rather than as a statement about Bob. Ann was able to gain the insight that she tended to accept responsibility for other people's actions in general, and to blame herself for the things that they did. She was able to trace this back to her reactions to her parent's marital distress. She was encouraged to become aware of times when she was making this formulation with the goal of eventually reframing such events.

The "sensate focus" homework assignments, which over the weeks became increasingly more sexual, included an emphasis on sexual communication training. The couple was encouraged to give and receive feedback about what felt good. As the assignments became more sexual, both Bob and Ann were encouraged to continue to notice any experiential signs of anxiety, and to try to determine what cognitive statements were behind these feelings. They were asked to express their worst fears about the sexual situation. By session 6 both Bob and Ann agreed that their fears were that Bob would lose his newly active desire and that his erections would not be maintained. In-session they were encouraged to communicate their thoughts and feelings to each other and to make empathic statements indicating that they understood and accepted each other's feelings. They were also asked to discuss with each other their thoughts about the sexual myths presented in *Male Sexuality* (Zilbergeld, 1978).

At session 7 Bob and Ann were asked to spend some time at home thinking of a sexual fantasy that each might like to try and to write an outline of it. At the next therapy session, they were asked to discuss their fantasies with each other. This assignment was designed to provide them with an opportunity to experience sex as a playful activity. Bob and Ann were able to share their fantasy outlines with each other and were quite comfortable in doing so. They continued to make excellent progress in communicating sexual wants to each other and in feeling comfortable about talking about sexual issues. The fantasies were restructured so that Ann and Bob could act them out at home, which they were able to do successfully.

At session 10 Ann was encouraged to try to trust Bob enough to ask for what *she* wanted sexually, even though she was concerned that any "pressure on Bob" would push him away. Bob was encouraged to be able to say "no" to Ann or "I'm just wanting to do some activity, but not have intercourse." Each was asked to take responsibility for his or her own initiation and refusal. For future homework assignments, they were told that they could do whatever they wanted sexually as long as they asked for what they wanted.

At session 11 Bob and Ann reported on one homework session, planned in advance, which found neither of them interested. After a while, they stopped their sexual activity. However, they were able to talk about the fact that this was not a time that either one of them wanted to have sex and that this was acceptable. Ann did not feel panicked and Bob did not feel the need to pull away and withdraw. They also described a session in which Bob became annoyed at Ann for asking him to search for a hair barrette in the middle of one of their sessions. His method of handling this annoyance was to withdraw and "turn off." Time was spent in this therapy session on assertion; that is, getting Bob to express his annoyance at Ann when it occurred, rather than simply withdrawing. Both Bob and Ann were able to talk freely about their feelings and vowed to be more directly assertive with each other in the future.

It also became apparent that Ann had a lot of difficulty expressing anger, often denying that she had any. Again, she was asked to notice her bodily sensations when a disagreement with Bob arose, to use these responses as cues to her cognitive responses, and then to assert herself. Ann and Bob were told to continue with sexual sessions as they wished, with one exception: Ann was asked to put some pressure on Bob during one of their sexual sessions. They were asked to then notice any bodily responses to this pressure and to examine what cognitions were associated with them. Finally, they were asked to make coping statements that might help them stay closer together and communicate instead of their usual practice of withdrawing from each other.

Ann and Bob returned for the following session (session 12) with a report of successful and varied homework sessions that included good communication. Ann was able to ask for what she wanted and to tell Bob how to touch her.

Although he felt a little awkward at first, he was able to make some coping statements to allow himself to enjoy pleasuring her. During one couple session, they both had manual orgasms. The couple labeled Ann's asking for what she wanted as pressure on Bob (which had been assigned). However, he did not withdraw, but was able to respond positively, and felt somewhat relieved that he knew exactly how to pleasure Ann, and did not have to wonder if he was "performing well."

Hypothesis 3: Pregnancy and Childbirth Issues

During the first four sessions of therapy, a considerable amount of time was spend exploring both Bob's and Ann's feelings and attitudes about having a family. While Bob's feelings were somewhat ambivalent, he indeed did want to have children, and along with Ann, was able to express some of his positive expectations about raising a family. Bob did not appear anxious about the prospect, and he was not able to identify any physical anxiety responses to the subject. As a result of these discussions, fear of pregnancy was removed from the list of factors hypothesized to be contributing to the low sexual desire.

Hypothesis 4: Low Desire Secondary to Other Dysfunctions

In the first homework assignment, Bob described a tendency to concentrate on his erections, which helped produce an anxious and negative effect. Ann found herself frightened during the sexual interaction and thinking about Bob's reaction. This kept both individuals from relaxing and enjoying what was happening. This focus on erections was introduced to the couple as a possible major reason for their sexual experiences becoming negative. Because Bob had been experiencing premature ejaculation when he did get erections, in session 3 he was introduced to the "pause and squeeze technique" (J. LoPiccolo, 1978) for the treatment of premature ejaculation. He was asked to practice this in individual masturbation sessions. Ann was given the assignment of looking at her own genitals at home. She responded to this with some embarrassment and anxiety, and was able to state, "I guess my feelings over the years have been to the point that my genitals were not mine to explore, and I was doing something wrong to touch them. I feel a little awkward and uneasy touching myself. However, I remembered to think about what you said about being in touch with your own body. I would like to be more comfortable with my own body, sexually speaking. As I continued, it was exciting and I felt slightly aroused at times."

At future sessions Ann learned to explore her own genitals for sensation and then for arousal. She was able to recognize the bodily sensations accompanying feelings of discomfort and anxiety and make coping statements to herself such as, "This is my body and I have a right to explore it," which subsequently allowed her to relax, to fantasize, and to experience pleasure during this exercise. Subsequently, Ann was able to become much more relaxed during the couple sessions, which reduced the anxiety level for both Ann and

Bob. Ann also learned to use Kegel's exercises to strengthen the vaginal musculature (J. LoPiccolo & Lobitz, 1978).

In the couple sessions the emphasis was taken off erection and placed on enjoying the sensuality and sexuality of other sexual experiences. Both Ann and Bob were able to recognize feelings of anxiety and make appropriate coping statements. By session 8 Bob was having full erections most of the time they were interacting sexually, and by session 9 they were able to have successful intercourse with a full erection and a satisfactory ejaculatory latency.

In her individual homework sessions, Ann learned to use "orgasm triggers" such as pelvic thrusting, breathing heavily, tensing muscles, and other responses usually associated with orgasm (J. LoPiccolo & Lobitz, 1978), and she was able to have an orgasm during most of her individual sessions. Bob and Ann continued to relax in their sessions together and would often precede them with a shared bath.

By session 11 they were routinely having intercourse with orgasm and no problem with erection. Bob did lose his erection partway through one session, but they continued stimulation and the erection returned.

Hypothesis 5: Guilt

Early in the therapy, the couple's learning history was jointly explored and they began to see how poor learning history and unresolved family of origin issues contributed to their sexual problems by making it difficult for them to deal with intimacy, to make themselves vulnerable, and to accept themselves fully as sexual beings.

After introducing the book *Male Sexuality* (Zilbergeld, 1978), the therapist spent time with the couple discussing the formation of male and female sex roles and how Ann and Bob acquired their own sex role attitudes. These were linked back to automatic irrational beliefs, and the couple began to recognize how they allowed certain beliefs and attitudes to influence their behavior, even though consciously they claimed not to still hold these beliefs and attitudes. For example, Bob recognized that one of his irrational beliefs was that "nice" women did not exhibit strong sexual responses and that this, indeed, contributed to Ann's holding back in a sexual situation. Ann's belief was that a man should always be ready, willing, and able to have sex, and if he could or would not then it meant that *she* was inadequate. Ann was helped to see how she tended to almost always take personal responsibility for the problem.

Some transactional analysis concepts were introduced to the couple and some of the rational restructuring was reframed within this conceptual framework. They were taught that they each had a strong "judgmental parent" and each needed to work on developing his or her "nurturing parent" (another way of stating that they needed to replace irrational beliefs by rational coping statements). They were also told that in order to be sexual, each of them needed to allow his or her "child" out to play, and to nurture the "frightened child" so that the "playful child" would be free.

Bob came to see that being sexual made him somewhat uncomfortable (through tuning into the bodily responses that signified anxiety), and he started to generate coping statements that would help him accept the sexual versatility and initiation that he claimed to want.

One behavioral assignment that was quite effective with Bob was asking if he could take a 5-min fantasy break each day, with at least half of these fantasies being about Ann. He was then asked to become aware of what in his fantasies produced anxiety responses. He recognized that totally uninhibited sex and intercourse were the two activities that were most troublesome. Coping statements allowed Bob to become "desensitized" to these activities in his fantasies and subsequently in the couple sessions, as well. Generating fantasies that could be acted out by the couple together provided desensitization as well.

By the eighth session Bob and Ann were given the assignment to role-play together being as aroused and excited as they could imagine. This was to include appropriate sounds and actions and the role play of orgasms. Actual orgasm was made optional. At the next session, the couple reported feeling somewhat strange about playacting their fantasies and exaggerating excitement. However, they were able to get past this and enjoy themselves. During the session in which they exaggerated their arousal, Bob was also able to have a manual orgasm. He had no erection difficulties during these sessions.

Major issues in session 9 centered around intercourse, intimacy, and letting go. The couple was shown an educational, explicit film, and Bob and Ann were able to discuss their reaction. Although both still felt somewhat uneasy viewing the film in each other's presence, this was much less so than in the case of the film shown earlier in therapy.

Bob was able to verbalize in session 9 that there was something about intercourse that made him somewhat uneasy, although he could not quite identify what. Even during solitary masturbation throughout his life, he would have difficulty fantasizing intercourse at the time of orgasm. This was reframed as a problem of intimacy, as intercourse is probably the situation in which a couple is most vulnerable and intimate. The couple was encouraged to keep exploring, letting go, and feeling free during sex. Within the transactional analysis framework, they were told to use, as a coping statement, "I'm going to let my child out to play."

As previously indicated, by session 12, the couple was having orgasm, no problem with erection, and was enjoying sexual activities together completely. At this point in therapy, it was decided to pause and evaluate the progress that had been made. Bob indicated that although he was feeling relaxed and enjoying his experiences with Ann, he was still not totally involved with the sexual experience. Part of him was still not comfortable being very sexual and having intercourse. Ann stated that she was much more relaxed and able to express her own wants and needs without fear that Bob would turn off and withdraw.

To help Bob deal with his continued discomfort with sexual behavior, a Gestalt exercise was introduced as part of the experiential phase of the program.

The empty chair technique was used, and Bob's sexual self was asked to talk to his nonsexual self, and vice versa. With the nonsexual self in the empty chair, Bob was able to describe this part of himself as very "puritanical, straight-backed, humorless, and function-oriented." He was able to tell this part of himself several things that were designed to assure "him" that Bob was not totally abandoing "him" by being sexual. With the help of the therapist, Bob generated rational coping statements that he could use to help himself "take care of" his nonsexual self. These statements included, "Just because I am being sexual with my wife does not mean I am sacrificing any moral standards you have for me," "I will not try to stop you from being so serious and goal-oriented in other aspects of our life if you do not stop me from trying to be free and spontaneous during my sexual activities," "Just because I allow myself to get totally involved in a sexual situation does not mean that I will lose control over my entire life."

Bob was then helped to learn to focus on his sensations further. An exercise in which he closed his eyes and was handed various objects that he was supposed to experience only through touch was used to help him in this endeavor.

Because Bob continued to report a degree of discomfort with sexual activity in spite of the fact that sex was enjoyable and functional, it was decided to return to the insight phase of therapy at sessions 13 and 14. The family histories of both Ann and Bob were reviewed with the goal of helping them see how these histories inflluenced their current feelings and attitudes. When Bob was asked to describe his father in detail, he described him as a very straight-laced puritanical man lacking in a sense of humor. It was pointed out to him how similar this description was to the description of Bob's own, nonsexual self that he had given 2 weeks previously during the Gestalt exercise. This realization had a tremendous impact upon Bob when he realized how thoroughly he had allowed his father's attitude to influence his own sexual behavior. Ann was helped to see how she was influenced by her mother, that is, always giving and never feeling free to express anger.

Armed with these new insights and the experiential, cognitive, and behavioral tools that had been developed, the couple was asked to go home prior to their last session and make a list of gains they had made during therapy, things they could do to maintain these gains, things their partner could do to help them maintain these gains, goals they still had, and things they could do to help them achieve these goals.

At the final session Bob and Ann reported that they had been much more involved in their sexual experience than they had previously, and they felt that they had made tremendous strides towards their goals. Bob wrote, "I feel that my whole attitude toward sex has changed. Before starting therapy, I had an almost puritanical view of it. I felt 'inside' that sex was dirty and something to be hidden from view. I equated sex with intercourse. If I had an erection, everything was fine, if not it was a disaster. Ann shared my misconceptions. When I failed to get an erection, she took it as my rejection of her. We both got very obsessed, which of course compounded the problem. Now I feel so much more comfortable with sex. I no longer have the pressure to perform. I also feel much closer to Ann than I have in quite some time."

In filling out a questionnaire, on the question, "Overall, how has your sexual behavior changed during your time of therapy?" both Bob and Ann rated the response "5" on a 5-point scale.

A follow-up phone call 3 months later indicated that Bob and Ann had maintained their goals and were continuing to have sex frequently and with much more involvement than had previously been the case.

Hypothesis 6: Lack of Attraction to Partner

It became clear late in therapy that lack of attraction to Ann was *not* a major contributor to Bob's low sexual desire. In fact, throughout therapy, he seemed to be quite attracted to her and was easily aroused by sexual contact with her. Most likely, Bob *concluded* that he was unattracted to Ann because of his low sexual desire, as a way of explaining his problem to himself.

Summary

Examining the original hypotheses, lack of attraction to partner and pregnancy and childbirth issues did not, indeed, play a major role in Bob's low sexual desire. Communication dysfunction clearly was a major issue for this couple. Both Bob and Ann were very uncomfortable telling each other what they liked sexually, and they found it difficult to let each other know what would be pleasing and arousing. This came from lack of skill in communication as well as anxiety and guilt about being sexually functioning individuals. Bob's performance anxiety was a major contributing factor and the behavioral desensitization that was part of their treatment significantly reduced this anxiety. Bob's erectile difficulties disappeared early in treatment and were clearly related to his performance anxiety. Helping Ann to be less inhibited in sexual functioning and helping Bob control his ejaculatory latency did help the couple function more successfully sexually. Guilt about being a sexual person produced a good deal of discomfort both in fact and in fantasy and did seem to be one of the major factors in maintaining the sexual dysfunction. Insight into how early learning history influenced these feelings, experiential/Gestalt exercises, learning new cognitive coping statements, and behavioral assignments all helped this couple overcome feelings of guilt and helped produce increased desire and more pleasurable sexual functioning.

Bob and Ann and their therapist were pleased with the therapeutic outcome. The couple's relationship was strong and basically intact to begin with. Basic behavioral skills such as communication and assertion helped this couple make gains. Working on their individual issues such as Bob's guilt and discomfort over intercourse and Ann's difficulty with displaying her sexual appetite also helped this couple make gains.

Assessment Data

The pre–post changes on the assessment battery also indicate a positive outcome (see Table 8-3). Ann and Bob's Locke–Wallace scores were in the happily married range both pre- and posttherapy. Bob's overall marital happiness score (from the Locke–Wallace MAT) was "very happy" both prior to and after therapy, while Ann rated her marriage "very unhappy" at intake and as "happy" posttherapy. Several measures from the Sexual History Form are also presented. Both Ann and Bob's ratings of their own overall sexual satisfaction went from "extremely unsatisfactory" at intake to "moderately satisfactory" posttherapy. Frequency of intercourse for this couple went from "not at all" prior to therapy, to "two times each week" posttherapy. Bob increased his masturbation from "not at all" at intake to "one time each week" posttherapy. Bob rated his overall frequency of desire at "once every 2 weeks" prior to therapy and at "three to four times each week" posttherapy. Bob rated his desire to initiate sex at "a few times each year" prior to therapy and as "two times each week" posttherapy.

At intake Sexual Interaction Inventory scales that were more than one standard deviation from the mean in the distressed direction were: frequency of dissatisfaction of the male and frequency of dissatisfaction of the female. Posttherapy no scales were more than one standard deviation from the mean in the distressed direction, with most scales tending toward the positive direction.

TABLE 8-3. Assessment Data Pre- and Posttherapy

	Intake	Post
Overall satisfaction measures		
Male Locke–Wallace score	115	121
Female Locke–Wallace score	107	121
Male overall happiness	Very happy	Very happy
Female overall happiness	Very unhappy	Happy
Male overall sexual satisfaction	Extremely unsatisfactory	Moderately satisfactory
Female overall sexual satisfaction	Extremely unsatisfactory	Moderately satisfactory
Desire measures		
Male's estimate of intercourse frequency	Not at all	2/week
Female's estimate of intercourse frequency	Not at all	2/week
Male's masturbation frequency	Not at all	1/week
Male's overall frequency of desire	Once every 2 weeks	2/week
Male's desire to have intercourse	3–4/week	2/week

CONCLUSION

The assessment and treatment of low sexual desire are still in the infancy stage. Sexual desire is not an overt, measurable behavior, but a truly subjective private experience. Therefore, we need to develop methods of tapping the subjective sexual experience of individuals. How do they *know* when they are experiencing desire? How do they *know* that their desire has actually changed? How do different individuals subjectively experience desire? Future work on the treatment of low sexual desire will need to address the issues of developing different and/or more sophisticated measures of this elusive construct. If paper and pencil measures are to be used, the same questions will have to be asked in several different ways. Therapist interview and rating scales may be the assessment of choice. Open-ended questions that ask individuals to describe their feelings and how they experience desire may be the most desirable measures.

The individual and relationship history assessments, described previously, are useful for generating hypotheses in cases of low desire. If the low desire is lifelong and global in nature, the focus should be on assessing the "deeper" individual reasons for the problem, such as displaced affect, guilt, and antipleasure bias. If the problem is lifelong but situational in nature (parnter specific), focus should be on idealized expectations, performance anxiety, deficient learning history, and object–choice conflict.

If the low desire is not lifelong and is relationship specific, all the relationship factors need to be considered as primary candidates for major contributors to the low desire. If the problem has not been exclusive to a particular relationship, issues of intimacy and vulnerability should be considered first. While the focus may vary, all hypotheses should be reviewed for all cases. The etiological factors can combine and interact in complex ways to produce different patterns of low desire. It is this extreme variability and lack of predictability that necessitates the multistage individualized assessment strategy as well as the multicomponent, highly individualized treatment approach. The conceptual framework presented here can help therapists approach the problem in a systematic manner.

The development of effective treatment techniques for low sexual desire lags far behind that for the other sexual dysfunctions. This is due to the elusive nature of the construct of "low desire," the complex etiology of low desire, and the repression, denial, marital discord, and lack of motivation for change that are present in many cases of low desire. Effective treatment of these cases will require an increased integration of techniques and concepts from cognitive–behavioral, psychodynamic, general systems, Gestalt, and other approaches.

References

American Psychiatric Association. (1980). *Diagnostic and statistical manual of mental disorders* (3rd ed.). Washington, DC: Author.
Bandura, A. (1969). *Principles of behavior modification.* New York: Holt, Rinehart & Winston.

Berne, E. (1964). *Games people play.* New York: Grove.

Broderick, J., Friedman, J. M., & Carr, E. (1981). Negotiation and contracting. In A. Goldstein, E. Carr, W. Davidson, & P. Wehr (Eds.), *In response to aggression* (pp. 66–109). New York: Pergamon.

DeAmicis, L. A., Goldberg, D. C., LoPiccolo, J., Friedman, J. M., & Davies, L. (1984). Three-year follow-up of couples evaluated for sexual dysfunction. *Journal of Sex and Marital Therapy, 10*(4), 215–218.

DeAmicis, L. A., Goldberg, D. C., LoPiccolo, J., Friedman J. M., & Davies, L. (1985). *Three-year follow-up of couples treated for sexual dysfunction.* Manuscript submitted for publication.

Derogatis, L. R., Lipman, R. S., & Covi, L. (1973). SCL-90: An outpatient psychiatric rating scale. *Psychopharmacology Bulletin, 9*(1), 13–28.

Ellis, A. (1962). *Reason and emotion in psychotherapy.* New York: Lyle Stuart.

Ellis, A. (1971). Rational–emotive treatment of impotence, frigidity, and other sexual problems. *Professional Psychology, 2*, 346–349.

Fagan, J., & Shepherd, I. L. (1970). *Gestalt therapy now.* New York: Harper & Row.

Friedman, J. M. (1983). *A treatment program for low sexual desire.* Unpublished doctoral dissertation, State University of New York at Stony Brook, Stony Brook, NY.

Goldfried, M. R. (1980). Toward the delineation of therapeutic change principles. *American Psychologist, 35*, 991–999.

Goldfried, M. R., & Davison, G. C. (1976). *Clinical behavior therapy.* New York: Holt, Rinehart & Winston.

Goldfried, M. R., Decenteceo, E. T., & Weinberg, L. (1974). Systematic rational restructuring as a self-control technique. *Behavior Therapy, 5*, 247–254.

Heiman, J. R., & LoPiccolo, J. (1983). Clinical outcome of sex therapy: Effects of daily versus weekly treatment. *Archives of General Psychiatry, 40*, 443–449.

Heiman, J., LoPiccolo, L., & LoPiccolo, J. (1976). *Becoming orgasmic: A sexual growth program for women.* Englewood Cliffs, NJ: Prentice-Hall.

Heiman, J., LoPiccolo, L., & LoPiccolo, J. (1981). Treatment of sexual dysfunction. In A. S. Gurman & D. P. Kniskern (Eds.), *Handbook of family therapy* (pp. 592–627). New York: Brunner/Mazel.

Hogan, D. R. (1978). The effectiveness of sex therapy: A review of the literature. In J. LoPiccolo & L. LoPiccolo (Eds.), *Handbook of sex therapy* (pp. 57–84). New York: Plenum.

Husted, J. R. (1972). Effect of method of systematic desensitization and presence of sexual communication in the treatment of sexual anxiety by counterconditioning. *Proceedings of the 80th Annual Convention of the American Psychological Association, 7*, 325–326.

Kanter, N., & Goldfried, M. R. (1979). Relative effectiveness of rational restructuring and self-control desensitization in the reduction of interpersonal anxiety. *Behavior Therapy, 10*, 472–490.

Kaplan, H. S. (1974). *The new sex therapy.* New York: Brunner/Mazel.

Kaplan, H. S. (1977). Hypoactive sexual desire. *Journal of Sex and Marital Therapy, 3*, 3–9.

Kaplan, H. S. (1979). *Disorders of sexual desire and other new concepts and techniques in sex therapy.* New York: Brunner/Mazel.

Kimmel, D., & Van derVeen, F. (1974). Factors of marital adjustment in Locke's Marital Adjustment Test. *Journal of Marriage and the Family, 29*, 57–63.

Kockett, G., Dittmar, F., & Nusselt, L. (1975). Systematic desensitization of erectile impotence: A controlled study. *Archives of Sexual Behavior, 4*, 493–500.

Kohlenberg, R. J. (1974). Directed masturbation and the treatment of primary orgasmic dysfunction. *Archives of Sexual Behavior, 3*, 349–356.

Laughren, T. P., & Kass, D. J. (1975). Desensitization of sexual dysfunction. The present status. In A. S. Gurman & D. G. Rice (Eds.), *Couples in conflict* (pp. 281–302). New York: Jason Aronson.

Lazarus, A. A. (1971a). Behavior therapy of sexual problems. *Professional Psychology, 2*, 349–353.

Lazarus, A. A. (1971b). *Behavior therapy and beyond.* New York: McGraw-Hill.

Lazarus, A. A. (1974). Multimodal behavior therapy: Treating the "Basic ID." In C. M. Franks & G. T. Wilson (Eds.), *Annual review of behavior therapy: theory and practice* (pp. 679–690). New York: Brunner/Mazel.

Linehan, M., Goldfried, M. R., & Goldfried, A. P. (1979). Assertion training: Skill acquisition or cognitive restructuring. *Behavior Therapy 10*, 372–388.

Lobitz, W. C., & Lobitz, G. K. (1978). Clinical assessment in the treatment of sexual dysfunctions. In J. LoPiccolo & L. LoPiccolo (Eds.), *Handbook of sex therapy* (pp. 85–102). New York: Plenum.

LoPiccolo, J. (1978). Direct treatment of sexual dysfunction. In J. LoPiccolo & L. LoPiccolo (Eds.), *Handbook of sex therapy* (pp. 1–17). New York: Plenum.

LoPiccolo, J., & Friedman, J. M. (1985). Sex therapy: An integrative model. In S. J. Lynn & J. P. Garske (Eds.), *Contemporary psychotherapies: Models and methods*. New York: Charles E. Merrill.

LoPiccolo, J., Heiman, J. R., Hogan, D. R., & Roberts, C. (in press). Single therapist vs. dual sex therapy team for the treatment of sexual dysfunction. *Journal of Consulting and Clinical Psychology*.

LoPiccolo, J., & Hogan, D. R. (1979). Sexual dysfunction. In O. F. Pomerleau & J. P. Brady, (Eds.), *Behavioral medicine: Theory and practice* (pp. 177–203)). Baltimore: Williams & Wilkins.

LoPiccolo, J., & Lobitz, W. C. (1978). The role of masturbation in the treatment of orgasmic dysfunction. In J. LoPiccolo & L. LoPiccolo (Eds.), *Handbook of sex therapy* (pp. 187–194). New York: Plenum.

LoPiccolo, J., & Steger, J. C. (1974). The sexual interaction inventory: A new instrument for assessment of sexual dysfunction. *Archives of Sexual Behavior, 3*, 585–595.

LoPiccolo, L. (1980). Low sexual desire. In S. R. Leiblum & L. A. Pervin (Eds.), *Principles and practice of sex therapy* (pp. 29–64). New York: Guilford.

LoPiccolo, L., & Heiman, J. R. (1978). Sexual assessment and history interview. In J. LoPiccolo & L. LoPiccolo (Eds.), *Handbook of sex therapy* (pp. 103–112). New York: Plenum.

Masters, W. H., & Johnson, V. E. (1970). *Human sexual inadequacy*. Boston: Little, Brown.

Mathews, A., Bancroft, J., Whitehead, A., Hackman, A., Julier, D., Bancroft, J., Gath, D., & Shaw, P. (1976). The behavioral treatment of sexual inadequacy: A comparative study. *Behaviour Research and Therapy, 14*, 427–436.

Munjack, D., Cristol, A., Goldstein, A., Phillips, D., Goldberg, A., Whipple, K., Staples, F., & Kanno, P. (1976). Behavioral treatment of orgasmic dysfunction: A controlled study. *British Journal of Psychiatry, 129*, 497–502.

Nowinski, J. K., & LoPiccolo, J. (1979). Assessing sexual behavior in couples. *Journal of Sex and Martial Therapy, 5*, 225–243.

Obler, M. (1973). Systematic desensitization in sexual disorders. *Journal of Behavior Therapy and Experimental Psychiatry, 4*, 93–101.

Perls, F. S. (1960). *Gestalt therapy verbatim*. Moab, UT: Real People Press.

Rimm, D. C., & Masters, J. C. (1974). *Behavior therapy: Techniques and empirical findings*. New York: Academic Press.

Schover, L. R., Friedman, J. M., Weiler, S. J., Heiman, J. R., & LoPiccolo, J. (1982). Multiaxial problem-oriented system for sexual dysfunctions: An alternative to DSM-III. *Archives of General Psychiatry, 39*, 614–619.

Semans, J. H. (1956). Premature ejaculation: A new approach. Southern *Medical Journal, 49*, 353–357.

Sharing orgasm (1977) [Film]. New York: Multifocus International.

Skinner, B. F. (1953). *Science and human behavior*. New York: Macmillan.

Steiner, C. M. (1974). *Scripts people live*. New York: Grove.

Stevens, J. O. (1971). *Awareness*. Moab, UT: Real People Press.

Strupp, H. H., & Hadley, S. W. (1977). A tripartite model of mental health and therapeutic outcomes: With special reference to negative effects in psychotherapy. *American Psychologist, 32*, 187–196.

Wolpe, J. (1958). *Psychotherapy by reciprocal inhibition.* Stanford, CA: Stanford University Press.

Zilbergeld, B. (1978). *Male sexuality: A guide to sexual fulfillment.* New York: Bantam.

Zilbergeld, B., & Ellison, C. R. (1980). Desire discrepancies and arousal problems in sex therapy. In S. R. Leiblum & L. A. Pervin (Eds.), *Principles and practice of sex therapy* (pp. 65–101). New York: Guilford.

Zilbergeld, B., & Evans, M. (1980, August). The inadequacy of Masters and Johnson. *Psychology Today, 14*(3), 28–43.

Zinker, J. (1977). *Creative process in Gestalt therapy.* New York: Vintage.

Zung, W. W. (1973). From art to science. The diagnosis and treatment of depression. *Archives of General Psychiatry, 29,* 328–337.

9

THE CHRONICALLY MENTALLY DISABLED: INDEPENDENT LIVING SKILLS TRAINING

CHARLES J. WALLACE, STEVEN E. BOONE, CLYDE P. DONAHOE, AND DAVID W. FOY

Few problems are more frustrating or have been more difficult to work with than those presented by chronic schizophrenics. As most of us are aware, a major problem for our mental hospitals and for society at large is the necessity to deal repeatedly with the chronic schizophrenic patient through numerous acute episodes and/or long-term custodial care. One of the major developments in behavioral treatment during the last decade has been the successful rehabilitation of chronic schizophrenics and other chronically mentally disabled patients through detailed and painstakingly structured intervention programs. In this chapter Wallace and his colleages describe one of the most advanced programs of its type for training the chronically mentally disabled in independent living skills. Everyone reading this chapter will immediately become aware of the years of work that went into the development of the specific and highly structured training "modules." Such details as when to stop the modeling videotape, what questions to ask, and the number and types of observations that the therapist must make are all specified in advance. Despite this highly structured format, this program of training modules is extremely amenable to individual application in the best tradition of behavioral analysis and therapy. Thus, from among these training modules one can structure a program for almost any chronically disabled patient.

What is also important about this program is that it includes not only the latest techniques for training behavioral performance, often referred to as "sending skills," it also includes training in "receiving skills" necessary to understand the requirements of a particular situation as well as "processing skills" enabling the client to problem solve situations as they arise. The comprehensive and detailed nature of this program makes it a model for programs of its type in the years to come.— D. H. B.

The purpose of this chapter is to describe a comprehensive set of techniques designed to rehabilitate schizophrenic clients by assessing and training their interpersonal, community living, and problem-solving skills. Although it is true that the use of neuroleptic medication has been a major advance in the treat-

Charles J. Wallace, Steven E. Boone, Clyde P. Donahoe, and David W. Foy. Rehabilitation Research and Training Center, UCLA School of Medicine, Los Angeles, California; West Los Angeles Veterans Administration Medical Center—Brentwood Division, Los Angeles California.

ment of schizophrenia, it is also true that it is no panacea. As summarized by Klein and Davis (1969), studies have consistently found that medication reduces the acute positive symptoms of schizophrenia—hallucinations, delusions, disordered thinking, agitation, and incoherence. However, not only do neuroleptics have disquieting and possibly damaging side effects, but by themselves they are ineffective in remedying the negative symptoms of schizophrenia—social withdrawal and inadequate interpersonal and community living skills. Thus, a comprehensive rehabilitation program for schizophrenic clients must include both pharmacologic and social rehabilitation components.

This two-pronged approach to the treatment of schizophrenia also springs from the theoretical model proposed by Zubin and Spring (1977). They view the development and outcome of schizophrenia as an interaction between a vulnerability to develop the disorder and the number and severity of environmental "challenges." Vulnerability is an unmodifiable characteristic of the individual that is both genetically and developmentally determined. The challenges to an individual are either endogenous or exogenous events; they create stress when there is a discrepancy between the demands posed by these challenges and the individual's perception of the adequacy of his or her responses to these demands. When faced with a challenge, the individual responds with coping efforts using his or her competencies to meet these demands. Zubin and Spring (1977) define coping efforts and competencies as follows:

[Coping efforts] refer to the attitudinal, motivational stance of an individual faced with a task; [competencies] refer to his abilities, skills, and accumulated know how in solving life's problems. Whereas coping represents the motive power of an organism, competencies refer to its capacities (pp. 111–112)

When the individual is faced with a challenge to which he or she may respond either by putting forth insufficient coping efforts or using incompetent responses, a schizophrenic episode may develop depending upon the individual's vulnerability. The more vulnerable an individual, the more likely an episode will occur. Thus, the individual's vulnerability is a trait-like characteristic that may develop into a state-like episode given certain combinations of stressful environmental events, insufficient coping efforts, and incompetent responses. The thrust of the techniques to be described in this chapter is to improve not only the individual's competencies, but also, via an increased sense of self-efficacy, his or her coping efforts.

MODEL OF TREATMENT

Treatment techniques focus on two types of competencies: the ability to perform the skills necessary to function adequately in the community and the ability to solve the problems that arise in using these skills. The following is a summary exposition of the treatment model; details will be explained and illustrated in a subsequent section of the chapter.

Community Living Skills

The community living skills taught in the program are organized into the 10 major groupings or "modules" listed in Table 9-1. These modules were identified in a survey of health care professionals who were asked to list areas of skill that they thought were essential to clients' successful adaptation to the demands of community living. Each module is composed of a set of skills, each of which is defined in terms of a set of component behaviors that are necessary for a successful performance of that skill. Table 9-2 lists the skills taught in each module.

These skills are trained with a combination of videotaped demonstrations, focused instructions, role-played rehearsals, social and videotaped feedback, and practice in the "real world."

Problem-Solving Skills

As clients perform these community living skills, they might encounter obstacles that make it difficult for them to achieve the outcomes they expected when they used these skills. Training in problem-solving skills is designed to teach clients methods that they can use to overcome these obstacles. The problem-solving model used as a basis for procedures is a five-step model that includes definition of the problem, generation of alternative responses to solve the problem, evaluation of these alternatives in terms of their potential positive and negative consequences, choice of an alternative based upon the evaluation, and implementation of the chosen alternative. Training is provided in methods of overcoming two types of obstacles: resource management problems and outcome problems.

TABLE 9-1. Training Modules

Topic	Description
Conversational skills	Beginning, continuing, and terminating a conversation
Vocational rehabilitation	Job exploration, seeking, and maintenance
Medication management	Managing an antipsychotic drug regimen
Self-care skills	Personal hygiene and clothing care
Personal information	Maintaining personal records
Home finding and maintenance skills	Finding and maintaining housing
Leisure/recreational skills	Identifying and sampling leisure activities
Food preparation	Planning, purchasing, storing, and preparing food
Public transportation	Using bus systems
Money management	Budgeting

TABLE 9-2. Skills Taught in Each of the 10 Modules

Conversational skills
A. Verbal and nonverbal active listening skills
B. Levels of self-disclosure
C. Identification of emotions
D. Open and closed ended questions
E. Topic identification

Vocational rehabilitation
A. Job-seeking skills
   1. Exploring job possibilities using the *Occupational Outlook Handbook*
   2. Exploring job possibilities using the *Dictionary of Occupational Titles*
   3. Recording job leads obtained from a job bulletin board
   4. Recording and using (telephoning employers) job leads obtained from the yellow pages
B. Job interviewing skills
   1. Introduction
   2. Handling difficult questions regarding psychopathology
   3. Closings
C. Job maintenance skills
   1. Accepting criticism from employers
   2. Accepting compliments from employers
   3. Accepting suggestions/instructions from employers
   4. Explaining a problem to Supervisor
   5. Initiating requests to Supervisor
   6. Refusing unreasonable requests from co-workers
   7. Initiating requests to co-workers
   8. Complimenting co-workers
   9. Making suggestions/instructions regarding job task to co-workers

Medication management
A. Basic information about medications
B. Techniques of self-administration
C. Medication side effects
D. Negotiating medication issues with physician
E. First aid: Stocking a home pharmacy
F. First aid: Handling minor medical emergencies

Self-care skills
A. Washing hair
B. Towel-drying hair
C. Blow-drying hair
D. Combing/brushing hair
E. Wash face
F. Shaving with electric razor
G. Shaving with safety razor
H. Trimming a beard
I. Brushing teeth
J. Showering
K. Clothing care

Personal information
A. Completing a written application for benefits
B. Verbally providing personal information to a professional
C. Filling out an application for banking accounts
D. Filling out a work history on a job application

(*continued*)

TABLE 9-2. (*Continued*)

Home finding and maintenance skills

A. Discovering resources for housing leads
B. Consideration in choosing an appropriate place to live
C. Calling housing leads using the classified ads
D. Moving and getting settled in a new home
E. Paying utility bills
F. Cleaning an apartment—kitchen
G. Cleaning an apartment—living area
H. Decorating the home

Leisure/recreational skills

A. Benefits overview
B. Sources of activities in the VA
C. Sources of activities in the community
D. Collecting information about an activity by asking an expert
E. Collecting information about an activity by reading books
F. Overviews of ways to learn an activity
G. Obtaining instruction from a friend
H. Obtaining instruction by enrolling in a class
 I. Evaluating an activity after having tried it

Food preparation

A. Nutritional needs (basic food groups)
B. Choosing appropriate serving size
C. Meal planning (constructing shopping lists)
D. Shopping
E. Storing foods properly
F. Setting up a kitchen (basic utensils, staples)
G. Kitchen maintenance (cleaning)
H. Kitchen safety and sanitation
 I. Recipe use
J. Precooking activities
K. Cooking activities

Public transportation

A. Asking questions on how to use public transportation
B. Choosing from available bus companies
C. Using the bus information number
D. Paying fares
E. Taking the right bus
F. Boarding the bus
G. Exiting

Money management

A. Keeping a budget/spending record
B. Opening a savings account
C. Using a checking account
D. Organizing bill payment
E. Spending and saving
F. Using a calculator

Resource Management Problems

The training in solving resource management problems is designed to teach clients methods of gathering or arranging the resources necessary to implement a particular community living skill. For example, even if an individual has the skills to perform competently during a job interview, he or she needs certain resources such as money, clothes, and transportation to obtain the interview. A predetermined set of resource management problems is presented during training of each skill of each module. These problems were generated based on interviews conducted with clients and with health care professionals. Resource management problems that are unique to a particular client can also be presented. The training methods are based on a model presented in Figure 9-1 of the

FIGURE 9-1. Flowchart for resource management problems.

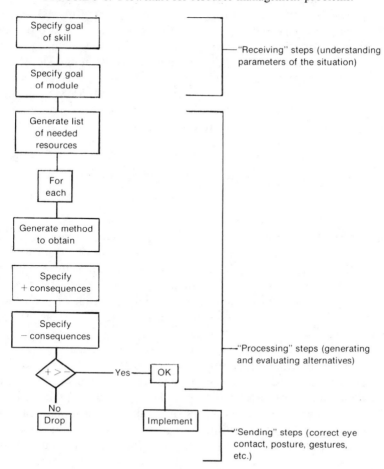

variables involved in successfully solving these problems. The training methods consist not only of role-played practices but also of questions designed to assess the accuracy of clients' consideration of the variables postulated to be involved in successfully solving resource management problems. Incorrect answers presumably indicate incorrect evaluations of the variables, and the trainer uses a series of ever more leading questions to prompt clients to evaluate the variables correctly. These training methods will be illustrated in detail in a later section of this chapter.

Outcome Problems

The training in solving outcome problems is designed to teach clients methods of responding when their environment has not provided the expected outcomes for the performance of a particular community survival skill. For example, if an individual arrives for a job interview, but the interviewer has unexpectedly gone for the day, what must be done to solve the problem? A predetermined set of outcome problems is presented during training of each skill of each module. Like the resource management problems, these were generated based on information obtained from clients and health care professionals. Outcome problems unique to a particular client can also be used in the training. The training methods are based on a model presented in Figure 9-2 of the variables involved in successfully solving these problems. The training methods are very similar to those used during the training in resource management problems, and will be illustrated in detail in a later section of this chapter.

TREATMENT CONSIDERATIONS

Setting

The methods of training community survival and problem-solving skills are currently used as the major therapeutic element in a day treatment program (Social and Independent Living Skills program, SILS) conducted at the West Los Angeles Veterans Administration Medical Center—Brentwood Division. The program staff consists of individuals from a spectrum of professional disciplines: psychology, psychiatry, nursing, social work, occupational therapy, vocational counseling, and human service work. The staff is employed both through the Veterans Administration and through federal grant support by the National Institute of Handicapped Research (NIHR). Clients (primarily outpatients) are referred by the various wards and treatment units of the 550-bed hospital, and therefore have access to its miscellaneous medical, psychiatric, and social support resources. The latter include programs for vocational rehabilitation, occupational therapy, and various other forms of veteran assistance.

The program requires, in addition to its multidisciplinary staff, physical space for conducting the various treatment services, videotape recording and

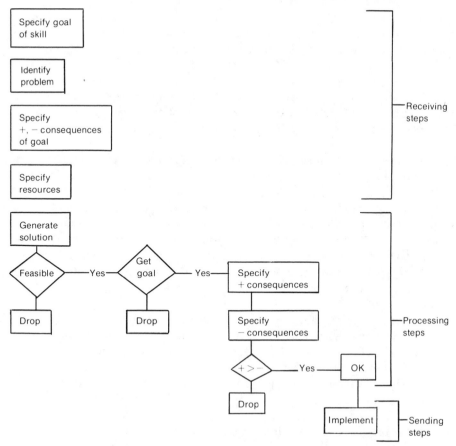

FIGURE 9-2. Flowchart for outcome problems.

editing facilities, miscellaneous supplies, secretarial and receptionist support, and transportation and support funds for the community activities that assist the clients in using their acquired skills in the community. Since the techniques are designed for the long-term rehabilitation of chronic schizophrenic clients, they are primarily suitable for settings that are oriented toward long-term rehabilitative treatment such as day hospital–day treatment programs and residential care facilities. Given the length of time required to train clients in this extensive set of skills, a setting in which the goal is a rapid turnover of clients would be an inappropriate one in which to conduct treatment.

Clients

Clients participating in the SILS program at Brentwood VA Medical Center constitute the population with whom the training procedures described in this chapter were developed. Predominantly male veterans ranging in age from 21–65 years, 60% of whom receive service-connected disability compensation, are referred from general psychiatric treatment units when acute psychotic symptoms have been stabilized. Most clients have protracted psychiatric histories (>5 years) with multiple hospitalizations, are unmarried or divorced, have no stable residential arrangements or live in a board and care facility, have minimal or no contact with family or origin, and have unstable vocational histories with transience and entry-level job skills as frequent concomitants.

There are several important considerations in the use of these training procedures with chronic psychiatric clients. Most important is that clients' psychotic symptoms (hallucinations, delusions, and other thought disturbances) be controlled, most often by a neuroleptic regimen, so that attentional or other cognitive aberrations do not obstruct the extensive learning and retention required (Hersen & Bellack, 1976). Additionally, procedures for chronic clients are more structured and repetitive in that more problem situations are trained; more trials in each situation are used; and more focused instructions, feedback, and prompting are required of the trainer. Modeling is frequently a critical training component for chronic psychiatric clients (Eisler, Blanchard, Fitts, & Williams, 1978).

Motivation for changing one's behavior by learning new skills in the appropriate training modules is necessary. Operationally, this means that the client must prioritize attendance and constructive participation in the daily training sessions above other competing activities during the 2-month course of the modules. Although this requirement is applicable to any population, special consideration must be given to chronic mental clients who are frequently characterized by poor attendance and lack of assertiveness to refuse competing demands on their time. For some chronic mental clients, external contingencies applied by staff or significant others are necessary to reinforce consistent attendance, punctuality, and participation in class or homework assignments. Negotiation between staff and client to reach agreement on which functional areas are to be trained is a vital activity.

Ability to participate in the small group training format is another client consideration. Occasionally, extreme shyness inhibits performance to the extent that assessment of the acquisition of the skills cannot be accomplished. In such cases initial familiarization with the videotaped role-playing format and preliminary training can be conducted on an individual basis until the client is prepared to join the group.

A final consideration is the client's potential for resuming some degree of personal autonomy in his or her living environment. If poor premorbid competence and living environment constrictions conspire against development or use of higher order skills, then training goals must be modified accordingly. For example, a client whose optimal residential placement is a board and care home may have to confine his or her food preparation interests and skills to occasional opportunities provided in the residential care setting.

Therapists

The therapists should have all the basic skills required of any good social skills therapist. They themselves should have excellent interpersonal skills, be familiar with basic behavior therapy principles, be enthusiastic about their work, enjoy working with people, be able to follow detailed procedures, know when to deviate from the procedures, and be able to collect behavioral data. They must be trained in all the basic social skills methodology: modeling, rehearsal, prompting, feedback, reinforcement, and homework assignments.

In addition, working with schizophrenic clients requires some special talents. Therapists must have a good deal of patience, be willing to train small increments of behavior, and tolerate progress that is slower than might be found with some other populations. Therapists must know how to respond to occasional episodes of unusual behavior and be familiar with the special medical requirements of these clients to help them keep their symptomatology under control. Therapists need to be able to give a considerable amount of social reinforcement to individuals who may be withdrawn and who may not always be "socially appropriate." Since a goal of the program is to rehabilitate clients for an enduring stay in the community, it is extremely helpful if the therapists are familiar with local community resources for assisting former mental clients with their independent living needs.

The therapists in the program described in this chapter need not have advanced professional degrees in psychiatry or psychology. In particular, the therapists have backgrounds in occupational therapy, human service work, social work, or nursing. Formal educational credentials are far less important than the considerations described above. Perhaps even more important are the intangible characteristics of enthusiasm, dedication, and patience.

Assessment and Treatment Planning

Referrals of clients to the program are made from inpatient and outpatient treatment units throughout the medical center. Once a referral has been received by the program's intake worker, a screening interview is conducted to determine the referred client's eligibility for the program based on the following criteria:

1. Not acutely ill
2. No evidence of organic brain syndrome
3. No continued drug or alcohol abuse
4. Deficient in at least two areas of community living skills

Although a specific diagnosis is not a criterion for eligibility, priority is given to clients diagnosed as schizophrenic, since the treatment techniques are, to some extent, designed to accommodate the unique attentional problems of these clients. The criterion of deficiencies in at least two areas of community living skills was established to ensure that the clients who participated in the program would need the program's long-term intensive services. Clients with few deficiencies would seem to be better served by brief highly focused interventions. The criterion of not being acutely ill was established to ensure that clients were admitted who could participate in the program's rather "attention-demanding" cognitive treatment techniques.

The screening process involves two levels of assessment. An initial interview is conducted by the program's intake coordinator to determine if the referred client meets the criteria previously described. This interview uses the semi-structured format presented in Figure 9-3. Clients that meet the criteria are then assessed in a more intensive manner using instruments that are designed to identify goals and deficits to be targeted during training. Client goals are assessed using a modified version of the self-anchoring Striving Scale (or Life Ladder; Cantril, 1965). This instrument asks clients to describe their "best and worst" possible lives and then to rank where they are at present, 5 years in the future, and 5 years in the past on a 10-point scale with their descriptions as end points. Client descriptions are coded in terms of life goals that the client is interested in achieving. A behavioral checklist (Figure 9-4) is administered to clients to assess their current performance of the community living skills taught in the program. The checklist is not directly keyed to any particular treatment module or set of modules. Rather, it was designed to fulfill the evaluation requirements of the medical center and to compliment a behavioral checklist of the clients' skills completed by clients' significant others.

Once the information has been collected about the clients' community living skills deficits, an Individual Rehabilitation Plan is written. The plan lists the training modules in which the client will participate and details any individualized behavioral treatment programs that will be developed to remediate excesses and deficits not taught in the modules. Specific role-play assessments of client performance in the skill areas of each training module are administered as necessary.

ASSESSMENT AND TREATMENT TECHNIQUES

A flowchart of the assessment and treatment procedures is presented in Figure 9-5 as an overall map of the program sequence. After the assessment clients are assigned to one or more training modules appropriate for remediating their deficits.

The procedures, techniques, and sequence of programming shown in Figure 9-5 are best illustrated with a typical case description. In the following text the formal procedural steps will be described, with each step demonstrated by a representative case transcript. Thus, the reader will be able not only to learn the program details but also to obtain an understanding of how the formal steps are actually implemented.

FIGURE 9-3. Screening Form.

Name: _____   Ward/Program: _____   Contact: _____
Date: _____   Interviewer: _____

Instructions: Please make a check mark ($\sqrt{}$) in the appropriate column after each question. Sources of
information can be the patient's chart, the patient, the treatment team member(s), and/or
your observation. A space for comments is provided after each question for any additional
information you feel is necessary in making an assessment.

Sources

	Yes	No	Not assessed	Chart	Patient	Treatment team	Observation

1. Psychotic symptoms in remission?
   Comments
2. Medically stable?
   Comments
3. Carry out assigned tasks and tolerate routine task-oriented
   activities?
   Comments
4. Has other commitments that will interfere with making and
   sustaining a voluntary commitment to our program?
   Comments
5. Likely to be placed in a setting such as a nursing home that
   deemphasizes independent living skills?
   Comments
6. Sufficient source of financial support for community? Or
   financial arrangement imminent? (circle one)
   Comments
7. Community living capacity?
   Comments
8. Management problems:
      Suicidal history and/or potential?
      Homicide history and/or potential?
      Assaultive behavior?
      Destructive to property?
   Comments
9. Severe legal problems?
   Comments
10. Acting-out problems (e.g., sexual behavior) that will disrupt
    the operation of the program?
    Comments
11. Months available for program (circle):
       1   2   3   4   5   6+
    Comments
12. Tolerate tutorial setting?
    Comments
13. Tolerate group activities?
    Comments
14. Support systems (circle as applicable):
       Family Friends Religious Vocational potential   Other (specify)
    Comments
15. Nonservice connected? or service connected (what %:)?
    Comments

(*Continued*)

FIGURE 9-3. (*Continued*)

	Yes	No	Not assessed	Chart	Patient	Treatment team	Observation
						Sources	

16. Need areas (circle):
    Social skills   Home finding
    Self-care skills   Food preparation
    Leisure and recreation   Vocational rehabilitation
    Medication management   Shopping, consumerism
    Personal information   Money management
    Community agencies   Friendship/dating
    Other services (specify)
    Comments

    Patient's perception of his needs

    Assessment of patient's overall motivation
17. Is the commute a problem? (circle)
    Yes   No   N/A

Client

The client to be presented in the transcript is "Ben," a 26-year-old black veteran who joined the army after dropping out of high school in the 11th grade. He served as a communication specialist, a job which he liked very much. He also completed his GED while in the service. Ben began to experience psychological problems during the latter part of his tour of duty and was discharged with a small disability pension.

Since his discharge Ben has lived in a variety of places including "the streets" and several board and care homes. He has been employed in several part-time jobs, all of which involved entry-level unskilled labor. He worked as a dishwasher and a cook in a fast-food chain, a clerk and a stockboy in a retail drug store, and, most recently, as a cab driver. He left these jobs for a variety of reasons, and he described his work experience as limited.

Ben's social support network has been limited. He has had few friends whom he visited "once every 2 or 3 months." Most of his family members live several hundred miles away and he only talks to them on the phone "once or twice a year." He has a sister who lives locally but he describes their relationship as distant. He does not have a girlfriend.

During the last 5 years, Ben was hospitalized twice for extended periods of time. His most recent hospitalization occurred 6 months ago and resulted in a 3-month inpatient stay. Upon admission he presented a number of acute primary symptoms and was diagnosed as chronic schizophrenic. He evidently had been

FIGURE 9-4. Behavioral checklist of social and independent living skills.

Date: _____ Interviewer: _____
Patient: _____ Inpatient: _____ Outpatient: _____

The purpose of this assessment device is to gather information about a patient's performance of social and independent living skills. Two types of information are gathered: (1) the patient's report of the performance of these skills in either the 30 days prior to the interview or "in general," and (2) direct observation of the "outcome" of these skills (e.g., how well groomed is the patient). Of course, not each type of information will be gathered about each skill.

I. SKILL AREA: Personal hygiene
   TIME FRAME: In the past 30 days
   A. PATIENT REPORT   N/A   YES   NO
      1. Do you bathe or shower using soap at least twice per week?
      2. Do you shampoo your hair at least twice per week [once per week for females]?
      3. Do you use deodorant daily?
      4. Do you brush or comb your hair daily?
      5. Do you shave or comb your beard daily [males only]?
      6. What do you use during menstruation [females only]? (Score yes if patient indicates pads or tampons.)
      7. Do you regularly clean your nails?
      8. Do you brush your teeth using toothpaste at least once a day?
   B. INTERVIEWER'S OBSERVATION
      9. Face, arms, hands, etc., appear clean.
      10. Hair appears clean.
      11. Hair appears neatly combed.
      12. Hair appears neatly cut.
      13. No body odor.
      14. Nails appear clean.
      15. Face shaven or beard appears neatly combed [males only].
                                     TOTAL NUMBER N/A _____   (Transfer to Col. B)
                                     TOTAL NUMBER YES _____   (Transfer to Col. D)

Please explain all items marked N/A (e.g., #—explanation): _____

II. SKILL AREA: Personal appearance and care of clothing
    TIME FRAME: In the past 30 days
    A. PATIENT REPORT   N/A   YES   NO
       1. Do you change your underwear at least twice a week?
       2. Do you buy your own clothing?
       3. Do you use soap when you wash your clothes?
       4. Do you fold or hang up your clothes after they have been washed?
       5. Do you neatly store your clothes after they have been washed?
       6. Do you store your dirty clothes in a place separate from your clean clothes?
    B. INTERVIEWER'S OBSERVATION
       7. Clothing appears neat and clean.
       8. Clothing appears appropriate for time of year.
       9. Colors and types of clothing appear appropriately coordinated.
                                     TOTAL NUMBER N/A _____   (Transfer to Col. B)
                                     TOTAL NUMBER YES _____   (Transfer to Col. D)

Please explain all items marked N/A (e.g., #—explanation): _____

III. SKILL AREA: Care of personal possessions
     TIME FRAME: In the past 30 days
     PATIENT REPORT   N/A   YES   NO
     1. Do you make your bed daily?

(Continued)

FIGURE 9-4. (*Continued*)

N/A   YES   NO

2. Do you keep your room clean?
3. Do you pick up your "clutter" and put back objects such as clothes, magazines, and cigarettes where they belong?
4. Do you wipe up something that spills on your furniture or carpet, such as coffee?
5. Do you vacuum (if you have carpet) or mop your floor?
6. Do you dust your furniture?

TOTAL NUMBER N/A _____   (Transfer to Col. B)
TOTAL NUMBER YES _____   (Transfer to Col. D)

Please explain all items marked N/A (e.g., #—explanation): _____

IV. SKILL AREA: Food preparation and storage
TIME FRAME: Usual lifestyle (not in hospital)
PATIENT REPORT   N/A   YES   NO

1. Do you eat at least one serving of a vegetable daily?
2. Do you eat at least one serving of a dairy product daily?
3. Do you eat at least one serving of a cereal or grain (bread, etc.) daily?
4. Do you eat at least one serving of either meat, poultry, or fish daily?
5. Do you prepare simple foods such as sandwiches, cold cereal, etc., that do not require cooking?
6. Do you prepare food that requires a small amount of cooking such as fried eggs, TV dinners?
7. Do you discard foods that have been spoiled?
8. Do you wash dishes after each meal?
9. Do you dry the dishes after they have been washed?
10. Do you put dishes away after they have been dried?
11. Do you buy your own groceries?

TOTAL NUMBER N/A _____   (Transfer to Col. B)
TOTAL NUMBER YES _____   (Transfer to Col. D)

Please explain all items marked N/A (e.g., #—explanation): _____

V. SKILL AREA: Health maintenance
TIME FRAME: Usual lifestyle (not in hospital)
PATIENT REPORT   N/A   YES   NO

1. Do you administer your own medication?
   (If not on medication, in the past when you were taking medication, did you administer your own medication?)
2. Do you take your medication every day exactly as prescribed? (If not on medication, in the past when you were taking medication, did you take the medication every day exactly as prescribed?)
3. If you do not administer your own medication, do you cooperate with the person who administers the medication? (Score yes if the person self-administers.)
4. Do you contact the appropriate person to renew your prescription? (If not on medication, in the past when you were taking medication, did you contact the appropriate person to renew your prescription?)
5. Do you treat yourself for minor physical ailments such as a cold?
6. Do you know the proper use of insurance or welfare coverage such as Medi-Cal and Medicare?
7. Do you smoke cigarettes safely (i.e., no holes in clothes, no cigarette burns on beds or furniture)? (Score N/A if person does not smoke.)

TOTAL NUMBER N/A _____   (Transfer to Col. B)
TOTAL NUMBER YES _____   (Transfer to Col. D)

FIGURE 9-4. (*Continued*)

Please explain all items marked N/A (e.g., #—explanation): _____

VI. SKILL AREA: Money management
TIME FRAME: Usual lifestyle (not in hospital)
PATIENT REPORT   N/A   YES   NO
   1. Do you manage your own money?
   2. Do you pay your own bills such as rent, utilities, and phone?
   3. Do you pay your own bills on time?
   4. Do you have a savings account (not a patient account)?
   5. Do you have a checking account?
   6. Do you fill out a budget or make a plan for expenses?
   7. Do you cash your own paycheck or SSI check?
   8. Do you purchase essential items such as rent and food prior to spending
      money on luxuries?
                              TOTAL NUMBER N/A _____   (Transfer to Col. B)
                              TOTAL NUMBER YES _____   (Transfer to Col. D)

Please explain all items marked N/A (e.g., #—explanation): _____

VII. SKILL AREA: Transportation
TIME FRAME: Usual lifestyle (not in hospital)
PATIENT REPORT   N/A   YES   NO
   1. Do you hold a valid California driver's license?
   2. Do you have and use your own car? (If yes, answer all other questions
      yes.)
   3. Do you use the bus?
   4. Do you read bus schedules?
   5. Do you call the bus company to get directions to someplace new?
   6. Do you ask others for directions to someplace new?
                              TOTAL NUMBER N/A _____   (Transfer to Col. B)
                              TOTAL NUMBER YES _____   (Transfer to Col. D)

Please explain all items marked N/A (e.g., #—explanation): _____

VIII. SKILL AREA: Leisure and recreation
TIME FRAME: Usual lifestyle (not in hospital)
PATIENT REPORT (weekly)   N/A   YES   NO
   1. Do you have a hobby on which you work regularly?
   2. Do you go to church/synagogue?
   3. Do you regularly listen to the radio or watch TV?
   4. Do you regularly write letters or visit friends or relatives?
   5. Do you regularly go to the movies?
   6. Do you regularly read books, newspapers, or magazines?
   7. Do you regularly attend meetings of veterans' organizations or other
      groups, such as Project Return?
                              TOTAL NUMBER N/A _____   (Transfer to Col. B)
                              TOTAL NUMBER YES _____   (Transfer to Col. D)

Please explain all items marked N/A (e.g., #—explanation): _____

IX. SKILL AREA: Job-seeking skills
TIME FRAME: In the past 30 days
PATIENT REPORT   N/A   YES   NO
(If the patient is currrently employed or has the job "waiting," score all
questions yes!)
   1. Do you read the classified ads one or more time per week to look for jobs?
   2. Do you contact potential employers to determine possible job openings?

                                                              (*continued*)

FIGURE 9-4. (*Continued*)

N/A   YES   NO

3. Do you contact friends and others such as employment agencies to obtain job leads?
4. Do you participate in job interviews?

TOTAL NUMBER N/A _____   (Transfer to Col. B)
TOTAL NUMBER YES _____   (Transfer to Col. D)

Please explain all items marked N/A (e.g., #—explanation): _____

X. SKILL AREA: Job maintenance
TIME FRAME: Usual lifestyle (not in hospital)
PATIENT REPORT   N/A   YES   NO
(If the patient has never been employed for a cumulative total of at least 1 year, score all questions N/A.)
1. Do you arrive on time for work?
2. Do you get along with your co-workers?
3. Do you get along with your supervisors?

TOTAL NUMBER N/A _____   (Transfer to Col. B)
TOTAL NUMBER YES _____   (Transfer to Col. D)

Please explain all items marked N/A (e.g., #—explanation): _____

COMMENTS (include any circumstances that may invalidate these assessments): _____

---

off his antipsychotic medication for some time, a recurrent problem from his medical records. To control these symptoms, an antipsychotic drug regimen was used, which included self-administered Prolixin for his primary symptoms and Cogentin for side effects. Prior to discharge and community placement, his ward treatment team referred Ben to the SILS program for evaluation and training of community living skills. Services provided by the SILS team began 1 month prior to his discharge and have continued on an outpatient basis since then.

Screening and Assessment

An initial screening interview was conducted by the intake coordinator in order to describe the training program and to identify skill areas to be trained. Ben felt he would obtain benefits from many areas including medication management, conversational skills, leisure and recreational skills, home-finding, and job-seeking skills. He appeared highly motivated to participate in the program and agreed to meet with the training groups as long as other obligations (such as obtaining a job) did not interfere.

Upon entry into the program, an intensive assessment of Ben's deficits and goals was conducted. Using the Life Ladder Ben identified three target areas—understanding more about his illness and medications, overcoming his shyness and improving his interpersonal communication, and obtaining and maintaining employment. These goals were operationalized in terms of skills deficits in

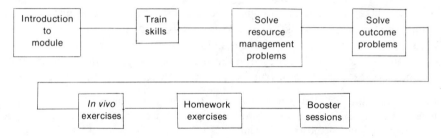

FIGURE 9-5. Components of the training model.

medication self-management, conversational skills and job seeking and mainte-nance skills. A behavioral checklist of community living skills involved in these areas also provided corroborative information for these deficits in Ben's skills repertoire. Based upon this information two areas were prioritized for initial skill training. Ben agreed to participate in the medication self-management and conversational skills training modules. This agreement was formalized using a behavioral contract explicitly dated as an Individualized Written Rehabilitation Plan (IWRP). In his IWRP Ben agreed to participate in the medication and conversational skills groups on a daily basis, 4 days a week. Each hour-long group would consist of a therapist, Ben, and one other client (George). Ben also agreed to be on time and actively participate in the training. Staff agreed to provide training in the best manner possible and also to be on time. Contingent upon attendance, Ben would be periodically rewarded with (1) coupon books that he could exchange in the local canteen and (2) leisure recreational activities conducted in the program such as outings and parties. Illustration of the training techniques will be given in the context of medication self-management training.

MEDICATION MANAGEMENT TRAINING

Training in medication management is designed to teach clients four sets of skills that are related to the use of antipsychotic medication (see Table 9-2). In addition to training in these skills, clients are taught problem-solving skills that may facilitate the implementation of the skills they have learned. Excerpts from each of the exercises involved in the training process will be presented to illustrate the training procedures.

Baseline Assessments

Prior to implementation of the training, baseline measurements are collected that not only assist in pinpointing each client's deficits but are also an essential first step in evaluating the effectiveness of the training. These baseline measurements are taken in analogue role plays designed to simulate situations in which clients should exhibit the skills to be learned. Given the limitations of role play assessments, *in vivo* data are also obtained whenever possible.

Ben was individually assessed in the specific skills scenes in the medication module. For example, the instructions for the physician negotiation scene are:

Ben, you take the role of a veteran on oral medication. For a couple of days your right hand has been shaking and causing you some discomfort. You think the problem is a side effect of your medication. Assume it is 9:00 a.m., and you have arrived for an appointment with your doctor. I'll play the doctor you have the appointment with. Your task is to enter my office from this corner and take appropriate action to deal with the problem that you have been suffering with for the last couple of days—the shaking of your right hand.

Since schizophrenic clients are typically deficient in "receiving skills," it is important to ensure the client understands the parameters of the situation. A common set of questions are asked across all scenes and all training modules to address this problem. These questions, illustrated with answers in the context of the medication example, include:

THERAPIST: What is your role in this scene?
BEN: A vet . . . with a side effect of my meds.
T: What is my role in this scene?
B: The doctor.
T: What is your task in this scene?
B: Tell about my problem.
T: Great, let's start!

The therapist then plays a prescribed role during the assessment. In this example, he or she sits down at a desk and pretends to be working on paperwork. When the veteran enters the therapist looks up but does not greet him. The therapist makes a reference to the veteran's last visit. If the veteran makes a request, the therapist provides a vague order for additional medication to deal with the problem. At the conclusion of the performance, the therapist thanks the client. It is important to reinforce the client for his efforts, no matter how poorly they may be: "Ben, nice job. We can make some improvements with training though. I really appreciate that you tried so hard." Figure 9-6 details the criteria used to score Ben's performance on this scene. As indicated in Figure 9-6, Ben performed 54% of the criterion behaviors. Figure 9-7 presents Ben's performances in each of the four skill scenes of the module. As may be seen in the figure, although Ben's performance varied across the four scenes in the module, he could stand improvement in all training scenes of the module.

Introduction to the Module

Following collection of baseline data for each skill scene, training begins with an introduction to the module. The purpose of this training component is to have clients actively identify the goal of the module, the consequences that will occur

Module: Medication management
Skill: Negotiating medication issues with physician
Patient: _____
Score: X if behavior is present

	Role play				
	1	2	3	4	5
Criterion behaviors					
1. Greets doctor	X				
2. Tells name	X				
3. Describes side effects	X				
4. Describes length of occurrence					
5. Describes extent of discomfort					
6. Requests action to deal with problem	X				
7. Repeats/asks questions to clarify order					
8. Asks question about expected effect (e.g., how long)					
9. Thanks doctor and leaves	X				
Response topography					
10. Eye contact					
11. Voice volume					
12. Speech fluency	X				
13. Posture	X				
Total (13)	7				
Percent	54%				

FIGURE 9-6. Criteria sheet for physician negotations scene.

FIGURE 9-7. Percentage of criterion behaviors performed in the four skill scenes of the medication module.

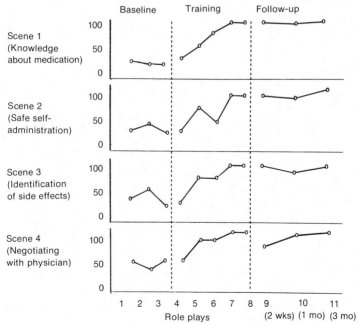

if the goal is achieved, and the steps necessary to achieve the goal, each of which represent skills that will be trained in the module. In addition, the exercise is used to introduce clients to the language that will be used in various aspects of training (e.g., consequences, resources).

Procedure

This exercise consists of a brief description of the module and the following set of questions:

1. What is the goal of this module?
2. What is the problem?
3. If you get [goal], what will happen?
4. Do you have time, money, skills, people to help?
5. What are the steps to get [goal]?

As in all components of training, the description and predetermined correct answers are written on a data sheet that the therapist uses to evaluate clients answers. Figure 9-8 presents the data sheet used in this component of the

FIGURE 9-8. Data sheet for medication management module introduction.

Today we are beginning the medication management module. The goal of this module is to provide you with the information and skills necessary for you to manage your medication properly and safely. This is important for you to know, since you are taking these medications. In the module you will see videotapes that present the important information to you. Pay close attention, because I will ask you questions whose answers will highlight the skills that are being taught.

Date: _____

Patient	Question	Correct answer	Number of trials
	Goal	Proper self-management of one's medication	
	Problem	Need clear understanding of purposes of medication	
	+, − consequences	+ Relief of symptoms	
		+ Improvements of thinking and concentration	
		+ Restoration of sound judgment and insight	
		+ Restores a sense of calmness and well-being	
		+ Fosters participation in therapy programs	
		+ Improves the course of emotional illness	
		− May cause unpleasant side effects	
		− May have to take medications for a very long time	
	Resources	Time: N/A	
		Skills: N/A	
		Money: N/A	
		People: help; no help	
		Miscellaneous: _____	
	Steps	1. Obtain information about purpose of medication.	
		2. Learn to take medication properly.	
		3. Evaluate your body's response to medication.	

medication management module. The data sheet provides a means of recording the information about the effectiveness of the training (in this case, the number of correct and incorrect answers), as well as a cue to the trainers regarding their activities during the exercise, thus enhancing intertrainer consistency.

Case Example

A typical session with the therapist and two clients (one of whom is Ben) is as follows:

THERAPIST: Today we are beginning the medication management module. The goal of this module is to provide you with the information and skills necessary for you to manage your medication properly and safely. This is important for you to know since you are taking these medications. In the module you will see videotapes that present the important information to you. Pay close attention, because I will ask you questions whose answers will highlight the skills that are being taught. . . . Ben, what is the goal of this module?
BEN: To learn about my medication.
T: Right! George, why would you need to learn this information?
GEORGE: Because I'm taking the meds and I need to know how to take them . . . tell me what they are supposed to do.
T: That's very good George. If you take your meds right, what positive consequences will happen?
G: I won't hear any voices, or see things.
T: Yes. How about you Ben?
B: They make me think clearer.
T: Excellent. What negative consequences may happen, Ben?
B: Well, I might have side effects, but my Cogentin is for that.
T: That's possible, but if you continue to take your Cogentin is that a problem?
B: No, at least not now.
T: George, what resources do you have to help you deal with your meds?
G: What do you mean? I mean, what is a resource?
T: Anything that can help you or you can use to help you . . . like money or people.
G: Oh, I guess I've got people, that's why I'm in the group to learn.
T: Right . . . do you have any other resources?
G: No, at least none I can think of.
T: OK. Ben, what steps do you need to know in order to properly manage your medications?
B: I need to know what they are supposed to do.
T: Right . . . what else?
B: Well how to take them.
T: That's good, can you add anything, George?

G: Well, I need to know when they aren't working right . . . you know, causing me a problem.

T: You mean like a side effect?

G: Right.

T: You guys have got all the things we are going to learn about . . . the benefits of your meds, how to take them . . . recognizing side effects and get help to deal with them. We'll learn all these skills during the training. Good job guys!

It is important to note that the major goal at this point is to get clients thinking and talking about the material they are to learn. Thus, the therapist is primarily concentrating on establishing a highly reinforcing environment for client effort rather than the correctness of information provided per se.

However, if clients respond incorrectly to any question, the trainer asks an additional set of ever more leading questions designed to prompt clients to give the correct answer. These additional questions are developed to some extent at the option of the trainer. Data are collected about the number of correct answers and the number of leading questions (number of trials on the data sheet, Figure 9-8) required to elicit a correct answer.

Training Skills

Following the general introduction to the module, training progresses through the various skills in the module that clients have just identified. Training includes a combination of behavioral techniques including role-played practices, social and videotaped demonstrations, and social and videotaped feedback. Following an introduction to the skill that emphasizes the relationship of the skill to overall goal of the module, training involves two basic sets of procedures.

First, clients view a videotaped demonstration (modeling tape) of the correct performance of the skill. The tape is periodically stopped and clients are asked questions to assess their attentiveness to and comprehension of the information conveyed in the demonstration. The questions to be asked and the correct answers are written on a data sheet; Figure 9-9 presents a data sheet used in one segment of the videotaped demonstration of negotations with physicians. Incorrect answers result in replaying the videotape and highlighting the information needed to correctly answer the question when it is repeated. Data are collected about the number of correct and incorrect answers.

In the second set of procedures, clients are asked to practice the skills they have just learned in a role play. This performance is videotaped for subsequent review by the client and therapist. In this review the therapist evaluates the performance for the presence and/or absence of behaviors identified on a checklist of criterion behaviors from the modeling tape. Positive feedback is provided for the performance of criterion behavior and suggestions for improvement to highlight absent criterion behaviors. The role play is then reenacted and the process is repeated until the client exhibits 100% of the criterion behaviors included in the skill scene.

Module: Medication management
Skill: Negotiating medication issues with physician
Date: _____

In viewing this videotaped scene, you will learn to present information about a side effect to your doctor in a way that will maximize your chances of obtaining positive action toward relief of the problem.

Patient	Question	Correct answer	Number of trials
	Goal (specific scene)	To take proper action to relieve side effects	
	Goal (module)	Self-management of one's medication	

Stop	Questions/answers	Trials to criterion
1	Q: Who is in this scene? A. Dr. Smith and Frank Brown Q: What did Frank do when he first met the doctor? A: 1. Said hello 2. Introduced himself Q: What was Frank's problem in the scene? A: Drowsy at work Q: What information did he tell the doctor about his drowsiness? A: 1. Degree of discomfort—bothering a lot 2. Length of occurrence—couple of weeks Q: What should you do after you describe the problem? A: Ask for help Q: Can you describe his nonverbal behavior when making his request for help? A: 1. Good eye contact 2. Strong voice volume/tone 3. Posture Q: Do you think he asked his question in a positive manner? A: Yes	

Break and review

FIGURE 9-9. Skill training data sheet.

Example

In order to illustrate the training process, excerpts from the scene on dealing with physicians are given below. Training begins with an introduction to the goals of the scene.

THERAPIST: In this scene you will learn to present information about a side effect to your doctor in a way that will maximize your chances of obtaining positive action toward relief of the problem. What is the goal of this scene?

BEN: To learn how to talk to a doctor about my side effects.

T: Right, and what is the goal of this module?

B: To learn how to manage my medication.

T: You got it! Let's watch the tape.

The modeling tape is shown to the group at this point. The tape depicts a client discussing a side effect of his medication with a doctor. For example,

CLIENT: Hi, Dr. Smith. Do you remember me? I'm Frank Brown.

DOCTOR: Sure Frank, it's been a while since I've seen you, though. On your last visit, things seemed to be going along quite nicely.

C: Yeah Doc, the nurse has been helping me with a lot of my problems, but I waited to talk to you about one of them.

D: OK.

C: I'm having a lot of trouble with being sleepy on the job. I'm so drowsy I can't hardly keep up with my work.

D: I see.

C: The problem has been getting worse for a couple of weeks now and it's so bad I'm afraid I might get fired. Is there anything you could do about it . . . I mean my drowsiness?

D: Are you sleeping at night?

C: Yes, I even tried to go to bed early, but that doesn't seem to help.

At this point, an edited pause would appear on the tape, and the therapist asks questions about what had just been demonstrated. Two kinds of questions are asked, some that are primarily attentional and others that highlight the relevant criterion behavior.

THERAPIST: Ben, who is in this scene?

BEN: A doctor and a veteran.

T: Right. George, do you remember their names?

GEORGE: Dr. Smith and . . . Frank.

T: Exactly right, you two are really paying close attention. George, what did Frank do when he first met the doctor?

G: Said hello to him.

T: Yeah, did you notice anything else?

G: He introduced himself.

T: Right! It's important to greet the doctor pleasantly and to be sure and introduce yourself, especially if the doctor hasn't seen you in a while or if he is a new doctor for you. Ben, what was Frank's problem in the scene?

B: He was drowsy at work.

T: Yes. What information did he tell the doctor about his drowsiness?

B: That it's bothering him a lot.

T: OK, was there anything else?

B: No.

T: How about you, George?

G: He just said he was drowsy and it was bothering him a lot.

T: Good. It's important to describe very carefully what the problem is and how much it's bothering you. But that's not all you should tell him. Let's view the tape again. Watch closely for all the information he tells the doctor.

As a correction procedure, the therapist would show the tape again and prompt the clients to look for any specific information they missed, in this case, how long the problem has been occurring.

THERAPIST: What else did he tell the doctor, guys?

BEN: That the problem had been going on for a couple of weeks.

T: Sure. When you describe a problem to the doctor, be sure and tell him how long it has been occurring and how much trouble it is causing you.

GEORGE: Alright, then I guess you should ask him for his help.

T: Exactly, you guessed my next question. What should you do after you describe the problem?

B: Ask for help so you are sure he knows what you want.

T: Right, Ben. Can you describe his nonverbal behavior when making his request for help?

B: He looked him directly in the eyes and spoke in a strong tone of voice.

T: Yeah . . . anything else you noticed, George?

G: Well, he sat in a chair close to the doctor and sat up straight.

T: So he had good posture. Do you guys think he asked his question in a positive manner?

G AND B: Yes.

T: Great! Let's review what we saw in the segment. Frank greeted the doctor and introduced himself. He told the doctor his problem, described how long it had been going on and how much discomfort it is causing him. He directly asked for help using good nonverbal behavior . . . eye contact, posture, good voice volume. Let's look at the next segment of the tape.

With this summary the process repeats until all segments of tape have been seen.

Clients are then asked to practice the skills they have observed in a role play. In this example these (instructions) are to describe the side effect and request action to help alleviate a side effect if possible. (The same instructions and criteria behavior that were described in the section on baseline assessments are used to set up the scene). Since client performance is videotaped, the therapist may serve as a confederate in the role play and then provide feedback regarding client performance while reviewing the tape. In addition, the use of videotape allows the therapist to involve the client and others in the group in the feedback process. This involvement may actually result in more variety in sources and types of reinforcers provided to the client as well as increase the overall involvement of all clients in the group. In many instances other clients provide extremely good suggestions for improvements in performance. The following excerpt illustrates a typical client performance and the way in which the therapist provides feedback to the client.

BEN: Hello, doctor. I wanted to talk to you about a problem I've been having that I think is a side effect of my medication.

DOCTOR: OK.

B: For a few days my right hand has been shaking. I can't seem to make it stop and it's really bothering me. Could you do something about it?

D: Let's increase your side effect medication to three tablets per day instead of one.

B: OK, how long should it be before the shaking stops?

D: Very soon . . . a day or two at the most.

B: I hope it works doctor. Thank you for your help.

While reviewing the tape, the therapist rates Ben's performance using the criteria previously identified.

THERAPIST: You did a really nice job there. Let's look at the tape and see how you did. Let's start with your nonverbal behavior. Your eye contact, voice volume, and speech fluency were excellent. In fact, I couldn't have done a better job myself. What do you think?

BEN: Well, I tried hard to remember the things we discussed. Looking at the tape, I wish I'd sat up straighter.

T: Yes, I agree. If you sat up straighter you might make a better impression on the doctor that you mean business and want some action. Let's look at the content of what you said. (*Plays tape.*) You greeted the doctor very nicely . . . and did an excellent job of describing your problem . . . how long it has been occurring, how much it's bothering you. Good request for help. George, what do you think up to this point?

GEORGE: Well, I like what he did. Aren't we supposed to tell the doctor our name just in case he doesn't remember it, though? Did you do that?

B: I don't think so. I'll try that next time.

T: Good idea. I only saw one other thing you left out. Remember about repeating the orders the doctor gave you to make sure you got them right?

B: Oh, yeah.

T: Let's try again. This time I want you to do everything you did that time and to concentrate on adding three more items: Your posture, reminding the doctor of your name, and repeating the doctor's orders. OK, let's go.

The scene is replayed until the client can perform all criterion behaviors in the role play on two successive trials. The therapist may go to other members of the group for similar practice and shaping or alternate among members of the group until each client exhibits all criterion behaviors. Figure 9-7 shows Ben's data for the acquisition of the skills in this scene, which clearly show improvements in his performance. This information was presented to him to concretely illustrate how well he was learning in the program. Subsequent assessments made on 2-week, 1-month, and 3-month follow-up intervals indicated Ben was retaining most of the information he had learned.

Problem-Solving Training

A major difficulty with skills training programs is an often noted lack of generalization of the skills to the client's natural environment. Two critical factors in facilitating generalization of skills are focused upon in specific training procedures. Clients may not implement the skills in their repertoires because they lack the resources that are required to put their skills into use. For example, it is impossible to exhibit good job interview skills if one is unable to obtain transportation to the interview. Thus, training should teach clients to identify and obtain needed resources.

Clients may also fail to implement skills because they run into obstacles in the environment that preclude their performance of trained skills. For example, one is unable to exhibit good interview skills when the interviewer does not keep the client's appointment. Thus, training should teach clients ways to deal with such obstacles. In the SILS program problem-solving training is used to teach clients ways to deal with these resource and outcome problems.

Resource Management Problems

After each skill has been correctly role-played, clients are taught to solve the resource management problems for that particular skill. The training procedures consist of the trainer's describing the skill and asking a series of questions designed to have clients actively consider each of the variables outlined in the model of a successful solution to this type of problem (see Figure 9-1). The questions are:

1. What is your goal in using this skill?
2. What is the goal of this module?
3. What resources must you have to [skill]?
   (For each resource mentioned in 3:)
4. How would you get [resources]?
5. If you were to get [resource] by [method in 4], what other positive consequences would happen?
6. If you were to get [resource] by [method in 4], what negative consequences might happen?
7. Do the positive consequences outweigh the negative consequences?

As detailed in Figure 9-10, all questions and the corresponding correct answers are written on a data sheet. The trainer compares clients' answers to those on the data sheet and institutes a correction procedure if any answer is incorrect.

Example

The following transcript illustrates the application of these exercises in the physician negotiation scene:

Module: Medication management
Skill: Negotiating medication issues with physician
Date: _____

Let's consider how you might use the problem-solving model to generate resources you might need to talk to a doctor about a side effect you are experiencing. This time, let's use the side effect of blurred vision that has persisted for 2 weeks on a sporadic basis. You've decided to discuss this problem with your doctor and want to find out how to get some relief from the problem.

Patient	Question	Correct answer	Number of trials
	Goal (specific)	To get information about appropriate action to take for medication side effects	
	Goal (general)	Self-management of one's medication	

Resources
Patient: _____ Doctor appointment: _____ (# GEN:)

#	Answer	# T	# +	# −	# T	+ > −	Role play Skills[a]
			Specify +, −			Eval +, −	
	Call and ask						NO, EC, VV, FL, PO, CONT
	Go to hospital ER						NO, EC, VV, FL, PO, CONT
							NO, EC, VV, FL, PO, CONT

Side effect monitoring data
Patient: _____ (# GEN:)

#	Answer	# T	# +	# −	# T	+ > −	Role play Skills[a]
	How get?			Specify +, −		Eval +, −	
	Collect/write down						NO, EC, VV, FL, PO, CONT
							NO, EC, VV, FL, PO, CONT
							NO, EC, VV, FL, PO, CONT

[a]NO = not role-played; EC = eye contact deficiency; VV = voice volume deficiency; FL = fluency deficiency; PO = posture deficiency; CONT = content deficiency.

FIGURE 9-10. Data sheet for resource management.

THERAPIST: Let's consider how you might use the problem-solving model to generate resources you might need to talk to a doctor about a side effect you are experiencing. This time, let's use the side effect of blurred vision that has persisted for 2 weeks on an on-and-off basis. You've decided to discuss this problem with your doctor and want to find out how to get some relief from this problem. What is your goal in this situation?

BEN: To find out how to get rid of my side effect.

T: Right, and what's the goal of the module?

B: To self-manage my medication.

T: What are all the steps you might need to gain information from your doctor to obtain relief from this side effect?

B: Well . . . I'd need an appointment with my doctor and a way to get there. I might also want to be sure and have information about my side effect and medication.

T: Great! Let's start with getting an appointment with your doctor. Can you name all the ways you might go about getting an appointment with the doctor?

B: Well, the easiest would be to just call and ask for one.

T: If you were to get an appointment by calling and asking, name as many positive consequences as you can think of besides getting the appointment.

B: Well, it's cheap since I have a phone.

T: Can you think of any other?

B: Well . . . it's convenient and doesn't take much time.

T: Yeah . . . if that's all you can think of, can you name as many negative consequences you can think of?

B: Well, there doesn't seem to be any . . . except I would have to talk on the phone, and it might be easier for someone to give me the brush off.

T: Yeah, there aren't really too many. Can you think of any others.

B: No.

T: Well, do the positive consequences outweigh the negative consequences?

B: I guess so. I think that's what I would do.

T: OK, let's practice calling and asking for an appointment.

A number of predetermined alternatives are evaluated for each scene. For example, in addition to the alternative just evaluated, the client may opt to go directly to the hospital where he or she could ask to see the doctor, or if the side effects were serious enough, try the emergency room. In each instance a chosen alternative would be practiced, especially if it involves an interpersonal situation.

If clients do not mention each of these predetermined alternatives, they are asked leading questions until each has been mentioned and evaluated in terms of its positive and negative consequences. There are no predetermined answers to evaluating each alternative; the only criterion is that the consequences generated by the clients be realistic and correclty evaluated in terms of their positive or negative value.

Once the client has solved the problem of obtaining a given resource, he or she would then proceed to apply the process to the next resource identified, in this case, transportation. A number of alternative methods could be used to get the appointment, such as walking, riding a bus, taking a cab, or borrowing a ride with a friend. Clients would evaluate each and choose one that they would then practice implementing in a role play. It is interesting to note that the therapist may use this opportunity to identify additional deficits in the client's skills and knowledge ranging from lack of information about public transportation to poor skills in initiating requests. Each practice session may be used to work on the content and response topography of the client's behavior based upon this information.

Outcome Problems

After clients have been trained to solve the problems involved in marshalling the resources necessary to perform a skill, they are trained to solve the problems that might occur when they use the skill and the environment does not respond in an optimal manner. The training procedures begin with the trainer's reading a description of the attempt to use the skill, the response made by the environment, and the resources available to solve the problem posed by the environment's response. Clients are then asked questions designed to have them actively consider each of the variables outlined in the model of a successful solution to this type of problem (see Figure 9-2). The questions are:

1. What is the problem?
2. Do you have time, money, skills, people to help?
3. What can you do to solve the problem?
4. Is [method in 3] feasible?
5. If you [method in 3], will you likely get your goal?
6. If you were to [method in 3], name as many positive consequences as you think would occur besides solving the problem.
7. If you were to [method in 3], name as many negative consequences as you can think of.
8. Do the positive consequences outweigh the negative consequences?

The scoring of clients' answers, the training of correct answers, and the collection of data are all performed in much the same manner as in the training of the solving of resource management problems. Figure 9-11 presents the data sheet used with one of several outcome problems presented in the physician negotiation scene. This problem involves the client's attempt to obtain relief from blurred vision, a side effect of medication. The physician in the problem is unresponsive to the client's requests for help. A number of predetermined alternatives are included in the solution to the problem. If clients do not generate all of these alternatives in response to the question about what can be done to solve the problem, they are asked a series of leading questions until they identify all four alternatives. Similarly, there are predetermined answers to the questions about each alternative's feasibility and likelihood of obtaining the goal. Incorrect answers again result in a series of leading questions designed to elicit the correct response. As in the resource management problems, there are no predetermined answers for generating the positive and negative consequences of each alternative. The trainer may ask clients to role-play their solutions for evaluation and practice of delivery skills such as eye contact, fluency, posture, and so on.

Example

The following transcript illustrates the application of these exercises in the context of the physician negotiation scene. Outcome problem exercises are set up with the following general instructions:

THERAPIST: I'm going to present you some problem situations that you may run into if you were to use the skills you have learned in the medication module. Each situation is related to the role plays you have been practicing . . . the only difference is that an obstacle will arise in the situation that will make it difficult for you to use the skills you have learned. You will have two tasks in these new role plays. First, you are to try to use the skills you have learned as best you can in the situation. Second, when you run into the obstacle in the situation, I would like you to use the problem-solving method we talked about to decide how to solve the problem. Do you have any questions?

BEN: Just act like I would if I was in the situation?

T: Right.

Following a description of the scene, clients are asked to role-play the scene and the obstacle is presented to the client. For example, in the physician negotiation scene:

FIGURE 9-11. Data sheet for outcome problems.

Module: Medication management
Skill: Negotiating medication issues with physician
Date: _____

You are a veteran on oral medications. You have self-administered your medications for the past 2 months and have been going for follow-up visits on a once-a-month basis. You have noticed some blurring of vision and dryness of mouth for the last week, which is causing you problems on your job. You have decided to report these symptoms to your doctor during your next visit, which is today. When you arrive for your appointment, you find that your usual doctor is out on an emergency call, and you have been scheduled to see the doctor who is filling in for him. I'll play the role of the new doctor. You enter and take appropriate action to deal with your side effect.

(Note: Therapist is nonresponsive; "Let's just monitor that for awhile.")

Patient	Question	Correct answer	Number of trials
	Problem	Doctor doesn't want to deal with side effect	
	Resources	Time: <u>now</u>, later, N/A	
		Skills: high, low, <u>N/A</u>	
		Money: high, low, <u>N/A</u>	
		People: <u>help</u>, no help, N/A	
		Misc:	

(*continued*)

FIGURE 9-11. (*Continued*)

Patient: _____
Alternative: Go to emergency room   (# Gen:)

Feasible		Likely		Specify +, −			Eval +, −	Role play
Answer	# T	Ans	# T	# +	# −	# T	+ > −	Skills[a]
Y N		Y N ?					Y N	NO, EC, VV, FL, PO, CONT

Assume: Unavailable

Patient: _____
Alternative: Wait as directed   (# Gen:)

Feasible		Likely		Specify +, −			Eval +, −	Role play
Answer	# T	Ans	# T	# +	# −	# T	+ > −	Skills[a]
Y N		Y N ?					Y N	NO, EC, VV, FL, PO, CONT

Assume: You need action now

Patient: _____
Alternative: Repeat request   (# Gen:)

Feasible		Likely		Specify +, −			Eval +, −	Role play
Answer	# T	Ans	# T	# +	# −	# T	+ > −	Skills[a]
Y N		Y N ?					Y N	NO, EC, VV, FL, PO, CONT

Assume: Doesn't work

Patient: _____
Alternative: Stop taking all medication   (# Gen:)

Feasible		Likely		Specify +, −			Eval +, −	Role play
Answer	# T	Ans	# T	# +	# −	# T	+ > −	Skills[a]
Y N		Y N ?					Y N	NO, EC, VV, FL, PO, CONT

Assume: You are afraid your original symptoms will return

Patient: _____
Alternative: Ask to see own doctor   (# Gen:)

Feasible		Likely		Specify +, −			Eval +, −	Role play
Answer	# T	Ans	# T	# +	# −	# T	+ > −	Skills[a]
Y N		Y N ?					Y N	NO, EC, VV, FL, PO, CONT

Assume: Unavailable

[a]See Figure 9-10 for explanation of abbreviations.

THERAPIST: You are a veteran on oral medications. You have self-administered your medications for the past 2 months and have been going for follow-up visits on a once-a-month basis. You have noticed some blurring of vision and dryness of mouth for the last week, which is causing you some problems on your job. You have decided to report these symptoms to your doctor during your next visit, which is today. When you arrive for your appointment, you find that your usual doctor is out on an emergency call, and you have been scheduled to see the doctor who is filling in for your doctor. I'll play the role of the new doctor. You enter and take appropriate action to deal with your side effect.

BEN: Good morning, Dr. Kimbal. I was supposed to see Dr. Smith today, but they told me to see you instead.

T: Yes, he's out on a call.

B: I'm having some trouble with my vision . . . it's always blurred and I can't see when I'm on my job. This problem has been going on for a week now. Could you do something about it?

T: (*Acting as physician.*) OK. Well, let's just monitor that for awhile, it could just be a matter of getting used to your medications. (*Stops role play.*) *Stop!* Let's solve that problem. . . . First, Ben, what is the problem?

B: I can't see well.

T: Right. That's the side effect you want the doctor to help you with. But what is the problem in the situation?

B: Oh, the doctor doesn't want to help me now.

T: That's the one I was interested in. Do you have time to solve the problem?

B: Well it's really bothering me so I want to get on with it. Not too much time.

T: OK. Do you have money to help you solve the problem?

B: Well, that's not really a factor . . . but I do have money.

T: Alright, do you have skills to solve the problem?

B: Yeah, I've been practicing talking with doctors for a long time.

T: Sure. . . . Do you have other people to help you solve the problem?

B: No, not in this situation. It's just me and the doctor. I guess I could ask others to help too though.

T: Yeah, it is good to remember there are others available sometimes. They may be helpful in identifying alternatives you could use to solve the problem. Well, what can you do to solve the problem?

B: Well, I guess I'd just do what he said. I mean he knows best.

T: Yeah . . . is waiting a feasible alternative?

B: I guess.

T: Yeah, if you waited, would you likely get your goal? I mean would it help with your vision?

B: Well . . . no, at least not for awhile.

T: Right! So maybe we should discard this one. What else could you do to solve the problem?

B: Well . . . I guess I could ask again and be sure the doctor knows how serious it was for me.

T: That's a better idea. Is it feasible?

B: Maybe.

T: OK. If you were to repeat your request and emphasize the seriousness of the problem, name as many of the positive consequences as you can think of that would happen besides solving the problem.

B: Well, it's easy to do. Since I'm already there it wouldn't take much time. It wouldn't cost me any bus money as it would if I had to come back.

T: Excellent. If you were to repeat your request, name as many negative consequences as you can think of.

B: Well, I don't know . . . it might make the doctor mad at me.

T: Well, maybe . . . can you think of others?

B: No.

T: Well, do you think the positive consequences outweigh the negative ones?

B: I think so.

T: OK. Let's try that one. Show me how you would repeat your request. [A role play is set up to let the client practice the request. Feedback regarding the performance is given to Ben.] Excellent job! You know, the way you asked was fantastic. You had excellent nonverbal behavior, especially your eye contact and voice volume. I really thought you meant business. Also, your request was put in a way that wouldn't make me mad. . . . I mean you emphasized the discomfort the problem is causing you and reminded the doctor how long you've been on your medication.

B: Well, I thought that might help. You know since he really doesn't know me very well.

T: Right. So that's an alternative you could certainly use. Suppose that didn't work . . . what else could you do to solve the problem?

B: I don't know. I guess I could ask to wait until the regular doctor came in.

T: Very good idea. Let's evaluate that alternative.

The process is repeated until the therapist and client have exhausted the pool of reasonable alternatives. During training clients are taught that when solving problems, as many alternatives should be presented as possible . . . more is better. A minimum of three alternatives are evaluated for each scene. Generation of consequences follows the same rule and clients are taught to identify at least two positive and negative consequences for each alternative. The choice of a particular alternative is left entirely up to the client, since the subjective weighting of various consequences may vary with individuals. However, the therapist does try to shape the client toward using alternatives that minimize expenditure of time, money, and resources. In addition, the therapist prompts the client to look at the interpersonal consequences of their behavior especially when they could result in benefits for the client such as meeting with others and potentially expanding the client's social network.

In Vivo Exercises

It is extremely important that the client is given the opportunity to practice the skills he or she has learned in his or her natural environment as an additional check and step toward programming for generalization. Skills that can only be used in the context of the laboratory are of little use to the client. In the SILS program *in vivo* exercises are used to facilitate this. Essentially, the client performs the skills in his or her world, but with a therapist who goes along in order to collect data regarding the performance as well as to provide feedback to the client. These exercises may be graded in terms of difficulty for the client, and his or her performance is assessed in these increasingly difficult situations.

An example in the medication management module may involve the client (and therapist) generating some questions regarding the client's own medication and then going to the program nurse to obtain answers. Following this task the client may be asked to try the same or similar questions with the ward physician or a local pharmacist. In each of these *in vivo* exercises, the therapist may help the client "fine tune" his or her performance as well as to problem-solve regarding resources or obstacles encountered during the performance. Ben and his therapist, for example, scheduled an appointment with Ben's nurse to discuss the side effects of his medication. All went smoothly during the interview, and the therapist decided to encourage Ben to expand the conversation to include general social topics. After being instructed to do so, Ben thought for a moment and then asked the nurse if she were a veteran. The nurse was understandably taken aback by the question, and the therapist suggested a more appropriate topic. Upon returning to the program, Ben and the therapist practiced introducing appropriate topics for conversation.

Homework Exercises

Finally, clients should be given the opportunity to independently perform the skills they have learned. Since it is the goal of the program to teach clients to function independently, this represents the ultimate step in training. Wherever possible, evaluation of these performances is made by looking at permanent products. For example, if the assignment is to obtain information from a pharmacist about one's medication, the client can verbally report to the therapist the information and bring back the pharmacist's business card. Therefore, the therapist has some indirect evidence for the performance of the skills. The role of the therapist in these exercises is to provide feedback to clients regarding their performance.

When planning homework assignments, it is important to anticipate and prepare clients for obstacles or undesired outcomes potentially encountered during the assignment. Despite these efforts, occasionally situations may arise where the "best laid plans" simply do not work. In light of this it is important for the therapist to provide clients with a sense of realism regarding the environment's potential response to client's efforts. An active problem-solving approach is used to deal with such situations and help clients redesign their assignment to ensure a more favorable outcome if necessary.

For example, Ben was assigned to locate a resource person regarding his medication outside of his regular therapist. He chose to talk to a pharmacist, and went to obtain information regarding the availability of time to discuss his medication. As a permanent product, he was to bring back a signed pharmacist's card with a list of hours when an appointment could be arranged and a phone number at which the pharmacist could be contacted in order to schedule an appointment.

Ben's attempt to complete the assignment was unsuccessful and he returned to the program confused and angry, stating "I did just like we planned and couldn't get the pharmacist to cooperate—this junk just doesn't work." On the surface the therapist identified that Ben had approached the pharmacist and implemented the "skills" he had learned. Only after careful questioning did the therapist learn that Ben had approached a female pharmacist and asked her for her phone number. Her reluctance was not surprising, since she had never met or seen Ben before. Using the problem-solving format, Ben decided on another alternative (to approach a male pharmacist) and subsequently carried out the assignment without problems.

Booster Exercises

The "booster" exercises are designed to refresh patient's skills after a period of inactivity. The exercises consist of the same or similar role-play, problem-solving, *in vivo*, and homework exercises used in the original training.

SUMMARY

The program described in this chapter makes considerable use of the methods typically found in other social skills programs: modeling, rehearsal, feedback, reinforcement, and homework. The efficacy of these methods in helping psychiatric patients—including schizophrenics—gain important skills has been demonstrated on several occasions. However, the previous social skills methodology has its limitations, and the Brentwood VA program incorporates several features not ordinarily found in social skills programs.

First, most programs focus on conversational skills, including nonverbal ones such as eye contact, voice volume, and posture, as well as simple content such as initiating a conversation or slightly more advanced content such as being assertive in difficult interpersonal social situations. The Brentwood program does include such skills training; one of the modules is exclusively devoted to training conversational skills. However, the conversational skills module is but one skill area; patients may also receive training in several or many other areas. The focus in the Brentwood program is on *independent living skills*, not only conversational skills. This approach has particular value for poorly skilled psychiatric clients. For example, it does a client little good to have appropriate conversational skills if the concomitant grooming skills are so deficient the patient is repugnant to others. The variety of skills modules provides clients with an opportunity to learn a comprehensive set of important living skills, which when combined with the usual conversational skills training, is more likely to lead to the possibility of increased independent living.

A fundamental feature of the SILS program is the heavy emphasis on a kind of information-processing model of social skills training. In recent years several investigators (McFall, 1982; Trower, Bryant, & Argyle, 1978; Wallace *et al.*, 1980) have proposed that social skills be conceptualized not only in terms of behavioral performance, but also in terms of abilities such as perceiving the requirements and goals of a situation, identifying the possible behavioral alternatives to solve the problem, identifying consequences of the alternatives, and selecting an appropriate alternative. In the Brentwood program each module trains not only *sending* skills (ability to perform a response) but also *receiving* skills (ability to understand the situation) and *processing* skills (ability to problem-solve the situation) (Wallace & Boone, 1983). Throughout the training procedure (of every module) patients are frequently asked such questions as "What is the problem? Who is in this scene? What did [the person in the scene] do?" (receiving skills training); and "What do you need to [implement the skill]? How would you get [the needed resources]? What are the positive consequences [if you performed a certain behavior]?" (problem-solving or processing skills).

This information-processing approach is especially important for social skills training with schizophrenic populations. It is not sufficient to assume these clients have only sending-skill deficits; it is important to be sure they learn to attend to relevant situational cues, understand the situational requirements, generate strategies for coping with the problem, evaluate the potential efficacy of each strategy, and have the skills to implement the selected strategy.

As can be seen from the program description, case example, and therapist forms, the modules are administered in a highly structured format. The training steps are very specific, and therapists are able to be consistent with such details as when to pause the modeling tape, what questions to ask, when to give prompts, and what behavioral criteria to observe and reinforce. This is not to say that the procedures are completely inflexible; sometimes patients do unexpected things not accounted for in the therapist's manual. The program does allow the therapist to vary from specified procedures as necessary to help patients who have individual needs or problems either in training or in their personal lives.

An important advantage of having specified training procedures, including comprehensive behavior checklists, is that program evaluation can be conducted simultaneously with ongoing clinical training. By evaluating pretraining skills, training progress, and posttraining skills with built-in data collection records, not only can patients' specific deficits be identified and remedied, but the program's procedures can undergo continuous troubleshooting, enabling the program to be frequently revised and improved. This latter point is especially important during the early periods of program development.

Evaluation has recently begun to test the effectiveness of the program's training modules. Preliminary data from the medication management module indicate the model described in this chapter is effective in the respect that the clients learn the skills content and that the skill acquisition is maintained for at least a period of 3 months after training has been completed. In addition to replicating these results with the other modules, future evaluation research will determine whether the skills acquired in treatment generalize to various natural environmental contexts. Research is also planned to "dismantle" the procedures to determine the relative therapeutic contributions of each of the procedural components. In particular, the problem-solving components—resource and outcome problem management—need to be evaluated to determine whether the cost of adding these procedures to a social skills training progress enhances the efficiency of the training.

Teaching chronically mentally disabled clients crucial social and independent living skills is a relatively new addition to available rehabilitation methods. Efforts to change their physical, family, and social environments to accommodate their disabilities are more familiar. For many mentally disabled individuals, a full range of traditional acute treatment and supportive services, in addition to environmental modification and independent living skills training, will be necessary over an extended rehabilitation period in order for quality of life improvements to be realized.

Acknowledgments

This research was supported (in part) by Research and Training Center Grant No. G-008006802 from the National Institute of Handicapped Research.

References

Eisler, R. M., Blanchard, E. B., Fitts, H., & Williams, J. B. (1978). Social skills training with and without modeling in schizophrenia and non-psychotic hospitalized psychiatric patients. *Behavior Modification, 2,* 147-172.

Hersen, M., & Bellack, A. S. (1976). Social skills training for chronic psychiatric patients: Rationale, research findings, and future directions. *Comprehensive Psychiatry, 17,* 559-580.

Klein, D. F. & Davis, J. M. (1969). *Diagnosis and drug treatment of psychiatric disorders.* Baltimore, MD: Williams and Wilkins.

McFall, R. M. (1982). A review on reformulation of the concept of social skills. *Behavioral Assessment, 4*(1), 1-34.

Trower, P., Bryant, B., & Argyle, M. (1978). *Social skills and mental health.* Pittsburgh: University of Pittsburgh Press.

Wallace, C. J., & Boone, S. E. (1983). Cognitive factors in the social skills of schizophrenic patients: Implications for treatment. In *Proceedings of the Nebraska Symposium on Motivation*. Lincoln: University of Nebraska Press.

Wallace, C. J., Nelson, C. J., Liberman, R. P., Aitchison, R. A., Lukoff, D., Elder, J. P., & Ferris, C. (1980). A review and critique of social skills training with schizophrenic patients. *Schizophrenia Bulletin*, 6, 42–63.

Zubin, J., & Spring, B. (1977). Vulnerability: A new view of schizophrenia. *Journal of Abnormal Psychology*, 86, 103–126.

10

PERSONALITY DISORDERS: APPLICATION OF THE EXPERIMENTAL METHOD TO THE FORMULATION AND MODIFICATION OF PERSONALITY DISORDERS

IRA DANIEL TURKAT AND STEPHEN A. MAISTO

As Turkat and Maisto point out in this chapter, personality disorders constitute up to 50% of all cases seen in some clinical centers, and yet are the most difficult and poorly understood disorders that clinicians are likely to face. Our ignorance of how to best deal with these disorders extends beyond treatment to more basic issues in classification and basic psychopathology. Working from a sample of 35 cases of various personality disorders recently interviewed and assessed, the authors are able to outline for practicing clinicians viable therapeutic interventions that differ significantly, depending on the type of personality disorder encountered and the behavioral formulation of the case. In fact, in view of the paucity of information concerning the nature of personality disorders, the authors correctly devote a significant portion of this chapter to describing presenting problem lists and subsequent behavioral formulations of the most frequently encountered personality disorders. In doing so, Turkat and Maisto provide a fascinating early glimpse of the core psychopathology found in personality disorders. This information in turn provides an important footing for clinical researchers to replicate these findings concerning maintaining factors in personality disorders in other centers with other patients. The authors also illustrate a unique approach with which clinicians can experimentally test their formulations on individual cases in their own offices.

Based on the social learning model of personality disorders suggested by these formulations, the authors illustrate a variety of specific treatment interventions that follow directly from their formulations. Clinicians will be particularly interested in descriptions of the treatment of compulsive personalities by social skills training with emphasis on adequate expression of emotions, or the treatment of dependent personality disorder by reducing anxiety concerned with independent decision making. Equally interesting are the treatment strategies proposed for the core problems of inability to delay immediate gratification in narcissistic personality

Ira Daniel Turkat. Department of Psychology, University of North Carolina at Greensboro, Greensboro, North Carolina.

Stephen A. Maisto. Department of Psychology, Vanderbilt University, Nashville,Tennessee.

disorder, hypersensitivity to criticism within the paranoid personality disorder, and the excessive need for attention combined with a failure to use appropriate social skills in order to achieve desired attention found in histrionic personality disorder. The clinical insights to be found in this chapter will be extremely important to all clinicians encountering these problems—D. H. B.

The construct of personality disorder has often stimulated discussion of questions concerning the operations and efficacy of behavior therapy. Such questions are basic and include whether there is such a thing as personality and, if so, whether disorders of personality are acquired behavior patterns or biogenetic manifestations. Another question is whether behavioral approaches are too narrow for modifying such complex phenomena. Unfortunately, there is not sufficient evidence bearing on these questions. In fact, there is such a paucity of sound scientific data on the personality disorders that speculation is the hallmark of the relevant literature (Turkat & Levin, 1984). Nevertheless, there is ample justification for including a chapter on the personality disorders in this volume.

INITIAL CONSIDERATIONS

In 1980 the American Psychiatric Association published the third edition of the *Diagnostic and Statistical Manual of Mental Disorders* (DSM-III), a radical departure from its predecessor, DSM-II (American Psychiatric Association, 1968). In DSM-III an attempt was made to be atheoretical, descriptive, and comprehensive in order to satisfy clinical and research needs. While many problems remain, the DSM-III is a major advance (Adams, 1981) and has been accepted for use by many prominent behavior therapists (e.g., Barlow, 1981).

The DSM-III personality disorders represent a major category in the diagnostic nomenclature (Millon, 1981). They also appear to represent a large percentage of the psychopathologic population. For example, an inspection of the data accumulated in the DSM-III field trials on interrater reliability indicates that *personality disorders were diagnosed in 50% or more of clinical cases* (Spitzer & Forman, 1979; Spitzer, Forman, & Nee, 1979). This finding is consistent with impressions of the prevalence of these disorders (Tyrer, Alexander, Cicchetti, Cohen, & Remington, 1979). Furthermore, while diagnostic reliability for the *class* of personality disorders is relatively poor (Frances, 1980), there is evidence that diagnostic agreement on *certain* personality disorders is acceptable. In fact, one study showed a kappa coefficient of 1.0 for diagnostic agreement on histrionic personality disorder (Strober, Green, & Carlson, 1981).

While the personality disorders may be seen frequently in clinical practice, there are hardly any convincing data on their etiology or treatment (Turkat & Levin, 1984). Further, the data and theories about the personality disorders that are available are rarely discussed in basic psychopathology textbooks (Turkat &

Alpher, 1983). Thus, we have a major problem of ignorance if it is accepted that half or more of the adults admitted for psychological treatment could be diagnosed as having a personality disorder. Given the high prevalence of the personality disorders, it seems appropriate to ask why our knowledge of these disorders seems relatively scanty. There are several reasons.

First, the construct "personality" has traditionally served as a catalyst for controversy. Almost 50 years ago Allport (1937) outlined 50 different definitions of personality. Today there is still no universally accepted definition. Accordingly, the term "personality" means different things to different people, thereby setting the stage for arguments about the nature and genesis of normal and abnormal personalities.

Second, the construct "personality disorder" has endured a similar history. While most theorists agree that personality disorders represent "maladaptive *patterns* of behavior," attempts to specify more distinguishing aspects reveal the chaos in definition. For example, personality disorders have been defined as maladaptive patterns of behavior, "which an individual develops to prevent anxiety" (Goldstein, Baker, & Jamison, 1980, p. 301), or as "stemming from an immature disordered personality structure" (Sue, Sue & Sue 1981, p. 383), or when "a particular personality style is overused" (Duke & Nowicki, 1979, p. 300). Contributing to the definitional chaos, DSM-II (American Psychiatric Association, 1968) defined personality disorders as "deeply ingrained maladaptive patterns of behavior that are perceptively different in quality from psychotic and neurotic symptoms. Generally, these are life-long patterns often recognizable by the time of adolescence and earlier (American Psychiatric Association, 1968, p. 41). This vague definition perpetuated confusion as to what qualified as a personality disorder and contributed to the low diagnostic reliability of the DSM-II category (Turkat & Levin, 1984).

In 1980 DSM-III was published, and the personality disorders were defined more specifically and given greater emphasis. In DSM-III personality traits were defined as "enduring patterns of perceiving, relating to, and thinking about the environment and oneself, and are exhibited in a wide range of important social and personal contexts. It is only when *personality traits* are inflexible and maladaptive and cause significant impairment in social and occupational functioning and subjective distress that they constitute *Personality Disorders*" (American Psychiatric Association, 1980, p. 305). This distinction between adaptive and maladaptive traits, as well as clearer specification of what the diagnostic system viewed as abnormal, contributed to the DSM-III recommendation that all cases be evaluated in regard to personality traits and disorders (as well as other categories/classes of mental disorders). Thus, DSM-III placed the personality disorders into a new and pronounced role in psychiatric classification.

The personality disorders in DSM-III represent a significant change from the DSM-II personality disorders. The number of titles of, criteria for, and explanations of the personality disorders have changed. However, the new system is only 4 years old (as of this writing); the findings on DSM-II personality disorders seem irrelevant to the current diagnostic entities, and the category as a whole still lacks evidence for acceptable levels of reliability and validity (Turkat & Levin, 1984). Useful scientific knowledge of these disorders still remains a promise of the future.

Given the high prevalence of the personality disorders, the lack of scientific knowledge about them, and the common *belief* that such disorders are valid psychological entities, it seems imperative that we begin to investigate such disorders thoroughly. Unfortunately, the personality disorders are encountered most often by the clinician who rarely has the resources available to conduct research with these patients and who has little if any scientific literature to guide clinical management of these cases.

The purpose of this chapter is to begin to address this problem by outlining a science-based approach to clinical management of the personality disorders that also allows the clinician to help develop scientific knowledge about them.

SCIENTIFIC APPROACH TO THE CLINICAL CASE

It is useful to review what is meant by "a scientific approach to the clinical case," and it is important first to distinguish between the process and outcome of science. In the former a hypothesis is created, experimentally tested, and then evaluated for its validity based on the results of the experimental test. Thus, the process of science (the experimental method) depends on the availability of a testable hypothesis. The outcome of science refers to the product (knowledge) generated by using the experimental method. Since our understanding of the personality disorders suffers from a lack of relevant scientific products, it makes sense to focus on the application of the experimental method to individual cases presenting personality disorders.

Clinical Hypothesis Testing

As mentioned above, science cannot proceed without testable hypotheses. Accordingly, it is important to discuss the type of hypotheses that should be evaluated if scientific knowledge of the personality disorders is to accrue.

If the history of how successful treatment methods for behavior disorders have developed is studied, it would be discovered that such methods rest on a foundation of a formulation or theory of the particular disorder. For example, Wolpe's (1958) development of systematic desensitization stemmed directly from his theory of how anxiety develops. While there is still debate about the adequacy of Wolpe's theory, the efficacy of his treatment procedure is well established (cf. Rachman & Wilson, 1980). Another good example among several is Yates's (1975) use of Hullian theory in the development of treatments for tics. The major point is that treatment procedure development depends, to a large extent, on an adequate formulation or theory.

Therefore, *developing formulations of the personality disorders should be the first step of creating effective interventions for their modification.* Accordingly, our discussion of applying the experimental method to the individual case will focus on case formulation. Procedures for testing the efficacy of treatment techniques already have been delineated (see Hersen & Barlow, 1976, and Barlow & Hersen, 1984, for excellent reviews).

The Experimental Case Approach

In the 1950s Monte B. Shapiro, a British clinical psychologist, outlined an impressive approach to application of the experimental method to single cases, which is relevant to the present discussion. The steps involved have been nicely illustrated (Shapiro, 1951a, 1951b, 1952, 1953a, 1953b, 1957, 1970; Shapiro & Nelson, 1955; Shapiro & Ravenette, 1959) and will be briefly reviewed here.

First, the patient is interviewed with the goal of identifying and describing the presenting behavior dysfunctions. Next, an attempt is made to measure these uncontrolled observations in a *controlled* manner. Following this, the clinician generates all possible theories that might account for the presenting dysfunctions and then systematically conducts experiments to eliminate untenable hypotheses. After such rigorous hypothesis testing, the most plausible *explanatory theory* is tested for its generality. In this respect the clinician has operated as a researcher by documenting the mechanisms of psychopathology in a way that leads to the development of relevant treatment techniques.

Impediments to the Experimental Case Approach

There is little question that Shapiro's approach to scientific clinical practice is one of experimental rigor. Its application has resulted in a considerable amount of scientific products (cf. Inglis, 1966) and has been incorporated in the training of numerous British clinical psychologists (Shapiro, 1955, 1962, 1969). Therefore, Shapiro's contributions to clinical psychology have been substantial, although as Yates (1975) has noted, he has rarely been given the credit that he deserves.

As is evident from the above description, the present authors have been greatly impressed with Shapiro's work. However, the elegance of Shapiro's approach cannot override numerous practical constraints that prevent *clinicians* from following the course of clinical research that Shapiro has outlined.

One of the major problems is the amount of time, energy, manpower, and resources required to carry out the type of thorough investigations advocated by Shapiro. Few psychologists in clinical practice have the luxury of such conditions. Another deterrent is the unwillingness of patients seeking immediate symptomatic relief to participate in such time-consuming investigations. While the efficacy of psychological therapy is, at present, limited to only a handful of behavior disorders (cf. Rachman & Wilson, 1980), many clinicians *and* patients seem to operate under the belief that psychotherapy is effective, thereby creating a resistance to engage in thorough single-case research. Another impediment is the lack of reliable, valid, and norm-referenced assessment measures, which are integral to single-case research.

In short, Shapiro's experimental approach to clinical problems is rigorous, elegant, and useful. Unfortunately, as Shapiro has noted (Shapiro, 1957), most clinicians could not meet the requirements for its implementation at that time. (For a complete discussion of the evolution of the role of the scientist–practitioner and newly developed practical and realistic experimental methods for use by clinicians with individual cases in the area of formulation, but with more emphasis on assessment and the evaluation of interventions, see Barlow, Hayes, & Nelson, 1984.)

Experimental Needs and Clinical Constraints: A Compromise Approach

Recognizing the merits of a scientific approach to individual cases as well as the practical impediments, the authors have developed a method that attempts to balance experimental needs and clinical reality in evaluating novel formulations (cf. Turkat, Maisto, Burish, & Rock, in press). In this approach the clinician interviews the patient with the primary goal of developing a behavioral formulation. The formulation is defined as a hypothesis that (1) specifies the mechanism that produces all the presenting problems of the patient; (2) details the etiology of these problems; and (3) provides predictions of the patient's behavior in future situations (Meyer & Turkat, 1979). In this respect *the clinician eliminates untenable hypotheses by systematic questioning in the interview*; a belief that does not meet the definition of a behavioral formulation is discarded in the interview (Turkat, in press).

Next, the clinician constructs tests of the validity of the formulation. In this regard several predictions are derived from the formulation and then subjected to empirical test. If the results obtained are consistently in line with the formulation, it is assumed that there is converging validity for it. Finally, once the clinician has provided objective evidence for the validity of his or her belief about a patient, a treatment program based on that belief is developed, implemented, and evaluated.

The primary assumptions underlying the case formulation approach may be listed as follows:

1. At all times, the clinician must be willing and able to specify in operational detail his or her beliefs about a particular patient.
2. These beliefs should be able to explain every symptom the patient presents, including their etiology, and if valid, should lead directly to a specific treatment.
3. These beliefs should provide testable predictions of future patient behavior.
4. Experimental tests of these beliefs should be conducted to determine the validity of the clinician's thinking.

5. The clinician cannot realistically investigate every plausible theory and thus should test, at minimum, the explanatory theory he or she has adopted for the particular patient.
6. The clinician who provides experimental data to support his or her beliefs about a patient has provided a more useful contribution than the clinician who operates on a belief without providing experimental support.
7. Such investigations should be viewed as pilot clinical research, since untenable hypotheses are eliminated by interview logic and not controlled experiments.
8. Such investigations should only be conducted with disorders that are poorly understood scientifically.

To clarify the importance of these assumptions, it seems appropriate to review how clinical work is traditionally conducted. Typically, a patient is interviewed, subjected to psychological tests, and then the clinician develops a belief about the patient's problems. This belief may or may not be specified to the patient. Further, the belief is rarely tested for its validity *after* the belief is developed. Finally, the particular belief may or may not lead to a specific treatment. *The major limitation in clinical implementation is the lack of objective evidence for the validity of the clinician's beliefs.*

In contrast, Shapiro advocates generating all potential beliefs that might explain the presenting dysfunctions and then systematically testing each. *The major limitation for the clinician is the need for extensive resources to evaluate clinical hypotheses.*

As a compromise position, the present authors advocate the need to develop a formulation of the presenting case by eliminating untenable hypotheses through systematic questioning. Then, predictions from this formulation are tested, and if consistent confirmatory evidence is obtained, the clinician's belief is judged as having some validity. *The clinician is limited only by his or her ability to arrive at an accurate behavioral formulation.*

It now should be apparent that the most important aspect of conducting clinical work is the formulation of the case. Without a formulation there is no hypothesis to test, and without a valid formulation it is unlikely that an appropriate treatment can be devised.

The Behavioral Formulation

A behavioral formulation is a *hypothesis* that identifies the mechanism responsible for the patient's behavioral complaints and their etiology and can generate predictions of the patient's behavior in future situations. Once a valid formulation is developed, the therapist can then devise an appropriate intervention, determine what type of therapeutic relationship to implement, and predict and avert resistances to treatment (Turkat & Meyer, 1982). A simple (non-personality disorder) case illustration will be helpful.

Mr. X has requested therapy for a problem with test anxiety. Upon further questioning it appears that the patient also is experiencing anxiety when giving speeches. Further, Mr. X reports having difficulty falling asleep at night and also feels depressed. After investigating the antecedents and consequences of these problems, the therapist decides upon the following treatment package:

- test anxiety: systematic desensitization to tests; study skills training
- speech anxiety: systematic desensitization to speeches; oral presentation skills training
- insomnia: stimulus control; progressive muscular relaxation
- depression: cognitive restructuring; activity/reinforcer increase

If the therapist were following the steps of many behavior therapists, he or she would become a supportive "reinforcing" agent by using relationship enhancement methods (e.g., Ford & Kendall, 1979) such as reflection of feeling (e.g., Goldfried & Davison, 1976). Clearly, the treatment plan seems comprehensive.

Now let us assume that the patient is following all of the therapist's prescriptions and by the fourth session feels that treatment is working. At the fifth session, however, the patient seems very depressed and all symptoms are worse than ever. The therapist checks all recent test and speech encounters and finds no sensitizing experience. The therapist asks the patient to explain why he is depressed, and he reports having no idea. How should the clinician proceed? The therapist has used his or her "bag of tricks" but to no avail. He or she is lost.

The preceding example helps to illustrate the importance of a good behavioral formulation. If one examines Mr. X's list of problems (which might suggest the DSM-III classification of social phobia), it appears that the basic *mechanism* of the patient's problems may be an overall fear of evaluation *of any kind*. This could explain the anxiety during tests and speeches, which perhaps causes ruminations about them at night (insomnia). As a result of these problems, the patient feels inadequate and depressed. Now, what are the advantages of hypothesizing this mechanism?

If the hypothesized mechanism is correct, then the clinician would be able to *predict other behavioral problems the patient experiences but does not report*. For example, if the patient is generally fearful of evaluation, he might be anxious during exposure to any of the following: talking to authority figures such as teachers; friends who have certain expectations of him; dating; sexual intercourse; meeting new people; trying new tasks; being watched. This list is by no means exhaustive. The problem may extend to practically any potential evaluation such as sipping soup too loudly in a restaurant or combing his hair the wrong way. Accordingly, exposure to an evaluation situation other than speeches or tests may have accounted for Mr. X's sudden relapse.

If Mr. X's problems were formulated, it might reveal that he was raised by perfectionistic parents who constantly criticized him. Accordingly, current parental criticism would be another source for anxiety.

Finally, if the mechanism is evaluation anxiety in general, the clinician would predict that the patient would be fearful of the therapist's rejection. Thus, the therapist would avoid criticizing the patient at all at first and then gradually become more critical in the therapeutic relationship, paralleling the treatment program (Turkat & Brantly, 1981).

This brief example should demonstrate the importance of having a good case formulation to guide the treatment process. Detailed accounts and illustrations of how to develop a behavioral formulation may be found in several sources (Meyer & Turkat, 1979; Turkat, in press; Turkat & Meyer 1982; Wolpe & Turkat, in press). It should be noted however, that the Meyer and Turkat (1979) criteria are just one set of rules for a behavioral formulation. Clearly, there are many different tyeps of formulations that might be considered behavioral in nature. Perhaps the *sine qua non* is a hypothesis of functional relationships (cf. Nelson & Barlow, 1981).

Testing Case Formulations

Once the clinician has developed a formulation of the patient's problems, he or she should be able to develop predictions of patient responses to future stimulus situations. If the formulation is valid, then these predictions should be accurate. Accordingly, the clinician should be able to isolate the treatment most likely to succeed among several alternatives, as well as identify the obstacles to successful treatment and the likelihood of success. A formulation that has no predictive power is a useless formulation.

Since therapists operate clinically on their case formulations, it is assumed that such beliefs hold predictive power. Unfortunately, few clinicians systematically test the predictive power of their clinical formulations. It would seem that much could be gained if clinicians tested the validity of their formulations of complex cases. First, if the clinician were able to demonstrate objectively that his or her formulation has predictive power, then both the patient's and the therapist's confidence in the treatment plan and its rationale would be increased. Second, with objectively demonstrated predictability, the clinician has become more accountable for therapeutic actions (i.e., he or she has evidence to support the value of a treatment approach to the patient). Third, if the formulation is shown to lack predictive power, the clinician has early evidence that his or her thinking on the problem is perhaps incorrect and thus he or she should reevaluate the problem before implementing a treatment.

Finally, testing a case formulation allows the therapist to communicate his or her findings to clinicians and clinical researchers, which makes it more likely that the generalizability of the finding will be assessed. As Campbell and Stanley (1963) noted, scientific discovery is a process of trying to disconfirm hypotheses by subjecting them to progressively more rigorous tests, and the "good" hypothesis is the one that survives this process. Therefore, by specifying and initially testing the formulation of a complex case, the clinician can play an active part in the *initial development* of scientific knowledge of psychopathologic disorders that are poorly understood (e.g., the personality disorders).

By clinicians testing case formulations we mean that a small number of predictions derived from the formulation are tested to see if evidence can be obtained for their validity, since most clinicians may not have the time or inclination for more rigorous experimentation. Experimental tests should be simple and take no more time than does administration of a traditional test battery (e.g., Minnesota Multiphasic Personality Inventory [MMPI], Wechsler Adult Intelligence Scale [WAIS], Thematic Apperception Test [TAT]). The type and range of formulation-based testing depends largely on the ingenuity of the clinician and the resources available (cf. Carey, Flasher, Maisto, & Turkat, 1984).

As a brief example, recall the case of Mr. X, the possible social phobic, whose text anxiety, speech anxiety, insomnia, and depression were formulated as manifestations of a hypersensitivity to evaluation. Several ways to test this hypothesized mechanism are possible. First, the clinician could administer the Fear of Negative Evaluation Scale (Watson & Friend, 1969) and compare the patient's response to norms. Second, the clinician can generate several evaluation scenes *other than the previous complaints* such as speeches or tests (e.g., trying a new and difficult task, meeting a new person) and several non-evaluation scenes, present them according to an A-B-A design and obtain anxiety measures (e.g., State Anxiety ratings, heart rate, electromyographic [EMG] levels, or skin conductance [GSR] responses) during a short time period. The possibilities seem infinite.

In the remaining portions of this chapter, we will illustrate more clearly our formulation-based approach to a variety of personality disorder cases. Our emphasis will be upon the case formulation and, where possible, the validity tests and treatment of these cases.

THE PATIENT POPULATION

The senior author previously directed a clinical psychology service in the Department of Medicine at Vanderbilt University, which is housed in the Diabetes Research and Training Center. The patients consist primarily of individuals with diabetes or their family members. To the senior author's benefit, several faculty and students have participated in the clinic's varied activities.

The majority of patients are referred by health professionals (i.e., physicians, nurses, dietitians) for a variety of reasons including overt psychopathology, suspected psychopathology, poor medical outcomes, or routine screening. A sizeable minority is self-referred. The sample of patients varies in demographic characteristics, and while many of them live in Nashville, a large percentage come from rural Tennessee and Kentucky.

Over 100 patients have been seen at the clinic over the past 2½ years. At the time of this writing, records on 74 patients are available. Of these, 35 cases or 47% received a personality disorder diagnosis. The distribution of diagnoses within the personality disorder category is presented in Table 10-1. These data

TABLE 10-1. Distribution of Personality Disorder Diagnoses among 74 Cases

Type	Number of cases	Percentage of personality disorder cases	Percentage of all cases
Antisocial	2	5.7	2.7
Avoidant	4	11.4	5.4
Borderline	1	2.9	1.4
Compulsive	6	17.1	8.1
Dependent	1	2.9	1.4
Histrionic	8	22.9	10.8
Narcissistic	2	5.7	2.7
Paranoid	8	22.9	10.8
Passive–aggressive	1	2.9	1.4
Schizoid	2	5.7	2.7
Schizotypal	0	0	0
Mixed	0	0	0
Atypical	0	0	0
Other	0	0	0
Total	35	100	47

show that the avoidant, compulsive, histrionic, and paranoid personality disorders represent 74% of all personality disorder cases seen and 35% of all psychopathologic cases who were seen in our center. However, it should be noted that, like other clinical settings, it generally was not possible to evaluate diagnostic reliability.

ASSUMPTIONS FOR CONCEPTUALIZING PERSONALITY DISORDERS

Before embarking on a detailed account of our clinical experience with personality disorders, it is important to briefly summarize our assumptions about these disorders.

First, diagnosing a patient as having a personality disorder means that the individual has displayed certain clusters of behavior that can be conveniently summarized and communicated by a descriptive label (i.e., psychiatric diagnosis). We do not assume that such disorders are diseases or the result of unconscious conflict. In fact, the data available in the literature do not suggest *any* clearly identified etiology. Diagnosis is used only for scientific classification purposes (cf. Adams, Doster, & Calhoun, 1977).

Second, we assume that the individual with a personality disorder behaves consistently across many different situations. This does not mean that such cases *always* behave consistently.

Third, we *believe* that behavior indicative of a personality disorder is under the control of relevant stimuli (both antecedent and consequential), like other behaviors. We assume that such behavior is a result of certain modeling and shaping experiences. Since this remains a hypothesis, we attempt to examine such patients' histories in light of this theoretical orientation. We recognize of course that retrospective investigations suffer from many threats to validity.

Finally, we believe that the etiology, treatment, and prognosis of most personality disorder cases are unknown. The present chapter attempts to begin addressing some of these issues.

SPECIFIC PERSONALITY DISORDER CASES

In this section we will provide several clinical illustrations of our approach to formulating personality disorder cases. In each, we will try to do the following:

1. Specify all the presenting complaints.
2. Hypothesize the basic underlying mechanism.
3. Detail the presumed etiologic sequence.
4. Outline relevant predictions.
5. Report results of predictions that were tested.
6. Discuss treatment strategies.

We will discuss any important generalities that were observed among the personality disorder cases that have been seen frequently (i.e., avoidant, compulsive, histrionic, paranoid). Certain disorders have been seen less frequently (e.g., dependent, narcissistic), but we will outline what we have learned. On the other hand, in certain cases (particularly for infrequently seen examples) we were unable to test predictions and/or implement treatment because of logistical problems or because we learned very little (e.g., schizoid, schizotypal, passive-aggressive, antisocial, borderline). Nevertheless, we hope that our case formulations will prove to be of value to the reader either in clinical application or in research on these disorders.

Finally, we assume that the reader is familiar with the DSM-III diagnostic criteria so that we do not have to discuss diagnostic decisions in detail.

Avoidant Personality Disorder

The avoidant personality disorder is a new category in the DSM nomenclature and was originally proposed by Millon (cf. Millon, 1981). According to DSM-III, the primary feature of this disorder is a hypersensitivity to potential rejection, humiliation, or shame. Concomitantly, the individual avoids social rela-

514 TURKAT AND MAISTO

tionships that lack guarantees of unconditional acceptance. The individual strongly desires affection and acceptance and generally has a low self-esteem.

Case Example

PRESENTING PROBLEMS

The patient was 17 years old at the time of referral. She was an attractive Caucasian in her junior year at high school. The primary reason for referral was chronic hyperglycemia with no apparent medical reason to account for it. The patient presented the following behavioral problems:

1. Upsetting family interactions. The patient reported that her mother frequently criticized her performance of daily household chores, irrespective of the quality of her performance. Further, the patient indicated that her older brother often teased her about many things, such as doing poorly on a test at school. Finally, she reported that her father was "overprotective" and restricted her social life. As a result, the patient reported withdrawing from family interactions and spending an inordinate amount of time alone in her room.

2. Upsetting interpersonal events. The patient indicated that her boyfriend broke up with her 6 months previously. When discussing this, she became tearful and related that she was still very upset by his rejection. The patient also indicated that she had a very small network of friends and that approximately 1 month earlier, one of these "turned" on her. She reported feelings of anxiety when she thought or spoke of or actually encountered either of these two individuals.

3. Test anxiety. The patient indicated that she gets extremely nervous when taking examinations at school, which interferes with her performance on such tests.

4. Speech anxiety. The patient reported experiencing excessive anxiety when speaking in front of a class or group.

5. Head pain. The patient reported experiencing daily dull, ache-like pain in the frontal area of her head, which varied in intensity and duration.

6. Poor self-concept. The patient reported many feelings of insecurity and viewed herself negatively.

7. Depression. The patient reported frequent bouts of unhappiness, crying, and feelings of ineptness and hopelessness, which were often associated with acute increases in food consumption.

ETIOLOGIC INFORMATION

The patient was the youngest of two children, who lived with their parents in a small town in rural Tennessee. Her mother was described as being an extremely moody individual who was very concerned about providing good social impressions. Further, she was reported to be "two-faced" in that she would frequently criticize the patient for a variety of things but would "show off" her "perfect beautiful girl" to outsiders.

The patient's father was seen as a "nice" man who was overprotective. She reported that he was more "accepting" of her than the mother but often was "too concerned" about the patient's well-being. As an example, he would restrict her social life because he was fearful of the patient being "kidnapped, raped, or attacked."

As far back as the patient could recall, she saw herself as a shy and insecure individual. She had had a small group of friends since early childhood and typically had "followed." The anxiety she currently experienced was in social, familial, test, and speech situations reported as "always being present" and not due to any particular traumatic events. Similarly, the patient's headaches and depression were seen as gradually acquired although only of recent origin (within the last 2 years).

FORMULATION

The patient's basic problem appeared to be a hypersensitivity to negative evaluation, which was acquired through early upbringing. Specifically, her mother served as a model for excessive concern about social evaluation and shaped the patient to develop this concern by punishing (i.e., criticism) her for poor performance while in the home and rewarding her for "looking good" to others. Concomitantly, the father's excessive concern for protecting the patient from any potential danger served to teach her to be cautious and fearful. Given this training, the patient developed into a shy, overly sensitive girl, fearful of doing the wrong thing and being negatively evaluated by others. Accordingly, this led the patient to restrict her social network (thus avoiding further potential rejection); become nervous when those she interacted with (i.e., family, friends, boyfriend, teachers, classmates) negatively evaluated or rejected her; and experience anxiety in situations where she could be potentially rejected, humiliated, or negatively evaluated (i.e., tests, speeches). As a result, the patient developed a negative self-image, was easily provoked to depression, and developed tension headaches in response to the stresses. Finally, there are data suggesting that stress of sufficient duration, frequency, and intensity can lead to increases in blood glucose levels in certain individuals (see Turkat, 1982a, 1982b), and this might account in part for the patient's medically inexplicable hyperglycemic reactions.

In short, the presenting symptoms of this patient were hypothesized to be a function of a general hypersensitivity to evaluation.

PREDICTIONS

Given the hypothesized mechanism of disorder as a general hypersensitivity to negative evaluation it was predicted that the patient would:

1. score high on a standardized measure of sensitivity to negative evaluation;
2. score high on a standardized measure of social avoidance and distress;

3. score low on a standardized measure of being direct or assertive with others;
4. score high on a standardized measure of defensiveness.

TESTS AND RESULTS

To test the first hypothesis, the patient was administered the Fear of Negative Evaluation Scale (FNE; Watson & Friend, 1969). The mean score on the FNE is 15.47 with a standard deviation of 8.62. The patient's score on this test was 30 (the maximum score), indicating 100% endorsement of items reflecting sensitivity to negative evaluation.

To test the second hypothesis, the patient completed the Social Avoidance and Distress Scale (SAD; Watson & Friend, 1969). The mean score on the SAD is 9.11 with a standard deviation of 8.07, reflecting a skewed distribution. Watson and Friend (1969) reported that the modal score on the SAD was zero and suggested that moderate to high endorsement of items represented serious psychopathology. The patient's score on the SAD was 18, representing a 64% endorsement of items reflecting social avoidance and discomfort.

In order to test the third hypothesis, the patient was administered the directiveness subscale of the Personal Relations Inventory (PRI; Lorr & More, 1979). A person high on directiveness would agree with PRI items such as "I am usually the one who initiates activities in my group." Centile ranks and T scores are provided by Lorr and More (1979) for each PRI subscale. The patient's raw score on the directiveness subscale was 5 (range of 0–20), yielding a centile rank of 18 and T score of 41.

Finally, to test the fourth hypothesis, the patient was given the defensive subscale of the PRI. Individuals who are highly defensive agree with PRI statements like, "I never resent being asked to return a favor." The patient's raw score on this subscale was 15 (range 0–20), which was a centile rank of 95 and T score of 66.

In sum, the patient performed on standard measures as predicted by the formulation in that she was highly fearful of negative evaluations, considerably avoidant of and distressed by social situations, deficient in directiveness behaviors, and highly defensive.

TREATMENT STRATEGIES

Given the mechanism of disorder in this case, it would seem that treatment aimed directly at modifying the patient's hypersensitivity to evaluation would result in elimination of the presenting symptoms (test, speech, interpersonal and familial anxiety, tension headaches, and depression). Because the patient lived beyond commuting distance to our center, she was referred to a more accessible location for treatment aimed at her hypersensitivity to evaluation. Over the next 2 years, anecdotal evidence revealed that her symptoms became steadily less severe and that her general functioning had vastly improved. Her medical records indicate significant improvement in glycosylated hemoglobin (a metabolic measure of diabetes status).

DISCUSSION

The clinical picture presented in this case seems similar to the three other avoidant personality disorder cases whom we have seen. All reported having at least one parent very concerned about social evaluation, and none could identify any particular traumatic event that precipitated all symptoms. Finally, hypersensitivity to evaluation seemed to be the mechanism for a style that intruded into most facets of the patient's life.

It is important to note that none of these cases reported a fear of evaluation as the reason for seeking treatment or as a presenting complaint. Rather, this hypersensitivity was *inferred* by the therapist from the presenting data. In this regard, judging the patient as meeting the DSM-III criteria for avoidant personality disorder required an inference; description alone would not have permitted such a diagnosis. Accordingly, it seems that certain DSM-III categories are not as operational as is desirable (Turkat & Levin, 1984).

Finally, the reader should recognize that we did not use psychological tests in the traditional fashion. Rather, predictions were derived from the formulation, and only psychological tests that could aid the evaluation of pertinent hypotheses were used (cf. Carey *et al.*, 1984).

Future research should determine if behavioral anxiety management procedures aimed directly at the general hypersensitivity to negative evaluation are effective in treating avoidant personality disorder cases.

Antisocial Personality Disorder

The literature indicates that this disorder is the most widely researched and discussed problem among the personality disorders (Turkat & Alpher, 1983), and the reader is referred to the excellent work by Sutker and her associates on sociopathy (see Brantley & Sutker, 1984; Sutker, Archer, & Kilpatrick, 1981). To date, effective treatment for such disorders has not been developed.

In our own clinic we have seen two cases that seemed to meet the DSM-III criteria for antisocial personality disorder. In both instances the patients were not interested in receiving psychological treatment; rather, they seemed to be trying to obtain the therapist's aid to get an important other in their environment "off their back." We therefore were unable to develop a behavioral formulation in accord with Meyer and Turkat (1979) criteria. As such, we have little to convey about understanding such cases or how to manage them clinically.

Borderline Personality Disorder

The borderline personality disorder is a new category in the DSM-III nomenclature although the term "borderline" has been used for decades (Hartocollis, 1980). Throughout the literature there are discussions of borderline patterns, states, characters, personalities, and schizophrenics (Spitzer, Endicott, & Gibbon, 1979), which has led some to view the term "borderline" as a "wastebasket" (Gunderson & Singer, 1975). Perry and Klerman (1980) have gone so far as to state that a borderline diagnosis can represent almost the entire spectrum of psychopathology.

In DSM-III the borderline personality disorder is characterized primarily by instability and unpredictability that pervade social, affective and self-image spheres. Such individuals are described as uncertain about their identity, having unstable and intense interpersonal relationships, and showing inappropriate anger, vacillating mood, and intolerance of boredom. Psychiatric tools for diagnosing these individuals are available (e.g., Kolb & Gunderson, 1980), but little is known regarding the etiology and treatment of borderline personality disorder.

In our center we have seen only one case that seemed to meet the DSM-III criteria for borderline personality disorder (cf. Turkat & Levin, 1984). The patient was a 29-year-old black woman who presented the following problems: (1) excessive eating that resulted in a need for a weight loss of 80 lb; (2) marital difficulties involving verbal and physical fighting; (3) vacillating social behavior, ranging from general pleasantness to rapidly induced temper outbursts; (4) unpredictable moody behavior at work; (5) uncertainty about long-term and short-term goals; (6) concern about who she "was" (not in the psychotic sense, but more in terms of her place in society and life); (7) frequent periods of boredom and an inability to tolerate it; (8) poor self-image; and (9) depression.

The patient was raised in a religious Christian home where her father taught her always to strive to achieve and to be productive, whereas the mother emphasized the need to always be patient, accepting, and understanding. Thus, she was presented with models emphasizing incompatible lifestyles: "Produce and achieve at all costs" versus "always turn the other cheek." Accordingly, it was hypothesized that this conflict led the patient to develop a *problem-solving deficit*, which perpetuated vacillating and unpredictable responses in social and occupational situations leading to mood swings, insecurity, and uncertainty. It was not possible to test this formulation, because the patient did not return to our center.

Unfortunately, we have little to offer the reader about validated formulations of borderline personality disorder.

Compulsive Personality Disorder

The compulsive personality has been discussed in the psychiatric literature throughout the twentieth century. It was officially recognized as a diagnostic entity by American psychiatrists in 1952, although previously it had been mentioned in the International Classification of Diseases (ICD), under the rubric of "anakastic personality," a label that still occasionally appears in the literature (Turner & Hersen, 1981). The DSM-III definition of compulsive personality disorder is strikingly similar to the definition of the anakastic personality that appears in the ninth revision of the ICD (World Health Organization, 1979).

The compulsive personality has been a favorite topic among psychoanalytic theorists, and it is often used interchangeably with the notion of "anal charac-ter." At times, compulsive personality disorder has been confused with individu-als experiencing compulsive rituals or obsessions. However, recent research in classification (cf. Adams, 1981; Sturgis & Meyer, 1981) and DSM-III show that individuals with a compulsive personality disorder do not necessarily display compulsive rituals or obsessional behavior, and that individuals experiencing compulsive rituals or obsessions do not necessarily have a compulsive personal-ity disorder.

The DSM-III characterizes the compulsive personality disorder by the individual's deficiencies in expressing warm and tender emotions, inability to grasp the big picture because he or she is preoccupied with trivial rules and details, insistence that others conform to his or her rules without recognizing the emotional reactions this behavior elicits in others, excessive devotion to work to the exclusion of pleasure, and indecisiveness.

A review of the compulsive personality disorder literature shows there are little empirical data on the etiology and treatment of this disorder.

Example

PRESENTING PROBLEMS

The patient was a 37-year-old Caucasian female who was referred to the senior author by her physician. The patient's husband was a diabetic of many years who had recently developed a variety of medical complications (retinop-athy, nephropathy, stroke) in a short time period that caused blindness, speech and motor difficulties, and renal problems. The patient became depressed over her husband's medical problems.

To arrange an initial interview the patient was called (at the physician's request) at a work number but could not be located. She returned the therapist's call, but stated that she was too busy to find enough time to meet, including on nights and weekends. However, a time to meet was arranged. At the interview (which is presented in detail in Turkat, in press) the patient said that she did not have the desire or enough time to go into and deal with her problems in therapy. However, she presented the following problems:

1. *Excessive responsibilities.* The patient indicated that she held a "stress-ful" job as a special education teacher for 11 different schools. This involved dealing with many different children, parents, teachers, and principals. In addition, she reported having many responsibilities and obligations, including a 1-year-old baby, a 14-year-old son, caring for her sick husband (she was now forced to be the breadwinner), her father (who was dying of cancer), financial obligations, and six credit hours remaining for completion of a college degree.

2. *Concern about priorities.* The patient reported that she had too little time to adequately think through how to handle priorities. She indicated that she typically required spending a few days thinking about her alternatives in order to develop solutions.

3. *Laziness.* The patient felt that she was lazy. She reported that she

recently had spent too much time reading novels to "escape." Further, she felt that she procrastinated too much, rendering her unable to keep up with her responsibilities.

4. *Marital difficulties.* The patient reported that she had recently come to pity her husband, which she found aversive (i.e., to pity). She particularly disliked having to "nurse" him. Further, she indicated that her husband had begun to "resent" her for being so involved in her job and course work and she had begun to resent him for not being supportive of her.

5. *Interpersonal difficulties.* The patient said that she was having a hard time listening to other people and their "crabby little complaints." She reported that what other people complained about and deemed important seemed unimportant to her. The patient stated that she was a "terribly honest" person and had learned to keep her "mouth shut." She stated that she did not let anyone know how she felt. She did not appear to have any close friends.

6. *Anger.* The patient reported feeling much anger toward others, which she could "admit" to herself. In addition to feeling angry at her husband for not supporting her, she reported similar feelings toward her mother-in-law because "she acted like a 10-year-old" in regard to the patient's husband's medical problems. Further, the patient felt that her mother-in-law should have helped out financially and resented her for not doing so. Finally, she felt anger toward those who complain about "little things" (e.g., someone losing a tooth) as well as those who asked her how her husband was doing.

7. *Excessive eating.* The patient expressed concern that she was eating too much "junk food," particularly sweets, and that this was upsetting because she usually tried to avoid eating junk food. She reported gaining 10 lb in the last month.

ETIOLOGIC INFORMATION

The patient was an only child whose father died shortly before her birth. When the patient was 2 years old her mother remarried.

The patient's mother was described as being very ambitious, overwhelmingly driven by obligations, possessive, and unemotional. The mother was reportedly very concerned with acting and being seen as a "good family."

The patient's stepfather was described as a workaholic who consequently was never at home.

The patient described her upbringing as one of having to follow her mother's rules regarding what the patient could and could not do. There reportedly was little of an emotional relationship.

The patient was an "A" student in elementary school (and throughout her school years), but did not have many friends, because her mother viewed other children as "poor white trash." In junior high school the patient became a cheerleader but was forced to begin a job at the age of 14 years.

In high school the patient described herself as a "wallflower" who was shy, naive, and dated rarely. In college she met a man whom she married because of "insecurity." She stated that she did not like him but felt that she would not get other offers. The patient reported that her husband used to beat her intensely and repeatedly. She stated that she could not remember how she felt after being beaten and that she never discussed it with anyone. The patient also reported that sex between them was unsatisfactory and that she once went to a physician because she had never had an orgasm. The husband was also reported to have been arrested for exposing himself to children. The patient decided to leave her husband after 9 years when her child was "old enough to say 'stop that daddy,' [then] I realized that it was more harmful for him to be in the home situation than it was to take him out of it."

A year later she married her present husband, an assistant principal, whom she met through the school system where she worked. She reported loving him because "we had a lot in common, we could talk . . . he was so encouraging of my ambitions." Social interactions were mostly restricted to structured events such as board meetings and classes. Her life was replete with responsibilities and work with little recreation or pleasure. She reported never having time for unstructured activities or fun.

FORMULATION

The present case of compulsive personality disorder was formulated in the following way. The patient was reared in a home that emphasized work, productivity, and rule-following and de-emphasized emotions and interpersonal relationships. The step-father worked continuously and was rarely at home. The most potent model and shaper of the patient's behavior was her mother, who inculcated the need to work, be productive, take on many obligations, and provided little training in identifying, expressing, and dealing with emotions in interpersonal relationships. Accordingly, the patient did not acquire empathy skills or the skill of interacting with others on an emotional basis.

As a result of this training, the patient excelled in work situations (e.g., school grades) but failed to learn how to deal with her own and others' emotions. This was reflected in her neglect of interpersonal relationships throughout her life; the patient had few friends. Furthermore, she had worked since she was 14 years old, and social interactions were restricted to structured situations. The patient married her first husband for rational reasons, and when he would beat her, which demands an emotional reaction, she could not recall it. Her decision to leave him was based on logic and not on emotion. She also married her second husband for rational reasons (in the interview she could not identify what "love" was). Like her mother, her energy was put into work and obligations, and this led to her taking on overwhelming responsibilities. When these responsibilities accumulated, the patient could not figure out rationally how to deal with them, which led for example, to procrastination and reading to escape. Because of this the patient perceived herself as lazy.

Before the second husband became ill, the patient felt that life was fine and was able to handle her many obligations. However, her husband's illness not only increased her responsibilities, but forced her to deal with highly emotional situations. Since the patient was deficient in this important social skill, she was unable to empathize and provide the emotional support her husband required. Accordingly, his resentment of her work angered the patient instead of understanding his need for emotional support. Similarly, she was angry with the mother-in-law for acting like a child (as opposed to understanding the emotions of a mother toward her ill child) and for not offering to help out financially (rather than discussing her feelings with the mother-in-law). Further, her empathy deficit precluded the patient's understanding and appreciating other people's life problems and their concerned inquiries about the status of the ill husband.

Given these problems, the patient became depressed (including the eating and weight gain) as her work and productive lifestyle could not adequately manage the current situations requiring emotional responses. Furthermore, it seems appropriate to become depressed in response to a spouse's critical illness.

In short, the patient developed a deficiency in emotion-related social skills from early upbringing, which led her to take on overwhelming responsibilities, have interpersonal and marital difficulties, and thus be vulnerable to depression when her productivity skills could not solve the current dilemma.

DISCUSSION

The formulation of this case suggested that if the patient learned how to develop good social skills (particularly, emotion related), she would be more able to handle most of her interpersonal and marital problems. Further, this should lead to a diminution in devotion to work and productivity and thus reduce many of the current stresses. However, it was apparent that the patient was so overwhelmed with responsibility, that taking on another (e.g., therapy) would not be in her immediate best interests. Simply put, she did not have time. Accordingly, she was offered the opportunity for treatment once time would permit (most likely, at the death of the husband). As such, no predictions were experimentally tested and treatment was not initiated.

This particular case illustrates nicely the importance of the behavioral formulation. First, it allowed the prediction that immediate therapy would not benefit the patient and perhaps would increase her current problems. Without the formulation, the therapist likely would have made the mistake of setting up an appointment to work on these problems. Second, the formulation suggested that treatment should be aimed directly at emotion-related social skills. Interestingly, a common approach to depression is that it is a result of irrational thinking. It seems unlikely that teaching this patient to think more rationally would be of help. Finally, while there is much literature on social skills training, little of it focuses on teaching patients to be empathic, to accept others' emotions, to identify their own emotions, be comfortable with them, and to express them appropriately.

We have noted certain commonalities among the five other compulsive personality disorder cases that we have seen. First, all had difficulties with emotions, which seemed to cause other symptoms. Second, all seemed to come from homes that emphasized the protestant work ethic and de-emphasized interpersonal relations and emotional behavior. Third, all reported at the initial interview that depression was the primary complaint. Fourth, almost all seemed to be angry about others not living up to their (i.e., patients') expectations and that other people were the cause of the problem. Fifth, none was seriously interested in changing his or her rational, productive approach to life. In fact, several of these patients found the idea of learning how to be more emotional and less rational to be rather frightening. Interestingly, they all agreed that the formulation was accurate.

In short, it appears that an appropriate treatment (i.e., social skills training) can be generated for compulsive personality disorder cases on a conceptual level, but few cases seem interested in learning what they agree that they need to learn.

Dependent Personality Disorder

The DSM-III classification of dependent personality disorder did not appear in DSM-II, although it is similar in certain respects to the DSM-I description of the "passive–aggressive personality, dependent type." Little research on this DSM-III category is available (Turkat & Levin, 1984).

In our center, we have seen only one such case, which has been reported in detail elsewhere (Turkat & Carlson, 1984) and is discussed below.

Case Example

PRESENTING PROBLEMS

Mrs. S was a 48-year-old married Caucasian female who was referred to the senior author by her family physician. Two months previously her 13-year-old daughter had been diagnosed as an insulin-dependent diabetic. Mrs. S presented the following behavioral difficulties.

1. Difficulty sleeping. She reported sleep difficulties including delayed onset, frequent awakening, and early awakening which varied from day to day. In addition, she reported muscle tension in her chest whenever she woke up and disturbing cognitions regarding her daughter's medical condition.

2. Anxiety around daughter. The patient reported that she experienced "nervousness" when interacting with her diabetic child, which concerned her greatly.

3. Anxiety in supermarkets. Mrs. S reported that she felt nervous and uncomfortable in supermarkets. Apparently, the need to buy certain foods for her daughter elicited disturbing cognitions about her daughter's condition and concomitant muscle tension in the chest.

4. Avoidance of reading materials. The patient related that she avoided any type of reading materials that concerned any aspect of diabetes. This included popular magazines that occasionally contained articles about diabetes and often contained fund-raising advertisements for diabetes organizations.

5. *Avoidance of social gatherings.* Mrs. S indicated that she was beginning to avoid certain social situations, which she identified as ones where she knew that someone would bring up the topic of her daughter's diabetes.

6. *Depressive feelings.* Mrs. S described her anxiety sensations as depressing but she did not report any experiences of agitation, psychomotor retardation, appetite changes, weight changes, or crying episodes.

HISTORY OF PRESENTING PROBLEMS

Mrs. S reported that the presenting problems originated when her daughter was diagnosed as having diabetes. Neither she nor her husband (who was interviewed with and without Mrs. S) could identify any other problems that Mrs. S experienced at present or in the past. According to both, everything was fine in their lives before the onset of the daughter's diabetes.

CONCEPTUALIZATION

Following several unsuccessful attempts to formulate the problem, the therapist explained to Mrs. S that he had no idea why she developed such a strong and unusual reaction (i.e., compared to the clinical norm), and that the only reasonable course of action was symptomatic treatment or referral. Mrs. S chose the former.

SYMPTOMATIC TREATMENT

Symptomatic treatment involved the following: (1) progressive muscular relaxation training; (2) development of a hierarchy (in this case, 15 items) of (imaginal and *in vivo*) diabetes-related anxiety-producing stimuli; (3) instruction in substituting adaptive cognitions (e.g., "there's nothing I can do about my daughter's condition, so it makes no sense to get upset about it") for anxiety-arousing ones and (4) practice in (bidirectional) anxiety management (see Meyer & Reich, 1978; Turkat & Kuczmierczyk, 1980).

Throughout treatment, Mrs. S worked diligently on learning anxiety management skills. Further, she frequently sought the therapist's reassurance that she was following instructions properly. She appeared very motivated to eliminate the presenting problem.

Mrs. S was seen weekly for 4 months, and it seemed that she had eliminated her presenting complaints. Accordingly, it was decided to move to a 2-week intersession interval so that the patient could be gradually faded from treatment. Following the first 2-week interval, the patient reported a complete return of her original complaints. No specific environmental trigger for the relapse could be identified.

ANOTHER ATTEMPT TO FORMULATE

The relapse suggested that a re-analysis of the problem was necessary. The following observations were available:

1. The patient's presenting complaints revolved around anxiety concerning stimuli associated with her daughter's diabetes.
2. She was very motivated to eliminate this problem.
3. She worked diligently on acquiring the necessary skills.
4. She consistently requested therapist reassurance regarding execution of treatment techniques.
5. She reduced her diabetes-related anxiety and avoidances to acceptable levels.
6. At the first instance of reducing the therapist's availability, a full relapse occurred.

Observation 4 suggested that receiving reassurance from the therapist was quite important to this patient. Similarly, the only identifiable trigger for the patient's relapse was reduced interaction with the therapist. Thus, a hypothesis emerged that the patient was anxious about coping independently with her problems.

This hypothesis suggested how the patient's presenting problems developed. Care of the insulin-dependent diabetic demands daily decision making regarding type, quantity, and timing of food intake, insulin, exercise, self-monitoring of glucose metabolism, and so on. Incorrect decisions can lead to life-threatening complications. If the patient's basic problem were a hypersensitivity to independent decision making, then her symptoms associated with diabetes should be eliminated if the anxiety about decision making were modified directly.

Given this new hypothesis of mechanism of disorder (i.e., anxiety about making independent decisions), it was expected that the patient experienced anxiety in situations unrelated to diabetes that required independent decisions. Further, it was also expected that the patient's history would reveal a developmental sequence of: (1) punishment for independent decision making and/or positive reinforcement for dependent behavior; (2) anxiety about independent decision making; (3) seeking out individuals who would be relatively independent and/or reassuring to the patient; and (4) avoidance of situations requiring independent decision making.

ETIOLOGIC INQUIRY

Following the patient's relapse she agreed to participate in a second attempt to formulate the problem. This began with scrutiny of current decision-making situations and was followed by a developmental analysis.

At present the patient reported (with the therapist's prompts) numerous decision-making situations that provoked anxiety and attempts to seek reassurance, related and unrelated to her daughter's diabetes. For example, buying food in the supermarket, deciding what to make for dinner, and buying furniture all provoked anxiety and attempts to seek reassurance from her husband. Further, she reported feeling anxious when her husband's reassurance was not available (e.g., when Mr. S was away and Mrs. S was responsible for the style of trimming the garden bushes and lawn). Finally, the patient related numerous anxiety-provoking instances in which decisions she made were initially approved by an authority figure (e.g., husband, physician) and then criticized by an important other (e.g., after following the instructions of her physician, she was criticized for doing so by a friend).

Assessment of early upbringing revealed the patient's lack of independent decision making and anxiety about it. The patient's father was a minister, and Mrs. S related that she viewed him with considerable respect. Further, she reported that "he always told me what to do" and "that he did not permit me to be independent at all." The father was viewed as fully in command of the family and responsible for all decision making. The patient's mother was described as subservient. Further, Mrs. S stated that her mother continually told her to be careful about what she did. The mother would frequently express her own anxiety about decision making by reminding her daughter "What would the parishioners think?" The patient described her upbringing as one in which her parents "mapped out what I was to do and not to do" and "left me with low initiative to make decisions when younger."

During her school years Mrs. S always wanted to be part of the "group" but felt uncomfortable because no one would explicitly point out that she did in fact, "fit in." Consistent with the above, her high school adviser noted on Mrs. S's record that she "lacked initiative."

When the patient went to college, she studied nursing because "a lot of people my age went into nursing." When the time came to choose between a university-based or hospital-based program, this was decided largely from the advice of another.

The patient's first job as a nurse went rather smoothly because she had readily available supervisors. Unfortunately, her second position did not fare well. Apparently, Mrs. S had trouble adjusting because she did not have "supportive" supervisors. She left this position after a short time.

Mrs. S did not have much of a dating history. Her husband was her first and only lover. She was greatly attracted to him because he was "very forceful" and an "independent decision maker."

Given the above, it appeared that the patient had significant modeling and shaping experiences that promoted an anxiety about independent decision making.

PREDICTIONS

In order to test these hypotheses, the patient was administered two subscales of the Interpersonal Dependency Scale (Hirshfeld et al., 1977): (1) Assertion of Autonomy, and (2) Emotional Reliance on Another Person. The correlation between these two subscales is $-.23$ (Hirshfeld et al., 1977).

The first and second hypotheses were tested by converting the patient's raw score on each subscale into Z scores, using normative data (cf. Hirshfeld et al., 1977). The third hypothesis was tested by creating a Z score based on the difference between Z scores for the first two measures. The formula provided by

Payne and Jones (1957) for this type of hypothesis testing with single cases was used.

The patient's score on the reliance measure was 54, almost two standard deviations above the mean score of a population of normal females. This yielded a Z score of 1.86 ($p < .04$; one-tailed). Mrs. S's score on the autonomy measure was 18. This score was exactly two standard deviations below the mean ($p < .03$; one-tailed). The discrepancy between autonomy and reliance scores yielded a Z score of 2.41 ($p < .01$; one-tailed).

FORMULATION-BASED TREATMENT

The formulation was presented to the patient, and a new treatment procedure was devised that capitalized on the patient's abilities that had been learned during the previous months of therapy. This treatment approach had several features. First, a 2-week interval for therapy sessions was maintained so as not to facilitate the patient's dependence on the therapist. Second, practice of anxiety management skills was emphasized. Further, a new hierarchy was developed. The new items included situations in which the patient had little experience or guidelines for her behavior and required her to make decisions without the support and advice of others. With the assistance of the therapist, the patient developed a 16-item hierarchy. Examples of items in this hierarchy included such things as planning supper with only the food in the refrigerator, seeking support from the husband when she felt ill but he did not provide it, and interacting with people who asked about the daughter's condition while being unsure as to what to say. At this time the patient was also asked to perform daily self-ratings on the hierarchy items (which appeared on a standard checklist) using a 1–6 scale where "1" represented "not anxious" and "6" represented "most anxious." Self-ratings were gathered for a 3-week baseline period, during the 2 months of treatment, and at follow-up periods of 2 weeks, 1 month, 4 months, and 11 months.

The patient's response to treatment was assessed primarily by daily self-monitoring of anxiety related to independent decision making. These data were analyzed across the three phases of therapy following the revised formulation (baseline, treatment, and follow-up), and the results indicated significant improvement. Anecdotal evidence revealed that the patient was able to manage independent decision-making situations that were not included on the treatment hierarchy. Further, the patient reported that she no longer experienced the anxiety, avoidances, and depression symptoms she initially experienced. These gains were maintained at an 11-month follow-up.

DISCUSSION

This case illustrates several important points regarding our approach to clinical cases in general and dependent personality disorder in particular. First and foremost, the case of Mrs. S demonstrates the importance of a good formulation. Symptomatic treatment was deceptively effective at first but relapse ensued because the *mechanism* of disorder had not been modified. After the validity of the hypothesized mechanism was confirmed, treatment aimed *directly* at this mechanism resulted in immediate and long-term benefit.

Second, the case of Mrs. S highlights the practical difficulties that occur when phenomena are presented that have not been investigated scientifically. If there were a substantial research literature on dependent personality disorder, it seems likely that the basic problem of this case would have been identified much earlier in the course of therapy.

Finally, the present case suggests that a behavioral approach to treat complex disorders, such as the dependent personality disorder, may be effective. Arguments regarding the "narrowness" of behavior therapy are questioned by the case of Mrs. S.

Histrionic Personality Disorder

The histrionic personality disorder as described in DSM-III has long been a favorite subject of psychodynamic therapists (cf. Adams, 1981). The histrionic personality disorder has been characterized in DSM-III as an individual who is lively and dramatic, seeks the center of attention, is overly reactive, emotionally labile, manipulative, bored easily, and superficial in interpersonal relations. Often it has been confused with "hysteria," "hysterical conversion," "hysterical neurosis," and other disorders (Turkat & Levin, 1984), which muddles much of the research literature. Currently, there is a lack of scientific evidence regarding treatment of this disorder (Adams, 1981).

We have seen eight cases of histrionic personality disorder in our center, but have not been able to treat any of them successfully. Elsewhere (Turkat & Levin, 1984), we have illustrated our attempt to treat such a case and how it failed. For the reader's interest we present another case.

Case Example

PRESENTING PROBLEMS

The patient, Ms. B, was a 30-year-old female Caucasian who was self-referred for treatment at our clinic. The initial interview revealed that Ms. B was experiencing problems in a number of areas.

1. Depression. This was Ms. B's primary complaint and her reason for seeking psychological treatment. She reported that she had been depressed for a few months and that she "just didn't feel like doing anything anymore." Ms. B also reported current suicidal thoughts, which had also occurred in the past. She reported that she had attempted suicide about 3 years ago.

2. Poor marital relationship. Ms. B had been married since she was 16 years old, because she was pregnant with her first child (a girl). Ms. B reported that she and her husband had little in common and never communicated with each other. Each had had extramarital affairs, for which Ms. B reported that she sometimes felt guilty. Further, Ms. B said that she had a high degree of dissatisfaction with her current sexual relationship with her husband. She was generally disinterested and nonresponsive to whatever sexual advances he made. Nonetheless, Ms. B insisted that she stay married, since she felt financially and otherwise secure with her husband.

3. *Disinterest in maternal behaviors.* Ms. B reported that she was bored with having to deal with her two children and with their demands on her. She was especially adamant about the 14-year-old daughter, whose early adolescence was trying Ms. B's patience. Ms. B reported that her daughter was "just like her old man" and that her son was "just like [her]—a bitch."

4. *Poor social life.* Ms. B reported that she had no close male or female friends. She reported that this was a long-standing problem, especially regarding females. Other women were seen as "competition" for attention. Currently Ms. B spent much of her leisure time alone. Ironically, she craved the attention of others, especially men.

5. *Inappropriate flirtatiousness.* Ms. B regularly frequented a tavern in order to meet, talk, and flirt with men and to get their attention. Apparently she would be seductive during these encounters, but, if the man responded, Ms. B almost always withdrew. She could not understand why she had difficulty finding a satisfying relationship with a man, which she claimed to desire very much.

6. *Easily bored.* Ms. B could not attend to any one task or project for long, since she invariably became bored with it if there were too much of a lapse in overt expressions of attention or praise from others.

7. *Excessive insecurity.* Ms. B was extremely insecure about what others thought about her. This extended into a variety of areas, including her maternal behaviors, her interactions with her father, mother, and five brothers, her work, and her behavior as a wife. Through these and other domains, Ms. B desired approval and acceptance of her behavior. This insecurity was a major reason for staying with her husband, despite their problems: she saw it as her "responsibility," and he provided for everything she needed.

8. *Temper tantrums.* Ms. B reported that when events did not go her way she frequently threw temper tantrums in order to manipulate others to give in to her.

9. *Labile mood.* Ms. B's mood state reportedly fluctuated all the time, with mood changes induced by apparently trivial events. She did not understand why her moods changed so much.

DIAGNOSIS

Based on the criteria specified in DSM-III, Ms. B's problems were diagnosed as symptomatic of a histrionic personality disorder. Specifically, she frequently had irrational, angry outbursts or tantrums, drew attention to herself, and craved activity and excitement. Furthermore, she was dependent, constantly sought reassurance and was prone to manipulative suicidal threats or gestures.

ETIOLOGIC INFORMATION

Ms. B was the eldest of six children (five brothers), and her mother left the family when Ms. B was only about 12 years old. Shortly after this event, Ms. B was placed in foster homes for a few years with her brothers and assumed much responsibility for their every activity and caretaking. Ms. B's mother had married when she was only 14 years old and was reported to have separated from her family because she could no longer "take it." Further, although Ms. B's mother remarried, Ms. B was not allowed contact with her stepfather for some time because her mother was jealous. Ms. B also reported that her mother liked to be the center of attention.

FORMULATION

Ms. B's problems were formulated as an excessive need for attention and a failure to use the appropriate social skills in order to achieve attention from others. Therefore, Ms. B was currently depressed because she was receiving little, if any, of the attention (reinforcement) that she desired because of her social ineffectiveness. Examples of her inappropriate behaviors included temper tantrums, teasing of men, and suicidal statements. It is likely that these same behaviors accounted in large part for her poor marital relationship and her failure to develop close personal relationships. Other women were a particular problem, since they were "competition." It also follows that anyone like Ms. B, who is overly dependent on others' attention, is likely to have frequent mood changes, because the social environment changes rapidly and the individual's mood with it. This same dependence on the social environment produced Ms. B's high degree of insecurity.

It also seems that Ms. B modeled a good part of her mother's social behavior, including a low tolerance of boredom and excessive attention seeking. Furthermore, due to her early management of her brothers, Ms. B was used to being in a position of control and the center of her brothers' attention. At the same time, she was clearly rejected by both parents at an early age of her life, which explained her fear of rejection from others. The combination of these factors therefore accounts in large part for Ms. B's excessive attention needs. It also appears that Ms. B had little opportunity (e.g., her mother's behavior, marriage at a very young age) to model or to otherwise learn more adaptive social behaviors that she could apply to get the attention from others.

TEST OF THE FORMULATION

Based on the formulation that Ms. B's problems were due to a high need for attention from others and the failure to use appropriate social skills to obtain that attention, two hypotheses were advanced:

1. Ms. B would tend to show negative mood during performance of a boring task only if she received no immediate social reinforcement for task performance.

2. Ms. B had poor empathy skills and, therefore, should perform lower than average on a task involving determining the moods and thoughts of others on the basis of verbal and nonverbal cues.

Hypothesis 1. The test of hypothesis 1 involved assessment of Ms. B's mood following different conditions of task performance. Specifically, Ms. B was instructed to perform a task of crossing out the *o*'s and *e*'s that appeared in each line of literary text. The conditions varied as a function of whether Ms. B received periodic social reinforcement (praise) from the therapist during task performance or whether she performed the task uninterrupted by the therapist. Each of the four task periods lasted 10 min and followed the sequence, task alone, task + social reinforcement, task alone, and task + social reinforcement in an A-B-A-B design. Ms. B's mood was assessed following each test period with the Nunnally Affect Inventory (Nunnally, 1980). The results showed that the mood variables measured did not change as a function of task performance conditions.

Hypothesis 2. The second hypothesis was tested in two ways. First, it was predicted that Ms. B would score below appropriate norms on a test of self-perception of ability to discriminate others' feelings by various verbal and nonverbal cues, and the self-perception of whether one gives those same cues to others to reveal one's feelings (Zuckerman & Larrance, 1979). The results showed that Ms. B scored in the normal range compared to a normative sample of adult females on both dimensions. Therefore, this test did not support hypothesis 2.

The other test of hypothesis 2 was developed especially for this experiment. In this regard excerpts were taken from a book of readings in abnormal psychology and sociology that concerned patients revealing their feelings. Excerpts were chosen that were evaluated by the experimenters as being "easy" to judge the character's feelings (six excerpts), and the remaining six excerpts were evaluated as being "difficult" to judge. Ms. B's task was to describe briefly what the character in each excerpt was feeling and why and then to rate how difficult she found it to make that judgment. Her difficulty ratings were compared to those made by a sample of five undergraduate students enrolled in a summer semester course in personality. Ms. B was given the 12 excerpts to rate and instructed to take all the time that she needed to complete the task. The results showed that Ms. B's ratings did not differ systematically from those of the undergraduate student sample. Further, her assessments of patients' feelings seemed appropriate. Therefore, the data from this test also did not support hypothesis 2.

DISCUSSION

These results led the authors to consider a difficult question: was our formulation incorrect or was our experimentation an insensitive test of our formulation? Two primary considerations guided us in dealing with this dilemma. First, we recognized that we could not answer this question because an alternate appropriate methodology was not available. Second, the welfare of the patient was of prime concern. Accordingly, we discussed the situation in all of its aspects with the patient, and her view was that the formulation was correct regardless of the test results. Unfortunately, during treatment she enjoyed flirting with us, but decided that it would be too much effort to change her ways. Thus, treatment was terminated.

Our experience with histrionic personality disorder cases suggests two things. First, we know little about formulating and treating such cases. Second, our experimental method approach is still in its infancy, and considerable effort will be required to eliminate its current shortcomings.

Narcissistic Personality Disorder

Narcissistic personality disorder is a new entry in the DSM-III, although the construct of "narcissism" dates back to some of Freud's earliest papers (Freud, 1911/1958, 1913/1955, 1914/1957). The DSM-III narcissistic personality disorder is characterized by a grandiose sense of uniqueness, self-importance, preoccupation with fantasies of unlimited success, exhibitionist need for constant attention, and interpersonal difficulties including an empathy deficit, feelings of entitlement, and exploitiveness.

In our review of the literature, we found little research on the assessment, etiology, or treatment of narcissistic personality disorder. In contrast, there is much psychoanalytic discussion of narcissism, which has little resemblance to the DSM-III description of narcissistic personality disorder (Turkat & Levin, 1984).

We have seen two cases of narcissistic personality disorder, but for present purposes, we will discuss the case of Ms. R.

Case Example

PRESENTING PROBLEMS

The patient, Ms. R, was an attractive but overweight 22-year-old Caucasian female. Ms. R was an insulin-dependent diabetic and was referred to the senior author for difficulty in adhering to her diabetic treatment regimen. Specifically, her diabetes was in poor control due to the patient's inability to adhere to a diet, to exercise daily, and to monitor her glucose levels at various times throughout the day. At the time of referral, the only aspect of the diabetes treatment regimen that Ms. R followed was daily injection of insulin (which if not followed would result in death).

The clinical psychologist began the interview by asking the patient how he could help her. Ms. R stated that she was not taking her diabetes seriously. Upon elaborating, Ms. R indicated that actually she was less concerned about improving her attitude toward her diabetes and more concerned about being 30 lb overweight. When asked to generate a list of all the problems she was experiencing, Ms. R provided the following.

1. Eating. The patient indicated that she had no control over urges to eat. When hungry she ate whatever she craved. All attempts at dieting were seen as futile.

2. Drinking. Ms. R reported that she drank alcohol every night at various bars and discos with a circle of "partying buddies." She indicated that she would often go out to the bars following work and frequently stay out drinking until two or three o'clock in the morning. Ms. R reported that she typically drank the equivalent of six, 12-oz beers a night.

3. Work difficulties. The patient reported that she hated working and preferred a lifestyle of just "play." Ms. R had changed jobs frequently over the 4-year period since graduating from high school. She viewed her present job as a sales clerk in a jewelry store as boring and financially unrewarding. The patient indicated that she often called in sick simply because she just felt like doing other things.

4. Financial problems. Ms. R indicated that she was constantly running out of money, and that bills were unpaid. She often did not have enough gasoline in her car to get across town, and cigarettes were frequently "bummed" from others. Ms. R reported that most of her money went to "partying" (i.e., drinking, eating, and, occasionally, drug use) and to buying clothes. Her parents (especially her father) frequently provided money to help her get by.

5. Dependence on family. Although the patient reported that she did not want to be financially dependent on her parents, she felt that her lifestyle forced her to be. Ms. R and her sister shared an apartment that was partially supported by her paretns.

6. Lack of a boyfriend. The patient reported that she currently did not have a steady boyfriend and that this was of great concern to her. While Ms. R was sexually active with a number of male friends, she viewed most of these relationships as only superficial. She felt that a wealthy lover would solve most of her problems. She felt that if she improved her physical appearance by losing weight, then her chances to attract such an individual would be enhanced.

Following generation of the above problem list, a variety of other areas were discussed. The following problems were identified by the interviewer and mutually agreed upon as problem areas.

7. Boredom. The patient reported that she was easily bored. For example, when Ms. R interacted in bars, if she was not the center of attention, she became bored. Ms. R indicated that if she wanted some excitement, often she would have to create it. For instance, she reported that she once bounced a check in order to create some excitement.

8. Concern about appearance. In addition to her concern about her weight, the patient reported feeling uncomfortable about being unable to wear the clothes she preferred at work. Further, she indicated that she only "hung out" with "cool" individuals. Although she claimed that all who knew her liked her, Ms. R seemed especially concerned about being seen with the "right" individuals.

9. Selfishness. Although the patient did not view herself as selfish, a review of her behaviors (e.g., bored when not the center of attention, calling in sick to engage in other self-rewarding activities, expressing disgust about her father's complaining about a recent injury that he incurred) led the patient to agree that she was rarely empathic and more often, self-absorbed. Further, she viewed herself as special in that she thought that she should not have to work for a living.

10. Excessive daydreaming. Ms. R indicated that each day she spent many hours daydreaming about having and spending endless amounts of money, going on shopping sprees, partying, and having power. Ms. R recognized that these were just dreams, but she reported that they made her feel good.

11. Lack of planning. The patient showed little ability to prepare for future responsibilities, such as paying bills. Further, she had no specific plans for preparing herself to gain some of the financial rewards that she dreamed about. The only future event that Ms. R "planned" for was to somehow get out of the "mess" that she felt she was presently in.

12. Depression. The patient reported frequent periods of depression that were brief (a few hours to a few days) and could be alleviated by such events as "partying."

13. Noncompliance with diabetic treatment. While Ms. R was not primarily concerned about managing her diabetes, she agreed that it was necessary to take better care of herself. However, since she perceived adhering to her treatment protocol as work with no apparent payoff, she felt little desire to comply.

ETIOLOGIC INFORMATION

The patient was the youngest of four children. She had two brothers and a sister. Both parents were musicians who taught their trade professionally. In describing her upbringing, the patient reported, ". . . by the time I came along my mother said 'do what you want; I give up.'" Ms. R described an upbringing that included few rules or regulations. Furthermore, chores or responsibilities were never assigned to her, and she rarely did homework or studied. Her parents paid little attention to her schoolwork and there were no contingencies enforced for achievement. In addition, bedtime was up to her, and she was allowed to choose her own activities. Ms. R reported that, as a child, she was given just about anything she asked for.

The patient viewed herself as popular and well liked by her peers. Ms. R reported that, as early as the sixth grade, her friends came to her house daily to "party." The patient's parents permitted their basement to be a "hangout" for Ms. R and her friends, where they would smoke tobacco and marijuana and drink alcohol even while Ms. R's parents were at home. The patient recalled that she had the most freedom among her peers and was told frequently that she had the "coolest parents around." The patient had no curfews.

Throughout junior high school and high school, Ms. R dated a variety of males in a series of short-term relationships. Ms. R moved out of her parents' house in the 10th grade and into a male's apartment. When asked to describe parental reaction to this she stated that "no one really noticed anyway." The relationship did not last long, and the patient continued her promiscuous ways.

When Ms. R was 16, she developed classic symptoms of diabetes (e.g., frequent urination at night, excessive thirst and hunger, weight loss) and was hospitalized in ketoacidosis. After Ms. R was diagnosed as an insulin-dependent diabetic and treated in the hospital, her physician emphasized that she needed to monitor her urine glucose throughout each day, take injections of insulin daily, and strictly follow a diet in order to avoid further illness and hospitalization. At first Ms. R complied with these instructions. However, she soon discovered that the diet and glucose monitoring seemed inconsequential, and that the only necessity was to take her insulin. Thus, she abandoned efforts to control her diabetes tightly through diet and monitoring procedures.

Following high school graduation, the patient held a variety of jobs, none lasting more than 1 year. These included work as a nurse's technician, attendant at two day care centers, clerk in a key and gift shop, and her present employment, salesperson in a jewelry store.

FORMULATION

Ms. R was reared in a home with few rules or regulations, and did not have responsibilities or chores as a child. Rather, she was exposed to an environment emphasizing enjoyment of life, pleasure seeking, and freedom from obligations. When she desired something it was generally provided for her. In this regard the patient could not present examples of having to earn pleasurable things. She also could not recall ever being punished for certain behaviors. Accordingly, it was hypothesized that the patient learned to be concerned with seeking reinforcers without having to work for them, which resulted in her development as an egocentric, self-indulgent, impulsive individual. This can be operationalized as a deficit in responding to delayed reinforcement schedules (or, conversely, excessive responding to immediate reinforcement).

Consistent with this hypothesis, excessive eating and drinking can be viewed as examples of immediately gratifying activity. Avoidance of work (i.e., noncompliance with medical regimen, calling in sick to employer, frequent job change) is immediately negatively reinforcing. Furthermore, Ms. R's desire to be the center of attention may be explained by her excessive concern for immediate reinforcement. An environment that did not offer such attention would seem aversive. Other consequences of this deficit in impulse control included easily induced boredom (since immediate reinforcers are not always available), excessive concern about appearance (since physical attractiveness increases the opportunities to gain attention and reinforcers from others), and superficial relationships and promiscuity (since close relationships involve sacrifice and effort). Accordingly, the patient could not develop plans for the future, spent money impulsively resulting in financial problems, and thus was depen-

dent on her family for support of her lifestyle. Finally, when immediate reinforcers were not available, Ms. R daydreamed about having them; when deprived of them for sufficient time periods she became depressed. Therefore, the
various presenting problems were formulated as behavioral manifestations of an
impulse control deficit that was learned from early upbringing.

In the three sessions following the initial interview, the patient participated
in two experiments and two controlled observations designed to evaluate the
validity of the behavioral formulation of a deficit in impulse control.

Hypothesis 1. It was predicted that the patient would choose an immediate,
smaller reinforcement over a delayed, larger reinforcement for performance on
a boring task.

Test of Hypothesis 1. During the first testing session, Ms. R was given a
work task that involved crossing out certain letters of the alphabet on a
typewritten sheet. She was given two choices: (1) crossing out all of the *o*'s and
e's that appeared in the text, with an immediate payment of 10 cents for each
line correctly crossed out, or (2) crossing out all the *i*'s and *a*'s that appeared, for
which she was to receive 20 cents for each correct line 1 month after the session.
The patient assumed that she could perform both options simultaneously,
despite the instructions to choose only one. Accordingly, over the 10-min
period, she crossed out all the specified *o*'s, *e*'s, *i*'s, and *a*'s on 17 lines, which
netted $1.70 immediately and $3.40 to be reimbursed later. To correct the
misunderstanding in instructions, the patient was retested in session 2, when the
work task was repeated with two minor changes. First, she was forced to make a
choice between option (1), immediate reinforcement (one reinforcer), and option (2), delayed reinforcement (three reinforcers). Second, instead of money,
cigarettes were used as reinforcement because they cost less and were identified
as strong reinforcers to the patient. A second trial of the work task involved a
choice between receiving one cigarette for each line immediately or a later
reinforcement of five cigarettes a line.

On the first trial the patient chose the immediate reinforcement (one
cigarette) over the delayed reinforcement (three cigarettes at the end of the
month) as predicted. On the second trial Ms. R chose delayed reinforcement
(five cigarettes a line) to the immediate reinforcement of one cigarette. On the
first trial she earned 35 cigarettes for 35 lines, and on the second trial she earned
185 cigarettes for 35 lines. Therefore, Ms. R performed as predicted on the first
trial, when she chose an immediate reinforcement that was one third the value of
the delayed reinforcement. On the second trial she chose the delayed reinforcement because, she said, "I already had earned enough cigarettes for today."

In order to replicate the original finding without confounding previous
earnings, the experiment was repeated in session 3. In this experiment a choice
to cross out *o*'s and *e*'s resulted in immediate payment of one cigarette. In
contrast, a choice of crossing out *a*'s and *i*'s resulted in payment of five cigarettes

a line at the end of the month. As predicted, Ms. R chose immediate reinforcement even though the delayed reinforcement paid off at five times the rate of immediate reinforcement. Accordingly, it was concluded that hypothesis 1 was supported.

Hypothesis 2. It was predicted that the patient would eat more desirable food following a period of no immediate social reinforcement compared to the amount eaten after immediate social reinforcement was provided.

Test of Hypothesis 2. During the first testing session, the patient was asked to list her favorite brands of snack foods such as crackers, cookies, and pretzels. During session 2, she was given a monotonous, boring task to work on for 20 min. The task consisted of completing a series of Symbol–Digit Modalities Test sheets. In this session Ms. R was given no encouragement and simply instructed to complete the task as quickly as she could. She remained alone in the room while completing the task. After 20 min, it was explained that a "taste test" (cf. Schachter & Rodin, 1974) would be conducted that had no apparent connection to the digit test. The experimenters placed three plates of crackers before the subject, and read the following instructions:

We have three types of crackers we would like you to taste. You are to rate each of them on the characteristics on this sheet [an adjective checklist including "tasty," "salty," etc.]. Eat as few or as many as you want—the only requirement is that you taste each one at least once. You will have 15 minutes to do this.

After the "taste test" was completed, the crackers were removed to another room and the quantity and weight of crackers consumed was determined. In session 3, the patient was given the same monotonous task to do for 20 min. However, every 5 min the experimenter entered the room and encouraged her by saying that she was doing well, working very quickly, and the like. At the end of 20 min, three plates of crackers (same quantity and quality as the first test but different brands) were brought in, and Ms. R was again asked to taste and rate three types of crackers. After 15 min, the crackers were removed, and the quantity and weight of crackers consumed was recorded.

During the no reinforcement condition (i.e., the first exposure), the patient ate a total of 42 g of crackers. During the attention condition (i.e., experimenter in the room attending to her) Ms. R ate only 20 g of crackers. Thus, as predicted, Ms. R ate more than twice the amount of crackers after the no-attention condition, compared to the attention condition. Both of the taste test sessions were run at 2:00 p.m. exactly 1 week apart. Ms. R arrived at each session without having eaten for 2 hr.

Hypothesis 3. It was predicted that the patient would score in the upper percentiles of the Sensation Seeking Scale (Zuckerman, 1979).

Test of Hypothesis 3. In order to test hypothesis 3, the patient completed the Sensation Seeking Scale, Form V, in Session 2. The patient achieved a total score of 27, which was at the 95th percentile for females in a normative sample of undergraduates enrolled in Introductory Psychology (Zuckerman, 1979). Thus, hypothesis 3 was supported.

Hypothesis 4. It was predicted that the patient would appear to be more impulsive compared to other individuals.

Test of Hypothesis 4. In order to test this hypothesis, the patient completed the MMPI during Session 2. The results indicated a 4–7–9 profile. As described by Lachar (1980), individuals with a 4–7 MMPI configuration demonstrate

. . . excessive insensitivity . . . these persons may act with little control or forethought, violating social and legal restrictions and trampling on feelings of others needlessly . . . excessive alcohol indulgence or stepping out/promiscuity. (p. 84)

Individuals with a 4–9 configuration are described in Lachar (1980) as

. . . always associated with some form of acting out behavior. The individual exhibits an enduring tendency to get into trouble with his environment . . . arousal seeking and inordinate need for excitement and stimulation . . . impulsive and irresponsible . . . untrustworthy, shallow and superficial in their relationships to others. They typically have easy morals; they are selfish and pleasure-seeking. Many temporarily create a favorable impression because they are internally comfortable and free from inhibiting anxiety, worry and guilt but are actually quite deficient in their role-taking ability. Their judgement is notably poor and they do not seem to learn from past experiences. They lack the ability to postpone gratification of their desires and therefore have difficulty in any enterprise requiring sustained effort. (p. 88)

Finally, a 7–9 configuration is described in Lachar (1980) as indicative of

[a] heightened energy level . . . patients often experience periods of impulsivity. . . . This patient may be somewhat self-centered and immature. (p. 133)

Accordingly, hypothesis 4 was supported.

The results of these experiments and controlled observations provide converging validity for the behavioral formulation of a deficit in impulse control, as each specific prediction was supported by the data. As hypothesized, the patient preferred immediate reinforcement over a delayed reinforcement of substantially higher value, ate more food following no attention compared to social attention, and scored as more sensation seeking and impulsive compared to norms on standardized measures.

TREATMENT

Before treatment began the results of the assessment and formulation and the rationale for treatment were presented as illustrated in the following (condensed) transcript.

DR. TURKAT: OK. Well, you've now gone through some interesting experiences with us. What have you been thinking about them?

MS. R: That I can't wait to find out why crossing out those letters really matters. I mean what can you learn from me about that?

DR. T: Yes. Basically, you are someone who has learned from your upbringing that when you want something, go get it and do it right now, and never had to learn, or were never given the opportunity to learn that we must do a, b, c, d, e, f, g for this, but this isn't going to come until much later on. It's been an upbringing of well, "I want this, I'm going to have this." And so you've never really learned how to control urges to get things. As you said, there were no rules, regulations in your home, you had no chores or responsibilities. Your father gave you everything, your mother gave up. You partied and never had to work—only to get things immediately. Act on your impulses. Thus you now have problems dealing with things that require you to do work without immediate reinforcement. Now similarly how to work for things that may not come immediately, OK? Which might help explain why it's hard to take care of your diabetes. There's nothing in it for you immediately. You won't drop over; you won't go blind; that may happen way down the road, maybe not, but immediately it doesn't. Well, going off a diet and sticking with it, well, "God that's going to take forever. It's much easier to sit and enjoy myself now and put the food in and eat the food I shouldn't, but it's easier." And these are some examples. Similarly in your job, I suspect that a lot of the fluctuations in terms of the way you go, you get bored with what you're doing, and the novelty wears off, and you're not getting a lot of things out of it immediately, but if you wake up and say "Ah, I don't want to go to work," you don't go to work because it's more immediately reinforcing to stay home as opposed to going and working and not getting the money for a week later. Or going to the mall, or the bars where you and your friend know you shouldn't spend the money, but screw it. "I'm just for right now." And so it all correlates to being impulsive, the inability to learn how to delay urges, acting on urges, and conversely, working for a goody that doesn't come immediately is difficulty to do. That all make sense?

MS. R: Uh-huh.

DR. T: OK. Basically, this problem with being impulsive is a learned kind of thing. All your life you were unstructured, whatever you wanted you got basically. And you never really had to work for anything that would come a lot later. And so in essence you learned this kind of routine, and now it's difficult to get under control because you've been practicing it for so long.

MS. R: I've been in it for years.

DR. T: OK. So what was the purpose of crossing out all those letters, earning cigarettes and money for such a boring task? We wanted to have a test that would help us see if in fact you are impulsive. And so we created a test to see if this would happen. So, for example, if you have this problem then you should respond to immediate goodies as opposed to goodies that are to come a long time from now. We would give you a choice if you do X amount of work, you do 10 problems, and after the 10 problems we're going to give you a choice. We'll pay you now or we're going to pay you later at a much higher rate. We predicted you'd go for now. Crossing out o and e is a very boring, monotonous task. We aren't concerned so much in how well you crossed out letters. We're concerned with what you would choose. OK? And you consistently went for the immediate. Even when the number of cigarettes was 5 to 1.

MS. R: Yeah.

DR. T: So that kind of supported the hypothesis. OK. Then we had a test. Now that was bizarre, wasn't it? One of the things that we predicted from the way I formulated this case was if you were working in a task that was boring,

OK, and nothing was going on except that task, and then you had an opportunity to eat, you'd eat a lot, as opposed to if you were working on a boring task, but someone was paying attention to you or giving you immediate goodies or reinforcement. You wouldn't eat as much after that. So what we did was we had you copy digits and symbols, which was also a very boring, monotonous kind of task.

MS. R: Tell me about it!

DR. T: We weren't interested so much in how well you copied the symbols. We then had you rate crackers, how salty, or which one was better. We were interested in how much you were going to eat.

MS. R: Oh. OK.

DR. T: We were predicting that given those situations where you did some work, a boring task, and then you'd eat afterwards. The only differences between the two times you did it was that one time you were in the room by yourself and had no reinforcement while you were doing the task. The other time Sue was in the room and commenting about your performance. Remember? So, we hypothesized that if someone else was in here, and you were getting a little bit of attention and reinforcement that you wouldn't eat as much after that. And we found you'd eat two times as much when she wasn't in the room.

MS. R: Gosh. Strange.

DR. T: Does that make sense?

MS. R: Yes it does.

DR. T: That again supported our hypothesis. Then we also gave you some standard questionnaires that are typically used in psychology, to see if your responses matched up with other people who have this kind of problem. And they do. OK? So in essence what we were trying to show was that the hypothesis that I had about you was accurate, so we wanted to test to see if in fact it was. And we think it is, because all of the data that we got suggest that this is probably correct. Now let me get your comments and thoughts on all that.

MS. R: Well, it all makes sense completely now. But I tell you I spent a lot of time trying to figure out what in the world those symbols, you know, sheet after sheet of those. I thought why give me one and then give me another one just like it. I've been trying real hard to figure out why.

DR. T: What did you come up with?

MS. R: I didn't come up with anything.

DR. T: And now you understand.

MS. R: Yes.

DR. T: Does it make sense?

MS. R: Yeah.

DR. T: OK. So in essence we think we have the way we understand the problem. I think it is correct or as close as you can get to correctness as we think. Now the question is what do we do? If our hypothesis is correct and you came in saying in essence, first you said, "Well I'm not taking my diabetes seriously." And you then clarified that. You're saying, "Look, I don't like being overweight.

I want to get my weight down, my appearance better. That's what I'm really concerned about. I don't care so much about the diabetes stuff." So how do we do that? Well, from our hypothesis and understanding and formulation of your problem it would seem almost impossible to put you on a diet and you'd just stick to it. OK? We'd say, here's a diet. And you had that experience before and there's no way you can do it. That's because doing a diet requires work with a delayed goodie or a delayed reinforcement. The weight loss comes much later. So by not eating you have an immediate urge to eat, competing with the urge to lose weight. But losing weight won't come for a long time later. And so given your training you're much more likely to go for the immediate. Similar with drinking, which is very high in calories. It's bad for your health if you're drinking too much and too often. It feels good and it tastes good—sometimes it doesn't taste good—but most of the time. But it's an immediate thing, and it's much more powerful than if you don't do it you're going to lose some weight 5 weeks from now. Alright? So given your training you're much more prone to develop a weight problem or a drinking problem or anything where the imme-diate reinforcement is very strong, and you're likely to get addicted to it. Does that all make sense?

MS. R: Yeah.

DR. T: Alright. Based on that, I would predict that there is no way in the world that our nutritionist could give you a diet and you're going to stick to it. Unless somehow, you're going to be able to work in the absence of immediate reinforcement, meaning two things. One, you can do a certain amount of work without getting anything out of it immediately. You're going to have to learn how to do that. Because if you don't then you're not going to be able to stick to anything that doesn't provide the immediate goodie. Are you following me?

MS. R: Uh-huh.

DR. T: OK. Similarly, when you have an urge, you're going to have to learn you can't act on it immediately to do something. See, we all have urges to do things. But many of us say, "OK, I'd really like to do it, but I know in the long run that's bad for me and I'm not going to do that." You can't do that. You've a hard time doing that. From your training you have a hard time doing that. It's not that you're crazy, or ill, or you're a terrible person. This is just how you learned to be. And so it makes it very difficult for you to be able to learn to delay acting on an urge, such that if you had no money and had to pay your rent and you just got paid and you're passing by a bar with a friend, and she says, "Let's go get a drink or seven," you go, "Oh, I'd love to do that, but I really need to save the money for the rent. Let's get drunk"—that's what you'd do. You're going to have to learn . . .

MS. R: You've been watching me!

DR. T: This just shows that my hypothesis about you is correct, as far as I can tell. I may be wrong, but I don't think so.

MS. R: I don't think you are either.

DR. T: OK. So you're going to have to learn how to control urges and delay acting upon them, and you're going to have to learn how to work and do things without getting reinforced for them immediately, before you can get to even lose weight. You have to have that filled before you can go on a diet. OK? You are not going to do it as you've learned. There's no quick way to lose weight. You've got to make a permanent change in your habits, your eating, your drinking, your exercising, and the reinforcement is delayed. It takes a long time before losing that fat. So when you first go on a diet, you might lose weight quickly after the 1st week, and then it's very slow. And that's always the hard thing for you. So somehow you have to be taught how to deal with that situation before we can even put you in that situation with a chance or hope for success.

MS. R: It's going to take awhile.

DR. T: It's going to take awhile. So what I'm saying is this: In order to help you lose weight, before we can do that, one first has to teach you how to control impulses and work in the absence of immediate goodies or reinforcements. And that is the first thing we have to do in treatment. If you can learn that skill, then you might be able to learn to lose the weight, and control drinking, and control your finances.

MS. R: Yeah.

DR. T: And, not have hassles at work. And not miss work and not jump from job to job. And, be able to get along with guys, because in relation to this hypothesis, someone has to be immediately reinforcing. If you're talking with a guy in a bar, I predict that as soon as you're not the center of attention you get bored and don't get turned on anymore. Is that fairly accurate?

MS. R: Yes.

DR. T: And so there's no way you're going to hook a guy that you really want unless he is immediately reinforcing you all of the time. You see what I'm saying?

MS. R: Uh-huh.

DR. T: Does that make sense?

MS. R: Yeah, it does.

DR. T: Do you think that's an accurate statement? So, I don't see this as just a way to control your weight. I see you have to learn that skill to control your weight, your drinking, your job, your behavior and social life.

MS. R: My whole life. I could use some help. I mean if I never lost a pound the rest of me still could use some help.

DR. T: Now, many of the things you've learned, you're not realistic in terms of say, doing any type of work; which is in essence the type of training your parents gave. That's been your history, hasn't it? You've never really had to do any work until after you got out of school. And all of a sudden "Whoa—I'm on my own, I have to produce some income and that means I have to work," and you have a very hard time keeping a job, getting along with supervisors, following the rules and regulations, and so in order for you to do that, you have to learn how to control these kinds of impulses and work in the absence of immediate reinforcement. Similarly, I would suggest that if you're not getting immediate reinforcement you're more likely to start daydreaming about having it, having money, running around, etcetera. And that's happened quite a bit I suspect. You spend a lot of time daydreaming about having money and shopping, and playing.

MS. R: Yeah, sure do.

DR. T: OK. That's just a daydream. And I suspect that when you're bored you like to think of that more, and particularly, if you're not in a situation where you're getting immediate reinforcement you're much more likely to get depressed. And so you have periodic moods where you get depressed. But when some people come in with some booze, some attention, your mood is better and depression goes, and so there are short periods of depression. They're not for weeks and weeks and weeks of your laying in bed.

MS. R: No.

DR. T: No. It's kind of like transient. Is that also correct?

MS. R: Yeah.

DR. T: Now let me stop. I've been talking quite a bit. What do you think about this?

MS. R: Well, it all sounds true. I would have stopped you if I thought you were wrong about something you said. But it sounds true and it scares the hell out of me. It sounds like such a major undertaking. It sounds like I couldn't do this. I'm not sure if I'm going to change. I mean I want to, but it sounds very hard.

DR. T: You're right. Now let me comment on that. Before you can work on a problem you've got to understand it and understand it correctly. Another question is can we treat it? That's another story. One thing you probably may have noticed about me is I'm relatively frank and straightforward. OK? And I'll tell you just what I think. I think that there's a possibility we might be able to do this. We might be able to teach you how to do this. But I don't know. We, I really don't know for the following reason. Given this history, you're going to want immediate results all of the time. Somehow we now both know that the results are not going to be immediate and that somehow we've got to create an environment or a treatment situation where you're getting something out of not getting something immediate. You see what I'm saying?

MS. R: Yeah. Uh-huh.

DR. T: So it's going to be difficult.

MS. R: Extremely.

DR. T: It doesn't mean it can't be done. Now, what it's going to require is a lot of hard work on your part, our part, close cooperation, and to give it the best try we can. And a lot of creativity. OK? I've got good people working with me. It's a very touchy thing what we're talking about, given the problem you've developed, that you've learned and how it's manifested, it creates a difficult way to go about treating it. That doesn't mean it can't be treated. But it doesn't mean that I guarantee success. And so what I'm saying to you, is I think that if we, both, us, you, give it the best shot we can, we might be able to do it. Or we might not. So I can't guarantee results. What I can guarantee is you can commit yourself to trying to do it. We will commit ourselves in trying to do it. It won't be able to be done once a week, no way. Now it won't be just talk but practicing.

So I would envision some kind of process of beginning in situations where you have difficulty controlling urges. We have you bring them on and then try to teach you ways to prevent acting upon them, and then trying to teach you to do it longer and longer. That's one approach, OK? Also, we will try to increase your ability to stay with doing the boring, monotonous task in the absence of getting something for it, because you've had trouble doing that. So these are the kinds of things I would say you would have to start working on first. Alright? And see if we can set up practice exercises for you. We'll all help to try to teach you how to get your impulses under control, etcetera. Then, you might start immediately noticing benefits. For all I know within 3 weeks you may start noticing you're really getting this under control. You may not. I can't predict it.

MS. R: Yeah, I understand.

DR. T: Everyone is different, your environment has a lot to do with it now. You've got all these people saying "Come on, let's go get drunk, come on, let's go stuff our face, get munched out," what are you going to do? And so we may have to arrange certain things with your sister, and your friends, and your mother and father. We wouldn't do anything you'd not be willing to agree to do. So overall what I'm saying is ideally we have a theoretical approach or a hypothesis about how we might treat it. Now we have to see if we can devise a practical way to implement what I think it ought to be. Now, in my thinking we need some kind of task to teach you how to delay acting on impulses. Ideally that sounds great, but what we can do is another question. So that will require hard work on our part with you, creativity, and commitment to try to do it. And, it's ultimately our responsibility to see if we can devise such a treatment.

MS. R: It sounds like you have it as hard as I do.

DR. T: We do. I never see treating somebody's problems as an easy job. It never is. It is never easy.

MS. R: I'm glad to hear you say that. I thought about Dr. _____ today that I saw for $60 an hour for months. He never said anything to me. I'd just go there and talk about nothing. We never even figured out what the problem was at all. I just sat there and talked. Then I wrote a check for $60. He didn't do anything at all. Ever. And so really, even through it, you know, something will come of it and something will have happened to me. So I'm willing to work.

DR. T: The only thing you have to lose by this right now is time. By committing yourself to a treatment program, the only thing you lose now is time. There's nothing detrimental or bad that will happen as far as we can see. OK? And, in fact, you'll be getting lots of attention, which you like.

MS. R: Right.

DR. T: OK. Questions, comments?

MS. R: Well, this is strange, but you may not be able to answer it. How do you know if it's not working? I mean, stop, you know this isn't working.

DR. T: Very clear. You at any point have the right to say, "I'm not coming back." Just say we have the right at any time to say, "Sorry we can't treat you." So, we each have the right to pull out at any time. One of the quickest ways you know whether it's working or not is if you see changes coming on in your life, you'll be aware of it. You'll say, "I've got more money in my pocket. Hey, I'm not eating as much. I'm handling work better." It will be very obvious to you whether you're progressing or not and it will be very clear-cut. Dr. Maisto and I will define very specific goals. You either reach them or not. If you're not reaching them, you're not improving. So you'll be very aware of whether or not you're improving. And, we'll say, "Ms. R, you're not doing what I'm telling you, you're not following it," or "We're not going to be successful." We'll tell you that. So, we'll be very straightforward, and frank, and honest. None of this not knowing what the goal is. We're going to make the goal very specific and keep changing the goal and making it more and more difficult. And so you'll know if you're reaching the goal. You'll see it in your behavior. We don't like seeing people who aren't changing. That makes us nervous. It's very punishing for us to put time in and we're not helping someone change. We are motivated to see some change, and if you obviously don't, there's going to be none of this just sitting and talking stuff, cause I don't believe that works. And it won't work in your case. Definitely won't work in my opinion.

MS. R: I believe that.

DR. T: You need to get impulses under control and how to work in the absence of immediate reinforcement. And if you can learn to do these two things, I think you may be able to get your weight, your drinking under control. You might be able to stay with a career.

MS. R: That would be nice.

DR. T: And work at it and enjoy it. You may be able then to start taking care of your diabetes and get that under control. And you may be able to get closer relationships to people. Superficial drinking and partying, there's no real emotional closeness. There's a lot of partying but no closeness. There's partying buddies and the same things with guys. You know, close relationships require work, efforts, sacrifice, or delaying reinforcement, thus part of your problem. Close relations requires work. And there's punishment in there and not always immediate reinforcement. So, if the plan works, you should start seeing changes in those areas. But the first step is the basic problem, which is impulse control and working in the absence of reinforcement. The first thing we have to do. Otherwise we can't touch the others. So we have to give it our best shot and see. If you're willing to do it, we're willing to do it. We'll try to help you in every way possible.

MS. R: OK.

DR. T: Well, what do you think?

MS. R: It sounds great, you know, and also scary, but I know there's no way I can do this by myself. It's nice, you know you're fighting this with me.

DR. T: Well, that's critical. If we didn't give you that impression, you would not be back here. Then we wouldn't be giving you reinforcement and attention, which you apparently are hooked on. Other comments and thoughts? Questions?

MS. R: I'm sure there will be some when I get home, on the way home.

DR. T: Anything else we should cover today?

MS. R: I guess not.

DR. T: Do you feel blown away?

MS. R: Yeah.

DR. T: You look blown away.

MS. R: Now, well, it's not real often that I'm speechless. I'm going to have to go to my Mom's house and let her enjoy it.

DR. T: Why does it make you speechless?

MS. R: It just gives me a lot to think about. I guess I'm bored so I daydream. I don't usually have such important matters such as the rest of my life to think about. Or I don't like to anyway, but this is, you know, this is encouraging to me. It makes for happy thoughts for me. A possible life. I used to say to myself, "What's it going to take with me? Why do I do these things? What is it going to take to finally make me realize that I have to stop eating and drinking." You know I didn't really realize that there was so much to it, that it was so deep and hard to deal with. I guess I thought I could, you know. I kind of thought it was stupid or ignorant or something for not stopping the things I was doing, so I'm glad to think of it because you know, it's hopeful.

DR. T: I can understand that. OK. Anything else?

MS. R: I guess not.

DR. T: OK. I'll have Dr. Maisto call you and you should hear from him either tomorrow or Friday, and if you don't by Monday, call me.

MS. R: OK.

DR. T: It's going to take a lot of hard work, but I think we understand the problem. I think you now have a decent understanding of what we think the problem is. I think it's an accurate understanding and a guide to how we'll treat it. Feel free to tell us when we're screwing up.

MS. R: OK. I will.

DR. T: Because we'll tell you if you're screwing up.

MS. R: I believe it.

DR. T: OK. Anything else? Good. You'll hear from him soon. I'll see you sooner or later. If you have any questions, give me a ring or get a hold of me. You have my phone number.

MS. R: Bye.

Given the validated mechanism of disorder, a treatment program was devised that aimed to teach Ms. R how to control impulses. Basically, imaginal and *in vivo* hierarchy items were developed, ranging from stimuli producing easily dismissible urges (e.g., imagining that her brother asked her to join him at a lounge for a few beers) to stimuli producing urges that could not be controlled and thus always acted upon (e.g., happy hours at a lounge with a favorite drinking buddy). The patient was taught distraction and other cognitive strategies (e.g., imagining long-term physical consequences of excessive eating and drinking) to use during exposure to such stimuli during and between sessions.

By the end of the 3rd month of treatment, the patient had reduced her drinking episodes to 1 night a week. Further, she reduced the quantity of her consumption to two drinks an occasion. She began paying bills, was able to save some money, and depression episodes were not occurring. She felt that her whole life was beginning to "turn around."

By the 6th month of treatment further gains were noted. She began volunteer work for a church, began to display more empathy for others, reported no longer becoming bored so easily, was complying with part of her diabetic treatment regimen (testing her blood sugar twice a day on weekdays and once daily on Saturday and Sunday), and was saving money. Finally, her daydreaming had diminished to less than 1 hr a day, and the content changed from spending money to working for money.

At this time, however, certain problems still existed and new ones developed. First, although the patient reported that she was controlling her eating, her weight did not change. Insulin dose adjustments were then made by her physician. Second, the patient quit her job and planned to go to a technical school. Finally, and most importantly, she met a man who was wealthy and who catered to her whims. Thus, within a short time, the patient had found her "wealthy lover" who sabotaged our treatment plans by taking her out frequently to dinner and bars, flying her around the country on vacations, and giving her just about anything she wanted. Ms. R's therapy was terminated shortly thereafter.

DISCUSSION

Our experience with the case of Ms. R led us to believe that the hypothesized mechanism of disorder was valid and that, when she followed the treatment program, the patient was improved markedly. However, as in all clinical work, when environmental events occur (in this case, a wealthy lover) that are incompatible with and stronger in immediate reinforcement value than the effects of treatment procedures clinical failure occurs.

We should also note that our second case of narcissistic personality disorder was formulated quite differently from the case of Ms. R. We do not yet have enough experience with these types of cases to offer any notable commonalities.

Paranoid Personality Disorder

There has been much theoretical discussion of paranoid behavior (cf. Adams, 1981; Colby, 1977; Ullmann & Krasner, 1975), but there is little research on paranoid personality disorder. The DSM-III characterization describes paranoid personality disorder as an individual who is pervasively mistrustful, suspicious without good cause, continually on guard for attack, secretive, easily slighted, unable to relax, and has restricted affect. We have seen eight such cases in our center. In a later section of this chapter, we detail our approach to assess, formulate, test the formulation, and treat such a case.

Passive–Aggressive Personality Disorder

The passive–aggressive personality has been classified under various labels in DSM-I, II, and III, and its criteria as a nosologic category have undergone numerous modifications. In DSM-III the disorder is characterized by a resistance to demands for adequate performance in occupational and social functioning that is displayed indirectly (e.g., forgetting, procrastinating). As a result, the individual shows poor social and occupational functioning.

The assumption that passive–aggressive personality disorder is common (Pasternack, 1974) has not been empirically validated (Turkat & Levin, 1984). Like many of the other personality disorders, it has been the subject of considerable psychoanalytic speculation (e.g., Whitman, Trosman, & Koenig, 1954).

We have seen only one case in our center who clearly met the DSM-III criteria for passive–aggressive personality disorder. Unfortunately, we were unable to develop a formulation of the case according to Meyer and Turkat (1979) criteria. Therefore, we are not yet able to contribute a useful conceptualization.

Schizoid and Schizotypal Personality Disorders

The DSM-III schizoid and schizotypal personality disorders are new nosologic categories. The former is characterized by emotional coldness, aloofness, indifference to others, and social isolation. Schizotypal personality disorder is characterized by odd thoughts, perceptions, speech, and behavior that are not severe enough to merit a schizophrenic diagnosis.

We have yet to see a patient who met the DSM-III criteria for schizotypal personality disorder. We have seen two cases whose behavior fit the criteria for schizoid personality disorder, but in each case we were unable to develop an adequate formulation. Thus, we have little to offer to advance understanding of these two personality disorders.

Atypical, Mixed, or Other Personality Disorder

This diagnostic category was devised to allow classification of individuals who seemed to have a personality disorder but cannot clearly meet the criteria for a previously specified disorder (atypical or other) or who show several features of at least two other personality disorders but cannot clearly meet the criteria for any one particular personality disorder (mixed). We have yet to see a patient who would be classified as meeting the criteria for atypical, mixed, or other personality disorder.

ILLUSTRATION OF AN ONGOING CASE OF PERSONALITY DISORDER

The purpose of this section is to illustrate the sequence of assessment–formulation validation–design and implementation of treatment by describing the methods and procedures used with an individual who is currently receiving treatment at our clinic. The patient's presenting problems and history, as he reported them in the initial interview, are used to construct a diagnosis and a case formulation. The procedures used to suggest that this formulation was valid are described along with the ensuing treatment design and implementation.

The Presenting Case

The patient, Mr. E, was a 52-year-old Caucasian male who was self-referred to the senior author.

The Initial Interview

At the beginning of the initial interview, the patient stated that he sought professional help because his wife would no longer have sex with him. Mr. E said that he had been married for 22 years and that 4 years ago his wife had had a hysterectomy. Mr. E reported that since that time his wife stopped sexual relations with him, because she considered him to be unattractive, overweight, and boring.

The patient was interviewed by the first author and subsequently was interviewed by the second author, who was blind to the information elicited in the earlier interview. The data collected in both interviews were similar. Ten presenting problems were identified, as follows.

1. Sexual problems. Mr. E reported that before his wife's hysterectomy, he and his wife would have sexual intercourse every night. He reported that each night both experienced multiple orgasms. As previously noted, after the hysterectomy she and Mr. E reportedly stopped having sex. Further, the patient indicated that he had had no sexual interactions with any other individuals during this period, but that he currently masturbated "1 to 4 times a week."

2. Marital problems. Mr. E said that his wife constantly criticized him. In particular, Mrs. E was reported as frequently reminding the patient that he was a failure in whatever he attempted. She also told Mr. E frequently that he was boring and unattractive.

3. Depression. The patient reported experiencing frequent bouts of depression. He often ruminated during these episodes about many topics that he found aversive. These will be elaborated upon below.

4. Family problems. Mr. E reported problems with his wife, three chilren, and mother. He said that his family was disturbed about his repeated ruminations and his discussions about the past 30 years, which they claimed considerably disrupted the family's life. Mr. E also told of several outbursts of violence with his children because of his preoccupation with the past.

5. Job dissatisfaction. Mr. E said that he was very dissatisfied with his present position as a clerk in a sheriff's department. At the time of the initial interview, Mr. E had been employed at that position for 11 years. He reported considerable distress about being passed up for promotion several times. Further, he felt that he deserved a position of higher status.

6. Ruminations about the past. The patient reported spending much of the day thinking about the past and said that he was unable to stop. These thoughts primarily concerned failures in the many academic and employment settings that had marked his life. There did not seem to be any one episode that dominated his ruminations.

7. *Loneliness.* The patient initially reported that he had many friends. However, further discussion revealed that he actually had no close friends and had no social contacts outside of work. Mr. E initially referred to his co-workers as friends, but later admitted that he did not spend any time outside of work socializing with them. Consequently, he felt very lonely.

8. *Obesity.* Mr. E was approximately 35 lb overweight at the time of the initial interview. He reported that he would eat more when he felt nervous, upset, or depressed.

9. *Smoking.* The patient reported excessive cigarette smoking, which also was correlated with feelings of anxiety and depression.

10. *Muscle twitching.* Mr. E said that he often developed involuntary muscle twitching in the face. These episodes occurred exclusively when Mr. E was alone at night and when he was ruminating about his past.

History

The patient reported that he was an only child who was rather large and fat. He described his mother as a "bitchy, spoiled woman" whom he found extremely difficult to get along with because she often criticized and picked on him. Mr. E's father divorced the patient's mother and left the house when Mr. E was 3 years old. Mr. E did not see his father again until he was 18 years old. When the patient's father moved out of the home, his maternal grandfather moved in and assumed the father role. Mr. E described his grandfather as a very successful judge and lawyer who was "loved by everyone who knew him." He also described his grandfather as the "perfect southern gentleman." Mr. E stated that he was reared in a very strict religious home. Both his grandfather and mother were affiliated with a fundamentalist religious denomination and followed its doctrines strictly.

Mr. E's social history was characterized by isolation and loneliness, and he described his grandfather as his only good friend. Mr. E reported that as a child and later on in life, he had always been the target of others' criticisms. For example, one of his nicknames was "fatty meat." Furthermore, the patient said that during childhood he was often smacked in the mouth by the other children (despite his large size) for "no reason at all." When he would go home to his mother for comfort, she would reply, "Don't bother me, fend for yourself." Mr. E reported that he always tried to be nice to everyone so that they would like him, but that it never seemed to work.

The patient did not do well academically. He said that after high school graduation he enrolled in and was expelled from eight different colleges and universities because of failing grades. In this regard Mr. E reported that while studying he felt extremely insecure and nervous, which resulted in his inability to learn the material. He also reported feeling so anxious during exams that he could not concentrate. Nevertheless, he continued to hold the achievement of a strong educational background as an important goal and aspired to earn a professional degree. Although Mr. E viewed his educational background as a series of failures, he liked to "impress" others by his "educational aspirations."

Mr. E related a similarly unstable job history. Over about the past 20 years, the patient had been hired and fired from numerous jobs, including salesman, dishwasher, taxi driver, and worker in a paint warehouse and drug store chain.

The patient's sexual history revealed that he had had no sexual encounters other than with his wife. As an adolescent, and in his early 20s, he reported having many offers for sexual activity but that he avoided them due to his religious beliefs and to his fear of being sexually inadequate. He indicated that at times he felt that his penis was too small and that he feared that others thought that he might be homosexual (although he denied being one). In fact, the patient reported that certain females had accused him of being homosexual because he had refused to have sex with them. Mr. E had dated his current wife only one time before he married her. The patient had not seen his wife for some time after the first date, when one day she approached Mr. E and asked him to "run off and get married." Mr. E felt that he would never have an opportunity to marry anyone so he accepted the offer.

At the initial interview the patient reported spending a considerable amount of time ruminating about his past. He continuously thought in detail about his failures in educational pursuits. Mr. E fluctuated between thinking that everyone was against him and thinking that perhaps he was a genius. He felt that being a genius might have made it impossible for him to learn in the typical academic environment. The patient also ruminated frequently about his grandfather. While he felt that his grandfather was "special" and was grateful that his grandfather "took him under his wing," Mr. E felt angry toward his grandfather for creating such high standards for him to meet. In this regard the patient spent much of his time ruminating about his special skills as a "perfect southern gentleman," like his grandfather. However, he also thought about times when people made critical comments about southerners in general, which led Mr. E to hate the fact that he was a southerner. Finally, the patient's ruminations about the past and his many failures led him to explain, even to acquaintances, the circumstances surrounding these episodes so that his goals or aspirations would not be misunderstood. As an example, Mr. E reported that while waiting to pay for an item at a drug store, he began explaining to another person whom he had just met in line much of his history and how he has been "screwed over."

Diagnosis

The presenting problems of this patient suggest a primary DSM-III diagnosis of paranoid personality disorder. Specifically, he was always on guard for others' misunderstandings of him and attempted to avoid any possible blame by explaining to others why things were against him. Further, he tended to be easily slighted, exaggerated the severity of his mistakes and was unable to relax. Finally, he tried to present an image of rationality and objectivity and he lacked a true sense of humor.

Formulation

The patient was an only child who had physical characteristics that made him a target of social criticism. Further, his mother appeared to be difficult to relate to, and she criticized the patient frequently. She did not provide any comfort or reassurance when the patient was humiliated or hurt by others, instead suggesting that the patient should learn to fend for himself. Since the father left the home when Mr. E was only 3 years old, it appeared that the grandfather served as the father model. In this regard the patient was presented with a "perfect southern gentleman." The grandfather was reportedly "loved and admired" by everyone, and the patient viewed him with considerable respect. The grandfather also was seen as "special" and treated the patient in a similar manner by "taking him under his wing." It appeared that, given the high standards of performance modeled by the grandfather, combined with the criticism from the patient's peers and his mother, and elicited by his physical characteristics, he developed appropriate self-evaluations of inadequacy and insecurity, and a fear of failure. Accordingly, the patient felt that he never could live up to the standards modeled by his grandfather. Nevertheless, he tried to become like his grandfather by pursuing academic training to become a professional. Unfortunately, he failed repeatedly.

As a function of this history, it was hypothesized that the patient developed a hypersensitivity to others' evaluations of him. This led to social isolation and, therefore, little opportunity to develop good social skills. As a result, a cycle was created in which the patient was afraid of others' opinions, attempted to make a good impression, but did so in such a way as to invite criticism, which caused even further isolation. During this isolation the patient ruminated about his failures and viewed himself as inadequate and persecuted. The variety and frequency of ruminations about his failures, combined with frequent actual failure experiences, led Mr. E to rationalize his predicament by viewing himself at first with persecution and later with grandeur.

Thus, it appeared that the patient's hypersensitivity to others' evaluations was the general mechanism accounting for his problems. The patient was so concerned about others' evaluations that he frequently tried to assure that others did not "misunderstand him" by going over his history, his failures, and how things were set against him. Obviously, this made him an undesirable social partner, a "boring" and irritating marital partner, and in combination with his large frame and obesity an unattractive sexual partner, which led to further social isolation. As a result, the patient felt lonely and depressed. While alone, he ruminated about his past to the extent that his face would become so tight with muscle tension that he would start twitching. When his anxiety increased, he would increase his eating and smoking. Finally, he was dissatisfied with his present job because it reminded him that he could never reach his aspirations.

Test of Formulation

The major hypothesis of mechanism of disorder in this case was the patient's hypersensitivity to others' evaluations of him, both explicit and implicit. Accordingly, it was predicted that if the patient were presented with explicit criticisms he would demonstrate heightened autonomic arousal and subjective anxiety. Further, if presented with subtle criticisms (i.e., relatively neutral stimuli that the patient perceived to be a criticism), then he also would demonstrate autonomic arousal and subjective anxiety. Accordingly, these hypotheses were investigated by monitoring the patient's autonomic and subjective arousal while he was exposed to such stimuli.

Mr. E was presented with neutral (A) and criticism (B) scenes alternated in an A-B-A design (Hersen & Barlow, 1976). During each phase EMG activity from the right masseter area was recorded. The patient also reported his current level of anxiety for each phase on a 0 (no anxiety, totally relaxed) to 10 (panic) scale. A total of eight criticism scenes were presented, four of which were considered "subtle," since they were not directly threatening to the patient, and four of which were considered "explicit," since they involved direct threats. The explicit stimuli (or scenes) were presented first and included, in order of presentation, (1) the image that Mr. E entered a tavern where he saw some colleagues sitting at a table having a beer and laughing, and that he had overheard the group talking about him, which had resulted in their laughter; (2) the image that Mr. E had received a letter from his fraternity rescinding his admission; (3) an image that the second author was telling Mr. E that he made many serious errors in the past; and (4) the image that there was a notice from the sheriff on the bulletin board at work that an employee had committed a serious error and that a meeting of all employees was being scheduled to discuss this.

The subtle stimuli included, in order, (1) a picture of Lee surrendering to Grant, taken from a book on the Civil War; (2) a current bulletin of the Vanderbilt University Law School; (3) a magazine picture of a male physician in a white coat with a stethoscope suspended from his neck; and finally (4) the instructions that the session would end with the experimenters teaching Mr. E how to operate the psychophysiological recording apparatus. These four subtle criticism scenes were an important part of the test of the formulation's validity. Although it could be argued that almost anyone might become anxious while imagining one of the explicit criticism scenes, it would be far less likely for someone who did not have a history and psychological characteristics similar to those of Mr. E to become aroused in response to the subtle criticism scenes.

The neutral scenes consisted of various images, enhanced by the experimenter's description, designed to relax Mr. E to baseline levels of arousal. The scenes included imagination of geometric forms such as a circle, triangle, and square, and the repeated inflation and deflation of a toy rubber balloon.

When Mr. E arrived at the laboratory for his appointment, he was met by his primary therapist, who took him to a soundproof, light-attenuated room and seated him in a reclining chair. The therapist then explained in detail the purpose of the session, including the fact that in order to complete the assessment of psychological functioning it would be necessary to record his physiological responses. Mr. E was told that a technician would soon enter the room and attach some physiological sensors. The technician then entered the room, cleansed the electrode sites with alcohol, and attached the electrodes. During this time the technician carefully explained to the patient what he was doing and that the electrodes would not cause any pain or discomfort. After the electrodes were attached, and the patient's questions were answered, the technician asked him to sit quietly and relax for approximately 15 min. The purpose of this adaptation period was to allow the patient to become accustomed to the experimental setting and to provide a baseline measure of his masseter EMG level. When the adaptation period was completed, the therapist entered the room and explained that the patient would be asked to imagine certain scenes and inspect certain materials during the rest of the session.

The patient was exposed to a neutral scene, which was followed by a criticism scene, and so on, for a total of 19 scenes in an A-B-A design. The nine criticism scenes included two presentations of the first explicit criticism scene and one presentation of the other criticism scenes. Each criticism scene was presented for 1 min. Neutral scenes were presented until (1) the EMG level returned to baseline levels and (2) three consecutive 15-s periods had passed in which there was not a consecutive increase or decrease in EMG response.

The patient's EMG responses were sampled throughout the session at 15-s intervals. The peak EMG response following return to baseline level during each neutral scene was scored for statistical analysis. The peak EMG response during the criticism scenes was also quantified for statistical analysis. EMG responses due to artifact (e.g., movement) were not quantified for analysis. The patient reported his level of anxiety following each neutral and criticism stimulus.

Statistical analyses revealed significant differences in EMG response among the explicit criticism, implicit criticism, and neutral scenes in the predicted direction. Responses to both the explicit and implicit criticism scenes significantly differed from the neutral scenes, but EMG response did not significantly differ across the explicit and implicit criticism scenes. Similar results were obtained on the self-report data.

Treatment

The results of this investigation were interpreted as suggesting that the formulation of Mr. E's problem was valid. Accordingly, Mr. E's treatment centered on his hypersensitivity to criticism. The formulation also suggested that Mr. E's social behavior resulted in an exacerbation of his fear of criticism. In particular, Mr. E's behavior toward others invited and worsened the criticism that he feared. Therefore, treatment was also designed to address Mr. E's deficits in social skills.

An important question in Mr. E's treatment concerned whether social skills training or anxiety (in response to criticism) management should be implemented first. It was decided that anxiety management should occur first because of the impairing effects that high levels of anxiety could have on social behavior. In this regard even if social skills training were administered first and seemed highly effective, there still might not be a significant change in Mr. E's behavior. That is, whatever social skills were acquired during time in treatment could be suppressed by a high degree of anxiety. The present formulation suggests that under such conditions the patient would show little, if any, improvement.

Anxiety Management Training

This treatment is designed to expose the patient to feared stimuli in order to *increase* his or her anxiety. The patient is then instructed to use various self-control strategies to help him or her *decrease* the level of anxiety while confronted with feared criticism-related stimuli. In particular the anxiety management training procedures used in treating Mr. E followed from a four-step model: (1) identification of anxiety-arousing stimuli; (2) identification of maladaptive reactions, such as autonomic arousal, avoidance behavior, and unadaptive cognitions; (3) training in adaptive coping responses, such as progressive muscle relaxation and adaptive cognitions; and (4) extratreatment practicing of skills acquired during therapy sessions. It was decided that the patient's problems warranted holding therapy sessions twice a week. Occasionally the patient was seen three times a week and, less frequently, once a week.

CONSTRUCTION OF THE FEAR HIERARCHY

The therapist worked with Mr. E in constructing a series of descriptions of situations related to criticism. These situations were defined in detail to include all important aspects of the setting, such as other persons and physical environment. Construction of the hierarchy was begun by asking Mr. E to describe the situation pertaining to personal criticism that he anticipated would elicit the most anxiety or panic. Mr. E was then asked to describe a setting involving criticism of him that would elicit very little or no anxiety. The remaining items, which were added until Mr. E could think of no other relevant situations, were designed to fall between these extremes on anxiety. Mr. E generated 26 items in four 1-hr therapy sessions. He was then asked to rank the items from "most anxiety arousing" to "least anxiety arousing." The complete list of hierarchy items is presented in the following list.

1. (*Least fearful*) A retired high school principal sees you smoking at church. He says, "I'll pray for you Mr. E, because you shouldn't be smoking."

2. The women at work ask you to give them your paycheck, and say they'll take care of your sexual needs.

3. You are criticized at work because you can't use one of the family cars for transportation to and from work.

4. A woman at work criticizes you because you weren't reared in the country and couldn't do farm labor work. You feel criticized because you're not from a rural background.

5. You're criticized by your mother for not doing the "little things," like neatness in the bathroom.

6. Judge _____ [who was in Mr. E's law school class] approaches you. You feel criticized because you compare yourself to him.

7. You're eating a sandwich at work in the morning, and the women there want to know what you're eating and what you eat at other meals.

8. It's Saturday morning, and you're preparing to come to _____. As you're leaving, your mother says, "I suppose you need cigarettes and don't have any money." She rants and raves, reminding you repeatedly that you're not supposed to smoke. In the end she gives you the dollar anyway.

9. A woman from corrections volunteers to type some of your school work. She says you can work at her house, since her husband isn't home. She says she'll meet you at the jail. You sit outside waiting for her in view of your co-workers. They ridicule you for sitting outside the jail. Three times this woman stands you up and you feel like a sucker.

10. Your immediate chief tells you that since you're living off the Democratic party, you're expected to vote Democratic.

11. Your wife fixes the same thing for dinner three times a week. When you complain she acts as if you were brought up with a silver spoon.

12. People at work tell you to shave off your mustache because it looks like Hitler's. However, you decide to keep it. People at work also tell you to keep on and take off your toupee.

13. You're on usher duty for the sheriff on a special occasion. A number of lawyers attend, and their wives are with them. You wish you were a lawyer and could afford the $50 entrance tickets and could afford to go to a formal social affair with your wife.

14. People leave food on your desk and say that the "human garbage can" will eat the food. You always eat it but then feel guilty.

15. You call crisis call and identify yourself. The woman volunteer says she's a member of your church and asks to speak to your wife. Your wife refuses and gets angry since she thinks that the "whole church" would know that you need help with solving your problems. She says this even though she suggested that you call the center.

16. The women at work suggest that you're inadequate sexually because you don't have sex with your wife.

17. You are sitting at your desk at work when you notice a beautiful blonde. The people at work tell you to get her a box lunch. When you return, they ask you to transport this prisoner to _____. The prisoner says, "I'm very hot, wanna take my clothes off, wanna have sexual relations." You think that the people at work are setting you up and having fun at your expense.

18. Women and men ask you whether you like _____, whether you find him attractive, implying that you're homosexual.

19. Women and men ask you whether you like _____, whether you find him appealing, implying that you're homosexual.

20. You're walking up to the desk of the dispatcher at work when he stops you and tells you you'll have to take the target shooting test.

21. Your mother is yelling and screaming at you for borrowing $1 to buy a pack of cigarettes.

22. You're at work and you run out of cigarettes. You spend your bus money to buy the cigarettes so you have to borrow money for carfare home. The chief tells you you're a "bum" because you never have any money.

23. The lawyers at the courthouse identify you as, "The jerk who carries the box."

24. Your eldest daughter wants to go to [a local college]. She goes to your mother's house to ask for tuition. You have to intercede to get your mother to pay 75% of the quarter's tuition. In the course of these discussions your mother says that, "If you were anything you'd be paying the tuition!"

25. Mr. Z calls from _____ and, in a mock southern drawl, asks you how everything is in _____. He then asks if you're still [working at two low-status jobs].

26. (*Most fearful*) You are sitting at your desk at work surrounded by warrant officers. [Your boss] approaches you and says, "You have been selected to be Chief Deputy." The warrant officers laugh, criticize you, say you're "unstable and can't make any decisions." When the laughing dies down [your boss] says, "By the way, you'll be getting a cut in salary."

RELAXATION TRAINING

Due to the high degree of muscular tension in Mr. E, it was decided to use progressive muscle relaxation as part of anxiety management training. In this regard it was hypothesized that Mr. E would complete the fear hierarchy more quickly if scene exposure began when he was in a relaxed state. This conclusion was based on our observation that Mr. E became considerably aroused physiologically and psychologically when he was exposed to criticism-related stimuli. Mr. E was taught progressive muscle relaxation according to procedures described by Bernstein and Borkovec (1973). These procedures entailed the typical progression from achieving relaxation through tension-release of single muscle groups, then to combined muscle groups, then to use of recall, and then to use of self-instruction. Specifically, Mr. E first was trained to relax by alternately tensing and releasing, in succession, 16 muscle groups. When Mr. E became proficient at this, the 16 muscle groups were combined into four larger groups, which he was told to tense and release to achieve relaxation. Upon succeeding at this stage, Mr. E was instructed to relax these same four muscle groups by identifying tension in the specific areas (by recall of that feeling from previous exercises) and then reducing it rather than by alternate tensing and releasing. After proficiency at this step, Mr. E could relax his entire body in less than a minute simply by instructing himself to do so. Mr. E reached this last stage of training, through daily 20- to 30-min practice sessions, in about 3 weeks.

ADAPTIVE COGNITIONS

The final step in preparing Mr. E for anxiety management training was developing a repertoire of adaptive cognitions that he could use to help reduce anxiety when he was confronted with fear-eliciting stimuli. The purpose of this aspect of training is to train the patient to interpret events in a way that helps to reduce anxiety, in contrast to his present anxiety-increasing interpretations. In one therapy session Mr. E generated a wide variety of adaptive self-statements. Some of these were, "People may be saying that I look foolish, but that's their opinion, not fact. So there's no reason for me to get upset about this." Another example was, "I'm sorry you think I'm doing a poor job, but I think I'm managing well and doing the best I can. So what do I have to get anxious about?" These and similar statements were designed to help Mr. E not to react to perceived criticism from others in his habitually anxious and defensive way, but to recognize that such criticism is only their opinion. As a result, more positive (to Mr. E) interpretations of the same event would probably be plausible. By this process Mr. E would be more likely, with practice, not to react indiscriminantly to perceived criticism from others with anxiety, but instead to consider the validity of their communications and then to behave according to a more reasoned interpretation of events.

PROCEDURES

When the components of hierarchy construction, relaxation training, and generation of a repertoire of adaptive self-statements were completed, anxiety management training began. The procedures were straightforward. As noted above, prior to the first training session Mr. E ranked the 26 fear hierarchy items from least fearful (1) to most fearful (26). He was asked to do this twice to establish consistency of the rankings. The first training session began by instructing Mr. E to lie down comfortably on a cot in the therapist's office. When he reported that he was in a comfortable position, Mr. E was instructed to use his progressive muscle relaxation skills to achieve a state of total relaxation. Achievement of this state was communicated to the therapist, which was his signal to begin presentation of the hierarchy items. The first item was the one ranked 1 by Mr. E—the least feared stimulus.

Mr. E was asked to imagine the stimulus and to report to the therapist when he had achieved a vivid image. The therapist then instructed Mr. E to signal to the therapist when he experienced anxiety. When Mr. E reported that he was feeling anxious, the therapist instructed him to maintain the image of the stimulus but to use adaptive cognitions and self-relaxation to help eliminate the anxiety. Mr. E signaled the therapist when his arousal level decreased to a relaxed state. Trials proceeded like this to the same hierarchy item until Mr. E reported that he *could not* become anxious when imagining the stimulus. It was hypothesized that, if the procedures were working as theorized, Mr. E should take a longer time to become aroused to a criticism scene and be able to eliminate that arousal more quickly with successive trials. Therefore, latency to arousal and to removal of arousal for the trials associated with each stimulus was recorded for hierarchy items 6–26 (due to therapist error, these latencies were not recorded for items 1–5).

In summary, training consisted of Mr. E's alternately arousing and decreasing anxiety while imagining a given criticism-related stimulus until he could no longer become aroused in response to it. The therapist measured the latencies associated with arousal and de-arousal as an internal check on the procedures. When an item no longer elicited anxiety in Mr. E, the therapist moved up one hierarchy item and repeated the anxiety arousal–reduction cycles. This was done until Mr. E had completed the 26 hierarchy items. He was also instructed to practice anxiety management skills outside of treatment by using imagined stimuli and by application to actual events.

OUTCOME

The anxiety management training procedures were completed in about 4 months of usually twice-a-week and occasionally three-times-a-week 1- to 2-hr sessions. At the end of training, Mr. E's physiological and subjective arousal (anxiety) to the stimuli used in validating the formulation were reassessed. The procedures that were used in the validation also were used in the outcome assessment.

The posttreatment EMG data were examined within and in relation to the pretreatment data. The mean levels of pretreatment and posttreatment masseter EMG responses to the three types of scenes are presented in Table 10-2. No significant difference was observed between the three scenes at posttreatment. As can be seen in Table 10-2, there was a substantial reduction between pretreatment and posttreatment assessments of EMG responses to the implicit criticism and to the explicit criticism scenes.

Mr. E's posttreatment reports of anxiety in response to each of the scenes revealed little variance in the data. Specifically, Mr. E reported anxiety in response to only one of the explicit scenes (a rating of 2), one of the implicit scenes (a rating of 1), and one of the neutral scenes (a rating of 1). In contrast, in the pretreatment test, Mr. E reported anxiety in response to three of the five explicit criticism scenes (range = 5–7), all four of the implicit scenes (range = 3–7), and four of the nine neutral scenes (range = 1–4). Therefore, Mr. E's decreased EMG response to the experimental stimuli was accompanied by a similar reduction in his reports of anxiety. Furthermore, Mr. E reported that he had significantly improved in his ability not to become anxious in situations outside of treatment involving criticism from others.

TABLE 10-2. Mean Pretreatment and Posttreatment Masseter EMG Levels in Response to Neutral, Implicit Criticism, and Explicit Criticism Scenes

Type of scene	EMG levels (μV)	
	Pretreatment	Posttreatment
Neutral	3.40	1.4
Implicit	8.63	2.58
Explicit	9.28	2.26

Social Skills Training

Upon completion of anxiety management training, social skills training was initiated. Mr. E continued to see the therapist for twice-weekly 1- to 2-hr sessions. This part of the treatment is currently in progress.

As noted earlier, the formulation of Mr. E's problems suggested that his interpersonal skills deficits invited criticism from others. Of course, such criticism resulted in exacerbating Mr. E's sensitivity to criticism. Therefore, improvement in Mr. E's social skills should result in a lower frequency of the kinds of reactions from others that maintained or worsened his difficulties.

MODEL OF SOCIAL SKILLS AND ASSESSMENT OF DEFICITS

Social skills were conceptualized as comprising four dimensions: Attention, processing (of social information), response emission, and type of and reaction to feedback from others. Based on the detailed information obtained from Mr. E during assessment and treatment sessions, it was determined that he had deficits in each of these areas. First, Mr. E did not attend well to the social environment, which often resulted in his missing cues that others would give to him in reaction to his behavior or in his selectively attending to inappropriate cues (i.e., potential criticisms). Second, Mr. E's processing of social information was not adaptive in that he tended to interpret a wide range of reactions in others as criticism of him. Furthermore, he frequently interpreted others' comments as having "special meaning" for him. This tended to increase his isolation and paranoia. Third, Mr. E's behavior and appearance often contributed to negative responses from others. For example, Mr. E bathed infrequently, did not regularly wear clean clothes, often neglected his personal hygiene, and was overweight, which resulted in a high rate of negative comments from others. In addition, Mr. E frequently could not have a conversation with others without somehow bringing the topic back to him and his concerns. This gave the impression that he had little interest in what others were saying or that he was not paying attention to what they were saying. Another deficit in this area was that Mr. E often engaged in excessive self-disclosure, even with people he barely knew. Finally, the negative feedback received from others increased his isolation and suspiciousness, which could be reversed by the positive feedback that would likely follow from an improvement in his social skills. Based on this assessment, several treatment interventions were initiated to improve Mr. E's social skills.

SOCIAL SKILLS TRAINING INTERVENTIONS

The social skills training interventions that were used with Mr. E follow. These interventions were classified according to the four-dimension model of attention, processing, response emission, and feedback.

Attention. Mr. E's attentional problems seemed related in part to his absorption with his own problems. One way to attack this problem seemed to be by improving Mr. E's communication skills. For example, Mr. E's wife frequently criticized him because he was self-absorbed (and consequently) boring.

Therefore, Mr. E was first taught how to focus on and describe cues that others emitted in social encounters. This was accomplished through role playing, feedback and prompting. Once Mr. E was attending better to cues, he was taught the concept of "reflection" so that he could convey an understanding of the other person's feelings or actions. These were practiced thoroughly with the therapist in role-play situations. Mr. E appeared to master these concepts.

Another aspect of communications skills that was addressed in treatment concerned the use of open-ended questions, or questions that encourage or prompt the other person to elaborate on a topic to extend the conversation. Open-ended questions also would require Mr. E to focus on the other person's area of interest instead of his own, the latter of which he was strongly inclined to do. Mr. E was asked to generate a list of common open-ended questions, such as "Could you tell me more about that?" and "What did you think of . . . ?" For homework Mr. E was instructed to notice the open-ended questions that other people used and to practice asking open-ended questions to people outside of treatment. Role-play sessions were enacted in treatment, in which the therapist introduced a topic and Mr. E asked open-ended questions. Mr. E also was instructed to introduce a topic in role plays and to follow it up with open-ended questions to sustain the conversation.

Role plays of asking open-ended questions also included videotaping to aid social skills training. In particular, the role plays were videotaped and immediately played back to Mr. E, with the therapist asking him to identify his appropriate and inappropriate verbal behavior. The therapist then critiqued Mr. E's verbal behavior and, where appropriate, suggested better statements and questions. Videotaping was a substantial aid to communication skills training and was used in the other components of social skills training, as described below.

Processing Information. One of Mr. E's social skills deficits involved poor processing of information in certain situations. For example, when a female co-worker invited Mr. E to play racquetball, Mr. E replied "I don't want to have an affair with you." His thinking was as follows: "she knows I'm unhappy with my wife and she's asking me to join her alone in a physical activity so she must want to have an affair. Even if she doesn't want to have an affair, I don't want her to misinterpret my intentions." This type of information processing (i.e., indicating special meanings) led to social behavior that invited others to ridicule Mr. E. Accordingly, much effort was expended on teaching Mr. E new ways to process social cues. This involved teaching Mr. E how to generate alternative explanations given particular social cues and then how to evaluate each potential interpretation. Of particular importance was an emphasis on Mr. E learning not to view himself and others' actions as having "special meaning." Prompting, behavioral rehearsal, and feedback were used.

Response Emission. This area has received the most emphasis so far in treatment and has involved several different interventions. As noted, Mr. E was deficient in some basic hygiene habits, which frequently resulted in criticism from others. His relative neglect of his personal hygiene also was sometimes apparent during therapy sessions. Mr. E neglected bathing, regular changes of clothes, and regular brushing of his teeth. Specifically, Mr. E reported bathing every other day (but his wife reported that he bathed only once a week). Therefore, the therapist instructed him to bathe once a day. He was also instructed to wear clean clothes every day. Finally, he was asked to begin brushing his teeth at least twice a day instead of his customary once a day. Mr. E currently reports that he is following the therapist's instructions.

The other aspect of Mr. E's physical appearance that has invited criticism is his obesity. As noted above, when treatment began Mr. E had been about 35 lb overweight, and his weight had not changed during the course of therapy. Furthermore, Mr. E rarely exercised. Accordingly, a goal of treatment was to reduce his weight to the normal range through a program of diet and exercise. A 1700-calorie-a-day diet was arranged for him in collaboration with the dietitian affiliated with the medical center where Mr. E was receiving treatment. The therapist also reviewed with Mr. E how to handle situations that posed a risk for his eating high-calorie foods, and he kept a record of his food intake for 2 weeks. His record was reviewed and critiqued during treatment sessions. Mr. E is currently losing weight. His baseline weight was 222 lb, and 4 weeks later he weighed 216 lb, a loss of 6 lb. The therapist weighs Mr. E once a week at the treatment program.

Mr. E's weight loss would be facilitated if he exercised more as well as dieted consistently. Before initiating his diet Mr. E reported that his exercise consisted of walking eight blocks during workdays (to and from the bus stop) and minimal walking on non-workdays. He was instructed to walk at least a mile in addition to his usual eight blocks on workdays, but he has not followed this instruction consistently. However, Mr. E reports that he now walks 1–3 miles on each non-workday.

Mr. E also has been instructed to eliminate two behaviors that had resulted in frequent criticism, which were borrowing money repeatedly from people at work and disclosing personal information to virtually anybody who would listen to him. Mr. E reports that he is following these instructions.

Finally, Mr. E's children have been a source of some criticism of him. In this regard Mr. E often invited this criticism by being critical of *them* and giving unsolicited or premature advice. Therefore, repeated role-playing enactments are being used to train Mr. E to ask questions that encourage elaboration on a problem without verbal attack and not to offer advice based on inadequate information.

Reaction to Feedback. Because Mr. E reported that his wife's criticism of him was persisting, the concept of "agreeing with part of a criticism" was introduced. First, Mr. E role-played with the therapist how he responded to his wife's criticisms. Typically, her criticisms triggered an argumentative response. Mr. E then was instructed in the method of agreeing, in part, with the criticism *without* denigrating himself. For example, if Mr. E's wife exclaimed, "You're a bore!," he could respond, "I guess I seem boring to you. I'm trying to be more active now. Do you have any suggestions?" As can be seen, this response involves agreeing in part with the criticism and then asking an open-ended question. So far Mr. E has found it difficult to suppress an argumentative response to his wife's criticisms but reports that he does much better with others, such as people at work.

Therapeutic Relationship. Given the formulation of this case, several aspects of the therapeutic relationship have been manipulated throughout treatment. First, Mr. E was assigned a male therapist who was very supporting and noncritical of the patient. As Mr. E became more comfortable with criticism, an attractive female took over as primary therapist (since Mr. E was terrified of humiliation by a female). She, too, played a supportive nonthreatening role, at first. Once Mr. E became more comfortable with her, she began to introduce critical judgments of the patient into their encounters, paralleling the treatment program. When he became anxious during these encounters, he was instructed to immediately reduce his anxiety via the self-control procedures Mr. E had learned. By the time Mr. E was midway through social skills training, he experienced little anxiety when the therapist criticized him. While we are unable to document the specific effects of this therapeutic relationship on Mr. E's progress, the important point is that the therapeutic relationship was structured to be consistent with the case formulation.

SUMMARY

The present model of social skills was used to guide assessment and design of treatment interventions to improve Mr. E's social skills. A number of specific interventions followed from this assessment, ranging from simple instructions to improve his personal hygiene habits to continuing complex social interactions and using videotaping apparatus to improve communication and other interpersonal skills. This part of treatment was still in progress as of this writing and will not terminate until improvement in all areas of social skills deficits are noted. Some progress seemed to have occurred, but further improvement is required. For example, Mr. E reported improved interactions with others in settings such as work and home, which suggests that he in part generalized the use of these concepts outside of treatment. However, his tendencies to monopolize conversations with his elaborations, self-defenses, premature advice, and criticism of others were still evident.

General Summary of Treatment Interventions

The present detailed description of the ongoing treatment of Mr. E illustrates the use of the case formulation to derive behavioral interventions. In particular, Mr. E's problems were formulated as a hypersensitivity to criticism from others that was exacerbated by his own frequently poor appearance and interpersonal behaviors. Accordingly, treatment included, first, substantially eliminating anxiety in settings that involved criticisms and learning how to cope adaptively with criticism-related anxiety if it did occur and, second, correction of problem social behaviors.

In order to assess Mr. E's general progress as of this writing (about 7 months after beginning treatment), he was interviewed about the 10 problem areas that he identified in the pretreatment interview. His current status in each problem area is reviewed below.

1. Sexual problems. Mr. E reported that he still was not having sexual relations with his wife. Although he and his wife no longer discussed this problem, Mr. E said that he felt better about it but that he would be "less tense" if he could have sexual relations. Mr. E reported that he was masturbating one to two times a week.

2. Marital problems. Mr. E said that he and his wife still did not do much together. He reported that he was still being criticized by her for being lazy (about his house chores), not following his diet, and failing to exercise, but he no longer was upset by her behavior. Mrs. E indicated that she had no desire to change her ways and did not want marital therapy. Mr. E was currently considering a divorce.

3. Depression. Mr. E reported that he experienced depression only "once in awhile." The degree of depression seemed mild, because work, sleep, and appetite were not disturbed.

4. Family problems. Mr. E reported improvement in this area. He said that he got along much better with his two daughters, whom he used to frequently argue with and receive criticism from. They have commented consistently on his improvement and said that he was "acting more like a father."

5. Job dissatisfaction. Mr. E said that he was "doing fine" at work and that he was "interacting beautifully down there." Although he was still somewhat demoralized about his job status, he tried to do "the best that I can at the job." Mr. E also reported that he recently had lunch with several judges without anxiety or animosity.

6. Ruminations. Mr. E reported that ruminations occurred only "sporadically." Their average duration was about 2 min. Mr. E said that he no longer went into his bedroom alone to ruminate for hours. When ruminations occurred they were related to Mr. E's not beginning a new career.

7. Loneliness. Mr. E said that he was not lonely at work but still was lonely outside of work. He said that he had no close friends but had developed a new relationship with another male. Mr. E reported that he had trouble "letting himself go" with people to get close to them, because he still felt that they might "screw" him. Mr. E said that he no longer self-disclosed excessively to acquaintances.

8. Obesity. Mr. E was dieting and had lost weight, as reported previously.

9. Smoking. Mr. E continued to smoke about a pack of cigarettes a day.

10. Muscle twitching. Mr. E reported that muscle twitches generally did not occur. The only time he said that they happened was during "extreme" arguments with his wife.

In conclusion, this recent assessment suggested that Mr. E made substantial improvements in the many problem areas that he identified during the pretreatment interview. He seemed to respond far more adaptively to criticisms, and he made some progress in social relations, especially with his children and his co-workers. However, Mr. E needed to work further on some of these problems, which still seemed to cause him some distress. It would appear that continued improvement in social skills areas as noted above would make positive reactions from others more likely, which in turn, should make it easier for Mr. E to feel that he can trust them.

PARANOID PERSONALITY DISORDER: DISCUSSION

The case of Mr. E highlights in many respects some commonalities we have noted in the various paranoid personality disorders that we have seen. Basically, these fall into three categories.

First, none of these patients announced in the initial interview, "Listen Doc, I'm paranoid" or "Everybody's out to get me." Rather, their interview responses and behavior revealed that they were tense, socially isolated, fearful of others' reactions to them, and proficient in supplying detailed rationalizations for their social isolation. To get at their paranoid thinking, stepwise questioning was often necessary, since such cases by definition are distrustful and defensive. The following sequence is typical:

1. Many people feel at times that they have not been treated fairly, have you ever felt this way? ("Yes"; get examples.)

2. Sometimes people feel that their behavior is misinterpreted at times or not understood. Has this happened to you at all? ("Yes"; get examples.)

3. Ever get the feeling that certain people were purposely unfair to you? ("Yes"; get examples.)

4. Ever feel at times that certain people pick on you? ("Yes"; get examples.)

5. It must be hard to trust these people? ("Yes.")

6. Ever try and figure out why some people seem unfair or seem out to get you? ("Yes.")

7. Well sometimes, we all get wild ideas about why people dislike us but sometimes they seem almost true. Have you had any of these? ("Yes"; get examples.) *or* Sometimes we feel that people act differently toward us because we are different or special. Have you ever felt different or special? ("Yes"; explain in detail.)

8. How are you different or unique from others?

9. I know it may seem weird at times, but do you ever get the sense that you have special talent or skill (or thoughts that others don't have? ("Yes"; please explain.)

Questioning along this line will often lead the paranoid personality to giggle, laugh, tense up, and so on. At times, such patients begin to worry that the clinician is reading their mind. An important point is that in most of these cases, one must attempt to draw inferences about the patients' behavior in order to elicit the necessary data to making a diagnosis of paranoid personality disorder.

A second commonality we have noted is that such patients seem to report a similar history. Most report having at least one parent who was a *perfectionist* and *especially sensitive to social evaluation*. Second, at some time in his or her early family life, the individual was *labeled as unique* in some ways (e.g., bright, better looking, etc. than others). Third, such patients seem socially "uptight" early on and often are seen by classmates as being different, resulting in harassment and derogatory remarks (e.g., "turkey," "computerhead"). Fourth, as they get older and physically mature, they become isolated socially and particularly terrified of the opposite sex. Fifth, while isolated, they spend much time thinking about why they are isolated, and persecutory explanations develop. Sixth, spending much time alone and ruminating about their predicament, they become anxious and then come up with grandiose explanations as to why people act "differently" toward them; by this point the individual is acting in a defensive way, trying to avoid social criticism and to find support for his or her paranoid explanations. This results in behaviors that others find "weird" and leads others to avoid him or her. Thus, a vicious cycle is created.

In short, our clinical observations suggest that paranoid personality may result from parental training in *evaluative uniqueness* (i.e., hypersensitive to social evaluation and feeling that he or she is unique), which sets the stage for acting "differently," avoiding others, and developing a paranoid thinking style. We are currently involved in testing this theory in a research setting.

The third commonality we have noted, is that treatment of such cases is relatively straightforward but very time consuming. Given the evaluative uniqueness hypothesis, treatment is aimed at reducing the patient's hypersensitivity to evaluation and eliminating social behaviors that make the person "stand out." Thus, behavioral treatment procedures such as anxiety management and social skills training seem to work quite well with paranoid personality disorder cases. Of course, strong experimental support for our clinical assertions is lacking.

In sum, our approach to formulating and treating the single case, using uncontrolled and quasi-controlled clinical observations, has led us to a potential theory about paranoid personality disorder development and an approach to treating such cases. Future controlled research will determine the viability of our hypothesis and how well our approach to involving the clinician in the process of generating knowledge scientifically will fare.

CONCLUSION

From the research literature and our clinical experience with 35 personality disorder cases, it is clear that much has yet to be learned regarding the etiology, mechanisms, and treatment of the personality disorders. It is our hope that the approach we have advocated will lead to advances in the clinical management of the personality disorders. At the very least, we hope that the reader has been sensitized to the importance of developing good case formulations and of articulating, testing, and acting upon them.

Acknowledgments

Work on this chapter was initiated while the senior author was at Vanderbilt University but was completed at the University of North Carolina at Greensboro.

The authors gratefully acknowledge indirect and direct contributions to this manuscript by some of our students (Michael Carey, Charlie Carlson, Lydia Flasher, Stephanie O'Malley, and Susan Snyder).

The approach to paranoid personality disorder and the model of social skills presented herein stem directly from ideas suggested by Dr. Henry E. Adams.

References

Adams, H. E. (1981). *Abnormal psychology.* Dubuque, IA: William C. Brown Co.

Adams, H. E., Doster, J. A., & Calhoun, K. S. (1977). A psychologically based system of response classification. In A. R. Ciminero, K. S. Calhoun, & H. E. Adams (Eds.), *Handbook of behavioral assessment.* New York: Wiley Interscience.

Allport, G. W. (1937). *Personality: A psychological interpretation.* New York: Holt, Rinehart & Winston.

American Psychiatric Association. (1952). *Diagnostic and statistical manual of mental disorders* (1st ed.). Washington, DC: Author.

American Psychiatric Association. (1968). *Diagnostic and statistical manual of mental disorders* (2nd ed.). Washington, DC: Author.

American Psychiatric Association. (1980). *Diagnostic and statistical manual of mental disorders* (3rd ed.). Washington, DC: Author.

Barlow, D. H. (Ed.). (1981). *Behavioral assessment of adult disorders.* New York: Guilford.

Barlow, D. H., Hayes, S. C., & Nelson, R. O. (1984). *The scientist–practitioner: Research and accountability in clinical and educational settings.* New York: Pergamon.

Barlow, D. H., & Hersen, M. (1984). *Single case experimental designs* (2nd ed.). New York: Pergamon.

Bernstein, D. A., & Borkovec, T. D. (1973). *Progressive relaxation training: A manual for the helping professions.* Champaign, IL: Research Press.

Brantley, P. J., & Sutker, P. B. (1984). Antisocial personality disorder. In H. E. Adams & P. B. Sutker (Eds.), *Comprehensive handbook of psychopathology.* New York: Plenum.

Campbell, D. T., & Stanley, J. C. (1963). *Experimental and quasi-experimental designs for research.* Chicago: Rand-McNally.

Carey, M. P., Flasher, L. V., Maisto, S. A., & Turkat, I. D. (1984). The a priori approach to psychological assessment. *Professional Psychology, 15,* 515–527.

Colby, K. N. (1977). Appraisal of four psychological theories of paranoid phenomena. *Journal of Abnormal Psychology, 86,* 54–59.

Duke, M., & Nowicki, S. (1979). *Abnormal psychology: Perspectives on being different.* Monterey, CA: Brooks/Cole.

Ford, J. D., & Kendall, P. C. (1979). Behavior therapists' professional behaviors: Converging evidence of a gap between theory and practice. *The Behavior Therapist, 2,* 37–38.

Frances, A. (1980). The DSM-III personality disorder section: A commentary. *American Journal of Psychiatry, 137,* 1050–1054.

Freud, S. (1955). Totem and taboo. *Standard Edition, 13,* 1–61. London: Hogarth Press. (Originally published 1913)

Freud, S. (1957). On narcissism. *Standard Edition, 14*, 69–102. London: Hogarth Press. (Originally published 1914)

Freud, S. (1958). Psycho-analytic notes on an autobiographical account of a case of paranoia (dementia paranoids). *Standard Edition, 12*, 9–82. London: Hogarth Press. (Originally published 1911)

Goldfried, M. R., & Davison, G. C. (1976). *Clinical behavior therapy.* New York: Holt, Rinehart & Winston.

Goldstein, M. J., Baker, B. L., & Jamison, K. R. (1980). *Abnormal psychology: Experiences, origins, interventions.* Boston: Little, Brown.

Gunderson, J. G., & Singer, M. T. (1975). Defining borderline patients: An overview. *American Journal of Psychiatry, 132*, 1–10.

Hartocollis, P. (1980). Affective disturbance in borderline and narcissistic patients. *Bulletin of the Menninger Clinic, 14*, 135–146.

Hersen, M., & Barlow, D. H. (1976). *Single case experimental designs.* New York: Pergamon.

Hirschfeld, R. A., Klerman, G. L., Gough, H. G., Barrett, J., Korchin, S. J., & Chodoff, P. (1977). A measure of interpersonal dependency. *Journal of Personality Assessment, 41*, 610–618.

Inglis, J. (1966). *The scientific study of abnormal behavior.* Chicago: Aldine.

Kolb, J. E., & Gunderson, J. G. (1980). Diagnosing borderline patients with a semi-structured interview. *Archives of General Psychiatry, 37*, 37–41.

Lachar, D. (1980). *The MMPI: Clinical assessment and automated interpretation* (6th ed.). Los Angeles, CA: Western Psychological Services.

Lorr, M., & More, W. M. (1979). *Personal relations inventory.* Copyright by M. Lorr.

Meyer, V., & Reich, B. (1978). Anxiety management: The marriage of physiological and cognitive variables. *Behaviour Research and Therapy, 16*, 177–182.

Meyer, V., & Turkat, I. D. (1979). Behavioral analysis of clinical cases. *Journal of Behavioral Assessment, 1*, 259–270.

Millon, T. (1981). *Disorders of personality.* New York: Wiley.

Nelson, R. O., & Barlow, D. H. (1981). Behavioral assessment: Basic strategies and initial procedures. In D. H. Barlow (Ed.), *Behavioral assessment of adult disorders.* New York: Guilford.

Nunnally, J. C. (1980). *Psychometric structures for attributed emotion: Lexical relations and trait attributions.* Unpublished manuscript.

Pasternack, S. A. (1974). The explosive, antisocial, and passive–aggressive personalities. In J. R. Lyon (Ed.), *Personality disorders: Diagnosis and management.* Baltimore: Williams & Wilkins.

Payne, R. W., & Jones, H. G. (1957). Statistics for the investigation of individual cases. *Journal of Clinical Psychology, 13*, 115–121.

Perry, J. C., & Klerman, G. L. (1980). Clinical features of borderline personality disorder. *American Journal of Psychiatry, 137*, 165–173.

Rachman, S. J., & Wilson, G. T. (1980). *The effects of psychological therapy* (2nd ed.). New York: Pergamon.

Schachter, S., & Rodin, J. (Eds.). (1974). *Obese humans and rats.* Potomac, MD: Erlbaum.

Shapiro, M. B. (1951a). Experimental studies of a perceptual anomaly: I. Initial experiments. *Journal of Mental Science, 97*, 90–110.

Shapiro, M. B. (1951b). Experimental approach to psychological diagnostic testing. *Journal of Mental Science, 97*, 748–764.

Shapiro, M. B. (1952). Use of psychological tests for the differential diagnosis of early dementia. *Proceedings of the Royal Society of Medicine, 45*, 375–376.

Shapiro, M. B. (1953a). Experimental studies of a perceptual anomaly: II. Confirmatory and explanatory experiments. *Journal of Mental Science, 98*, 605–617.

Shapiro, M. B. (1953b). Experimental studies of a perceptual anomaly: III. The testing of an explanatory theory. *Journal of Mental Science, 99*, 394–409.

Shapiro, M. B. (1955). Training of clinical psychologists at the Institute of Psychiatry. *Bulletin of the British Psychological Society, 8,* 1–6.

Shapiro, M. B. (1957). Experimental methods in the psychological description of the individual psychiatric patient. *International Journal of Social Psychiatry, 111,* 89–102.

Shapiro, M. B. (1962). A two-year course for the training of clinical psychologists at the Institute of Psychiatry. *Bulletin of the British Psychological Society, 15,* 30–32.

Shapiro, M. B. (1969). Recent trends in the training of clinical psychologists in Great Britain. *Bulletin of the British Psychological Society, 22,* 13–17.

Shapiro, M. B. (1970). Intensive assessment of the single case: An inductive–deductive approach. In P. Mittler (Ed.), *Psychological assessment of mental and physical handicaps.* London: Methuen.

Shapiro, M. B., & Nelson, E. H. (1955). An investigation of an abnormality of cognitive function in a cooperative young psychotic: An example of the application of experimental method to the single case. *Journal of Clinical Psychology, 11,* 344–351.

Shapiro, M. B., & Ravenette, A. T. (1959). A preliminary experiment of paranoid delusions. *Journal of Mental Science, 105,* 295–312.

Spitzer, R. L., Endicott, J., & Gibbon, N. (1979). Crossing the border into borderline personality and borderline schizophrenia. *Archives of General Psychiatry, 36,* 17–24.

Spitzer, R. L., & Forman, J. B. W. (1979). DSM-III field trials: II. Initial experience with the multiaxial system. *American Journal of Psychiatry, 136,* 818–820.

Spitzer, R. L., Forman, J. B. W., & Nee, J. (1979). DSM-III field trials: III. Initial interrater diagnostic reliability. *American Journal of Psychiatry, 136,* 815–817.

Strober, N., Green, J., & Carlson, G. (1981). Reliability of psychiatric diagnoses in hospitalized adolescents. *Archives of General Psychiatry, 38,* 141–145.

Sturgis, E. T., & Meyer, V. (1981). Obsessive-compulsive disorders. In S. M. Turner, K. S. Calhoun, & H. E. Adams (Eds.), *Handbook of clinical behavior therapy.* New York: Wiley.

Sutker, P. B., Archer, R. P., & Kilpatrick, D. G. (1981). Sociopathy and antisocial behavior: Theory and treatment. In S. M. Turner, K. S. Calhoun, & H. E. Adams (Eds.), *Handbook of clinical behavior therapy.* New York: Wiley.

Sue, D., Sue, D. W., & Sue, S. (1981). *Understanding abnormal behavior.* Boston: Houghton Mifflin.

Turkat, I. D. (1982a). Glycosylated hemoglobin levels in anxious and nonanxious diabetic patients. *Psychosomatics, 23,* 1064–1066.

Turkat, I. D. (1982b). The use of EMG biofeedback with insulin dependent diabetic patients. *Biofeedback and Self-Regulation, 7,* 301–304.

Turkat, I. D. (in press). The behavioral interview. In A. R. Ciminero, K. S. Calhoun, & H.E. Adams (Eds.), *Handbook of behavioral assessment* (2nd ed.). New York: Wiley Interscience.

Turkat, I. D., & Alpber, V. S. (1983). An investigation of personality disorder descriptions. *American Psychologist, 38,* 857–858.

Turkat, I. D., & Brantley, P. J. (1981). On the therapeutic relationship in behavior therapy. *The Behavior Therapist, 4,* 16–17.

Turkat, I. D., & Carlson, C. R. (1984). Symptomatic versus formulation based treatment: A case study of dependent personality disorder. *Journal of Behavior Therapy and Experimental Psychiatry, 15,* 153–160.

Turkat, I. D., & Kuczmierczyk, A. R. (1980). Clinical considerations in anxiety management. *Scandinavian Journal of Behavior Therapy, 9,* 141–145.

Turkat, I. D., & Levin, R. A. (1984). Formulation of personality disorders. In H. E. Adams & P. B. Sutker (Eds.), *Comprehensive handbook of psychopathology.* New York: Plenum.

Turkat, I. D., Maisto, S. A., Burish, T. G., & Rock, D. L. (in press). Evaluating case formulations of psychopathology. In H. Lettner & B. Range (Eds.), *Handbook of behavioral psychotherapy.* Sao Paulo, Brazil: Editorn Pedagogica e Universiteria.

Turkat, I. D., & Meyer, V. (1982). The behavior-analytic approach. In P. Wachtel (Ed.), *Resistance: Psychodynamic and behavioral approaches.* New York: Plenum.

Turner, S. M., & Hersen, M. (1981). Disorders of social behavior: A behavioral approach to personality disorders. In S. M. Turner, K. S. Calhoun, & H. E. Adams (Eds.), *Handbook of clinical behavior therapy.* New York: Wiley.

Tyrer, P., Alexander, M. S., Cicchetti, D., Cohen, N. S., & Remington, N. (1979). Reliability of a schedule for rating personality disorders. *British Journal of Psychiatry, 135,* 168–174.

Ullmann, L., & Krasner, L. (1975). *A psychological approach to abnormal behavior* (2nd ed.). Englewood Cliffs, NJ: Prentice-Hall.

Watson, D., & Friend, R. (1969). Measurement of social evaluation anxiety. *Journal of Consulting and Clinical Psychology, 43,* 384–395.

Whitman, R. N., Trosman, H., & Koenig, R. (1954). Clinical assessment of the passive–aggressive personality. *Archives of Neurology and Psychiatry, 72,* 540–549.

Wolpe, J. (1958). *Psychotherapy by reciprocal inhibition.* Stanford, CA: Stanford University Press.

Wolpe, J., & Turkat, I. D. (in press). Behavioral formulation of clinical cases. In I. D. Turkat (Ed.), *Behavioral case formulation.* New York: Plenum.

World Health Organization. (1979). *Manual of the international statistical classification of diseases, injuries, and causes of death* (9th rev., Vol. 1). Geneva: Author.

Yates, A. (1975). *Theory and practice in behavior therapy.* New York: Wiley.

Zuckerman, M. (1979). *Sensation seeking: Beyond the optimal level of arousal.* Hillsdale, NJ: Erlbaum.

Zuckerman, M., & Larrance, D. T. (1979). Individual differences in perceived encoding and decoding abilities. In R. Rosenthal (Ed.), *Skill in nonverbal communication.* Cambridge, MA: Oelgeschlager, Gunn & Hain.

AUTHOR INDEX

SUBJECT INDEX

r